BRITAIN'S SEA SOLDIERS

A RECORD OF THE ROYAL MARINES
DURING THE WAR 1914-1919.

COMPILED BY
GENERAL SIR H. E. BLUMBERG, K.C.B.,
ROYAL MARINES

Series Editor
Colonel Brian Carter OBE RM

ROYAL MARINES HISTORICAL SOCIETY
SPECIAL PUBLICATION NO 42

BRITAIN'S SEA SOLDIERS
A RECORD OF THE ROYAL MARINES
DURING THE WAR 1914-1919.

Copyright © Royal Marines Historical Society 2014

First published in 1927 at Devonport by
SWISS &: Co., Naval and Military Printers and Publishers,
111 and 112 Fore Street.

All Rights Reserved

No part of this book may be reproduced in any form
by photocopying or by any electronic or mechanical means,
including information storage or retrieval systems,
without permission in writing from the copyright owner.

ISBN
978-1-908123-10-7

First published 2014 by the
ROYAL MARINES HISTORICAL SOCIETY
Royal Marines Museum
Eastney
Southsea
Hants PO4 9PX
United Kingdom

Cover, design and layout
Tim Mitchell
www.tim-mitchell.co.uk

Printed and bound in Great Britain by
CPI Antony Rowe Ltd, Chippenham and Eastbourne

PREFACE

In presenting this record of the deeds of the Royal Marines in the War of 1914-1919 to my comrades, I wish to thank one and all for the great assistance they have so generously afforded me. Wherever possible an account has been obtained from an officer or man who took part in each incident and thus it is hoped to present a more intimate picture than would be possible from the official account alone.

H.M. the King, our Colonel-in-Chief, has graciously given permission for his portrait to be published as a frontispiece of this volume.

I am greatly indebted to the Adjutant-General, Major-General A. R. H. Hutchison, C.B., C.M.G., D.S.O. and the Staff of the Royal Marine Office for their assistance in enabling me to collate the official diaries and also to present so complete a record of the decorations and awards gained by members of the Corps.

Also to Colonel J. A. Tupman, O.B.E., who has undertaken the whole task of gathering subscribers and without whose able assistance this volume would never have seen the light.

I am much indebted to the author of the "History of the Royal Naval Division" and also to the two books "The Navy Everywhere" and "The Navy in East Africa" by Conrad Cato for several accounts of incidents that are not generally known and also to the numerous correspondents of the *Globe and Laurel,* mostly anonymous, whose records of interesting events often written at the time, I have shamelessly copied.

I am very grateful to those officers, who, like Colonel Channer, have hunted up individuals and induced them to write an account of their experiences: also to all those who at the sacrifice of much of their leisure time have written me most interesting accounts of the various units, among whom are Colonels R. Temple, J. A. M. A. Clark, ; Lieut.-Colonels A. G. Little, Pryce Peacock, G. L. Raikes, C. D'O H. Harmar, G. Carpenter, M. Filmer-Bennett, H. Ozanne, H. Channer; Majors C. Graham, C. F. Jerram, P. Sandilands, C. H. Coode, J. P. Nind, P. W. Malcolm, J. F. Ellison, A. L. Forster, E. J. Huskisson, G. H. Littleton, L. D. Briscoe, C. Attwood; Captains F. R. Jones, C. T. Brown, H. A. C. Webber, E. J. Noyes, L. S. Wilkinson, C. M. Sergeant, R. W. Spraggett, H. M. Leaf, A. E. Rann, S. Bucknall, R. C. Glunicke, R. H. P. West; Lieutenants C. A. Pearce, H. Gardner, P. R. Smith-Hill; Sergeant-Major J. Bach; Q.M.S. G. L. Barfield; Cr.-Sergt. W. Meatyard ; Sergeants Tucker, Cook, F. T. Jordan; Corporal C. Hoite; Private T. Grinham.

Lastly I wish to express my grateful thanks to Colonel Field not only for his sketches but also for his invaluable help in preparing the illustrations and also to Mr. de Lacy for so kindly allowing us to reproduce his picture of H.M.S. *Vindictive* at Zeebrugge, the original of which is now in the Officers' Mess at Deal.

The Controller of H.M. Stationery Office has also granted permission for the reproduction of the Maps which have been printed by the Ordnance Survey, and the Director of the Imperial War Museum has permitted the publication of some most interesting photographs.

January, 1927.

Royal Marines in the War of 1914-1919

H.M. King George V., Colonel-in-Chief, Royal Marines

Contents

PART I.

CHAPTER 1.   REINFORCEMENT OF THE PERSONNEL OF THE ROYAL NAVY.   Page, 3
Mobilisation - Recruiting-Ship's Complements - Naval Examination Service - Wireless Staffs - Naval Staff Officers - Transport Staffs - Special Orderlies - London Picquet.

PART II.
THE WAR AT SEA.

CHAPTER 2.   ACTIONS AND INCIDENTS, 1914-1916   Page, 11
Pursuit of Von Spee's Squadron-Chase of *Goeben* and *Breslau* - Sinking of *Konigin Luise* - Battle of Heligoland Bight - Duke of Cornwall's Light Infantry serve as Marines – Tsingtau - *Cap Trafalgar* - Sinking of *Aboukir, Cressy* and *Hogue* - Experiences in a Cruiser on patrol - *Pegasus* and *Konigsberg* – Bombardment of Dardanelles - Battle of Coronel - Battle of Falkland Islands - Armed Merchant Cruisers - Tanga, East Africa-Air Attack on Cuxhaven - Walfisch Bay-Battle of Dogger Bank - Destruction of *Koenigsberg* - Loss of H.M.S. *Hampshire*.

CHAPTER 3.   THE DARDANELLES - PER MARE   Page, 24
Naval Attack decided on - The Base at Mudros - The preliminary Bombardments - Landing of demolition Parties - The attack of 18th March - Preparations for the landing - Disposition of the Naval Forces - The landings - The feint landing at Bulair - Submarines - Albion ashore – R.N.A.S. - Monitors - Evacuation of Suvla - Evacuation of Helles - Honours and Rewards.

CHAPTER 4.   THE BATTLE OF JUTLAND   Page, 40

CHAPTER 5.   ACTIONS AND INCIDENTS, 1916-1919   Page, 52
Action in North Sea, August, 1916 - Guns at N. Foreland - *Swift* and *Broke* - Training of Royal Marines afloat - the Adriatic - Cruiser action North Sea, November, 1917 - Sortie of *Goeben* and *Breslau* - Award of Albert Medal to Lieut. Day – Armistice - Passage of Fleet to Constantinople - Surrender of German Fleet - King's Message to Royal Navy and Royal Marines - Honours and Rewards – Post - Armistice Operations.

CHAPTER 6.   BOMBARDMENTS   Page, 63
Belgian Coast, 1914 - Support of Expeditionary Forces - Palestine.

CHAPTER 7.   THE ANTI-SUBMARINE WAR   Page, 66
Defensively Armed Merchantmen - "Q" Boats - The *Baralong* - Defended Bases – Convoys - 5th R.M. Battalion.

CHAPTER 8.   RIVER OPERATIONS   Page, 71
Capture of Modyuski Island - River Dwina, North Russia, 1918-19 – Ussuri River, Siberia – Armoured Train, Siberia and Russia, 1918-19 – Kama River, Siberia, 1919.

APPENDIX TO PART II. Admiralty Orders re Medal Clasps   Page, 90

PART III.
NAVAL STRIKING FORCES.

CHAPTER 9.   FORMATION OF RM. BRIGADE AND EXPEDITION TO OSTEND   Page, 95

CHAPTER 10.   R.M.L.I. BRIGADE AT DUNKIRK AND ANTWERP   Page, 98
Re-organisation of RM. Brigade - The "Motor Bandits" - Dunkirk - Cassel - Action at Lierre - Antwerp - Retirement from Antwerp – Casualties - Honours and Rewards - Re-organisation of the Brigade-Staff of the Royal Naval Division.

CHAPTER 11.   THE DARDANELLES. PER TERRAM   Page, 111
Attachment to the Mediterranean Fleet - Landing of 4th March, 1915- "Y" Beach - Anzac - Kemal's Third Attack - Lance Corporal Parker gains the Victoria Cross - The Chessboard - Second Battle of Krithia - Third Battle of Krithia - Action of 12th and 13th July - Amalgamation of R.M. Battalions - The Evacuation of Helles- Stavros – Macedonia – Casualties - Honours and Rewards. - Officers of the Battalions.

CHAPTER 12.   ZEEBRUGGE - 4th BATTALION ROYAL MARINES   Page, 159
Formation of the Battalion – Training - Inspection by H.M. the King - Plan of the operations - Embarkation - Battalion Orders - List of Officers - First Attempts - H.M.S. *Vindictive* - The Operation on the Mole – Incidents - H.M.S. *Iris* – Casualties - Award of Victoria Cross - Honours and Awards - Letter from His Majesty - Dispersal.

CHAPTER 13.   ROYAL MARINES IN NORTH RUSSIA   Page, 182
H.M.S. *Glory* at Murmansk - H.M.S. *Cochrane* at Pechenga - Action with the White Finns - Operations in the White Sea – R.M. Field Force - Finnish Legion – Murmansk - Kem and Kandalaksha - Training on Skis - Actions at Maselskaya and Medveyja Gora - 6th R.M. Battalion - Actions at Ussuna - Koikori.

PART IV.
SHIPS' DETACHMENT LANDING PARTIES.

CHAPTER 14.   MEDITERRANEAN AND RED SEA   Page, 201
Coast of Syria.- H.M.S. *Doris*, 1914-15-Long Island, Smyrna.-Gulf of Akaba.

CHAPTER 15.   ROYAL MARINES IN GREECE   Page, 205
Occupation of Lipso Island-Athens, 1st December, 1916.

CHAPTER 16.   RED SEA   Page, 211
Action at Salif

CHAPTER 17.   PERSIAN GULF   Page, 213
Landing at Fao - Dilwar, 1915 - Bushire, 1915

CHAPTER 18.   THE CAMEROONS, 1914 - 1916   Page, 217
H.M.S. *Cumberland* at Victoria - Base at Suellaba Point - *Dwarf* and *Nachtigal* - Surrender of Duala - Action at Japoma Bridge - Edea Expedition - Buea Operations - Nyong River Operations - Campo River – Kribi - Nyong and Campo Rivers, 1915 - 1916.

CHAPTER 19.   COASTAL OPERATIONS IN EAST AFRICA   Page, 225
Tanga - Bweni Bluff – Sadani - Bagamoyo - Coastal operations August to September, 1916 - Lindi, etc. 1917 – 18 - Quilimane - Port Amelia.

PART V.
ADVANCED BASES.

CHAPTER 20.   THE SCOTTISH BASES   Page, 235
Cromarty – Aultbea - Inverness Firth - Kyles of Loch Alsh - Corpach.

CHAPTER 21.   ORKNEYS AND SHETLANDS   Page, 237
Scapa Flow-Shetlands.

CHAPTER 22.   ADVANCED BASES ABROAD   Page, 242
The Aegean Islands (Lemnos, Imbros, Tenedos)-3rd R.M. Battalion - The West Indies - St. Helena - Ascension.

CHAPTER 23.   THE CASPIAN NAVAL FORCE   Page, 253
Journey from Basra to the Caspian - Commissioning of the Squadron - Actions in the Sea - Naval Base at Petrovsk.

PART VI.
UNITS ATTACHED TO THE ARMY.

CHAPTER 24.   THE HOWITZER BRIGADE, ROYAL MARINE ARTILLERY   Page, 259
6-inch B.L. Batteries - Formation of Howitzer Brigade - Description of Howitzer and Mounting - Technical details - Personnel - Table of Battles and Actions in which Brigade was engaged - List of Commanding Officers - Summary of Diaries - Honours and Rewards.

APPENDIX TO CHAPTER 24. Services of Brigadier-General F. W. Lumsden, VC., C.B., D.S.O. and three Bars, R.M.A.   Page, 280

CHAPTER 25.   THE ANTI-AIRCRAFT BRIGADE, ROYAL MARINE ARTILLERY   Page, 283
Formation of Brigade – Equipment - Arrival at Dunkirk – Ypres - Formation of additional Batteries- "C" Battery   attached to Third Army - "B " Battery at Nieuport - Disbandment of Brigade - "B" Battery at Dunkirk - Formation   of Special Battery - Honours and Rewards.

CHAPTER 26.   R.M.L.I. BATTALIONS IN FRANCE, 1916 - 1919   Page, 293
Arrival in France – Re-organisation - Souchez Area - Trench Routine - Preparation for Beaumont Hamel - Wounding of General Paris - Battle of the Ancre - Operations on the Ancre, 11th January to 13th March, 1917 - Grandcourt – Miraumont - Battle of Arras - Second Battle of the Scarpe - Capture of Gavrelle - Battle of Arleux - Capture of Gavrelle Windmill - The Gavrelle Sector, 1917 - Machine Gun Company - Trench Mortar Battery - Battles of Ypres, 1917 - Second Battle of Passchendaele - Welch Ridge - Flesquieres Salient - March Retreat - First Battle of the Somme - Battle of St. Quentin - First Battle of Bapaume - Rearguard at Bertincourt - Crossing of the Ancre - Aveluy Wood - Aveluy Wood, April - Amalgamation of Battalions – Training - Second Battles of the Somme -Battle of Albert - Logeast Wood – Loupart Wood and Le Barque - Second Battles of

Arras - Battle of Drocourt - Queant Line - Attacks on the Canal du Nord - Battle of the Canal du Nord – Anneux – Cambrai - Battle of Cambrai – Niergnies, - The Pursuit to Mons - The Armistice - Official Entry into Mons – Demobilisation - Return to England - Speech of H.RH. the Prince of Wales – Dispersal - List of Honours.

CHAPTER 27. ROYAL MARINE BATTERIES IN EAST AFRICA Page, 362
Formation of the Batteries - Action at Salaita – Latema – Reata - Advance down Pangani River - No. 15 Battery to Morogoro - The Rufigi River - No. 16 Battery in Myanna Column - Four-inch gun at Lindi - Actions at Tandamuti Hill and at Narunyu - Advance on Nyangao - Honours and Rewards – Numbers.

CHAPTER 28. ROYAL MARINE MOTOR TRANSPORT COMPANY Page, 371
Formation – Antwerp - St. Omer – Ypres – Inventions – Disbandment - Honours and Rewards.

CHAPTER 29. ROYAL MARINES ATTACHED TO ROYAL GARRISON ARTILLERY Page, 375
Siege Batteries in France - Coast Defences in England.

PART VII.
MISCELLANEOUS.

CHAPTER 30. THE ROYAL MARINES IN SERBIA Page, 381
Arrival in Serbia – Distribution - Battle of Belgrade-Retreat to Salonica - Retreat to San Giovanni di Medua - Honours and Rewards.

CHAPTER 31. ROYAL MARINE ARTILLERY BATTERY IN EGYPT, 1915-1916 Page, 386
Alexandria – Mersa Matruh - Sollum.

CHAPTER 32. SOUTH AFRICAN HEAVY ARTILLERY, R.M.A. CONTINGENT Page, 388
Organisation - Campaign in German South - West Africa - Formation of the South African Heavy Brigade - Services in France.

CHAPTER 33. ROYAL MARINE BATTALION IN IRELAND, APRIL-MAY, 1916 Page, 391

CHAPTER 34. ROYAL MARINE ARTILLERY, HEAVY SIEGE TRAIN AT DUNKIRK Page, 394
Evolution of Train – Incidents - Nieuport, 1917 - 0stend, 1918 - British Offensive, 1918 - Honours and Rewards.

CHAPTER 35. VARIOUS INCIDENTS Page, 402
Dardanelles, 1918 – Sevastopol - Bosphorus - Buda Pesth - Singapore, 1914 - New Guinea.

PART VIII.
SPECIAL UNITS.

CHAPTER 36. ROYAL MARINE SUBMARINE MINERS Page, 409

CHAPTER 37. ROYAL MARINE UNITS IN THE ROYAL NAVAL DIVISION Page, 411
Divisional Engineers - Divisional Train - Medical Unit.

CHAPTER 38. ROYAL MARINE LABOUR CORPS Page, 422
France - Home Service.

CHAPTER 39. ROYAL MARINE ENGINEERS Page, 427

PART IX.
ADMINISTRATION AND TRAINING.

CHAPTER 40. ADMINISTRATIVE ARRANGEMENTS OF THE CORPS AT HOME Page, 433
Numbers - Royal Marine Office - R.M. Headquarters – Mobilisation - R.M. Acts, 1914 – 1916 – Officers - Recruiting - Records, Pay, etc - Bands – W.R.N.S. - Equipment - Prisoners of War Comforts Fund. - Table of Strengths.

CHAPTER 41. TRAINING ARRANGEMENTS Page, 442
Recruit Courses - R.M.A. Brigade Depot - 1st Reserve Battalion, R.M.L.I .- Courses at Headquarters - Physical Training School - School of Musketry - Blandford.

APPENDICES.

1. CASUALTIES FROM 4th AUGUST, 1914 TO 5th APRIL, 1919 Page, 448
2. SERVICES OF ROYAL MARINES WITH UNITS OTHER THAN ROYAL MARINES Page, 449
3. DECORATIONS, BRITISH AND FOREIGN Page, 454

INDEX Page, 464

Royal Marines in the War of 1914-1919

ILLUSTRATIONS.	PAGE
Frontispiece - H.M. King George V., Colonel-in-Chief, Royal Marines	vi
No. 1. Gallipoli-" V" Beach and Sedd-ul-Bahr Fort; "W" Beach,	33
No. 2. Major F. J. W. Harvey, V.C., R.M.L.I.	43
No. 3. Major-General Sir A. Paris, K.C.B., R.M.A.	105
No. 4. Lance-Corporal W. R. Parker, V.C., R.M.L.I.	123
No. 5. Anzac - Shrapnel Valley; Walker's Ridge	125
No. 6. Brigadier-General C. N. Trotman, C.B., R.M.L.I.	129
No. 7. Gallipoli - View of Anzac; Achi Baba Nullah	133
No. 8. Gallipoli - Troops of R.N. Division attacking, 1915; General view of Helles Sector looking towards Achi Baba	140
No. 9. Brigadier-General D. Mercer, C.B., R.M.L.I.	147
No. 10. Officers, 4th Battalion, Royal Marines	167
No. 11. Boat Deck of H.M.S. *Vindictive*	169
No. 12. H.M.S. *Vindictive* and *Daffodil* alongside the Mole at Zeebrugge (from the painting by Mr. de Lacey)	175
No. 13. H.M.S. *Iris* (from a sketch by Colonel C. Field, R.M.L.I.)	177
No. 14. Captain and Brevet Major E. Bamford, V.C., D.S.O., R.M.L.I.	179
No. 15. Sergeant N. A. Finch, V.C., R.M.A.	183
No. 16. Scapa Flow in winter, Holm Battery; Alexandria, 4-inch gun in Battery.	241
No. 17. Mudros Harbour, Lemnos	248
No. 18. Lieut.- Colonel G. R. Poole, C.M.G., D.S.O., R.M.A.	263
No. 19. France - 15-inch Howitzer preparing to fire; 15-inch Howitzer in action	266
No. 20. Brigadier - General F. W. Lumsden, V.C., C.B., D.S.O., R.M.A.	283
No. 21. Lieut.- Colonel A. R H. Hutchison, C.B., C.M.G., D.S.O., R.M.L.I.	302
No. 22. France - Troops resting prior to an attack; Troops returning from front line, Ypres Salient, 1917	312
No. 23. France - Troops resting in a support trench; Troops waiting to attack in the Canal du Nord	344
No. 24. East Africa-4-inch gun in action; RM. Battery crossing the Rufigi River	tt
No. 25. Dunkirk - Mounting the guns of the Heavy Siege Train	400
No. 26. France - Transport crossing the Canal du Nord; Men of R.M. Medical Unit with captured German Doctors	420
No. 27. Lieutenant - Colonel H. E. Blumberg, A.A.G., R.M.	440

PLANS.	PAGE.
No. 1. The Dardanelles Forts	25
No. 2. Panorama Sketch of " V " Beach (Lieut. C. H. Congdon, R.M.L.I.)	32
No. 3. North Russia, 1918-19	72
No. 4. River Dwina, Russia	72
No. 5. General Map of Eastern Russia	82
No. 6. Russia and Siberia - River Kama	85
No. 7. Gallipoli - Trench Map - Helles Area Right Sector	129
No. 8. Gallipoli - Action 13th July, 1915	135
No. 9. "V" Beach and Evacuation Rendezvous	140

Illustrations

No. 10. Positions of 2/R.M.L.I. at Evacuation of Helles	142
No. 11. The Mole, Zeebrugge	160
No. 12. North Russia Operations at Ussuna, Koikori. Etc.	194
No. 13. Athens - 1st December, 1916	208
No. 14. Red Sea - Salif	212
No. 15. Persian Gulf, 1915	215
No. 16. The Cameroons	219
No. 17. East African Campaign	227
No. 18. East Africa - Capture of Bagamoyo	229
No. 19. France - Capture of Gavrelle Windmill	308
No. 20. France - Battle of Passchendaele, 26th October; 1917	313
No. 21. France - Breaking of Drocourt - Queant Line and attacks on Canal du Nord	342
No. 22. Belgium - Position of 1st R.M.L.I. at Armistice, 11th November, 1918	354

EDITOR'S NOTE

General Blumberg's book has been reproduced as closely as possible to the original. I have kept his spelling and punctuation, which may seem a little strange to today's reader, but this is the way he wrote it and was obviously the custom of the time. Where the spelling in the sketches differs from the text I have used the spelling in the text. Because this book has been much reduced in size from the original many of the sketches became virtually unreadable and so many thanks to Tim Mitchell for producing typed labels for many of the more complex sketches. However a few of the sketches in the original 1927 edition were already illegible and so regrettably they inevitably remain so in this edition. Tim is also responsible for bringing this book down to a more manageable size.

The reader will find references to Maps 1-7, which were included in an envelope on the inside of the original's hardback cover. These maps were printed in the 1920s and contained no military positions or lines from the many battles on the Western Front. They have not been reproduced in this edition for reasons of cost, but the purist may still find them in the original versions. I have left the references in for authenticity.

Reproducing Blumberg's book has been an immense labour that has taken the team over eighteen months. I am indebted to members of the RMHS who have assisted; scanning the original document was undertaken by Alastair Donald, Paul Whitehead and John Rawlinson whilst John Gilbert completed the first draft of corrections. The index is entirely new and for which I am most grateful to Colonel Michael Reece OBE and Mr Leslie Rawlinson. Tim Mitchell's design has transformed the readability of this book. The original book remains an outstanding research document, but now thanks to the team at the RMHS it makes the information within more accessible and easier to read.

Brian Carter
August 2014

CHRONOLOGICAL INDEX.
1914.

AUGUST-
2	Mobilisation of Pensioners and Reserves
	Commencement of Formation of RM. Brigade
4	War declared with Germany. King's Pardon to Deserters
6	Action in North Sea. H.M.S. *Amphion* mined
	Engagement between H.M.S. *Bristol* and *Karlsruhe*
7	R.M. Brigade concentrated at Eastney and Gosport
8	Declaration of War with Austria
11	Goeben and Breslau chased into the Dardanelles
12	Capture of the Spreewald by *H.M.S. Berwick*
20	R.M. Battalions return to their own Divisions
25-31	Expedition to Ostend
26	H.M.S. *Highflyer* v. *Kaiser Wilhelm der Grosse*
28	Battle of Heligoland Bight
	Detachment of 2/D.C.L.1. embarked as Marines in China
	Royal Marines Act, 1914
	Reinforcement of garrison at Ascension

SEPTEMBER-
2	Attack on Tsingtau commenced
4	Landing party at Victoria, Cameroons
9	Bombardment and Landing at Suellaba Point, Cameroons
11	200 R.M.A. and R.M.L.I. to Dunkirk for service with Motor Cars of R.N.A.S.
12	R.M.L.I. Brigade concentrated at Walmer
14	H.M.S. *Carmania* v. *Cap Trafalgar*
19	R.M.L.I. Brigade embark for Dunkirk
20	H.M.S. *Pegasus* v. *Koenigsberg* at Zanzibar
	Grant of Temporary Commissions for the War authorised
	Recruiting for duration of the War opened
22	Sinking of H.M.S. *Aboukir*, *Cressy* and *Hogue*
25	Col. A. Paris, R.M.A. assumes command of the R.M. Brigade
27	Occupation of Duala, Cameroons
	Reinforcement of garrison at St. Helena

OCTOBER-
1	Affair at Douai, France
2	Action at Japoma Bridge, Cameroons
3-4	R.M. Brigade arrive in Antwerp
4-10	Defence of Antwerp
6	First attack on Jabassi, Cameroons
12	R.M.L.I. Brigade return to England
14	Occupation of Jabassi, Cameroons
15	H.M.S. *Hawke* sunk in the North Sea
	R.M. Motor Transport Company lent to the Army at St. Omer
17	Undaunted and Destroyers in action with German T.B.D.'s
18-26	Bombardments of the Belgian Coast
	Landing from the Monitors
19- 22 Nov.	First Battle of Ypres
20-26	Expedition to Edea, Cameroons
21	R.M.A. Contingent for South African H.A. leave England
26	German Attack on Nieuport broken by H.M.S. *Venerable*
27	H.M.S. *Audacious* sunk
30	Location of *Koenigsberg* in Rufigi River
31	H.M.S. *Hermes* sunk
	Formation of Divisional Engineers commenced

NOVEMBER-
1	Declaration of War with Turkey
	Battle of Coronel
3	German Raid on East Coast of England
	Bombardment of the Dardanelles Forts
	Attack on Tanga, East Africa
	Armoured Car Detachment return to England
4	Operations at Akaba
7	Capitulation of Tsingtau
7-8	Landing at Fao, Persian Gulf

Chronological Index

9	Sinking of *Emden* by H.M.A.S. *Sydney*
12-18	Buea Operations, Cameroons
17	Lieut.-Colonel Harris assumes command of Defences at Scapa Flow
19	Capture of Sheik Said, Red Sea
	Air Raid on Airship sheds at Dusseldorf
	R.M.A. Contingent arrive in South Africa
26	H.M.S. *Bulwark* blown up at Sheerness
28 & 30	East Africa-Bombardments of Dar -Es - Salaam
	Formation of Divisional Train, Royal Marines, commenced
	Formation of Medical Unit, Royal Marines, commenced
	Replacement of *Edgar* Class Cruisers by Armed Merchantmen

DECEMBER-
1	C. II. Battery S.A.H.A. to Luderitzbucht
8	Battle of the Falkland Islands
16	German Raid on Hartlepool and Scarborough
19	Occupation of Nyong, Cameroons
20	Occupation of Kribi, Cameroons
20-27	Occupation of Campo, Cameroons
25	Air Raid on Cuxhaven
	Landing of General Botha's Force at Walfisch Bay
	C.I. Battery, S.A.H.A. to Walfisch Bay
27	R.N. and R.M. Detachment leave Malta for Serbia
31	H.M.S. *Doris* on Syrian Coast
	Skirmish at Akaba

1915.

JANUARY-
1	H.M.S. *Doris* on the Syrian Coast
	Sinking of H.M.S. *Formidable*
6	Operations in Campo Area, Cameroons
7	Naval and Marine Detachment arrives in Belgrade
24	Battle of the Dogger Bank, North Sea

FEBRUARY-
2-5	Turkish Attacks on the Suez Canal
5	Formation of R.M. Submarine Miners authorised
6	R.M.L.I. Brigade less Portsmouth and Deal Battalions leaves for the Mediterranean
15-23	Mutiny at Singapore
19-20	Bombardment of Dardanelles Forts commenced
21	R.M.L.I. Brigade arrive at the Dardanelles
25-26	Bombardments continued
26	Fleet landing parties at Dardanelles
25	Actions at Nonidas and Goaknontes, G.S.W. Africa
	R.M. Garrison, Kribi, Cameroons

MARCH-
1	R.N. Division embark for the Dardanelles
	R.M.L.I. Brigade less Portsmouth and Deal Battalions to Imbros
3	Bombardments resumed
4	Landing at Dardanelles by Plymouth Battalion
5	Bombardment of Smyrna
6	First Howitzer, R.M.A. fired in France
6-7	Bombardments renewed
7	Action between *Lord Nelson* and *Agamemnon* with Forts at the Narrows
8	*Dresden* chased to Juan Fernandez
10-13	Battle of Neuve Chapelle, France
11	Bulair Lines bombarded
13-14	H.M.S. *Amethyst* at the Dardanelles
14	*Dresden* sunk in the Pacific
16	Demonstration by *Canopus* at Gaba Tepe, Dardanelles
18	Grand Attack by Fleet on Dardanelles
18	H.M.S. *Dreadnought* sinks German submarine in North Sea
19	Demonstration off Gaba Tepe
26	No. 3 Howitzer, R.M.A. Embarks for France
29- 7 April	R.M.L.I. Brigade in Egypt

APRIL-
11	Renewal of Bombardments at the Dardanelles
11-13	Advance of Jaunde R.M. Operations at Kribi, Cameroons
12	No. 3. Howitzer, R.M.A. leaves France for Dardanelles

14	No. 4. Howitzer, R.M.A. Embarks for France
18	Bombardment and Reconnaissance of Forts, Dardanelles
22	Sinking of Austrian Monitor on the Danube
23	Headquarters and "B" and part "C" Batteries, A.A. Brigade, R.M.A. Reach Dunkirk
24	Fleet leaves Mudros for Dardanelles
25	LANDINGS AT GALLIPOLI
	Plymouth Battalion at "Y" Beach
25-26	Feint Landings at Bulair
26	Action at Trekkopjes, G.S.W. Africa
28	R.M.L.I. Brigade less Plymouth and Deal Battalions at Anzac
28	"B" Battery, A.A. Brigade, R.M.A. In action for first time
29	1st R.N. Brigade with Deal Battalion land at Anzac
30	Turkish attacks at Anzac
	Lance-Corporal W. R. Parker gains the Victoria Cross
	Staff and Officers of Royal Marine Battalions in Gallipoli

MAY-

1	Turkish attacks at Anzac
2	Message from H.M. The King to the Forces in Gallipoli
3	Attacks on the Chessboard, Anzac. Black Monday
4	Landing at Gaba Tepe
6-8	Second Battle of Krithia
7	*Lusitania* sunk off Queenstown
8-13	Battle of Frezenberg Ridge
9	Bombardment of Dardanelles and Smyrna
	Battle of Aubers Ridge
10	Affair at Quin's Post, Anzac
	Turkish counter attack at Helles
12	Sinking of H.M.S. *Goliath*
	R.M.L.I. Brigade leaves Anzac for Helles
13	1st R.N. Brigade leaves Anzac for Helles
15	Battle of Festubert, France
16	Volunteers from Officers, R.M. Afloat to replace casualties in the R.M. Brigade
17	First German Submarine arrives at Dardanelles
19	Second Squadron left Dardanelles for Adriatic
23	H.M.S. *Albion* and *Canopus* at Gaba Tepe
24	A.A. Guns gassed at Ypres
	Night Advance and construction of Mercer Road, Dardanelles
26	H.M.S. *Triumph* sunk
27	Night Advance by R.M. Brigade and construction of Trotman Road, Dardanelles
	H.M.S. *Majestic* sunk

JUNE-

4	Third Battle of Krithia
6	Action at Kanli Dere
16	A.A. Brigade in action at Ypres
20	France-First Battle of Bellewarde
21	Gallipoli -Third Action of Kereves Dere
22	Action at Kalkfeldt, G.S.W. Africa
23	Dardanelles. The Rectangle
24-25	Gallipoli - Construction of Parsons' Road, Helles

JULY-

6-11	East Africa-Action with *Koenigsberg*
8-15	Operations in Nyong River, Cameroons
12-13	Gallipoli. Action of Achi Baba Nullah
16	Belgium. Action at Nieuport

AUGUST-

2	"A " Battery, A.A. Brigade formed
	R.M. Brigade organised into two Battalions
6	Gallipoli. Landing at Suvla Bay
6-7	Gallipoli. Action of Krithia Vineyard
	Operations on Campo River, Cameroons
9-14	Operations at Dilwar, Persian Gulf
15	Gallipoli. RN. Division takes over left section of line
24	One gun of "C" battery A.A. Brigade destroyed at Ypres
28	South African Heavy Artillery leave for England

SEPTEMBER-

Chronological Index

9	Defence of Bushire, Persian Gulf
19	Gallipoli. First leave party for Imbros
25-28	France. Battle of Loos
26-28	France. Second Battle of Bellewarde
28	"D" Battery, A.A. Brigade, R.M.A. Completed
	Cameroons - Operations on Campo River

OCTOBER-
3-8	Serbia, Battle of Belgrade
5	First troops landed at Salonica
6	Serbia. Battle of Semendria
	Cameroons. Affair at Moloko Post
16	R.M.A. Battery for Serbia leaves England
21	Bombardment of Dedeagatch, Bulgaria
22	France. "C" Battery, A.A. Brigade to Louvencourt
24	Serbia, Commencement of the Retreat
26	"A" Battery, A.A. Brigade, bring down Aviatik plane at Ypres
	Gallipoli. Heavy enemy shelling
	Scapa Flow. Increase of Garrison

NOVEMBER-
3-11	Rear Guard Actions in Serbia
5-6	Cameroons. Affairs at Metum and Mbula
10-19	Lord Kitchener at the Dardanelles
13	Commands and Staff in R.M. Brigade
21	Serbia. Detachments reach Salonica
27-28	Great Blizzard in Gallipoli and Salonica

DECEMBER-
2	Destruction of Kavak Bridge. Gulf of Xeros
8	Action at Nieuport, Belgium
12	Gallipoli. RM. Battalions take over French Sector
13	Nos. 5 and 6 Howitzers, R.M.A. arrive in France
19	Gallipoli. Evacuation of Anzac and Suvla
25	Gallipoli. Bombardment of Achi Baba
	Belgium. Action at Nieuport
26	Egypt. R.M.A. Guns at Mersa Matruh
27	Serbia. R.M. Detachment reach San Giovanni di Medua
31	H.M.S. *Natal* blown up (Errata)

1916.

JANUARY-
3	Dardanelles. Bombardment of Asiatic Coast
6	H.M.S. *King Edward VII*. Sunk
8-9	GALLIPOLI. EVACUATION OF HELLES SECTOR
28	Occupation of Fort Touzla, Salonica
	Dardanelles Campaign. Officers' Casualties
	Dardanelles Campaign. Honours and Rewards

FEBRUARY-
11	H.M.S. *Arethusa* sunk
14	East Africa. Formation of R.M. Batteries
22 - 16 April	Macedonia. R.M.L.I. Battalions at Stavros
29	H.M.S. *Alcantara* v *Greif*

MARCH-
8	East Africa. Action at Salaita
10	East Africa. Action at Latema-Reata
16	Egypt. R.M.A. Gun at Sollum
25	North Sea. Light Cruiser Action

APRIL-
1	Cameroons. Withdrawal of British Forces
16 - 27 May	Smyrna. Occupation of Long Island
22	France. No.8 Howitzer R.M.A. Arrives
25	Bombardment of Lowestoft
27	H.M.S. *Russell* sunk in the Mediterranean
	Irish Rebellion. Portsmouth Company arrive Queenstown
27 - 15 May	RM. Battalion in Ireland

XV

	Dunkirk. " Dominion" 12-inch gun mounted
MAY-	
4	Air and Cruiser Raid on Tondern
5	Zeppelin brought down at Salonica
19-20	R.N. Division arrives in France
27	France. German attack on Vimy Ridge
31	BATTLE OF JUTLAND
	Award of Victoria Cross to Major F. Harvey, R.M.L.I.
	Formation of 190th Machine Gun Company
JUNE-	
5	Loss of H.M.S. *Hampshire* and death of Lord Kitchener
7	East Africa. Occupation of Tanga
24	R.M. Cyclist Company disbanded
	Headquarters, A.A. Brigade, R.M.A. Return to England
JULY-	
1	Battle of the Somme commences
1-13	Battle of Albert
13	France. 1/R.M.L.I. Take over trenches for the first time
14-17	Battle of Bazentin Ridge
15 - 3 Sept.	Battle of Delville Wood
20	R.N. Division renumbered 63rd (R.N.) Division
22-26	East Africa. Capture of Bweni Bluff and Pangani
23 - 3 Sept.	France. Battle of Pozieres Ridge
27-29	East Africa. Capture of Mkwadja
	Royal Marines Act, 1916
	Formation of 1st Reserve Battalion, R.M.L.I.
	Institution of RM. School of Musketry
AUGUST-	
1	East Africa. Occupation of Sadani
10	H.M.S. *India* torpedoed
15	East Africa. Capture of Bagamoyo
17	France. Reconnaissance Patrols at Angres
19	North Sea. Cruiser Action
21	East Africa. Bombardment of Dar-Es-Salaam
26	East Africa. Occupation of Morogoro
SEPTEMBER-	
2-5	East Africa. Occupation of Dar-Es-Salaam
3-6	France. Battle of Guillemont
7	East Africa. Occupation of Kilwa Kiwinte and Kilwa Kisiwane
9	France. Battle of Ginchy
13	East Africa. Mikindani
15-22	France. Battle of Flers-Courcellette
17	East Africa. Occupation of Lindi
18	East Africa. Occupation of Kiswere
25-28	France. Battle of Morval
26-28	France. Battle of Thiepval Ridge
OCTOBER-	
1-18	France. Battle of the Transloy Ridge
10 - 11 Nov.	Battle of the Ancre Heights
11	Greece. Occupation of Lipso Island
13	France. General Paris wounded. Major Sketchley killed
NOVEMBER-	
13-15	BATTLE OF THE ANCRE-BEAUMONT HAMEL
24	Aegean Islands. 3rd R.M. Battalion takes over the garrison
	France. First R.M. Band sent to France for temporary duty
DECEMBER-	
1	Greece. Landing Party at Athens

1917.

JANUARY-

Chronological Index

1-2	East Africa. Action at Mgeta
	H.M.S. *Cornwallis* sunk in the Mediterranean
12	Red Sea. Capture of Salif
22	Destroyer Action in North Sea

FEBRUARY-
2	Formation of Heavy Siege Train. R.M.A.
	France. Formation of R.M. Labour Corps
6-7	France. Occupation of Grandcourt
17-18	France. Action of Miraumont
25	German Torpedo Boats bombard Margate

MARCH-
16	Sinking of German Raider *Leopard*
	Dunkirk. "B" Bn. A.A. Brigade armed with 3-inch guns
	N. Foreland. 6-inch guns mounted by R.M.
	Divisional Engineers R.M. transferred to Royal Engineers

APRIL-
7	Major F. W. Lumsden. R.M.A. gains the Victoria Cross
9-14	France. Battle of Vimy Ridge
9-14	France. First Battle of the Scarpe
21	H.M.S. *Swift* and *Broke* v. German Destroyers
28-29	France. Battle of Arleux
28	CAPTURE OF GAVRELLE WINDMILL

MAY-
3-4	France. Third Battle of the Scarpe
5-17	France. Battle of Bullecourt
15	Adriatic. Cruiser action
12	RM. Detachments leave England for West Indies
20 - 16 June	Actions in the Hindenburg Line

JUNE-
3-25	France. Souchez River
7	Battle of Messines
26-29	France. Capture of Avion
28	Capture of Oppy Wood and First Attack on Bullecourt
28	France. Lord Charles Beresford inspects R.M.L.I. Battalions
June-July	East Africa. Port Amelia

JULY-
9	H.M.S. *Vanguard* blown up
10-11	Belgium. German Attack on Nieuport
10	No. 12 Howitzer in Ypres
15	North Sea. Cruiser Action
18	France. New trench dug in front of Gavrelle Windmill
31	Belgium. Ammunition Dump blown up at Nieuport

AUGUST-
1-2	Flanders Battle of Pilkem Ridge
3	East Africa. Affair at Tandamuti
15-25	Flanders. Battle of Hill 70
16-18	Flanders. Battle of Langemarck
18	East Africa. Affair at Narunyu
	West Indies. Guns ready for action

SEPTEMBER-
9	Flanders. Affair at Nieuport
20-25	Flanders. Battle of Menin Road
	Scapa Flow. Further increase of garrison

OCTOBER-
4	Flanders. Battle of Broodseinde
9	Flanders. Battle of Poecapelle
	Treaty of Brest-Litovsk
12	First Battle of Passchendaele
26 - 12 Nov.	Second Battle of Passchendaele
27	Palestine. Third Battle of Gaza

Royal Marines in the War of 1914-1919

NOVEMBER-
- 3 — North Sea. Light Cruiser Action
- 17 — North Sea. Light Cruiser Action
- 20 - 3 Dec. — France. Battle of Cambrai
- 30 — France. No. I Howitzer R.M.A. at Gouzeaucourt
  - Aegean Islands. Royal Marines take over charge

DECEMBER-
- 16 — RM. Labour Company takes over duty at Granton
- 30 — France. Action of Welch Ridge

1918

JANUARY-
- 3 — Bombardment of Yarmouth
- 20 — Dardanelles. Sortie of *Goeben* and *Breslau*
- 21 — East Africa. R.M. Batteries leave for home
  - Shetland Islands. Increase of R.M. Garrison

FEBRUARY-
- 14 — France. Brigades of R.N. Division reorganised into three Battalions
- 21 — Zeebrugge. 4th RM. Battalion concentrated at Deal
  - Formation of 5th RM. Battalion commenced

MARCH-
- 1 — RN. Division Machine Gun Battalion formed
- 7 — Inspection of Depot, Royal Marines, Deal by H.M. the King
- 9 — France. Trench Raid by 2/R.M.L.I.
- 18 — Dunkirk. Bombardment of Carnac Battery
- 21 — France. Battle of St. Quentin, Commencement of the Retreat
- 22 — 2/R.M.L.I. beat off attack in Havrincourt Wood
  - No.1 Howitzer R.M.A. near Metz
  - No. 10 Howitzer R.M.A. in Havrincourt Wood
- 24-25 — First Battle of Bapaume
- 24 — Action at Bertincourt
- 25 — Rear Guard Action at Thiepval - Martinpuich
- 26 — No.6 Howitzer at Neuville Vitasse.
  - R.N. Division withdraws across the Ancre River
- 27 — Counter attack by 188th Brigade in Aveluy Wood
  - Casualties in the Retreat
  - Formation of Royal Marine Engineers commenced

APRIL-
- 3 — Siberia. Landing Party at Vladivostock
- 5 — France. Counter-attack by R.M.L.I.; Battalions in Aveluy Wood
- 8 — Orders for attack on Zeebrugge Mole
- 10-11 — Flanders. Battle of Messines
- 10 — Flanders. N0.5 Howitzer, R.M.A. at Kemmel
- 11 — Zeebrugge. First Attempt
- 15 — Cruiser Raid on Kattegat
- 23 — ST. GEORGE'S DAY. ZEEBRUGGE-OSTEND
- 29 — Flanders. Battle of Schepenberg Ridge
  - Amalgamation of 1st and 2nd Battalions, R.M.L.I.
  - Recruits, Royal Marines, lent to R.G.A.
  - Zeebrugge. Casualties
  - Bases established at Kyles of Loch Alsh and Inverness, etc.

MAY-
- 3 — No. 527 Battery mobilised
- 7 — No. 525 Battery mobilised
- 8 — Blocking of Ostend
- 8-10 — North Russia. Affair at Pechenga
- 9 — No. 526 Battery mobilised
- 10 — No. 528 Battery mobilised
- 18-19 — France. Outpost raid by 1/R.M.L.I. at Hamel
- 20 — North Russia. R.M. Field Force embarks
- 24-25 — France. Raid on German Trenches, Ancre Valley
- 31 — North Russia. R.M. Field Force lands at Murmansk

JUNE-

Chronological Index

8	North Russia. R.M. Contingent sent to raise Finnish Legion
29-30	North Russia. Disarmament of Bolsheviks
29	Siberia. Disarmament of Bolsheviks at Vladivostock
	Landing and Fortification of Quilimane, East Africa
	Special A.A. Battery to Dunkirk

JULY-
7	White Sea. Affair at Soroka
17	North Russia. Finnish Legion in action
31	North Russia. Allied Force leaves for Archangel
	R.M. Guard at Corfu

AUGUST-
1	White Sea. Capture of Modyuski Batteries
8	France. Commencement of the British Offensive
8-28	Siberia. Ussuri River Operations
11	North Sea. Action off the Frisian Coast
	Naval and Marine parties leave Basra to join the Dunster Force
18	Flanders. Action of Outsteen Ridge
	Formation of No. I Siege Battery, R.M.A.
21-23	Battle of Albert; Logeast Wood
25	France. Action at Grevillers and Le Barque
26 - 15 Sept.	Caspian. Defence of Baku
29	Siberia. Armoured Train leaves Vladivostock for River Volga
31 - 2 Sept.	Second Battle of Bapaume

SEPTEMBER-
2-3	BATTLE OF DROCOURT-QUEANT LINE
4	Attacks on Canal du Nord
5	Guns and Royal Marines leave Ruz for Caspian Sea
12	France. Battle of Havrincourt
14	North Russia. Action at Chamova, River Dwina
18	France. Battle of Epehy
27	France. Battle of Canal du Nord. Capture of Annuex
28	Flanders. Offensive. 9.2 inch gun on Railway Mounting
28-29	France. Bridging of Canal de L'Escaut
28 - 3 Oct.	Battle of Ypres
29	France. Seizing of Crossings of the Escaut
29-30	France. Attacks on Cambrai
30	Armistice with Bulgaria
29 Sept - 20 Oct.	Battle of St. Quentin Canal

OCTOBER-
1	Attack on strong point at Cambrai
7	Formation of "A" 'Hun' Battery
8-9	Battle of Cambrai. Capture of Niergnies
10	Dunkirk. A.A. Battery at Nieuport fired last shot
11	South Russia. Armoured Train at Ufa
12	Formation of No.2 Siege Battery. R.M.A.
14-16	Offensive in Belgium
17-25	Battle of Selle
31	Armistice with Turkey
	Commissioning of ships on the Caspian

NOVEMBER-
4	Armistice with Austria
5-11	Pursuit to Mons
5-7	Battle of the Sambro
6	Caspian Reconnaissance of Fort Alexandrovsk
9	H.M.S. *Britannia* sunk
11	Capture of Mons
	ARMISTICE WITH GERMANY
	H.M. the King's Message to the Fleet
12	Occupation of Forts in the Dardanelles
12	Allied Fleet passes through the Dardanelles
14	Occupation of the Forts in the Bosphorus
14	Guard of Honour at Constantinople
15	Official Entry into Mons
16	Armoured Train in action on River Volga
21	SURRENDER OF GERMAN HIGH SEA FLEET

Strength of the Corps at the Armistice

DECEMBER-
1	Sevastopol. Detachment of H.M.S. *Temeraire* landed
9	Occupation of the town by the 3rd R.M. Battalion
8	Action in the Caspian Sea
17	Royal Marine Field Force concentrated at Kandalaksha, North Russia
19-24	Armoured Train reaches Tisidma, European Russia and in action
29	Caspian Sea. Bombardment of Star-Tchernaya
30	Sevastopol handed over to the French

1919.

Feb-Mar.	Baltic. Operations at Libau and Riga
13 Feb.	West Indian garrisons return to England
21	Caspian. Opening of Base at Petrovsk
10 Mar.	North Russia. R.M. Field Force training at Kem
25	North Russia. H.M.S. *Glory's* Detachment to Knabja Ghuba
20 Jan - 17 Mar.	Detachment from H.M.S. *Suffolk* in garrison at Omsk, Siberia
15 April	Siberia, Royal Marines from *Kent* relief *Suffolk's*
17-22	Crimea. Operations off Sevastopol
19	Caspian. Cruiser Action
3 May	North Russia. R.M. Field Force advance and capture Maselskaya
6	Siberia. Commissioning of *Kent* and *Suffolk* at Perm
14	Siberia. Affair on Viatka River
17-18	North Russia. Capture of Medveyja Gora
21	Caspian. Bombardment of Fort Alexandrovsk
24	Siberia. Action at Elabouga
29-30	Siberia. Action at Bielaya River
June	Operations in Crimea
3	Siberia. Action at Sarapoul
4-10	Siberia. Engagements on Kama River
6	Inspection of Details, R.N. Division by H.R.H. the Prince of Wales
14-15	Details of R.M.A. Howitzer Brigade return to Eastney
19-21	North Russia. Actions at Topsa and Troitsa
28	Siberia. *Kent* and *Suffolk* dismantled at Perm
8 July	North Russia. Action at Troitsa, River Dwina
16	North Russia. R.M. Field Force embark for England
1 August	Crimea. Bombardment of Kinburn
1-8	South Russia. Operations on River Bug and River Dnieper
1	6th R.M. Battalion embarks for North Russia
10 Aug.	North Russia. Action on Selmenga River, River Dwina
17	North Russia. Action on Railway
30	North Russia. First Skirmish at Koikori
2 Sept.	Caspian. Force leaves Petrovsk
8-10	North Russia. Action at Ussuna and Koikori
16	North Russia. Affair on Vaga River. River Dwina
30	North Russia. Evacuation of Archangel
8 Oct.	North Russia. 6th R.M. Battalion embarks for England

NOTE.-The following witnessed the signature of the Treaty of Peace at Versailles on 28th June on behalf of the Royal Marine Corps-

Act.-Sergeant W. H. Beirne, Chatham R.M.L.I.
Act.-Sergeant G. H. Locker, Plymouth R.M.L.I.

INTRODUCTION.

In presenting this record of the doings of the Royal Marines, in the War of 1914-1919, the great difficulty has been to decide what form it should take. To attempt to give an account in chronological order would almost have amounted to writing the Naval, Military and Air Force history of the War, because there was practically no theatre or activity of the War in which the Corps was not represented.

It has, therefore, seemed best to strike out a new line, and to group their deeds under the several headings of characteristic "Marine" operations which perhaps whilst serving as a record of the past, may be of use as a guide to future training and policy in the development of the Corps.

The following headings have therefore been selected and an effort made to give the outlines of the work performed, together with such personal experiences as it has been possible to obtain.

PART I. In the first place comes the traditional role of the Corps, the reinforcement and supplementing of the personnel of the Navy.

PART II. The War at Sea, comprising the several battles, actions, bombardments, and operations in which the Corps took part.

PART III. The Naval "Striking" Forces, provided on a larger scale to extend the power of the Navy over the land, and thus help them to carry out the enterprises on which they were engaged, or to consolidate their success.

PART IV. Ship Detachment Landing Parties to effect a definite object followed by re-embarkation, when that object was attained.

PART V. The creation and occupation of advanced bases to further the action of the Fleet.

PART VI. Units for service with the Army.

PART VII. Miscellaneous.

PART VIII. (a) Provision of special units for the performance of Admiralty work in close conjunction with other services; which units, whilst remaining at Admiralty disposal, were subject to the disciplinary and in some cases the tactical control of other services.

(b) Special auxiliary units for the Royal Naval Division.

PART IX. The administrative and training arrangements of the Corps at home.

APPENDICES. Casualties.
Services of Royal Marines, with units other than Royal Marines
Honours and Awards.

PART 1.

Mobilisation, Etc.

Royal Marines in the War of 1914-1919

MOBILISATION

CHAPTER 1.

Mobilisation - Recruiting-Ship's Complements - Naval Examination Service - Wireless Staffs - Naval Staff Officers - Transport Staffs - Special Orderlies - London Picquet.

With the commencement of the War the Corps took up at once the traditional role, which it has performed in every war for the last three hundred years, and for which indeed it had been originally raised in 1664, that is to say the reinforcement of the personnel of the Royal Navy.

The mobilisation passed off smoothly according to plan; the telegram to mobilise Reservists was dispatched at 2-30 a.m. on 2nd August, 1914, and by 8-0 a.m. those living near the barracks were coming in. In the course of the next two or three days, practically all those in the United Kingdom had reported for duty, and had been allotted to their various appropriations, as far as they had been foreseen in peace time.

Fortunately, after this had been done, there remained a good surplus of Reservists, for no sooner was the mobilisation proper completed than demands began to pour in for personnel for various Fleet services, most of which had not been foreseen in the pre-war arrangements. Added to this came the demands of the Royal Naval Division and the R.M.A. Batteries, which were very insistent both then and throughout the War. Though no doubt the batteries and battalions considered that they were not receiving the reinforcements that they required, it must never be forgotten that the reinforcement of the Fleet was the first consideration to which all else had to give way. The demands of the Fleet became larger and more urgent every month, and the Corps can make the proud boast that in no single instance did they fail to meet the Naval requirements as they arose. The effect of the demand is shown by the fact that the numbers actually afloat (exclusive of shore garrisons, battalions, batteries, etc.) at the commencement of the War were 10,047, whilst at the close the same figures were 16,494, in spite of the heavy casualties and replacements due to sickness.

In the very early days numerous war vessels, building for foreign powers in the United Kingdom were bought by the British Government, and commissioned as soon as completed. At the same time the British programmes were considerably accelerated.

It may be of interest to recall the method of providing the R.M. detachments at that time. The detachments of all Dreadnought battleships and battle cruisers, together with cruisers that carried more than four 12-inch or 9.2 inch guns were fifty per cent. R.M.A. and fifty per cent. R.M.L.I. All other armoured cruisers and battleships, unless they were flagships on foreign stations, when they followed the above rule, carried R.M.L.I. only as did all the light cruisers, monitors, gun-boats and dispatch vessels. The armed merchant cruisers on mobilisation were allotted equally to all the Divisions, but later on they were all manned by R.M.L.I. On mobilisation however, battleships of the Albion class, owing to the number in reserve, were allotted R.M.A. Reservists in the same proportion as Dreadnoughts.

The Corps at once opened recruiting to the fullest extent; training was speeded up and carried out with redoubled vigour, and was modified as necessary owing to the introduction of new weapons and methods of fighting.

At the outbreak of War the voted strength was 16,900 R.M.A. and R.M.L.I. with 1,450 R.M.B. (R.N. School of Music); but the actual serving numbers were 3,393 R.M.A., 13,425 R.M.L.I. and 1,442 R.M.B. Recruits flowed in at once and the Order-in-Council establishment of 1902, viz: 19,845, which had been the constitutional limit for many years, was soon passed and the resources of the Depots were strained to the uttermost.

The Reserves consisted of four classes; 401 Immediate Class, 1,676 R.F.R. (Class A), 2,984 R.F.R. (Class B), and 1,790 Pensioners under 55 years of age.

The total strength at the Armistice in 1918 was :-

R.M. Artillery	307 Officers	7640 N.C.O.s and Men.
R.M. Light Infantry	648	24444
R.M. Band	3	1592
Reserves and Pensioners	59	6618

The other R.M. Units at the same date were :-

R.M. Submarine Miners	54 Officers	375 N.C.O.s and Men.
R.M. Labour Corps	57	5625
R.M. Engineers	130	7314
Labour Co. (H.S.)	1	131
Divisional Train, R.M.	31	799
Medical Unit, R.M.	4	980
Ordnance Unit, R.M.	1	3

Owing to the calling out of the Pensioners as well as the R.F.R., there was a considerable excess of N.C.O.s; these were most valuable because some relieved serving N.C.O.s on the clerical and instructional staffs at headquarters; others were lent to the Naval Battalions of the R.N. Division, where several were granted commissions, whilst others held positions as Sergeant-Majors, Instructors, etc. of whom many fell in Gallipoli and France. Some were lent to the Army as Instructors to the new armies and were worth their weight in gold and gained great kudos both for themselves and the Corps; many of these also were given commissions in the Army. Others filled an even more typical role; on mobilisation all the Naval Training Establishments had been closed, but it was soon realised that the country was engaged in a war of uncertain duration, and that it would be necessary, not only to reopen all training establishments, but also to increase their capacity; practically all the Petty Officer Instructors had been drafted to sea and were no longer available, so that in this difficulty the Admiralty called on the Royal Marines and many of the Pensioner N.C.O.s rendered invaluable service in these establishments.

MOBILIZATION.

Prior to the War the complements of many of the fighting ships, particularly the battle cruisers, had been drawn up on a very meagre scale, and it was soon found that they were insufficient to meet the double strain of day and night defence; as all the available seamen were required for destroyers and vessels of that type additional Royal Marines were embarked in each ship to augment the guns' crews; and for a similar reason Royal Marines were embarked in the recently purchased ships, e.g. *Agincourt* and *Erin*, in increased proportions.

As the War progressed and the new programmes came forward for commissioning, it became an urgent problem to obtain sufficient trained soldiers to form the nucleus for the recruit detachments; this was solved by arranging for a monthly relief in the Grand Fleet of a proportion of old soldiers by recruits, which worked well from the general point of view, but must have been very annoying to the officers commanding detachments.

Certain services for which practically no provision had been made in peacetime, caused a heavy drain on the Corps resources; firstly the Armed Merchant Cruisers of which great numbers were commissioned for the 10th

Cruiser Squadron and other duties; secondly the Armed Boarding Steamers, and thirdly the Defensively Armed Merchantmen. For the first two the seamen and stoker portions of the crews were almost entirely R.N.R. as were most of the officers, but the Royal Marine detachments, whose strength varied from 45 to 25, according to the class of ship, had to be provided; as far as possible Reservists were detailed but the numbers were insufficient and recruits were also embarked, although it was an unsatisfactory service on which to employ such lads; the N.C.O.s in charge of the detachments were deserving of every credit for what must have been a difficult task. These ships had their full share of the fighting and the losses from mine and torpedo were very heavy, in addition to the several single ship actions that took place; many of the R.M. were decorated for their services in these patrol cruisers, which included work such as armed guards for ships sent in to be searched, prize crews for captured ships, and in some cases engagements with enemy raiders and submarines. Among others the following incident is related: "when H.M.S. *Otway* was torpedoed on 21st July, 1917 Private W. C. Brown (Ch.) was severely wounded, his left arm being almost severed, he displayed extraordinary courage and endurance, insisting that the other wounded should be attended to before him, and his fortitude and cheerfulness during the whole night were the admiration of the commander and the doctors; the Admiralty directed that he was to be promoted to Corporal."

The work of these Armed Merchant Ships was greatly extended as escort ships when the system of convoys was introduced in 1917, and the Royal Marine signallers of these ships were found a very useful reinforcement to the Naval signalmen.

The work of the Corps in the Defensively Armed Merchantmen is described in Chapter 7.

EXAMINATION SERVICE.

The signallers of this service stationed at the various ports maintained their monotonous duties continuously throughout the War, and took over additional ports as the need arose; this service was very arduous and entailed hard and trying work in all weathers, which was most conscientiously and loyally performed, and it seems hard that this service did not qualify for prize money or the overseas medals; this was work for which members of the Corps were particularly useful as those employed were conversant with both Army and Navy signalling procedure.

WIRELESS STAFFS.

Very valuable services were rendered by the R.M. officers borne for Wireless duties on the staffs of many of the Admirals. The majority of these officers were experts who had had considerable experience of wireless telegraphy from its introduction, and whose technical skill and knowledge were invaluable.

Major and Brevet Lieut.-Col. B. C. Gardiner, R.M.L.I., served throughout the War on the staff of the Commander-in-Chief of the Grand Fleet and his services were recognised by the award of a C.B.

Captain R. C. S. Waller, R.M.L.I. was the wireless telegraphy officer of the Fourth Battle Squadron and was specially brought to notice by Admiral Sturdee after the Battle of Jutland, as was Captain H. M. Franks, R.M.A. who was wireless telegraphy officer of the *Lion* in all her engagements, and of whom Sir D. Beatty reported that he had shown great skill and resource in maintaining the vitally important wireless telegraphy communications throughout the battle; both were awarded the Brevet of Major, whilst Captain A. G. W. Grierson, R.M.L.I. the wireless telegraphy officer of the 2nd Battle Cruiser Squadron was also commended for service. Major E. Gillespie, R.M.L.I. was throughout the wireless telegraphy officer of the 10th Cruiser Squadron and for his most important work was awarded both the D.S.O. and the Brevet of Major, whilst among those in the Dardanelles Captain J. Geldart was awarded the D.S.C.

There were also several high powered stations at home and abroad where Royal Marine Officers were in charge, notably at Gibraltar, where Lieut.-Col. R. ff Willis, R.M.L.I. was awarded the C.B. As the War developed, it was discovered that it was also necessary to have a number of medium powered stations, in order to control the activities of raiders and submarines by furnishing early information; Captain C. G. Crawley, R.M.A., who had retired before the War to become the wireless expert at the General Post Office, was in charge of the erection of these stations and was largely instrumental in their successful development; further it became necessary to increase the number of wireless telegraphy operators in the Mercantile Marine; these men were drawn from the Post Office and enrolled in the R.N.V.R. In order to give them the necessary training Captain Crawley instituted a school in the R.N. Depot at the Crystal Palace in 1916. Even Ascension was equipped with a station by Major Malden who had been wireless telegraphy officer in North America and at the Falkland Island Battle. At the beginning of the War a considerable number of retired Royal Marine Officers were employed as wireless telegraphy censors at the several large stations in the United Kingdom; but gradually all those fit for service in the field were withdrawn for more active employment, and were replaced by older Naval and Royal Marine officers, who continued to carry out this monotonous but essential duty until the end of the War.

NAVAL STAFF OFFICERS.

Before the War, staff officers, who in many cases were Royal Marine officers, were stationed at all the principal coaling stations abroad. Their work was many-sided and comprised many duties that would not seem to be connected with their staff work. As the War developed and the control of merchant shipping in the face of the submarine dangers became more important, many more R.M. officers were added for this work, and towards the end these duties absorbed a large number of the regular officers of the Corps, to the efficiency of whose work the rewards in the *London Gazette* bear ample evidence.

Some like Major and Brevet Lieut.-Col. W. W. Godfrey, R.M.L.I. in the Mediterranean were employed on operational staff work; others found that their work, whilst principally connected with shipping, brought them into touch with local affairs and intelligence; and some like Major W. L. Huntingford, R.M.A. with the French Fleet in the Mediterranean and Lieut. J. C. Farmer, R.M.L.I. with the Russian were employed as liaison officers with the Fleets of the Allies. Nor should mention be omitted of the valuable work performed in the Trade Division at the Admiralty by Lieut.-Col. T. H. Hawkins, R.M.L.I. and Lieut.-Col. A. Peel, R.M.L.I. in the Intelligence Division, whilst on the re-organisation of the Admiralty War Staff at the end of 1917, Lieut.-Col. L. S. T. Halliday, V.C., R.M.L.I., was called to the Admiralty as Assistant Director of Plans.

TRANSPORT STAFFS.

A secondary service, that eventually absorbed a considerable number of N.C.O.s and men was also provided by the pensioners. In peace time there had always been a few RM. orderlies on the Naval Transport Staff at Southampton to help to settle the troops in their ships; but now the Corps was called on to provide parties for the Transport Staffs at all ports at home and abroad. They proved most useful and their presence at the ports of embarkation and disembarkation and even at frontier stations, such as Modane on the Italian frontier, was very welcome to stray individuals and parties of the Corps, who were grateful for the willing help afforded them in a strange land by their old comrades.

SPECIAL ORDERLIES.

No account would be complete without mention of the dozen or so Royal Marine orderlies, specially selected from men with experience as wardroom officers' servants, who accompanied the various King's Messengers, etc.

to most of the countries of Europe, and whose experiences of foreign capitals, revolutions and other adventures would form, an interesting chapter could it be told. The manner in which they performed their duties was much appreciated and all the Government departments were most anxious to obtain their services.

LONDON PICQUET.

Owing to the increase in the size of the Navy and the number of naval ratings passing through London, especially at the great London Termini, a Naval Provost Marshal was stationed in London, with a staff of Royal Marine Reservists (who had served in the Police) to carry out the duties usually performed at the Home Ports by the naval patrols; their tact and discipline rendered very useful service in rather difficult situations and they were very highly regarded, all being promoted as a reward for their services.

PART II.

The War at Sea.

Royal Marines in the War of 1914-1919

CHAPTER 2.

ACTIONS AND INCIDENTS, 1914-1916.

Note.- It is not proposed to give in this record any detailed account of the various battles and actions at sea, which have been already so eloquently described in the Official History. The following chapters only give a general account of the Naval Actions, etc. in order that any events of particular Corps interest may be followed; therefore many important and gallant actions are omitted, because no members of the Corps were engaged.

In the war at Sea was engaged the largest proportion of the Regular Active Service Ranks of the Corps and the Reservists. There were many officers and men who served continuously afloat throughout the four years that the War lasted, of whom many remained in the same ship. With the exception of destroyers, submarines and mine sweeping sloops the R.M. detachment formed part complement of every class of ship.

On the eve of the declaration of War, the Battle Fleet consisting of 1st, 2nd, 3rd and 4th Battle Squadrons, the Fleet Flagship, H.M.S. *Iron Duke*, the 1st Battle Cruiser Squadron with the Torpedo Boat Destroyers, Auxiliary and Repair Ships slipped quietly away on 29th July from Portland to the Northern Bases, whilst the Second Fleet of pre - Dreadnought nucleus ships, having embarked their balance crews, took their place at Portland and became the Channel Fleet.

The Examination Services, the signalling personnel of which were provided by the Corps, were put in force and the garrison of Cromarty was brought up to strength, as well as those of other bases manned by Royal Marines.

As soon as the 3rd and 4th Fleets of older battleships and cruisers were mobilised with their Reservists, they were scattered far and wide over the Seven Seas, some to reinforce the foreign stations, others to form patrols at the mouth of the Channel and across the North Sea, whilst to others were allotted the miscellaneous duties that fall to the lot of the Navy, chief among which was the escort of the convoys of troops to and from the British Isles.

On 3rd August Sir John Jellicoe hoisted his Flag as Commander-in-Chief of the Grand Fleet.

Immediately on the declaration of War the China Squadron started in pursuit of Von Spee's Squadron of fast Cruisers, which had been last heard of at Manila; gradually other squadrons were drawn into the chase, which culminated at the Falkland Islands. Each foreign station was also concerned with the location of the few German cruisers that were on the seas; and steps were taken to prevent the entry into hostile activity of German Armed Merchant Cruisers, because it was known that the enemy had made preparations for converting many of their liners into warships, a course very menacing to British commerce. To guard against these activities close watch had to be kept on the ports where they were known to be lying. The convoy of troops from the Dominions and Colonies to the United Kingdom, added to the hunt for enemy cruisers, brought a great strain on the available cruisers.

In the Mediterranean, the *Indefatigable, Indomitable* and *Dublin* sighted the German *Goeben* and *Breslau* at 10 a.m. on 4th August and followed them to the eastward, the *Dublin* keeping them in sight and tracing them to Messina; the two battle cruisers were outpaced and at dusk turned to the westward to guard the French Transport Route; (War between France and Germany had been declared on 1st August). The First Cruiser Squadron, consisting of *Defence, Warrior, Black Prince* and *Duke of Edinburgh*, was off the Straits of Otranto, because at that time the attitude of Italy, who was one of the Triple Alliance, was very uncertain.

At 5-0 a.m. on 5th the Battle Cruisers with *Weymouth, Chatham* and *Gloucester* rendezvoused off Pantellaria Island and spread to the westward to guard the French Transport Route, until at 6 p.m. the *Dublin* reported that the Germans were leaving Messina; but at this time all the cruisers were very short of coal, which was one of the problems of the moment.

The German commander, who had been given a free hand as to his movements, decided to run for the Dardanelles; the *Dublin* and *Gloucester* followed and shadowed them, but the First Cruiser Squadron could not leave their watch of the mouth of the Adriatic where were the Austrian Fleet of battleships, etc., whilst the Battle Cruisers, except those coaling at Malta, were unfortunately to the westward. Though the small *Gloucester*, Captain W. A. H. Kelly, in the best spirit of Grenville's *Revenge*, hung on like a terrier and even engaged the Germans at long range to try and delay them, they had too long a start. On 8th August, when the chase was in full cry, the declaration of War with Austria was received to complicate matters, and caused further delay; but by the 11th the three Battle Cruisers with *Weymouth* and *Chatham* were off the entrance of the Dardanelles, expecting that the German ships, which had anchored at Chanak on the night before, would be obliged to come out. Under the camouflage that they had been sold to Turkey, the two German ships passed up to Constantinople and, as war was not yet declared with Turkey, the British ships were refused permission to pass the Straits, an event which had far reaching consequences in the World War.

The patrols in the North Sea at once became active, particularly the Harwich Force. On 6th August, H.M.S. *Amphion* with her flotilla of destroyers encountered the *Konigin Luise*, which had been laying mines off the Thames and sank her after a short fight; the *Amphion* however, was shortly afterwards sunk by a mine, when 14 men were killed; Captain Fox commanding the *Amphion* reported the gallant behaviour of Private John Brown-King (Plymouth), one of the gun layers. Brown-King fired the first shot at the *Konigin Luise;* "he was proud of having brought down the German flag; he was badly injured (by the explosion of the mine), his face and hands being shockingly burnt and both eyes gone. At one time he had a glimmer of sight in his right eye and exclaimed 'Thank God it is the gunnery eye.' In all his pain, which was very great, he set an example of courage and endurance. No one heard him complain and he was always thanking people for what they did for him. He was conscious to the end which he met as a man and a Christian should." He was buried in Shotley Churchyard. (Letter to the Adjutant-General, Royal Marines).

On the same day H.M.S. *Bristol* had an indecisive fight in the West Indies with the *Karlsruhe*, which escaped in the darkness to be a cause for anxiety for many months, until definite information was obtained that she had blown up somewhere in the West Indies. In these waters the *Spreewald*, an armed merchant cruiser, was captured by the *Berwick* on 12th September.

On 26th August the *Highflyer*, Captain H. T. Buller, found the *Kaiser Wilhelm der Grosse*, a converted merchant cruiser, coaling at Rio d'Oro (Coast of Africa) and summoned her to surrender, which she refused to do; she was therefore sunk after an unequal fight of one and a half hours. It must have been some satisfaction to Captain B. F. Trench, R.M.L.I., the Marine officer, to have an opportunity of paying some of the score of his long imprisonment in Germany, after being captured in Borkum, before the War.

The first important action took place on 28th August in the Heligoland Bight, when an operation planned for the light cruisers and destroyers, developed into a major operation in which the Battle Cruisers were also engaged; the Armoured Cruisers *Euryalus* and her consorts, after landing the Chatham Battalion at Ostend (see Chapter 9) also hurried off to take part. H.M.S. *Arethusa* was severely handled and suffered several casualties, but the German cruisers *Mainz, Koln,* and *Ariadne* with Torpedo Boat Destroyer *V187* were sunk. The *Lion, Princess Royal, Invincible, New Zealand,* with the light cruisers *Nottingham, Lowestoft, Falmouth, Southampton,*

Actions and Incidents, 1914-1916

Birmingham, Liverpool, Arethusa and *Fearless* were engaged in these operations. This action synchronised with the landing of the Royal Marine Brigade at Ostend, but the two operations were not connected.

In September the operations in the Cameroons, described in Chapter 18, commenced.

On 2nd September the Japanese commenced the attack on Tsingtau, in which the British were represented by one British battalion (South Wales Borderers) some Native Troops and H.M.S. *Triumph*. The latter participated in the bombardments and useful lessons on bombarding forts from the sea were learnt. Tsingtau which was garrisoned by the German Marines, eventually capitulated on 7th November and the British Forces were later employed at the Dardanelles. The Russian Cruiser *Askold*, which we shall meet again as *Glory IV.*, was also present (vide Chapter 13).

The *Triumph* had been commissioned at Hong Kong by Captain M. S. Fitzmaurice with the crews of the river gunboats, the R.M.L.I. detachment of H.M.S. *Tamar* under Captain J. G. Horne and other details. To complete the complement three officers and 115 other ranks of the 2nd Battalion Duke of Cornwall's Light Infantry from Hong Kong were embarked as Marines and took their share of detachment duties, but after three weeks they were disembarked because the Battalion was ordered to England.

On 14th September there took place off the coast of Brazil one of the few single ship actions of the War; after an engagement fought in the old style H.M.S. *Carmania* (armed merchant cruiser), Captain N. Grant, sank the *Cap Trafalgar*, also an Armed Merchantman; among the rewards for this action the D.S.M. was given to Sergeant W. S. Dyer, R.M.A., Gunner R. B. Branske and Private W. Wadsworth (Portsmouth).

On 22nd September the German Submarine *U9* under the celebrated Weddigen, attacked the cruisers of the Broad Fourteens Patrol and sank the *Aboukir, Cressy* and *Hogue*. The *Aboukir* was torpedoed first, and as the others were rescuing the ship's company, they were in turn sunk by torpedoes. Captain C. Field, R.M.L.I. of the *Aboukir* and 200 N.C.O.s and men Royal Marines, were drowned; Captains C. Williams and H. Ozanne, R.M.L.I. with the remainder of the detachments, about 100, were rescued, the former officer being picked up by a Dutch trawler.

During the early days of the War there were no secure bases for the Grand Fleet, so that they were obliged to be constantly on the move, returning to their bases only to coal: whilst the base itself was constantly being moved. Harbours on the west coast of Scotland, which were beyond the reach of the submarines of that time, were often utilised for coaling and rest. The Fleet also made use of Lough Swilly in the north of Ireland, and it was whilst proceeding to this harbour that the *Audacious* was sunk by a mine off Tory Island on 27th October, 1914, fortunately without loss of life.

The 3rd Battle Squadron, consisting of the *King Edward* class of battleships, which all carried exceptionally large detachments of Royal Marines who had been embarked just before the War to release seamen for the newer ships, formed part of the Grand Fleet, but their speed was a serious obstacle to their employment with the Dreadnought squadrons; after a time they were based on Rosyth, and later on, after the raids on the East Coast of England, were moved to the mouth of the Thames.

At this time also several of the *Albemarle* class of battleship were included in the Grand Fleet, and they usually preceded the Fleet out of harbour, to be the first, so it was said, to bump the mines. They were popularly known as "Uriah the Hittite" Squadron.

The strain on officers and men was very great, and for many months many of them never set foot on shore; even when the ships were in harbour, they were at such short notice to proceed to sea, that there were no opportunities for recreation, and the facilities for exercise and amusement, that were developed later, had not yet been devised.

The following account of the experiences of a Royal Marine officer in a ship of one of the Cruiser Squadrons patrolling the North Sea in the early days is of interest.

"Cabin doors were got rid of, the oilcloth was removed from the decks, boats were landed; rafts were supplied in place of boats. For the first five months after the outbreak of war we had little rest, being almost continuously at sea, usually in very bad weather, patrolling and reconnoitring in the North Sea. At this time the War Watch system had not been introduced; officers and men spent long periods at the guns, as the routine was that which had been carried out during manoeuvres lasting only three or four days, and was not adapted for a long period as was now the case. My duties were to keep watch by night in the maintop with the full benefit of the funnel smoke. I was in charge of the after guns and searchlights, sharing the watch with the Gunnery Lieutenant, each of us taking half the night; the nights in these northern latitudes are very long in the winter, and I was frequently on duty for eight hours. On returning to harbour we coaled ship, an operation often lasting 24 hours and then proceeded to sea again. By day at sea there were constant false alarms, 'Action Stations' being frequently sounded off, so that very little sleep was possible. After some months a better routine was adopted; my position was on the fore bridge, where I had complete control of the guns and one could move about a little. In addition to these duties I had my detachment of 100 men to look after, and also had charge of the confidential books and documents, a very onerous task, owing to the numerous changes received which arrived immediately we got into harbour and which prevented any possibility of going ashore."

The Fleet was constantly at exercises and gunnery practice, and the newly commissioned ships such as the *Tiger, Erin* and *Agincourt* had hard and dangerous work in obtaining the necessary target practice to work up the ships' companies.

As regards their training, the Royal Marines were too busily occupied during the early period with their gunnery and in perfecting the drill and organisation of the turrets, secondary armaments and night defence, to be able to devote much time to the Military part of their training, but this was to come in due course.

Efforts were made to defend Scapa Flow; Captain Raikes, R.M.A. was sent up with some R.M.A. Reservists to man the 12-pounders that had been landed at the entrances by the Fleet (see Chapter 21); the *Magnificent* and *Hannibal* were sent up to guard the entrances, relieved later by the *Royal Arthur* and *Crescent*. They themselves, having parted with their turret guns to the new monitors, were sent to the Mediterranean, where as transports carrying masses of troops, they did yeoman service at the evacuation of the Dardanelles and at Salonica; and the *Hannibal* afterwards became guardship at Alexandria.

The submarine attack was becoming serious, and up to date there was no effective reply. The *Hawke*, one of the Edgar class was sunk on 15th October whilst on patrol in the North Sea, and the *Hermes*, the ship of the R.N.A.S. in the Channel on 31st October.

On 17th October, however, the *Undaunted* with her flotilla of destroyers from Harwich encountered four German Torpedo Boat Destroyers who were on patrol off the Dutch Coast and all the enemy vessels were sunk.

Meanwhile in the Indian Ocean the search for the *Emden* and *Koenigsberg* was being actively prosecuted; on 20th September the *Koenigsberg* came into Zanzibar harbour, where the *Pegasus* was lying under repair; the *Helmuth*, tug failed to warn the *Pegasus* in time and the Germans opened fire at 9,000 yards; the *Pegasus* was quite outranged and in fifteen minutes all her broadside was disabled. After a lull of five minutes the Germans again opened fire for fifteen minutes, the *Pegasus* being still unable to reply; 24 men were killed and 55 wounded, nearly all the casualties occurring on the upper deck. The British flag was shot down twice, but was held up by hand by Corporal W. R. McIntyre, Plymouth R.M.L.I. who died of wounds. Efforts were made to beach the *Pegasus*, but she capsized and sank. The town was not touched, and the guns and crew of the ship afterwards rendered good service in the Field in East Africa (see Chapter 27).

This action brought the hunt on to the *Koenigsberg*, and on 30th October, she was located by H.M.S. *Chatham*, at Sarari in the Rufigi River. The salvoes from the *Chatham* drove her further up the stream, but were unable to destroy her. On 10th November, the collier *Newbridge* commanded by Commander Fitzmaurice, R.N., was sunk in the channel under a hot fire.

The *Weymouth* and *Dartmouth* also closed in, and the *Koenigsberg* was blockaded in the river; *Hyacinth*, *Fox* and *Kinfauns Castle* also co-operated for a time, and many gallant attempts to get at her were made, though a landing party to cut her out in the old style does not seem to have been attempted. Later in February, 1915, it was proposed to send out Admiral Wemyss in charge of an expedition, including the Portsmouth and Deal Battalions, R.M.L.I. to dig her out. The transports were prepared and special equipment was obtained, but this plan was cancelled on the inception of the Dardanelles expedition. The *Koenigsberg* landed her 4.1-inch guns which afforded very material assistance to the Germans throughout the East African Campaign (see also Chapter 27).

On 1st November, 1914, hostilities were declared against Turkey, and on 3rd November there was a ten minutes bombardment of the outer forts of the Dardanelles, in the hope that it might cause a re-action against the German influence in Turkey; the firing took place outside the range of the Turkish guns. The ships present being *Indefatigable*, *Indomitable*, *Dublin*, *Gloucester*, *Blenheim*, and 12 Destroyers, with the French Battleships *Veriti* and *Suffren*, but the light cruisers did not open fire.

As the Indian convoy with the 29th Indian Brigade was passing up the Red Sea on 19th November, the Brigade under General Cox was landed at Sheikh Seyd opposite Perim, covered by the bombardment of the *Duke of Edinburgh*, and drove the Turks out of the forts, which were then destroyed by a naval demolition party. One of the regiments was commanded by an old R.M.L.I. officer (Lieut-Col. Rarding of 69th Punjabis).

On 3rd November, the German Light Forces made their first 'tip and run' raid on the English coast; when returning however the German Cruiser *Yorck* was sunk through striking a mine.

On 9th, the long hunt for the *Emden* was ended off the Cocos Islands, where she was sunk by H.M.A.S. *Sydney* (Captain Glossop).

On 1st November, the country was startled by the news of the Battle of Coronel in the Pacific. The *Good Hope*, *Monmouth*, *Glasgow* and *Otranto*, under the command of Rear-Admiral C. Cradock, were off the coast of Chili on the look out for the cruisers of Von Spee's squadron that had escaped from China. The *Glasgow*, which had gone into Coronel for telegrams, returned with the information that the enemy cruisers were in the vicinity. The squadron then spread and proceeded northwards; the enemy squadron was sighted steaming south at 4-15 p.m. The *Gneisenau* and *Scharnhorst*, were at once engaged by the *Good Hope* and *Monmouth*, whilst the *Leipzic* and another light cruiser were engaged by the *Glasgow*; the *Otranto*, being only an armed merchantman, had been ordered to keep out of the way. The squadrons engaged steaming south and as the sun set were in close action. The German ships, besides being heavily armed, were the best shooting squadron of the German Navy; the *Good Hope* and *Monmouth* on the other hand were old and lightly armed, and had only been commissioned on mobilisation largely with reservists, and the British ships were sadly over matched.

The *Good Hope* was soon on fire, and shortly after 7-45 p.m. there was an explosion amidships and she was not seen again; the *Monmouth* and *Glasgow* fought on, but could only fire at the flashes of the enemy's guns; the *Monmouth* was very badly damaged and on fire, which doubtless showed her up and enabled the enemy to see their target. The *Glasgow* made an attempt to draw the Germans off and as she passed the *Monmouth*, the latter's crew on the quarter deck cheered her. The *Glasgow* soon after heard guns and saw searchlight flashes and it was clear that the *Monmouth* was still being attacked; she was eventually sunk[11]. The *Glasgow*, owing to her speed, made good her escape to the Magellan Straits and informed the *Canopus*.

The Corps lost Captain C. B. Partridge and Lieutenant H. S. Walker (W/T officer), R.M.L.I. of *Good Hope* and Captain G. M. Herford, R.M.L.I. of *Monmouth* with 192 N.C.O.s and Men. No one was saved from these two ships, so there is no record of the awful experiences that the crews of the doomed ships must have undergone, as they were both out-ranged and out-gunned. The *Glasgow* was fortunate to escape with slight injuries.

They were soon avenged at the Battle of the Falkland Islands on 8th December.

Admiral Sturdee with *Invincible* and *Inflexible* from England was joined by *Kent, Cornwall, Carnarvon, Glasgow* and *Bristol*, of the S.E. Coast of America Squadron. They rendezvoused at the Falkland Islands, to which place the *Canopus* had proceeded after Coronel and had established herself with a view to denying the use of the harbour to the Germans should they make for it; as was apparently their intention, when they approached the island on the morning of 8th December and were greeted by a salvo from the 12-inch guns of the *Canopus*. At the same time the glimpse of the tripod masts of the Battle Cruisers over the land must have given the Germans warning of their approaching doom.

The British ships, which had just completed coaling, left the harbour at 9-15 a.m. and started to chase, with the *Glasgow* leading; at 1-30 p.m. *Invincible* opened fire and soon the big ships were engaged. The *Scharnhorst* and *Gneisenau* were speedily disposed of by the Battle Cruisers, both being sunk; only a few survivors were rescued from the *Gneisenau*, while the Battle Cruisers suffered no material damage. The light cruisers *Nurnberg, Leipzic,* and *Dresden* made off, hotly pursued by the *Carnarvon, Cornwall, Kent,* and *Glasgow*. The *Cornwall* and *Glasgow* sank the *Leipzic* at dusk after she had refused to surrender. The destruction of the *Nurnberg* by the *Kent*, is one of the epics of the War. How she chased her, exceeding her trial speed by several knots in spite of her age, burning the wood of her fittings to feed the boilers and though her 6 inch guns were outranged by the 4.1 guns of the enemy, sank the German ship is a well known story. Meanwhile the gallant deed of Sergeant C. Mayes (Portsmouth), R.M.L.I. added another leaf to the laurels of the Corps. A shell burst and ignited some of the cordite charges in the casemate; a flash of flame went down the hoist into the ammunition passage. Sergeant Mayes picked up a charge of cordite and threw it out of the way; he then got hold of a fire hose and flooded the compartment, extinguishing the fire in some empty shell bags, which were burning. The extinction of the fire saved a disaster which might have led to the loss of the ship. He was awarded the Conspicuous Gallantry Medal. Six N.C.O.s and men were killed and four wounded in the action, mostly in the *Kent*. The *Dresden* escaped by means of her superior speed and returned into the Pacific. After a long hunt, and having been chased to the Island of Juan Fernandez by the *Kent* on the 8th March, 1915, she was finally sunk on 14th March by the *Kent, Glasgow* and *Orama*.

BATTLE OF FALKLAND ISLANDS.

Invincible (Flag)	Major R C. Colquhom, R.M.L.I.	107 N.C.O.s and Men.
	Lieutenant J. Le Selleur, R.M.L.I.	

---

1. From an eye-witness' account in the Globe and Laurel.

	R.M.Gr. C. Catley.			
	Captain C. H. Malden, (W/T), R.M.L.I.			
Inflexible	Major J. B. Finlaison, R.M.L.I.	107	"	"
	Captain R Sinclair, R.M.L.I.			
	R.M.Gr. J. Cameron.			
Carnarvon (Flag)	Major E. Wray, R.M.L.I.,	92	"	"
	Captain A. J. Mellor, (W/T), R.M.L.I.			
Cornwall	Captain H. R Brewer, R.M.L.I.	92	"	"
Kent	Captain R J. Laing, R.M.L.I.	92	"	"
Canopus	Captain G. S. Hobson, R.M.L.I.	105	"	"
² *Glasgow*		29		
² *Bristol*		29		

On 26th November occurred the first of those mysterious explosions which caused the loss of so many ships, both British and Allied; H.M.S. *Bulwark*, lying in Sheerness Harbour, was blown up and the Corps lost two officers, Captain H. C. Morton and Lieutenant H. J. Lock, R.M.L.I. and about 95 N.C.O.s and men of the Portsmouth Division R.M.L.I.; Sergeant A. J. Budd having a miraculous escape, being blown clear of the ship and picked up in the water.

During November the old cruisers of the Edgar class, forming the 10th Cruiser Squadron, were found to be unequal to the task of facing the storms and rough seas that were their lot on the patrol line near the Orkneys and Shetlands; therefore they were replaced by a large number of Armed Merchant Cruisers, that belonged to the Atlantic trade, which were more fitted for the work of keeping the seas and examining the vessels that passed the patrol line. As all the old cruisers carried large detachments of R.M.L.I., this step was of considerable assistance to the manning question. It did not however, end the career of these old ships, for after being fitted with 'bulges' they rendered valuable services in bombarding on the flanks of the various Expeditionary Forces (see Chapters 3 and 6).

On 16th December the enemy made a raid on Scarborough and the Hartlepools; unfortunately the raiders got clear away after sinking H.M.S. *Patrol*, but Nemesis overtook them shortly.

In East African Waters on 3rd November, the Indian Expeditionary Force, detailed for the purpose, was landed at midnight to attack the German port of Tanga. At daylight the next day, they were met with fierce opposition and were unable to force their way through the thick scrub; so that by 8-0 a.m. the attack was broken off; other transports arriving with reinforcements, a general advance was made at noon, covered by the fire of the *Fox* and six mountain guns of the Royal Artillery mounted in the transport *Bharata*, but the force, although they entered Tanga, were obliged to retire at nightfall and to re-embark; H.M.S. *Fox* had bombarded the place a few days previously, and consequently the enemy were on the alert.

This was followed on 28th November by the *Goliath* and *Fox* accompanied by two smaller ships the *Dupleix* and *Helmuth*, visiting Dar-es-Salaam, the principal German town, in order to put the German merchant ships lying there out of action and to secure lighters, etc. The Germans on shore hoisted white flags, but when the steam pinnaces went in followed by the *Helmuth* and *Dupleix*, they were received with a heavy fire from both banks and suffered several casualties. In spite of the enemy fire (though the Germans kept the white flag flying all the time), demolition parties were put on board and destroyed the *Konig*, *Feldmarschall*

---

2. No Officers R.M. were borne.

and *Kaiser Wilhelm II*. and several lighters were brought off. The greatest gallantry was shown by all concerned and Commander H. P. Ritchie was awarded the V.C. The parties eventually returned under cover of the fire of the *Goliath* and *Fox*; four officers and eight men were missing, who had been put on board the *Konig* and *Feldmarschall*,. the boats were so injured that they could not return for them. On 30th November *Goliath* and *Fox*, after landing the wounded at Zanzibar, returned to Dar-es-Salaam and systematically bombarded the place. The enemy did not reply as the place had evidently been deserted.

The North American Squadron had maintained a ceaseless patrol off the North American coasts until the German Squadrons and outlying ships had been accounted for; they prevented many German liners from escaping and converting themselves into armed ships and captured others. The crews and detachments of these ships *Suffolk*, *Lancaster*, *Berwick* and *Essex* were very restless at their seeming inactivity in the great events taking place in Europe, and such was the spirit of the men, that many deserted in order to join the Canadian Forces proceeding to France.

At the end of 1914 H.M.S. *Jupiter*, which had been gunnery firing ship at Plymouth in the early days, was sent to the Tyne as guardship, because the Military authorities were not satisfied with the defences at Tynemouth. To aid the defences Major A. M. Connolly, R.M.L.I. (retired) was landed with some 12 pounder guns and a portion of the detachment and the guns were mounted on the north side of the entrance.

At dawn on Christmas Day the daring raid of the aircraft on Cuxhaven took place, in which destroyers, submarines and cruisers participated. Seven aeroplanes made the attack, escorted by the *Arethusa*, *Endeavour* and Destroyers. Bombs were dropped on important places and in return the British Squadron was attacked by Zeppelins, seaplanes and submarines.

Six seaplanes returned safely, the pilot of the seventh was rescued by a trawler and taken to Holland. Among the pilots were Captain C. F. Kilner, R.M.L.I. who was awarded the D.S.O. and Lieutenant C. H. Collet, D.S.O., R.M.A., who had been awarded the D.S.O. for his gallant attack on the Zeppelin sheds at Dusseldorf in November.

At the end of November H.M.S. *Albion* was sent to Walfisch Bay in S.W. Africa to protect the piers for the landing of General Botha's Force for the South-West Africa campaign; they found that the settlement had been destroyed, but the piers were left intact, as the Germans evidently expected to use them for their Reservists from S. America. A Royal Marine Guard under Lieut. Congdon, R.M.L.I. was landed daily and occupied themselves in putting the place in a state of defence as far as possible in the time available, which proved of use later for the landing. After the Battle of the Falkland Islands and the destruction of Von Spee's squadron extra vigilance had to be observed, as the piers being no longer of any use to him, the enemy tried to destroy them. After providing a covering party for the landing H.M.S. *Albion* left for the Cape; part of General Botha's Force was landed on Christmas Day, covered by the *Hyacinth* and *Astraea*; some of the Royal Marines of the *Hyacinth* under Lieut. Glunicke manned a 3-pounder gun mounted in a tug to cover the landing inshore, but as related in Chapter 32 the landing was unopposed. Some of the boats landing the covering force were manned by Royal Marines.

On the last day of 1914 H.M.S. *Natal* was destroyed by another of the mysterious explosions, the Corps losing 63 N.C.O.s and men.

1915.

The year opened inauspiciously with the loss of H.M.S. *Formidable*, which was torpedoed in the Channel, when cruising with the Channel Fleet off West Bay; though a gale was blowing, the boats were got out, but a large number of men went down with the ship; the magnificent discipline of the Navy was fully maintained and Captain A. N. Loxley, R.N. went down with his ship; the pinnace having picked up all the men that she could, drifted ashore at Lyme Regis; two officers and 69 men, after twelve hours in the cutter were rescued by a magnificent display of seamanship on the part of the Brixham trawler *Providence*, commanded by Captain Pillar. The Corps lost Captain J. C. Deed (retired) and Lieutenant G. V. Hathorn,. R.M.L.I. with 84 N.C.O.s and men of the Chatham Division; 10 N.C.O.s and men were among the saved. The senior surviving officer reported the exemplary conduct of Lieutenant G. V. Hathorn during the sinking of the ship, and Bugler S. C. Reed (Chatham) worthily upheld the traditions of the Corps; one of the survivors related that he saw Bugler Reed, after all the boats had left, standing on the quarterdeck and asked him how he felt; Reed replied 'alright,' he then suggested to Reed that he should use his drum to keep himself afloat when the ship sank, Reed replied that he had thought of it, but that he had given it to one of the bluejacket boys for that purpose, as the boy had nothing to keep him afloat in the heavy seas, and that he himself did not feel very nervous. The narrator did not see Reed again and the bugler was among those drowned, he was only 16 ½ years old.

THE DOGGER BANK ACTION.

On 24th January, the German Battle Cruisers in attempting a third raid on the English Coast met with due retribution. Admiral Sir D. Beatty with the *Lion* (Flag), *Tiger, Princess Royal, New Zealand* and *Indomitable*, was at sea with the light cruisers *Southampton* (Broad Pennant), *Nottingham, Birmingham*, and *Lowestoft*. The Harwich Force under Commodore Twyrrhit with *Arethusa, Aurora, Undaunted* and the Destroyer Flotillas were also in company.

The Harwich Force and light cruisers, were ahead at 7-25 a.m., when the *Aurora* reported sighting the enemy battle cruisers and was at once ordered to chase to the south east, followed by the battle cruisers. The enemy were now made out to be the three battle cruisers *Derfflinger, Seydlitz* and *Moltke*, together with the *Blucher* (armoured cruiser) six light cruisers and some T.B.Ds. The enemy was steering north west, but on sighting the British ships altered course to the south east; touch was, however, maintained as there was very good visibility with a north easterly wind. A long stern chase commenced, the speed being 28 ½ knots and at 9 a.m. the *Lion* made her first hit on the *Blucher*. The British gradually overhauled the enemy and by 9-45 a.m., the *Lion* was engaging the leading ship, *Princess Royal* was engaging No.3, the *Tiger* No.1, and *New Zealand* No.4. The second ship in the enemy line was apparently not engaged and she was believed to have fired the shot, which entering the *Lion's* feed tank, disabled the starboard engine, so that the flagship fell out of the line about 11 a.m.

At this time the leading enemy ship and No.3 were on fire, and the *Blucher* badly damaged was falling astern, being left to the *Indomitable* and the light cruisers to finish off. Admiral Beatty, having made the signal for 'close action' by flags, which apparently was not read, transferred his flag to the *Attack* and eventually to the *Princess Royal*. The other battle cruisers continued the pursuit of the Germans until the course to which they had turned to avoid submarines, prior to the *Lion's* falling out, carried them out of range of the enemy, when they returned to the *Blucher*, which was sunk; her survivors were rescued by the British ships. The *Lion* was towed home by the *Indomitable* and very quickly repaired, the British casualties were slight, only one Royal Marine being wounded in the *Tiger*.

Besides the loss of the *Blucher*, the *Derfflinger* and *Kolberg* were badly damaged and the *Seydlitz*, seriously injured, only made port with difficulty.

The following extract of a letter from the *Tiger* is of interest, especially as this ship had not long been commissioned.[3] "The turret's crew worked without a hitch and had the satisfaction of seeing a magnificent hit at 6000 yards burst at the foot of the *Blucher's* tripod mast, and observing the fore part of that ship in a sheet of flame, and next of seeing from the roof of their turret the final plunge of the doomed enemy ship. The 6-inch guns, also did good work in the final phase. One small bugler 15 years and 5 months old, and 4 feet ll ½ inches high, did powder monkey in regular Trafalgar style. He told himself off to fill the tubs for the rammers of the 6-inch guns, and because he was not big enough to carry a mess kettle full of water, he towed it along the battery fore and aft at the end of a piece of string."

In January, 1915, as the ice breaker in the White Sea had broken down, the *Jupiter*, (Captain D. St. A. Wake), was sent to keep open the route to Archangel, which was so important for the supply of munitions to Russia. She sailed within a few hours of the receipt of the orders, without any arrangements having been made for heating, or for any special supplies of clothing, etc. After herculean efforts to force a way through the ice, she eventually proceeded to Alexandrovsk, on the west shore of the White Sea, which was ice free and where there was a cable to Peterhead in Scotland. Shortly afterwards the S.S. *Thracia*, with aeroplanes and motor cars for Archangel, got stuck in the ice, and the *Jupiter*, going in search of her had to ram her way through the ice. The *Thracia*, was found and taken in tow; in spite of the tow breaking continually and very considerable hardship from the cold, the *Jupiter* succeeded in towing her to Archangel. With the aid of a Russian ice pilot they returned to Alexandrovsk, where for many days the Royal Marine detachment were employed in burying the cable to Scotland in the frozen and rocky ground. The ship was able to return in May, sadly battered, and the following winter H.M.S. *Vindictive* was sent to do the work. Lieutenant N. K. Jolley, R.M.L.I., was awarded the order of St. Stanislas (Russian).

By the 28th January, the Turks from Palestine were advancing in force on the Suez Canal, and on 2nd February delivered their first attack at Kantara, Toussoum and other places; they were repulsed with heavy loss by the troops stationed on the Canal, assisted by H.M.S. *Swiftsure*, *Minerva*, and the R.I.M. ship *Hardinge*. The attack was renewed on 3rd and 4th without success and again on 5th at Suez, when the enemy finally withdrew.

Events were now leading up to the Dardanelles expedition for which the ships were gathering from all over the world (see chapters 3 and 11).

On 18th March, H.M.S. *Dreadnought*, cruising with the squadron in the North Sea, sighted and rammed a submarine. Lieutenant-Commander B. H. Piercey, who had sighted her, was able to direct her navigating officer and she caught U. 29 amidships. The submarine stood on end, rubbing along the *Dreadnought's* side, and finally sank astern.

About this time it was arranged that squadrons of the Grand Fleet should visit Cromarty in turn for four weeks each, to give rest and recreation to the crews. This was much appreciated, and the Royal Marine detachments were frequently landed for exercises, which were made as varied as possible. Vice-Admiral Sturdee, commanding 4th Battle Squadron, gave a prize for a marching and shooting competition, in which the whole detachment of each ship took part. This was won by H.M.S. *Vanguard*, Captain H. W. Miles, R.M.L.I, commanding the detachment.

The Royal Marines of the 4th Battle Squadron under Lieutenant-Colonel C. E. Collard, R.M.L.I. (Ret), of H.M.S. *Benbow*, a musketry enthusiast, constructed a 200 yards range on the Calf of Flotta at

---

3. From Globe and Laurel.

Scapa Flow, and later also a revolver range. A short course of musketry with the Japanese rifle, with which the corps afloat was now armed, was instituted; Lieutenant-Colonel Collard being appointed Inspector of Musketry in the Grand Fleet.

The constitution of the squadrons was now changing considerably, as the new ships were being completed and brought forward for commission, whilst the older ships were paid off or relegated to less important duties.

There were several losses among the Armed Merchant Cruiser patrols, among them being the *Bayano*, when 21 N.C.O.s and men were drowned, and the *Viknor*. On 12th April, one of the last of the German merchant cruisers, the *Kronprinz Wilhelm*, arrived at Newport News (North America), and was interned.

The war at sea was now entering on its next phase, the stern and protracted struggle against the submarine. With the exception of the *Koenigsberg*, all the German cruisers were accounted for, and the High Seas Fleet was not displaying any very great eagerness to meet the British Fleet.

On 7th May, the *Lusitania*, the large liner, was sunk off Queenstown, and the anger and horror aroused by her fate sealed the doom of the Germans.

Although all attention was concentrated on .the Dardanelles, the blockade and interception of supplies to the enemy were maintained by the cruiser squadrons, whilst frequent sweeps in the North Sea were made by the Grand Fleet and the light forces from Harwich, which effectively controlled the movements of the German Fleet and, combined with the destroyer patrols, ensured the safe passage of the troops to France.

In July, 1915, the operations against the *Koenigsberg* were resumed, the monitors *Severn*, Captain E.]. Fullerton, and *Mersey*, Commander Wilson, with two whalers *Echo* and *Fly* and a tug the *Childers* having arrived on the scene. The Admiral of the station (King-Hall) flew his flag in the *Tweedmouth* and the *Weymouth* and *Pyramus* also formed part of the squadron. There were two aeroplanes which operated from Mafia Island under Major R. Gordon, R.M.L.I, Squadron Leader, R.N.A.S. and Commander Cull, R.N.A.S.

On 6th July H.M.S. *Weymouth* bombarded the *Koenigsberg*, which was lying up the river screened by trees and swamps, whilst the two monitors moved up the river under a hot fire from pom-poms and 3-pounders. In the afternoon the monitors opened fire and secured a hit, but withdrew after both aeroplanes had broken down. The enemy's observation post in a tree had however been destroyed.

The attack was renewed on 11th July and at 12-20 p.m. the *Severn* opened fire; Commander Cull and Sub-Lieutenant Arnold spotting from the aeroplane; a hit was scored at the eighth salvo, but unfortunately the aeroplane was hit by A.A. gun fire and was forced to descend; nine salvoes, all hits, were got in, before the aeroplane finally fell into the water, the pilot and observer fortunately being rescued. An explosion was heard on board the *Koenigsberg* and both monitors, still firing, closed in to 7,000 yards, when the enemy was seen to be on fire fore and aft, and finally she blew up; the *Mersey* putting in the final salvo. Unfortunately she had already landed several of her 4.1-inch guns and a number of her crew, which proved a very valuable reinforcement to the German forces in East Africa. Private E. Redhead (Plymouth) of the *Mersey* was awarded the D.S.M. for these operations.

The dispatches showed that the Corps was represented not only on the water but also in the air; the R.N.A.S. personnel were worked to the limit of endurance. Squadron Leader R. Gordon (R.M.L.I.) in command of the Air Squadron, who was indefatigable in his work and ran great risks in spotting and reconnoitring, was awarded the D.S.O.; Lieutenant A. G. Bishop, R.M.L.I. of H.M.S. *Hyacinth* volunteered to observe during the second attack though he had no experience of flying and was mentioned in dispatches.

These two officers with their party went on to Mesopotamia and were present at the Battle of Ctesiphon.

About the middle of 1915 the defences of Scapa Flow were approaching completion, so that the Grand

Fleet was able to lie at this base without the constant anxiety that had been such a strain on the Commanders; the old cruisers *Royal Arthur* and *Crescent*, which had been assisting to guard the entrances, were withdrawn when the batteries were completed. It was therefore possible to afford the crews of the Fleet more opportunities for recreation and exercise; a certain amount of rifle shooting also took place and schools for education were started.

On 5th October, the first troops were landed at Salonica, and from now on the support of this force became one of the onerous duties of the Navy as the transports had to be escorted through the dangerous waters of the Aegean, whilst ships and monitors were also necessary to guard the boom and carry out the duties of S.N.O.

After the Battles of Kosturino and Doiran near the Greek frontier, the French and British forces fell back to the hills encircling the town, where entrenchments were constructed, stretching from the Vardar River through Hortakoi to the Gulf of Rendina at Stavros; the battleships at Salonica, *Exmouth, Prince George* and *Albion* were anchored so that their guns might cover the passes leading to the town, and the *Albion* landed two 6-inch guns which were mounted at the Derbend Pass, but manned by the R.G.A. As soon as Stavros was established and the net laid the 'Blister' ships, usually the *Grafton* or *Endymion* and the monitors were stationed there to cover the right flank of the army and a naval observation station under Major G. H. Seath, D.S.O., R.M.L.I., was established ashore.

1916.

On 6th January H.M.S. *King Edward VII.*, when returning to the base was sunk by a mine, but all the crew were rescued.

In January, 1916, after the evacuation, the operations at the Dardanelles ceased except for the regular patrol by destroyers, submarines and aeroplanes, supported by a squadron of battleships at Mudros, which patrol was maintained off the Straits from now on to the end of the War. The battle squadron was later considerably reduced and replaced by a French squadron, and as the Air strength increased constant bombing attacks were made on Constantinople and the Narrows.

The return of the old battleships and cruisers to England released the personnel, who were required for the ships of the new construction, which were now coming forward for commission in large numbers; whilst the East Indian squadron was reconstituted for the support of the Egyptian, Mesopotamian and East African campaigns.

On 19th January the *Hibernia* and *Zealandia* which had been lent to the Mediterranean, were ordered back to England, but Admiral Fremantle remained in charge of the Aegean squadron, whilst Rear-Admiral S. Nicholson was at Salonica with his flag in the *Exmouth*.

On 28th January as the attitude of the Greeks at Salonica was so uncertain, it was decided to occupy the Touzla Fort on Kara Burnu, which was armed with heavy guns and which completely commanded the harbour and Bay of Salonica. The *Prince George*, which had come from the Dardanelles, was to assist in case of trouble; a French force was dispatched to occupy the Fort, but when they approached with all due military precautions and entered the Fort, they found the *Prince George's* marines under Captain Toulmin and Lieutenant Strugnell, R.M.L.I. already comfortably in possession, they having landed and taken over from the Greeks a couple of hours before. The R.M. remained in charge until 28th May, 1916.

On 11th February the *Arethusa*, when 'carrying out a sweep in the Bight was sunk by a mine, and on 29th off the coast of Norway occurred another of the single ship actions, when H.M.S. *Alcantara*, Captain T. E. Wardle, an armed merchant cruiser, met the *Greif*, one of the German raiders, returning to Germany: a sharp action followed in which the *Alcantara*, after being hit by a torpedo, was sunk; but she had so damaged the *Greif* that she also was sinking and was quickly finished off by H.M.S. *Andes* and *Comus*, who appeared on the scene at the close of the action and rescued the survivors. The R.M.L.I. casualties were seven killed, one died of wounds and two wounded.

On 25th March, H.M.S. *Cleopatra* (Commodore Twyrrhit) and *Undaunted* cruising with the Flotilla from Harwich, encountered some German torpedo boat destroyers on patrol; the *Cleopatra* (Captain Loder Symonds) at once rammed and sank one of the enemy and the remainder made off; the battle cruisers and light cruisers which had come out in the hopes of meeting the German forces were disappointed.

On 25th April the enemy bombarded Lowestoft but managed to elude the British Forces on their return, although the Grand Fleet was at sea.

On 27th April H.M.S. *Russell* was sunk in the Mediterranean by a mine; Major W. Esson R.M.L.I., a noted rifle shot and a valuable officer was killed and Lieutenant T. E. Marsh, R.M.L.I. died of wounds with nine N.C.O.s and men of the Chatham Division.

On 4th May, an air raid was made on the Zeppelin sheds at Tondern. As it was considered probable that it might draw out the High Seas Fleet, it was supported by the whole of the Grand Fleet. Though the raid was successful, the enemy refused to be drawn and there were no further results; at 10 a.m., however, H.M.S. *Galatea* and *Phaeton* brought down the Zeppelin "L 7," by gun fire. On the next day away in the Aegean, H.M.S. *Agamemnon* also brought down a Zeppelin, which had previously bombed Salonica; the airship fell in the Vardar Marshes, where it was destroyed.

On 31st May, off the Horns Reef took place the long hoped for battle with the High Seas Fleet, which was given the name of the Battle of Jutland, and is described in chapter 4.

A few days later, on 5th June, the Empire sustained an irreparable loss, when H.M.S. *Hampshire*, which was conveying Lord Kitchener and his staff to Russia, struck a mine off the Orkneys and was lost with all hands, except a few who were rescued from a raft. The Royal Marines in the batteries at Hoy (Orkneys) found themselves helpless spectators and could only watch her sinking, and search the shore for any survivors who might have been washed ashore in the rough seas. Captain C. S. Hazeon, R.M.L.I. (who had narrowly escaped being blown up in H.M.S. *Natal*), and 63 N.C.O.s and men (R.M.L.I.), were drowned.

HONOURS AND REWARDS.

Besides those mentioned in the text, a certain number of rewards were given to members of the Corps for services during this period, necessarily few from the nature of the work.

D.S.O - Captain E. Gillespie, RM.L.I. (see Chap. 1).

D.S.M.-(a) *Services in Patrol Cruisers, where they were engaged in the hard and dangerous work of boarding and armed guards of the suspected ships.*

Colour-Sergeant T. W. Boffey, (Plymouth).   Sergeant W. S. Elliott, (Plymouth).
Colour-Sergeant W. Seabrook, (Portsmouth).   Colour-Sergeant G. Burley, (Portsmouth).
Corporal G. Finch, (Plymouth).   Lance-Corporal R Emmett, (Chatham).
Private W. Reynold, (Plymouth).

(b) *For Operations on the Belgian Coast-*
Corporal S. Morriss, (Portsmouth).

(c) *For Work at Suda Bay-*
Private F. G. Clarke, (Chatham).

CHAPTER 3.

THE DARDANELLES PER MARE.

Naval Attack decided on - The Base at Mudros - The preliminary Bombardments - Landing of Demolition Parties - The attack of 18th March - Preparations for the landing - Disposition of the Naval Forces - The landings - The feint landing at Bulair - Submarines - *Albion* ashore – R.N.A.S. - Monitors - Evacuation of Suvla - Evacuation of Helles - Honours and Rewards.

(See Plan I and Map 4.)

At the end of 1914 and the beginning of 1915, it became evident that closer touch with Russia must be established. Communication by the White Sea was blocked in the winter and early spring, and it was necessary not only to provide the Russians with munitions, but also for the Allies to avail themselves of her vast reserves of men and grain. It was clear, too, that owing to the stalemate in the West, the Germans would shortly make an attack on Russia in order to finish her off quickly and release the German troops for the Western Front.

It was further necessary to deter Turkey from her evident intention of attacking Egypt, which attack actually took place in February, 1915, and to occupy her armies, which were also threatening Russia in the Caucasus.

Under these circumstances some point at which to attack Turkey, and force a communication with Russia was sought; the Dardanelles were selected. Unfortunately both the lessons of history and the considered decisions of the Committee of Imperial Defence were overlooked, and though no troops could be provided to support the action of the Fleet, it was decided to make a purely naval attack on the forts, and endeavour to force a passage through the Straits.

An elaborate plan was drawn up by Vice-Admiral Carden (who had relieved Admiral Milne in command of the station), which received the approval of the Admiralty.

During January and February the ships were gathering from all quarters of the Globe to take their part in the operations, together with the store, ammunition and repair ships, necessary for the maintenance of such a large naval force.

As there was no base nearer than Malta, the harbour of Mudros in the island of Lemnos was taken over from the Greeks, and the ships were accommodated there with subsidiary bases at Imbros and Tenedos. These islands had formerly belonged to Turkey, but they had been seized by Greece in the Balkan War of 1912-13, and retained, though the treaty had never been ratified. The base at Mudros was organised by Rear-Admiral Wemyss, as S.N.O. and Military Governor, and the difficulties encountered and the measures to deal with them are related by him in his most interesting account of "The Navy at the Dardanelles." A full account of the base and the share of the Royal Marines, is given in chapter 22.

The ships detailed at first were mostly those which had been commissioned on mobilisation largely with reservists, and nucleus crew ships of the Second Fleet, which were completed with active service crews.

On 31st January, as there seems to have been some idea that it might be necessary to secure the forts after they had been reduced by the Fleet, the H.Q. of the Royal Marine Brigade with the Chatham and Plymouth Battalions under Brigadier-General Trotman, were sent out, arriving at the Dardanelles on 21st February (see chapter 11).

On 19th February, the attack opened with the bombardment of the outer forts, Nos. 1, 3, 4 and 6, on both sides of the entrance to the Straits. The squadron consisted of *Inflexible* (Flag), *Vengeance* (Flag),

THE DARDANELLES

PLAN 1

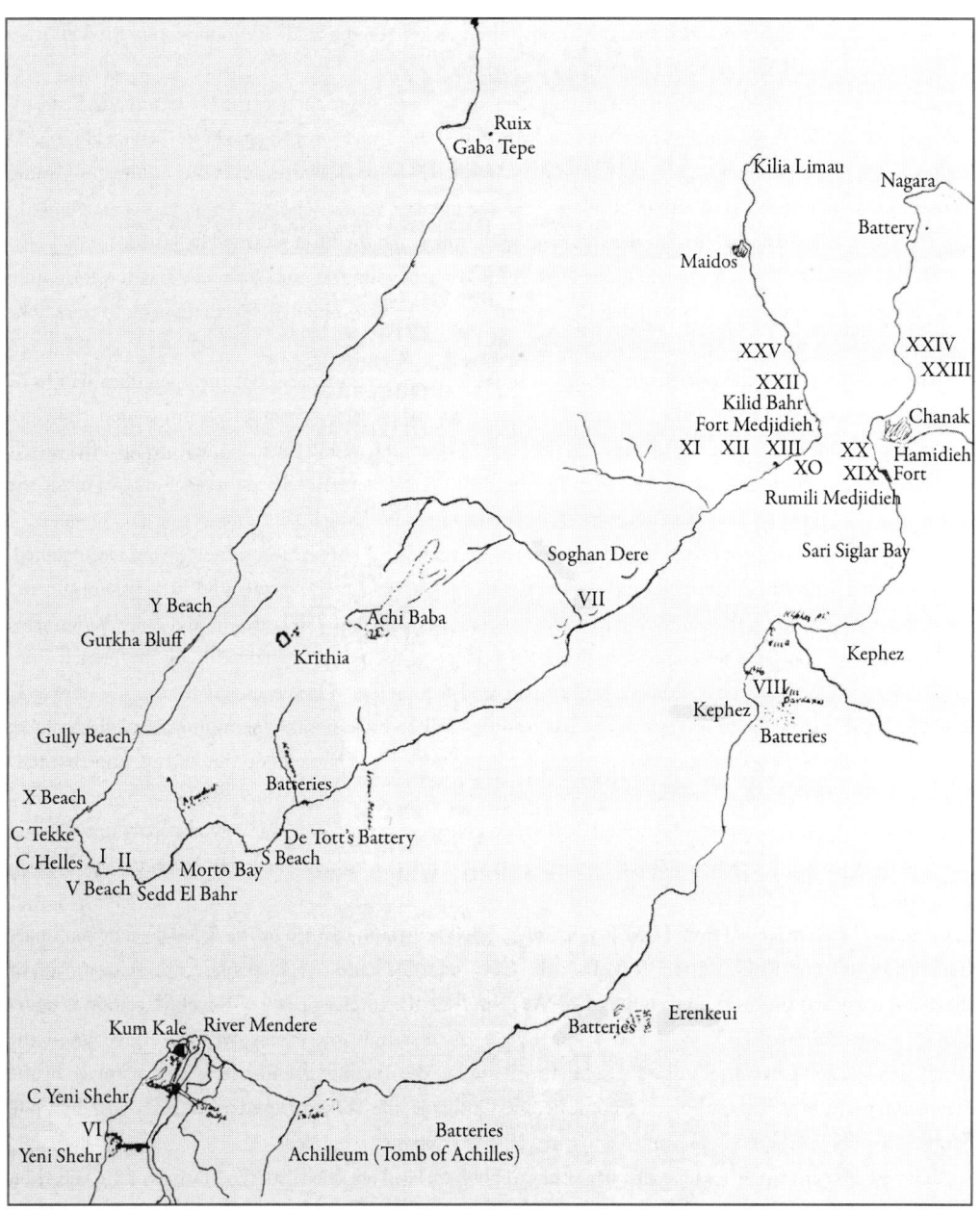

SKETCH MAP OF DARDANELLES.
Showing position of Forts.

Albion, Triumph, Cornwallis and *Irresistible* battleships, with the cruiser *Amethyst* and destroyers, also three French battleships.

The stonework of the forts was considerably damaged, but the material damage was very slight, and the enemy casualties were small. There was no damage to the Allied squadron. The forts made no reply until the afternoon. The Official History says, "By 5-15 p.m. the *Inflexible* was engaging Orkhanie, (Asiatic Shore) with the result-so good was her practice-that the Turkish fire quickly became wild." 19 rounds were fired all from "Q" Turret, the Royal Marine turret, between 5-15 and 5-26 p.m.

In the afternoon the *Agamemnon* arrived, and at 5 p.m. was ordered to support the *Cornwallis*, off Sedd-ul-Bahr, whilst the *Vengeance* attacked fort No.4, at Kum Kale. The *Agamemnon* engaged No. 3 (Fort Helles). At 5-20 p.m. the ships withdrew, but by the end of the day it had become clear that direct hits on the guns would be necessary to put them out of action.

The *Queen Elizabeth* arrived after the ships had withdrawn, and the Fleet returned to Tenedos.

During the next few days preparations were made for renewing the bombardment and the forts were reconnoitred. The aeroplanes reported that the guns in fort No.1 were uninjured, but that owing to the smoke the damage to the other forts could not be ascertained.

The next day (20th) the bombardment of the inner forts was commenced, but the operations had to be suspended on account of bad weather. Meanwhile mine sweeping was being energetically prosecuted, this work had to be performed under the fire of guns and the blaze of searchlights, and the fishermen crews of the vessels were replaced by officers and men drawn from the Fleet. By great gallantry and perseverance an area inside the Straits was swept up which enabled the battleships to enter and attack the inner forts.

On 25th February *Queen Elizabeth* and *Agamemnon* engaged No. 1 Fort at Helles; the *Agamemnon* anchored, but after being badly hit, she weighed and kept on the move. *Queen Elizabeth* having knocked out one gun and the *Agamemnon* the other, they shifted to Fort No.3 and about 12-48 p.m. the *Vengeance* and *Cornwallis* started their run against the same forts and were firing till 1-15 p.m. The firing was taken up by the French ships *Charlemagne* and *Suffren* from 2-20 p.m. to 2-35 p.m. and then by the *Triumph* and *Albion* from 3-10 to 3-37 p.m.; the last ship closed in to 1000 yards and according to their observations the enemy guns were dismounted.

On 26th *Albion, Vengeance* and *Majestic* were sent in to attack Fort Dardanus on the Asiatic shore, but they were frequently hit by hidden batteries of howitzers, whose positions could not be located; the enemy now retired from the forts at the entrance, and Admiral de Robeck, considering that there was a good opportunity to send in demolition parties of seamen, covered by small parties of Royal Marines asked permission to do so, which was granted.

A party therefore landed from H.M.S. *Irresistible* at Sedd-ul-Bahr, covered by the R.M. detachment under Captains Panton and R. G. Burton, R.M.L.I.; the guns, six 6-inch and two 12-pounders, were destroyed by the Naval party and they withdrew unmolested. At Kum Kale the covering party of Royal Marines was under Major G. M. Heriot, D.S.O., R.M.L.I. of the *Vengeance*; they drove the enemy over the bridge across the River Mendere and partially destroyed it. Two 4-inch guns at the Tomb of Achilles were also destroyed by the demolition party, as well as the guns at Kum Kale, and Orkhanie; the Turks attacked as the party withdrew and Sergeant Turnbull (Chatham) was killed and three N.C.O.s and men wounded.

It is perhaps permissible to consider what results might have been obtained if all the Marines of the Squadron had been landed on the Gallipoli Peninsula as soon as the firing ceased, as was done at Alexandria in 1882. At least 1,200 Royal Marines were available, to whom could have been added the 2,000 men of the Royal Marine Brigade with their Headquarters and it does not seem to have been beyond the bounds of possibility that supported by the guns of the Fleet they might have been able to seize a covering position (from their own accounts the Turks were concentrated on the Asiatic Shore) and hold it until reinforced by the 5000 Australians who were landed at Mudros on 4th March.

Some idea of this sort seems to have been in the minds of those responsible, because the transports carrying the Royal Marine Brigade were ordered to Imbros on 28th, but it was then too late, as a violent gale from north east caused them to stand off and on, and they anchored at Imbros on 1st March; proceeding to Tenedos on 2nd, and the landing described in Chapter 11 took place on 4th, but the enemy were now fully alarmed and reinforcements were arriving.

The bombardments were suspended until the afternoon of 3rd March owing to the weather; though this was still unfavourable the *Irresistible, Albion, Prince George* and *Triumph* renewed the attack on Fort Dardanus (four 5.9 inch guns) and the concealed guns at Erenkeui and round the bay.

It was now decided to attack the forts at the Narrows by indirect fire. The Narrows were defended at their entrance by the forts at Chanak, and Kilid Bahr, the principal of which were Fort Rumili Medjidieh (two 14-inch, six 9.4 inch) and Hamidieh, in front of Chanak (three 14 inch, six 9.4-inch). Further up at Nagara Point is Fort Nagara and the group of batteries between there and Chanak all heavily armed.

The *Queen Elizabeth* fired 29 rounds with aeroplane spotting and the *Inflexible* and *Prince George* also supported the attack; the fire was observed from inside the Straits by *Irresistible, Canopus, Cornwallis* and *Albion*, known as the "Live Bait Squadron" who also engaged the forts.

The magazine at Fort Medjidieh blew up, and the other forts were damaged. The *Sapphire* meanwhile had been operating against the Turkish troops in the Gulf of Adramyti. Also to effect a diversion on 5th March the East Indies Squadron under Vice-Admiral Peirse with the *Swiftsure, Goliath, Triumph* and *Euryalus* (Flag) bombarded the forts at Smyrna including Fort Yenikale and did considerable damage.

To cover the landing of the Plymouth Battalion R.M.L.I. on 4th March the ships were stationed as follows: H.M.S. *Irresistible* off Kum Kale, *Cornwallis* off the Mendere River, *Agamemnon* off Fort No.4, *Amethyst* and *Dublin* off Yeni Shehr, and on the other side *Queen Elizabeth* off No.3 Fort, *Triumph* in Morto Bay, *Lord Nelson* off Cape Helles; the *Canopus* and *Dartmouth* were off Besika Bay.

The bombardment was continued on 5th March and on 6th Dardanus and the Forts surrounding it were attacked by *Vengeance, Albion, Majestic, Prince George* and *Suffren*, whilst the *Queen Elizabeth, Agamemnon* and *Ocean* again fired across the Peninsula at Forts Hamidieh and Medjidieh with aeroplane spotting and observation by the "Live Bait Squadron." The *Queen Elizabeth* was, however, hit by six-inch howitzers mounted on the Peninsula near Gaba Tepe.

On 7th *Lord Nelson* and *Agamemnon* had a duel with Forts No. 13 (Rumili Medjidieh) and No. 19 (Hamidieh). Steaming on a triangular course within the Straits, they engaged the forts at 12,000 to 14,000 yards; the fight lasted for two hours. At 1-10 p.m. the magazine of No. 13 blew up; *Lord Nelson* having also started a fire in No. 19, there was an explosion at 1-15 p.m. the fort ceased firing for five minutes, but then recommenced. There was a second explosion in Fort No. 13 at 2-0 p.m.; *Agamemnon* then fired a salvo of all four 12-inch and five 9.2-inch from her port side and one gun of No. 13 leapt out of its mounting; the forts ceased firing at 2-30 and by 2-50 p.m. No. 17 had also been silenced. Both the ships were hit, but they were principally troubled by the howitzers and field guns at Erenkeui and Soghan Dere. The French squadron covered them from the fire of the forts at Kephez, but it could not locate the mobile guns.

On 10th and 11th March the Turks mounted guns near Morto Bay, which were attacked and the Lines at Bulair were also shelled.

Bad weather again supervened causing the suspension of the bombardments but the sweeping for mines and the operations of the submarines continued. On the night 13-14th the *Amethyst*, whose nightly work was covering the minesweepers and shooting at the searchlights, was at last found by the searchlights and received several hits causing heavy casualties. On the 16th H.M.S. *Canopus* made a demonstration to the north of Gaba Tepe, putting her R.M. detachment into the boats and firing, but did not actually land them.

The main attack was made on the 18th March; Admiral Carden had been invalided and the command devolved on Admiral de Robeck, who shifted his flag from the *Vengeance* to the *Queen Elizabeth*. At 10-45 a.m. *Queen Elizabeth*, *Inflexible*, *Agamemnon* and *Lord Nelson* from inside the Straits bombarded the forts at the Narrows, whilst the *Triumph* and *Prince George* on their flank engaged the forts just before the Narrows. The enemy again opened fire with howitzers and field guns, which worried the ships, particularly the howitzers at Soghan Dere. The fore control of the Inflexible was hit and all ships received hits during this part of the action. At 12-20 p.m. the French squadron advanced to engage the forts at closer range and at 1-25 p.m. the forts had ceased firing.

The *Vengeance, Irresistible, Albion, Ocean* and *Swiftsure* advanced to relieve the *Queen Elizabeth* squadron; as the French ships were withdrawing the *Bouvet* struck a mine in the bay below Erenkeui Village and sank in three minutes with heavy loss; the *Inflexible* also in withdrawing struck a mine in the same spot and was so severely damaged, that she was with difficulty sufficiently repaired to enable her to reach Malta and she took no further part in the operations. The relieving battleships renewed the attack on the forts, which again opened fire, whilst the minesweepers were again called into requisition. About 4 p.m. whilst bombarding, the *Irresistible* struck a mine in Kephez Bay and sank in deep water at 5-50 p.m., her crew being rescued by destroyers; Captain R. G. Burton, R.M.L.I. and one private were hit by shell fire and died of wounds on their way to Malta.

At 6-15 p.m., the *Ocean* also struck a mine and sank shortly afterwards in deep water, her crew were rescued by the destroyers under a hot fire from the enemy.

The attack ceased at dusk and was the last serious attempt to force the passage by the Navy alone. The menace of the mines impeded the movements of the battleships, and there were not at that time the means of dealing with them, which were evolved later; whilst their presence also rendered any attempt to rush the Narrows an operation foredoomed to failure. It was now realised that the task could not be carried out by the Fleet alone, and that the assistance of troops was necessary, particularly to deal with the howitzers and mobile guns of the Turks.

In this action the numbers of the Corps were 20 officers, 2 W.Os. and 1118 N.C.Os. and men.

The troops were now beginning to arrive. General Sir Ian Hamilton was present at the bombardment of the 18th, and whilst the Army went to Egypt to reorganise the troops and the stowage of their gear, the Navy continued their preparations for the landing: collecting lighters and small craft, organising the beach parties and attending to the many details essential to a combined operation of this magnitude. During this period reconnaissances were made for suitable landing places and a constant watch was kept on the movements of the enemy. Minesweeping was continued under protection of battleships each night, and occasionally the enemy camps and Krithia were bombarded, but bad weather constantly interfered with the operations.

The Turks employed the interval in strengthening their defences, and bringing up their reinforcements, but as there was no indication of where the blow would fall, they could only concentrate their forces in certain areas.

The duties entailed on the Navy absorbed a very large personnel for boats crews, beach parties, working parties, etc., and the crews of the *Irresistible* and *Ocean* were fully employed. The Royal Marine detachments of those ships, under Major R. C. Temple, R.M.A., who was appointed Military Governor, were detailed to garrison Tenedos; where an aerodrome had been established and where in Dimitri Bay was an advanced base for the ships to lie screened from the forts.

The R.M.A. detachment of the *Inflexible* were sent from Malta to man the six-inch howitzers, with which some of the ships had been equipped, but as they had been found useless afloat, it was proposed to land them with the troops. The detachment however, was not utilised for this purpose and after a short period manning the batteries at Buda and Lemni (Mudros) they returned to their ship, The howitzers were later utilised by some of the *Ocean's* Marines and R.N. Division, under Lieutenants H. J. Pace, R.M.A. and Lieutenant G. Crick, R.M.L.I

The *Queen* and *Implacable*, left England on 19th March, to replace the *Irresistible* and *Ocean* and were followed soon after by the *London* and *Prince of Wales*, who arrived at Lemnos on 29th March.

On 11th April, operations were resumed, the forts being again bombarded, and mine sweeping was carried out inside the Straits. *The Prince of Wales* fired over the hills with aeroplane spotting and scored several hits.

On 18th, the transport *Manitou* on her way to Mudros, was attacked by a Turkish destroyer and some casualties were caused. The destroyer was chased ashore and destroyed by the *Minerva* and some T.B.Ds. On the same day the *Swiftsure* and *Majestic* again bombarded the forts; the divisional and brigade staffs of the 29th Division with the captains and gunnery lieutenants of the covering ships were embarked in the *Swiftsure*, to reconnoitre the landing places and make themselves acquainted with their characteristics.

Meanwhile the naval and military staffs, under Rear-Admiral R. Wemyss and General Sir I. Hamilton, were working out the detailed orders and plans for the landing and in seeing that everyone was conversant with the part that he had to play. The troops were trained in embarking in the ships' boats quickly and silently, and the ships were told off, each for its particular duty.

The object of the expedition was to capture the Kilid Bahr Plateau, on the Gallipoli Peninsula, and thereby dominate the forts at the Narrows. This would involve also the destruction of the enemy's concealed mobile batteries. The enemy's strength was estimated at 40,000 men and strong opposition was expected.

At last on 24th April all was ready, and that afternoon, with loud cheers, the Fleet accompanied by the mass of transports, sweepers, hospital ships, etc., left Mudros for the great attack on the morrow.

The actual command of the arrangements for the landing were under Rear Admiral Wemyss, with his flag in the *Euryalus*, whilst the commander-in-chief in the *Queen Elizabeth*, was in supreme command of the forces afloat.

The attack was divided into four sections, the first the main attack on the Southern landing places, to be carried out by the 29th Division to which the Plymouth Battalion R.M.L.I., and Anson Battalion of the R.N. Division were attached. The second by the Australians at Gaba Tepe, with the object of seizing the plateau above Kilid Bahr, from the flank. The third a demonstration by the R.N. Division in their transports off Bulair, to make the enemy believe that a landing was to be attempted there. The fourth an attack by the French on the Asiatic shore at Kum-Kale, to occupy the enemy on that side.

Each section was allotted a proportion of battleships, cruisers and destroyers, with trawlers and drifters attached. The squadrons were divided into "*attendant*" ships, destroyers and trawlers, to land the covering troops and the "*covering*" ships for bombarding. The *Queen Elizabeth* was the fleet flagship.

For the Southern landings the First Squadron consisted of:-

ATTENDANT SHIPS.- *Euryalus.* "W" Beach (Lancashire Landing).
Cornwallis. "S" Beach (De Tott's Battery).
Implacable. "X" Beach.

At "V" Beach the troops were landed from the *River Clyde* a specially prepared transport.

COVERING SHIPS.- *Swiftsure.* "W" Beach.
Vengeance. off Kereves Dere.
Albion. "V" Beach.
Lord Nelson. off Morto Bay to prevent movement between Sedd-ul-Bahr and De Tott's.
Prince George. to neutralise the Asiatic Batteries.
Talbot.
Minerva.
Dublin. "X" Beach.
8 T.B.Ds. and 6 Fleet sweepers.

At Gaba Tepe the Second Squadron :-

ATTENDANT SHIPS.- *Queen.*
Prince of Wales.
London.

COVERING SHIPS.- *Triumph.* 2600 yards west of Gaba Tepe.
Bacchante. about 1 mile from centre landing place.
Majestic. to the Northward of Fishermen's huts to prevent reinforcements coming from Biyuk Anafarta.
Ark Royal. aeroplane ship.
Manica. balloon ship.
8 Fleet sweepers.

At Bulair, The Third Squadron:-

COVERING SHIPS.- *Canopus.*
Doris.
Dartmouth.

At "Y" Beach, The Fourth Squadron :-

ATTENDANT SHIPS.- *Amethyst.*
Sapphire.
12 Trawlers.

COVERING SHIP.- *Goliath.*

Inside the Dardanelles, The Fifth Squadron:

Agamemnon.
12-16 Destroyers for mine sweeping.
3 French Mine-sweepers.
2 Net Trawlers.
10 Drifters.

The object of this squadron was to cover the mine-sweepers, and to prevent mines drifting down on the bombarding ships; also to prevent forts 7 and 8 (Dardanus), interfering with the landings.

At Kum-Kale, The Sixth Squadron:-

The French.

At Smyrna, The Seventh Squadron:-

Triad.

2 T.B.Ds.

To supplement the working parties the "Anson" Battalion of the Royal Naval Division had been distributed to the principal beaches, but in the event under Lieutenant-Colonel Morshead, D.S.O., R.A., of the West African Forces, they contributed very materially with their rifles to the eventual success.

As so large a percentage of the seamen were required to man the boats, etc. for landing the troops, the R.M. Detachments of the Fleet were employed at their gun stations, afloat, and except at De Totts Battery as related below took no part in the actual landing. The numbers of the Corps afloat on this great day were approximately 37 officers, one warrant officer, 1,908 N.C.O.s and men.

Dealing with the landings in order from the right, "S" Beach was in Morto Bay below De Totts Battery; the South Wales Borderers, less one company, were detailed: to take the Battery covered by the *Cornwallis*, Captain A. P. Davidson; Captain Davidson had been directed to render all the assistance he could, and this he interpreted to mean, not only to cover the landing with his fire, but he also lent 36 of his Royal Marine Detachment under Major W. W. Frankis and Lieutenant E. M. Parker R.M.L.I. to replace the company of the South Wales Borderers and himself accompanied the boats crews with 25 seamen. The South Wales Borderers on approaching the shore, jumped into the water up to their middle as a hot fire was opened on them; they at once made for the two pre-arranged points of attack, the steep cliff and the slope on the left; this well trained battalion worked its way methodically up to the top of the battery from both sides and established themselves there, with the loss of two officers and 14 killed and three officers and 57 wounded. The *Cornwallis* detachment arrived as the right flank was half-way up the cliff and the Royal Marines followed the soldiers advance; the seamen having beached the boats of the other party seized their rifles and joined in the attack; meanwhile the *Cornwallis* was ordered round to "V" Beach to assist, but it was some considerable time before her parties could be collected and brought off.

The main landing was intended to be at "V" Beach which was the beach just under the old ruined fort at Sedd-ul-Bahr. It had been strengthened by every means known to field fortification and its natural slope in the shape of an amphitheatre gave its defenders every opportunity of rendering it impregnable; it still remains a mystery how the gallantry of the 29th Division triumphed over the obstacles. H.M.S. *Albion* and her consorts poured in a concentrated fire but they could not crush the machine guns dug into the cliffs on either side and fire had to be stopped when the boats were close inshore for fear of hitting our own men. Here the Royal Munster and Royal Dublin Fusiliers, to be followed by the Hampshire Regiment, had been detailed to attack and they were carried in the S.S. *River Clyde*, which had been specially prepared, whilst parties of the covering troops were landed from the ships boats. The *River Clyde* was successfully grounded, but there is no space in this chronicle to detail the gallant deeds of these famous regiments or to relate the gallantry of Commander Unwin and the Officers and seamen of the Royal Navy, who by their heroic efforts enabled the troops to land and earned undying glory by effecting the apparently impossible.

In the evening the *Albion* closed in and destroyed a machine-gun post on the left, and the following morning another one in the old Fort of Sedd-ul-Bahr which helped the troops to advance. During the night the troops made good the lodgment that had been made in the early morning, and by dawn the village and heights had been captured and the beach was secured.

At "W" Beach, for which the 1st Battalion Lancashire Fusiliers formed the covering troops, the landing was covered by the *Euryalus* and *Swiftsure*; the regiment landed from open boats in spite of a very fierce fire and the wire entanglements which were stretched in the water, and by the greatest gallantry secured the beach, which here as at "V" Beach slopes gently down to the water's edge, but fortunately the cliffs on either side afforded a certain amount of cover up which the assailants climbed and consolidated their position.

At "X" Beach the covering troops were provided by the Royal Fusiliers to be followed by the Royal Inniskilling Fusiliers and the Border Regiment; the covering ship was the *Implacable* and here the bold handling of his ship by Captain Lockyer, who ran her in to 500 yards from the beach and deluged both it and the cliffs with shell fire until the troops were landed enabled them to land without loss and the position was consolidated. The *Implacable* brought her broadside of four 12-inch, six 6-inch, and eight 12-pounders to bear, the larger guns firing on the cliffs and beach and the 12-pounders sweeping a ridge to starboard, from which rifle fire reached the ship; the fire was also supported by the *Dublin*. After the troops had advanced the *Implacable* placed a barrage ahead of them until it was stopped by the Admiral, because it was getting too close to the troops coming from "W" Beach; at noon these ships assisted to smash up the Turkish counter attack. In the afternoon the *Implacable* and *Swiftsure* assisted in an attack on Krithia and afforded continuous support to the troops. They were called on again at 11-40 p.m. to support the troops against another counter attack, and were in action until 1-30 a.m. The attack was renewed and the ships' 6-inch guns (the Royal Marine Group) remained in action until 3-30 a.m. Support was continued all the next day and the ship also assisted in the re-embarkation of the "Y" Beach troops. Captain L. Norcock, R.M.L.I. was mentioned in dispatches for the handling of his group of guns.

At "Y" Beach the landing was unopposed, but the *Goliath* and cruisers were in action during the attacks in the afternoon and on the following morning covered the withdrawal, the events at this landing are fully described in Chapter 11.

The troops to be landed at Gaba Tepe embarked in the *Queen, London* and *Prince of Wales* at 12-30 p.m. on 24th leaving Mudros at 1-30 p.m. The rendezvous off Gaba Tepe was reached at 12-30 a.m. on 25th, where the position was marked by the *Triumph*; the troops then got into the ships' boats, which were towed in by picket boats (this had been well practised at Mudros) and the 'tows' proceeded towards the beach at five knots. The *Queen* was to land her troops just north of Gaba Tepe, the *Prince of Wales* four cables to the north of her and then the *London*. The covering troops disembarked without discovery, but about 2 miles north of the proposed place, for it was then discovered that there was a four-knot current setting along the shore; the mistake was a fortunate one as the

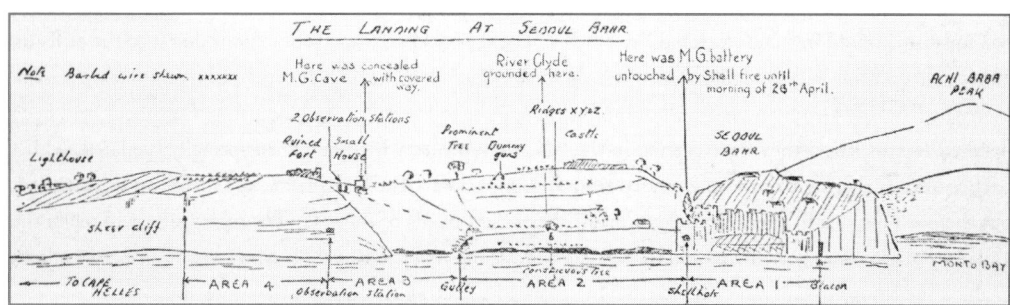

PLAN 2 PANORAMA SKETCH OF "V" BEACH BY LIEUT. C. H. CONGDON, R.M.L.I.
For use of Officers of Quarters, H.M.S. Albion.

The Dardanelles

"V" BEACH AND SEDD-UL-BAHR FORT

FIRST CAMP AT LANCASHIRE LANDING ON "W" BEACH

correct place was later found to have been heavily fortified.

After landing, musketry and howitzer fire commenced to which the ships replied with 6-inch guns. By 9 a.m. it was reported that the landing was successful and that the Australians were holding the ridge and had captured three Krupp guns.

At 9-30 a.m. some 12-inch shells, probably from the *Goeben* lying in the Narrows, dropped close to the squadron, which weighed and shifted billet. The. resistance on shore increased and by 4-30 p.m. the Australians had been driven back over the crest. The troops reported that the fire from the covering ships was short, it was therefore stopped, but at 5 p.m., aeroplanes having become available for spotting, fire was re-opened and three enemy guns were knocked out; for two hours the reverse slope of the hill was bombarded. Complaints were received from the troops of lack of support, but owing to the height of the ridges and the scrub covering them it was very difficult for the ships to assist the troops in their close and fierce fighting with the Turks, especially as no observers had yet been landed to control the ship fire from the shore.

At daybreak the next day the bombardment was continued at Anzac; the *Queen Elizabeth* using her 15-inch guns, assisted by the *Majestic*, with the aid of spotting from the kite balloon of the *Manica* silenced the enemy howitzers; during the night of 25/26 searchlights were kept on the beach to facilitate the work of tending and removing the wounded, and the naval surgeons were also lent to the transports.

At 9-30 a.m. on 27th a heavy bombardment was opened by the Second Squadron, including the *Queen Elizabeth*, because 5-inch shrapnel from the enemy howitzers had fallen close to the ships, and during the day an advance of about a mile was made by the troops supported by bombardment from the ships. Rifle and artillery fire continued throughout the night 27/28th April, but owing to lack of means of observation support could not be afforded at night by the ships. On 28th some ships embarked ammunition, which was rather a dangerous proceeding, so close to the enemy positions, and the *Prince of Wales* with the *London* as observing ship, bombarded an enemy battery during the forenoon.

During this period, in the Southern area the ships supported the attacks on Krithia, and during the forenoon of the 27th the *Implacable* shelled the village, which was full of troops and was followed by the *Goliath*. In the afternoon *Implacable* again shelled Krithia with her 12-inch guns and the village was soon a mass of smoke and dust.

On 28th the First Squadron was engaged in supporting the troops in the First Battle of Krithia, and on 29th they themselves came under the fire of enemy battleships from somewhere near the Narrows.

The feint landing of the Royal Naval Division, less Plymouth and Anson Battalions was carried out at the head of the Gulf of Xeros. The covering ships *Canopus*, *Dartmouth* and *Doris* carried out a prolonged bombardment, and the feint was then made just before dark. 1,200 men, one company from each battalion, were put into boats and towed in by trawlers; the feint was made at three contiguous beaches north of Xeros Island, near the village of Karachali; the boats remained off the shore till 9-30 p.m. without drawing any fire; they were then withdrawn and a Naval party was sent in to light flares on the beach-Lieutenant Freyberg, R.N.V.R. of the Hood Battalion swam in and lighted the flares-so as to attract the enemy's attention. The lines of Bulair appeared to be so deserted that Captain Grant of the *Canopus* hoped that he might receive orders to carry out a real landing the next day, but at midnight on the 25th he was ordered to leave the *Dartmouth* with the transports, whilst the *Canopus* and *Doris* collecting all the boats were to join the *Majestic* to protect the Anzac left.

The Royal Naval Division transports hung about till 27th and at dawn on 28th the *Dartmouth* and *Amethyst* made a further demonstration; the feint this time being made further to the westward before the little port of Ibriji, but no troops were seen and after destroying the sheer-legs and some lighters they withdrew and the

Headquarters of the Royal Naval Division went to Helles.

General Paris having been ordered to place one Brigade at General Birdwood's disposal at Anzac, the Royal Marine Brigade, less Plymouth and Deal Battalions was detailed on 28th followed on the next day by the 1st Royal Naval Brigade less the Drake[4].

The fighting on shore continued fiercely, the ships rendering continuous support in breaking up the Turkish attacks, and in silencing the Asiatic batteries; observation became more organised and the results obtained were correspondingly improved; the ships worked to a routine with the necessary visits to Mudros or Imbros to coal and ammunition.

At Anzac, as at the Southern landings, bullets and shrapnel reached the ships and caused some casualties; the bombardment was continued on 29th and some big shells fell near the 2nd Squadron at 5 a.m., two hitting the *Majestic*; which showed that Turkish battleships were somewhere near the Narrows. The bombarding ships were using a great deal of ammunition, for instance one 6-inch gun fired 87 rounds in one afternoon's bombardment.

On 29th a large fire was seen to be burning across the Peninsula, which proved to be Maidos village, and the next day the *Lord Nelson* set Chanak on fire.

On 30th, coinciding with Mustapha's third attack (see Chapter 11), the *Goeben* was reported in the Narrows and the British ships off Anzac each got off two rounds of 12-inch shell and she decamped; on this day one account relates that the *Prince of Wales* coaled ship and fired at the same time.

On 1st May the 2nd Squadron exchanged shots with two enemy battleships across the Peninsula, but without any damage to either side. On 2nd May, however the same squadron caused heavy casualties to a column of Turkish troops, whilst the *Agamemnon* with the aid of the kite balloon, the observer of which was a trained spotter knocked out three enemy guns; the Turks retaliated on the *Prince of Wales* which had to shift billet.

On 1st May the *Implacable* and other ships were engaged in landing the Indian Brigade and as an observation station was being made on shore Lieutenant Seath, R.M.L.I. of that ship was sent ashore as one of the spotters. This squadron also supported the actions on the Eski Hissarlik line which were fought on 1st and 2nd of May, the *Prince George* and other ships supporting the French on the right. A German aeroplane attacked the ships, but was driven off by rifle fire and A.A. Guns.

The following message was received from His Majesty the King on the 2nd May:

"*To Vice-Admiral de Robeck and General Sir Ian Hamilton.*

"*It is with intense satisfaction that I have heard of the success which, in the face of determined "resistance, has attended the combined Naval and Military operations in the Dardanelles. Please "convey to all ranks, including our Allies, my heartfelt congratulations for this splendid "achievement."*

In the afternoon of 2nd the *Bacchante* and *Dartmouth* at Anzac succeeded in wiping out a battery on shore.

At 4-15 a.m. on the 4th *Triumph, Bacchante, Dartmouth* with the destroyers *Colne* and *Chelmer* landed about 120 men at Gaba Tepe to ascertain if the place was held; the beach was found to be a mass of wire entanglements defended by about 500 Turks and three machine guns; the party could therefore do nothing and most were re-embarked between 5 and 6 a.m.; the ships then bombarded the place which cleared out the Turks and the wounded were re-embarked.

Firing continued on all points until the 10th May, but aeroplanes were difficult to obtain for spotting and no very great results were obtained, until later in the operations.

---

4. The Official Naval History says "No part of this reserve was used except the Drake and part of the Anson." As is described in Chapter 11 the R.M. Brigade landed that night, followed the next day by the 1st Brigade and 14 days severe fighting belies the 'quiet' of the Official Historian. The "Drake's" landed at Helles and the "Anson's" formed the beach parties as already described.

On 11th May, the Royal Marine detachments of the Fleet surrendered their short rifles for the use of the reinforcing three battalions of the Royal Naval Division, which were due from England, and on 16th volunteers were called for, from the officers of the Royal Marine detachments afloat to replace casualties in the Royal Marine Brigade, and practically all names were sent in. But the Captains of the ships in most cases declined to allow them to go without relief, and the reliefs, second lieutenants from England, could not arrive for some time; however, a few were landed and proved a welcome reinforcement to the depleted battalions.

On 9th May, Smyrna was again bombarded by the ships of the East Indian Squadron, and on this day an attack was made at Cape Helles, covered by the ships. The *Agamemnon* engaging Kephez, *Vengeance*, *Goliath* and *Albion* firing in turn on the right flank. *Swiftsure* off Cape Tekke, *Lord Nelson* in Morto Bay, *Implacable* and *Cornwallis* at "X" and "V" beaches, also co-operated.

As soon as possible a Naval observing station had been estalished on shore at Cape Helles, above "V" beach, under Commander Collard and Lieutenant Bent, R.N., assisted by artillery officers to direct the fire of the supporting ships, and two ships were always kept on the right flank until after the *Goliath* was sunk.

Once the troops were ashore the duties of the Navy were largely concerned with their maintenance and support, and the handling and supervision of the mass of small craft and transports required. Ships were detailed to cover the flanks of the troops and to assist their attacks wherever possible, a duty which gradually increased in importance, and which eventually attained to such great efficiency. In carrying out this duty on the evening of 12th May, *Goliath* lying in Morto Bay, was torpedoed by a Turkish torpedo boat, and was sunk with heavy loss; among them being Captain J. Barber, R.M.L.I., and 8 N.C.O.s and men, Royal Marines.

On 23rd May, the *Albion* and *Canopus* had an exciting adventure. The former when bombarding, went ashore off Gaba Tepe and the *Canopus* attempted to tow her off. The Turks at once opened fire from the heavy batteries and howitzers and shelled both ships; then large shells from the *Barbarossa*, a Turkish battleship, above the Narrows, fell close to the ships. On the arrival of the *Lord Nelson*, her fire across the peninsula drove off the enemy ship, whilst the *Albion* and *Canopus* themselves kept down the fire from the shore batteries, and eventually the *Albion* was hauled off into safety. During the time the *Albion* was on shore, the enemy registered 240 direct hits on her and over 2000 holes (luckily none below the water line) were repaired at Malta.

One shell struck "X1" casemate (the Royal Marine quarters) and caused several casualties, Sergeant Brown, R.M.L.I. was killed and Corporal Collier, R.M.A., severely wounded. Gunner Druce, R.M.A., carried the corporal from the casemate to the dressing station, crossing the open deck, under very heavy fire and was awarded the D.S.M. Private Robins, R.M.L.I., was also awarded the D.S.M. ; he was employed in removing empty cartridge cases from "X1" casemate, when he saw that the 12-pounder cartridges of the night defence guns had caught fire, he at once threw them overboard so preventing an explosion and was wounded in doing so.

At last after many false alarms a submarine was definitely sighted off Mavro Island on 17th May, and it became necessary to reconsider the position of the battleships. The *Queen Elizabeth*, which was already under orders to return to England, at once did so, being relieved by the *Venerable*, fresh from her bombarding experiences on the Belgian coast. Whilst as Italy was on the point of declaring war on the Central Powers, the *Queen, Prince of Wales*, *London*, and *Implacable* with *Dartmouth* and *Amethyst*, were withdrawn from the Dardanelles, leaving Mudros on 19th May, and proceeded to Malta, where they were prepared for their new duties. The submarines soon made their presence felt, as on 26th May the *Triumph*, whilst firing off Anzac, was torpedoed and sunk by one of them, most of her crew being saved, among them Captain J. G. Horne, R.M.L.I. The following day the *Majestic*, though lying among the transports off Cape Helles, was sunk with a loss of several N.C.O.s and men. It was obvious that large ships and transports could no longer lie off the peninsula, and they were withdrawn to Mudros and Imbros, where anti-submarine nets were laid, and it was necessary to bring all supplies, reinforcements, etc., by means of small craft, mine sweepers and trawlers, among these were many of the pleasure steamers so well known on the south coast of England.

The support by gunfire of the troops was therefore for a time carried out by destroyers (whose low velocity guns were very suitable for the purpose) and cruisers, until during the summer the monitors, the mountings of whose guns admitted of high elevations, and the "blister" cruisers of the Edgar class, became available.

Throughout the operations the units of the R.N.A.S., under Commander Samson, R.N. and Major E. L. Gerrard, R.M.L.I., had rendered invaluable service in spotting and reconnoitring. Colonel F. H. Sykes, of the Royal Flying Corps, was given a temporary commission in the Royal Marines, as colonel for charge of the air units. Captain C. H. Collet, D.S.O., R.M.A., was killed at Imbros, in an accident and Captain C. E. Robinson, R.M.L.I., was brought down in November in the Dardanelles and captured when making a reconnaissance, he died of wounds in Turkey. Major Gerrard was awarded the D.S.O. and Colonel Sykes the C.M.G.

Smyrna had been bombarded on 6th and 22nd of April, and on 9th May, by the East Indian Squadron, but no landing took place, and operations were henceforth confined to masking the place.

The big land attack on 4th June (third Battle of Krithia), was supported by six battleships and cruisers, who deluged Achi Baba for two hours with shell, and on the 18th, *Prince George* and *Humber*, engaged the Asiatic shore. On 2nd July, the *Venerable*, with the *Chatham*, bombarded the Bulair Lines from the Gulf of Xeros, with satisfactory results. Covering fire was again provided during the actions of 12th and 13th July (action of Achi Baba Nullah).

Among the heterogeneous duties that fell to the Corps, was the task of keeping order among the crews of the mass of transports at Mudros, who were drawn from every nation under the sun, and armed Marine Guards from the ships in harbour soon quelled any desire to give trouble.

At the end of June the monitors commenced to arrive. The *Humber*, with her six-inch guns, *Roberts*, *Raglan*, *Abercrombie* and *Havelock*, with fourteen and fifteen-inch guns. The "blister" ships were also added to the squadron (*Theseus*, *Endymion*, *Grafton* and *Edgar*), and the support of the troops was taken over by them, the battleships only being utilised for special tasks. The *Vengeance*, whose boilers were worn out left for England and was replaced by the *Exmouth*.

In August and September enteric fever showed itself among the personnel of the Fleet, who had not hitherto been inoculated, and henceforward all Naval and Marine personnel for foreign stations were inoculated.

At the end of July preparations were being made for the landing at Suvla, and the Fleet was drawn on largely for beach parties, boats, etc.

The actual landing was to be in the form of a surprise and the covering troops were therefore landed in silence and darkness, by means of the new "K" lighters, each carrying 400 men and fitted with special landing platforms. Troops were also embarked in the *Theseus* and *Endymion*, and the covering ships were the *Bacchante* and *Talbot*. At daybreak on 6th August, the ships together with the fourteen-inch monitors opened a heavy bombardment. A net boom with nets was laid around the landing place to cover the bombarding ships, and from this time three ships were told off to cover the troops at Suvla, two being on duty, and one resting at Mudros. A shore observation station was also established to direct their fire. On one day, when bombarding, the *Swiftsure* wiped out a whole Turkish column and during the fighting here, she, the *Bacchante* and *Talbot* all received hits as did the *Glory*, which had now joined the squadron.

In October the Salonica expedition commenced, and drew off troops from the Peninsula. The *Magnificent*, *Mars*, *Hannibal* and *Terrible*, which had surrendered their turret guns to the new monitors, were utilised as transports. The first troops of the 10th Division, were landed at Salonica on 5th October.

On 17th October, the *Chatham* took General Sir I. Hamilton to Marseilles, on relief by General Sir H. Monro.

On the 21st, as Bulgaria had definitely joined the Central Powers, the port of Dedeagatch was bombarded by the *Doris, Endymion, Theseus* and two monitors, with the Russian *Askold,* and the French *Kleber.* A good deal of material and many public buildings were destroyed and the breakwater was damaged.

On 10th November Lord Kitchener arrived in the *Dartmouth,* and remained until the 19th. Discussions took place as to the future policy in the Dardanelles, but nothing definite was apparently settled. On 24th November, Admiral de Robeck. proceeded on leave to England, and Rear-Admiral Wemyss assumed command; it was under his command that the subsequent evacuations were carried out.

On 2nd December the *Agamemnon, Endymion,* and *M. 33* with protecting drifters proceeded to the mouth of the Kavak River at the head of the Gulf of Xeros and destroyed the bridge over the river, thus cutting one of the important lines of supply of the Turks in the Peninsula.

In view of the evacuations Admiral Fremantle with *Hibernia* and *Russell* arrived from England, and about the same time the *Dublin* left. The Turks were now getting more ammunition and heavier guns, and the intensity of the fire on the troops was increasing, so that support from the ships, which had now been effectively organised under Captain D. L. Dent, R.N., became increasingly necessary.

The difficulties of the evacuation were increased by this activity, but the Navy were able to afford great help by a special organisation of supporting ships under the general charge of Admiral Fremantle, which included the regular covering squadron under Captain Dent. In the Aegean to support the left flank were the *Edgar, Theseus, Abercrombie* and two destroyers'; to keep down the Asiatic fire was the Rabbit Island Squadron, off Mavro, consisting of *Sir T. Picton, Earl of Peterborough, Roberts, M. 18,* and *M.31.* At Imbros Admiral Fremantle held in reserve the *Hibernia, Russell, Grafton, Raglan* and *Havelock* which were not required during the intermediate stage of the evacuations.

On 19th December Anzac and Suvla were finally evacuated; a marvel of organisation on the part of both Army and Navy and the ships and small craft were safely withdrawn. On the morning of 20th all available craft opened fire on Suvla and Anzac and must have punished the Turks severely.

The following account from *The Globe and Laurel* gives an interesting picture of the scene from a different point of view.

"By the 17th December, 100,000 men had been withdrawn from Suvla and Anzac during the hours of darkness ;- about 41,000 were due to leave on Saturday 18th and the remainder, rather fewer, on the 19th; the weather was ideal, but the moon was very bright.

"The escorting ship arrived with 20 empty transports at Mudros at dawn on 17th; the ship had two beaches to work from; and Suvla beach was absolutely commanded by the Turkish guns. On Friday night 17th we left Imbros after dusk in absolute darkness and at 7 p.m. were anchored close in to the beach at Suvla in order to help as much as possible. All the boats of the Fleet were away, manned and armed to bring off the troops; and soon we were stowing them away, waiting on the officers and doing all that we could to make things go; officers and men were crowding on board all through the night; whilst the guns of the ships and the Turks were strafing continually, but without any casualties. We left at 3-0 a.m., the last ship, following in rear of all sorts of craft and by 4-0 a.m. the landing at Imbros had commenced. A submarine was sunk by a trawler during the afternoon on Sunday. On the 19th we crossed again to Suvla, but were not observed by the Turks and the troops came on board at 1, 2, 3, and 4 o'clock; the hay on shore was then set alight, and then all were off except the sappers and rearguard; we were longing to drop shells into the Turkish trenches, but silence and darkness were the order of the night: but below decks, food, drink, blankets and warmth, with cabins for the first forty eight, after that the deck for all. At 5-0 a.m. the next day they were landed at Imbros and the evacuation was completed.

On 25th December all available ships bombarded Achi Baba and again on 27th the *Agamemnon* had another shoot at the howitzers at Soghan Dere, which had been so difficult to locate all along.

Preparations were now in hand to evacuate Cape Helles and constant bombardments and demonstrations were made by the ships; on 3rd January, *Russell* and *Hibernia* with the monitors bombarded the Asiatic Coast and on 5th and 7th Russell with the 'blister' ships again attacked Achi Baba. As described in Chapter 11, the evacuation was successfully completed on the night of 8/9th January, 1916, and the next morning the monitors, which from the neighbourhood of Mavro Island had silenced any Turkish guns that fired during the night, bombarded Achi Baba and the beaches for two hours.

On 9th January, all ships, with the captive balloon to look-out for mines, and trawlers to guard against submarines, left Kephalo, Aliki and Sunday Bays in Imbros for Mudros.

The great adventure was over, and the high hopes with which it had been undertaken by the Fleet were disappointed; but the record of the gallantry and devotion of the Combined Services will remain for ever as a monument of what can be accomplished by skill and courage in conquering impossible conditions.

The work allotted to the Corps afloat did not admit of many opportunities of gaining individual distinction but the following rewards were gazetted:-

C.M.G. Major W. W. Godfrey, R.M.L.I., who served throughout on the staff of the Admiral, Commanding-in-Chief; both the official dispatches and all published accounts speak of the valuable services of this officer; he was also awarded the Brevet of Lieutenant-Colonel.

Major R J. Saumarez, RM.L.I. (Ret.), of *Bacchante* who was senior RM. Officer afloat.

D.S.O. Lieutenant G. H. Seath, RM.L.I., *Implacable*, for observation station on shore.

D.S.C. Lieutenant F. H. Thomas, RM.L.I., *Talbot*, liaison with the troops.

Lieutenant J. Geldart, W/T officer, RM.L.I.

D.S.M. Sergeant H. R Kimber, RM.A.

Private C. D. Brace (Plymouth).	Sergeant W. Perkins, R.M.A.
Gunner J. S. Druce, RM.A.	Private E. Throssell (Portsmouth).
Private T. Robins (Plymouth).	Private J. H. Westall (Chatham).

Mentioned in Dispatches.

Lieut.-Colonel St. G. B. Armstrong, RM.L.I., A.A. and Q.M.G., Lines of Communication Army.

Major G. M. Heriot, RM.L.I., *Vengeance*.	Major A. E. Bewes, RM.L.I., Plymouth Battalion
Major W. T. C. Jones, D.S.O., RM.L.I., Beach Staff, "X" Beach	
Major L. Norcock, RM.L.I., *Implacable*.	Sergeant H. R Jeffcoate, (Chatham).
Major W. W. Frankis, RM.L.I. (Ret.), *Cornwallis*.	
Major W. W. Godfrey, RM.L.I., *Queen Elizabeth* and later *Lord Nelson*.	
Sergeant H. R Kimber, R.M.A.	Gunner S. C. Parker, R.M.A.
Private E. Trollope, (Chatham).	Gunner J. Bell, R.M.A.

CHAPTER 4.

THE BATTLE OF JUTLAND

NOTE. - No attempt has been made to give a detailed description of the battle, but its general course is indicated in order to connect the several incidents.

INFORMATION had been received that the German High Seas Fleet was likely to be on the move, and in accordance with the policy of trying to entice the enemy into a Fleet action one of the periodical sweeps in the North Sea was commenced on 30th May, 1916.

The great battle, which had been so eagerly sought, was now imminent, and all were anxious to test the culmination of so many years continuous effort. The long days of tactical exercises at sea, the many weary hours spent in turrets and control tops, the drills and loading competitions, were now to bear their fruit; whilst the skill of the control officers, gunlayers and crews, were to be tested in the fiery furnace.

Admiral Beatty with the Battle Cruiser Fleet and the 5th Battle Squadron left Rosyth, with orders to meet the Grand Fleet, at a given rendezvous, about 2 p.m. on 31st May.

His Fleet comprised the 1st and 2nd Battle Cruiser Squadrons[5], the 5th Battle Squadron, the 1st, 2nd and 3rd Light Cruiser Squadrons, the 1st, 9th, 10th and 13th Destroyer Flotillas. At the same time the Second Battle Squadron, under Vice-Admiral T. M. Jerram, left Cromarty.

The Main Battle Fleet, 3rd Battle Cruiser Squadron, 4th Light Cruiser Squadron with the attached cruisers *Chester* and *Canterbury*, the 4th, 11 th and 12th Destroyer Flotillas left Scapa Flow for the rendezvous.

The 1st Cruiser Squadron (Rear-Admiral Sir R. Arbuthnot), the 2nd Cruiser Squadron (Rear-Admiral H. L. Heath), 4th Light Cruiser Squadron (Commodore Le Mesurier) were scouting about eight miles ahead of the Battle Fleet, with the *Chester* and *Canterbury* 20 miles ahead; the attached cruisers *Active, Boadicea, Blanche* and *Bellona* were on the flanks of the Battle Fleet.

At 2-25 p.m. on 31st May the *Galatea* of the 1st Light Cruiser Squadron sighted two enemy vessels boarding a neutral steamer, and Admiral Beatty at once turned towards the Horns Reef to get between the enemy and his base; shortly afterwards the *Galatea* reported smoke, as if from a Fleet steering north, on which the Light Cruisers at once formed to the eastward to form a screen and engaged the enemy Light Cruisers at long range; at 3-30 p.m. the *Southampton*, Commodore Goodenough, sighted the enemy Battle Cruisers, which were sighted by Admiral Beatty a minute later and a seaplane was sent up from the *Engadine* to reconnoitre; the 5th Battle Squadron was following the Battle Cruisers on the starboard quarter about five miles off. The enemy Battle Cruisers altered course and made off pursued by the British Battle Cruisers, who were trying to cut them off. At 3-48 p.m. the action opened at 18,500 yards; on both sides fire was effective at once, the range at 4 p.m. being 16,000 yards.

At this moment the roof of "Q" Turret of H.M.S. *Lion* was blown off and the second Victoria Cross gained in the War by a member of the Corps was earned by Major Francis Joseph William Harvey, R.M.L.I. in charge of the turret. The shell exploded in the gun house, killing or mortally wounding all the crew in the gun house and control position, Major Harvey who had been mortally wounded, both legs being shot off, was heard to give the order to flood the magazine in case the fire which had started in the turret should reach the magazine, the order was at once obeyed by the magazine parties. Bombardier Brown, in charge of the working chamber took charge and the crews of the two after 4-inch gun batteries under Lieutenant F. R. Jones, R.M.L.I., hearing that "Q" Turret was out of action,

---

5. For composition of Squadrons see Table at end of Chapter.

went forward to see what they could do, and as there was insufficient pressure to work the hoses they formed a party to pass buckets of water into the turret until it was reported that the fire was under control and they had to return to their station. Shortly after there was a second explosion in "Q" Turret which was caused by some smouldering material falling on a half charge in the cage, which exploded and killed all the loading chamber numbers, and also exploded a charge in the cage in the main trunk which passed down the trunk and killed all the magazine and shellroom parties who had collected at the foot of the trunk, "it passed down and right through the turret in a great sheet of flame," but owing to Major Harvey's foresight the magazines had been closed and flooded as the *Gazette* puts it "with great presence of mind and devotion to duty, saving the ship." He was awarded the Victoria Cross posthumously, which was presented by His Majesty to his widow. The Corps casualties in the ship were 47 killed and two wounded.

At 4.6 p.m. the *Indefatigable* was hit and an explosion followed, when she fell out of the line; she was again hit forward and blew up, Captain P. M. C. Wilde, R.M.A., R.M.Gunner G. H. Field and 89 N.C.O.s and men being killed.

Many hits were being obtained on the .enemy ships and the fighting was very fierce. At 4-15 p.m. a gallant attack was made by the British Destroyers, which resulted in a destroyer action with the enemy Torpedo Boat Destroyers and a light cruiser; both sides lost two destroyers, but *Nestor* and *Nomad* under Commander Bingham got home their attack and forced the enemy Battle Cruisers to turn away.

By 4-18 p.m. the third enemy ship in the line was on fire and the Fifth Battle Squadron which had come into action was inflicting and receiving hits. At 4-26 p.m. the *Queen Mary* was hit abreast of "Q" Turret; a terrific explosion occurred and the fore part of the ship instantly disappeared, the after part blew up in a second explosion alongside the *New Zealand* as the latter was passing, only a few survivors being rescued by the destroyers; Major G. C. Rooney, R.M.L.I., R.M.Gunner C. Catley and 115 N.C.O.s and men were killed.

At 4-38 p.m. the *Southampton* reported that she had sighted the enemy Battle Fleet steering north, and at 4.42 Admiral Beatty also sighted them; he at once recalled his destroyers and, turning 16 points tried to draw the enemy Fleet towards his own Battle Fleet; the enemy Battle Cruisers continued their course to the south and for twelve minutes the Squadrons were fighting on opposite courses, when the enemy cruisers turned also to the northward course.

The 5th Battle Squadron followed the Battle Cruisers round, the two leading ships *Barham* and *Valiant* engaged the Battle Cruisers and the *Malaya* and *Warspite* engaged the enemy Battle Fleet. Fire ceased at about 5-10 p.m. owing to the mist, but was reopened at 5-40 p.m. The mist, aided by the smoke, was now thickening and visibility was getting very low; the *Barham* had been hit and the *Malaya* and *Warspite* had both suffered severely; in the *Malaya* at 5-30 p.m. a shell from an enemy battleship burst inside the starboard battery and wrecked it starting a fire and causing 102 casualties, the Corps losing eight killed, nine died of wounds and nine wounded.

The Battle Fleet was now approaching the scene of action formed in columns of Divisions.

LINE OF ADVANCE

1st Division.	2nd Division.	3rd Division	4th Division	5th Division	6th Division
King George V.	*Orion*	*Iron Duke*	*Benbow*	*Colossus*	*Marlborough*
Ajax	*Monarch*	*Royal Oak*	*Bellerophon*	*Collingwood*	*Revenge*
Centurion	*Conqueror*	*Superb*	*Temeraire*	*Neptune*	*Hercules*
Erin	*Thunderer*	*Canada*	*Vanguard*	*St. Vincent*	*Agincourt*

Consequent on the rapid and continuous turning movements of the ships engaged with the enemy, there was a discrepancy in the positions reported and the Battle Fleet found itself in proximity to the enemy rather sooner than it expected.

At 4 p.m. the 3rd Battle Cruiser Squadron under Rear-Admiral Hood had been ordered to reinforce the Battle Cruiser Fleet and proceeded with some destroyers, *Chester* and *Canterbury*. At 5-30 p.m. the *Chester* turned south-west to investigate the firing heard in that direction and Captain R. N. Lawson sighted a light cruiser with some destroyers and closed her; he then sighted two or more light cruisers astern of the first ship and was immediately hotly engaged at about 6,000 yards; the enemy's fourth salvo hit the *Chester* and put No. 1 gun port out of action, killing and wounding a large proportion of the crews of Nos. 1, 2, 3 guns port; Captain E. Bamford, R.M.L.I. of this ship was in the after control, when it was blown to pieces by a shell; he was slightly wounded in the leg, but he at once assisted to work one gun with a much reduced crew and controlled another gun; he also assisted in extinguishing a fire and in general showed great coolness, power of command, judgement and courage when exposed to a heavy fire and was awarded the D.S.O. Of the 20 R.M.L.I. who manned one gun on each side of the ship, eight were killed, and 10 wounded, yet the two guns remained in action throughout; when the men at the top of the ammunition hoist became casualties Privates Patterson and Smith rushed up from below to keep up the supply, both were unfortunately killed; out of 28 Royal Marines "commended for good service" in the *London Gazette* for this Battle five belonged to this small cruiser with a detachment of 40 all told[6]. It was in this ship that Boy Cornwell, R.N. was awarded the V.C. and there were 70 casualties altogether; Captain Lawson though wounded, after 19 minutes of this unequal fight, zigzagged into the last fall of shot and so defeated the enemy gunnery lieutenants and saved his ship.

Admiral Hood coming up with his squadron passed between her and her opponents and opened fire on the enemy light cruisers at 5-55 p.m. This was followed by another gallant destroyer fight with enemy light cruisers and destroyers.

Reverting to the line of the First and Second Cruiser Squadrons, firing was heard at 5-40 p.m. and the squadrons formed single line ahead; at 5-47 p.m. the *Defence* sighted three or four enemy light cruisers, which she at once engaged; about 6 p.m. the *Wiesbaden*, which had been severely damaged by the 3rd Battle Cruiser Squadron, was also evidently crippled by the fire of the *Defence* and *Warrior*. In his eagerness to close her Sir R. Arbuthnot in the *Defence* passed close across the bows of the *Lion* about 6-5 p.m.; she was followed by the *Warrior*, but the *Duke of Edinburgh* and *Black Prince* of that squadron could not cross and had to turn away; at 6-10 p.m. *Defence* and *Warrior* came under the fire of the enemy Battle Cruisers and Battle Fleet and at 6-15 p.m. the *Defence* was hit by two salvoes from the *Frederich der Grosse* and blew up; Lieut. A. D. P. Hamilton and 83 N.C.O.s and men, Royal Marines, being killed. The Warrior was also badly hit and disabled at the same time; Captain Molteno succeeded in bringing his ship out of action, and she was taken in tow by the *Engadine*, but during the night the tow had to be abandoned owing to the rising wind and the crew were taken off by the *Engadine*.

A R.M. officer in a turret of a battleship of the 6th Division relates that he saw a salvo hit the *Defence* aft and the turret blew up, almost immediately afterwards another salvo hit her forward, the fore turret seemed to explode. And the remaining turrets went off in a 'ripple' from forward to aft[7].

The sinking of the *Warrior* enabled the Corps once more to exhibit its qualities of steadiness and discipline; the behaviour of the detachment under Major H. St. G. Morgan, R.M.A. being very favourably reported on by

---

6. From the *Globe and Laurel*.
7. The senior RM. Officer of Defence, Major G. R S. Hickson, RM.L.I., escaped the fate that befel his ship, as he was visiting the trenches in France. A curious incident occurred in connection with this Officer; a few months after the battle a Norwegian trawler reported having recovered in her trawl, the drawer of a writing table containing some receipt notes for confidential books and some coins, which on enquiry proved to belong to Major Hickson and were returned to him.

[Photo by Russell & Sons, Southsea.]
MAJOR FRANCIS JOHN WILLIAM HARVEY. R.M.L.I. OF H.M.S. Lion.
Killed at Battle of Jutland. Awarded Victoria Cross posthumously.

the Captain; the Sergeant Major, Colour Sergeant Abraham Spooner, R.M.A. was awarded the Conspicuous Gallantry Medal for showing the greatest gallantry and initiative in rescuing wounded in dense smoke and gas fumes from the mess deck.

About 6-10 p.m. Admiral Hood sighted Admiral Beatty's Squadron and at 6-16 p.m. turned to take station ahead of the *Lion*, a movement magnificently executed; at once they were involved in a fierce action and the *Invincible* was observed to be hitting with her salvoes, but at 6-34 p.m. she was heavily hit and blew up as the *Indefatigable* had done and disappeared; the Commander, Dannreuther, and a few who were in the control top were saved, but the Corps suffered a great loss in the death of Major R. C. Colquhoun, R.M.L.I. who had been for many years the Captain of the Corps Rifle team and a noted shot himself, with him Lieutenant T. Ie Selleur, R.M.L.I., R.M.Gunner E. A. Nixon, and 106 N.C.O.s and men were killed.

The *Inflexible* then became the leading ship and turned twice to starboard to close the enemy, but as this class were considerably slower than the *Lion* and her sisters, she and the *Indomitable* were ordered to take station astern of the *New Zealand*.

Meanwhile at 5-55 p.m. the *Marlborough* had reported to the *Iron Duke* that she could see gun flashes of cruisers in action and at 6 p.m. Admiral Burney in the *Marlborough* sighted the *Lion* steering east; at 6.8 p.m. the Battle Fleet were steering south east and at 6-14 p.m. Admiral Beatty reported having sighted the enemy Battle Fleet bearing S.S.W. and at the same time a similar report was received from the *Barham*. The 5th Battle Squadron had been reported in sight at 6.7 p.m. and at 6.15 p.m. the *Marlborough* reported that the enemy Battle Fleet was bearing S.S.E.

At 6-15 p.m. therefore the Battle Fleet was ordered to form single line ahead on the port wing column with the *King George V.* leading, the course being set S.E. by E.

The *Lion* and Battle Cruisers went on to get ahead of the Battle Fleet and the 5th Battle Squadron, which up to then had only seen the *Marlborough* Division, also turned to follow the Battle Cruisers, but on sighting the rest of the Battle Fleet had to turn away and form astern of them; in turning the helm of the *Warspite* jambed and she became the target of the enemy ships; in turning round, however, she helped to screen the *Warrior*, which was lying helpless and fortunately by clever manoeuvring she managed to get herself clear, though very severely damaged and was ordered to return independently to Rosyth.

The deployment of the Fleet was effected by 6.38 p.m. and the speed was then17 knots.

From 6.14 p.m. the enemy shells had been falling amongst the 1st Battle Squadron and three minutes later the *Marlborough* Divison became engaged with ships of the *Kaiser* Class at 13,000 yards.

At 6-30 p.m. as soon as the Battle Cruisers had drawn clear ahead the 5th Division of the Battleships also opened fire. The rear ships of the line now made out the enemy's Fleet steering to the eastward, four ships of the Konig Class in the van; then ships of the *Kaiser* class and then the *Helgoland's*, but the rear of the line was invisible.

Between a quarter and half past six a three-funnelled enemy cruiser was fired at by the Battle Fleet and sunk. As soon as the Battle Cruisers had got sufficiently far ahead the 3rd and 4th Divisions of the Battle Fleet opened fire in succession, on the enemy's *Konig* Division and inflicted heavy damage. The 1st and 2nd Divisions opened fire as soon as their range was clear. "The flash, smoke and roar of the opening salvoes of the three great Battle Squadrons was a thing to be remembered. In some ships the second guns of the turrets were brought to the 'ready' so quickly that the Director fired all guns practically simultaneously and the hydraulic pumps had the time of their lives.[8]"

---

8. From the Globe and Laurel.

Visibility was very bad, though rather better at the rear end of the line than in the van and centre, but the smoke and mist were very patchy and visibility varied sometimes from 15,000 to 9,000 yards. The enemy's fire was now very ineffective and only the *Colossus* received a hit.

It is related by a turret officer that the *Revenge* engaged one of the *Konig* class on the starboard side and their first salvo blew all their blast screens away, and then fell short, as did the second; after several salvoes the mist blotted out the enemy; "the transmitting station was howling for ranges, but they could not obtain them in the mist,"; "fire was then shifted to the third ship to the right, apparently a *Kaiser* class, but the mist kept on intervening; after checking fire to let the *Defence* and *Warrior* go past all battleships fired a few salvoes at an enemy ship which was drifting down the line." (probably the *Wiesbaden*).

At 6-35 p.m. under cover of the mist and smoke the enemy, who were suffering from the effects of the fire, turned away 16 points to the westward and their destroyers made an attack to cover them, whilst Admiral Jellicoe by successive alterations of course was seeking to close.

About ten minutes to seven the *Marlborough* was hit by a torpedo, but she was able to keep her place in the line, and re-opened fire, and by seven o'clock scored a hit with a salvo on one of the *Konig* class. An account from the *Revenge* says that just after clearing the attack by torpedoes the *Revenge* felt a bump, and almost immediately a large circular pool of oil rose alongside, abreast of the Royal Marine Turret, with a certain amount of wreckage in the centre; the *Revenge* claimed to have rammed a submarine[9]. About this time the *Lutzow*, the flagship of the enemy battle cruisers, was badly disabled and fell out of the line.

At 6-55 p.m. the enemy seems apparently to have thought that he had shaken himself free, and that he might be able to slip past the rear of the Grand Fleet, for he altered course again to the eastward to endeavour to get away to the Horns Reef and the channels swept clear of mines, and so be enabled to reach his base; but as a matter of fact he had miscalculated and was actually heading straight into the arc formed by the British Fleet. Heavy fire was re-opened on him as soon as he appeared and from 7 to 7-30 the fire of the Fleet at varying ranges was very effective; at 7-12 the *Hercules* and *Colossus* obtained hits on the *Lutzow* and *Derfflinger* and by 7-15 the guns of practically the whole Fleet had joined in; the *Calliope* reporting that two of the *Konig* class were heavily on fire.

This was too much for the Germans, who turned away again to the westward, sending their destroyers and battle cruisers to make an attack to cover the retreat of their battleships. The attack was most gallantly made by the destroyers and twenty torpedoes crossed the British Line as they turned away to avoid them, turning back again as soon as they were clear. There was a second destroyer attack at 7-25 p.m. which was defeated by gunfire, not only from the British Light Cruisers and Destroyers, but the 6-inch and 4-inch guns of the Battleships joined in and many of the enemy boats were disabled and three sunk.

Under cover of this attack the German Fleet escaped to the westward, helped by the smoke screens, though the rear of the British line was intermittently in action up to 7-55 p.m. when fire practically ceased although course had been altered to the westward. The Battle Cruisers however, who were out of sight of the *Iron Duke*, continued the pursuit and were in action up to 8-30 p.m.

At 8 p.m. the *Calliope* was hit by a heavy shell from an enemy battleship at 6,500 yards, but retaliated with a torpedo and a fire was observed on a ship of the *Kaiser* class. A writer in the *Globe and Laurel* describing some of the experiences of the light cruisers sums up the matter by saying "next time he hopes to be in a big ship."

---

9. The Official History says: "that no German submarine was sunk during the battle."

At 8-30 p.m. when the light was failing, the British Fleet was between the enemy and his base, for he had been driven off to the westward and the Battle Cruisers were reluctantly abandoning the chase.

At 9 p.m. the four squadrons of the Battle Fleet were formed into four parallel columns at an interval of one mile apart, on a southerly course; the Battle Cruisers and Cruisers were to the westward of the Fleet; with the 2nd and 4th Light Cruiser Squadrons to north and south of the Fleet; the destroyers were formed five miles astern, whilst the *Abdiel* was dispatched to lay mines off the Horns Reef.

Whilst the Fleet was proceeding to the southward the enemy made their effort to escape by crossing the rear of the British Fleet; his ships were much scattered and squadrons were constantly appearing out of the darkness. The night was rendered immortal by the gallant work of the British destroyers, who attacked continuously and gained considerable successes.

About 10 p.m. the *Castor* sighted three enemy battle cruisers, who opened fire, disabling her wireless apparatus, but the 11th Flotilla retaliated by firing torpedoes at them. About 10-20 p.m. the 2nd Light Cruiser Squadron was engaged by five enemy vessels, who opened a concentrated fire on the *Southampton* and *Dublin*, inflicting heavy loss on these two ships, but the *Frauenlobe* was sunk during this action. At 11-30 p.m. the 4th Flotilla sighted and attacked the enemy cruisers who were on a south easterly course, and again about midnight this flotilla encountered the enemy Second Battle Squadron and sank the *Pommern*. At 1-45 a.m. the 12th Flotilla, which was about 10 miles astern, owing to the 1st Battle Squadron being also astern of station due to the injury to the *Marlborough* encountered a squadron of the *Kaiser* class and most gallantly torpedoed two of them. Unfortunately Commodore Stirling's report of his discovery of the German Battle Fleet miscarried and did not reach Admiral Jellicoe.

At 12-30 a.m. the enemy encountered the 9th Flotilla and at 2-35 a.m. the 13th Flotilla attacked a squadron of *Deutschland* class and torpedoed one of them.

The *Black Prince* which had been cut off when the *Defence* attacked and had evidently failed to join another squadron was reported to have been sunk by a German Battle Squadron about 11 p.m. Captain A. W. Delves-Broughton, Lieut. G. R. Steinthal, R.M.L.I. and 77 N.C.O.s and men were killed.

In the Battle Fleet, the crews were kept closed up at action stations, but food was passed round at 9 p.m. and during the night a few at a time were allowed on the tops of the turrets, etc. for a little fresh air; in some ships from these positions they were able to watch the destroyer actions.

Owing to the injury to the *Marlborough*, her speed was so much reduced that her squadron fell considerably astern of station, consequently at 2-30 a.m. on 1st June Admiral Burney shifted his flag to the *Revenge* and the *Marlborough* was detached to the base escorted by destroyers. At 2-37 a.m. the Fleet altered course to the north and formed a single line ahead in the following order, 2nd Battle Squadron, 4th Battle Squadron, 1st Battle Squadron (less the 6th Division) the 5th Battle Squadron which was also astern of station rejoined at 3-30 o'clock and took station ahead of the 2nd Battle Squadron. About this time the *Revenge* sighted a Zeppelin and as her guns were loaded with A.P. Lyddite fired two salvoes at her as the quickest way of emptying the guns for the shrapnel, on which the airship promptly sheered off.

The Grand Fleet patrolled the area till noon on 1st June, but there were no signs of the enemy. The search was reluctantly abandoned, and the Fleet returned to its bases to refuel and make ready for any service that might be required of it.

And so ended the great battle; as was so often the case in this war, both ashore and afloat, the weather seemed to be on the side of our enemies and robbed us of our complete victory. If, in spite of the gallantry and devotion of all ranks, the battle may have yielded results that did not attain to the high standards of the

Royal Navy, which aim at nothing less than the total annihilation of its opponents, yet the words of one of the best known writers in Germany on Naval subjects should not be forgotten: "the losses sustained by our (German) Fleet were enormous, in spite of the fact that luck was on our side; and from June, 1916, it was clear to everyone of intelligence that the fight would be and must be the only one to take place. Those in authority have often admitted this openly."

The enemy losses were concealed, but it is known that the *Pommern* and *Lutzow* were sunk, whilst the *Derfflinger* and *Seydlitz* reached port in a sinking condition; four light cruisers *Wiesbaden, Elbing, Rostock* and *Frauenlobe* with five Destroyers were sunk and at least ten large ships were under repair for many months.

The British losses were very heavy and the Corps lost a large number of officers and men;

Killed. - 3 Majors, 2 Captains, 3 Lieutenants, 4 RM. Gunners, 514 N.C.O.'s and Men.
Died of Wounds. - 12 N.C.O.'s and Men.
Wounded. - 1 Captain, 50 N.C.O.'s and Men.

The officers killed were :-

Majors. - R C. Colquhoun, F. J. W. Harvey, G. C. Rooney, all RM.L.I.
Captains. - P. M. C. Wilde, R.M.A., A. W. D. Broughton, RM.L.I.
Lieutenants. - T. Le Selleur, A. D. P. Hamilton, G. R Steinthal, all RM.L.I.
Royal Marine Gunners. - C. Catley, J. H. Goss, G. H. Field, E. A. Nixon.

The total number of the Corps engaged were: 93 Commissioned Officers, 39 Warrant Officers, 5,700 N.C.O.s and Men-a total of 5,832 and the total casualties were 589 or approximately 1 in 10.

A comparison with Trafalgar shows as follows :-

Numbers engaged. –
Trafalgar	90 Officers	3,600 N.C.O.'s and Men.
Jutland	93 Officers	39 Warrant Officers 5,700 N.C.O.'s and Men.

Casualties (killed.) –
Trafalgar	4 Officers	113 N.C.O.'s and Men.
Jutland	8 Officers	4 Warrant Officers 526 N.C.O.'s and Men.

Wounded. –
Trafalgar	13 Officers	212 N.C.O.'s and Men.
Jutland	1 Officer	50 N.C.O.'s and Men.

A list of British ships engaged with the names of Royal Marine Officers and the numbers of the Royal Marine detachments are given in Table" A." The German ships are given in Table" B " at the end of this chapter.

HONOURS AND REWARDS.

The list of honours awarded to members of the Corps was long and in marked contrast to that of Trafalgar when only one Brevet Majority was awarded to Captain T. Timmins, the senior Royal Marine Officer. As the *Gazette* notices illustrate many of the phases of the Corps' varied duties they are given in full.

Major and Brevet Lieutenant-Colonel C. E. Collard, R.M.L.I. (retired) was the senior Royal Marine Officer afloat in the Battle; he had retired, but having rejoined for the war had volunteered to serve afloat; he was awarded the C.B. for very materially assisting in controlling the gunfire of H.M.S. *Benbow* from an exposed position in the control top.

The award of the Victoria Cross to Major F. J. W. Harvey, R.M.L.I. has been already described; as has the award of the D.S.O. to Captain E. Bamford, RM.L.I

The D.S.O. was also awarded to Captain H. Blount, R.M.A. of H.M.S. *New Zealand* for excellent service as officer of "Q" turret at Jutland, as well as in action off Heligoland Bight, 28th August, 1914, and at the Dogger Bank, January, 1915.

Major A. G. Troup, R.M.A. of H.M.S. *Cochrane* was awarded the Brevet of Lieutenant Colonel for good service in action.

Captain R. E. Kilvert, R.M.A. was promoted to Major for command of "X" Turret of H.M.S. *Neptune* during the action and as commanding officer of the Royal Marine Detachment, he was recommended as having specially contributed to the efficiency of the ship.

Captain R. C. S. Waller, R.M.L.I., wireless telegraphy officer on the staff of Admiral Sir D. Sturdee was awarded a Brevet Majority for his work in charge of the wireless organisation of the 4th Battle Squadron since the commencement of the war; the squadron consisted of ships of various types and the work of bringing the wireless installations of ships designed for Foreign Powers into .effective working order was carried out entirely satisfactorily and he was reported as having rendered valuable assistance to the Admiral commanding.

Lieutenant H. M. Franks, R.M.A. was promoted to Captain and Brevet Major for his valuable services as wireless telegraphy officer on the Staff of Admiral Sir David Beatty, who reported that Lieutenant Franks had shown great resource in maintaining the vitally important wireless communications throughout the action, despite the fact that the aerials were shot away and required constant repair.

Lieutenant H. L. McCausland, R.M.L.I. of H.M.S. *Conqueror* was noted for good service and awarded a Brevet-Majority on promotion to the rank of Captain.

Promoted to Lieutenants R.M. for good Service
R.M. Gunner George Allan, H.M.S. *Temeraire*
R.M. Gunner J. E. Flower, C.G.M., H.M.S. *Indomitable*.

Commended for Services in action
Major A. P. Grattan, RM.L.I., H.M.S. *Orion*.
Captain A. G. W. Grierson, RM.L.I., WIT Officer of H.M.S. *New Zealand*.

Conspicuous Gallantry Medal
Colour-Sergeant Abraham Spooner, R.M.A., H.M.S. *Warrior*.

Distinguished Service Medal-
Sergeant Walter Henry Fairs, R.M.A.
Musician A. G. S. Flippence, RM. Band.
Sergeant H. R Lucas, R.M.A.
Acting Bombardier J. Mulraney, RM.A.
Colour-Sergeant L. D. Roberts, (Portsmouth) R.M.L.I.
Sergeant H. Ross, (Portsmouth), RM.L.I
Sergeant E. W. Weston, R.M.A.
Lance-Sergeant H. Waterloo, (Portsmouth)

Commended for good Service in action -
Sergeant A.W. Balcome, (Chatham),R.M.L.I.
Gunner Ch. Beard, R.M.A.
Corporal W. Broadbridge, R.M.A.
Sergeant H. C. Barlow, R.M.A.
Sergeant J. Clerk (Plymouth), R.M.L.I.
Gunner E. A. Crawley, R.M.A.
Corporal J. Mulligan (Plymouth), R.M.L.I.
Colour-Sergeant R Magson, R.M.A.
Sergeant A. E. Murrell (Portsmouth), R.M.L.I.
Sergeant E. J. Nichol, R.M.A.
Corporal A. Phipps (Portsmouth), R.M.L.I.
Colour-Sergeant W. H. Potter, R.M.A.

Sergeant F. Cox, R.M.A.
Colour-Sergeant W. W. Finnegan
    (Portsmouth). R.M.L.I.
Sergeant W. T. Hunt (Plymouth), R.M.L.I.
Private W. A. Hamilton (Chatham), R.M.L.I.
Private A. J. Jenner (Plymouth), RM.L.I.
Lance-Sergeant T. Keirby (Portsmouth), R.M.L.I.
Lance-Sergeant J. R King (Chatham),
Bandmaster H. Lodge, RM. Band. R.M.L.I.
Sergeant F. Lefevre (Plymouth), RM.L.I.

Private W. J. Patterson,(Portsmouth). R.M.L.I.(killed).
Sergeant J. Reid (Portsmouth), R.M.L.I.

Sergeant A. E. Stevens, R.M.A.
Sergeant W. E. Shaw, R.M.A.
Private W. Smith (Chatham), R.M.L.I. (killed)
Sergeant H. L. Vale, R.M.A.
Private H. Willows (Plymouth), R.M.L.I.
Lance-Sergeant G. R Westlake (Plymouth), R.M.L.I.
Private A. V. Whatley (Plymouth), R.M.L.

LIST OF SHIPS CARRYING ROYAL MARINES AT BATTLE OF JUTLAND, 31st MAY, 1916.

NAME OF SHIP.	APPROX. No OF N.C.O.s AND MEN	NAMES OF OFFICERS.	CASUALTIES
1st Battle Squadron:			
Marlborough	135	Major F. L. Dibblee, R.M.A., Lieut. C. A. Lucas, R.M.L.I, R.M.Gr. W. Gazeley.	
Revenge	147	Capt. E. Jukes-Hughes, Lieut. C. H. Congdon, R.M.L.I., R.M.Gr. H. W. Edmunds.	
Hercules	107	Capt. P. H. Colley, R.M.L.I., Lieut. E. L. Bishop, R.M.A., R.M.Gr. S. T. Washburn.	
Agincourt	171	Capt. E. K. Fletcher, Lieuts. H. A. Webber and R C. Mackenzie, R.M.L.I., R.M.Gr. C. W. Ryman.	
Colossus (Flag.)	100	Capt. C. E. Hill, Lieut. R L. de Strother, RM.L.I., RM.Gr. G. Seyd	One wounded
Collingwood	99	Capt. A. S. Cantrell, R.M.A., Lieut. O. M. Haworth-Borth, R.M.L.I., R.M.Gr. E. H. Taylor.	
Neptune	97	Capt. R E. Kilvert, Lieut. H. J. Hamilton-Cox, R.M.A., R.M.Gr. F. C. Waters.	
St. Vincent	99	Capt. H. S. D. Went, Lieut. E. J. B., Noyes, R.M.L.I., R.M.Gr. H. Maconochie.	
2nd Battle Squadron:			
King George V (Flag.)	107	Major. A. G, Ridings, R.M.A., Capt. H. R. H. Haines, R.M.L.I., R.M.Gr. Robson.	
Ajax	97	Major J. Hazel, R.M.L.I., Lieut. J. Wood-Roberts, R.M.L.I., R.M.Gr. R Brooks,	
Centurion	97	Capt. C. A. Tennyson, Lieut. J. A. Bath, R.M.L.I., R.M.Gr. H. R Horne.	
Erin	149	Capt. F. C. Willes, R.M.A., Lieut. R A. Stewart, R.M.A., Lieut. R H. Campbell, R.M.L.I., R.M.Gr. Puxley.	
Orion (Flag.)	98	Major A. P. Grattan, R.M.L.I., Capt. F. A. Hamer, R.M.A., R.M.Gr. W. E. Petley.	
Monarch	97	Capt. G. H. Kendle, R.M.A., Lieut. R G. Sturges, R.M.L.I., B. M. N. Walker, R.M.Gr. J. Murdoch..	
Conqueror	97	Capt. J. McNair-Smith, Lieut. H. L. M. Causland, R.M.L.I., R.M.Gr. C. R Lane.	
Thunderer	97	Capt. G. L. Parry, R.M.L.I., Lieut. E. E. Johnson, R.M.A., R.M.Gr. M. Clarke.	
Iron Duke (Fleet Flag.)	134	Capt. G. Rutledge, R.M.A., R.M.Gr. B. King, B.M. A. Moffatt.	
4th Battle Squadron:			
Royal Oak	147	Capt. H. E. Gillespie, Lieut. R A. Neville, R.M.L.I., R.M.Gr.] , Porteous.	
Superb (Flag.)	96	Capt. H. F. P. Rees, R.M.L.I., Lieut. R Matthews, R.M.A., R.M.Gr. J. Creedon.	
Canada	156	Capt. H. E. Ravenshaw, Lieuts. N. K. Jolley and N. B. Ward, R.M.L.I., R.M.Gr. A. V. Kemp	
Benbow (Flag.)	133	Lieut.-Col. C. E. Collard, R.M.L.I., Capt. C. T. Brown, R.M.A., R.M.Gr. F. Buckland.	
Bellerophon	96	Capt. S. Cruddas, R.M.A., Lieut. S. A. Field, R.M.L.I., R.M.Gr. F. C. Wyld.	
Temeraire	96	Major H. Filmer-Bennett, R.M.L.I., Lieut. E. W. Husey, R.M.A., R.M.Gr. G. Allan.	
Vanguard	69	Capt. H. W. Miles, R.M.L.I., Lieut. C. H. Blunt, R.M.A., R.M.Gr. W. A. Young.	

LIST OF SHIPS CARRYING ROYAL MARINES AT BATTLE OF JUTLAND, 31st MAY, 1916.

NAME OF SHIP.	APPROX. No OF N.C.O.s AND MEN	NAMES OF OFFICERS.	CASUALTIES
5th Battle Squadron:			
Barham (Flag.)	147	Capt. N. S. Clutterbuck, Lieut. E. St. V. Ryan: R.M.L.I., R.M.Gr. F. O. Botterill.	1 died of wounds, 3 wounded.
Warspite	139	Major H. Ozanne, Lieut. R A. Poland, R.M.L.I., R.M.Gr. W. B. Tapper.	1 wounded.
Valiant	139	Capt. H. E. Iremonger, R.M.A., Lieut. E. J. Eastman, R.M.L.I., R.M.Gr. W. Greig.	
Malaya	139	Major G. H. Jollye, R.M.A., Lieut. D. H. Kitchin, R.M.A., R.M.Gr. E. G. Thornton.	8 killed, 9 died of wounds, 9 wounded.
1st Battle Cruiser Squadron:			
Lion (Flag.)	94	Major F. J. Harvey, Lieut. F. R Jones, R.M.L.I., R.M.Gr. J. H. Goss.	47 killed, 1 died of wounds, 2 wounded.
Princess Royal (Flag)	88	Major F. J. Tanqueray-Willaume, Lieut. V. D. Thomas, R.M.A., R.M.Gr. J. Masterton.	7 killed, 13 wounded.
Tiger	115	Capt. A. G. Bourne, Lieut. C. W. Adair, R.M.A., RM.Gr. R J. Gumm.	1 Killed
Queen Mary	115	Major G. C. Rooney, R.M.L.I., R.M.Gr. C. Catley.	113 killed.
2nd Battle Cruiser Squadron:			
New Zealand	86	Capt. H. Blount, Lieut. H. M. Brown, R.M.A., RM.Gr. A. E. Elliott.	
Indefatigable	89	Capt. P. M. C. Wilde, RM.A., RM.Gr. G. H. Field.	89 killed.
3rd Battle Cruiser Squadron:			
Invincible (Flag.)	106	Major R C. Colquhoun, R.M.L.I., Lieut. T. Le Selleur, R.M.L.I., R.M.Gr. E. A. Nixon.	86 Killed.
Inflexible	86	Capt. R Sinclair, R.M.L.I., Band.-Master H. Reeley, R.M.B., R.M Gr. J. Cameron.	
Indomitable	86	Capt. L. D. Briscoe, R.M.A., Lieut. C. P. Sparrow, R.M.A., R.M.Gr. J. E. Flower, C.G.M.	
1st Cruiser Squadron:			
Defence (Flag.)	83	Lieut. A. D. P. Hamilton, R.M.L.I.	83 killed.
Duke of Edinburgh	96	Capt. G. E. Wainwright, Lieut. L. C. Holles, R.M.L.I.	
Black Prince	77	Capt. A. W. D. Broughton, Lieut. G. R Steinthal, R.M.L.I.	77 killed.
Warrior	82	Capt. H. St. G. Morgan, R.M.A.	
2nd Cruiser Squadron:			
Minotaur (Flag.)	108	Capt. T. L. Hunton, Lieut. A. Rendell, R.M.L.I.	
Cochrane	82	Capt. W. A. Jolley, R.M.A	
Shannon	98	Major A. E. Troup, R.M.A., Lieut. E. J. Williams, R.M.L.I.	
Hampshire	80	Capt. C. S. Hazeon, R.M.L.I.	

LIST OF SHIPS CARRYING ROYAL MARINES AT BATTLE OF JUTLAND, 31st MAY, 1916.

NAME OF SHIP.	APPROX. No OF N.C.O.s AND MEN	Remarks	NAME OF SHIP.	APPROX. No OF N.C.O.s AND MEN	Remarks
1st Light Cruiser Squadron:			Destroyer Flotillas		
Galatea (Flag.)	31	Lieut. G. T. Newbold, R.M.L.I.	Castor	33	One killed, one wounded. Inconstant
Inconstant	33		Fearless	22	Seven killed
Cordelia	33		Tipperary	12	
Phaeton	31		Broke	12	
			Faulknor	12	
2nd Light Cruiser Squadron:					
Southampton (Flag.)	29	Two killed, five wounded			NOTE- In the Battleships and Cruisers the Detachments consisted of approximately 50% R.M.A. And 50% R.M.L.I.
Birmingham	31				
Nottingham	29				
Dublin	29	Three wounded			
3rd Light Cruiser Squadron:					In the Light Cruisers and Destroyer Flotilla ships all R.M.L.I.
Falmouth (Flag.)	29	Lieut. J. S. Hicks, R.M.L.I.			
Birkenhead	42				
Gloucester	29				
4th Light Cruiser Squadron:					
Calliope (Flag.)	33	Two killed, one died of wounds, [2 wounded			
Caroline	33				
Comus	33				
Constance	33				
Royalist	31				
Attached Ships:					
Active	20				
Boadicea	20				
Bellona	22				
Blanche	20				
Chester	42	Capt. E. Bamford, R.M.L.I. [8 killed, 10 wounded			
Canterbury	33				

TABLE "B."

LIST OF GERMAN SHIPS ENGAGED.

Ships	Speed	Armament
Konig *Grosser Kurfurst* *Kronprinz* *Markgraf*	23 knots	10 12-inch. 14 5.9-inch. 5 Torpedo tubes.
Kaiser *Kaiserin* *Prinz Regent Luitpold* *Frederich der Grosse* (Fleet Flag)	21 knots	10 12-inch. 14 5.9-inch. 5 Torpedo tubes.
Helgoland *Ostfriesland* *Thuringen* *Oldenburg*	20.5 knots	12 12-inch. 14 5.9-inch. 6 Torpedo tubes.
Nassau *Posen* *Rheinland* *Westfalen*	20 knots	12 11-inch. 12 5.9-inch. 6 Torpedo tubes.
Deutschland *Hessen* *Pommern (sunk)* *Hannover* *Schlesien* *Schleswig Holstein*		4 11-inch. 5.9-inch.
Derfflinger	28 knots	8 12-inch.
Lutzow (sunk)		14 5.9-inch; 4 Torpedo tubes.
Seydlitz	26.7 knots	10 11-inch; 12 5.9-inch; 4 Torpedo tubes.
Moltke	27.5 knots	10 11-inch; 12 5.9-inch; 4 Torpedo tubes.
Von der Tann	26 knots	8 11-inch; 10 5.9-inch; 4 Torpedo tubes.

LIGHT CRUISERS.

Frankfurt *Elbing (sunk)* *Hamburg.* *Rostock (sunk)*	*Wisebaden (sunk)* *Stettin* *Fraunlobe (sunk)* *Regensburg*	*Pillau (sunk)* *Munchen* *Stuttgart*

Destroyers 72.

CHAPTER 5.

ACTIONS AND INCIDENTS, 1916-1919.

Action in North Sea, August 1916-Guns at North Foreland - *Swift* and *Broke* - Training of Royal Marines Afloat - The Adriatic - Cruiser Action, North Sea, November 1917 - Sortie of *Goeben* and *Breslau* from Dardanelles - Award of Albert Medal to Lieut. Day - Armistice - Passage of Fleet to Constantinople - Surrender of German Fleet - King's Message to the Royal Navy -Honours and Awards-Post Armistice Operations.

AFTER the Battle of Jutland many changes took place in the Grand Fleet; the squadrons were re-organised and made more homogeneous; the *Revenge* class with 15-inch guns were now coming into commission and the 12-inch guns ships, except the *Agincourt*, were all placed in the 4th Battle Squadron; the 2nd Squadron consisted of the *King George V.* and *Orion* classes with 13.5 inch guns together with the *Erin*. The *Queen Elizabeth* class formed the 5th Squadron and all the others were drafted into the 1st Squadron. When the *Repulse* and *Renown* became available, the Battle Cruiser Fleet was also re-organised into two squadrons.

The 3rd Battle Squadron had left the Thames to participate in the Battle of Jutland, but they arrived too late, and after the Battle were gradually paid off; in consequence of the experience that had been gained during the war their main deck guns were removed and many of this class afterwards rendered good service in the Mediterranean and in lieu of cruisers in the convoy patrols off the West Coast of Africa, etc.

About this time too the squadrons ceased to visit Cromarty for recreation, as the facilities at Scapa had been improved. Recreation grounds had been made and other facilities provided, and later on a canteen ship fitted with a stage where entertainments could be given was added, which went alongside the ships in turn.

In August, 1916, we find the Grand Fleet making another sweep into the Heligoland Bight, and on 19th touch was almost gained with the enemy, but the High Seas Fleet had no desire for a repetition of Jutland and avoided contact and returned to harbour. On the 20th "E 23" torpedoed the *Nassau* twice, but she managed to reach her base. The British Light Cruisers however, had encountered the enemy submarines and light forces, and on the 19th about 6 a.m. the *Nottingham*, screening ahead of the Battle Cruisers, was hit by two torpedoes; she was hit again by a third torpedo about half-past six and her crew were taken off by destroyers; torpedoes were also fired at the *Dublin* and the destroyers during the rescue but without effect. Zeppelins were numerous and active and evidently warned the Germans of the presence of the Grand Fleet, so that the enemy squadrons kept out of reach. At about 5 p.m. the *Falmouth* of the 3rd Light Cruiser Squadron was hit by two torpedoes and was escorted home by the *Chester* and destroyers, but when off Flamborough Head she was again hit twice and though taken in tow by tugs she sank on the 20th; the *Pelican* dropped depth charges on the submarine and reported that she was sunk and the *Porpoise* also rammed the one that made the first attack.

At 6 pm. on the 19th the Commodore with the Harwich Force was following the enemy's heavy squadrons, but the conditions were unfavourable for a night attack and the pursuit was abandoned.

On 10th August, H.M.S. India had been torpedoed by a submarine when several N.C.O..s and men were lost and the survivors were interned in Norway. The Harwich Force, together with the constant blockade maintained by the 10th Cruiser Squadron (Armed Merchant Cruisers) were continued, but it was evident that the High Seas Fleet would not seek another engagement, and the British efforts were concentrating on the submarine danger, which both in home waters and in the Mediterranean was assuming serious proportions. On 7th November, Commander Laurence in "J. 1" torpedoed two battleships of the *Kaiser* Class in the Bight, but they limped back to port.

On 28th November, Admiral Sir John Jellicoe relinquished the command of the Grand Fleet in order to become First Sea Lord and to grapple with the submarine dangers, which he so fully realised; considerable changes consequently took place in the Grand Fleet. Admiral Sir David Beatty became Commander-in-Chief with his flag in the *Queen Elizabeth* in place of the *Iron Duke*. Admiral Sir C. Madden from Chief of the Staff assumed command of the 1st Battle Squadron with his flag in the *Revenge* and was succeeded as Chief of the Staff by Rear Admiral Sir O. de B. Brock. Admiral Sir W. Pakenham assumed command of the Battle Cruiser Fleet, Major Cantrell, R.M.A. was appointed to the *Queen Elizabeth* and Major and Brevet Lieut.-Colonel B.C. Gardiner, R.M.L.I. transferred to her to continue his duties as Fleet wireless telegraphy officer and carried out also many of the duties of S.O.R.M. The actual senior R.M. Officer afloat was Major A.G.Little, R.M.L.I. of the *Revenge*.

In the Mediterranean the Naval Forces were occupied with the protection of the Merchant Shipping and the transports of the Expeditionary Forces in Salonica, Egypt and Mesopotamia. This duty, added to the necessity for guarding the entrances to the Dardanelles and Adriatic by aircraft, destroyers and trawlers, with their supporting Battle Squadrons stationed at Mudros and Taranto, absorbed a considerable number of ships and personnel.

In the autumn in conjunction with the French Fleet, the *Exmouth, Duncan* and other ships were engaged at Athens as described in chapter 15.

1917.

The Grand Fleet, particularly the battleships, now found itself faced with the problem which has confronted the battleships in every great Naval war. Shortly stated, it is the question of maintaining the efficiency of the ships, whilst ensuring the contentment and proper fitness both mental and physical, of the personnel during the long and dreary months of waiting for an enemy to show himself; complicated in modern days by the fact that the Fleet must necessarily lie for long periods in harbour without even the conflict with the elements that was such a potent factor in the old sailing days in moulding the Fleets.

Many officers and men of the Corps served continuously through the War in the battleships of the Grand Fleet, because the ordinary terms of recommissioning were suspended, and all the diaries record the intense boredom of the year 1917, when there was little hope of a Fleet engagement.

In January the *Cornwallis* was sunk in the Mediterranean and the loss of ships employed in the escort of convoys increased throughout the year.

On 22nd January there was a destroyer fight in the North Sea when one German and one British boat were sunk. On 25th February the enemy destroyers bombarded Margate and Broadstairs and again in March, Ramsgate was bombarded when a certain amount of damage to property was done. To prevent a recurrence two 6-inch guns were mounted at the North Foreland and two more at Foreness, to the north of them. The work was done under the supervision of Commander Lewin of the Dover Patrol in a remarkably short space of time; considerable help was given by one of the tractors of the Royal Marine Artillery Howitzer Brigade under Captain Shadwell, D.S.C., R.M.A.; the working parties being provided by the recruits from Deal under Captain Pinkerton, R.M.L.I.

When the guns were mounted they were manned by 120 N.C.O.s and men, R.M.A. and R.M.L.I. (principally invalids) under Brevet-Lieut-Colonel A. Troup, R.M.A. and when he was invalided by Captain A. L. Durst, R.M.L.I. (retired) other officers being Captain L. S. Wilkinson, and Lieutenant M. H. Spicer, R.M.L.I.

and Capt. Shadwell, R.M.A. Adjutant. An anti-aircraft gun was mounted as they were the object of several air raids, but escaped without casualties. On 21st April, 1917, there took place the destroyer fight off Ramsgate when the *Swift* and *Broke* (which carried 12 Royal Marines) fought their very gallant action with six German destroyers attempting to bombard Dover; the enemy escaped with the loss of two vessels; among the honours awarded for this action Sergeant R. Jinks (Chatham) was mentioned in dispatches. The North Foreland guns were also in action on this occasion.

On 16th March, H.M.S. *Achilles* cruising off the Shetlands with the armed boarding steamer *Dundee* encountered a suspicious-looking craft which was stopped by the *Dundee*. She proved to be the *Leopard*, a German raider, returning to Germany; the Germans at once opened fire and sank the *Dundee*, fortunately the *Achilles* was close at hand and sank the raider with a few rounds.

Early in 1917 the Commander-in-Chief of the Grand Fleet assembled a conference of the senior officers Royal Marines on board the *Emperor of India* to discuss the question of carrying out some form of Military Training for the Royal Marines embarked. The Committee consisted of Major E. Wray, R.M.L.I. (*Emperor of India*) Major A. P. Grattan, R.M.L.I. (*Orion*), A. G. Little, R.M.L.I. (*Revenge*), A. W. Ridings, R.M.A. (*King George V.*), M. F. Bennett, R.M.L.I. (*Hercules*), B. C. Gardiner, R.M.L.I. (*Queen Elizabeth*) and in consequence of their proposals arrangements were made in April for parties of 60 N.C.O.'s and men to undergo a course of field training lasting about 21 days; all subaltern officers attended when training was in progress and with the assistance of Vice-Admiral Sir F. Sturdee good work was accomplished particularly in the 4th Squadron. The range at Scapa was much improved, huts were erected and a training staff, consisting of Captain R. W. Bagot, R.M.L.I., one quarter-master-sergeant instructor, two sergeants and one corporal were supplied from Headquarters for the musketry, and bombing instruction, whilst great attention was paid to the bayonet fighting. A training staff under Lieutenant M. H. Spicer, R.M.L.I. and two N.C.O.s was also supplied for the detachments at Rosyth. It later became part of the weekly routine for the Royal Marines of the Fleet to land as a Battalion every week and even coaling was not allowed to interfere with these landings by Admiral Sturdee and his successor in the 4th Squadron, Admiral Sir M. E. Browning.

As examinations for promotion had been suspended on the outbreak of war, it became necessary to give the N.C.O.s opportunities to improve their knowledge and with the assistance of the Admirals afloat, classes were established at the Depot, Royal Marines, Deal, to which N.C.O.s from the Fleet were sent for a period of instruction of about six weeks, which had most beneficial results. Classes were also established to train men for Physical Training Instructors and for training men for the higher gunnery ratings at Headquarters, which were regularly attended by men from the Fleet.

Further a musketry school was established at Browndown under Major F. E. Chichester, R.M.L.I. which was attended by men from the Fleet, and those who qualified were noted as passed for Musketry Instructor; all these facilities had a very good effect on the general training and keenness afloat. Attention was paid to education and examinations for certificates were re-introduced afloat, and the opportunities offered were eagerly embraced by N.C.O.s and men.

Recreation was not forgotten; boat races and other competitions were constantly held; in 1917 the Challenge Cup for Royal Marine cutters was lost when H.M.S. *Vanguard* blew up. To replace it a cup was presented by the Royal Marine officers of the 4th Battle Squadron called the" Miles" Cup in memory of Major H. W. Miles, R.M.L.I. of H.M.S. *Vanguard* who was killed on that occasion; this cup is now competed for on the Mediterranean Station.

On 15th May three Austrian Light Cruisers attacked the drifters guarding the Adriatic Barrage and in spite of the gallant defence made by these tiny vessels 14 were sunk in the Straits of Otranto. The *Dartmouth* and *Bristol* at once started in chase with some Italian Torpedo Boat Destroyers; on overhauling the Austrians the ships opened fire at 9.30 a.m. and the foremost enemy cruiser was soon on fire; the engagement continued for two hours, but as the enemy found the range of the *Dartmouth* she was obliged to ease speed to allow the *Bristol* to come up ; *Dartmouth* then fired a torpedo, but was herself hit several times and was also attacked by enemy seaplanes. At 11-30 a.m. enemy battleships were sighted and the British ships had to turn away, at which time one of the enemy cruisers was in a sinking condition and the two others had received many hits. About half past one the *Dartmouth* was hit by a torpedo fired by a submarine and after great difficulties was towed into harbour.

On 9th July H.M.S. *Vanguard* was destroyed by one of those mysterious explosions that caused so many losses to the Allies and which were the cause of the loss not only of material but the much heavier loss of valuable officers and men. Major H. W. Miles, R.M.L.I. was killed with approximately 90 N.C.O.s and men; Lieutenant Blunt, R.M.A. and several officers were fortunately visiting another ship at the time.

On 15th July there was a light cruiser and destroyer action in the North Sea in which one German destroyer was sunk.

On 3rd November, some of the British light cruisers encountered and sank a German auxiliary cruiser and 10 patrol boats. On the 17th, a raid into the Bight by light forces, including the new large cruisers *Courageous, Furious,* and *Glorious*, resulted in a running fight with the Germans. There was a calm sea, with an easterly wind and some haze, when the 6th Light Cruiser Squadron, consisting of *Cardiff, Caradoc, Calypso, Cassandra,* and *Ceres*, came into action about 80 miles south west of the North Dogger Lightship, and surprised and sank some small German ships. The enemy proved to belong to the *Stralsund*, and *Konigsberg* classes, and when sighted were about 20,000 yards off. The German cruisers at once altered course 16 points and fled down the swept channel, opening fire, as they did so. They were promptly followed by the British, and the fight lasted about two and half hours, until the ships were about thirty miles, N.N.W. of Heligoland, where they came under fire from some *Bayern* class battleships, and had to turn away in succession, under heavy fire, which was fortunately drawn off the light ships by H.M.S. *Repulse*, that had come up. After dark the squadron rejoined the Grand Fleet. The bugler (Timmins), of the *Cardiff* was among the killed. When the German Fleet surrendered in November, 1918, there was a 15-inch shell on board the *Konigsberg*, which the Germans said had come on board in this action, fortunately for the Hun, it had not exploded.

The German forces, having been beaten off the high seas, the fighting at sea died down, but the raids into the Bight and the patrols to prevent the egress of raiders went on continually. The Harwich Force had now been strengthened by the addition of six new light cruisers, and consequently the number of Royal Marines enabled to take part in their exploits, under their gallant commander, Commodore R. Y. Twyrrhit, was increased. Captain B. Dowding, R.M.L.I., was the senior officer (Royal Marines), and served continuously in the flagship, being awarded a Brevet Majority for his services.

Bombardment of the enemy batteries on the Belgian Coast, was systematically carried out and the largest monitors, mounting 15-inch guns, were employed for this service.

1918.

On 3rd January, Yarmouth was bombarded for the third time, and the raiders unfortunately again escaped punishment.

During all the War, the Dover Patrol, first under Rear-Admiral Hood, and then under Admiral Bacon, had been carrying out their magnificent work of safeguarding the passage of the transports to and from France; ensuring the safe passage of our shipping to the Thames, and watching the Belgian Coast, where the Germans had created an enormous defence organisation, to guard their submarine bases at Zeebrugge and Ostend.

From the nature of the work, the Corps had been able to take very little part except in the monitors employed in bombarding. Though in September, 1914, an effort had been made to deal with the air raiders, by embarking small parties of the Corps in trawlers to try and bring them down by rifle fire, an attempt which was soon abandoned. In 1918, however, under Admiral Sir Roger Keyes, their opportunities were increased. Commencing with small beginnings, in 1917 the R.M.A. Heavy Siege Train at Dunkirk, grew to a large and efficient organisation (see chapter 34). The Royal Marine Submarine Miners, also extended their activities, and new stations were opened in the command. In April, the 4th Royal Marine Battalion, took part in the immortal exploit at Zeebrugge (see chapter 12), and as the year wore on and the activities of the patrol developed, the 5th Royal Marine Battalion, under Lieutenant-Colonel R. H. Morgan, R.M.L.I., came into existence, but the Armistice arrested its development, which had only just begun (see chapter 7).

On 20th January the *Goeben* and *Breslau* at last broke the veil that had hung over the Dardanelles, and in the early morning, aided by the mist, made a sortie; they were not seen by the post at Mavro Island and the first intimation of their presence was given by the shells falling on the Lighthouse Post and in the camps of the 3rd Royal Marine Battalion at Kephalo, Imbros. The Germans pushed on to Kusu Bay at the north east corner of the Island and there sank the monitors H.M.S. *Raglan* and M. *28* causing several casualties. Returning towards Tenedos the *Breslau* struck a mine and was sunk, most of her crew being saved by the British; the *Goeben* also struck a mine and was attacked by the British destroyers *Tigress* and *Lizard*; she however, made good her escape into the Straits, but grounded at the Narrows. The R.A.F. Squadrons from Imbros and Mudros made gallant efforts to destroy her by bombing, under the orders of Wing Commander R. Gordon, D.S.O. (late R.M.L.I.) but she was eventually refloated and escaped to Constantinople.

On 15th April the British Light Forces and aircraft made another raid on the Kattegat, and again on 11th August there was a fight off the Friesian Coast north of the island of Ameland.

Early in 1918, owing to the Treaty of Brest-Litovsk and the penetration of Russia by the German Forces, coupled with the activity of the Bolsheviks and disaffected Finlanders, great anxiety was felt about the White Sea Route and the possible use of the ice free bases by submarines. A British ship had always been stationed in these waters and H.M.S. *Glory* had been in the Kola Inlet for the past year as Depot Ship; she carried a very large detachment of Marines, 176 N.C.O.s and men, many borne in lieu of seamen for the purpose of landing strong detachments to quell any local disturbances; also six Lewis gun detachments were sent out in April, 1918, under Lieutenant J. D. Morris, and in May a Field Force of Royal Marines under Lieut.-Colonel R. Paterson, R.M.A. as described in Chapter 13. The river operations on the River Dwina are described in Chapter 8.

In 1918 the American Battle Squadron consisting of the *New York, Florida, Wyoming, Texas* and *Arkhansas* joined the Grand Fleet and became the Sixth Battle Squadron. These vessels all carried detachments of the sister Corps, the United States Marine Corps, the senior officer being Major N. P. Vulte, U.S.M.C.

In July, General Foch had commenced his hammer blows on the Western Front and on 8th August General Sir D. Haig struck his first and as it proved decisive blow. During the next three months his Armies were pushing on, the Howitzers of the R.M.A. and the 1st R.M.L.I. Battalion, with the R.M. Siege Batteries (Chapter 28) taking part in the advance as described in Part VI.

Following desperate and most bitter fighting on the Doiran Front the Bulgarians retreated and the

Actions And Incidents, 1916-1919

Armistice with that Power was signed on the Salonica Front on 30th September. No sooner was this completed than preparations to continue the attack on the Turks were at once pushed on and Mudros became again a scene of activity.

The Commander-in-Chief of the Mediterranean, Sir Somerset Gough-Calthorpe and Vice-Admiral M. Culme-Seymour commanding in the Aegean were busily engaged in arranging for the transport of troops and the sweeping up of mines along the mainland coast; because owing to the breaking of the railways and the state of the roads, it was necessary to convey the greater part of the French and British Troops by sea in destroyers from Salonica to Dedeagatch. In spite of the bad weather, during which the destroyers, each carrying 500 troops had to shelter at Thaso, this was successfully carried out and on 30th October the British and French troops were in position on the River Maritza ready to cross the river and invade Turkey when the news of the Armistice arrived.

Following on the great victories of General Allenby in Palestine, the Turks had notified Admiral Gough-Calthorpe, that they wished to send out envoys to discuss terms and they were brought from Smyrna to Mudros in H.M.S. *Liverpool*, this ship also brought General Sir C. Townshend[10] who had been liberated by the Turks, and after some discussion the Armistice was signed at 5 p.m. on 30th October in the fore cabin of H.M.S. *Agamemnon* at Mudros to come into force at noon on 31st October.

H.M.S. *Superb* and *Temeraire* had by this time arrived from the Grand Fleet. There had been rumours of an intended sortie by the *Goeben* reinforced by the Russian Black Sea Fleet, the strength and condition of which was unknown, and it was therefore deemed advisable to strengthen the Aegean Squadron which only consisted of the *Lord Nelson* and *Agamemnon* and some scouts, in addition to the French Squadron of battleships of the *Diderot* class.

Although the Armistice was signed on the 31st October there were many preparations required before the Fleet could pass up the Dardanelles to Constantinople. Major R. C. Temple, R.M.A. with other officers proceeded to the Dardanelles to obtain the plan of the minefields and the defences; a channel for the Fleet had to be swept and as described in chapter 37 the Forts were occupied by the Royal Marines of the 3rd Battalion on 11th November. The areas on both sides of the Straits were garrisoned by the 28th British Division and by French troops. Royal Marines of the 3rd Battalion were also detailed to man the forts in the Bosphorus to guard against any possible hostile action by the Russian Black Sea Fleet; at last all was ready, and on 12th November headed by the *Superb* flying the flag of Sir Somerset Gough-Calthorpe, followed by the *Temeraire*, *Lord Nelson* (flag of Sir M. Culme Seymour) and *Agamemnon* with six French battleships under Vice-Admiral Amet and the Italian Cruiser *Piemonte* also the Greek ships *Lemnos* and *Averoff*, the Allied Fleet passed up the Straits saluted by guards of Marines mounted on the Forts on the Peninsula and by Indian Troops on those at the Narrows and anchored the following morning off the Golden Horn at Constantinople. The next day the Fleet went to Ismid and anchored off the town. The *Superb* returned to Constantinople on the 14th and provided a guard of honour of Royal Marines to receive General Milne, G.O.C. of the Salonica Army and later of the Army of the Black Sea, and then the Guard marched through Constantinople creating a very good effect.

The subsequent operations of the Black Sea Fleet as it was now called are described later.

On 4th November the Armistice with Austria was signed.

On 9th of the same month H.M.S. *Britannia* which had been patrolling on the routes west of Gibraltar

---

10. Formerly R.M.L.I.

when passing Cape Trafalgar was torpedoed by a submarine and sunk. Lieutenant H. M. Day, R.M.L.I. displayed great gallantry and was awarded the Albert Medal; after the ship was hit there was an ammunition explosion and fires were started, resulting in the spread of fumes and smoke. Lieutenant Day went down to the wardroom to look for wounded, he heard groans coming from forward of the wardroom but found the heavy wooden door leading forward was jambed and immovable. He then burst open the trap hatch to the wardroom pantry and climbed through; he here found Engineer-Lieutenant S. F. Weir and a wardroom steward alive and conscious but unable to move. He climbed back into the wardroom and up to the quarter deck, where he got hold of two or three stokers and returning to the wardroom carried the dying officer and man on deck to the forecastle. During his first visit to the wardroom Lieutenant Day was alone in the dark, the ship had a decided list and the fire was close to the 12-inch magazine; whilst carrying out the rescue work he inspected all scuttles and deadlights in the wardroom and cabins before it, and ascertained that they were properly closed before leaving; the cordite fumes were very strong and his life in danger throughout; his courage and resource were beyond praise.

On 11th November the glad news of the signing of the Armistice in France was flashed throughout the Empire, and the dead weight that had lain on men's hearts for so many weary years was lifted. The Navy rejoiced with the rest, but for them there was as yet no rest; many German submarines were at sea and until it was ensured that they had reached their bases all precautions had to remain in force; and then followed the perilous and weary task of sweeping up the mines, that were blocking the fairways, and rendering for many months the passage of the seas dangerous to shipping.

There was yet to come the great surrender of the High Sea Fleet; a humiliation such as had never before fallen to a Great Power. H.M.S. *Hercules* proceeded to Wilhelmshaven, where Admiral Sir M. Browning made the arrangements for the surrender and ascertained the condition of the German Fleet and munitions.

At last " THE DAY " dawned, and the Grand Fleet left its anchorage early on 21st November to meet and escort to an anchorage in the Firth of Forth the ships of the German High Seas Fleet. Included in the Grand Fleet was the American Battle Squadron. The Allies were also represented; the French by the *Admiral Aube* and two torpedo boat destroyers; the Italians by an Admiral on board H.M.S. *Hercules*.

[11]The Fleet steamed out in two lines each formed in single line ahead to meet the approaching Germans. All ships were ready for instant action with guns trained fore and aft; though there was little possibility of the Germans showing fight at the eleventh hour, still no risks could be taken with such an enemy.

At last through the haze appeared H.M.S. *Cardiff* with her kite balloon followed at three cables astern by the *Seydlitz* (Flag), *Moltke*, *Derfflinger*, *Hindenburg* and *Van der Tann*, following them were the five battleships of the *Kaiser* class, next the *Bayern* (15-inch guns) and last, three battleships of the *Konig* class; the leading battleship the *Friederich der Grosse* flew the flag of Rear Admiral Von Reuter.

Three miles astern with the *King Orry* in between came H.M.S. *Phaeton* leading the seven light cruisers *Karlsruhe, Emden, Nurnberg, Coln, Frankfurt, Brumme* and *Bremse*.

Three miles astern came the 120 British Destroyers headed by Commodore Tweedie in H.M.S. *Castor* escorting 49 German Destroyers formed in five lines (one had been sunk by a mine on the way over) and those who saw the triumph of the British Destroyers thought of the long arduous work, which had been their lot throughout the war, affording protection to every class of craft, as one account says "they are the salt of the earth, some day Britain will know, perhaps how well they have performed their part."

---

11. *From an account in the Globe and Laurel.*

Actions And Incidents, 1916-1919

SOUTHERN LINE.	MAY ISLAND.	NORTHERN LINE.
7th Light Cruiser Squadron (4)		4th Light Cruiser Squadron (5).
2nd Battle Cruiser Squadron (4)	*Cardiff.*	*Lion*
1st Battle Squadron (9)	German Battle Ships and Battle Cruisers.	1st Battle Cruiser Squadron (4)
4th Battle Squadron (5)		Queen Elizabeth.
Furious		2nd Battle Squadron (9).
Minotaur.	*King Orry.*	6th Battle Squadron (5) U.S.A.
2nd Light Cruiser Squadron (4)	*Phaeton*	5th Battle Squadron (4).
3rd Light Cruiser Squadron (4)	7 German Cruisers.	1st Cruiser Squadron (2).
	Castor and Destroyers.	6th Light Cruiser Squadron (4).
	German Destroyers.	1st Light Cruiser Squadron (4).

Blonde, Boadicea, Fearless, and *Blanche* were between as linking ships.

When the German Squadron was hemmed in on both sides by the British, each British Squadron turned outwards 16 points and then the whole Fleet proceeded to Rosyth in the following order.

After passing May Island, the Southern Line except the 7th Light Cruiser Squadron turned 16 points to port and took station astern of the German destroyers. At the same time H.M.S. *Queen Elizabeth* with the Commander-in-Chief dropped out of the line and watched the passage of the Grand Fleet to the anchorage. Headed by H.M.S. *King George V.* (flagship of Sir J. de Robeck) the 2nd Battle Squadron, in passing the *Queen Elizabeth,* gave three cheers for the Commander-in-Chief and this spontaneous tribute to a great sailor was repeated by all passing ships.

After passing Fidra Gap the Germans formed up for anchoring, and at a given signal anchored off Inch Keith, together with the 1st Battle Squadron, 2nd Battle Cruiser Squadron and 2nd and 3rd Light Cruiser Squadron who were detailed to guard them. There were also present three airships and some aeroplanes.

The approximate numbers of Royal Marines present at the surrender were 86 officers, 44 warrant officers, 4,818 N.C.O.s and men.

Owing to the low visibility it was impossible at times even to see the Northern line from the Southern, and no words could do adequate justice to the display of the might and power of sea power on "THE DAY."

At noon the Commander-in-Chief made the following signal "The German Flag will be hauled down at sunset to-day (21st) and will not be hoisted again without permission" and later another signal was made. "It is my intention to hold a service of Thanksgiving at 6-0 p.m. to-day for the victory which Almighty God has vouchsafed to His Majesty's Arms and every ship is recommended to do the same."

The next day the escorting squadrons commenced the search of the German ships, all shells and explosives in accordance with the terms had already been removed. The spirit of the Germans, ruled by permission of a Council of two Petty Officers, one Army Sergeant and a civilian, was listless and bored, and their existence seemed devoid of all outlook. The officers ran some sort of routine by means of orders franked by the Council; the fire control had been dismantled, but the turrets were clean which is more than can be said for the living quarters. The Fleet left in small contingents for Scapa Flow, the last contingent consisting of the *Bayern, Grosser Kurfurst, Kronprinz,* and *Markgraf* arriving on 27th November and the Royal Marine garrisons of the Batteries at last had a glimpse of the enemies for whom they had waited so many weary months.

The Harwich Force had received the surrender of the submarines and these were escorted to their port of interment at Harwich by that force.

His Majesty's message to the Fleet was published on 11th November and was gratefully received by all ranks of the Royal Navy and Royal Marines.

"11th November, 1918."

"Now that the last and most formidable of our enemies has acknowledged the triumphs of the Allied Arms on" "behalf of right and justice, I wish to express my praise and thankfulness to the Officers, Men and Women of the" "Royal Navy and Royal Marines, with their comrades of the Fleet Auxiliary and Mercantile Marine, who for" "more than four years have kept open the sea, protected our shores and given us safety. Ever since that fateful 4th" "August, 1914 I have remained steadfast in my confidence that whether fortune smiled or frowned, the Royal Navy" "would once more prove the sure shield of the British Empire, in the hour of trial. Never in its history has the Royal" "Navy, with God's Help, done greater things for us, nor better sustained its glories and the chivalries of the seas." "With full and grateful hearts the peoples of the British Empire salute the White, the Red and the Blue Ensign," "and those who have given their lives for the Flag. I am proud to have served in the Navy. I am prouder still to be" "its head on this memorable day."

(Signed) GEORGE R.I."

After the Armistice certain honours were awarded to Royal Marine Officers in conjunction with Naval Officers for their services afloat in the Grand Fleet.

C.B. - Major and Brevet Lieut.-Colonel B. C. Gardiner, R.M.L.I., who had been Fleet W/T Officer since August 1914.

C.M.G - Major A. G. Little, R.M.L.I., Senior Officer, RM., afloat since 1916.

O.B.E. - Major H. E. Gillespie, R.M.L.I.   Captain H. R Haines, R.M.L.I.
Major G. H. Jollye, R.M.A.   Captain C. A. Lucas, RM.L.I.
Captain E. J. Jukes-Hughes, R.M.L.I.

M.B.E. - RM.Gunner J. Cameron.   R.M.Gunner F. O. Botterill.
"   E. Kimber.   Bandmaster J. G. Welsh.

During the period dealt with in this chapter the following rewards were gained by members of the Corps afloat.

D.S.M. - Sergeant W. H. France, R.M.A.	Miscellaneous.
Gunner A. Fenton, R.M.A.	Miscellaneous.
Sergeant A. V. Proctor, R.M.A.	Mediterranean.
Lance-Corporal R D. Hale, (Portsmouth), R.M.L.I.,	Patrol Cruisers.
Private R Burns (Portsmouth), R.M.L.I.	Patrol Cruisers.
Colour-Sergeant N. Sears (Portsmouth).	Patrol Cruisers.
Lance-Corporal G. Short (Plymouth),	Patrol Cruisers.
Sergeant A. B. Cox (Portsmouth)	Miscellaneous.
Sergeant. J. Dix (Portsmouth),	Patrol Cruisers.
Private F. S. Paull (Plymouth),	Mediterranean.
Colour-Sergeant F. M. Thompson (Chatham),	Mediterranean.
Private J. Wilson (Portsmouth).	Patrol Cruisers.
Sergeant A. E. Bowen (Chatham),	Egyptian Division.
Sergeant W. H. Padwick (Portsmouth).	Egyptian Division.
Sergeant H. Hayes (Chatham).	Aegean.

Sergeant F. W. Ladd (Chatham).	Belgian Coast.
Private J. M. Stevenson (Plymouth).	Miscellaneous.
Sergeant B. W. Hatcher (Portsmouth).	Dover Patrol.
Private W. Marriott (Portsmouth).	Dover Patrol.
Private T. H. Wigley (Plymouth).	Aegean.
Private W. G. Geary (Portsmouth).	Miscellaneous.
Corporal D. Griffiths (Plymouth).	North Russia.
Corporal W. J. Last, R.M.A.	North Russia.
Sergeant A. Levett (Portsmouth)	North Russia.
Private W. E. Lewington (Portsmouth).	North Russia.
Private W. E. Peters (Portsmouth).	North Russia.
Sergeant E. C. White (Portsmouth).	North Russia.

SOME POST ARMISTICE OPERATIONS.

As has already been said the Armistice did not put an end to the activities of the Navy and with them the Corps was also busy.

The situation in Russia and the East, and later in Turkey, continued to give cause for their employment in warlike operations, some of which are described in Chapters 8, 13, 23 and 35, whilst various operations were carried out by the cruiser squadrons and the Black Sea Fleet.

One of the first places to be visited was the Baltic and the 6th Light Cruiser Squadron was dispatched to open up the routes, enforce the terms of the Armistice and assist the so-called Baltic Barons against the Bolsheviks. After a great reception by the Danes at Copenhagen, the squadron proceeded to Libau with a view to forming an advanced base; this project was, however, abandoned, owing to the shallow water in the harbour and the hostility of the inhabitants. The squadron then sailed for Reval, but on the way H.M.S. *Cassandra* was lost through striking a mine. Captain Reading, R.M.L.I. displayed great gallantry in rescuing a Royal Marine who was left on board unconscious, the survivors were rescued by the destroyers and the squadron returned to Copenhagen.

The *Ceres* and *Princess Margaret* were sent to Riga; Captain H. A. C. Webber, R.M.L.I. of the *Cardiff* was lent to the *Princess Margaret* and given the local rank of Lieutenant-Colonel and Captain Craig, R.M.L.I. that of Major; their duty was to raise and train a body of volunteers to act against the Red Forces. In this they were successful and in addition the Royal Marine Detachment of the *Ceres* was landed every night for over a week to patrol the town in bitterly cold weather when they encountered much hostility from the Germans.

After a time the so-called White Regiments mutinied, in consequence of which the *Ceres* bombarded their barracks and quickly quelled the outbreak. The Reds soon after advanced against Riga and the volunteers were sent out against them; as the local authorities could not be trusted the *Ceres* did not land any of her parties. In the Red Orders of the Day it was ordered that Captains Webber and Craig were to be shot at sight, which fortunately for them was not obeyed and they were later awarded the O.B.E. for their services. The Reds captured the town which had therefore to be evacuated. The weather was bitterly cold and the scenes were heartbreaking as the refugees were mostly in a starving condition.

Meanwhile H.M.S. *Caradoc*, whose Royal Marine Officer was Captain E. M. C. Parker, R.M.L.I. was having similar experiences at Libau.

The Squadron was then withdrawn and was sent to the Mediterranean where re-named the 3rd Light Cruiser Squadron, it was actively engaged in the AntiBolshevik operations in the Black Sea.

After the surrender of Turkey the attention of the Mediterranean Fleet was concentrated on the possible action of the Russian Black Sea Fleet under its new masters-the Bolsheviks. The Aegean Squadron had been strengthened by the *Superb* and *Temeraire* and later the *Marlborough* and *Emperor of India* were also added with the 3rd Light Cruiser Squadron, as before stated. The occupation of Sevastopol is described in chapter 35, but this was only the commencement of the work. At the beginning of April, 1919, owing to the advance of the Bolshevik armies the *Caradoc* and her sisters were employed evacuating refugees from Odessa and as the advance was threatening the Crimea, where the Dowager Empress of Russia, the Grand Duke Nicholas and other notabilities had taken refuge at Yalta, the *Marlborough*, *Lord Nelson* and *Cardiff* went to that place and took off the Royal Personages who were very reluctant to go and would only consent to do so when the Red Armies were close to the town.

The White Army then took up a position across the Kertch Peninsula and was supported on both flanks by the British ships, and the Greek troops who had been at Odessa retired into the Crimea via Perekop and arrived at Sevastopol where were the French and Greek battleships and H.M.S. *Calypso*. All the mines, torpedoes and seven submarines in the Arsenal had been rendered useless.

On the 14th April, the Red Army halted outside the town and on 16th M 17 was sent up the harbour to defend the magazine and waterworks and opened fire. The Reds opened fire on the town on 18th and on 19th there was an armistice; the next day there took place a mutiny of the French troops and the Allied troops evacuated the town between 28th and 30th; the White Army withdrew to Theodosia where they were supported by the *Emperor of India*, *Calypso* and *Centaur*.

Meanwhile the *Caradoc* was supporting the Kertch position and was in action on 17th and 22nd of April and crushed the Red attack. The *Iron Duke* and *Emperor of India* came up and fired two salvoes of 13.5 inch shells on Vladislavka which destroyed the Red headquarters and the railway station. The *Caradoc* left for Malta on 5th May and was relieved by the *Marlborough*.

On 18th June the White Army made a successful attack after a bombardment by the battleships, and the ships getting under weigh followed up the coast and cleared out the machine gun posts; Theodosia and Vladislavka were reoccupied, the Reds retiring to Simferopol.

The White Army pushed right on through Yalta to Sevastopol and then advanced up to Perekop, the ships following up and assisting as much as possible. The advance on Ganischensk failed as the ships could not get in close enough. Eventually General Denikin drove the Reds across the River Dnieper, but was unable to follow up owing to the want of heavy guns.

The thrust of the Bolsheviks to cross south of Kertch and to penetrate to the Caspian and Persia, where the British Forces were engaged, see chapter 23, was frustrated by the work of the Fleet.

On 1st August the *Caradoc* with some monitors and destroyers bombarded Orklahoff (Kinburn) and in the afternoon went in again and was heavily fired on and hit, but she dismounted two of the enemy guns by direct hits. Later on she engaged the batteries again and passed in armed barges which attacked the forts around Kherson in order to get into the River Dnieper and assist Denikin; this was repeated on several nights and the Crimean Army were enabled to cross the river and capture Kherson.

Nicolaieff was also captured and the Bug River crossed, an operation which threatened the communications between Odessa and Kieff and opened the estuary of the Bug. On 18th August the *Caradoc* and her flotilla returned to Sevastopol.

The operations in the Black Sea continued throughout the remainder of 1919 and in 1920, but as this history does not deal with events subsequent to 1919 the interesting operations in the Black Sea and Bosphorus are left for a future volume.

CHAPTER 6.

BOMBARDMENTS FROM THE SEA.

WITHOUT venturing on the vexed question of Ships versus Forts, a few points stand out as valuable lessons for the future. In the first place the futility of bombardments unless an adequate landing force is available to complete and exploit the success was shown by the Dardanelles, Tanga, etc.; whilst when this condition was fulfilled the satisfactory results obtainable are illustrated by Tsingtau, and the numerous landings described in Part IV.

Secondly in addition to the spotting by aeroplanes the importance of a shore observation station. Thirdly the small effect of high velocity guns on mountings which did not admit of high elevation.

But if the attack on Forts is controversial, an outstanding feature throughout the War was the support rendered to forces on shore by the fire of the Fleet.

The science and factors governing this employment developed greatly as the years went on, and the aid rendered was invaluable.

In the first days of the War the Admiralty purchased the three small monitors, *Humber, Mersey* and *Severn* armed with 6-inch guns building for the Brazilian Government. These vessels rendered most valuable service in nearly every theatre of war and were the precursors of many more built by Lord Fisher, with guns from 15-in. downwards. Each of these small ships carried their detachment of Royal Marines in the same proportion as their larger sisters.

After the fall of Antwerp when the Belgian Army was falling back to Dunkirk and the race for the Sea between the adversaries was taking place leading up to the first great Battle of Ypres, the Dover Patrol under Rear-Admiral Hood was very active. On 18th October, 1914, H.M.S. *Attentive, Adventure, Foresight* and *Sapphire* with *Humber, Severn and Mersey* and some British and French destroyers attacked the flank of the German Army advancing on Lombartzyde, rendering great assistance to the French and Belgian troops. The three monitors each landed 10 Royal Marines, with maxims under Lieutenant Wise, R.N. to assist in the defence of Nieuport; Lieutenant Wise was killed, gallantly leading his men and the Corps sustained a loss of one killed and two wounded.

On the 19th the monitors opened fire again and were joined by the Gunnery School Tenders, armed with a miscellaneous collection of guns, the *Hazard, Bustard, Vestal, Rinaldo, Wildfire, Sirius*, so well known to the gunnery classes at Headquarters, who were employed for a week and checked the Germans most effectively.

On 20th October, the Germans attacked again with heavy batteries; the monitors knocked out one battery and to divert the others Admiral Hood led the destroyers close in and so diverted their fire. The Belgians evacuated Lombartzyde on 20th and the ships opened fire on the town on 21st. This caused the Germans in the town to evacuate it and it was re-occupied on 23rd by the Belgians, when the attack died away so that the Allied left was left unmolested, whilst the German trenches were taken in reverse by the ships. On 26th the enemy attacked again, but H.M.S. *Venerable* with her 12-in. and 6-in. guns broke the attack in an hour and the enemy howitzers were turned on her. Throughout the remainder of 1914 the *Venerable* was constantly bombarding the German right, assisted later by the *Revenge*, re-named the *Redoubtable*, and these bombardments continued till the submarines and the erection of the powerful long range batteries by the enemy forced the ships to keep at a distance beyond the range of their guns.

The place of the battleships was taken by the monitors as soon as they were ready, but after the bombardment of the Docks at Ostend in September, 1915, it was clear that as long as the 'Tirpitz' Battery of four ll-in. guns with a range of 30,000 yards was unhampered no great results could be obtained; accordingly guns were landed and mounted on shore by Admiral Bacon commanding the Dover Patrol, for counter-battery work, and the Royal Naval Siege Guns came into existence under Captain F. C. Halahan, R.N. (see Chapter 34).

The monitors however, in conjunction with the aeroplanes from Dunkirk, kept up constant attacks, throughout the four years, on the coast and enemy establishments, and developed methods of control which rendered their fire more and more effective.

Several awards were made to the Corps for these operations: T/Lieutenant J. H. D' Albiac, R.M.A. was awarded a D.S.O. for his services as an aeroplane observer and spotter, whilst the D.S.M. was awarded to Corporal S. Morriss (Portsmouth) Sergeant W. A. Arnold (Plymouth), and Sergeant F. W. Ladd (Chatham) beside many mentions in dispatches.

The bombardments of the Dardanelles Forts are described in Chapter 3, but though observation was made by other vessels inside the Straits, the equipment of aeroplanes and observation balloons was insufficient for all the calls made on them. When the troops had landed, it was found possible to establish observation posts on shore from which the fire of the ships could be controlled. The post at Cape Helles under Commander Collard and Lieutenant Bent was established at once and later under Commander Swabey and Lieutenant G. H. Seath, R.M.L.I. (from H.M.S. *Implacable*) served throughout the operations until the evacuation and rendered valuable service. Lieutenant Seath was awarded the D.S.O.; later, posts were established both at Anzac and Suvla.

The importance of close support by ship fire was shown by the successful landing at "X" Beach, where H.M.S. *Implacable* not only plastered the beach and cliffs before the landing and landed her troops without any casualties, but also fired a barrage of her whole broadside ahead of them to cover their advance inland, and a somewhat similar service was rendered at De Totts Battery, whilst in the same way the *Sapphire*, *Amethyst* and *Goliath* covered the re-embarkation at "Y" beach.

During the Dardanelles operations Lieutenant F. H. Thomas of H.M.S. *Talbot* was mentioned for his good service in keeping close touch from the shore between the troops and the ship, whilst the latter was supporting the Army and was awarded the D.S.C. and several other officers were similarly employed.

The organisation of the ship fire under Captain D. L. Dent, R.N. reached a very high standard, and the troops were able to call on them for assistance in repelling attacks with every confidence. In the great attacks at Suvla and Sari Bair in August the ships covered the attacking troops; unfortunately as illustrating the difficulties of control and observation, shells from one of the ships fell on the troops just as they had gained the ridge at Sari Bair. At the evacuation of Cape Helles the monitors lying off the Mavro Island by their fire soon silenced any fire of the Turks which might have interfered with the embarkation. Both in the chapter on the Dardanelles and in many of the succeeding ones the fatal effects of shots from the ships falling among our own troops will be noticed and shows the necessity that this supporting fire should be controlled by officers in close liaison with the infantry and in communication with the ships.

The landings at Salif, Bagamoyo and the operations of H.M.S. *Doris* on the Syrian Coast (see Part IV.) illustrate what a dominating part the effectively controlled fire of the covering ships play in this type of operation.

After the evacuation of Gallipoli, the supporting ships moved to Stavros to cover the right flank of the Salonica Army; the Naval observation party now under Brevet-Major Seath, D.S.O., R.M.L.I. also proceeded there and took part in the operations on the Struma River until the Armistice; one of the "blister ships" *Endymion* or *Grafton* was always stationed there with several monitors ; and as no heavy shore artillery could get round there, whilst the range was very great for the field guns and howitzers of the R.F.A., the troops were very dependent for support on the fire of the ships, which the existence of the observation post made very accurate.

In the Palestine campaign, where the left flank of the Army was on the sea as at Gaza, the monitors were enabled to render most useful service in breaking up enemy attacks and in covering the British attacks; Major and Bt. Lieut.-Colonel T. B. Luard, R.M.L.I. in conjunction with Lieut.-Commander Haselfoot, R.N. established observation posts before Gaza, and was in charge of the spotting officers and men, and rendered valuable services in authorizing fire. As the dispatch says "the accuracy and success of the sea bombardment was largely due to Major Luard's organisation"; he was awarded the D.S.O. and Sergeants A. E. Bowen (Chatham) and H. Padwick (Portsmouth) R.M.L.I. were also awarded the D.S.M. for these operations.

The account of the River operations in Chapter 8 is yet another example of the good effect of the supporting fire from ships when properly controlled, an experience which was confirmed by the Mesopotamia operations; in all of these except in Mesopotamia the Corps had a considerable share.

The duty of shore observation officer would appear to be one peculiarly suited to the Royal Marines, as their military training teaches them to understand the requirements of the troops, particularly the Infantry whom they are supporting; whilst their Naval Gunnery training keeps them in touch with the difficulties of the ships, and their technical knowledge of the ships methods of fire enables them to render efficient assistance.

CHAPTER 7.

THE ANTI-SUBMARINE WAR.

Defensively Armed Merchantmen - "Q" Boats - The Barralong - Convoy Duties - 5th R.M. Battalion.

PRIOR to the War, the possibilities of the submarine do not seem to have been accurately gauged, though a few of the Merchant Fleet, principally the larger liners, had been armed with a gun mounted right aft. This was more as a protection against surface commerce-raiding cruisers, and trust was placed in the speed of the liners, to enable them to escape. With the advent of the submarine, conditions altered, and early in 1915, owing to the increasing activities of the enemy in this direction, it was decided to extend the practice of arming merchantmen. A start was made with the ships of the coastal trade, but then arose the difficulty of obtaining trained men to handle the guns.

Consequently, another call was made on the Corps, who rose to the occasion, and the difficulty was surmounted by relegating selected volunteers from the Royal Marine Reservemen to the Reserve, who signed on as part of the crew in the ordinary way. This was the beginning of the vast organisation, built up as the War progressed, and known as the D.A.M.S. (Defensively Armed Merchant Ships), and eventually over 2000 Royal Marines were so employed, besides an even larger number of R.N. and R.N.V.R.

As experience was gained, the men were put through a short gunlaying course at the Royal Marine Headquarters, and volunteers were also taken from the active service ranks. At first they were armed with light guns, 3 and 6 pounders and 12 pounders, but gradually the calibres increased. 4-inch, 4. 7-inch, and even 6-inch guns were employed, and later still, howitzers, throwing large bombs were included in the armament, and the arming was extended to all classes. At first two men were allowed per gun, but when howitzers were added, they carried three. The remainder of the crew being formed from the merchant seamen, whose gallantry and devotion to duty, in the face of deadly and hourly peril, throughout the War, exceeded all the records of even their own magnificent past, in the history of the Empire.

This service gave great scope for the peculiar individual characteristics of the rank and file of the Corps, who as usual justified the confidence reposed in them when "on their own; " and there was never any lack of volunteers for this duty, in spite of its hardships and dangers. Although the temptations and opportunities were many, the standard of discipline and courage was uniformly high.

Numerous decorations and mentions in dispatches, were earned by the men employed in this service; among which the following are some of the outstanding instances. Private J. E. Brown, R.M.L.I., was serving in the S.S. *Rhydwen*, at Genoa, when a fire broke out in the ship's magazine. Brown went below with another man, unlocked the door of the magazine and got a hose to the seat of the fire; water was then played on the magazine, the ammunition was taken out on deck, and owing to the prompt action of the ship's crew, the fire was extinguished. Brown was awarded the Albert Medal, which was presented by His Majesty, to his wife, because Brown was unfortunately killed, when his ship was torpedoed later. Lance-Corporal W. Brown (Chatham), while serving in a ship which was torpedoed, disabled his gun by throwing the striker overboard and smashing the sights; he then saved and returned the two gunsight telescopes of the 4.7-inch gun.

The following account of the action of the S.S. *Tremorvah*, with a submarine, on 11th April, 1917, illustrates the nature of the work which was done in this service. The submarine was sighted on the starboard beam, about six miles off. The captain at once altered course to bring her astern and prepared for action. The submarine opened fire at 4 p.m., at a range of five miles. Five minutes later, the *Tremorvah's* gun replied.

The submarine fired about 150 rounds and hit the *Tremorvah*, about twenty times and damaged her. The *Tremorvah* fired seventy-six rounds, but they all went short, and the smoke screen was too low. After a running fight of two hours and fifteen minutes, the crew had to abandon their ship, the master and the two gunners (acting Corporal G. D. Wright and Private E. White (Chatham), were taken prisoners by the submarine, the two Royal Marines, were mentioned in dispatches, for their work. On 10th March, the S.S. *Otaki*, with her one 4.7-inch gun fought the German raider *Moewe*, with four 5.9-inch guns, four 4.1-inch and smaller guns. The fight raged at a range of 1000-2000 yards, and the *Otaki*, scored several hits causing considerable damage to the German and starting a fire, which lasted three days. The *Otaki*, had several casualties and was much damaged. Lieutenant A. B. Smith, R.N.R., in command of *Otaki*, ordered the boats to be lowered to give a chance to the crew to be rescued. He himself went down with his ship, with his colours still flying, and his enemy described the action as "a duel as gallant as Naval History can relate." Lieutenant Smith, was awarded the V.C., posthumously.

The enemy later adopted the practice of taking prisoners the captains and gunners of the ships which they sank, and taking them to Germany, after putting the rest of the crew into their boats. Many of the corps were made prisoners, in this manner.

The line in the *London Gazette* "For service in action with enemy submarines," was constantly repeated and many members of the corps figured in these lists; as they did also in the casualty lists.

Those awarded the D.S.M., included:

Lance-Corporal S. W. Barford (Portsmouth)   Lance-Corporal H. W. Roberts (Portsmouth)
Corporal A. E. Reed (Portsmouth) *since killed*.   Lance-Corporal H. Winwood (Plymouth).
Lance-Corporal H. Walley (Portsmouth) *killed*   Private B. Trowse (Chatham).
Lance-Corporal W. Brown (Chatham).   Gunner S. W. Brattle, R.M.A.
Private A. E. Allen (Plymouth).   Lance-Corporal W. S. Clements (Chatham).
Gunner J. N. French, R.M.A.   Gunner A. T. Peckham, R.M.A.

Those mentioned in dispatches were more numerous still:

Private R S. Nash (Portsmouth).   Acting-Bombr. T. C. Westall, RM.A.
  " T. Keating (Portsmouth).   Lance-Corporal J. H. Hill (Plymouth).
  " J. W. Phillips (Plymouth).   " G. D. Wright (Chatham).
  " G. W. Thorne (Portsmouth).   Private E. White (Chatham).
Lance-Bombr. W. Horton, R.M.A.   " G. H. Cunnington (Portsmouth).
Private J. Epton, (Chatham).   " R Taylor (Portsmouth).
  " F. J. Morrison (Plymouth).   Corporal F. W. Groves, R.M.A.
  " G. H. Attryde (Plymouth).   Lance-Corporal H. E. Facer (Portsmouth).
  " S. E. Benning (Portsmouth). *killed*.   " J. Marchant (Portsmouth)
  " H. H. Dunn (Chatham).   *Good Shooting.*
Lance-Corporal A. Grant (Chatham).   Private H. Ellis (Portsmouth).
  " A. Jameson (Chatham).   Acting-Bombr. S. W. Curtis, R.M.A.
Private A. Leith (Portsmouth).   *Good work when S.S. "Persia" was sunk.*
  " A. W. Lidstone (Portsmouth).   Gunner A. Wellington, R.M.A.
  " G. Wainwright (Portsmouth).   *Good work when S.S. "Persia" was sunk.*
  " C. F. Clerk (Portsmouth).   Lance-Corporal L. Peach (Portsmouth).
  " F. Dockett (Plymouth).   Private E. Hopps (Plymouth).

Private D. Wilson (Plymouth).
" J. Gill (Plymouth).
Acting-Bombr. W. Dauber, R.M.A.

Private W. G. Skerry (Portsmouth).
" W. Robinson (Portsmouth).

The Corps were able to take but a small part in the other aspects of this phase of the War; but they were employed in the "Q" ships. at the beginning. In fact, the first attempt in this line was made by embarking the musketry staff of the Chatham Division, R.M.L.I, in one of the Flushing steamers, taken up for the purpose, and sending them to cruise in the Channel, in the hopes that their expert marksmanship would enable them to deal with the submarine, when found. But they had no luck in encountering any.

In the well known incident of the *Baralong*, so graphically described in the Official History, the Royal Marines bore their part. The historian relates that one submarine was firing into the defenceless *Nicosian*, which was full of mules, at 1000 yards, and a second was believed to be present from the appearance of things. When the *Baralong* approached, the enemy submarine ceased firing and trimmed down to attack, but Lieutenant Herbert steered towards the *Nicosian's* boats, as if to pick up the survivors, on which the submarine manned her gun and steered so as to cut him off from the boats. Steering so as to place the *Nicosian* between himself and the submarine, Lieutenant Herbert hoisted the White Ensign, cleared away his 12-pounders and trained them on to the bow of the *Nicosian*, and as soon as the submarine appeared, Lieutenant Steele, R.N.R., opened fire at 600 yards, as did the ten Marines, with their rifles. The *Baralong's* crew consisted mainly of R.N.R. men, with one corporal, one lance-corporal, and eight privates of the Chatham Division, R.M.L.I. The surprise was crushing, and after the *Baralong* had fired thirty-four rounds, the submarine heeled over twenty degrees, and the crew jumped overboard; thus "U 27" went to the bottom. The Baralong started to save the *Nicosian's* boats, when about a dozen of the submarine's crew were seen to be swimming to the *Nicosian*, and to be swarming up her sides. The situation was serious, for the other submarine was still unaccounted for, whilst the *Nicosian*, full of mules and fodder, could easily be set on fire. To save the ship it was necessary to act at once. Fire by the guns and Royal Marines was at once re-opened, but a number of the Germans succeeded in getting on board. Lieutenant Herbert placed his ship alongside as soon as possible and sent his Royal Marines to board the *Nicosian*, and recover possession, "It was a piece of service desperate enough to test the stoutest nerve." (*Official History*). The Germans were nowhere to be seen and they made no sign of surrender, whilst rifles and ammunition had been left readily accessible, in the chart house. After a short search, the Germans were found in the engine room, "the Marines in hot blood and believing that they had to do with the men, who had so wantonly sunk the *Arabic* (*with her women and children*.-ED.), in the morning shot them all at sight" (*Official History*). The *Nicosian* was then brought safely to port. The corporal was awarded the D.S.M. and the lance-corporal was promoted for their services in this ship.

As related elsewhere, the Royal Marine Submarine Miners also took a share in this submarine war. The establishment of the numerous small bases in the West Indies, Falklands, Coast of Scotland, etc. manned by the Corps, described in Part V. were due to the necessity to counteract the activities of the enemy submarines, whilst numbers of the Corps spent many weary hours in the look out stations in the Aegean, Orkneys, Shetlands, and Cromarty, watching for these pests of the sea to reveal themselves.

When the system of convoys for merchant shipping was introduced in 1917, cruisers and armed merchant cruisers were employed on escort duty, and a large number of the Corps steamed many thousands of miles and spent many anxious hours on watch to guard against submarine attack. They performed many useful functions in connection with this work, including the provision of signallers. As related before, though the seamen portion of the crews of the merchant cruisers were largely R.N.R., the Royal Marines were regular members of the Corps, and the *London Gazette* bears witness that their services were appreciated.

The following notes by an officer of the Corps who was employed on the escort duty with convoys are interesting as illustrating the nature of the work.

"We left Milford Haven for Sierra Leone, with a convoy of transports. Two days afterwards, just before dark, and in a thick mist, a suspicious looking steamer approached, which did not answer signals. We chased but could not open fire, for fear of hitting the convoy, and at last had to give up the chase for fear of losing our charge. On comparing charts later, the steamer was found to have been the *Moewe*, returning from her cruise.

Our work on the West Coast of Africa consisted in taking convoys north and then handing them over to the light cruisers, forming convoys at Sierra Leone or Dakar, etc. For a month we did guardship at Monrovia, because the presence of a submarine had been reported, and the Germans in Monrovia were known to have machine guns and ammunition. Arrangements were made for our Royal Marines and a party from the French cruiser to land, on which the arms were surrendered.

I then turned over to an armoured cruiser and commenced convoying to Plymouth, doing four runs. Then we were transferred to the North American run, (the temperature at Sierra Leone was about 100 degrees, and on arrival at Halifax there was 20 degrees of frost in my cabin, the temperature ashore was 10 degrees below zero).

We did four runs on the North Atlantic route, for three of them, we held a full gale most of the way. On our first return journey, we lost every boat in the ship, and there was so much water in the engine room, that only one set of boilers could be kept going. There was insufficient pressure to work the pumps and every officer and man baled ship by bucket throughout one night. On the fourth trip, we were torpedoed seventy miles north east of Rathlin Island. We got into Belfast Lough with the whole of the ram out of water, and the quarter deck submerged. When we finally docked at Liverpool, the hole, all below the water line, measured thirty five feet by twenty five feet.

When well at sea convoying was easy work, but it was very trying inside of forty-eight hours of England, and on the North Atlantic run, there is no doubt that it told on officers and men."

In 1918, the 5th Royal Marine Battalion, was formed for anti-submarine and anti-aircraft duties in the Dover Patrol, under the Admiral of Controlled Mining. It consisted of a headquarters and twenty platoons; Colonel R. H. Morgan, R.M.L.I., was appointed to command with Major A. P. Grattan, as second in command, Captain C. P. Goodden, adjutant, and Lieutenant G. H. Ilton as quartermaster.

The strength of the battalion was fixed at 64 officers and 863 other ranks with medical and pay staff attached. They were borne on the books of the depot ship at Dover, where the headquarters were established in September, in an old hotel near the docks. The personnel consisted of a nucleus of reservists for each platoon, with specially commissioned officers and enlisted men drawn from the older men of 45 years of age and over, who were called up in that year. A proportion of the officers were trained electrical engineers, and the recruits included many electricians and members of nearly every known profession. Each platoon was self-contained and consisted of three officers, an anti-aircraft gunnery section, a searchlight section, and an anti-submarine section, with a signaller. Only one station with two platoons, had been established, when the Armistice stopped any further developments. The other platoons were formed at the Royal Marine headquarters and underwent their training there, all officers and men being put through a special electrical course. An equal number of platoons had been allotted to each division, to be raised and trained. Captain G. Bullock, R.M.L.I., who had done such good work in Serbia, was in charge of the first station and did invaluable work in getting it into working order. In January, 1919, "orders were issued for the battalion to be disbanded, and this was completed by the end of February. The battalion in the short period of its existence earned a good name for itself, for its discipline, energy and keenness.

CHAPTER 8.

RIVER OPERATIONS.

Capture of Modyuski Island-River Dwina, North Russia, 1918-19 - Ussuri River, 1918 - Armoured Train in Siberia and Russia, 1918-19 - Kama River, Russia, 1919.

1 - River Dwina, 1918.

CONSEQUENT on the Russian Revolution, and the Treaty of Brest-Litovsk, whereby Russia withdrew from the War against Germany, anxiety arose in the Allied countries, as to the large stores of munitions at Murmansk and Archangel, and as German forces were reported to be pressing up to the north, it was feared that these places might become depots and bases for submarines and be more difficult to control than those already existing.

In Chapter 13, the measures to deal with this menace are described. This chapter deals with the river operations, which have a peculiar nature of their own, entailed by the counter-revolution of the White Russians. The latter were supported by the Allies against the Bolsheviks, who were supported by the Germans.

H.M.S. *Glory* (flagship of Rear-Admiral Kemp), had, as has already been told, spent the winter of 1917-1918, at Murmansk, and the British Military Mission, under General Poole, had also arrived there. In April, 1918, H.M.S. *Attentive*, Captain Altham, was dispatched to Murmansk; the other ships present, being the French *Admiral Aube*, the U.S.S. *Olympia*, trawlers, drifters, etc. In May, Colonel Paterson's Royal Marine Field Force (see chapter 13), arrived. In June, General Maynard and his troops, the Syren Force, arrived and took over the Murmansk Railway. Summer was now coming on rapidly, and the *Attentive*, set to work to train a landing party, including her small detachment of Royal Marines.

The attitude of Finland at that time was an unknown quantity, but the country was known to be infested with Germans, and a considerable force of German troops, was believed to be there. The country was very difficult; whilst under snow movement of troops and supplies is possible, but when the thaw comes, the country turns into a swamp and becomes impassable. The enemy's movements were therefore, restricted more or less to the railway line, and in consequence, the British established strong garrisons at salient places, such as Kandalaksha, and later at Kem. On 1st July, the *Attentive* left for the White Sea, and had to force her way through the ice. She kept along the western shore, and on 3rd, went up the Gulf of Kandalaksha, and anchored off that place, leaving the next day for Kem, which town is about seven miles up the river, on which it stands. The idea was to strengthen the Anti-Bolshevik Russians, and so checkmate the German manoeuvres, whilst at the same time helping British and other refugees, who were coming to Murmansk, from the south.

The position at Archangel, where there were large stocks of munitions, was serious, for it had become Bolshevik in 1917, and as troops were now arriving, preparations were made for the occupation of Archangel and the *Attentive* returned to Murmansk.

On 31st July, an urgent telegram was received from Archangel, saying that the Counter-Revolution was about to commence, and asking for Allied support.

The troopships could not get away in time so *Attentive*, *Nairana* (the seaplane ship) and *Admiral Aube* (French), who could all steam 15 or 16 knots, were ordered to leave that night. *Attentive* embarked 100 French troops, *Nairana* (flying Admiral Kemp's Flag) another 200, *Admiral Aube* embarked 200 French and 96 Royal Marines under Lieutenants Merchant and Harries, R.M.L.I. of Colonel Paterson's Force. Navigation was difficult and much hampered by fog. *Attentive* and *Nairana* made the lightship off the bar next morning,

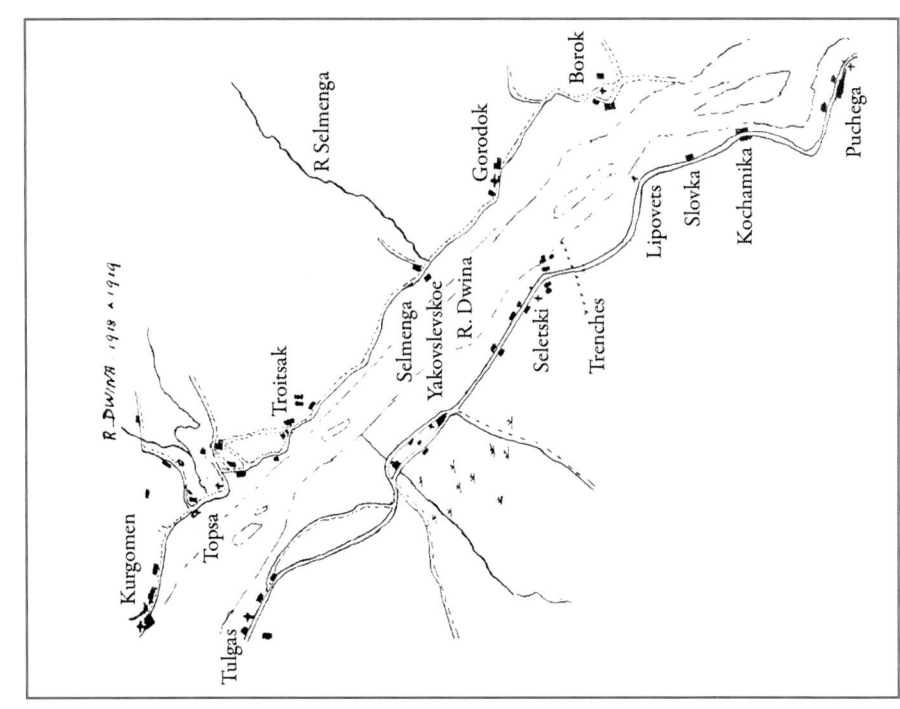

PLAN 4 — RIVER DWINA, NORTH RUSSIA

PLAN 3 — SKETCH MAP TO ILLUSTRATE OPERATIONS IN CHAPTER 8 AND 13

but the *Admiral Aube* went ashore. Abreast of the lightship is Modyuski Island (see Plan No.3) running approximately north and south; in the middle of the island were the batteries of four 6-inch guns, four 6-inch howitzers, and a partially completed 4-inch battery. It was reported that there was a station to control the observation minefield at the southern end of the island. The Captain of the *Attentive*, boarding the lightship, from which ran a telephone to the battery, summoned them to surrender, giving them half an hour to reply. After a lot of delay the enemy agreed to surrender, but on the ships steaming in they refused. *Attentive* then anchored 5,000 to 6,000 yards from the forts and opened fire with her whole broadside of one 6-inch and two 4-inch guns. The forts replied and a hot action ensued, in which the seaplanes from the *Nairana* with their bombs took a share; after a time the batteries ceased fire and the French troops were landed in the ships' boats, the ships searching the trees at the north end of the island with their fire, just before the troops landed. On the boats reaching the beach Frenchmen, Marines and signalmen jumped out and started to clear the island from north to south which was completed by the evening.

The French troops occupied the batteries, the Bolsheviks having bolted; traces of the Germans were found in them. On the ships approaching the minefield the cables were found, but they were out of action.

Next morning the ice-breakers were found to have been sunk in the channel, but they had failed to block it and a clear passage was left, through which the *Attentive* passed as well as some trawlers; meanwhile the *Admiral Aube* had been refloated and arrived, and her troops were transferred to trawlers at the bar. The ships passed up and anchored off Archangel, where they were received with cheers by the populace and the Russian officers were able to appear in uniform again; the ships in harbour were flying the old Russian Mercantile Flag, the Red Flag having disappeared. Each ship was cheered, particularly the trawler carrying the khaki-clad British troops - The Royal Marines. The Admiral and General landed and were greeted enthusiastically.

The next morning the *Attentive* stood across the harbour and secured Bakaritsa, the terminus of the Archangel-Petrograd Railway, where there were deep water quays and storehouses. A naval detachment of some 70 men and a small party of Royal Marines were landed under the 1st Lieutenant of the *Attentive* and entraining proceeded up the line to the next station Isarko Gorka. When the naval detachment detrained and advanced the Bolsheviks were advancing from the south, but a four-inch shell from the ship forced the enemy to take cover and they were soon in full flight. The naval detachment then advanced and secured the embankment, and on some French troops coming up the whole advanced and secured the station and the wireless telegraphy station.

Although a good deal of the stores had been taken away there were still quantities in the storehouses at Bakaritsa; that night the naval party were relieved by British troops, who proceeding down the line, secured all the approaches until the landing of the troops was completed.

The Bolsheviks had removed most of the best river steamers, together with the guns and ammunition, so that the problem in front of the naval authorities was to create a river flotilla to support the Allied troops, who had meanwhile gone about 150 miles up the river and met with strong resistance.

Two gunboats the *Advokat* and *Gorodok* antique paddle steamers, with thin sides and decks were armed with a 12-pounder at one end and a pom-pom at the other, whilst a third gunboat named the *Razlyif*, was got ready by the crew of *Glory IV.*, late the Russian Cruiser *Askold* (see Chapter 13). Arriving off Bereznik (see Plan 3) the *Advokat* and *Gorodok* became hotly engaged in support of the troops and drove off the Bolsheviks. A few days later, proceeding up the river, they fell into a trap off Troitsa and came under a heavy fire, sustaining some casualties, a lesson in the danger of ships pushing on too far, unsupported by troops to move up the banks.

The country consisted of large tracts of forest land, stretching for miles; so that small forces moving through, were always vulnerable on their flanks and rear.

No roads except rough tracks existed, as the River Dwina is the main artery of communication. The river is full of shifting sand-banks and is very winding, it varies in width from 400 yards to a mile, but in many places is narrowed to a hundred yards by long islands. The banks in places are steep cliffs of alabaster, pink and white, which glow in the sun, whilst across the river the bank is flat with a village; the banks which were rarely of the same level changed their character with regularity. The forest always grew to the edge of the cliff. Ambushes which constantly hampered the transport, were laid by the Bolsheviks, who opened fire from the tops of the cliffs and they also sank barges across the channels. Even on the low-lying banks the forest only receded about two miles and in those open spaces were found the villages. In these circumstances it was necessary for the Army and Navy to work in close touch and the flotilla advanced up the river with the troops on either bank.

Captain R. Burton, R.M.L.I. was appointed adjutant of the Allied Naval Brigade, consisting principally of Russians, who formed part of the Flotilla.

The British Army staff had now taken over command and an attack on Troitsa was planned. Russian and French troops were to outflank the position and endeavour to seize the batteries, whilst the gunboats were to move up stream in support; it was hoped to surprise the enemy flotilla, but the enemy gunboats after an exchange of shots fled up the river and as the troops were delayed the enemy convoy escaped, but the batteries were captured. A couple of days later an enemy gunboat with a long range gun engaged the boats which were employed in escorting a convoy and after a hot fight the enemy was driven off. In the meantime the Bolsheviks brought up 500 men and worked them round the weak British Force on the right bank, their guns threatened to cut off the flotilla and also made movements on the left bank precarious. By skilful handling and gallantry on the part of the gunboats, the troops were re-embarked and though subjected to a heavy fire from the right bank, they successfully effected their retirement to Bereznik, the gunboats anchoring off the mouth of the River Vaga (Plan 3). H.M.S. M. 25, armed with a 7.5 inch gun, had now arrived, which had an immediate effect on the natives. Some motor launches had also arrived and the Senior Naval Officer embarking in *M.L 2* went up to Bereznik, where the 10th Royal Scots had now arrived. Bereznik became the base; the barges, tugs and *Retvisan* (the Army Headquarters Ship) were tied up to the left bank, where there was a collection of wooden houses. The village itself was further off inland and the intervening space was used as an aerodrome.

A few days later M. 25 with the three gunboats, went up stream and when abreast of the village of Borka, the enemy opened fire with rifles, machine guns and some guns of 3 or 4-inch calibre, to which a vigorous reply was made. One shell passed through the wardroom of M. 25 and exploded on the Captain's cabin door. It put the entire 12-pounder gun's crew on the quarter deck out of action, the gun was at once manned by a spare crew and with the aid of the 7.5-inch gun the enemy's guns were soon silenced. M.25 sustained seven casualties and the surgeon although very severely wounded himself, displayed the greatest gallantry, in attending to the wounded.

On 1st September, as it was reported that 300 Bolsheviks and 15 machine guns were advancing on Siskoe, where there was only a slender force, all the French troops with a small party of Royal Marines (about 40 of the Royal Marine Field Force under Lieutenant Harries had accompanied the flotilla up the river), with the *Advokat* as escort were sent back as it was feared that the enemy might reach the banks of the river and cut the communications of the force.

River Operations.

There was now in the flotilla a steel barge, which carried two small singleseater seaplanes from the *Nairana*, which performed valuable work in reconnaissance.

M.*25* was established off the mouth of the Vaga River, where there was a deep water berth off an island christened Monitor Island; a rifle range and recreation ground were constructed on the island; and the Senior Naval Officer hoisted his flag in the *Kathleen*, a steam yacht.

On 12th September the American Battalion, 1000 strong, arrived and the advance commenced on 14th; the flotilla comprised the M. *25, Radzlyff, Advokat*, and M.L's *1* and *2*. Two miles below the village of Chamova, M. 25 engaged a large paddle steamer the *Magoochy* and disabled her by a shot in the engine room, on which her crew jumped into the water and the ship sank. The flotilla then pushed on to Chamova, where all was quiet. It had been intended that the troops should cut off a large party of the enemy in the angle between the Vaga and the Dwina, but as they were two hours late, they could not arrive at Chamova before mid-day; the enemy however, had been warned by the arrival of the flotilla, which was now in an awkward bend of the river, where the cover of the forest trees behind the village allowed the enemy to open fire on the ships without exposing themselves; it was therefore necessary either to withdraw or else secure the village and its approaches by a landing party until the arrival of the troops; accordingly a naval landing party of 50 men with eight Lewis guns of the Royal Scots were landed under the Captain of M.*25*; the enemy gunboats appeared as the party was landing and a battery near the church also opened fire; the monitor's guns however soon put the gunboats to flight and silenced the battery; the landing party advanced in three sections, one forming the right flank guard, one moving directly on the village and pushing through it, the third section covering the flank; suddenly fire was opened from the surrounding woods, and the ships had difficulty in supporting the party until it was ordered to fall back to the river bank, when the ships were soon able to silence the enemy fire. Later on the enemy brought up a gun and commenced shelling the flotilla which was still waiting for the arrival of the troops; the landing party was therefore recalled and the flotilla stood up the river and met the enemy ships who were advancing; the enemy bolted as soon as the British ships opened fire, but a concealed battery on shore opened on the flotilla and they were caught between two fires. At 4 p.m. as there were no signs of the troops, the flotilla returned down the river and ran the gauntlet of the batteries which the fog had hidden in the morning; M.*25* knocked out one in passing and the ships returned to Monitor Island. The troops who were much delayed, marched into Chamova that night and found it deserted; the action had a good effect as the enemy never made another determined stand either ashore or afloat. A few days later M.*25* sank another Russian ship which came down to Chamova, to which place the flotilla and transports had now moved. On 19th the discovery of mines in the river occasioned a check in the operations; M.L *3*, in which were the Senior Naval Officer and other officers had her stern blown off; mine sweeping operations were therefore undertaken, which proved to be a most risky business; owing to the brown colour of the water, it was not possible to see more than a foot below the surface; however when 40 had been swept up the way was found to be clear.

The troops had now fought their way forward to Troitsa, and the flotilla arrived at that place on 23rd. A sweep up to Seltzo (Seletski) found the way clear and this was the furthest point reached; the troops were established on the line Gorodok-Seltzo for the winter, as it was necessary, in order to avoid being iced in that the flotilla should return down the river not later than October 7th; several guns were landed and when the Navy had done all in their power to help the troops the ships proceeded down the river to Archangel and the personnel rejoined their ships and the naval work of that season came to an end.

The position held by the 'Elope' Force and the Russian Battalions with British Officers was about

350 miles up the river. It was strengthened by blockhouses, but the climatic conditions were very trying; whilst the summer had been passed in steaming forests and malaria infested swamps, during the winter the thermometer was 40 degrees below freezing point.

Captain R. Burton, R.M.L.I. was awarded the D.S.C. for his services as Adjutant of the Allied Naval Brigade, where he carried out very difficult work in a most successful manner. He was relieved as Adjutant by Major H. R. Brewer, R.M.L.I. who was sent from England at the beginning of December with four N.C.O.s and 20 Privates to assist in the preparation of the River Expeditionary Force for the following year, which job was now seriously taken in hand. This party was quartered in the Naval Barracks south of Archangel. Captain Burton and his 250 Russians returned from service with the Army about the beginning of February and they were then fitted up as sailors and taken in hand for instruction. The barracks were now called the Royal Naval Barracks and became the Depot for the Expedition which started up the river in the following summer; Major Brewer being placed in charge of the Depot. During the winter Captain Merchant and Lieutenant Harries, R.M.L.I. with their party of 100 of the Royal Marine Field Force came into the barracks for a short time; this party was continuously employed on operations to check the Bolshevik advances, in which they performed splendid services; they continued to serve on this front until July, 1919. Lieutenant Harries, who became A.P.M. at Archangel and remained there until the final evacuation, was awarded the O.B.E.

Major Hammond, the Naval Store Officer, also held a temporary commission in the Corps and rendered most valuable service, being awarded the O.B.E.

The following rewards were gazetted for service in North Russia:-

Meritorious Service Medal.

Cr.-Sergeant A. G. Squibb (Portsmouth). Private J. W. Smith (Plymouth).
Sergeant L. A. Scott (Portsmouth). " A. J. Still (Chatham).
Private G. J. Friend (Chatham). " H. L. Weaver (Plymouth).
" F. A. J. Parsons (Plymouth). " W. Wolstenholme (Plymouth).

Mentioned in Dispatches

Sergeant M. W. Minter, D.S.M. (Portsmouth).

Distinguished Service Medal. (For List see Chapter 13.)

1919.

In the spring of 1919 arrangements were made to relieve the Garrison Battalions who were serving on the Archangel front and elsewhere, and as soon as the Russian White Forces were organised and equipped to evacuate the Allied Troops in North Russia.

The British troops detailed for the relief, comprised two weak Infantry Brigades, each of two Battalions with a proportional force of artillery, machine guns and auxiliary services: the Brigades were commanded by Brigadier-Generals Grogan, V.C. and L.W. Sadleir-Jackson.

The Naval Force to proceed up the river was commanded by Captain E. Altham, C.B. and comprised the following vessels; H.M.S. *Humber*, H.M. *Monitors, 23, 25, 27, 28, 31, 33*, with the river gunboats *Glow-worm, Cricket, Cicala, Cockchafer, Moth, Mantis*; the *Hyderabad* was the depot ship for the coastal motor boats with the *Cyclops* for repair ship. A river paddle steamer the *Borodino* which rather resembled a Thames houseboat in appearance, was the Senior Officer's Ship. Lieutenant C. M. Sergeant, R.M.L.I. was appointed to the Staff of the S.N.O. as Intelligence Officer, but as there were plenty of Intelligence

River Operations.

Officers on shore, he took command of all the Royal Marines, which as each ship carried from five to fifteen R.M.L.I. amounted in the aggregate to a respectable force. In addition there were four minesweepers *Sword Dance, Step Dance, Morris Dance* and *Fandango*.

The Royal Air Force had 12 seaplanes and three observation balloons; their materiel and personnel were accommodated in three large Flemish barges with the *Pegasus* as Depot ship.

The Bolsheviks disposed of considerably more troops than the Allies, but of more importance they owned a fine flotilla of paddle steamers, each mounting two guns, 3-inch, 5.9 inch or 8-inch calibre; the smallest of these out-ranged the British 6-inch by 2,600 yards; as they were up stream they were able to float mines down on to the British flotilla and they always covered their retirement with a minefield.

The object of the White Russian Force was to advance south up the River Dwina and capture Kotlas, about 700 miles from Archangel, which was an important road, river and railway junction which the Bolsheviks used as a base and Dockyard.

Captain Altham arrived at Murmansk in the *Fox* on 9th May and at once pushed on to Archangel, in company with the ice breaker *Sviagator*, but the ships were jambed in the ice in the White Sea and finally arrived at Archangel on 16th, when the Senior Naval Officer and his Staff with the Royal Marine Detachment transferred to the *Borodino* and a fortnight was spent in fitting out.

Some of the monitors and other vessels had spent the winter at Archangel and others were arriving; some ships had already been sent up the river to assist the troops and to check the enemy flotilla.

When ready, the Senior Naval Officer and his escort started up to the front (350 miles away) on 31st May, and after an eventful journey arrived on the Tulgas-Kurgomen Line on 3rd June.

This front was the River Dwina front. There were other fronts, principally the railway front on the Archangel- Vologda-Moscow Railway (chapter 13). The Pinega front, on the river of that name, on the right bank of the Dwina, about 100 miles from Archangel. The Vaga front, which was on a large tributary river, running into the left bank of the River Dwina, 25 miles below the main position, and six miles above the advanced base Bereznik. During the winter our troops had been driven from the Gorodok-Seltzo (or Seletski) position, and had fallen back to below Tulgas. By the end of May, the monitors, etc., that had already arrived, in conjunction with the troops, had regained the village of Tulgas, on the left bank.

On 6th June, Lieutenant Sergeant was sent to establish a naval observation post, in Tulgas village. This was required, because owing to the intervening islands and the windings of the river, only the masts of the Bolshevik ships were visible. The left bank at Tulgas, rose high and sheer from the river. On the right bank, the British held high ground, facing a more or less level plateau, ending in the red cliffs of Topsa and Troitsa, which were in enemy hands and dominated each reach of the river. There was also an extensive enemy minefield, under cover of their batteries.

An excellent observation post was found on the top of a prominent house on the cliff, whence they could see everything, and unfortunately also be seen; luckily for the party, when the house was hit, it was on the other end, whence they were able in future to watch through the holes in the roof. Their duty was to watch for the enemy gunboats, and to spot and correct the fall of shot from our ships. This they did by means of a telephone to the foot of the cliff, whence it was signalled off to the ships. When later, the wire was cut, it was found possible to shout the corrections from the top of the cliff to the gunboat, below.

At this time there was practically no darkness, and spotting was possible at night up to five or six miles. As the Bolshevik vessels were continually advancing and retiring, the work became too much for one officer, and a lieutenant, R.N., was sent up to assist after a fortnight.

The troops were now arriving, and it was decided to make an attack. The advance was to be made from Kurgomen. The Russians were detailed to attack Topsa, on the right bank. Colonel Sherwood-Kelly's battalion, after a march through the forest, was to make a flank attack on Troitsa, five miles beyond Topsa. On the left bank, the other battalion was to make a frontal and flank attack on Yakoslevskoe, about six miles forward.

On the afternoon of the 19th June, before the attack, Lieutenant Sergeant noticed people carrying gear into a big barn, in the main Topsa village, which he surmised might be ammunition. A shoot was accordingly arranged with H.M.S. *Glowworm*; the third shot was a direct hit, which was followed by a terrific explosion that set the whole village alight, and all the enemy's artillery ammunition was destroyed. Under cover of a bombardment, ashore and afloat, Topsa and Yakoslevskoe, were attacked at 4 a.m. on the 20th, and the attacks were successful. The naval observation post, therefore, was moved to Topsa, and was established in the belfry of the church, about noon. Meanwhile the attack on Troitsa had not been carried through, with the result that during the night of 20-21st, the enemy heavily counter-attacked Topsa, and the Naval Flotilla were busily engaged in repulsing the attack. The Bolsheviks brought down some 5.9-inch guns mounted in barges, which were made fast to the bank. These guns outranged the guns of the British Flotilla, so that the gun boats were unable to reach the Bolshevik ships. The counter-attack, which had been made with Chinese troops drove the White Russians out of Topsa, and to increase the difficulties, the British batteries, were running short of ammunition. The gunboats opened fire on positions indicated by the observation post, but the belfry was soon hit by a 5.9-inch shell and brought down, the party, luckily escaping unhurt. The counter-attack was finally beaten off, and by a vigorous pursuit, Troitsa villages were also captured. The flotilla then moved up to Tulgas, and for the next week was busy mine sweeping.

On 7th July, a mutiny occurred among the White Russian troops, at Troitsa, and the Chief of the Naval staff, landed with all the available seamen and Marines. The mutineers decamped after murdering their seven British officers, but the General Headquarter Staff, held out in their house, until the arrival of the Naval Brigade. The Naval party then took up a defensive position, which they held until relieved by General Sadleir-Jackson's Brigade, two days later.

An attack planned for the 8th July, was undertaken to cover the relief of Grogan's Brigade by Sadleir-Jackson's, as the former was proceeding to Murmansk, leaving detachments on the Vaga and Pinega fronts. After a heavy bombardment by the flotilla and the artillery on shore, the Slavo-British Legion attacked, but when the White Russian infantry advanced, they joined with the Reds and all together advanced on Troitsa.

The Naval observation post, therefore, found themselves exposed to heavy machine gun fire and had to throw everything, except maps and telephone, into the standing corn and make the best of their way back through the forest, until they arrived abreast of H.M.S. *Humber*, where they went on board and informed the captain of what had occurred. After reporting on board the *Borodino*, Lieutenant Sergeant was sent to take command of the Royal Marines, who had landed with the Naval Brigade, owing to the aforementioned mutiny.

The White Russian troops were now in full flight, the seaplanes were there¬fore sent up and bombed the enemy, until they ran out of bombs. At the same time the enemy flotilla were pressing hard, and several of the monitors were hit. About 11 a.m., the front line had withdrawn to within 1200 yards of the fringe of the wood, and as the White Russians were still retiring, a small force of British infantry were sent up to hold the exits of the wood, and a Naval machine gun section, consisting mostly of officers from the Coastal Motor Boats held the right flank.

River Operations.

As the enemy's advance threatened the flotilla, the tugs and depot ship were sent down the river to a safe place, whilst the fighting ships took up their positions. The *Cricket* was badly hit, the *Humber* therefore moved up to take her place and was soon hotly engaged, but by 7 p.m. the fighting had died down. During the night M *27, 31,* and *33,* carried out several heavy bombardments to prepare a counter-attack by the White Russian troops, but the latter were not inclined to advance. The following day, General Sadleir-Jackson's reinforcements arrived and quickly stabilised the whole position.

Meanwhile a mutiny had broken out at Onega, but with the aid of the monitors left at Archangel, the situation was neutralised. Mine sweeping in the river was carried on, and by 27th July, a passage had been cleared for the flotilla up to Troitsa. As soon as they advanced they were received by a barrage of fire from the enemy, but pushing on they anchored under the cliffs at Troitsa, which became the advanced base for the remainder of the time.

Shortly after this, Admiral Kolchak's advance from Siberia was checked, so that the main object of effecting a junction with him at Kotlas was defeated, and orders for complete evacuation were issued.

In order to cover the withdrawal, it was necessary to attack and disorganise the enemy. The plan was therefore to attack on both banks; on the right bank the following positions were to be attacked, Selmenga River-Gorodok- Borok-Slovka-Kochamika-Puchega. The flotilla was to bombard and cover the frontal attack, whilst Puchega and the further positions were encircled. The British troops were relieved from all places except the front positions and concentrated for the attack, and were replaced by seamen and Marines. On 1st August, the Royal Marines, 60 in number, were allotted to the defence of Troitsa, where General Headquarters were stationed. The Royal Marines remained here for a fortnight, and during that time, as there was only one trained Lewis gunner in the party, all were put through a course, which proved very useful later on.

The Russian position was a line of 16 blockhouses at intervals of about 200 yards on the southern crest of a wide open valley, in which flowed the Selmenga River. The troops marched through forests and swamps for three days and were forced to leave the artillery behind owing to the swamps; the machine guns and ammunition being carried forward by hand. Zero hour was fixed for noon on August 10th. With the exception of Seletski, all objectives were carried at the first assault. Seletski was then bombarded for two hours by every available Naval and Military gun, and was taken at the second attempt.

The Royal Marines were then ordered to leave a detachment of 10 men in Troitsa, and cross the river to take over Seltzo (Seletski). As the tug conveying them (one officer, 50 N.C.O.s and men and five Lewis guns), ran aground they did not arrive until 8 p.m. The White Russians were all drunk and there was no one to guide them to the position. Lieutenant Sergeant was eventually shown the position on a map and given a guide. The position to be taken over was four miles long, consisting mostly of trenches with occasional Bolshevik blockhouses. Fortunately they met an English machine gun sergeant (an ex-officer, with the D.S.O. and M.C.), who knew the ground, and with his assistance eight blockhouses were occupied, with a small reserve at Seletski Church. The arrangements were re-organised in daylight the next morning.

The Bolshevik casualties had been heavy, 3500 killed and wounded and 1000 prisoners, whilst those of the Allies had been light.

These defences were held by the Royal Marines until 10th September; the Bolsheviks who had brought up more troops were becoming more aggressive and made raids on 6th, 7th, and 8th September, which were beaten off and on 9th the enemy commenced a new attack, which was awkward, as the final withdrawal was fixed for 10th. The detachments were recalled to their ships on 10th September and Lieutenant Sergeant left with a detachment of 21 men for Bereznik.

Lord Rawlinson had arrived on a visit of inspection on 5th, and the Naval Brigade took part in the parade.

The river was falling fast and in places was only three feet deep; as two of the monitors drew seven feet and others four feet, it was necessary to commence the evacuation without delay and the ships were dispatched down the river. Mines were laid in the river above Troitsa, the first big mine field being completed on 28th August. Every means was taken to lighten the ships, guns were put into barges, and armour plates removed. Although working day and night the job took nearly a month, finally only H.M.S. *Humber* and M *27*, whose draught after stripping bare was still too great, were left. The *Humber* was got away by blowing up the sand bars with depth charges and towing her over before the sand closed the channel, but at last on 16th September, M *25* and M *27*, had to be blown up as it was impossible to get them any further.

After Lieutenant Sergeant and his party arrived at Bereznik, a rising of the peasants in a village on the Vaga River gave some trouble, so he was dispatched with his party of 21 Royal Marines and five Lewis guns to Ust Vaga, 16 miles up the River Vaga, which they reached by march from Bereznik, which entailed a march of 21 miles through the forest. There was a fair road but as it was of loose sand, progress was slow so that leaving at 9 p.m., they did not reach their destination till 6 a.m. the next morning. It was found that the trouble had stopped, but the Royal Marines were ordered to take up a position for defence of the village, whilst the forward troops fell back. On their arrival the Royal Marines returned to Bereznik, marching back on the night of 15th-16th September, where they arrived at 11 a.m.

On 16th September, as the infantry were proceeding down the river in small barges, the first was fired at from the mouth of the Vaga River, the troops sustaining 17 casualties. General Sadleir-Jackson who was present in a coastal motor boat, requested the Senior Naval Officer to hold up all further craft till this party was cleared out. If the two other barges, each containing 300 or 400 men had passed, they must have sustained heavy casualties. On the arrival of General Jackson at Bereznik, he ordered Lieutenant Sergeant and his party, who had just marched in, to proceed up stream in a small tug, with a small boat and dislodge the Bolsheviks.

Arriving about a mile below the ambush, Lieutenant Sergeant landed with 10 men and two Lewis guns in the small boat covered by the remainder in the tug. When the boat grounded, they waded ashore and took up a position to cover the landing of the remainder. The party then advanced up a road parallel to and about 50 yards from the river bank, with dense scrub on one side and forest on the other. The enemy position was found to be empty, so they followed up the road for about a mile, passing through several open places. On entering one of these, the scouts stopped and when the officer went forward to investigate, he was closely followed by the main body. Fire was at once opened on them from all round. The men were ordered to lie down and the four Lewis guns were set to fire at each quadrant of the circle; the reserve was then brought up by Lieutenant Sergeant, on the inland side of the scrub, shouting and making as much noise as possible and firing the Lewis gun from the hip. As soon as the Bolshevik fire ceased, the main body were got out of the clearing into the scrub on either side, and covered by a Lewis gun, the officer and some rifle men charged the far side of the clearing. Here only one man was found, the rest having decamped. As the party was now well round the mouth of the river, the officer decided to hold the ground they had taken, and signalled off to the tug to signal "all clear" to Bereznik, and the barges, etc., passed safely down the river.

The ambush had been cleverly laid, a machine gun was hidden on either side of the road through which they passed, in front were two Russian Lewis guns, and another on the left hand side. About half a company had been posted on either side. The two machine guns had been left, together with three dead and 15 wounded Bolsheviks. Superiority of fire had fortunately been obtained by the Royal Marine Lewis gunners, who only had one man wounded, though three of the advanced Lewis guns had been smashed by direct hits. Just after firing ceased, a machine gun opened on the party from a small island in the Vaga River, this however, was soon silenced by the two remaining Lewis guns.

The party then withdrew, but as the small boat was sunk by the tug in taking off the first party, the remainder had to march nine miles down the river bank, arriving at 11.30 p.m. Lieutenant Sergeant was awarded the D.S.C. for his services.

Bereznik was evacuated the following morning, leaving the White Russians in a good position, which they lost within 12 hours, but as the river had been heavily mined above Troitsa, pursuit by the Bolshevik gunboats was prevented.

As the Bolshevik troops were now in full pursuit, along the river banks, H.M.S. *Sword Dance*, was blown up in deep water, and the remainder of the evacuation proceeded uneventfully, all arriving at Archangel on 27th September,

The Royal Marine detachment remained under the orders of General Sadleir-Jackson, for any rearguard work, until they arrived at Archangel on 20th September and on leaving were thanked by him for their services at Vaga River, because, as he said, if the Bolsheviks had not been turned out of that position the British battalions, the Senior Naval Officer's staff and the personnel of the remaining vessels would have been cut off.

The party left Archangel on 30th September and arrived at Devonport. The men had had a very hard time, as they were ashore for a long time under most miserable conditions and for some time received their rations from the ships, which were insufficient and unsuitable for work on shore, but their conduct had been exemplary throughout.

In addition to Lieutenant Sergeant, Sergeant E. Randell (Chatham), Sergeant F. A. Albury (Portsmouth), Privates J. G. Hudson (Portsmouth), J. W. Watson (Chatham), were mentioned in dispatches.

Major Brewer and his party from Archangel, were among the last to be evacuated, when the barracks were finally handed over to the Russians.

II. ARMOURED TRAIN ON USSURI FRONT. ARMOURED TRAINS ON VOLGA FRONT EUROPEAN RUSSIA.

In January, 1918, the *Suffolk* was sent to Vladivostock, and in view of the conditions in that city where the Bolsheviks were making trouble, landing parties were held in readiness to land, and on 30th March British refugees from Petrograd and Moscow were received and sent on to England.

On 3rd April in consequence of the murder of some Japanese subjects, the Allies landed parties, and at 1-30 p.m. the first party of Royal Marines from the *Suffolk* landed to protect the British Consulate. On the 28th the first contingent of Czecho-Slovaks reached Vladivostock. These were originally prisoners of war from Austria, but this race loathed the Austrians and Germans and took the first opportunity of. deserting, even whole Divisions going over. They served with the Russians until after the Revolution and then arrangements were made to transfer them to the Western Front, and in consequence of these arrangements they were being sent to Vladivostock and by 6th June 12,000 of them had arrived; but owing to the behaviour of the Bolsheviks, under the influence of the Germans, every obstruction was put in their way and they were murderously attacked at Irkutsk on 25th May: they therefore joined with the White Russians and remained in Siberia fighting against the Bolsheviks.

On 22nd May more seamen and Marines were landed, but by June 29th affairs had become so serious that it was decided to disarm the Bolsheviks in the town and to take charge of the telegraph, railway station, etc.

All the armed parties from the *Suffolk* were therefore landed with the Japanese and patrolled the town and completed the disarming, except that of 200 to 300 Bolsheviks who in the afternoon took refuge in a building, which was attacked by the Czechs and did not surrender till 6 p.m. after a severe fight.

The *Suffolk* parties were then employed in dockyard guards, guards for German and Austrian Prisoners of War and getting the barracks ready for the 25th Middlesex Regiment under Colonel John Ward, M.P. who arrived on 3rd August; on the 9th, 800 French troops arrived and on 15th a U.S.A. contingent, followed on 17th by the Japanese.

On the 14th August the ship mounted two 12-pounders in a railway truck for use on the Ussuri River; the guns manned by a detachment of R.M.L.I. under Captain J. A. Bath left for the front on 16th and the ship commenced mounting two more with which Commander Wolfe Murray left for the front on 21st. On the 22nd the ship commenced to mount a 6-inch gun in a railway truck.

Captain Bath was awarded the D.S.C. for his direction of the 12-pounders against superior enemy forces in the battles on the Ussuri Front. The detachment returned to the ship on 28th.

On the 29th the 6-inch and 12-pounder guns left for the Volga front. The crews consisted of Captain J. A. Bath, Sergeant J. P. Cridland, Corporal C. Hoit, E. F. Wallis, J. A. Purdie and C. Kingdom with 12 Privates, R.M.L.I. all of the Plymouth Division with Mr. Moffatt, Gunner, R.N.

The train started on its long journey of 6,105 miles and arrived at Nicholsk on 30th, where the wheels and bearings of the truck carrying the 6-inch gun had to be changed owing to overheating and the 12-pounders went on. They arrived at Harbin on 1st September and the 6-inch rejoined on 2nd with Commander Wolfe Murray, R.N. They remained here until 14th when another truck was obtained for the 6-inch which took them a week to fit up.

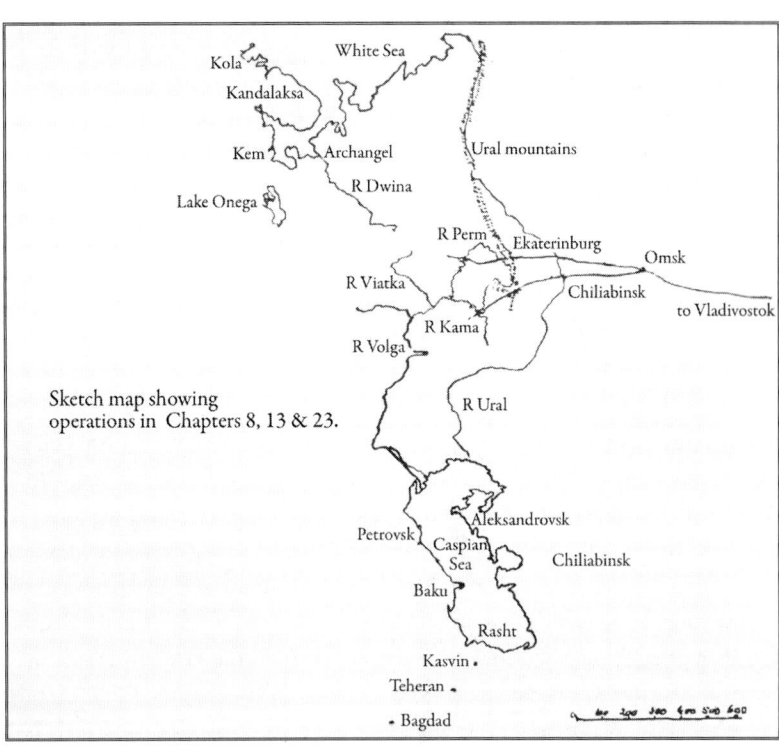

PLAN 5 GENERAL MAP OF RUSSIA AND WESTERN SIBERIA.
To illustrate Operations in 1918 and 1919.

River Operations.

Leaving Harbin on 21st September they arrived at Manchuria Station on 23rd after passing through beautiful scenery; at Iron Bridge the bridge had been blown up and the trains crossed on a temporary pontoon bridge which was rather a risky business as the river had an 11 knot current. On 28th they reached Lake Baikal with its magnificent scenery and were running round the Lake all day passing through 34 tunnels. They reached Irkutsk on 30th, but as the place was crowded with German prisoners of war who threatened to blow up the train, it was taken on five versts and an additional guard of Czechs was mounted. Leaving there on 6th October they reached Krasnoyarsk and on 11th the 6-inch left for the front at Ufa.

On 20th Colonel Ward and the Middlesex Regiment arrived and 300 of the Manchester Regiment and on 3rd November they experienced their first fall of snow.

On 5th November the 12-pounders left for Omsk where they arrived on 7th; they note that this was a nice place with fine churches. They reached Chiliabinsk on the 9th and then left for Ufa in European Russia passing through the Ural Mountains amidst magnificent scenery. They arrived at Ufa on 12th November and heard of the Armistice on 13th.

On 16th the 6-inch gun went into action at Blagavad but the 12-pounders remained at Ufa until 18th December and then were sent to Tisichma which they reached on 19th; this was the furthest point reached by the Allied troops who went across Siberia and 6,105 miles from their starting point and this small detachment of Royal Marines had the honour of being those troops. (See Plan 5).

On 20th the guns went into action, with the temperature 42 degrees below zero; to which the Bolsheviks replied; their shooting was bad, but one shell burst over the train, luckily without doing any damage. They remained in action until 24th but then, as it was impossible to act with the White Russians, they had to retire, "for the Russians would leave their trenches to watch the guns firing and the Bolsheviks would come along and take them. The guns also would blow up villages occupied by the Bolsheviks and set them on fire but the Russians would not advance to occupy them and the Reds would re-occupy them."

A Bolshevist officer who was captured had a paper saying that any English captured were to have their throats cut, he was shot.

The 12-pounders retired with the Russians, the 6-inch having been sent back three days before. All went well till Christmas Day, when there was a block on the line owing to trains colliding and the 12-pounder train had to wait so that the engine ran out of water; the detachment carried buckets to fill her up from 5 p.m. to midnight whilst the Bolsheviks were closing in on them and they only just escaped, the trains behind them being captured.

Ufa was reached on 27th and on 31st they had to water the engine with handfuls of snow until they could reach a watering place where the detachment turned to and pumped for five hours with a temperature of 31 degrees below zero and snowing all the time.

The New Year was celebrated by the snapping of the coupling of one of the trucks as they were going up a steep incline and 20 trucks went dashing down the hill and collided with an engine; luckily no one was injured and the eight trucks of ammunition were safe.

Chiliabinsk was reached on 8th January where they remained until 20th when they left for Omsk where the temperature was 50 degrees below zero; here they went into barracks with the Middlesex Regiment.

On 17th March they re-embarked in the train and on 11th April mounted a new 6-inch gun from H.M.S. *Kent* which had been brought up by the Canadians.

It was then decided to withdraw the *Suffolk's* detachment and replace them by Royal Marines of H.M.S *Kent*; they left on 13th April for Vladivostock and met the relieving party at Novo-Nicholas on 15th.

85

Vladivostock was reached on 6th May after a total railway journey of 12,210 miles.

In addition to the D.S.C. Captain Bath was awarded the French Croix de Guerre and Sergeant J. P. Cridland who had already done good work in the Cameroons (see Chapter 18) was awarded the D.S.M., as was Private F. Stevenson (Plymouth) and Corporal E. F. Wallis was mentioned in dispatches.

III. NAVAL EXPEDITION TO SIBERIA AND RUSSIA. APRIL-JUNE, 1919.
(See Plan 6).

H.M.S. *Kent* relieved H.M.S. *Suffolk* at Vladivostock in January, 1919, and when permission was given to withdraw the Suffolk's Royal Marine detachment from Omsk where they had spent the winter, it was decided to replace them from H.M.S. *Kent*.

The officers of the Naval detachment were, however to remain as a Naval Mission to assist Admiral Kolchak, who was leading the Anti-Bolshevik forces, in forming a flotilla on the River Kama as soon as the ice permitted of navigation.

It was also decided to take the 6-inch gun and the four 12-pounders out of the armoured trains and to place them in two ships of the Russian Naval Flotilla at Perm.

Volunteers were called for from the Royal MarineDetachment of H.M.S. *Kent* and at the beginning of April, Captain T. H. Jameson and 34 Royal Marines, one mate, one surgeon-lieutenant, one warrant officer, one armourer and one sick berth attendant, R.N., proceeded to Perm arriving on 27th April on which day the ice broke and started to flow down the river.

Attempts to wreck the train were made by the Red Bands and many were hanged along the railway; whilst typhus also was prevalent throughout Siberia. The party reached Omsk and proceeded with the rest of the Naval Mission to Perm; stopping for a short time at Ekaterinburg where the Tsar and his family were murdered. The Naval Mission remained first at Perm and then at Omsk whilst the Naval Force under command of Captain Jameson, R.M.L.I. joined the Flotilla.

Practically all the ice had disappeared by the 1st May and they were introduced to Admiral Smirnoff, C.M.G., in command of the Russian Flotilla and were handed the two ships to be gunned and manned by the British.

The Flotilla consisted of three Fighting Divisions, 1st and 3rd at Perm, the 2nd at Ufa; these had been prepared during the winter.

Each Division consisted of:-
(a) Six fighting ships carrying 3-inch or 4.7-inch guns and four machine guns; light armour sheeting being provided as a protection against rifle fire.
(b) A barge with one or more 6-inch guns.
(c) One ship with A.A. guns.
(d) Minelayers and auxiliary tugs.

Each Division had also its base ship, repair ship, and barges to carry fuel and kite balloons.

The Flotilla base had headquarters staff ship, liaison ship, hospital ship, etc.

The British were allotted to the Third Division commanded by Captain Fierdoroff; the ships allotted to them were a fast oil driven tug and a barge. The 12-pounders were mounted in the tug which was christened the *Kent* and the 6-inch in the barge named the *Suffolk*.

The British Force was distributed as follows:-

Kent.-Captain T. H. Jameson, R.M.L.I., Mate H. N. Barnes, R.N. Act.-Sergeant G. H. Odey,

Corporal F. E. Hill, three lance-corporals and 16 privates, R.M.L.I. and one sick berth attendant, R.N.

Suffolk.-Gunner C. W. Clark, R.N., Sergeant A. Taylor, Corporal P. F. Eveleigh, 5 privates, R.M.L.I. one P.O. armourer, R.N. .

Russian volunteers made up the necessary gun numbers where required and Captain Jameson supervised both ships. Surgeon H. C. Joyce was in the base ship.

The *Kent* was 170 feet long, 40 feet wide over the paddles and drew four feet six inches. The decks had to be strengthened to take the guns, and as the 12 pounders had only half their pedestals these had to be made before they could be mounted. The pedestals were made of five discs of wood each three inches thick, cemented together, with four 6-inch bolts passing through them and the deck to secure the guns. The *Kent* was equipped with wireless telegraphy and light armour plating placed over the gun platform, wheelhouse and wireless telegraphy cabin, whilst living quarters were also constructed. As there were few workmen available, most of the work was carried out by the detachment themselves. *Kent* carried out her trials after six days work and at 10 p.m. 7th May, having completed with stores and ammunition left Perm to report to Admiral Smirnoff at Elabouga. Only four ships of the 1st Division were ready, and as none of the Third Division had yet been completed *Kent* was ordered to join the First Division temporarily and proceeded to Kotlovka, a village four versts east of the junction of the Kama and Viatka Rivers.

The Viatka River marked the battle front, the Reds holding the right bank and a line running due south on the other side of the Kama River.

The *Suffolk* was prepared with all speed, a platform was built across the centre of the barge and the deck strengthened underneath with props; with magazines and living quarters for the British and Russian crews. The work was completed on 11th May and after passing her trials she left to join the flotilla down stream. On 13th two more ships of the Third Division arrived and the *Kent* and *Suffolk* joined their own Division.

On 14th *Suffolk* at Elabouga was bombed by two seaplanes but was uninjured whilst both planes were brought down and surrendered. The same day the Bolshevist Flotilla appeared west of the confluence of the Rivers Viatka and Kama and opened fire on the guard ship, which was holed and had to be beached; the flotilla of six ships at once proceeded down stream from Kotlovka and engaged the enemy, but they were outranged and the high ground commanding the junction of the rivers was strongly fortified with enemy artillery; the Reds had a well chosen position as regards both light and background whilst the flotilla offered an ideal target. The Flagship and *Kent* tried to close the enemy, but as they had to keep to the channel they were subjected to close fire from the enemy's shore batteries, and it was decided to withdraw. The *Suffolk* now arriving opened fire with her 6-inch gun on the

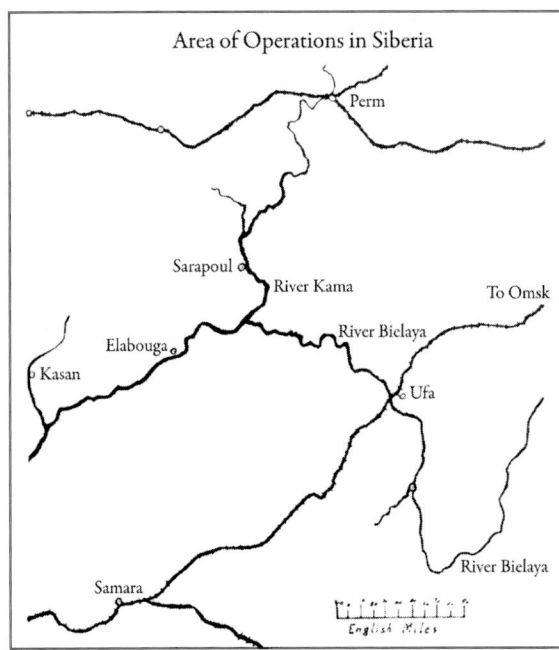

PLAN 6 OPERATIONS ON KAMA RIVER, 1919.

battery concealed by the church and put it out of action and then opened on the Red ships which promptly retired down stream. The 6-inch gun gave a lot of trouble in running out, and had to be run out by hand after each round.

The Bolsheviks now managed to cross the river Viatka and as the Siberian Army to the south of the Kama River were also retiring to the eastward, the Flotilla withdrew to Elabouga.

The river was now falling rapidly about one foot a day and great care had to be exercised in manoeuvring. On 18th May *Suffolk* proceeded to a position below Piani Bohr and opened fire at a range of 8,500 yards on to the right bank of the river obtaining good results.

At this time reports were received of further reverses to the south and that the Red Army was rapidly approaching the Bielaya River.

On 21st the flotilla proceeded to the Bielaya River to help the Army and prevent the Reds from crossing, but as no operations were observed and no fighting was seen they returned the next day to the Kama River, and received instructions to complete with fuel and proceed after dark at 11 p.m. to Elabouga and that "as the Reds were in possession of the left bank they must expect trouble." They proceeded at full speed, and reached Elabouga at 3-40 a.m. on 24th without being molested; the Bolsheviks were quite deceived for the return of the flotilla to Elabouga was unknown to them, to which was largely due the success of the subsequent operations.

At 1 p.m. the Red flotillas appeared steaming up stream to help their army on the left bank to capture Elabouga. At 1-30 p.m. the Allied flotilla weighed anchor the Third Division leading, in single line ahead, *Kent* being 3rd ship, followed by the First flotilla and *Suffolk* (in all seven ships and one barge) and proceeded down stream at full speed. Under heavy fire the flotilla got within range, and the *Kent* opened fire at 8,000 yards. Observation was difficult and the gunlayers had to lay at the enemy flashes; in a short time their fire compelled the leading ship of the enemy the *Terek* to beach herself in a burning condition. Eleven ships of the enemy were in action, but after this loss the remainder returned down stream at full speed.

Kent then fired at the second ship of the line, at first one of the after guns could bear by firing over the land on the inside of the curve and then the two foremost guns. Repeated hits were made at 4700 yards, and this ship the *Roosal*, the enemy flagship, was beached in a sinking condition and burning fiercely; the crew being dealt with by machine guns, as they jumped ashore. One of the flotilla tried to salve the *Roosal*, whilst the Flagship and *Kent* continued the chase, but rounding the next curve, the enemy flotilla, which had superior speed, went out of sight, except one small vessel, which after being fired on also ran ashore. The flagship and *Kent*, then proceeded round the next bend, where the flagship was received with a hot fire at close range, from the enemy concealed behind the high ground and was hit badly, a shell knocking the two foremost guns out of action. She turned up stream and ordered the *Kent* to retire and form a rearguard. The *Kent* turned astern of her, and with her oil fuel formed a smoke screen, whilst she burst shrapnel on the high ground, thus enabling both ships to retire up stream without further trouble.

The *Suffolk*, owing to her slow speed, had been ordered to open fire from a position five versts below Elabouga, but not to go further. The fight therefore soon passed out of her range, but until it did the fire of her six-inch gun greatly assisted the flotilla and demoralised the enemy. *Kent* fired 288 rounds and *Suffolk* 42.

H.M.S. *Kent* had sent a range finder for her small namesake, but it was delayed at Perm, and they had to do without it.

On 25th May, the *Suffolk* opened fire on some artillery, that fired at her from the left bank, and put two batteries out of action with three rounds.

River Operations.

The flotilla then retired up stream to Ekeskoia and Ust Kia, but as the troops were still falling back, the flotilla had to follow.

At 9.15 a.m. on 27th, the enemy flotilla appeared round the bend, about five versts off. The *Kent*, which was acting as guardship, straddled them with the third salvo and then tried to draw them on towards the base. The Allied flotilla advanced, but the shore observation party ordered the *Suffolk* and the other six-inch barge to open fire too soon, with the result that the Bolsheviks put such a strong barrage on the bend, that it was impossible for the flotilla to advance, and they were compelled to withdraw. Advancing again in the afternoon, the Bolshevik flotilla retired and the Allied flotilla could not get within range of them, without coming under the fire of the enemy's land batteries.

On 29th, Admiral Smirnoff hoisted his flag in *Kent* and proceeded down stream to where a minefield was being laid by the First Division, but it was found necessary to retire, and all ships were ordered to proceed north to the junction with the Bielaya River. With the *Kent* leading, the mouth of the river was reached shortly after dark.

Here the Reds had fired some barges, and from another barge and some houses on the bank, they opened an ineffective fire. As soon as they were located, *Kent* stopped and opened fire with machine guns, sweeping the barge and houses, and put up a smoke screen, under cover of which the remainder of the flotilla and their auxiliaries passed in safety. *Kent* after sinking the barge by gunfire and shelling the houses, followed and arrived at the new base at 6 a.m. the following morning.

On 30th May, *Suffolk* approached the mouth of the Bielaya River and after a considerable bombardment, during which she was subjected to heavy fire, silenced three enemy batteries at a range of 7500 yards, one being totally destroyed.

The *Kent's* engines now required repair, the work being carried out by the repair ship, after which she was able to steam 11 knots against the stream and 15 knots with it.

As the Army were still retreating, the flotilla retired up river and the new base was fixed at Sarapoul ; where the running out springs of the six-inch gun, which had been giving so much trouble were repaired.

The *Kent's* refit was completed on 2nd June and she rejoined the flotilla at Nikola Berezooka, about 25 miles down the river, arriving at 4-30 p.m. An hour later, Admiral Smirnoff arrived and informed them that Sarapoul had fallen at 5.15 p.m., and that the army had been completely surprised and defeated.

Sarapoul was a large town, on the right bank of the river; two miles below the town was a large six span bridge, only one arch of which was navigable for the flotilla.

At 10-15 p.m., *Kent* and *Grogin* of Third Division, were ordered to proceed to Sarapoul at full speed to guard the bridge, and if it had been broken to force a channel through one of the other arches. They were not molested on their way up stream and arriving at 3-25 a.m. on 3rd June, they found the bridge intact and passed above it. At 5-25 a.m., the flotilla appeared, and whilst the First Division engaged the enemy artillery on the right bank, the flotilla passed under the bridge and with *Kent* and *Grogin* leading pressed on at full speed towards the town. The enemy now opened heavy fire, shells falling in barrages across the river, and the volume of gunfire increased as they advanced.

The flotilla replied at 6-15 a.m., and the town hall was soon demolished; but they were now subjected to machine gun fire from the houses on both banks. At 6-35 a.m., one of the ships astern was hit so badly that she began to sink and *Kent* and *Grogin* turned back to help her. The crew were taken off by a ship astern and the ship herself sank in deep water. *Kent* turned into line again and destroyed a white house, from which a field gun was firing through an open door at 50 yards range. A large number of wooden houses at the eastern end of the town, containing Red troops with machine guns, were destroyed by gun fire; the trenches in the foreground were swept by the ship's machine guns. The Bolsheviks had 16 batteries in position and the flotilla, although all ships were hit, were lucky to escape serious damage, and to lose only one ship. The *Kent* was hit twice below her port paddle wheel, but the wheel was not put out of action.

The base was now formed at Galova, the terminus of the railway from Vodinski factory, where the workmen were strongly anti-Bolshevik. In 1918, they had defended themselves until, after a long siege, they were compelled to surrender, when the Bolsheviks murdered several thousands of them out of hand, a feat which they repeated in 1919.

The flotilla was now employed between Galiani and Galova, in providing artillery support to the army, and the *Suffolk* was kept very busy.

On 4th June, *Kent* went down stream to shell an enemy position, about 6000 yards inland, the army providing observation. She was however, so heavily shelled, that she had to weigh anchor and move to a more concealed position. Galiani changed hands several times, but was definitely lost on 7th June. On 7th, 8th, 9th, and 10th, *Kent* and *Suffolk* engaged enemy's infantry and field batteries and drove them back, but the morale of the Siberians was so bad that they made no use of the efforts of the flotilla.

The river was now normal, and the heavier base ships went back to Perm, because their draught was too great to permit of safe navigation. The Bolshevik flotilla was also hung up at the mouth of the Bielaya River, until the autumn.

The Siberians were deserting and retiring almost daily, and the Bolsheviks quickly gained access to the wheat country in the Urals, which was their main objective; the harvest was just ripe and the best for some years, when it fell into the hands of the Reds.

Food was very bad, and mosquitoes though not of the malarial variety, were very troublesome; the health of the detachment however, remained good.

The front troops were now falling back to a line 15 miles west of Perm and in view of the base falling, it was decided to disarm the First and Third Divisions, the Second remaining at the front.

On 26th June *Kent* proceeded to the magazine, near which was the British Naval armoured train and commenced to dismantle, placing armour, guns, ammunition and stores in the train; on this day the *Suffolk* engaged the enemy in the Veltanka district, and again the next day at the village of Stralka she routed large numbers of the enemy at close range. She fired 256 rounds and having expended all her ammunition was recalled to Perm, arriving at Motavaileka Works on 28th.

As no workmen could be obtained the crews of the two ships were obliged to dismantle the ships themselves; in order to dismount the 6-inch gun it was necessary to extend the light railway by building out a staging and running two small trucks out to reach the barge. The only available crane would lift five tons, whereas the gun alone weighed seven tons; the crane had therefore to lift one end at a time, and swing the gun on to the trucks; with the aid of 70 women the gun was then towed through the works, a considerable distance; about half-way the foremost trolley fell through between the rails, which everywhere needed repair and the two jacks in their possession were quite inadequate to lift such a weight. Time was precious and the situation was becoming critical, for they had no demolition gear to destroy the gun; however by means of wedges and chocks the truck was eventually lifted and the gun brought to an arch crane over the main line.

In the meanwhile the crew of the *Kent* had loaded some hundreds of rounds of 6-inch and 12-pounder ammunition from a sinking barge into the train.

During this time endeavours were being made at Perm to obtain an engine to join the 6-inch truck to the main train, and to take the whole train to Perm about two miles distant. With the greatest difficulty this was achieved, thanks to the help of the British Railway Mission, and the train reached Perm Station at 7 p.m. on 28th the same day that the *Suffolk* had arrived from the front.

The work of loading the train with guns, ammunition and material amounting to 225 tons was entirely carried out by the crews of the two ships. A fine performance.

All material, except 200 rounds of ammunition for which there was no accommodation, was brought away, whilst these rounds were sunk in the river.

Perm was expected to fall that night, confusion was everywhere, the station was overflowing with refugees and every train was loaded to the fullest extent; the engines were in appallingly bad repair and the traffic organisation was pitiable until the arrival of the British Railway Mission under the command of General Jack, C.B., C.M.G., C.B.E. The town itself was congested with refugees and wounded, and everywhere was panic.

As a last resort they searched the repair shop for an engine and took the only one available, which the Russians reluctantly gave them; it was only just capable of drawing the train and they eventually left Perm at 6 a.m. on 29th June.

The Bolsheviks had cut the railway south of Perm and completely surrounded the town of Kunger an important position on the railway; however a northern line from Perm running eastward and then south to Tiumen had recently been completed and all trains had to use this single track.

The party of 37 of all ranks was crowded into two wooden trucks and travelling was very slow; their rations consisted of the biscuit and beef of their reserve rations. On arriving at Omsk they volunteered to form the British Naval Armoured Train but the offer was not accepted, as there were already so many of these trains which could not be used.

The Admiralty then decided to withdraw the force altogether and they proceeded in two waggons to Vladivostock arriving there on 18th August having taken 52 days to complete the journey from Perm. A few days before leaving Omsk there was a case of small pox which had to be isolated by building a partition across one waggon causing still further congestion; the line was continually being broken and there were constant delays owing to trains in front being wrecked and the stations burnt; there were also strikes of the railway employees between Manchuria and Harbin. They were taken on board H.M.S. *Carlisle* and with the exception of one case of typhoid and one of consumption, transferred at Shanghai to H.M.S. *Colombo*, reaching England on 10th November, 1919[12].

Captain T. H. Jameson, R.M.L.I. was awarded the D.S.O.; Mate H. N. Barnes and Gunner C. W. Clark, R.N., the D.S.C.; Sergeant A. Taylor (Portsmouth) R.M.L.I. the D.S.M.

The Meritorious Service Medal was given to Corporal (Acting-Sergeant) G. H. Odey and Privates J. Brown, A.Haile, J. Netherway, D. G. Stepney, E. N. Stevenson and J. Williamson, all of Portsmouth Division R.M.L.I.

Surgeon H. C. Joyce was mentioned in dispatches.

---

12. The above account is taken from an article in the Globe and Laurel by Captain Jameson, D.S.O.

APPENDIX TO PART II.
THE FOLLOWING BATTLES, ETC., WERE NOTIFIED BY THE ADMIRALTY AS RANKING FOR ISSUE OF CLASPS TO THE WAR MEDAL SHOULD THESE BE APPROVED.

A. GENERAL ACTIONS AT SEA.

Heligoland	28th August, 1914.
Falkland Islands	8th December, 1914.
Dogger Bank	24th January, 1915.
Jutland	31st May, 1916.

B. SINGLE SHIP ACTIONS.

Cap Trafalgar,	14th September, 1914	(H.M.S. *Carmania*)
*Emde*n		(H.M.A.S. *Sydney*).
Koenigsberg,	July, 1915,	(H. M.S. *Mersey, Severn, & Aeroplanes*).
Leopard,	16th March, 1917,	(H.M.S. *Achilles* and *Dundee*).
	21st April, 1917,	(H.M.S. *Swift* and *Broke*).

C. FIGHTING AT SEA IN PARTICULAR AREAS.

North Sea.	1914-1918.	Arctic	1914-1918.
Narrow Seas	1914-1918.	Baltic	1914-1918.
Home Seas	1914-1918.	Mediterranean	1914-1918.

D. SPECIAL SERVICES NOT CONFINED TO PARTICULAR AREAS.

Mine Sweeping.	Baltic Submarines.
Mine Laying.	Heligoland Bight Submarines.
"Q" Ships.	Marmora Submarines.
Submarines.	

E. ACTIONS WITH ENEMY LAND FORCES.

Belgian Coast.4th August,	1914-19th October, 1918.
Dardanelles.	February 18/19th, 1915-March 18/19th, 1915.
Gallipoli Landing.	24/25th April-26/27th April, 1915.
Gallipoli.	
Tsingtau.	
Suez Canal	February 2nd-4th, 1915.
Zeebrugge-Ostend.	
Ostend.	10th May, 1918.

F. OPERATIONS IN CONNECTION WITH THOSE ON LAND.

Red Sea.	Pacific Islands.
Mesopotamia.	Cameroons.
German East Africa.	German S.W. Africa.

G. SERVICE IN SERBIA, RUSSIA & POST ARMISTICE OPERATIONS.

North Russia, 1918-19.	Siberia, 1918-19.
Eastern Baltic, 1918-19	Black Sea, 1918-19
Serbia, 14th Dec. 1914-1st Jan.1916	Caspian, July, 1918-27th August, 1919.
Russia.	Mine Clearance, 1918-19.

River Operations.

PART III.

Naval Striking Forces.

CHAPTER 9.

FORMATION OF THE ROYAL MARINE BRIGADE. EXPEDITION TO OSTEND.

NOTE. - The Royal Marine Brigade later became the 3rd (R.M.L.I.) Brigade of the Royal Naval Division. and then the 2nd Brigade of that Division, in Gallipoli; on arrival in France it was renumbered as the 188th Brigade 63rd (R.N.) Division and completed with other units. Its movements in France are dealt with in Part VI. Units attached to the Army, (see Chapter 26). (See Map 2).

ON 2nd August, 1914 the Admiralty ordered the formation of the" Flying Column" Royal Marines. Plans for this force had been drawn up under the directions of Admiral Prince Louis of Battenberg, the First Sea Lord, by an Admiralty Committee in 1912-13, but no steps had been taken to put their recommendations into force, except that fifty per cent. of the detachments of the 3rd and 4th Reserve Fleets were in future to consist of Royal Fleet Reserve so that a proportion of Active Service Royal Marines could be released for service in the Column, which was to be completed by reservists.

In the rush of general mobilisation little progress could be made at first, but the Royal Marine Artillery and Chatham Division R.M.L.I. were able to provide sufficient personnel to form a battalion each, though these battalions were very short of officers; later, as the Fleet mobilisation cleared up, Portsmouth and Plymouth R.M.L.I. were each able to provide their battalion.

Major General E. L. McCausland, R.M.L.I. was appointed to command with Major and Brevet Lieut.-Colonel H. D. Farquharson, R.M.L.I. as Staff Officer.

The Battalion Staffs were as follows:

	R.M.A.		CHATHAM R.M.L.I.
C.O.	Lieut.-Col. G. M. Campbell.		Lieut.-Col. C. McN. Parsons.
2nd in Comd.	Lieut.-Col. C. A. F. Osmaston.		Lieut.-Col. F. R Godfrey.
Adjutant	Capt. A. L. Forster.		Capt. W. H. P. Richards.
Q.M.	Lieut. A. Gibson.		Lieut. J. Hammond.
	PORTSMOUTH R.M.L.I.		PLYMOUTH R.M.L.I.
C.O.	Lieut.-Col. F. W. Luard.		Lieut.-Co!. G. E. Matthews, C.B.
2nd in Comd.	Lieut.-Col. E. G. Lywood.		Lieut.-Co!. F. T. Phillips.
Adjutant.	Capt. E. F. P. SketcWey.		Capt. R H. D. Lough.
Q.M.	Lieut. E. Sullivan.		Lieut. J. Battin.

The Divisions were deprived of their Adjutants and Third Quartermasters to provide these officers for the Battalions.

The greatest difficulty was experienced in obtaining equipment and khaki clothing was not obtainable until after the return from Ostend. Some 12-pounder guns, on specially designed fixed mountings, were included in the equipment of each battalion, in the event of their being required for advanced base work, and there were also a few .45 and .303 Maxim guns; in other respects all battalions were equipped as infantry.

The Brigade, by great exertions on the part of all concerned, was concentrated at Portsmouth on 7th August, 1914, the R.M.A. and Chatham at Eastney, Portsmouth and Plymouth at Forton and Browndown.

Training commenced and the organisation was getting into shape, though it was found that considerable numbers of the Reservists were too old, whilst there was also too large a proportion of Reserve N.C.O.'s, in fact it was reported that one platoon was entirely composed of N.C.O.s and the shortage of officers amounted to nearly 50 per cent. of the establishment.

Suddenly, for some unexplained reason, the Admiralty ordered the Battalions to be returned to their own Headquarters and the Brigade Staff was dispersed on 20th August.

Training continued at Headquarters until 7-0 p.m. on 25th August, when orders were received from the Admiralty through the Adjutant-General Royal Marines that the Brigade was to proceed to Ostend that night; no hint was given as to the service for which the Brigade was required, and consequently the Battalions could not be informed as to the equipment that they should take; with the result that they were considerably overloaded with all the stores that had been collected for a totally different purpose.

Brig.-General Sir Geo. Aston, K.C.B., R.M.A., who had been attached to the Operations Division of the Admiralty, was appointed to command and proceeded that evening to Chatham to take over.

The Chatham Battalion was embarked that night at Sheerness in the cruisers of the Southern Force, *Euryalus* and *Aboukir* under Admiral A. H. Christian (having marched in from Gravesend to Chatham) and was disembarked at Ostend at 3-30 a.m. on 27th.

The Royal Marine Artillery and Portsmouth Battalions were embarked in H.M.S. *Prince of Wales, Venerable, Formidable* and *Irresistible* under Rear Admiral Curry of the 7th Battle Squadron and were disembarked at Ostend during 27th. The Plymouth Battalion, embarking in *Vengeance, Goliath, Prince George* and *Caesar* under Admiral Bethell, landed on the morning of 28th.

Some airships and aeroplanes of the R.N.A.S. under Commander Samson, R.N. were attached to the Force, and arrived before dark on 27th; as the Brigade had not been warned of their coming they were very nearly received with a hostile reception.

No staff had been detailed, so General Aston appointed the Adjutant of the Portsmouth Battalion, Captain Sketchley, as Brigade Major; he was replaced as Adjutant by Captain M. C. Festing, and Major Farquharson on his arrival a few hours later took over the duties of D.A.Q.M.G.

Local transport was hired, and deficiencies made good as far as possible, whilst 50 bicycles were obtained: the inhabitants proving helpful if rapacious.

There was no time to reconnoitre properly the outskirts of the town, therefore from the map an outpost line, clear of the houses, which was about seven miles in extent, was indicated to the Battalions. The line was intersected by big canals which necessitated round-about routes for lateral communications. Beyond the houses the high sand dunes screened the country inland from seaward, so that no dependence could be placed on support from the guns of the squadron; the battleships had to lie about nine miles out owing to the shallow water, whilst the destroyers could not engage targets inland owing to the height of the dunes.

The line ran from Mariakerke-Bruges Railway-Bassin de chasse-Seacoast. The roads leading out of Ostend were occupied and cyclist patrols were pushed out to try and gain touch with the Germans; machine guns and their crews were dug in to cover the roads and the posts were wired.

By 1-0 p.m. on 28th General Aston was able to report to the Admiralty that they were established, and that, as regards the enemy, Bruges and Dixmude were clear of hostile troops; that the enemy main columns were using the Brussels -Renaix-Tournai Road and that cavalry had been at Ypres and Menin on 26th. (Note.-The Battle of Le Cateau was fought on 26th). On this day news of the atrocities at Louvain reached the civilian population, who were very anxious that Ostend should be declared an open town like Brussels, unless it could be held in real strength. On 30th the remnants of the 4th Belgian Division, which had retired from Namur with the French, and had then been sent to Havre, arrived by sea and was sent on to Antwerp.

The 29th and 30th were spent strengthening the position, organising the services and reconnoitring. Some motor cars of the R.N.A.S. had arrived; one car with an officer and a small guard approached close to Menin where there were still German troops and one actually ran through Thourout. At 10 p.m. on 30th General Aston reported that the country between the sea and the line Dunkirk--Lille-Tournai-Ghent was clear of the enemy.

Meanwhile the position of the 7th Battle Squadron was causing anxiety, exposed as it was to submarine attacks. As the Royal Marine Brigade could not effect anything more at the moment, the Admiralty issued orders at midnight on 30th that they were to return to England as soon as possible. German accounts published since the war show that they had created the impression that they were the Advanced Guard of a larger force, which had a decidedly disturbing effect on the German plans.

The orders to return were received at 4-0 a.m. on 31st and in the next strenuous 12 hours, stores and personnel were embarked from the quay with the help of one small crane; all ranks, in spite of their hard work and sleepless nights since landing, working with unflagging energy; they were all embarked by 5 p.m. on 31st and sailed for their home ports. On the way over the Battalions assisted the guns crews of the ships in repelling an attack on some of the ships by enemy submarines.

The Admiralty issued the following Order-

" The whole operations has been carried out in such a way as to be a credit to the Marine Corps."

CHAPTER 10.

ROYAL MARINE BRIGADE AT DUNKIRK AND ANTWERP.

Reorganisation of R.M. Brigade - The "Motor Bandits" -Dunkirk - Cassel - Action at Lierre - Antwerp - Retirement from Antwerp - Casualties - Honours and Rewards - Reorganisation of Brigade - Staff of Royal Naval Division.(See Map 1).

O N returning to England the Royal Marine Artillery Battalion was withdrawn from the Brigade and absorbed in the Howitzer and Anti-Aircraft Brigades (see Part VI.). The R.M.L.I. Battalions were ordered to be formed into a Brigade with the Establishments laid down for the Army; a fourth Battalion, the Deal, was formed by taking one company and one platoon from each of the others, Lieut.-Colonel R. D. Beith was in command with Lieut.-Colonel E. G. Evelegh as second, Captain E. J. B. Tagg as Adjutant, and Lieutenant T. H. Burton as Quartermaster.

The Battalions were for a short time numbered Nos. 9, 10, 11 and 12, but soon reverted to the titles Chatham, Portsmouth, Plymouth and Deal.

All men with gunnery ratings were withdrawn, together with the older reservists, whilst some of the regular officers were withdrawn for sea service; being replaced by Reserve officers and those promoted from the ranks, with the addition of some recruit officers.

The Battalions were ordered to be raised to a strength of 750 each; this could only be done by drafting in recruits from Deal from the senior squads who had not completed their training; 605 were so drafted of whom 265 were under 18 years of age. Although the R.M.A. had been withdrawn, Sir Geo. Aston remained in command with Major Sketchley as Brigade Major, and Lieut.-Colonel H. D. Farquharson as D.A.Q.M.G.

The Brigade was concentrated at Freedown, Walmer, on 12th September, and settled down to assimilate its recruits and get on with its training; clothing and equipment were also beginning to come in, though no transport was yet available. It was now known as the Third Brigade of the Royal Naval Division.

To add to its difficulties as regards personnel, 150 picked men were ordered to be sent to Dunkirk to man the armoured cars of the R.N.A.S.

"THE 'MOTOR BANDITS."

150 N.C.O.s and men with Major H. G. B. Armstrong, Captain C. F. Graham, Lieutenants C. H. Coode and G. P. Lathbury, R.M.L.I. were selected from the Battalions, to whom were added 50 R.M.A. under Lieut. M. Williams; this force was known familiarly as the "Motor Bandits."

The party assembled at Chatham on 10th September and embarked in the *Empress*, the R.N.A.S. ship; after coaling and storing ship they left for Dunkirk on 11th.

On arrival they went into camp at St. Pol, Dunkirk, which was the aerodrome of the R.N.A.S. who were operating under Commander Samson, R.N. with Major C. Risk, R.M.L.I. in charge of the cars.

The Royal Marines were to assist to man the cars as a support to the Air Squadrons. The cars (some of which were armoured, but the majority were not) were armed with Vickers machine guns. Their instructions were very vague, and no definite object seems to have been assigned to their operations, but they carried out various motor expeditions from St. Pol and later from Morbecque. A large extent of country was covered in the endeavour to gain touch with the German cavalry, with whom they had several encounters. In the main theatre of the war this was the period of the Battle of the Aisne.

As a rule the column consisted of nine cars, but no one except the leader, generally Commander Samson, knew the object of the expedition; no spares were carried, no food and no maps, whilst the party were lucky if the car did not break down. When the cavalry were encountered the Germans generally scattered at full gallop, so that identifications could not be obtained; the usual plan was to distribute a small number of the Royal Marines in each column, the remainder of which consisted of R.N.A.S. Men. A connected account of their operations is therefore not available and it is only possible to describe certain incidents from officers' diaries.

On 12th September a column arrived at Savy at 4 p.m. en route for Arras, when a local inhabitant reported that hundreds of the enemy were in the village. The column turned down a side road leading into the village which lay in a valley, and halted at the entrance, on finding that the main street was barricaded. After a conference the Marine officer with the column decided to reconnoitre the situation and the main body was withdrawn to the cross roads, whilst the Royal Marine car went forward and drew up in a small cutting; the four Royal Marines and the officer then crawled to the top and discovered a cavalry patrol advancing at a walk, the patrol was unfortunately sighted by the main body at the same time, which at once opened fire, luckily high, as the Marine patrol was in the direct line of fire.

The patrols inflicted a certain amount of damage on the enemy and created an impression of greater strength than really existed. On another occasion a Royal Marine officer with three N.C.O.s and 18 men R.N.A.S. and Royal Marines with four cars was sent to St. Amand; he was informed that there were 10,000 Germans in the place, the party however, got back all right.

On 1st October a party proceeded to Douai, where the enemy were found attacking the town with artillery, and one Royal Marine car was sent to defend the Valenciennes Gate. On arrival however, they found a company of French Territorials, with a mitrailleuse in an armoured car, taking cover. Sniping was coming from the houses down the street, so the two cars proceeded up the street backwards, firing the machine guns at the windows of the houses; on arriving near the railway station heavy fire was opened on the cars and one Royal Marine was hit; as they could make no progress, they withdrew again to the Gate, Lieutenant Coode, R.M.L.I. appealed to the French infantry to secure the Park; Lieutenant Coode then led one half company and Private McMillan (Portsmouth) the other 50 French soldiers, and the far side of the Park was consolidated under heavy infantry fire. Private McMillan behaved most gallantly, he had repaired his machine gun under fire and then led on the French troops; after the action he assisted to dress the wounded, and would not have his wound attended to until all the others were settled. He was recommended for gallantry and was rewarded by promotion to unpaid Lance-Corporal, he was killed later in Gallipoli.

In one of the raids under Commander Samson, Lieutenant Williams, R.M.A. was wounded.

On 3rd October the party struck camp at Morbeque, being relieved by the Oxfordshire Hussars at that time attached to the Royal Naval Division. With a convoy of 150 motor'buses (see Chapter 28) they proceeded to Antwerp by road via Dunkirk and Bruges arriving on 4th; here they were attached to the Royal Marine Brigade on the 5th October as described later.

Captain Graham with his section of cars was detailed to escort Mr. Churchill into Antwerp on 3rd, but as the orders did not reach them in time, Mr. Churchill went into Antwerp by aeroplane. Captain Graham's section arrived in Antwerp that evening, being the first British troops to arrive; this section acted as escort to the First Lord during the Antwerp operations, but were left very much to themselves, they however, escorted him out of Antwerp for about 20 miles and then returned.

The machine guns of the other sections were attached to the Royal Marine Battalions and placed as desired by the Commanding Officers; when getting his gun into action with Major Shubrick's company of the Chatham Battalion, Lieutenant Coode was seriously wounded. The parties remained with the Brigade and shared their duties until it returned to Ostend, when they were ordered to Dunkirk; Captain Graham's section leaving Ostend the day the Germans entered it. Major Armstrong and Lieutenant Lathbury with about half the company then went to Poperinghe and Captain Graham with the other half remained at Dunkirk.

About the middle of October Major Armstrong and half the company were recalled to England to rejoin their Battalions.

About 16th October Captain C. Graham was sent from Poperinghe by Commander Samson with a section of three cars and 20 men to report to Sir T. Capper, commanding 7th Division, who sent them to reconnoitre and get in touch with the German Cavalry; this they did well in front of the Menin-Roulers road. On 18th they went out again and got into action at 50 yards range, losing two men killed; fortunately the cars had been turned about and approached their objective backward, so that they were able to pick up the men and effect their escape, whilst the 7th Division Artillery demolished the objective, a mill; the killed were buried in a field near Bercelaere. (See Map 5).

Sir T. Capper wished to employ the cars the next day, 19th, in an attack by one of his Brigades, but Commander Samson did not concur in the employment of the cars for this work; the attack did not succeed and the cars were employed elsewhere. Meanwhile Lieutenant Lathbury and his section had attached himself to the 3rd Dragoon Guards (3rd Cavalry Division) and served with them through the First Battle of Ypres.

The remaining parties were withdrawn finally on 3rd November to England, and rejoined their units.

DUNKIRK.

Returning to the Brigade, the force was not left long at Walmer, for at midnight 18/19th September, orders were received from the First Lord of the Admiralty that the Brigade was to embark for Dunkirk the following morning.

According to the Official Naval History, they were sent to create the impression on the enemy that they were the Advanced Guard of a larger British Force, which would threaten the enemy communications. In his instructions, General Aston was reminded that his force was too weak for anything but demonstrations, and that the enemy could bring to bear overwhelming forces, if he wished, but that if he forced them to concentrate for such an eccentric movement, he would achieve his object. He was to act in conjunction with the R.N.A.S. and the Oxfordshire Hussars Yeomanry and a small detachment of Royal Engineers was added to the force.

Arrangements were made hurriedly that night, the recruits exchanged their 'Drill Purpose Arms' for service rifles and equipment, less the entrenching tools of which there were not enough to supply all.

At noon on 19th the Battalions embarked at Dover in the *Lake Michigan* and *City of Edinburgh* and crossed to Dunkirk; they disembarked there on Sunday morning the 20th and were billeted in Dunkirk for four days and then went under canvas on the Champs de Manoeuvre, where they continued training. The machine guns were brigaded under Captain G. Barker, Lieutenants Conybeare, Foote and Mead. Before the war, machine-gun training in the Corps was carried out in the Naval Gun Batteries by the gunnery instructors, who naturally had no time to study the tactical handling or the difficulties of keeping the gun going in the field; a few months before the war this part of the instruction was transferred to the musketry instructors, but the mechanical part of the instruction remained in the hands of the gunnery instructors.

Fortunately Major F. Chichester and Lieutenant Lathbury had become experts in this weapon and the latter became Brigade Machine Gun Officer in the Dardanelles.

Colonel Ollivant, Royal Artillery (War Office Liaison Officer at the Admiralty) of the Administrative Staff of the Royal Naval Division under the orders of the First Lord was in charge of the Staff arrangements; Lieut.-Colonel Chaytor of the New Zealand Forces, who afterwards commanded the Divisional Train, was Base Commandant. On this occasion the Brigade Pay Office, under Colonel Barrett, R.M.L.I. accompanied the Brigade overseas.

Some transport had been provided; the staff of the R.N.D. had purchased some 90 'buses in London and sent them to Dunkirk; they travelled by road to Dover or Southampton, where they were shipped across the Channel (see Chapter 28 for account of this unit). There were also 50 motor owner drivers, who were given commissions as Honorary 2nd Lieutenants, Royal Marines and sent over with their cars, these proved very useful as additional transport. Lieutenant Wilding, the celebrated Lawn Tennis Champion, was one of these and he was killed during the Antwerp operations. There were also several who became well known in the Division later.

On 25th September Sir Geo. Aston was placed on the sick list and was invalided to England, being replaced by Colonel A. Paris, C.B., R.M.A., who afterwards commanded the Royal Naval Division with so much distinction.

On 27th Colonel Paris removed his headquarters to Cassel, concentrating the Chatham, Deal and Plymouth Battalions there; the Portsmouth Battalion going on 28th to Lille to cover the retirement of some French detachments at Douai, Tournai, and Orchies.

The recruits, except those of the Chatham Battalion, were left at Dunkirk under Lieut.-Colonel F. Godfrey; whilst at Cassel reconnaissances were made towards Lille by two or three small columns; the scouts and signallers being mounted on bicycles and the main body following in the 'buses.

On 30th September the main armies, in their efforts to outflank each other, were approaching the sea coast, whilst at the same time the Germans in Belgium were closing on Antwerp. On this date the outer line of the Antwerp Forts was broken through and the Belgian Field Army fell back to the line of the River Nethe. In consequence the Belgian Government was preparing to withdraw the Field Army to prevent its being locked up in the fortress.

The fall of Antwerp and the Belgian Coast would involve great danger to the Channel Ports, which it was essential should be kept open for the supply of the British Army, St. Nazaire having proved most unsatisfactory as a base for the Expeditionary Force.

The British and French Government had promised assistance to the Belgians, and in consequence the British 7th Infantry Division and 3rd Cavalry Division under General Sir H. Rawlinson were preparing to embark for Ostend and Zeebrugge; the loss of Antwerp would imperil these plans and as the Official Naval Historian puts it "It was a position, which for Naval reasons alone, could not be accepted without an effort to prevent the breakdown of our plans."

It was also of the first importance that the huge oil supplies and the shipping in the harbour should not fall intact into the German hands.

ANTWERP.

In view of these considerations Mr. Winston Churchill was sent over to Antwerp, on behalf of the British Government, to try and delay the withdrawal of the Field Army and to prolong the defence of the town.

The Belgian Government assented to his proposals, provided that they received some Allied assistance. Mr. Churchill at once ordered General Paris to bring his Brigade into Antwerp, thus the Royal Marine Brigade was launched on an enterprise that showed the need of adequate forces at Admiralty disposal for Naval purposes.

It is interesting to speculate as to what might have been the effect on the submarine campaign, with all its suffering and loss, if the Admiralty had been able to retain their hold on Ostend and Zeebrugge, even after the fall of Antwerp, so as to prevent their use as submarine bases which, having regard to the unsuspected strength shown by field defences during the war, might not have been so impossible as it appeared then.

General Paris received his orders early on the morning of 3rd October; the Brigade entrained in cattle trucks at 8-30 a.m. and travelled via Dunkirk and Bruges, machine guns were mounted in the trucks in case of attack. Arriving outside Antwerp they detrained at 11 p.m. at Vieux Dieux, which is about six or seven miles east of the town and went into billets at Edyghem about 4-0 a.m. (see Map 2).

Early on morning of 4th October they moved along the Lierre road to relieve the much exhausted 21st Belgian Regiment in the trenches north of the Petit Nethe, in accordance with the following orders (as these orders led to the first active operations of the Brigade they are given in full).

OPERATION ORDER No. 1.
By BRIGADIER-GENERAL A. PARIS, C.B., R.M.A.

Reference Map Scale 1/40,000. NEAR R. OF ROUTE D'ANVERS,
ANTWERP, 4th October, 1914.

1.-INFORMATION: (a) Belgian advanced posts along River Nethe were engaged with German Patrols last night.
(b) Belgian Artillery near Linthe is engaged with enemy on South side of Nethe to-day.
2.-INTENTION: The Royal Marine Brigade and 7th Regiment Belgian Infantry will hold the line of defence from Lisp to the road junction just North of Hof Van Lacheren.
3.-The Royal Marine Brigade and 7th Infantry Regiment will relieve the 21st Regiment now holding the line at 11 a.m.
4.-SECTORS: The line will be divided into Sectors as under :-
No.1 SECTOR.-(Lieut.-Col. Delorbe, 7th Infantry Regiment).
From road junction near L just N. of Hof Van Lacheren to the de of
Chemin de Fer Railway line East of Turnhout inclusive.

No.2 SECTOR.-(Lieut.-Col. C. Parsons (Chatham), R.M.L.I.)
From de of Chemin de Fer railway line E. of Turnhout, exclusive, to the bend of the road 400 yard; South East of K. of Klaplaar, exclusive.

No.3 SECTOR.-(Col. G. E. Matthews, (Plymouth) R.M.L.I.)
From road running S.E. of Klaplaar inclusive to the road near De of Deplas Fme, exclusive.
No.4 SECTOR.-(Col. R D. Beith (Deal), R.M.L.I.)
From road just S. of De in Deplas Fme, inclusive to the river at Lisp.
Each Sector Commander will form his own local reserve.

5.-ADVANCED POSTS: Each Sector Commander will push out advanced posts to the river and arrange to resist any movement of the enemy to cross the river. These advanced posts will be strongly entrenched, and communications established between them and the main line.

[Photo by Swaine.]
MAJOR-GENERAL SIR ARCHIBALD PARIS, K.C.B., R.M.A.
Commanded R.M. Brigade September, 1914 and Royal Naval Division from 4th October, 1914 to 13th October, 1916; Severely wounded 13th October. 1916; Awarded K.C.B. and promoted Major-General for Distinguished Service in Gallipoli.

6.-THE RESERVE WILL CONSIST OF: (a) lstCarbineers who will remain on left of the outpost line.
   (b) Portsmouth Battalion at R. of Route D'Anvers.
   (c) Machine guns of Royal Naval Air Service Department at R.of Route D'Anvers.

7.-ARTILLERY: [13] The Artillery groups will remain in their present positions, these will be communicated confidentially to Sector Commanders, who will take steps to get into touch with Artillery Commanders in their Section of Defence.

8.-ENGINEERS: † The RE. Detachment will place the advanced ports in a state of defence.

9.-In case of attack in strength the position of the main line will be held at all costs.

10.-No smoking, lighting fires, or cooking will be allowed in advanced posts.

11.-Countersign is *Arlon*.

12.-Section Commanders will submit rough sketches of their dispositions to G.O.C. by 4 p.m.
13.-Reports to house N. of road near R. of Route D'Anvers.

(Signed) GEO. S. RICHARDSON, ‡ *Major, Staff Officer.*

The trenches to be manned were wide and bad, 6 feet broad and 3 feet deep with no dugouts, they afforded no cover from shrapnel and high explosive shell to which they were fully exposed and the Brigade set to work at once to improve them. They were so sited as not to command the crossings of the river and artillery support was not too good. The position in which they found themselves formed, with the line of the Scheldt up to Termonde, the key of the Antwerp Defences, because it covered the gap where the Germans had broken through the outer line of forts. As long as the line of the rivers was held the enemy could not get his guns into position to bombard the city.

Each Battalion, Deal, Plymouth and Chatham from left to right found one company as an advanced post to hold the crossings of the river.

The Deal company was commanded by Major W. H. Pryce Browne (who had retired before the War to enter the Church, but had rejoined) and held the third crossing; Major Pryce Browne was mortally wounded during the forenoon and there were a few other casualties.

The advanced post of Plymouth (No.3 Company, Major A. E. Bewes) was so placed in the village of Lierre that it commanded the bridge over the River Nethe. This post was attacked by a large party of Germans who came under fire of the machine guns at this point and lost about 200 of their number, then the Germans brought up a field gun and blew the post to pieces and it had to be evacuated. The Chatham advanced post was commanded by Major Shubrick and the machine guns of this Battalion had been pushed on by motor lorry under Lieutenant Foote to come into position at the canal bridge covering the road into Lierre. This Battalion had a good deal of fighting with rifle and machine guns and suffered several casualties. The Deal machine guns under Lieutenant Mead were discovered by the German Artillery and the buildings occupied by them were blown to pieces.

During the afternoon of the 4th, Fort Kessel was abandoned and destroyed by the Belgians and half the Portsmouth Battalion were also sent into the trenches.

---

13. Belgian Artillery.
   † The small detachment under Captain Rooke, R.E.
   ‡ Major Richardson was an Officer of the New Zealand Forces who was given a temporary Commission in the Royal Marines for the Staff of the Royal Naval Division. He afterwards became the A.A. and Q.M.G. of the Division. A most able Officer who rendered most valuable services for the Division which he only left in Gallipoli on appointment to the Staff of the 12th Corps at Salonica.

During the night 4/5th October the Germans brought field guns up to the bank of the river and opened fire at short range, so the advanced posts were ordered to retire to the main position. Lierre was burning and with the fires in Antwerp behind made a weird spectacle, and bayonets were kept well under the parapet so that the glint of the light on them should not show.

Early next morning, the 5th, the enemy succeeded in crossing the river and forced the 7th Belgian Regiment to evacuate their trenches; the 2nd Chasseurs and 7th Regiment made a gallant counter attack and drove the Germans back across the river at 4-30 p.m. Portsmouth Battalion also joined in the counter-attack and the Belgians re-occupied their trenches; two companies of Portsmouth being left in the trenches, the other two returning into reserve; the 5th October was passed in the same trenches. The night 5/6th October passed with occasional sniping and the usual artillery fire. During this night the 1st and 2nd Naval Brigades arrived in Antwerp, and Brig.-General Paris was appointed G.O.C. of the Division with the temporary rank of Major-General. He took with him Major Sketchley as G.S.O. 2, the vacancy as Brigade Major was filled by Captain Festing and Major Burge became Adjutant of Portsmouth Battalion. Colonel Ollivant, Royal Artillery and Major G. S. Richardson of the Royal Naval Divisional Staff were part of General Paris' Staff and there appear to have been present also a number of unofficial Staff Officers and politicians who attached themselves to the staff and gave orders to the troops[14].

Colonel A. E. Marchant, C.B. was appointed to command the Royal Marine Brigade, but he did not arrive from England until late on 6th; Lieut.-Colonel Parsons acting as Brigadier until his arrival. Lieut.-Colonel H. D. Farquharson, R.M.L.I. the A.A. and Q.M.G. had with great difficulty organised a supply service and the Brigade received their rations fairly regularly.

At dawn on 6th the Germans attacked the Belgians on the right of the Brigade in great force and drove them from their positions in the vicinity of Boomlaar and De Holst; the Belgians counter-attacked at 8-0 a.m. and recovered the trenches at Boomlaar, but failed at De Holst and the position at 9-50 a.m. was very serious. The First Naval Brigade was sent up to reinforce, but before they arrived the Belgians had been forced to retire to a prepared line west of Donk. During the 6th October the trenches of the Brigade were subjected to a very heavy shelling, causing a great many casualties, and in the afternoon they became untenable; as there was now no support on the right flank, the Royal Marine Brigade was withdrawn and retired about four miles to the line Vremde-Boschoek, where the Belgian Engineers were digging a defensive line and the Royal Marine Brigade were ordered to dig in here. In withdrawing they had to crawl back to the hedge along the road and one of the signallers relates a yarn very typical of the old time Marine; when retiring he had to crawl back to the hedge but whilst in one hand he carried his signalling gear, in the other he clutched a Belgian canteen of butter! The retirement was carried out in good order, with rearguards of one company from each battalion; there was no infantry pursuit, and the line was taken up at dusk under the orders of Lieut.-Colonel Parsons, the order being from the right Chatham, Plymouth, Portsmouth and Deal; the right rested on the Route D'Anvers, the 1st Royal Naval Brigade were on the right of Chatham. The Germans followed up' and marked down the position; their patrols could be heard calling to each other with night birdcalls, using an instrument called an ochorina, one of which was taken from a prisoner.

---

14. On 2nd October the Administrative Staff of the R.N.D. was replaced by the Adjutant General Royal Marines and his Staff, so that matters proceeded on more normal Admiralty lines; Lieut.-Colonel H. E. Blumberg, R.M.L.I. became A.A. and Q.M.G.; and Major R F. Foster, R.M.A., although appointed as G.S.O. performed the duties of D.A.A. and Q.M.G.; Colonel C. G. Brittan, R.M.L.I. (Retired) was for a few days Brigadier-General i/c Administration, but resigned owing to ill health. Majors and Quartermasters J. Simpson and J. H. Mitchell, R.M.L.I. (Retired), was also appointed to this Staff.

Entrenching tools were short, but some sort of trenches were contrived. About two hours before dawn on 7th, they were suddenly ordered to evacuate the trenches and retire to the inner defences of the city. "At dawn, the German artillery made mincemeat of the trenches they had just vacated." General Rawlinson, had visited the position on the 6th, and incidentally had condemned these trenches, as they ran along a well defined road.

It was now clear that the 7th Division and the cavalry of the Third Army could not arrive before the 8th, and the Belgians commenced to withdraw their Field Army, less the 2nd Division. When this became known, the effect on the morale of the remaining Belgian fortress troops was so great, that General Paris had no option but to withdraw his troops to the inner line of forts.

The Royal Marine Brigade, withdrew into reserve near the Cinema Film Factory at Chateau Rouge, Waes Donk, whilst the Royal Naval Brigades occupied the trenches and forts of the inner line in conjunction with the Belgian fortress troops. The 7th passed fairly quietly for the Royal Marine Brigade, but the town was heavily shelled, and the enemy appeared to have an uncanny knack of searching out General Paris' headquarters. During that day and the next, heavy casualties were caused in the city, and the oil tanks of the American Petroleum Company, were set on fire.

The line which the Naval Brigades were now holding was very strong, wired trenches between the forts, with a field of fire up to 500 yards. The right was protected by the River Scheldt, and the left by inundations. To hold it meant to impose delay on the enemy, and force him to bring up his heavy guns, or else compel him to assault the line of the Scheldt, which was held by the Belgian Field Army, before they would be able to cut off the retreat of the garrison.

On the evening of 7th, the Germans, after severe fighting with the Belgians, secured a footing across the Scheldt, at Schoenande, and during the night 7/8th threw a bridge across. Therefore at 7 a.m. on 8th, General Paris informed General Rawlinson, that he would probably be forced to retire that night. There appeared to be no immediate hurry, the Royal Naval Brigades had taken over the guns in the forts, and it was desirable to prolong the defence as long as possible. The Royal Marine Brigade had spent the night 7/8th, at the factory, but as it was dangerous to occupy the buildings, had bivouacked in the fields. Fires were lighted in the middle of the field, to deceive the enemy spies, who were very numerous in Antwerp, and the troops moved later to a wood, returning to the prepared trenches at daybreak. On the right, however, the Belgian fortress troops had retired, so at 7 a.m., Chatham Battalion took over the redoubt line from the Scheldt to redoubt No.6, inclusive. At 2 a.m., Lieutenant Curtin, with a platoon of this battalion, had been sent to take charge of the bridge of boats across the Scheldt, in case of a retirement becoming necessary.

During the afternoon of 8th, it was clear that the Belgian fortress troops would not stand much longer, and it became necessary, in order to prevent the British Force being shut up in the town and forced to capitulate, to withdraw across the river; at 5 p.m., this decision was made and sent by telephone to the First Lord. The order for the withdrawal was issued between 5-30 and 6 p.m. The 1st Royal Naval Brigade to go by the Malines Gate to the City Pontoon Bridge, and then to rendezvous at Zwyndrecht. The 2nd Royal Naval Brigade and the Royal Marines, to go by direct routes to the Pontoon Bridge at Burght and thence direct to Zwyndrecht.

General Rawlinson's staff made what arrangements were possible for trains to meet the Division outside Antwerp. Meanwhile at 7 p.m., Portsmouth Battalion was ordered to reinforce the 1st Royal Naval Brigade, as the Belgians, on their right were hard pressed, and then to act as rearguard to that Brigade, moving off in rear of all details.

All brigades were to move off, on receipt of the orders. This was obeyed by the Royal Marine Brigade, the 2nd Brigade, and the Drake Battalion of the 1st, but owing to the mistake of a staff officer, it was not made clear to the Commodore of the First Brigade, that they were to move immediately, an error which led to their ultimate internment in Holland. Only verbal orders reached Colonel Luard, of the Portsmouth Battalion, to occupy the trenches, carry out some firing and then follow the First Brigade. In consequence of the delay of the 1st Royal Naval Brigade, this battalion did not move off until shortly after 10-30 p.m.

With Chatham and Deal Battalions leading, followed by the 2nd Royal Naval Brigade, and Drake Battalion, they moved off soon after 7-30 p.m. An account from the rearguard battalion says "huge fires were observed and by the light one could see the long column swerving from one side to the other to keep as far as possible from the huge tottering and burning buildings. Also one could not help noticing a slight but regular movement as large shells came near and exploded in the next street or near by. There was hardly a whole window left and broken glass crunched under one's feet, also there were numerous obstacles such as fallen trees, dismantled tramway wires, dead horses, etc., and these added to the hard cobbles, made marching difficult." They eventually reached Zwyndrecht, and after a short rest they marched to St. Gillaes Waes, where they entrained for Ostend, after a most exhausting march, as the roads were encumbered with refugees, Belgian transport and troops. They arrived at Ostend soon after daybreak on 9th.

Plymouth Battalion was told off as rearguard to the 2nd Royal Naval Brigade. The bridge, which they had to cross was in such a shaky condition, that it had to be passed with intervals of six paces between men. On reaching the other side, there were no connecting files left by the main column, and therefore Colonel Matthews took his own route to St. Gillaes Waes, as the Germans were reported to the westward. The roads were blocked with refugees and the Battalion had to proceed in single file, the men helping the wretched women along by carrying their babies and giving food to the children. On arrival at the station, Colonel Matthews commandeered a train, already half full of refugees. On reaching Bruges, they were stopped to allow the trains with the 7th Division to go through and finally reached Blankenbergh, whence they marched into Ostend, 16 miles, arriving very footsore.

Portsmouth Battalion followed the 1st Brigade, which lost its way, in the long march through the city, and arrived at the river, where there were neither boats nor a bridge. Colonel Luard found a bridge further up, had it cleared of refugees, and got the 1st Brigade and his own Battalion over just before dawn. Their correct time for crossing was 10 p.m. They fortunately lost no men from shell fire, which was continuous, and the last bridge was blown up as soon as the Portsmouth Battalion, had crossed.

On arrival at St. Nicholas about 5 p.m., 9th October, 12 miles the other side of the river and 24 miles since starting, the Battalion halted to rest and requisition food, as the men had had no rest or food for 24 hours. Whilst thus engaged, information was received, that the Germans were in action in the next village, to the westward, Lokeren, about five miles away, and the firing could be heard.

The Battalion, therefore started off again northwards without waiting for their food, in order to reach a railway line about eight miles to the north, where there was a service of refugee trains to Ostend; the march was continued after dark. After marching 32 miles in all, they arrived at a small station called Kemseke. Colonel Luard had sent on to telephone for a train, and they entrained about 8 p.m., on 9th. The train consisted of a long line of open trucks, already filled with refugees, women, children, and Belgian soldiers. The Battalion, about 400 strong together with 600 stragglers from the 1st Royal Naval Brigade, whom they had picked up, was crammed into the train, being much scattered.

After the train had been going about 20 minutes, it was fired on from both sides of the line, and then about a mile or so further on, the engine driver and stoker disappeared. They were replaced by a leading stoker, and an A.B. of the Naval Brigade, who restarted the train, but after about 10 minutes, it pulled up in a side track at Moerbeke, about 10 p.m. The Germans had put over the points and removed a rail, so that the leading trucks were derailed.

Rifle fire broke out in all directions, and it was clear that they had fallen into an ambush. The officers got out the Royal Marines companies as best they could. The scene was terrible, women and children screaming and clinging to every one, and the confusion was extreme.

Major A. French and Lieutenant D. J. Gowney organised a party, being joined by Lieutenant Crossman, R.N. and a few R.N.V.R. and drove off the Germans, who were advancing in close order. Half-a-dozen of the enemy were killed and as many wounded, on which the remainder bolted, several prisoners were taken; firing then began from all sides, but Colonel Luard and the officers had got as many as possible out of the train and they replied vigorously; after a quarter of an hour the enemy's fire died down, but the train was immoveable. Some of the women and children and some of the men had been wounded and a few of the women killed. Surgeon-Lieutenant L. Greig was captured whilst attending to the casualties.

The officers then tried to get the men formed up near the head of the train and about 100 were collected together with 12 of the R.N.V.R., but many were too exhausted to leave the train, and having taken off their boots were unable to get them on again: whilst others getting out of the wrong side of the train and mistaking the direction, fell into the hands of the enemy. About 300 N.C.O.s and men Royal Marines and seven officers and 600 R.N.V.R. were captured, including Lieutenant Crossman who had been wounded.

Colonel Luard with the remainder marched on down the track, covered by Major French's party and reached Selsaete eight miles further on, or 40 miles in all, at dawn on 10th, where they obtained a train to Bruges and also their first food and water for 48 hours. They rejoined the Brigade at Ostend. The train itself was brought in later on. On the 10th Belgian troops passed over the line, which showed that it can only have been a raiding party, which held up the train and its exhausted defenders.

On 9th October, Colonel Parsons again took over command of the Brigade vice Colonel Marchant placed on sick list. By this time the 3rd British Army had occupied Ghent, the Belgian Army had completed its withdrawal and rested, and the left wing of the Expeditionary Force had reached Bailleul.

On 12th October the Brigade embarked for England and proceeded to the respective Headquarters.

The losses were Major W. Pryce Browne killed, Lieutenant Foote died of wounds, Lieutenant C. H. Coode and 2nd Lieutenant A. R. Chater wounded, and Lieutenant and Qr.-Mr. J. Hammond wounded and taken prisoner. 23 N.C.O.s and men were killed, 103 wounded and 311 missing.

Several wounded were left behind in Antwerp, and were taken by the Germans. A Belgian woman, Marie Somers, was most helpful in nursing and taking care of them, a fact which was gratefully acknowledged by the Corps.

After the Royal Marine Brigade was sent into Antwerp and the Royal Naval Brigades had also crossed the Admiralty ordered further reinforcements of Royal Marines to be sent to Dunkirk; these consisted of about 300 Royal Marine Artillery under Lieut.-Colonel G. M. Campbell, including a battery of 12 pounder 8-cwt. guns drawn by three ton lorries, which had been organised by Lieut.-Colonel C. A. F. Osmaston, with 150 R.M.L.I. This party embarked at Portsmouth, but owing to the difficulties in embarking the guns and lorries, they were late in getting away; and arrived too late to get through to Antwerp; after the Brigade was withdrawn from Ostend they returned to England together with the R.M.L.I. recruits who had been left at Dunkirk.

The following honours and rewards were given for the Antwerp operations.

D.S.C. Major A. H. French, R.M.L.I.

D.S.O. Lieutenant D. J. Gowney. R.M.L.I.
Distinguished Service Medal.

Sergeant-Major J. T. Galliford (Chatham).
Qr.-Mr.-Sergeant J. Kenny (Chatham).
Sergeant G. H. Bruce (Chatham).
Lance-Corporal T. C. Franks (Chatham).
Lance-Corporal W. J. Cook (Plymouth).
Private G. H. Hall (Chatham).
" C. J. Fleet (Chatham)
" S. Lang (Chatham).

Mentioned in Dispatches.
Major-General A. Paris, C.B.
Lieut.-Colonel C. Mc N. Parsons.
" E. G. Evelegh.
Major A. H. French.
" J. A. Tupman.
" A. E. Bewes.
" C. L. Shubrick.
" W. H. Pryce Browne. (*killed*).
" Captain M. Festing.
" W. H. P. Richards.
" G. Barker.
Lieutenants D. J. Gowney.
" C. G. Foote. (*died of wounds*).
" G. Rutherford.
" M. Curtin.
Lieut. & Qr.-Mr. J. Hammond.
" E. Nobbs (*Hood*)
Lance-Corporal. W. J. Cook (Plymouth).
Sergeant R. Hill (Plymouth).
Corporal E. Martin (Plymouth).
Colour-Sergeant T. Cunningham (Chatham).

RE-ORGANISATION.

On the return of the Battalions to England they were sent to their own Headquarters to be re-equipped, reorganised and brought up to strength.

Colonel 2nd Commandant C. N. Trotman, R.M.L.I. was appointed to command the Royal Marine Brigade with Major M. C. Festing as Brigade Major and Captain C. F. Jerram as Staff Captain.

Short Service Recruits and new entry officers were drafted in and some of the older Reserve Officers withdrawn. They also received a draft of "Kitchener" recruits from the Army, 600 in number and mostly from the North Country Regiments.

Several officers were taken for duty with the Naval Battalions. Colonel D. Mercer, A.A.G., R.M. was appointed to command the 1st Royal Naval Brigade with Captain F. S. Wilson, R.M.L.I. as Brigade Major.

Lieut.-Colonel Evelegh was appointed to command the "Nelson" Battalion with Captain R. J. Carpenter as his Adjutant. Lieut.-Colonel R. N. Bendyshe (retd.) replaced Evelegh as 2nd in command of Deal and in a similar capacity Major C. H. Hoskyns-Abrahall (retd.) was appointed to Portsmouth Battalion and Major H.D. Palmer (retd.) to Plymouth Battalion. Captain C. E. H. Morton was appointed Adjutant of the Portsmouth Battalion and Captain G. Barker of the "Drake" Battalion.

A cyclist company was also formed under Major A. H. French with Major N. O. Burge as Second. The N.C.O.s and men were volunteers from the R.M.L.I. and were concentrated at Portsmouth, the other officers were Lieutenants T. H. Jameson, F. C. G. Stock, K. A. Puckle and F. C. Bowen with Lieutenants G. R. Curtis and W. S. Jessup, R.N.V.R.

STAFF OF THE ROYAL NAVAL DIVISION.

G.O.C. Major-General A. Paris, C.B., R.M.A.
G.S.O.1. Lieutenant-Colonel A. H. Ollivant, RA.
G.S.O.2. Major E. F. P. Sketchley, RM.L.I.

G.S.O.3. Captain A. C. Paris, Oxford and Bucks Light Infantry. (*Temporary Captain, R.M.*).

A.A. and *Q.M.G.* Lieutenant-Colonel G. S. Richardson, New Zealand Forces. (*Temporary R.M.*).

D.A.A. and *Q.M.G.* Major Hon. E. Twystleton-Wykeham-Fiennes, Oxford Hussars. (*Temporary Lieutenant-Colonel R.M.*).

A.P.M. Major G. T. Walmesley, Berkshire Yeomanry.

A.D. Medical Services. Surgeon-Commander A. Gaskell, RN.

D.A.D.M.S. Captain F. Casement, RA.M.C.

D.A.D.O.S. Major Lord Bangor, RA. (*Temporary Lieutenant-Colonel R.M.*).

Financial Adviser. Mr. A. Foot. (Admiralty).

FIRST ROYAL NAVAL BRIGADE.

G.O.C. Brigadier General D. Mercer, R.M.L.I.

Brigade Major. Major F. S. Wilson, R.M.L.I.

Staff Captain. Major R Wilberforce, Royal West Kent. (Temporary R.M.).

SECOND ROYAL NAVAL BRIGADE.

G.O.C. Commodore O. Backhouse, R.N.

Brigade Major. Major W. L. Maxwell, Indian Army. (Temporary R.M.).

Staff Captain. Major M. Saunders, Indian Army. (Temporary R.M.).

THIRD ROYAL MARINE BRIGADE.

G.O.C. Brigadier-General C. N. Trotman, R.M.L.I.

Brigade Major. Major M. C. Festing, R.M.L.I.

Staff Captain. Major C. F. Jerram, R.M.L.I.

CYCLIST COMPANY.

C.O. Major A. H. French, D.S.O., R.M.L.I.

DIVISIONAL ENGINEERS.

C.R.E. Major A. B. Carey, RE. (Temporary Lieutenant-Colonel, R.M.).

Signal Company. Major G. H. Spittle, R.M.

No.1 Field Co. Major A. J. Chivers, R.M.

No.2 Field Co. Major S. R Adams, R.M.

No.3 Field Co. Major T. C. Aveling, R.M.

MEDICAL UNIT.

1st Field Ambulance. Staff-Surgeon A. F. Fleming, R.N.

2nd Field Ambulance. Staff-Surgeon C. E. Stanford, R.N.

3rd Field Ambulance. Fleet-Surgeon E. J. Finch, R.N.

Those officers who did not belong to the Royal Navy or Marines were given temporary commissions in the Royal Marines, as the Royal Naval Division was administered under the Naval Discipline Act, being borne on the books of H.M.S. *Victory*. The Royal Marine Brigade and Divisional Train, though borne afloat, were placed under the Army Act for discipline in conformity with Admiralty Instructions on that point; whilst the Divisional Engineers and Medical Unit were borne on the shore strength of the Corps.

CHAPTER 11.

THE DARDANELLES.   PER TERRAM.

Attachment to the Mediterranean Fleet - Landing of 4th March, 1915 -"Y" Beach – Anzac - Kemal's Third Attack - Victoria Cross - The Chessboard - Second Battle of Krithia - Third Battle of Krithia - Action of 13th July - Amalgamation of Royal Marine Battalions - The Evacuation - Stavros, Macedonia.
NOTE.-For Lists of Officers, Casualties, etc., see Appendices at end of Chapter.
(See Maps 3 and 4).

AFTER the return from Antwerp, the Battalions went into strict training. Short service recruits and temporary officers, were drafted in, and the Battalions were gradually raised to the war establishment strength of approximately 1000 of all ranks. Clothing and equipment were received, and the Battalions remained at their own headquarters. Chatham at Gravesend, Portsmouth at Browndown, Plymouth at Tavistock, and Deal at the Depot with Brigade Headquarters, also at Deal. Here they absorbed their recruits and new officers and completed their organisation until the end of January, 1915.

The machine gun sections were reorganised, equipped and thoroughly trained. The regimental transport sections were formed, and N.C.O.s and men were trained for first line transport duties.

During the last week of January, they were ordered to concentrate at Blandford, but as there was no accommodation in the Royal Naval Division Camp, they were billeted in Shillingstone, and the neighbouring villages.

Hardly were they concentrated, before the Brigade Headquarters, with Chatham and Plymouth Battalions were ordered to embark for special service in the Mediterranean, at the disposal of the Naval Commander-in-Chief.

These Battalions embarked at Plymouth, on 6th February. The Headquarters, with the Plymouth Battalion and the signal section of the Divisional Engineers, in the *Braemar Castle*, and the Chatham Battalion, in the *Cawdor Castle*. Only first line limbered waggons were taken without mules, as the service on which they were to be employed was uncertain and it was considered that these could be obtained at Malta, if required. All arrangements were made by the Adjutant General, Royal Marines, as they were to be employed with the Royal Navy.

A great deal has been written about the unpreparedness, with which the 29th and Royal Naval Divisions were embarked in their transports for the Gallipoli Expedition, but this did not altogether apply to the Royal Marine Brigade. It was known that they were to be employed with the Fleet, probably in landing parties, so that it was arranged, after some difficulty with the Transport Department, that each Battalion should be embarked as a complete unit, with its officers, transport, etc. This was also the case with the Portsmouth and Deal Battalions, for whom the arrangements were also made by the Adjutant-General, Royal Marines, when they were ordered to the Rufigi River, East Africa. The Portsmouth Battalion embarking in the *Gloucester Castle*, at Portsmouth, and the Deal Battalion in the *Alnwick Castle*, at Avonmouth. This expedition was cancelled, as Lord Wester Wemyss has related, and they were diverted to the Dardanelles. The Cyclist Company embarked in the *Somali*, but the subalterns of the Deal Battalion were diverted into the *Franconia*, in which ship the Headquarter Staffs of the Royal Naval Division took passage, on 1st March.

ROYAL MARINE BRIGADE WITH THE MEDITERRANEAN FLEET.

Brigade Headquarters, with Chatham and Plymouth Battalions, arrived at Malta on 14th February. Having completed with stores, they left there on 19th, and arrived at Tenedos on 21st, proceeding to Lemnos on 24th. On 25th they left Lemnos and were off the Dardanelles during the bombardments of 25th and 26th, but were not called upon to land, though the Royal Marine detachments of the *Irresistible* and *Vengeance* did so, to cover the demolition parties. The transports returned in the evening to Tenedos, and on 27th, the force was warned to be ready to land at Kum Kale and Sedd ul Bahr the next day, but owing to the gale which sprang up on 28th these orders were cancelled. The transports lay off Imbros till 2nd March, when they proceeded to Tenedos, but returned to Imbros on 3rd.

On 4th March, the projected landing took place. Plymouth Battalion carried out the landings, whilst Chatham lay off Mavro (Rabbit) Island. The Headquarters of the Brigade were at first in the *Inflexible*, and later transferred to the *Wolverine*, a destroyer.

No.4 Company, Captain C. Andrews, was detailed for the landing at Sedd ul Bahr, under Major H. D. Palmer. Their task was to act as a covering force to a demolition party, who were to destroy any guns left serviceable by the bombardment, and to allow the officers of the Air Force to reconnoitre for a site for an aerodrome.

Five patrols were ordered to search the ground, including the old fort. When these reported all clear, an escort under Lieutenant T. Edwards, of 12 men with the demolition party was to move up and make good the fort. The patrols were to move out about half-a-mile in advance of the platoons. Three platoons, each about 46 strong, were to cover the ground in front of the village. The right of the line was to rest on the cliff, in front of the old fort, and the line to be taken up was Hill 141 - Cape Helles Batteries - Hill 138, the left overlooking what was later known as Lancashire Landing. The machine guns were to be on the right, and one platoon was in reserve. When the 'Retire' was signalled, the withdrawal was to commence from the left. The companies were transferred to two destroyers, and when half-a-mile from the entrance, into ships' boats, five in each tow, and were taken in to their respective landings. When about 100 yards from the beaches, the boats were slipped and they rowed in. The Fleet bombardment continued until the destroyers moved in. *Triumph* and *Lord Nelson*, covered the company at Sedd ul Bahr, whilst the *Cornwallis*, *Irresistible*, *Agamemnon*, *Amethyst* and *Dublin* covered that at Kum Kale, by bombarding the Mendere River and Yeni-Shehr; *Canopus* and *Dartmouth* meanwhile bombarded Besika Bay.

No. 4 Company landed at Sedd ul Bahr, in the small boat camber, at the foot of the cliff, and with the exception of long range artillery fire the landing was unopposed, until the men of the leading patrol started to debouch from the path up the hill into the road, between the fort and the village. Here they were met by rifle fire, and took cover behind the drinking fountain, whilst the remainder closed up. The party detailed for the fort entered it without any trouble. As the advance by the road was held up, the platoon on the right moved up the face of the cliff, and got among the houses, where they came under fire. The machine guns, under Lieutenant A. N. Williams, then came into action from the foot of the hill, but as the troops attacking the village were hung up, the ships were requested to open fire and the platoons were temporarily withdrawn. As soon as the bombardment ceased, they again advanced through the village without meeting any further opposition, but finding a few dead Turks. The houses were searched, but as the time allotted was drawing to a close, the order was given not to go beyond the village. On reaching the further end, they therefore turned back, and the demolition party having completed their work, they re-embarked at 2-30 p.m., bringing off their killed and wounded, covered by intense fire from the ships.

No.3 Company under Major Bewes and with the Commanding Officer, Colonel Matthews, C.B., had a much more trying experience. The object of their landing was to form a covering party for the Fleet demolition parties, who were to destroy any guns which had escaped the bombardment of the week before. As soon as Fort Kum Kale had been made good, it was the intention to advance to the village of Yeni-Shehr, about two miles distant, reconnoitring en route for an aeroplane base and then to deal with Fort No.8 as with Kum Kale.

Lieutenant J. F. May with a strong patrol was to search Kum Kale first, and then to examine the village of that name, and report whether it was occupied. The machine guns were ordered to land with the first platoon; the remainder of the company to remain in reserve and to form the party intended to advance on Yeni-Shehr. On rowing in to the long pier, it was found to be most unsuitable as a landing place, and only eighty men were landed there. The remainder, landing on the beach, reached the fort practically unopposed. The Fleet covered the landing by firing on the fort and village, but there were a few casualties in the boats before they landed. The machine guns were also landed at the pier; the parties came under fire from two windmills close to the fort and were therefore ordered to take cover under the fort, leaving the guns on the pier. Sergeant Cook, D.S.M. and Private Threlfall volunteered to rescue the guns and ammunition, but Cook was dangerously wounded after a gallant attempt to save his guns; at a second attempt the party succeeded in bringing in one gun and a box of ammunition, and the remaining gun and ammunition were brought off in a cutter manned by seamen and the Royal Marine machine gunners about ten minutes after the first attempts.

Lieutenant May's patrol met with strong opposition, but succeeded in entering the- fort and reported all clear; the fort was then thoroughly searched.

The advance on Yeni-Shehr was commenced in attack formation. When about half way to their objective, they came under very heavy rifle fire and it was realised that the enemy was in great strength, rendering a further advance inadvisable. The machine guns from the top of Fort Kum Kale assisted to cover the withdrawal which was successfully carried out but with considerable loss. The Fleet, in response to a signal, bombarded the enemy positions and rendered invaluable assistance. During the retirement a Marine was seen carrying another on his back, shots were fired at him by the Turks and the man tried to take cover; in an instant he was up again, struggling with his load, when more shots rang out; the gallant effort was repeated several times until he fell not to rise again; the man he was carrying was afterwards recovered unconscious; it has not been possible to identify the rescuer[15].

As soon as the company had returned to Kum Kale, it was decided to re-embark, this was effected without further opposition at dusk; volunteer boats' crews of seamen and Marines from the *Irresistible* brought off any wounded remaining except three missing, at 7-15 p.m. The companies sustained a loss of 22 N.C.O.s and men killed and 22 wounded.

The next day the transports with the Brigade proceeded to Tenedos, the dead being buried at sea, and returned to Lemnos, where they remained until 18th March. On 18th March, the day of the great attack, 200 of the Chatham Battalion were ordered to be ready to land and their transport lay off Rabbit Island during the operation, but they were not utilised and returned in the evening to Mudros. The Royal Naval Division had commenced to arrive at Lemnos on the 12th and the Brigade came again under the G.O.C. The Portsmouth Battalion having arrived on 11th, the Brigade was reformed, but Deal Battalion was lent to complete the First Naval Brigade, until the end of May.

---

15. From the Globe and Laurel

On 19th the transports carrying the Royal Marine Brigade made a demonstration off Gaba Tepe, but returned without effecting anything; they remained at Lemnos until the Division sailed on 24th for Alexandria to reorganise. Arriving at Port Said on 26th and 27th they were landed and went into camp on 29th, where they remained until the 7th April. Whilst the Brigade was on shore at Port Said, the transports and gear were re-stowed; the battalions, when not employed on working parties were at training and took part in a review for General Sir Ian Hamilton, the Commander-in-Chief. The Deal machine guns however, with other detachments went to El Kantara on the canal under General Mercer as the Turks were expected to renew the attack on the Canal, which however did not materialise. The Division returned to Mudros on 11th and 12th April, where Brigade Headquarters transferred to the *Gloucester Castle* on 13th. From 17th to 24th April the Royal Naval Division were at Trebuki Bay, Skyros, training in landing operations. Whilst in Egypt, Lieutenant-Colonel R. D. Beith commanding Deal Battalion went to hospital and was succeeded by Lieut.-Colonel R. N. Bendyshe (retired), Major J.. A. Tupman becoming second in command and also commanding "D" Company.

Except for the supply details and a certain number of drivers, the bulk of the Divisional Train were left at Alexandria, where a base depot was formed for the reception of reinforcements and convalescents, together with a base record office.

Another unit of the Corps was also represented in the Division, the Drake Battalion being accompanied by its Royal Marine Band under Bandmaster Faithful who had been with them in Antwerp and also served all through the Gallipoli operations.

All was now ready for the great attack on the Peninsula, but except for the Plymouth Battalion, the Brigade was employed on the feint landing at the Bulair lines off Xeros Island as described in Chapter 3. They were thus occupied on 25th and 26th but at daylight on 27th they were off Cape Helles.

At 5-0 p.m. on 28th the *Gloucester Castle* and *Cawdor Castle* were dispatched to Anzac Cove and landed their troops as described later.

LANDING OF THE PLYMOUTH BATTALION AT "Y" BEACH.

On 25th April, the day of the Great Adventure, Plymouth and the R.M.L.I. detachment of the *Cornwallis* (see Chapter 3) were the only R.M. units actually landed, but the members of the Corps in the Fleet were fully employed in manning the batteries of the covering ships, and in various other duties; included among the Beach Masters was Lieut.-Colonel W. T. C. Jones, D.S.O., R.M.L.I. at "X" Beach.

Plymouth R.M.L.I. were detailed to land with 1st King's Own Scottish Borderers and one company 2nd South Wales Borderers at "Y" Beach, which was apparently intended for a demonstration, as they were told that they would only have to hold on for six hours and then join with the "X" Beach Force, where the other Battalions of the 87th Infantry Brigade were landing. In the event they were actually on shore for 30 hours during which time they received no orders, nor were they supported. Colonel Matthews, C.B. as the Senior Officer was in command.

"Y" Beach consisted of a narrow strip of beach at the foot of high and steep cliffs, about 200 feet in height, covered with shrub, up which ran a small steep gully. It was situated about 6,000 yards from "X" Beach where the Royal Fusiliers were landing as a covering force supported by the Royal Inniskilling Fusiliers and Border Regiment of the 87th Brigade.

The object of the landing was to attack the Turks in rear, engage his reserves, and when he was driven back from the Southern landings to endeavour to cut him off.

The covering ships were the *Goliath, Dublin, Amethyst* and *Sapphire*.

Plymouth R.M.L.I. were transferred from the *Braemar Castle* to trawlers, which took them inshore, where they transferred to ship's boats and landed at 5-45 a.m. The landing was unopposed and the King's Own Scottish Borderers, who had landed from the *Amethyst* and *Sapphire* quickly gained the crest of the cliff, followed by the R.M.L.I.; the K.O.S.B. at once commenced to dig in on the top of the cliff, together with Nos. 1 and 4 Companies, R.M.L.I., who were on the left facing the north east. Nos. 2 and 3 Companies, R.M.L.I. advanced inland, in a south east direction to reconnoitre and locate a supposed Turkish gun; they crossed Gully Ravine which is about 100 feet deep, "fell most of the way down and crawled up the other side" as one account says, and when about 1200 yards inland they started to dig in and wait for the advance from the south to develop; they met with no opposition and captured two Turks on patrol.

The Turks, were, however, soon reported to be advancing on the left and the R.M.L.I. were ordered to attack. As they moved off they were shelled by one of the British ships in Morto Bay, before the mistake was discovered; the Turks however, still made no sign. About 1-30 p.m. the edge of the cliff over "Y" Beach was shelled by a few heavy Turkish high explosive shell fired apparently from an east or south-east direction and there being still no sign of an advance from the south, Colonel Matthews decided to withdraw to the cliffs and entrench a position covering the approach to the beach. At about 2-30 p.m. Nos. 2 and 3 companies were shelled by shrapnel and long range sniping, opened on them as they were withdrawing, caused a few casualties. Major Palmer was wounded at this time. The withdrawal commenced about 2-30 p.m. and was completed just before 4 p.m. when the dispositions were as follows: the position was a rough semi-circle Nos. 1 and 4 Company, R.M.L.I. on the left or northern flank, the King's Own Scottish Borderers in the centre, the South Wales Borderers' company on their right and then Nos. 2 and 3 Companies, R.M.L.I. on the south flank. As the trenches were dug entirely with entrenching implements in no case were they deeper than three feet on the left and centre and about two feet on the right when the first attack commenced.

During the afternoon, touch was gained with "X Beach" by means of the helio, and it was learned that matters were not going too well on the other beaches, and that the force would have to remain more than the six hours, provided for in their instructions. About the same time an aeroplane reported that two Turkish Battalions were advancing from Krithia. Sergeant Meatyard, the Battalion signal sergeant, relates that by lying on the slope of the cliff to avoid bullets coming over, and using a large flag, they were able to communicate with the ships, the helios being useless for the purpose, but that when it got dark they had no signal lamps; however by using the Commanding Officer's pocket torchlight lamp, they were able to signal off the necessary more urgent signals.

At about 4-30 p.m., a Turkish field battery near Krithia, opened on the position with shrapnel and at about 5-30 p.m., there developed the first of a series of attacks, which continued until daybreak 26th, increasing in pressure as it grew dark. The night was very dark, with showers of rain, and the Turks were able to assemble in Gully Ravine, which ran close to the left centre. During the night, they kept up a continual fire and bomb attack, with occasional bayonet assaults, but the line remained unbroken. The Turkish field battery also kept up a spasmodic shelling. The assaults were directed against the centre, left centre and on the left actually on the beach. On the right no actual bayonet assaults were made, but the troops lost heavily through being exposed to enfilade and reverse fire, with very slight cover.

At about 9 p.m., owing to the gravity of the position in the left centre, where the pressure was heaviest, No.3 Company, R.M.L.I. (Major Bewes) was taken from the right flank to support the left centre, and the right flank (No.2 Company) under Captain Knight was thrown back about 100 yards and dug in again, so as not to lose touch with the South Wales Borderers. At dawn, the situation looked serious, the troops were tired, the casualties very heavy, and there was a considerable shortage of ammunition. Colonel Matthews, therefore decided to shorten his line by withdrawing his flanks, as the position was too long a frontage for his troops. At about 6-30 a.m., the Turks were seen assembling for a further attack which materialised at about 6-45 a.m.

Unfortunately at the same time two six-inch shells from our own ships fell into the left centre of our line causing about a dozen casualties and the line broke. The Turks were actually trickling through, but a counter attack by two platoons of No.3 Company, R.M.L.I. which was in support, was initiated by Colonel Matthews and his Adjutant, Captain Lough, and the broken line rallied and the position was restored by a bayonet charge, the Turks retiring in disorder. In this counter attack, Lieutenant J. F. May was killed and Lieutenant F. C. Law distinguished himself, being later awarded the D.S.C. for this service.

The Turks who were evidently as tired as the British, and had lost severely, now appeared to have had enough and only occasional shots were fired.

There were still no signs of other troops advancing from the south, and the King's Own Scottish Borderers had lost practically all their officers. Of the R.M.L.I., Major H. D. Palmer, Major Bewes, and Captain Knight were wounded, the cliff and beach were crowded with wounded, whilst both ammunition and water were short.

Signals were sent to the covering ships to send boats for the wounded and for supplies of ammunition and water. At about 7-30 a.m., Colonel Matthews, who throughout the night had been everywhere and seemed to bear a charmed life, signalled his appreciation of the situation, but no orders or instructions were received from the Divisional Commander.

The boats were sent in by the ships, and without Colonel Matthews knowledge, in fact it was rumoured that he had been killed, the Kings Own Scottish Borderers, South Wales Borderers, and right flank Company R.M.L.I., were ordered to re-embark. When Colonel Matthews, who was on the left flank observed the movement at about 8 a.m., he sent his Adjutant, Captain Lough to ascertain the facts, but by the time he arrived, the line was deserted and most of the troops had reached the beach, and re-embarked as soon as the boats arrived. It is not known by whom the order was given, but at the Dardanelles Commission, Colonel Matthews accepted full responsibility for the action, owing to the lack of orders and reinforcements.

At 8-30 a.m., Colonel Matthews with Nos. 1 (Captain Tetley) and 4 Companies (Captain Andrews), R.M.L.I., and a few K.O.S.B. were still in position and were disposed round the head of the watercourse, running down to "Y Beach" by 9 a.m. Patrols were sent to front and flanks, a few wounded were found and taken to the beach, but the only signs of Turkish activity was occasional sniping. About 10 a.m., the companies retired to the beach unmolested, and by 11 a.m., the last troops re-embarked ; Colonel Matthews being the last man to leave.

The casualties were K.O.S.B. 296, and nearly all their officers.

R.M.L.I. 14 officers, 317 N.C.O.s and men.

When the original official dispatch was forwarded, these facts do not appear to have been fully known as various corrections were published subsequently.

At 1 a.m., on 27th, the Battalion transferred to their own transport, from the *Goliath*, and a memorial service was held for those who had been left on the field, the bagpipes of the K.O.S.B. playing the lament, and at 6 a.m., they landed at Lancashire Landing and were employed on working parties, etc.

It was unfortunate that this landing, which apparently was Sir Ian Hamilton's own idea, was not exploited, when the glories of Quebec in 1759, where the terrain much resembled "Y Beach," might have been repeated.

The Dardanelles

ROYAL MARINE BRIGADE AT ANZAC.

Turning now to the movements of the Royal Marine Brigade, and the other Royal Marine units, it may be as well to consider the composition of these Battalions before describing the operations, and these remarks apply equally to the Plymouth Battalion.

The Australian Official Historian says "they looked strangely young and slender." This was only too true; these battalions were different from the usual Marine Battalions who had served in Egypt and other wars, composed of seasoned long service soldiers. As we have seen the bulk of the serving ranks of the Corps were afloat, and the ranks of the Battalions had been filled up with recruits, both long and short service, many of them lads between 17 and 18 years of age (see page 112)-the Army had fixed 19 years as the age for draft overseas). Most of the regular subalterns were very young, fortunately a goodly number of the Reserve Officers were still young and active and many had only recently retired from active service, whilst there was a magnificent backing of officers promoted from the ranks since the commencement of the war; but a considerable number of the platoon officers were Second Lieutenants who had entered the service in August, 1914, or temporary officers commissioned on or subsequent to 20th September.

The considerable sprinkling of Reservists in the ranks, particularly the R.F.R. N.C.O.s provided a fine nucleus of experienced and determined men; it might be said roughly that the composition was about 75 per cent. recruits, 20 per cent. reservists, and five per cent. active service.

These Battalions had never been given the opportunity of steady training afforded to the Kitchener and Territorial Battalions to which they were really comparable; no sooner were they formed than they were sent to Ostend, and within three weeks of returning from that expedition, after what was practically a re-organisation, they were sent to Dunkirk, where training was impossible; then came the Antwerp operations, in which heavy casualties in proportion to their numbers were incurred. On their return to England they received more recruits to raise the numbers from 700 to 1000 per Battalion; Deal Battalion which had been formed by drafts from the other Battalions had an even larger percentage of recruits. For company and Battalion training there were only available the three winter months of short days (November, December and January), because as we have seen they embarked at the end of January for the Mediterranean; it should not be forgotten that, except for the short re-organisation in Egypt and a few landings for drill, Chatham and Plymouth Battalions had been afloat in their transports for practically three months; Portsmouth and Deal Battalions had also been partially re-organised in February in view of the proposed operations in the Rufigi River and they also had been afloat since the 1st March.

It is well to remember .these facts when reading the description of the gallant manner in which they carried out the difficult tasks that were set to them, when they were flung into the desperate and almost chaotic conditions described in the Australian Official History. The gallantry of officers and men and the strong *esprit de corps* enabled them to meet each new situation with success.

The Brigade Headquarters, Chatham and Portsmouth Battalions with No. 1 Field Company, Divisional Engineers, Royal Marines, and the Bearer Division of the 3rd Field Ambulance, landed at Anzac on 28th April, the disembarkation being completed at 8-0 p.m.

Portsmouth R.M.L.I. were the first to land; only a few stores and no kits were taken as it was understood that they were to be ashore for only 48 hours, they were actually 14 days.

The Brigade was placed under the orders of Major-General W. T. Bridges commanding the First Australian Division and was at once ordered to take over No.2 Sector of the Defences, to relieve the 1st and 3rd Australian Brigades on McLaurin's Hill and the Northern part of the Lone Pine Plateau. The historian of the Royal Naval Division thus describes the terrain "the sides of the gully were rocky and what in the wet season was the bed of a mountain torrent, was now the only path, which the landscape offered; on the upper slopes, thickly covered with arbutus, dwarf oak and other shrubs, the passage of men had indeed worn narrow tracks, but these were not serviceable and merely showed the least dangerous line of advance for individuals to the firing line."

According to one eye witness account, "they moved up a large gully, about half a mile wide, Shrapnel Gully, with steep slopes on either side, which ran up to a well defined ridge; there was a watercourse at the bottom of the Gully."

It was a cold and stormy evening with black storms of rain and as the Australian History says "they were led over the top to the worst sectors of the line; to trenches, of which those who had held them for days did not realise the badness-isolated potholes-on the edge of the plateau."

The ground in front of the trenches was covered with thick scrub, broken by small depressions; on the enemy side was another gorge similar to the gully which formed the centre of the Anzac position, where the Turkish Reserves were posted.

An Australian guide led them up; after going some distance he evidently mistook the way, for they turned back for some distance and then turning off they started to climb up the side of the gully by a steep track and they reached the ridge as it was getting light, and the relief of the Australians was completed by 4-0 a.m[16].

Portsmouth R.M.L.I. were on the right and Chatham on the left; owing to the extent of front to be covered, it was not possible to relieve all the Australians and isolated parties of the 9th and 12th Australian Battalions remained in the centre trenches.

Chatham R.M.L.I. Had "C," "A," "B," and "D" Companies in line from left to right with the machine guns to right and left of "B" Company, the Battalion Headquarters being in rear of that company. Portsmouth R.M.L.I. were in the same formation "P" Company (Major Clark) "placed three platoons in front line and one in reserve; the trenches were only shallow scrapings and the men were ordered to dig in at once with their entrenching implements; by daylight they had a rough shallow trench; next day a few picks and shovels were sent up and made use of the following night, only faint hearted attacks were made by the enemy on this day. The helmets and packs were found to be a great nuisance, the former were replaced as soon as possible by the soft Australian hats."

Another officer thus describes the position: "In some places there were two lines of shallow trenches with a fair field of fire up to 400 yards; in others no field of fire and only a few feet from the edge of the slope; the slope was too steep to climb without the aid of a man-rope (made from rifle slings) and one had to haul oneself up hand over hand; it was in such a place that Captain Hatton was killed in leading a party to recover a trench. The trenches were quite isolated with 30 or 40 yards of open ground between them, under an accurate and close range fire; it was one of the most advanced of these that was held by Lieutenants Empson and Alcock."

At 9-0 a.m. a company of the Motor Maxim Squadron of the R.N.A.S. Under Major C. E. Risk, R.M.L.I. attached R.N.A.S. was placed in reserve to the Brigade.

During the day the Battalions, who were occupied in improving the trenches. were subjected to small attacks all along the front.

On 29th April, Brigadier-General D. Mercer with Headquarters of 1st Royal Naval Brigade, Deal and

---

16. It is curious to compare the following account of their severe fighting with the statement in the Official Naval History that General Birdwood made no use of the Brigade lent to him.

Nelson Battalions were also landed about 8-0 p.m. and Deal Battalion came up into line with the other R.M.L.I. Battalions, the Nelson Battalion being placed in reserve. Deal R.M.L.I. crossed Shrapnel Gully and "D" (Major Tupman), "A" (Major Muller), "B" (Captain Bush) moved up Victoria Gully, "C" (Captain Lawrie) up Wantiss Gully and after a long climb reached the edge of Lone Pine Plateau and relieved the Australians holding the Western Edge, the relief being completed by 3-30 a.m. on 30th.

Chatham and Portsmouth Battalions, were holding the old line of the 3rd Australian Brigade on McLaurin's Hill, and also that of 19th Battalion on the north part of Lone Pine Plateau, the line south of this being held by Deal. By the night of 29/30th, most of the Australians had been relieved. General Trotman's headquarters were at Scott's Point, on the southern shoulder of McLaurin's Hill; this part of the line included the important position of Courtney's Post.

The ground held by the R.M.L.I., included half of the eastern front and was

too long, for these battalions. They worked hard at improving the trenches, but those on the plateau were under heavy shell fire, and little improvement was possible. The ground in front of Deal fell away into hollows and ravines, in which the Turks formed for their attacks about 100 yards in front of the British lines.

KEMAL'S THIRD ATTACK.

On the 30th, the Turks, who had massed in Wire Gully, renewed the attack, and the pressure from Courtney's Post, southwards became very great. The 14th Australians relieved the Royal Marines at Courtney's Post, and the Royal Marine supports were brought up. It was found that the trenches which had been prepared at the head of Wire Gully, could not be occupied, owing to enemy machine gun fire.

At 5 p.m., an attack was made on Chatham R.M.L.I., and part of "B" Company (Captain Hatton), was driven out of its trenches, but gallantly hung on to the edge of the slope. Captain Hatton rushed out single handed to stop the Turks, and was instantly killed, but his effort had a great effect in checking the enemy and Major Graham, who was in reserve, seeing what was happening through his glasses, at once rushed his company up the "rifle sling" pathway to reinforce. The Turks were driven out of the trenches, which were reoccupied by "B" Company; "D" Company being put back into reserve. ("D" Company had been relieved in the line earlier in the afternoon by some Australians, who also took part .in this counter attack.) Lieutenants Simpson, Dallas-Brooks and Macdonnell of "B" Company, rendered good service on this occasion, after Captain Hatton was killed.

All along the line, the front line companies were employed in repelling attacks. On the Deal front, Lieutenant Moxham was killed in the trenches, during the evening at 9-30 p.m. Reinforcements were sent to "C" Company but returned shortly after into reserve. In this battalion, Major Muller was killed in the trenches, the next day.

During this period, Lieutenants Empson and Alcock with two platoons of Portsmouth, were in occupation of one of the isolated trenches, which they held with the greatest gallantry. Lieutenant Empson, who was in command, was wounded early on 30th April, and was killed the next day. Lieutenant Alcock was finally compelled to withdraw after having held the ground for four nights and three days. During this time, no food or water could be conveyed to the trench and at one time ammunition was reduced to about 15 rounds a man. For his conduct on this occasion, Lieutenant Alcock, was awarded the D.S.C. The strength of the platoons was about 60 men.

LANCE-CORPORAL W. R. PARKER GAINS THE VICTORIA CROSS.

It was in connection with this defence, that the first V.C., awarded to a Royal Marine in the war, was gained by Lance-Corporal Walter Richard Parker, of the Portsmouth Division, R.M.L.I. He was a short service recruit and his deed is thus described in the "Gazette." On the night of 30th April/1st May, a message was received from the isolated trench at Gaba Tepe (really Lone Pine Plateau) asking for water, ammunition, and medical stores. A party of N.C.O.s and men were detailed to carry up water and S.A.A., and in response to a call for volunteers from among the stretcher bearers, Parker at once came forward. He had during the three previous days, displayed conspicuous bravery and energy under fire, whilst in charge of the battalion stretcher bearers. Several men had been killed in a previous attempt to bring assistance to the men holding the fire trench. To reach this trench, it was necessary to traverse an area at least 400 yards wide, which was completely exposed and swept by rifle fire. It was already daylight when the party emerged from shelter, and at once one man was wounded. Parker organised a stretcher party and then going on alone succeeded in reaching the fire trench, all the ammunition and water carriers being either killed or wounded. After his arrival in the trench, he rendered assistance to the wounded, displaying extreme courage and remaining cool and collected in very trying circumstances. When the trench was finally evacuated, Parker helped to remove and attend the wounded, although he himself was seriously wounded during the operation.

Private Thomas Henry Hoskins, Chatham R.M.L.I., was awarded the Conspicuous Gallantry Medal, for volunteering on 30th April and moving across the open under very heavy and close range fire to another sector of the line, with an urgent message for ammunition and water. Having delivered his message he courageously attempted to return to his unit and was twice wounded in doing so.

On 1st May, the Turks attacked again at 4 a.m., but this was broken by fire. Another attack was made at 4 p.m., along the front of Quinn's Post and Lone Pine trenches. The Turkish attack came across Johnston's Jolly and 1000 Turks attacked Chatham R.M.L.I., who opened rifle and machine gun fire, which broke the Turkish attack when about 200 yards off, and by 6 p.m., the enemy had retired. Lieutenant J. Cheetham was awarded the D.S.C., for his courage and initiative in the defence of this position. Private (acting Sergeant) C. J. Braddock (Chatham), the well known heavy-weight boxer, was awarded the Conspicuous Gallantry Medal, for volunteering, in company with Lieutenant Cheetham and one other man to counter attack the enemy on a flank, in the open under a heavy fire, thus assisting to clear the line. Lieutenant M. Curtin, in charge of the machine guns, was killed and the Regimental Sergeant-Major A. F. Hayward, who had been made temporarily a lieutenant in "D" Company, was mortally wounded, his loss being a very severe blow to the Battalion.

Fighting continued on the front all through the 1st May, and during the night 1/2nd May, whilst going the round of the trenches, about dusk, Lieutenant-Colonel R. N. Bendyshe, who had returned to service from the Reserve, one of the best loved officers in the Corps, was killed. He was succeeded by Major J. A. Tupman.

At 1 a.m. on 2nd, the Turks rallied at the head of the valley, and attacked again on the right, as soon as the moon rose. Sweeping past the left of the Australians on Bolton's Hill, they attacked the Deal Battalion. At 2 a.m., masses of the enemy were seen in front of "D" Company, (Major Tupman) on the right and an attack was launched by them shortly afterwards. The Marines were kept under cover, until the Turks could be seen charging in the dim light, when orders were given to stand up and fire. The attackers were mown down by rifle fire, and only a few reached the parapet, where they were shot down by rifles and revolvers over the top. Attacks were also made on "A" and "C" companies of this Battalion, and they were also able to

LANCE CORPORAL W. R. PARKER, V.C.
Royal Marine Light Infantry.

enfilade the attack on the Portsmouth Battalion, whilst the artillery at 700 yards range, assisted in repelling the attack. No more direct attacks were made but movement of considerable bodies was seen, and fire was opened on them.

As the Australian History says, "The Marines bore the brunt of Mustafa Kemal's third attack; though better timed and delivered than the last, it completely failed."

On the morning of 2nd May, the Royal Marine Brigade was relieved in the trenches by the 1st Australian Brigade, which had been rested and reorganised, and the Marines moved into bivouacs. Deal moved down to the beach at the bottom of Victoria Gully and were then ordered to dig trenches in Monash Valley.

"Thus from April 29th, to Saturday, 1st May a considerable portion of the Anzac line was in the hands of the Royal Marines" (Official Australian History).

The losses of the Battalions during this period were very serious, particularly in officers. Chatham lost, killed: Captain Hatton, Lieutenants Herford, M. Curtin, C. S. Grinling and A. F. Hayward. The Portsmouth losses were, killed: Captain J. C. Teague, Lieutenants W. H. Empson, J. C. Black and 2nd Lieut. H. G. Ferguson-Davie. Deal: Lieutenant Colonel R. N. Bendyshe, Major G. F. Muller, Lieutenants J. F. Moxham and K. A. L. Higgins.

Chatham and Portsmouth Battalions sustained 337 casualties and Deal about 40.

ACTION OF 3RD MAY. ATTACK ON THE CHESSBOARD.

On 2nd May at 8-0 p.m. an attack on Pope's Hill at the head of Monash Valley, was commenced by the 4th Australian Brigade, consisting of the Otago Battalion, New Zealand, with 13th and 16th Australians, the Nelson Battalion (Colonel Evelegh, R.M.L.I.) in support.

Although very carefully planned, with a view to improving the position the ground was very difficult and the movements complicated; the 13th Battalion was obliged to follow the 16th and deploy on their left with the result that this movement was never completed. The attack developed into three isolated eccentric attacks; two of the Nelson companies becoming involved on the left of the 13th Battalion. In spite of the most gallant efforts, the attack, after carrying two lines of trenches, failed to advance any further and the Australians were hanging on precariously to the edge of the slopes and in places were driven off the edge. At 2.0 a.m. on 3rd May the R.M.L.I. Battalions were ordered to dig behind the 4th Australian Brigade and support them at the head of Monash Valley. They moved off at 3-30 a.m. and proceeded to the head of the gully to support the Australians in the advanced trenches; Portsmouth moved along the eastern ridge and Chatham along the western. The Battalions advanced in single file and as they passed a certain point were issued with picks and shovels.

The advance was led by " D" Company, Portsmouth; this Battalion had been ordered to entrench on the support line, but on approaching, the trenches were observed to be crowded, and messages were received from the front line that the fire trenches were full and no further reinforcements could be received. "D" Company (Major Clark) was therefore ordered to move to the right, but as it did so, "A" Company (Captain Stockley) passed through with entrenching tools. As it got light, messages were received from the firing line,that they were in difficulties, but the orders to entrench on the support line were explicit, so Colonel Luard decided to adhere to his orders for the present; he continued to allot his companies to their positions. Suddenly the men in the firing line were observed to be coming out of the trenches about 40 to 50 yards ahead and retiring into the ravine below. Though only the leading portions of "D" and "A" Companies were in sight, Colonel Luard ordered 'Charge,, which was repeated; by all officers present: The Royal Marines at once charged most gallantly up the slope, and many of the Australians charged with them, and so probably averted a panic in the crowded ravine below. When the 16th

The Dardanelles

[By permission of Altieri Pidure Service.]
GENERAL VIEW OF SHRAPNEL VALLEY, ANZAC.

[By permission of Altien Picture Service.]
WALKER'S RIDGE. ANZAC.

Australians were driven out of their trenches, they carried part of the Portsmouth Battalion with them, but these were gallantly rallied by the Brigade Major (Major Festing) and led up again to the charge. The Battalion was met by a withering fire of shrapnel and machine gun fire which caused heavy casualties. Of those who reached the ridge, some advanced and gained the line of the trenches out of which the Australians had been driven. The men of "D" Company were directed to incline to their left, and continue the advance on the left of the ravine, where a projecting spur gave some cover from the enfilade fire. "A" Company had already taken up the charge in this direction and "C" Company (Captain Syson) from further below, gained the spur further to the left; on the extremity of which the Portsmouth machine gun section under Captain Lathbury was in position. "B" (Major Armstrong) moved up the edge of the slope afterwards known as the 'Razor Back' (in the map - Deadman's Hill). The trenches were found to be untenable, as they were overlooked by the Turkish machine gunners and the men were withdrawn during the day and the following night. In the charge Colonel Luard was wounded in the knee and as Major C. H. Hoskyns-Abrahall had already died of wounds, Major Clark from "D" Company assumed command. The attack had been very costly, and the strength was reduced to seven officers and 350 other ranks, who were re-organised into two companies, No 1 (Major Armstrong) and No.2 (Captain Syson).

Meanwhile, Chatham made a fine attack on the trenches in front. "B," "C" and "D" Companies advanced up the minor gullies leading off to the east of the main gully, and Captain Richards, the Adjutant led a brilliant charge up the 'Razor Back' Hill, and gained the ridge; Captain Richards was killed, but the machine guns were got up and brought into action on the top; two lines of trenches were taken and held at first, but as no support was forthcoming, after a gallant defence of six hours they were driven off the ridge by enfilade fire from the left flank and the old line was re-occupied. Q.M.S. C. White and Sergeant Oakey particularly distinguished themselves in the attack. Chatham lost 300 killed and wounded in this attack. By the death of Captain Richards, the Battalion suffered a very heavy loss, he was a most gallant officer, and a most valuable adjutant and was well-known for his fine horsemanship. In addition to those already named Lieutenant W. H. Sanders (the noted Corps rifle shot) J. F. Hyland, J.H.C. Fulton and 2nd Lieutenants F. A. Erskine and T. A. Deane of Portsmouth Battalion were killed, and the Adjutant, Captain C. E. H. Morton was wounded and died at Alexandria.

The Australian History sums up the attack as follows: "the attempt to improve the defective position at the head of Monash Valley had definitely failed, the throwing in of the Marines at daybreak to retrieve a battle already lost resulted only in the slaughter of many brave officers and men, and the disorganisation of these already overstrained battalions."

The Battalions cannot have been so 'disorganised,' because on this same day Brig.-General Trotman was detailed to command the 3rd Sector with the Chatham and Portsmouth Battalions now only 1,100 strong all told, and the 4th Australian Brigade, which was the freshest of the Australian troops. This sector they held for the next nine days until 12th May. The position comprised Pope's Hill on the left, Quinn's Post in the centre and Courtney's on the right.

From 4th to 8th May the trenches were re-organised and improved but casualties still occurred, Major H. Armstrong being killed on 6th, and Captain Syson the remaining Company Commander of the Portsmouth Battalion was wounded.

On 4th May, Bugler Ernest Sillence of the Chatham Battalion gained the Conspicuous Gallantry Medal for throwing back enemy bombs into their lines at great personal risk, thereby saving the lives of many of his comrades.

On 10th May took place the affair of Quinn's Post in which Chatham battalion participated and occupied the Turkish front line in front of the Post on the night 9/10th; they were forced to withdraw at 9 a.m. on 10th to the old line.

The period to the 12th May was one of severe and continuous fighting and the position was most difficult to hold. To quote again the Australian History "Monash Sector was the most difficult of the line. Few positions of the nature of Pope's Hill and Quinn's Post were held by any troops during the War" and as the historian of the Royal Naval Division says: "In general great resolution and a very high degree of gallantry distinguished the defence of the posts by the R.M.L.I. Battalions."

The Deal and Nelson Battalions under General Mercer had meanwhile relieved the Australian and New Zealand troops on 5th May by taking over the left flank of the position at Anzac, being placed on Russell's Top and Walker's Ridge; here the enemy positions were rather further off and the fighting was less severe. Two companies of the Nelson and two companies of Deal under Lieut.-Colonel Evelegh were on the left and two companies Nelson and two companies Deal under Major Tupman were on the right on Walker's Ridge, but at the suggestion of the higher command one company of Nelson and one of Deal were sent to reinforce Major Tupman. General Mercer had his headquarters half way up the ridge. From 5/13th May there were no attacks, so the companies carried out ordinary trench routine, being relieved on 13th May by the New Zealanders and the Battalion embarked in the *Alnwick Castle* at 6 p.m., disembarking at Helles the next day strength 23 officers and 845 other ranks.

On 12th May, Chatham and Portsmouth were relieved by the Australian Light Horse Brigade from Egypt; they re-embarked in the *Cawdor Castle* and were transferred to the Helles Sector and rejoined the Royal Naval Division; the Field Ambulance and 1st and 2nd Field Companies of the Divisional Engineers embarked with the Deal Battalion.

So that at last General Paris had his whole division again under his command, which was almost the first time since Antwerp.

The embarkation state of 3rd or Royal Marine Brigade was:

Brigade Headquarters	5 Officers	18 Other Ranks.
Chatham	12 "	559 "
Portsmouth	7 "	424 "
3rd Field Ambulance, R.M.	10 "	113 "
4th Section Signal Company, R.M.	1 "	19 "
Divisional Train, R.M.	2 "	40 "

The Brigade casualties from 25th April to 13th May were:

	Killed.		Wounded.	
	Officers.	Other Ranks.	Officers.	Other Ranks.
Brigade Headquarters		2	1	1
Chatham	4	68	7	206
Portsmouth	10	98	7	305
Plymouth	3	39	11	212
Deal	4	10	3	40

The Missing included:

Chatham	28 Other Ranks.
Portsmouth	28 "
Plymouth	66 "

THE HELLES SECTOR.

Plymouth Battalion after re-embarkation on 26th April as already described, was detailed for duties on the beach to land stores etc.; On the night 28/29th April the Corps lost a fine officer in Captain G. Barker, R.M.L.I. (Reserve of Officers) who was killed when acting as Adjutant of the Drake Battalion.

From 6th to 8th May, Plymouth Battallion formed part of the Composite Brigade, consisting of the Drake and Plymouth Battalions of the Royal Naval Division and 1st Lancashire Fusiliers under Lieut.-Colonel Casson, which together with the 2nd Royal Naval Brigade and an Australian and New Zealand Brigade had been formed into a Composite Division under General Paris, as his own Division had been so scattered.

SECOND BATTLE OF KRITHIA.

On 6th May, it was decided to attack before the enemy had settled in his trenches; the 29th Division less the 86th Brigade, a Brigade of 42nd Division and the 29th Indian Brigade were to be on the left, the Composite Division less the 2nd Royal Naval Brigade in the centre, and the French Corps with the 2nd Royal Naval Brigade attached on the right. Three objectives were assigned, the last being Achi Baba. The Commander-in-Chief had suggested a night attack, but the Corps Commander (Sir A. Hunter Weston) who was in charge, determined on a daylight operation.

General Paris' task was to advance up the Krithia nullah on the left centre with the 2nd Royal Naval Brigade on his right. The Lancashire Fusiliers were to lead, followed by the Drake and Plymouth Battalions to consolidate any success. The advance was slow and came to a standstill at 3-30 p.m. The Plymouth Battalion advanced in artillery formation at 3 p.m. But after a short distance were halted and did not move again until 4 p.m., when they came up into the support trenches for the night.

Fighting was resumed at 4-45 p.m. on 7th, but no material advance was made. On 8th May on the front of the Composite Division, the Australians delivered the main attack at 5-0 p.m. and achieved an advance of 600 yards, whilst the French seized the southern edge of the Kereves Dere and the Redoubt; The 2nd Royal Naval Brigade came up on the left of the French and two companies of the Drake at 8-15 p.m. closed the gap between their left and the Australians where the Turks were beginning to break through in force. At 1-15 a.m. on 9th, Plymouth also came up into line between the Drake and Australians and consolidation was carried out during the night and the next day. The Turks were about 500 yards off, and during the day they opened a heavy fire but were stopped from an advance by fire. To fetch water for the trenches the parties had to go to a well some distance away.

At dawn on 10th May, a Turkish counter attack was delivered on the French and Naval Battalions on their left, for a short time the situation was critical, but the position was restored on the front of the Composite Brigade by Captain Tetley, R.M.L.I. Who counter attacked with No. 1 Company of Plymouth as the enemy were on the point of breaking through and threw them back.

Captain C. B. Andrews of No.4 Company (who had returned from Australia to rejoin his old Corps) and Lieutenant J. S. Barnes were killed during this counter attack and Lieutenant E. B. Carpenter was specially promoted for his good work on this occasion. The Battalion was relieved on the 11th.

On 12th May, the Composite Brigade was relieved by the 42nd Division and withdrew to bivouac south west of Achi Baba Nullah, where they were joined by the Battalions from Anzac and the Royal Marine Brigade was reformed, though the Deal Battalion did not rejoin till 30th.

A conference of Royal Marine Officers was held on 16th to discuss the question of amalgamating the Battalions owing to the weakened strength, but no decision was arrived at.

[Photo by Swaine.]
BRIGADIER-GENERAL CHARLES N. TROTMAN, C.B., R.M.L.I.
Commanded R.M. Brigade and 2nd Brigade, R.N.D.,
November, 1914 to October, 1916;
Major-General, 1921; Lieut.-General, 1922; General, 1923;
Awarded K.C.B., 1922.

From now until the 24th May the Brigade was in bivouac in rest camp, being employed on fatigues, improving communications, etc. Rest Camp at Helles did not mean the same as on other fronts: because the camps were fully exposed to the view and fire of the enemy in the trenches on Achi Baba, which looked down on the slope and the plain at its foot, in fact one account says "I have known the Battalion to be in the line for a week with only eight casualties, whilst there were 18 casualties from stray bullets in rest camps."

Night advances were carried out by the Royal Naval Division on 18th, 22nd, 24th and 27th May, which advanced the line for half-a-mile and brought the Division within 200-300 yards of the main Turkish defensive position across the peninsula, Achi Baba and Krithia Nullahs; the advance on 24th May was made by the 1st Royal Naval Brigade under General Mercer, including the Deal Battalion, when "Mercer Road" was constructed. That on 27th was made by the Royal Marine Brigade.

On 24th when visiting the trenches Major F. S. Wilson, R.M.L.I, Brigade Major of the 1st Royal Naval Brigade was killed, and the Corps lost a very fine officer, who was Adjutant of the Depot at the outbreak of War but relinquished it to become Adjutant of the Drake Battalion at Antwerp. He was buried at Backhouse Post which was the Headquarters of the Brigade in the line. Major J. A. Tupman from Deal Battalion became Brigade Major in his place and was succeeded by Lieut.-Colonel F. R. Godfrey (from Chatham Battalion) in command of Deal, on 30th. About this time volunteers were called for from officers, Royal Marines serving in the Fleet to reinforce the Royal Marine Brigade; but as stated in Chapter 3, very few were allowed to leave their ships, however Major G. M. Heriot, D.S.O. and Lieutenants J. C. Farmer, H. Wilby, R. L. Sturges and C. H. Congdon, all R.M.L.I., were landed for this purpose.

On 25th May the Royal Marine Brigade relieved the 1st Royal Naval Brigade in the Royal Naval Division sector of the line, the mud being over the knees and up to the thighs in places when going up to the line, and on the night 27/28th they made an advance of 210 yards, Chatham being on the right, Portsmouth in the centre and Plymouth on the left, two companies of each were in the line; "C" Company of Deal Battalion made the communication trench and the Divisional Engineers pegged out the line with white pegs and also made the traverses. The right came under fire from the Turkish redoubt, and Corporal Rapkin, in charge of the Chatham scouts, who had done splendid work at Anzac was mortally wounded. One account says that the men started digging with equipment and everything on, but they all finished the same "in their shirt sleeves." The trench was made six feet deep and machine gun positions were constructed; the General Commanding praised their work and the trench was afterwards known as "Trotman Road."

Lieutenant C. White, of Chatham, was killed. in making good the machine-gun position; one of the gunners thus describes the incident: "Lieutenant White selected two positions and set us to work as it was getting light; one man, a volunteer went over the parapet and built up the position with sandbags, filled from the trench, covering them with earth and shrubs, crawling to the front to test its visibility in daylight. He got back safely and went out again to take ranges of roads, trenches, etc. in front; Lieutenant White then being satisfied, went to report to the Adjutant how much ground was covered, but to get a good view, it was necessary to climb out of the trench and in so doing he was killed." Many officers and men became casualties in a similar manner and later in June, Captain Billing was killed whilst watching the effect of the machine gun fire.

On 30th May reinforcements were received for the Division, those for the Royal Marine Brigade consisting of Major J. Grover, Captain R. N. White, H. Channer, C. G. Billing, C. E. Eagles, A. K. Evans with seven Lieutenants nine sergeants, eight corporals, and 472 privates. The Royal Naval Division also received the Benbow Battalion (Colonel J. R. H. Oldfield in command with Major F. D. Bridges as second), Collingwood Battalion (Commander A. Y. Spearman, R.N.) and Hawke (Lieut.-Colonel L.

PLAN 7.

Wilson, D.S.O., M.P., R.M.L.I.) and the 3rd Field Company Divisional Engineers.

Owing to shortage of numbers each of the R.M.L.I. Battalions were reorganised into three Companies (Plymouth into two only). Captain Channer became Adjutant of Portsmouth Battalion vice Morton died of wounds, and Lieutenant A. R. Chater of Chatham Battalion vice Richards killed in action.

It may be of interest to note that they only had office type telephones and "all the signallers were able to get was a shock," later they were supplied with Stevens' telephones and finally with 'D3' which were the best.

THIRD BATTLE OF KRITHIA.

On the 4th June, when the Royal Naval Brigades lost so heavily and behaved so gallantly, the R.M.L.I. Battalions were in reserve. The attacking troops had pieces of biscuit tin sewn on their backs so that the reflection might show how far they had reached.

Of the officers of the Indian Army, who were serving with the Royal Naval Brigades with temporary commissions in the Royal Marines, Major Sparling was killed and Major Kennedy-Craufurd-Stuart was wounded, the latter was awarded the D.S.O.

The casualties sustained on this day necessitated a reorganisation of the Royal Naval Brigades, the Benbow whose Commanding Officer, Colonel J. R. H. Oldfield, R.M.L.I. was wounded, and the Collingwood Battalions were broken up and the Brigades were each formed of three Battalions as before. Major F. D. Bridges, R.M.L.I. being transferred to command of Anson Battalion on 10th June, 1915. On this day the orders for the Royal Marine Brigade were that they were to advance and occupy Krithia and hold a line running due south from that place to the foremost line of the Royal Naval Division, but owing to the failure of the attack they were not required.

During the attack by the Naval Battalions, the junction between the French and the Royal Naval Division was along the top of a ridge, which had enemy strong points at the northern end, with the result that it was not clear who was responsible for dealing with these points: their possession by the enemy made it impossible for the 2nd Royal Naval Brigade, who had carried the Turkish trenches in their front, to maintain their hold and also prevented reinforcements reaching them. When the 2nd Brigade fell back to their original line, the left of the 42nd Division was left in the air, and it was entirely due to the gallant attack led by Colonel Evelegh, R.M.L.I. and his Adjutant, Captain R. J. Carpenter, R.M.L.I. of the Nelson Battalion belonging to General Mercer's 1st Brigade that a diagonal trench was made during the night of 4/5th June, joining the flank of the 42nd Division with that of the Royal Naval Division. The patrols, which were covering the digging parties, had hand to hand fighting with the Turks: this trench was given the name of Nelson Avenue.

During May and June, the Cyclist Company was utilised to reinforce the Royal Marine Battalions, but later in the month were converted into the Divisional Bombers and the personnel were trained in the use of catapults, bomb guns and trench mortars.

On 6th June, Chatham Battalion were sent to reinforce the 42nd Division: when moving up the Kanli Dere they were caught by enfilade fire and had several casualties. They were attached to the Reserve Brigade at Clapham Junction and "D" Company was sent to reinforce the Brigade in the front line. The next day a reconnaissance was made with a view to an attack, the task assigned to the Battalion being to clear the East and West Krithia Nullahs. The attack was timed for 7-0 p.m. but "C" Company were not available as they had been scattered by the Battalion to which they had been attached. "D" Company made good progress, but came under heavy fire from the Vineyard and was hung up, where they were reinforced by a platoon

[By permission of Imperial War Museum.]
GALLIPOLI.-ANZAC FROM THE SEA.

[By permission of Alfieri Picture Service.]
ACHI BABA NULLAH.

of "A" Company, but at 9 p.m. the force retired to the junction of the two nullahs. Artillery support was called for to enable them to push forward and help the Manchesters on the right, but as none was available the Brigadier postponed any further advance. On the 8th the Battalion rejoined the Royal Naval Division at 8-30 p.m.: during these operations four officers (Captain Stoddart, Captain J. Cheetham, Lieutenants Garrett and C. Q. Parsons) were wounded, and 130 others became casualties.

On 7th June, Portsmouth relieved the Hawke in the trenches; At this time advances were being made by sapping forward, two saps at a time, and when they had gone the required distance turning inwards to meet one another thus forming another bight forward, and in pursuance of this on 10th No. 2 Company, Captain Gowney, constructed a new fire trench connecting up the heads of two saps which had been run out about thirty to forty yards from the parapet on the left of the line held by the Battalion; this operation was a great success, and the new work was known as The Rectangle. On this night also Plymouth dug a new communication trench which led to the firing line adjoining the old communication trench thus making a triangle to relieve the congestion during reliefs, this trench was christened "Plymouth Avenue."

On 17th June, Major Festing, the Brigade Major, went sick and as he was invalided to England, Major C. F. Jerram was appointed Brigade Major dated 1st August and Major Lough from Adjutant of Plymouth became Staff Captain.

On 21st June, Chatham and "A" Company of Deal were sent to act as a Reserve to the French in the Third Action of Kereves Dere, but rejoined the Division the next day, when the Royal Marine Brigade relieved the 1st Brigade in the trenches. At this time a company of Deal Battalion was attached to each of the other Battalions. One account relates that on the Peninsula if they dug deep in constructing dug outs they generally came to water, not more than four feet below the surface unless the weather was very dry, this was of great assistance to the water supply and some good wells were dug especially by the Divisional Engineers, Royal Marines, which were guarded by sentries.

On 23rd June, a very gallant and daring night advance was attempted by : "A" Company, Portsmouth, under Major Grover; opposite the centre section of the Divisional front, at the Rectangle, was an advanced Turkish trench, which it was considered could be easily captured and which it would be useful to hold in order to permit of the line being pushed on to a more favourable position for a further advance. The Hawke had carried the trench on 19th, but after holding it for six hours had been compelled to evacuate it, as there was no adequate field of fire and they were enfiladed from the enemy's main position.

At 10 p.m. on 23rd the attacking party led by 2nd Lieut. P. L. Jermain, carried the trenches at the point of the bayonet, Major Grover following with the supports. It had been arranged that Major Grover should fire a Very's Light as soon as the trench had been taken, as a signal for the machine guns to open fire and prevent any interference during the consolidation. Unfortunately Major Grover was killed before he had given the pre-arranged signal, a great loss, as he was a most gallant and able officer. The Turks rallied and counter attacked, bombing our men heavily to which no effective reply could be made. After holding the trench for an hour and a half the company was forced to retire with the loss of Major Grover, 2nd Lieutenant Jermain and 31 killed and wounded, and 22 missing.

The D.S.M. was awarded to Sergeant E. C. Bonnet (Chatham) for gallant conduct on this occasion; although wounded by the same bomb which killed Major Grover, he remained at duty with his men and kept up a steady fire while the wounded were being removed to the rear, he himself carried Major Grover's body for some distance, and until the head of the sap was blocked. Sergeants Colan and Hunt (Portsmouth) also displayed great coolness in rallying the men and holding the sap head under the direction of Captain and Adjutant Channer, who had gone forward and taken charge.

On the night 24/25th June a trench was dug 70 to 100 yards in front of the fire trench held by Portsmouth and Chatham Battalions. The Chatham trench was sited by Captain R. N. White, who, in the absence of the Divisional Engineers, laid out the cord; the digging was successful in spite of the full moon and there were no casualties, though the enemy were only 70 to 100 yards off; this was due to the silence and quietness of the men. This trench and its prolongation by Portsmouth was known as "Parsons Road." The Portsmouth sector was constructed by No. 1 Company (Lieutenant Sitwell) ,and "A" Company, Deal (Lieutenant G. P. Y. Mascall) which was temporarily attached. The right portion was completed during the night, but the left had to withdraw owing to heavy fire from the enemy and this part was completed during the next two days. The Turks never exposed their machine guns during the day unless to support or repel an attack as they were immediately shelled.

On 28th June, Colonel Parsons of Chatham Battalion was wounded and Major C. L. Shubrick succeeded to the command., he was, however, invalided on 11th July and Lieut.-Colonel F. R. Godfrey, who had just returned from hospital assumed command, Colonel Parsons was awarded the C.B. for his successful command of the Chatham Battalion. On 11th July, Plymouth Battalion was organised into two companies owing to the reduction in strength due to dysentery and jaundice.

On 8th July, General Paris proceeded on leave to Imbros and Brig.-General Trotman was temporarily in command of the Royal Naval Division, Colonel F. Luard commanding the Royal Marine Brigade; the latter had just returned from Alexandria after being wounded at Anzac.

ACTION OF ACHI BABA NULLAH. 12TH-13TH JULY.
See Plan No. 8.*[17]

A big attack was planned for the 12th July, which was to be carried out by the 52nd Lowland Division, together with the 1st and 2nd French Divisions on the right. The plan shows the position of the trenches, etc. The Royal Marine Brigade was in Corps Reserve.

The 52nd were to advance from their right and were only to advance on the left, if the right attack succeeded. The attack by the French and 155th Brigade from the right of Parsons Road began at 7-30 a.m. on 12th and was generally successful, as was also the advance on the left of the 157th Brigade. The Division captured the line E11-J-EI3a-FI2a, but the position in the centre was not clear. By the evening on the extreme right of the French the attack was completely successful, but in the centre the attack had not yet advanced beyond the first two lines of trenches and the whole of the Divisional Reserves had been used up. At noon Chatham were sent to Backhouse Post in support of the 52nd and at 4 p.m. Portsmouth and Plymouth were also ordered to the same place, Chatham later moving on to the continuation of Parson's and Trotman's Road to the east, in support of the right flank of the 52nd. The 155th Brigade having gained the line T-S-P these battalions were sent to occupy the old front line, Plymouth in support of 6th Highland Light Infantry west of the Nullah, and Portsmouth to Trotman Road with its left on Oxford Street. The Turks were still holding out in the communication trenches, rendering reconnaissance difficult; it was obvious, however, that there was great confusion and heavy loss, and the 52nd Division which had carried

---

17. *The line P-J was shown on all maps as a trench and was ordered to be occupied as such. In actual fact it was a very slight bank, not noticeable to men advancing, and the 52nd Division attack on this part failed owing to the attackers not recognising the objective, they continued the advance up the smooth glacis and this portion of the attackers was annihilated.*

out a most gallant attack, found itself at nightfall with few officers and in strange surroundings, and by the next morning a great deal of the ground gained had been lost. Colonel Matthews of the Plymouth Battalion was wounded by a stray bullet and Captain Weller assumed command.

As the exact line held by the 52nd Division on the morning of 13th was unknown, Major Sketchley, G.S.O. 2, and Major Jerram of the Royal Marine Brigade were sent up in different directions to reconnoitre. On the west of the Nullah Plymouth found themselves in the morning in sole occupation of the captured trenches, which they held up to F12a the 157th Brigade having been withdrawn to Nelson and Plymouth Avenues. East of the Nullah the 157th Brigade communications with the remainder of their Division were very precarious, and an attempt to get into touch with the troops behind them led to a temporary retirement which was followed up by the Turks. Plymouth drove off this attack being able to enfilade the Turkish attack and taking 12 prisoners and two machine guns. Major Sketchley, R.M.L.I., who was in Parsons Road was able to stop the withdrawal and gallantly led the men back; with the aid of same Royal Marines of Plymouth Battalion he led them over the parapet and reoccupied some of the trenches which had been lost, he himself only carrying a fly whisk in his hand. He was awarded the D.S.O., and his orderly, Lance-Corporal J. G. Way, R.M.L.I. the Conspicuous Gallantry Medal for their gallantry on this occasion.

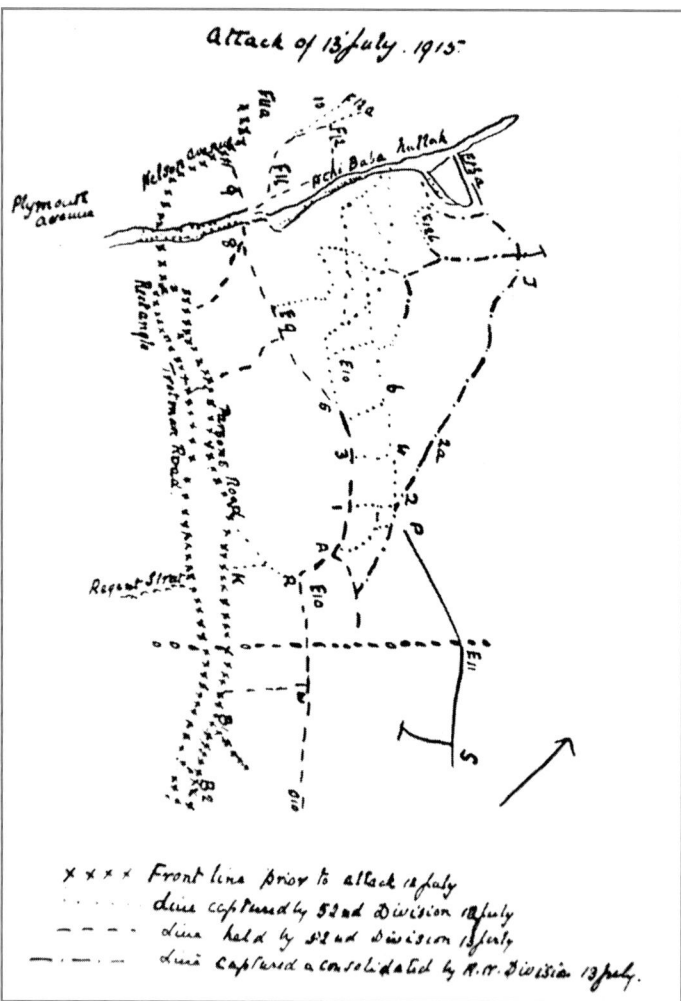

PLAN 8.

During the night of 12/13th the Nelson and Drake Battalions had arrived and were attached to the Royal Marine Brigade, the Nelson being sent up in support between Portsmouth and Plymouth.

The left was, however, dangerously isolated and the Turks were still holding their third line; in these circumstances it was necessary either to advance or retire. Brigadier-General Trotman (who had resumed command of the Royal Marine Brigade at 2-0 p.m.) was ordered to regain the lost ground, with the Chatham, Portsmouth and Nelson Battalions. The objective was the line T-S-P-E12-E13a. The attack was at first ordered to commence at 2 p.m., which was later altered to 4-30 p.m.

At 3 p.m. General Trotman

met his Commanding Officers at the junction of Regent Street and Trotman Raad and issued his orders. Chatham on the right were to attack the line T-S to track at E11. Portsmouth to attack the line from this track to 2a, Nelson to attack line from 2a to Nullah. Plymouth were to hold their position and assist by fire. The French on the right were also to have attacked and joined up.

The attack was to commence at 4-30 p.m., moving over the open ground to the present front line at 4-15 p.m.

The Battalion Commanders left the conference at 3-40 p.m. and the Brigadier returned to his Headquarters leaving the Brigade Major at the telephone at the junction.

At 4-0 p.m. the French Artillery opened to. support the attack, to which the Turks immediately replied causing heavy casualties in the communication trenches, which were very congested, especially in the Chatham area. This Battalion in trying to gain the jumping off line suffered very severely, and the trenches became impassable so that the Battalion was late in arriving at its place; at zero the only company of Chatham in position made endeavours to attack, but the French on the right, who had not yet received their orders would not advance until they did so; the Chatham Battalion therefore worked forward into the two lines of trenches already captured and held by details of the 52nd Division, and consolidated them, but in doing so lost touch with Portsmouth Battalion. Lieutenant L. F. Tayler was wounded and Lieutenant J. S. S. Thorneley died of wounds:

On the centre and left the Commanding Officers of Portsmouth R.M.L.I. and the Nelson Battalion were only able to give hurried orders to their companies and at 4-30 p.m. led their Battalions over the parapet. The attack was made with the greatest gallantry, but they were met by a perfect hail of shrapnel and machine gun fire. In spite of heavy losses, they captured and consolidated the left of the objective and gained touch with the 5th Highland Light Infantry in the neighbourhood of Achi Baba Nullah, but the Nelson suffered a great loss by the death of their gallant Commanding Officer, Lieut.-Colonel E. G. Evelegh, R.M.L.I., who. was killed with five other officers of the Nelson.

Portsmouth R.M.L.I. who advanced in two lines, the first from Parsons Road and the second from Trotman Road, found that their objective the third Turkish line was unrecognisable, as explained before, and advanced beyond it. Many advanced beyond E12 until all were killed and the remnants of the Battalion fell back, but dug in on a line in advance of the Turkish Third Line (which proved to be a narrow ditch 18 inches deep; one platoon under Lieutenant Murdoch Browne remained isolated in advance even of this position. The line was now 400 yards in front of Parsons Road.

These advances were most brilliant, but were obtained at a terrible cost; Portsmouth had only one officer untouched, Captain Gowney, D.S.C., and he was wounded the next day. Colonel Luard who had led the attack so gallantly was killed together with Lieutenants S. D. Wilmot-Sitwell, E. B. C. Dougherty, F. J. Sutcliffe (the great Corps Cricketer), whilst Major J. A. Clark, Captains H. Channer, W. de T. L. Clark, Lieutenants M. Browne, E. Harden, C. F. Woolley, and M. H. Spicer were wounded. The total casualties in the Battalion being four officers killed and seven wounded, with 32 N.C.O.s and men killed, 140 wounded and 54 missing afterwards reported killed. Lieutenant M. Browne was awarded the D.S.C. for his services in this action.

Colonel Luard was buried at Backhouse Post, the Battalion losing a most gallant commander, and many of the others were buried at Brown House. Colonel Evelegh was buried near the Post.

At nightfall the Nelson Battalion was dug in in tolerably deep and traversed trenches, but without any safe communications; the remnants of Portsmouth were clinging to and digging in on an undefined line, running back from the right of Nelson to a point some 200 yards in advance of the line held by Chatham, even for this flank there was no safe communication with the old line. The isolated little groups were collected as far as possible under Captain Gowney by Major Jerram, who had been sent up to reconnoitre, but they were without supports. The Drake Battalion whose Headquarters were at Brown House were sent up and 1st Royal Naval Brigade Headquarters under General Mercer went up at midnight to connect up Nelson and Chatham Battalions. Under the orders of General Mercer the Drake found and consolidated the line and by dawn of 14th a trench had been dug across from the right of the Nelson Battalion at "J"" to the left of Chatham at a point about 50 yards south of "P" Lieut.- Commander King (now Captain H. D. King, R.N.V.R.) commanding the Drake did splendid work and was awarded the D.S.O.

General Paris had resumed command of the Royal Naval Division on 13th. There was still a portion of the Turkish Third Line on the left of the French, which had been the objective of 155th Brigade, but which had not yet been captured, but General Paris decided, that as the line now held was the best from a military point of view that the Division had yet held, that it should be consolidated and reorganised. The first step was the withdrawal of the remnants of the 52nd Division on the following day. The new sector was divided into two sections, the 1st Brigade Headquarters with Chatham, Hawke and Plymouth on the right, and the Royal Marine Brigade with Nelson, and Drake, on the left; Plymouth digging a new trench on 14th.

The next few days were spent in consolidating and strengthening the trenches. Lieut.-Colonel F. R. Godfrey was invalided on 19th and Captain R. N. White assumed command of Chatham Battalion temporarily. On 18th July Captain E. F. Trew, who was appointed Acting Adjutant of Plymouth,with three officers, two acting warrant officers and 159 N.C.O.s and men arrived as reinforcement, but these numbers could not replace the heavy losses, to which, had to be added the numbers suffering from dysentery, jaundice and other gastric troubles due to the heat and other causes incidental to trench life on the Peninsula, which were causing a very severe depletion of the fighting strength of the Brigade.

The losses of the Brigade from 18th June to 30th July, were:-

Killed	5 Officers	99 N.C.O.s and Men.
Wounded	14 "	360 "
Missing	1 "	74 "(afterwards reported killed.)

It was consequently decided to reorganise the Royal Marine Brigade into two Battalions, Chatham and Deal forming the 1st R.M.L.I. and Portsmouth and Plymouth the 2nd R.M.L.I. Captain White remained in command of 1st R.M.L.I. and Colonel Matthews in command of No.2. Colonel Matthews had been slightly wounded on 12th but rejoined on 27th, Plymouth being commanded by Captain B. G. Weller in his absence. This reorganisation was carried out on 2nd August.

The losses in the Royal Naval Brigades had also been heavy, whilst in addition 300 stokers were withdrawn for service in the Fleet; at the same time Commodore Backhouse commanding the 2nd Brigade was withdrawn for a sea appointment. The Royal Naval Division were therefore reorganised into two Brigades, the 1st under Brig.-General D. Mercer was composed of Drake, Hawke, Nelson, and Hood Battalions; the 2nd under Brig.-General C. Trotman consisted of 1st and 2nd R.M.L.I., Howe and Anson.

The Cyclist company under Major A. H. French started a bombing school to train battalion bombers, the first class assembling on 12th July and thus formed the first school that was instituted on the Peninsula. The bombs were known as "Tickler's Bombs" as they were made from tins of that firm's jams, filled with explosive, they were fired from a catapult, which had wooden legs six feet high ; they carried a distance of 90 yards, but the elastic was constantly breaking.

Major N. O. Burge, R.M.L.I. of the Cyclist company succeeded Colonel Evelegh in command of the

Nelson. The Adjutants of the new battalions were Captain E. J. B. Tagg of 1st, and C. G. Farquharson of the 2nd.

On 28th July Lieut.-Colonels E. J. Stroud and J. B. Pym arrived to replace Colonels Parsons and Luard. Colonel Stroud assumed command of 1st R.M.L.I. but Colonel Pym was invalided for heart disease very shortly after, and when Colonel Matthews was invalided for eye trouble on 30th August, Lieut.-Colonel A. R. H. Hutchison, who had just arrived, assumed command of 2nd R.M.L.I.

It was noted at the end of July that the telephones were working well, but as they had earth returns they gave away a lot of information on account of the large amount of induction. On the 29th they fired a *feu de joie* for a victory in Palestine. On 13th August parcels were received from Her Majesty Queen Alexandra.

In the operations at Suvla the 2nd Field Ambulance was the only Royal Marine unit besides the beach parties from the Fleet that took part; but a considerable number of Royal Marine Officers were employed in various capacities.

In the attack in the Helles sector on 6th and 7th August (the Actions of Krithia Vineyard) made by the 29th and 42nd Divisions in conjunction with the Suvla operations, the 1st and 2nd R.M.L.I. were in reserve and during that month they were taking their turn in the trenches. During the summer months the plague of flies became unbearable and contributed very much to the sickness. Whenever possible, the troops went for a swim in the sea; which really was a parade and no one missed it, so that they could overhaul their clothing and get rid of the insect pests.

On 2nd September, Major F. J. Saunders, D.S.O., two officers and 242 N.C.O.s and men were received as reinforcements. This draft brought with them a large number of the Maxim guns that had been collected from the Grand Fleet, with a view to strengthening the fire power on the Peninsula, as reinforcements of men with rifles could not be provided in adequate numbers.

The Royal Marine Brigade had made great use of their machine guns. Captain Lathbury of the Portsmouth Battalion, had become an expert in this weapon and was appointed Brigade Machine Gun Officer, and had developed the tactics of the gun, which at that time were not too well understood; he was awarded the D.S.C. for his services. The machine gun sections had throughout done splendid work, and had incurred heavy losses. When Captain Lathbury was invalided, he was succeeded by Captain C. B. Conybeare. The officers of the sections on landing were :

CHATHAM: Lieutenant M. Curtain (killed) ; H. Watts (*wounded*).

PORTSMOUTH: Captain Lathbury (invalided); M. Adamson (*wounded*); Sergeant-Major C. Priscott.

PLYMOUTH: Lieutenant C. B. Conybeare (*wounded*) but *rejoined*; Sergeant-Major Staughton (*killed in France*).

DEAL: Lieutenant H. Millet (invalided); K. L. Higgins (*killed*).

On 15th August, the Royal Naval Division took over from the 29th Division the line between Gully Ravine and Krithia Nullah, which in consequence of the fighting on 6th August, was in a very bad state and entailed heavy work to put in order. The Royal Marine Battalions were in the firing line from 16th to 23rd August and again from 30th August to 8th September. In this sector, there were two barricades, the northern and the southern, which consisted of a widening at the end of the trenches, making it into an opening about 20 feet square, and sandbagged all round to about 12 feet high. It was possible for the catapult to throw bombs over the parapet. There was also a hole dug forward with a loophole plate at the end, just large enough to enable a sentry to crawl in and lie down, to watch No Mans Land. On 17th August,

[By permission of Imperial War Museum.]
GALLIPOLI. TROOPS OF ROYAL NAVAL DIVISION ATTACKING.

[By permission of the Imperial War Museum.]
GENERAL VIEW LOOKING TOWARDS ACHI BABA.

Captain E. Carpenter was severely wounded, from the effects of which he died later.

It was not until 19th September, that the first party of 100 from the Royal Marine Brigade was sent to Imbros for a rest. The Royal Naval brigades having had their turn in July and August.

Sickness was now taking a heavy toll of the Brigades, and the strength of the Battalions fell rapidly, in spite of the devoted efforts of Surgeon-Commander E. J. Finch, of the 3rd Field Ambulance, and Surgeons McBean-Ross and Payne, the medical officers of the battalions.

During September and October, the 1st and 2nd Brigades were relieving each other regularly in the trenches.

On 26th September, two French 10-inch guns took on "Asiatic Annie" the big Turkish gun, that worried the troops so badly all through, and after a spirited duel, "Annie" piped down.

During October, the Rest Camp was removed to the left of the Peninsula, in rear of the Divisional Sector, whilst efforts were made to prepare for the winter, but very little material, in the shape of timber and corrugated iron was available. In this month the weather in the Aegean commences to break, and rains and storms may be expected. On 1st and 2nd October, it was noted that there was a marked improvement in the enemy shells. On 4th October, the diary recorded that the 2nd Brigade was holding 1861 yards of front with 1286 rifles. On 11th October, the Plymouth Battalion relate that they started to prepare the dug-outs for the winter, and in the afternoon played their league football match with the Howe Battalion, which they lost by four goals to one, the game having to be stopped twice, owing to shells falling on the pitch. There is also a note that on the 26th, they saw large flocks of birds passing over evidently migrating.

On 27th October, Captain V. D. Loxley, five second lieutenants and 210 other ranks joined as reinforcements.

On 13th November General Trotman was placed on the sick list, and Lieut.-Colonel E. J. Stroud was appointed to command the Brigade, from 24th November till 26th January, 1916, so that he was in command during the period of the evacuation. Major F. J. Saunders took over the command of 1st R.M.L.I, until Lieut.-Colonel Mullins, who had been disembarked from *Lord Nelson*, for command of Tenedos and later of the Bomb School, was appointed on 27th December to the command, and Major Saunders became Brigade Major vice Jerram to the Divisional Staff as D.A.A. and Q.M.G.

On 27th November, the terrible storm of that year broke over the Peninsula; torrential rain and sleet for 24 hours turned to snow and frost and was followed by the blizzard of the 28th with a wind, the bitterness of which had to be felt to be realised. The troops in the trenches suffered cruelly, and the casualties were very numerous. There were 24 cases of frostbite in 1st R.M.L.I. alone; and there was totally inadequate protection against such cold. Fortunately on 1st December, the weather improved and the first week in December was normal; but as usual in that part of the world, December was a month of heavy rain and gales, which caused considerable anxiety as to the safety of the piers, besides rendering the task of landing supplies very difficult.

General Sir C. Monro had relieved General Sir Ian Hamilton on 28th October, and the Corps Commander of the VIII. Corps at Helles, to which the Royal Naval Division belonged, was General F. J. Davies, who had relieved Sir A. Hunter-Weston on 8th August.

During December, the Turkish bombardments became much heavier, and it was expected that the Austrian heavy artillery would be brought to the Peninsula, as the lines through Serbia were now open to the enemy, affording direct communication with the Central Powers.

Two gallant actions were reported in October and November.. Private Mark Turner (Portsmouth) of 2nd R.M.L.I., was working the catapult on 31st October, when a live bomb failed to clear the barricade and fell inside, Turner immediately picked it up and threw it over the parapet, where it exploded, and so saved what might have been a serious accident. On 27th November, Lance-Corporal E. A. Grindey (Portsmouth), 2nd

PLAN 9.

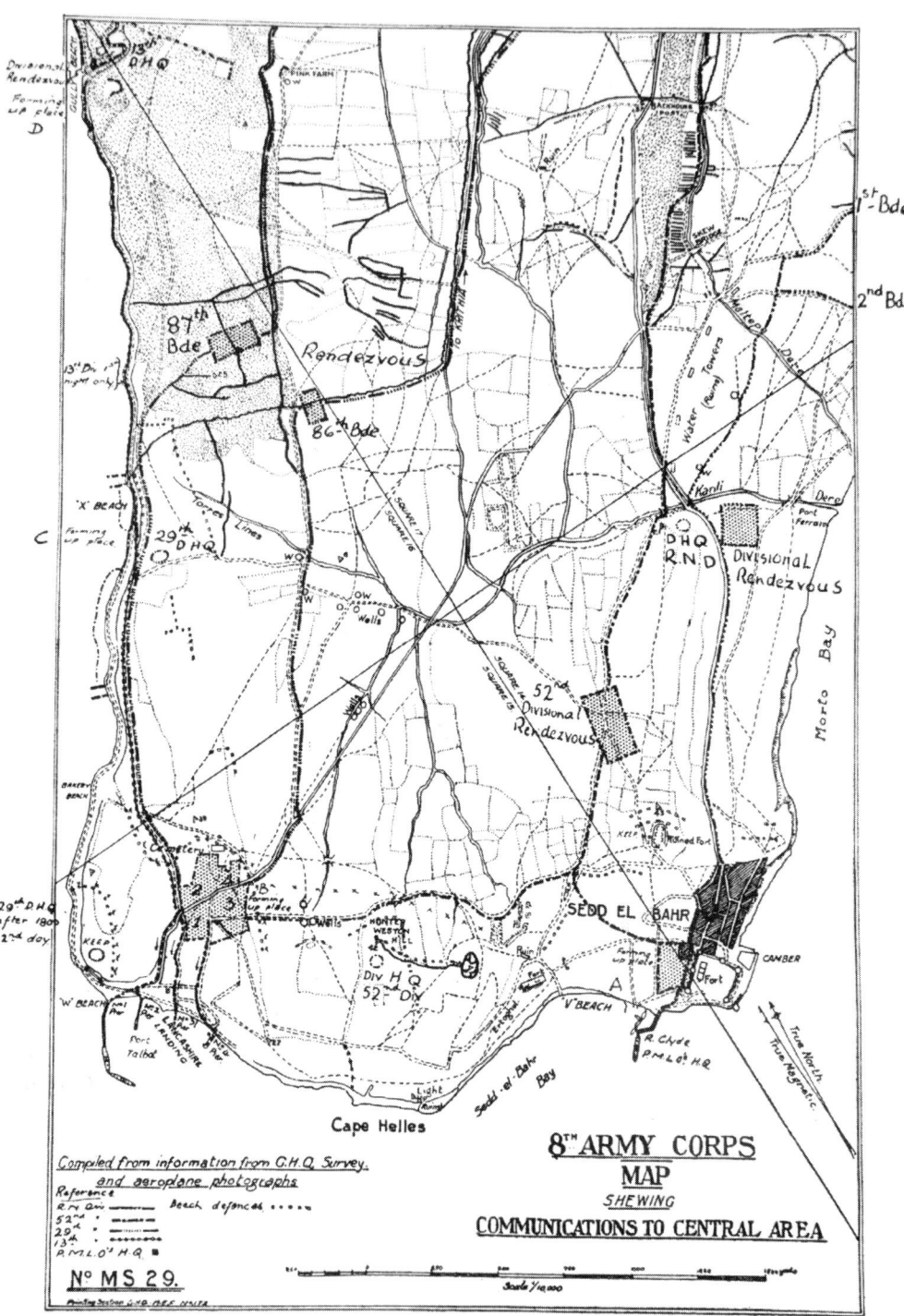

R.M.L.I., in the northern barricade, was firing a catapult, when a live bomb jambed in the pocket, with great coolness and courage,. he placed his hand on the burning fuse and pinched it until it was extinguished, he then removed the bomb and threw it over the parapet. Both were awarded the Conspicuous Gallantry Medal, as was Corporal F. Pilgrim (Portsmouth), who threw a live Turkish grenade out of the trench on 20th November.

On 24th December, General Birdwood, who had been appointed Commander of the Dardanelles Army in November, General Monro having been appointed to the command of both Gallipoli and Salonica, received orders to prepare, in case orders for immediate evacuation should be issued.

Suvla and Anzac had been evacuated on 19th December, but the Royal Naval Division took no part in this, though many Royal Marines from the Fleet were employed in various capacities.

On 30th December, General Paris received orders to prepare for early evacuation. Orders had already been issued, with a view to deceiving the enemy, that silence was to be observed for about four hours every night, and this commenced on 25th December. In order to reduce the number of formations to be finally evacuated, the 42nd and French Divisions were relieved on the nights of 31st December and 1st January. As the Royal Naval Division was on the right of the British Line, the 2nd Brigade had taken over part of the French sector, on 12th December, and on the evening of 1st January extended their flank to the sea on the Dardanelles. The 1st Brigade, General Mercer, was on the left and 2nd Brigade, Colonel Stroud, on the right. The French artillery remained in their positions to support them. In the 2nd Brigade, 1st R.M.L.I. and Howe were in the front line and 2nd R.M.L.I. in reserve in the Eski Line. The 13th Division were on the left of the line and the 29th and 52nd in the centre. At this time, each of the Naval Brigades had a battalion of the London Regiment (Territorials) attached to them.

The 1st R.M.L.I. took over the right section of the French Line on one of the last days of December; the French had held this line since it was first captured. The front line ran along the west bank of the Kereves Dere, except that a work called the Ouvrage Matillo had been pushed out on the east bank of the stream; from the north west corner of this work, there was an ascent by steps, which led up to a hole in the parapet of the front line, just in front of the Source Labarsouque, where Colonel Mullins had established his headquarters. Communication trenches ran back to the second line, which were more or less in view of the Turks, whose communications were equally exposed and there was a tacit agreement that firing was not to take place and the Battalion accordingly maintained this arrangement. French uniforms were also sent up, which were worn in the trenches to still further deceive the Turks. The Brigade Headquarters were established at Ferme Vermesche.

The 1st R.M.L.I. were disposed in line as follows, on the right "C" Company (Captain Loxley, Lieutenants Tuckey and Hanson), in the centre "B" Company (Captain Hoare, Lieutenants Cohen and Donne), in the Ouvrage Matillo (Captain A. K. Evans, Lieutenants Fiennes and Nourse) the Grenade Company (Lieutenant J. Pearson) held the steps, whilst "A" Company (Captain M. C. Browne, Lieutenants R. H. West and Kyle) with the machine guns (Captain Bastin) were partly in the 2nd line and partly in the Ligne de Repli; the strength of the Battalion at this time was about 630, the Adjutant was Captain Tagg, and the Quartermaster, Lieutenant T. H. Burton.

On 13th December, Lieutenant C. F. Mead, who had served with his battalion since the beginning and had been twice wounded, was killed. It was in memory of this officer, who was a very good and keen cricketer, that his father presented to the Corps the Cricket Challenge Cup, which is competed for annually by the Divisions and Depot. He received his commission in the Corps on 30th September, 1913.

On 2nd January, "A" and "B" Companies of 1st R.M.L.I. were reduced to six N.C.O.s and 18 privates each, "C" Company to 90 N.C.O.s and men, "D" Company to 65 N.C.O.s and men; the Grenade Company to 10, Machine Guns to 24 and Headquarters to 13; the remainder were ordered back to the Ligne de Repli, ready to go back to the Rendezvous, and to be employed on working parties; but by the 4th the strain on those left in the line was found to be too much, and a large proportion were again sent up to the front line.

The date of the evacuation was provisionally fixed for the 8th January. As soon as the 42nd and French Divisions had withdrawn, the bulk of the artillery, horses, supplies and transport followed; then the baggage of Divisional and Brigade Headquarters, battalion records and regimental stores.

"X" day was the 6th January and on this day the front line and reserve trenches were held in full strength, but the artillery were reduced to a minimum. On the night 6/7th January the 2nd London Regiment attached to the 2nd Brigade and the excess numbers of battalions were embarked and by the morning of 7th the total strength of the Division of all arms was only 4,400. Of the 1st R.M.L.I. one officer and 272 other ranks were withdrawn before the last day leaving 17 officers and 357 other ranks to be withdrawn on the last day.

Lieut.-Colonel Hutchison, commanding 2nd R.M.L.I. was at first nominated to be Officer Commanding "W" and "V" Beaches for the final withdrawal, but later the line was divided into two sectors, under Brig.-General Tufnell, G.O.C. Covering Force. The right sector, covering "V" Beach, was to be held by the 2nd R.M.L.I. with 400 of all ranks and 3 machine guns, the front to be from the Dardanelles to Hunter-Weston Hill exclusive; the left sector covering "W" Beach was held by 600 of all ranks and three machine guns of 29th Division under Lieut.-Colonel Pollard, 1st Borders.

Lieut.-Colonel Hutchison issued the following orders on 7th January. "A," "B," "C," and "D" companies were each to detail 94 of all ranks by name and the machine gun section 20 all ranks to form the Beach Defence party.

During 7th and 8th these men were occupied in improving the line and keeping out of the sight of enemy aircraft. (*The sketch show the positions*)

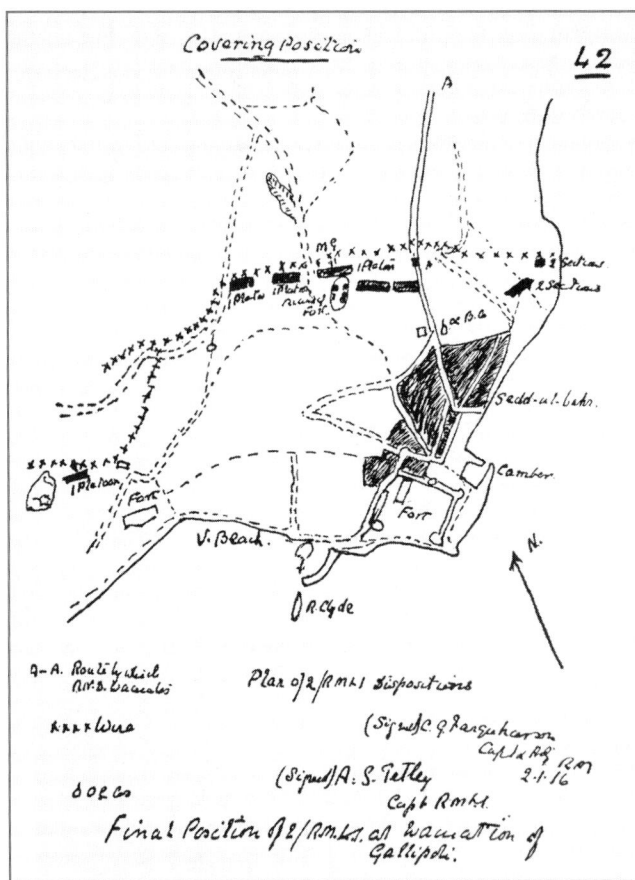

PLAN 10.

ORDERS BY LIEUTENANT-COLONEL HUTCHISON.
COMMANDING RIGHT SECTOR OF BEACH DEFENCES.

7th January, 1916.

1. - The Companies detailed for Beach Defence will occupy the Line as follows:
    "C" Company. (Captain. Tetley), from Dardanelles to Cemetery Road, inclusive.
    "B" Company. (Captain Eagles) from Cemetery Road to Bivouac Road, both exclusive.
    "A" Company. (Captain Edwards), Bivouac Road to Orchard Valley, both inclusive.
    "D" Company. (Captain D. J. Gowney), from this point to Hunter Weston Hill.
2. - "C" Company will provide a reserve of 1 Officer and 40 men at the small Cemetery in Sedd-ul-Bahr to be at my disposal.
3. - Troops to be in position by 1800 to-night. They will be withdrawn later by my orders with the exception of 1 Officer and 25 men of "C" Company, who will be withdrawn later by order of General Officer Commanding Embarkation. This Officer will be responsible for maintaining telephonic communication with P.M.L.O. and "V" Beach.
4. - On the order to withdraw, Companies will proceed to the Rendezvous as quickly and quietly as possible; the Rendezvous will be at the small Cemetery in Sedd-ul-Bahr, where first aid post will be established.
5. - Each Company will provide one orderly to report at Battalion Headquarters; this orderly will know the nearest way between Company Headquarters and Battalion Headquarters.
6. - All Officers and N.C.O.s must make themselves acquainted with the way to the Rendezvous.
7. - Smoking and striking lights are strictly forbidden. Electric torches will only be used by order of a M.L.O.
8. - Fire is only to be opened by word of command of an Officer.
9. - Absolute silence is to be maintained except for the issue of necessary orders.
10. - All ranks are to be warned that no wounded man, who can walk, is to be accompanied by other men to the rear.
11. - Officer Commanding "A" Company will detail an Officer to report to the P.M.L.O. on "V" Beach and to be at his disposal. This Officer is to make himself acquainted with the position of Battalion Headquarters; the name of this Officer is to be reported.
12. - All ranks are to be in possession of the unexpended portion of the day's ration, 1 Iron Ration and filled Water bottles.
13. - Each man to be in possession of 220 rounds Small Arms Ammunition. Each Machine Gun, 2,000.
14. - Battalion Headquarters will be established at the telephone box outside Sedd-ul-Bahr Fort.

(Signed), C. G. FARQUARSON, *Captain and Adjutant.*

On the same day Divisional Headquarters issued their final instructions. Each Brigade in the front line was to retain 800 rifles and four machine guns in front line; 150 rifles and one machine gun in Ligne de Repli; 230 rifles and one machine gun in Eski Line. Each Brigade was to leave one machine gun in position until 10 p.m. the remainder in front line being withdrawn with the troops leaving at 8-0 p.m., those in the Ligne de Repli and Eski Line being withdrawn at the same time as the troops in those lines for the 10-30 trip.

Each Brigade was to garrison the Ligne de Repli with 150 from the garrison of 380 men in the Eski Line. To be withdrawn for 10-30 trip. The troops were to pass the wire fence at the gateway, which is on the Sedd ul Bahr

Road about 200 yards north east of the ruined fort, land unless orders were received to the contrary the evacuation would be carried out the next night in accordance with orders already issued. No further order would be issued for its commencement.

At 2 p.m. on the 7th the Turks opened the heaviest bombardment so far experienced and made a heavy attack on the 13th Division on the left; "The Last Turkish Attack"; but fortunately the guns of the supporting squadron under Captain D. L. Dent, R.N., were able to keep up a counter bombardment and helped to smash up the attempted attack and all was quiet by 5 p.m.

On the night of 7/8th January the Hawke and 2nd R.M.L.I. left the trenches for the last time, and moved into bivouac in support. They were relieved in the Eski Line by detachments from the front line. The final allocation of troops for firing line, support and Eski Line was firing line 845 all ranks and eight machine guns. Immediate support 300 all ranks and two machine guns. Eski Line 460 all ranks and two machine guns[18].

These troops were drawn from the Hood and Drake of 1st Brigade and 1st R.M.L.I. and Howe of the 2nd. All other arms were proportionately reduced, except the Medical Unit, Royal Marines, which retained 210 of all ranks. The position was 3,000 yards in extent which was defended by 2,000 men. The road to the Beach was picketed and control posts established, who were furnished with the exact numbers of the parties to pass through; each party was scheduled to the exact minute and their arrival at each post was telephoned to the next and so on till the beach was reached, in order that the boats could be loaded to full capacity as there were no margins.

The Divisional Rendezvous had been fixed between the two bridges in front of the Caesar's Camp Spur, where units were to be collected and passed on to the forming up places near the Beach. Lieut.-Colonel Burge, R.M.L.I, of Nelson Battalion was in charge of the Rendezvous and all units had to report to him; Major A. E. Rombulow-Pearse, R.M.L.I was in charge of the forming-up places whence the troops were passed on to the beach.

At 6-15 p.m., the troops in bivouac moved off and there is a moving description of the scene by the historian of the Royal Naval Division. The actual evacuation commenced at 8 p.m., when the strength of the trench garrisons was reduced to skeleton numbers, who finally left the trenches at 11-45 p.m., and proceeded through the control posts to the embarking places on the beach.

The final withdrawal went according to schedule, without any difficulty. A battalion commander remarks that the forming up places were practically cut out, so that from 10 p.m. onwards, the back of the beach became rather crowded with men in fours waiting to be taken off. The enemy fired a few shells at the beach, fortunately without doing any harm, and they were immediately silenced by the heavy fire of the monitors lying off Mavro Island.

The weather got steadily worse from 8 p.m. onwards, and by 11 p.m., it was blowing fresh, and by 4 a.m., blowing hard. The Headquarters of the 1st and 2nd Brigades and Divisional Headquarters of the Royal

---

18 1st R.M.L.I. during the first period up to 8 p.m., 8th January had :-
  (a)   8 Officers 18 N.C.O.s 165 Men in Firing Line and Control Post.
  (b)   4   "   14   " in 2nd Line.
  (c)   3   "   112   " Ligne de Repli.
  (d)   2   "   51   " in Eski Line.
For the second period of the withdrawal from 8 to 10 p.m. these were reduced to (a) three officers 92 men; (b) one officer five men; (c) one officer two men; (d) one officer, two men. For the last period from 10 to 11-45 p.m. (a) three officers 80 men; (b) one officer five men; (c) one officer two men; (d) one officer two men.

[Photo by Swaille.]

BRIGADIER-GENERAL DAVID MERCER, C.B., A.A.G. Royal Marines,
1911-Dec. 1914.
Commanded 1st Royal Naval Brigade, 1915-16; Appointed Adjutant General, Royal Marines, 22nd June, 1916 and promoted to Major-General; Created K.C.B., 1917; Died 1st July, 1920, whilst holding appointment of Adjutant-General.

Naval Division, embarked in H.M.S. *Prince George*, at 12-30 a.m., 9th January and also the Headquarters of 1st R.M.L.I. This ship embarked 2000 men, who were taken off to the ships in the 'K'. motor lighters, each holding 400 men. The ship then got under weigh and proceeded to Mudros; it was reported that she had been struck by a torpedo at 2 a.m., which fortunately did not explode.

Lieutenant-Colonel Hutchison and the 2nd R.M.L.I, remained as the final party to leave, and his report is as follows :-

"I have the honor to report that the 2nd R.M.L.I was employed as follows, on the night of 8/9th January, during the evacuation of Cape Helles. Two posts, each of 29 rifles and one machine gun, under an officer were found at Zimmerman's Farm and near De Totts Battery. These two posts mounted during the forenoon of 8th and were withdrawn by Brigade Orders, 400 of all ranks with three machine guns took up a line from the Dardanelles to Hunter-Weston Hill, forming the right section of the beach defences. They were in position at 6 p.m. on 8th, and were withdrawn after all other troops had passed down to the beaches at about 2-30 a.m. on 9th, without any interference from the enemy. They embarked in H.M.S. *Grasshopper* and left the shore at 3-30 a.m. One officer and 25 rifles (No. 12 Platoon of "C" Company), were left as a covering party; this party was withdrawn by order of the General Officer Commanding Embarkation, very shortly after the remainder had withdrawn[19].

Colonel Hutchison also brought to notice the conduct during the evacuation of Captain A. S. Tetley, Private (acting Sergeant) S. J. Hutchings and Private F. S. Paull, both of Plymouth.

An eye witness describes the retirement of the last platoon- "By half past three in the morning, all were through and hence our task was done, so with mingled feelings, we reluctantly turned our backs for the time being on Achi Baba. With complete silence, we marched to the beach and boarded the waiting tug, which immediately got under weigh for Imbros. We had not proceeded far before we noticed that all the stores, which could not be got off, were a mass of flames. Still the Turks were sending up their customary signals, and holding an imaginary enemy; and now thoroughly awakened, but too late, the Turks shelled the beach heavily. Thus ended the grand finale to the campaign on Turkish Territory, where the 'Royals' (barrack-room term for Royal Marines), were the first on and the last off."

It is interesting to recall that the Plymouth Battalion were the first troops to attempt a landing on 4th March, 1915, and that it was the remnants of the Plymouth Battalion, now in the 2nd R.M.L.I., who were the last to leave. Further, that after the Armistice it was the Royal Marines of the 3rd Battalion, who were the first to take over the Turkish Batteries on the Peninsula on 11th November, 1918.

The question of the disposal of the Royal Naval Division now became acute. The Admiralty had no immediate use for a body of this description, and the Army were not desirous of retaining its services. However, it was judged necessary to retain possession of the islands of Lemnos, Imbros, and Tenedos, as a support for the Dardanelles patrol. The Headquarters of the 1st Brigade, Lieutenant-Colonel L. Wilson, D.S.O., R.M.L.I., temporarily in command, with the Hawke and Drake Battalions were sent to garrison Imbros, a company of the Hood was sent to Tenedos, whilst the Divisional Headquarters, the 2nd Brigade, remainder of 1st Brigade, and the Divisional units remained at Lemnos. The G.S.O. 1, Colonel Ollivant went to England on leave, and did not rejoin the Division; the A.A. and Q.M.G., Colonel Richardson had been appointed D.A. and Q.M.G. of the 12th Corps at Salonica. General Paris proceeded on leave to England, as did Brigadier-General Mercer, who was shortly after nominated to succeed General Sir W. Nicholls as Adjutant-General, Royal Marines.

---

19. *This party was under the command of Lieutenant B. G. Andrews with Colour-Sergeant J. Devitt. Sergeant W. Rimmer, Corporals B. French, G. Eddisbury and F. Jones, .all Plymouth, with 19 Plymouth and 5 Portsmouth Privates.*

Reinforcements had arrived, and training was carried out under the supervision of General Trotman, who had resumed command of the 2nd Brigade on 26th January, Colonel Stroud reverting to 1st R.M.L.I.; Lieutenant-Colonel Mullins proceeded to Malta, to take charge of the Royal Naval Division details there.

Before leaving for England on 16th February, General Paris visited Salonica and arranged for the 2nd Brigade, with attached units to be sent to Stavros, where they were attached to the Salonica Army in the defence line. On arrival in England, General Paris, seconded by the efforts of the numerous friends of the Division, arranged for its transfer to France, where numbered as the 63rd (Royal Naval) Division, it gained undying glory. Its adventures in France are dealt with in Part VI, "Units attached to the Army."

STAVROS, MACEDONIA.

On 22nd February, the 2nd Brigade Headquarters, with 1st and 2nd R.M.L.I., Howe and Anson Battalions, 3rd Field Ambulance and 3rd Field Company Engineers embarked for Stavros, on the right flank of the Salonica Army. The Battalions embarked at one and a half hour's notice, and landed at Stavros, the next day, here they were attached to the 27th Division in the sector of the 80th Brigade. The 2nd R.M.L.I. went up the mountains and relieved a battalion of the Rifle Brigade. They were holding the sector from the sea, in the Gulf of Orfano to the Beshik Geul (Lake). The 27th Division were holding the line up to the eastern end of the next lake, the Langaza Geul. The troops had moved to this sector by sea, but pack transport and the guns had managed to march across the hills, along the most difficult tracks, as there were then no roads from Salonica; good roads were made later. The Brigade was employed entrenching a position on the hills; sleeping billets were made of sticks and waterproof sheets. About 20 miles in front, was a Greek Division, but no one knew which side they were going to take, and at that time the Bulgarians were hesitating on the frontier; there was no line of retreat, as the hills behind were impassable and the only tracks ran parallel to the front. Supplies came by sea from Salonica, and were landed at a pier, which was several times washed away. As related in Chapter 6, the bay was netted, so that monitors and ships bombarding could lie in safety from the submarines.

The hill air and good climate, at that time the malaria of the Struma Valley had not shown itself, did everyone a lot of good, after their trying experiences on the Gallipoli Peninsula. On 3rd April, the Battalion returned to the shore and was inspected by the Divisional General on 8th; returning to the line on 12th. They remained here until they were recalled to Mudros, to prepare to go to France, the 1st R.M.L.I. embarking on 13th and 2nd R.M.L.I. on 17th. General Trotman had gone back to Mudros a short time before to take command of the Royal Naval Division, during the absence of General Paris on leave, and Colonel Stroud remained in command of the Brigade.

During this time the Cyclist Company had resumed their training as cyclists, but in April, they were armed with two 18-pounder field guns and commenced to train as Royal Field Artillery. Under Lieutenant B. F. Scott, R.M.L.I., the two guns were sent to Smyrna Bay for some contemplated operations, but as these were abandoned, the role of Royal Field Artillery was dropped. (see also chapter 14, Long Island).

Training and football filled their time, until they embarked for France, and their further adventures are dealt with in chapter 26.

APPENDIX 1.
OFFICERS OF THE STAFF AND BATTALIONS, ROYAL MARINES, WHO LANDED IN GALLIPOLI, ON 25TH, 28TH AND 29TH APRIL, 1915.

*NOTE.-*Present at Evacuation.* For dates of Casualties see Appendix 2.

DIVISIONAL HEADQUARTERS.

G.O.C. *Major-General A. Paris, C.B., R.M.A.
G.S.O. 2. *Major E. F. P. Sketchley, RM.L.I.

1st ROYAL NAVAL BRIGADE.

G.O.C. *Brigadier-General D. Mercer, R.M.L.I.
Brigade Major. Major F. S. Wilson, R.M.L.I. (*killed.*).
"Nelson" Battalion. C.O. Lieutenant-Colonel E. E. Evelegh, RM.L.I. (*killed*).
Adjutant. Captain R. J. Carpenter, R.M.L.I. (wounded).
"Drake" Battalion. Adjutant. Captain G. Barker, R.M.L.I. (*killed*).
Q.M. Lieutenant J. Carron, R.M.L.I. (*wounded*).
"Hood" Battalion. Q.M. Lieutenant E. Nobbs, R.M.L.I. (*wounded*).

CYCLIST COMPANY.

C.O. *Major A. H. French, R.M.L.I.
*:Major N. O. Burge, R.M.L.I.
Lieutenant T. H. Jameson, R.M.L.I. (*wounded*).
Lieutenant G. R Curtis, R.M.L.I. (*wounded*).
* Lieutenant K. A. Puckle, R.M.L.I.

3rd ROYAL MARINE BRIGADE.

G.O.C. Brigadier-General C. N. Trotman, R.M.L.I. (*wounded and invalided*).
Brigade Major. Major M. C. Festing, R.M.L.I. (*invalided*).
Staff Captain. * Major C. F. Jerram.

CHATHAM BATTALION (R.M.L.I.)

C.O. : Lieutenant-Colonel C. Mc N. Parsons (*wounded*).
Lieutenant-Colonel F. R. Godfrey (*invalided*).
Adjutant: Captain W. H. P. Richards (*killed*).
Q.M.: Lieutenant C. H. Smith (invalided).
Transport: Sergeant-Major J. T. Galliford (*invalided*).
Surgeon: Surgeon M. Onslow-Ford, R.N.
Sergeant-Major: A. F. Hayward (*killed*).

"A" Company	Major C. L. Shubrick	(*invalided*).	(Reserve of Officers).
	Lieutenant A. R Chater	(*invalided*).	
	" B. H. Herford	(*killed*).	(*Temporary*).

	" C. A. Stock	(wounded).	
	" G. J. Kenny,	(wounded).	
"B" Company	Captain E. A. Hatton	(killed).	
	Lieutenant H. W. Simpson	(wounded).	
	" R A. Dallas-Brooks	(wounded).	
	" R McDonnell	(invalided).	
	" G. D. Garrett(wounded).	(Temporary).	
"C" Company	Captain S. A. Stoddart	(wounded).	(Reserve of Officers).
	Lieutenant E. G. M. Roe	(invalided).	
	" J. Cheetham	(wounded).	
	" J. H. Haddon	(wounded).	
	" L.F. W. Tayler	(wounded).	(Temporary).
"D" Company	Captain C. F. O. Graham	(wounded).	(Reserve of Officers).
	Lieutenant C. S. Grinling	(killed).	
	" J. S. S. Thorneley	(died of wounds).	
	" E. Simonds	(wounded).	
	" G. Rutherford.		
	Acting Sergt.-Major C. D. Willsher	(killed).	
Machine Guns	Lieutenant R H. Watts	(wounded).	
	" M. Curtin	(killed).	

PORTSMOUTH BATTALION.

C.O.	Lieut.-Colonel F. W. Luard	(wounded and later killed).	
	Major C. H. Hoskyns-Abrahall	(killed).	(Reserve of Officers).
Adjutant	Captain C. E. H. Morton	(died of wounds).	
Q.M.	Lieutenant E. J. Sullivan	(invalided)	
Sergeant-Major	J. F. Sutcliffe	(killed).	
Transport	Lieutenant L. W. Woodroffe	(invalided).(Temporary).	
Surgeon	Surgeon B. A. Playne, R.N.	(invalided).	
"A" Company	Captain H. H. F. Stockley	(wounded). (Reserve of Officers).	
	Captain J. C. Teague	(killed).	(Reserve of Officers).
	Lieutenant J. E. Hyland	(killed).	
	" J. H. C. Fulton	(killed).	
	" S. D. Wilmot-Sitwell	(killed).	
	" J. H. Willoughby	(invalided).	
"B" Company	Major H. G. B. Armstrong	(killed).	
	*Lieutenant D. J. Gowney	(wounded).	
	" C. Brooke-Short	(wounded).	
	" F. G. Ferguson-Davie	(killed).	(Temporary).
	" C. J. T. Black	(killed).	
	" T. A. D. Deane	(killed).	(Temporary).

"C" Company	Captain A. E. Syson	(wounded).	(Reserve of Officers).
	Lieutenant R H. Empson	(killed).	
	" B. F. Alcock	(wounded).	
	" H. N. Pearse	(invalided).	(Temporary).
	" C. H. F. Woolley	(wounded).	(Temporary).
	Acting Sergt.-Major J. F. Wingfield	(wounded).	
"D" Company	Major J. A. M. A. Clark	(wounded).	
	Lieutenant C. G. T. Domville	(invalided).	(Temporary).
	" E. C. D. Dougherty	(killed).	
	" R C. Mackenzie	(invalided).	
	" W. H. Sanders	(killed).	
	" F. A. Erskine	(killed).	(Temporary).
	Acting Sergt.-Major C. J. Gibbs	(wounded).	
Machine Guns	Captain G. P. Lathbury	(invalided).	
	" M. C. Adamson	(invalided).	
	Acting Sergt.-Major F. O. Priscott (invalided).		

PLYMOUTH BATTALION.

C.O.	Lieut.-Colonel G. E. Matthews, C.B.	(wounded).	
	Major H. D. Palmer	(wounded).	(Reserve of Officers).
Adjutant	*Captain R H. D. Lough.		
Q.M.	Lieutenant J. Battin	(invalided).	
Surgeon	Surgeon R W. Mellor, R.N.		
Sergeant-Major	W. J. Stuart	(invalided).	
No.1 Company	*Captain A. S. Tetley	(wounded).	(Reserve of Officers).
	Lieutenant J. F. Ellison, D.C.M.	(wounded).	
	" E. B. Carpenter	(died of wounds).	(Temporary).
	" O. D. Bissett	(wounded).	(Temporary).
	" J. C. Barnes	(killed).	
No.2 Company	Captain J. H. Knight	(wounded).	
	Lieutenant C. P. Tuckey	(wounded).	
	" M. H. Spicer	(wounded).	
	" D. B. Carter	(invalided).	(Temporary).
	" N. E. Burton-Fanning	(invalided).	(Temporary).
No.3 Company	Major A. E. Bewes	(wounded).	
	Lieutenant F. C. Law	(wounded).	
	" *M. C. Browne	(wounded).	(Temporary).
	" J. F. May	(killed).	
	Acting Sergt.-Major G. Wheeler	(killed).	

No.4 Company	Captain C. B. Andrews	(*killed*). (*Reserve of Officers*).
	*Lieutenant A. N. Williams	(*wounded*).
	" J. F. Richards	(*invalided*).
	" C. R.W. Lamplough	(*wounded*).
	" *T. Edwards	(*wounded*). (*Temporary*).
Machine Guns	*Lieutenant C. B. Conybeare	(*wounded*).
	*Sergeant-Major A. W. Staughton	
	" T. A. Goldring	(*invalided*).

DEAL BATTALION.

C.O.	Lieutenant-Colonel R N. Bendyshe (*killed*). Reserve of Officers.	
	*Major J. A. Tupman	(*wounded*).
Adjutant	*Lieutenant E. J. B. Tagg	(*wounded*).
Q.M.	* " T. H. Burton.	
Surgeon	Surgeon F. B. Eykyn	"
	Sergeant-Major J. Britton	" invalided.
"A" Company.	Major G. F. Muller	(*killed*).
	Lieutenant G. P. Y. Mascall	(*invalided*).
	" R. J. T. Thomson	(*wounded*).
	" E. A. Marshall	" (*Temporary*).
	Acting Sergeant-Major T. H. Clarke	(*invalided*).
"B" Company.	Captain J. Bush	(*wounded*).
	Lieutenant G. S. Perkins	(*died of wounds*).
	" S. H. E. Inskip	(*invalided*).
	" G. W. M. Grover	(*invalided*).
	" E. J. Harden	(*wounded*).
	" C. W. Fiennes	
"C" Company.	Captain F. B. A. Lawrie	(*lent to Army*).
	Lieutenant C. F. Mead	(*twice wounded and killed*).
	" J. F. Moxham	(*killed*).
	" C. P. Goodden	(*invalided*). (*Temporary*).
	" F. W. Dewhurst	(*invalided*).
	" R.H.Quill	"
	Acting Sergeant-Major A. C. Miller	(*wounded*).
"D" Company.	*Major J. A. Tupman (see above).	
	Lieutenant W. F. B. Lukis	(*wounded*).
	" E. C. Fawcett	(*invalided*). (*Temporary*).
	" S. J. Tracey	" "
	" H. L. Frossard	(*twice wounded and invalided*).
	" C. Q. Parsons	(*wounded*).
	Acting Sergeant-Major W. A. Pinkerton (*invalided*).	

Machine Guns. Lieutenant H. Millet (*wounded and invalided*). (*Temporary*).
" K. A. Longuet-Higgins (*killed*).
*Acting Sergeant-Major E. Bastin.

APPENDIX 2.
OFFICER CASUALTIES IN DARDANELLES.
KILLED IN ACTION.

R.M.L.I.

Major H. G. B. Armstrong	6/5/15	Anzac.
Captain C. B. Andrews	11/5/15	Helles.
Major C. H. Hoskyns-Abrahall	3/5/15	Anzac.
Lieutenant-Colonel R. N. Bendyshe	1/5/15	"
Major C. F. Barber	13/5/15	H.M.S. *Goliath*.
Captain R. G. Burton	18/3/15	H.M.S. *Irresistible*.
" C. G. Billing	16/6/15	Helles.
" G. Barker	29/4/15	"
Lieutenant M. Curtin	3/5/15	Anzac.
" E. B. Carpenter	. . .	Helles.
" J. C. Barnes	11/5/15	"
" H. C. T. Black	3/5/15	Anzac.
" T. A. Deane	3/5/15	"
" F. G. Ferguson-Davie	3/5/15	"
" E. C. B. Dougherty	13/7/15	Helles.
" F. A. Erskine	3/5/15	Anzac.
" R. W. H. Empson	30/4/15	"
Lieutenant-Colonel E. G. Evelegh	13/7/15	Helles.
Lieutenant J. H. C. Fulton	3/5/15	Anzac.
" C. S. Grinling	3/5/15	"
Major J. Grover	23/6/15	Helles.
Lieutenant A. F. Hayward	3/5/15	Anzac.
" K. L. Higgins	2/5/15	"
" B. H. Herford	3/5/15	"
Captain E. A. Hatton	30/4/15	"
Lieutenant J. E. Hyland	3/5/15	"
Second-Lieutenant P. L. Jermain	23/6/15	Helles.
Colonel F. W. Luard	13/7/15	"
Lieutenant J. F. May	25/4/15	"Y" Beach
" C. F. Mead	13/12/15	Helles
Captain C. E. H. Morton	3/5/15	Anzac (*Died of wounds at* [*Alexandria*).
Major G. F. Muller	1/5/15	"
Lieutenant J. F. Moxham	30/4/15	"
" G. S. Perkins	23/6/15	Helles (*Died of wounds* [23/11/15).

Captain W. H. P. Richards	3/5/15	Anzac
Lieutenant C. E. Robinson	8/11/15	Dardanelles, attached R.N.A.S.
" E. St. V. Ryan	____	H.M.S. *Swiftsure*. (*Died of Disease*)
" W. H. Sanders	3/5/15	Anzac .
Captain J. C. Teague	30/4/15	"
Lieutenant J. S. S. Thornely	24/7/15	Helles (*Died of wounds*).
Major F. S. Wilson	24/5/15	" (*Brigade Major, 1st [Brigade.*)
Lieutenant C. White	27/5/15	Helles.
" W. D. Wilmot-Sitwell	13/7/15	"
Surgeon F. H. Rees, RN. (Portsmouth)		" (*Died of wounds*)
Sergeant-Major C. D. Willsher	25/5/15	Helles.
Sergeant-Major G. Wheeler	13/5/15	"

R.M. Artillery.

Captain C. H. Collet, D.S.O.	19/8/15	Imbros., attached R.N.A.S
" H. J. Pace	9/8/15	Helles. (*Died of Disease*)

Divisional Engineers.
  Lieutenant H. C. Amos.
    " A. M. Oakden. (*Died of wounds*).
    " R O. Tollast. (*Died of wounds*).

WOUNDED.

R.M.L.I.

Lieutenant E. L. Andrews.		
" B. F. Alcock	1/5/15	Anzac.
" O. D. Bisset	25/4/15	"Y" Beach.
Major A. E. Bewes	25/4/15	"
Lieutenant M. C. Browne	11/4/15	Helles.
Lieutenant & Qr.-Master J. W. Carroll	29/5/15	"
" C. G. Conybeare	25/4/15	"Y" Beach.
" G. R Curtis	29/5/15	Helles.
" J. Cheetham	6/6/15	"
Captain W. de T. L. Clark	13/7/15	"
Major J. A. M. A. Clark	13/7/15	"
Lieutenant E. B. Carpenter	11/4/15	"
Captain H. Channer	13/7/15	"
Lieutenant R.A. Dallas-Brooks	18/6/15	"
" T. Edwards	25/5/15	"
" J. F. Ellison	11/4/15	"
Major C. F. Graham	3/5/15	Anzac.
Lieutenant D. J. Gowney	14/7/15	Helles.

" J. H. Haddon	30/4/15	Anzac.
" C. Brooke-Short	30/4/15	"
" H. L. Frossard (twice)	19/5/15 & 11/6/15	Helles.
" T. H. Jameson	4/6/15	"
" G. J. Kenny	13/6/15	"
" A. G. Kyle	____	"
Captain J. H. Knight	25/4/15	"Y" Beach.
Lieutenant F. C. Law	25/4/15	"
" C. R W. Lamplough	25/5/15	Helles.
Colonel F. W. Luard	3/5/15	Anzac.
Lieutenant W. B. F. Lukis	15/6/15	Helles.
Lieutenant G. D. Lowdell (twice)		
" E. A. Marshall		Anzac
" H. Millett	____	
" A. C. Miller	12/6/15	Helles.
" C. F. Mead (twice)	19/5/15 & 2/10/15	"
Colonel G. E. Matthews	12/7/15	"
Lieutenant & Qr.-Mr. E. Nobbs (twice)	23/6/15	"
Major H. D. Palmer	25/4/15	"Y" Beach.
Lieutenant-Colonel C. Mc N. Parsons	28/6/15	Helles.
Lieutenant C. Q. Parsons	6/6/15	"
Colonel J. R. H. Oldfield	4/6/15	"
Major C. E. Risk, attached R.N.A.S.	1/5/15	Anzac.
Lieutenant W. J. Stuart	9/7/15	Helles.
Captain A. E. Syson	6/5/15	Anzac
" H. F. Stockley	3/5/15	"
" C. A. Stock	30/4/15	"
" S. A. Stoddart	6/6/15	Helles.
Lieutenant M. H. Spicer (twice) 1	1/4/15 & 13/7/15	"
H. W. Simpson	4/5/15	Anzac.
Brigadier-General C. N. Trotman	16/5/15	Helles.
Captain A. S. Tetley	11/4/15	"
Major J. A. Tupman	21/12/15	"
Lieutenant A. N. Williams	11/4/15	"
" H. W. Wilby	27/6/15	"
" L. F. Tayler	13/7/15	"
" R. H. Watts	30/4/15	Anzac.
" E. Simonds	30/4/15	"
Second-Lieutenant L. A. Unwin	8/11/15	Helles.
" C. H. F. Woolley	13/7/15	"
Sergeant-Major J. Britton	____	
" F. J. Wingfield	3/5/15	Anzac.

	C. J. Gibbs	14/5/15	Helles.

Divisional Engineers.
    Lieutenant J. S. Marshall   Helles.
          "   A. H. Roe   ——   "

Divisional Train.
    Lieutenant E. C. Lovatt   ——   Anzac.

APPENDIX 3.
HONOURS AND REWARDS FOR GALLIPOLI.

Victoria Cross.   Lance-Corporal W. R Parker (Portsmouth), R.M.L.I.

K.C.B.   Colonel (Temporary Major-General) A. Paris, C.B., R.M.A., and promotion to Major-General for Distinguished Service.

C.B.
Brigadier-General C. N. Trotman, R.M.L.I.
          "   D. Mercer, R.M.L.I.
Lieutenant-Colonel C. Mc N. Parsons, R.M.L.I.

C.M.G.
Colonel G. E. Matthews, C.B., RM.L.I.
Lieutenant-Colonel E. J. Stroud, R.M.L.I.
          "   A. R.H. Hutchison, RM.L.I.
          "   L. Wilson, D.S.O., M.P., R.M.L.I.
Colonel F. H. Sykes, R.M. attached R.N.A.S.
Major A. E. Bewes, R.M.L.I.

D.S.O.
Major E. F. P. Sketchley, R.M.L.I.
Captain R.D. Lough, R.M.L.I.
Lieutenant-Colonel Kennedy-Craufurd-Stuart, R.M. (Indian Army).
Captain H. N. Laws, R.M. Medical Unit.
Captain E. L. Gerrard, RM.L.I. attached R.N.A.S.
Major J. H. Howell Jones, R.M.A. attached Ordnance Corps.

D.S.C.
Lieutenant B. F. Alcock, RM.L.I.
      "   F. C. Law, RM.L.I.
      "   M. C. Browne, R.M.L.I.
      "   J. Cheetham, R.M.L.I.
Captain G. P. Lathbury, R.M.L.I.
      "   B. G. Weller, R.M.L.I.

Brevet Lieutenant-Colonel.
>Major J. A. Tupman, R.M.L.I.
>" J. A. M. A. Clark, R.M.L.I.
>" N. O. Burge, R.M.L.I.

Brevet Major.
>Captain M. C. Festing, R.M.L.I.

Conspicuous Gallantry Medal.
>Private T. H. Hoskins (Chatham), R.M.L.I.
>Sergeant C. J. Braddock (Chatham), R.M.L.I.
>Bugler E. Sillence (Chatham), R.M.L.I.
>Lance-Corporal E. A. Grindey (Portsmouth), R.M.L.I.
>Private M. Turner (Portsmouth), R.M.L.I.
>Lance-Corporal J. G. Way (Portsmouth), R.M.L.I.
>Corporal F. Pilgrim (Portsmouth), R.M.L.I.

Distinguished Service Medal.
>Corporal J. McDowell (Plymouth), R.M.L.I.
>Sergeant A. H. Hunting (Portsmouth), R.M.L.I.
>Corporal A. R Grainger (Chatham), R.M.L.I.
>Private F. Hunt (Portsmouth), R.M.L.I.
>Private C. R. Bell (Chatham), R.M.L.I.
>Sergeant E. C. Bonnet (Portsmouth), R.M.L.I.
>Sergeant J. C. Dunn (Portsmouth), R.M.L.I.
>Private R E. Owens (Plymouth), R.M.L.I.
>" M.W. Minter (Portsmouth), R.M.L.I.
>Sergeant J. J. Hughes (Portsmouth), R.M.L.I.
>Lce.-Corpl. D. G. Denyer (Portsmouth), R.M.L.I.
>" A. E. Hawkes (Portsmouth), R.M.L.I.
>Private Harry Mills (Plymouth), R.M.L.I.
>Private (Acting Sergeant) F. E. V. Wilcox (Portsmouth), RM.L.I.
>" Percy Berry (Plymouth), R.M.L.I.
>Col.-Sergt. F. Wolstenholme (Plymouth), R.M.L.I.

Medaille Militaire.
>Col.-Sergt. A. Woolbridge (Portsmouth), R.M.L.I.
>Private W. T. Ingram (Portsmouth), R.M.L.I.
>" R Milne (Portsmouth), R.M.L.I.
>Lce.-Corpl. Griffiths (Portsmouth), R.M.L.I.
>Corporal. A. E. Gannor (Portsmouth), R.M.L.I.
>Acting Sergeant-Major R Bell.
>Lce.-Corpl. R McDowall (Portsmouth), R.M.L.I.
>Private G. Smith (Plymouth). R.M.L.I.
>" R. D. Crowborough (Portsmouth), R.M.L.I.
>" R McDowall (Portsmouth), R.M.L.I.

Private S. Hillsley (Portsmouth), R.M.L.I.
" T. E. Jones (Portsmouth), R.M.L.I.

Mentioned in Dispatches. (*All R.M.L.I. except otherwise noted*).

Maj.-Gen. Sir A. Paris, RM.A. (three times).
Brig.-Gen. D. Mercer (twice).
Brig.-Gen. C. N. Trotman.
Capt. M. C. Festing.
Capt. C. F. Jerram.
Capt. F. S. Wilson (killed).
Lieut.-Col. E. G. Evelegh (twice); (killed).
Maj. J. A. Tupman.
Capt. & Adjt. W. H. P. Richards.
Lieut. J. Cheetham.
Lieut. C. White.
Sergt. L. Oakey.
Corpl. W. Munday (Chatham).
Bugler E. Sillence (Chatham).
Pte. E. Berry (Chatham).
Pte. C. J. Braddock (Chatham).
Pte. F. Farmer (Chatham).
Col. F. W. Luard (twice); (killed).
Maj. J. A. Clark (twice).
Maj. H. St. G. B. Armstrong (killed).
Capt. D. J. Gowney.
Lieut. W. H. Sanders (killed).
Lieut. B. W. H. Empson (killed).
2nd-Lieut. A. B. F. Alcock.
Capt. H. W. Channer.
Capt. A. E. Syson.
Actg.-Sergt.-Major C. J. Gibbs (Portsmouth).
Sergt. E. J. Lamacraft (Portsmouth).
Sergt. J. J. Welsh (Portsmouth); (Died of wounds.)
Sergt. F. Wilcox (Portsmouth).
Pte. H. Moss (Portsmouth).
Col. G. E. Matthews.
Maj. A. E. Bewes.
2nd-Lieut. C. B. Conybeare.
Lce.-Cpl. W. Kirbell (Plymouth).
Sergt. G. E. Wills (Plymouth),
Pte. J. C. Morgan (Plymouth).
Lieut. H. Millett.
Capt. A. S. Tetley.
Lieut. J. F. May (killed).
Sergt. Maj. G. Wheeler.
Sergt. G. V. Ollier (Plymouth).
Sergt. W. A. Sherwood (Plymouth).
Pte. A. R Duckworth (Plymouth).
Pte. E. Owen (Plymouth).
Pte. E. Stockham (Plymouth).
Capt. R D. H. Lough.
Capt. E. J. B. Tagg.
Maj. N. O. Burge.
Lieut. C. A. Hepburn.
Lieut. E. Bastin.
Sergt.-Maj. A. Hurford (Plymouth).
Bd.-Mtr. W. E. Faithful (Drake).
Lieut. R J. Carpenter.
Lieut.-Col. L. Wilson, D.S.O., M.P.
Clr.-Sergt. E. E. Marlow (Chatham).
Col. C. Mc N. Parsons.
2nd-Lieut. A. R. Chater.
Cr.-Sergt. G. H. Bruce (Chatham),
Cr.-Sergt. H. Hoare (Chatham).
Pte. W. Daborn (Chatham).
Capt. H. H. F. Stockley.
Actg.-Sergt.-Maj. W. Gwynne.
Sergt. J. L. Pickering (Plymouth).
Cr.-Sergt. F. Masters (Chatham).
Pte. S. Downey (Chatham).
Lieut. E. G. Roe.
Lieut. R A. Dallas-Brooks.
Lieut. L. C. T. Room.
Lieut. G. Rutherford.
Capt. C. G. Farquharson.
Capt. V. D. Loxley.
Sergt. S. J. Hutchings (Plymouth).
Pte. F. S. Paull (Plymouth).
Cpl. R J. Staite (Portsmouth).
Sergt. W. Rimmer (Plymouth).

Cr.-Sergt. A. Yarrow (Portsmouth).
Pte. S. W. V. Butt (Plymouth).

Pte. H. Atkins (Plymouth).
Lieut.-Col. St. G. B. Armstrong.
Lieut.-Cot. E. J. Stroud (twice).
Capt. A. K. Evans.
Lieut.-Col. A. R H. Hutchison.
Cpl. R McDowell (Portsmouth).
Pte. Geo. Smith (Plymouth).
Sergt. A. H. Hunting (Portsmouth).
Actg.-Sergt. Major R Bell (Plymouth).
Cpl. E. A. Grindey (Portsmouth).
Pte. M. Turner (Portsmouth).
Cpl. F. Pilgrim (Portsmouth).
Pte. T. H. Hoskins (Chatham).
Maj. E. F. Powys Sketchley (twice).
Capt. G. J. T. Walmesley.
Actg.-Sergt.-Maj. W. J. Darlow (Chatham).
Lieut. J. A. Gates (Nelson).
Lieut. & Qr.-Mr. E. Nobbs (Hood).
Maj. F. J. Saunders D.S.O.
Q.M.S. W. White (Chatham).
Pte. J. J. Whelan (Chatham).
Lieut.-Col. G. J. Mullins.

Capt. T. H. Burton.
Capt. J. C. Farmer.
Lieut. T. A. Goldring.
Lieut. C. W. Fiennes.

Lieut. F. W. Dewhurst.
Lieut. J. Pearson.

Maj. A. H. French, D.S.O.
Cr.-Sergt. C. W. E. Baker
    (Portsmouth); Cyclist Co.
Lieut. T. H. Jameson.
Sergt. G. Gardner (Chatham).
Sergt. P. R McLeish, R.M.A.; Cyclist Co.
Maj. Hon. A. V. Peel.
Capt. G. P. Lathbury.
Bd.-Cpl. J. Allen (Drake).
Pte. R McIlveny (Chatham).
Pte. E. Dowson (Chatham).
Lieut. C. H. F. Woolley.
Lieut. F. A. Erskine (killed).
Lieut. E. C. B. Dougherty (killed).
Sergt. J. C. Dunn (Portsmouth).
Sergt. M. W. Minter (Portsmouth).
Pte. C. R Bell (Portsmouth).
Pte. R H. Johnson (Portsmouth).
Capt. B. G. Weller.
Lieut. M. C. Browne, D.S.O.
Lieut. F. C. Law.
Cpl. A. R Grainger (Chatham).
Pte. J. McDowall (Plymouth).
Pte. J. H. Wilks (Plymouth).
Pte. P. E. Brugnier (Plymouth);
    (Died of wounds).
Pte. A. Prince (Plymouth); (Died of wounds).
Pte. W. Scott (Plymouth); (killed).
Pte. H. Mills (Plymouth); (Died of wounds).
Lce.-Sergt. F. Wolstenholme
    (Plymouth); Cyclist Co.
Lce.-Cpl. W. A. Wilson (Portsmouth).

CHAPTER 12.

ZEEBRUGGE. 4th BATTALION ROYAL MARINES.

Formation of the Battalion - Training-Inspection by H.M. the King-Plan of the Operations - Embarkation-Battalion Orders - List of Officers - First Attempts - The Operation on the Mole - Incidents - H.M.S. Iris - Casualties - Award of Victoria Cross - Honours and Awards - Letter from His Majesty - Dispersal.

IN November, 1917, owing to the disturbed state of Ireland, another Battalion was ordered to be raised, to be composed of one Company Royal Marine Artillery and one from each of the R.M.L.I. Divisions; but they were not employed at that time; and though the Battalion was nominally in existence, officers and men were taken for general draft. In December, owing to the requirements of the Royal Marine Artillery Brigades, the Commandant, Royal Marine Artillery requested that the Royal Marine Artillery Company should be disbanded - which was done.

The plans for the blocking of Zeebrugge and Ostend were, however, now beginning to take shape at the Admiralty, and on 11th January, 1918, the proposals for employing the Royal Marines in the operation were discussed between the First Lord, First Sea Lord and the Adjutant General, Royal Marines. Orders were therefore issued that drafting was to cease from the Battalion, and that the three R.M.L.I. Companies should be completed to strength and placed under training at the several Headquarters. Lieut.-Colonel F. E. Chichester, R.M.L.I.. was appointed to command and drew up the scheme of training.

The actual orders for the formation of the Battalion were issued on 6th February, Major B. N. Elliot, D.S.O. was appointed second in command, Captain A. R. Chater, Adjutant, and Lieutenant F. J. Hore, Quartermaster. Regimental Sergeant-Major C. J. Thatcher (Ports)[20].

On 10th February, Lieut.-Colonel Chichester to his bitter disappointment, was found to be medically unfit and Major Elliot was appointed to the command, being relieved as second in command by Major A. A. Cordner.

On 13th February the Headquarters were ordered to assemble at Chatham, but left for Deal on 21st, where the Battalion was concentrated.

Meanwhile information was received that volunteers for the Battalion from the Royal Marine Detachments of the Grand Fleet were being sent to Headquarters; these consisted of two Officers and 50 men, Royal Marine Artillery and two Officers and 80 men, R.M.L.I. The R.M.L.I. were incorporated in the companies of their own Divisions and the Royal Marine Artillery were formed into a Trench Mortar Section under their own officers.

The strength of the Battalion was fixed at:-

Battalion Head Quarters	4 Officers,	1 Warrant Officer,	46 N.C.O.s and Men.
Machine Gun Section	2 "		56 R.M.L.I.
Trench Mortar Section	2 "		51 R.M.A.*[21]
Chatham Company "A"	6 "		165 R.M.L.I.
Portsmouth Company "B"	6 "		165 R.M.L.I.
Plymouth Company "C"	6 "		165 R.M.L.I.
Medical Staff	2 "		6 R.N.
	28	1	654.

---
20. With the exception of Captain Dallas-Brooks and Lieut. Rigby, all Officers and Warrant Officers were R.M.L.I.
21. Added to later by two crews of Royal Marine Light Infantry consisting of one Officer and 30 N.C.O,s and men.

The Trench Mortar Section under Captain R. Dallas-Brooks with Lieutenant C. N. Rigby consisted of :-

R.M.A. One crew for 11 inch Howitzer.
Two crews for 7. 5 inch Howitzers.
Two crews for 1 ½ pr. Pom-poms.
Two crews for "Stokes" Trench Mortars (after the accident on 1st April, one crew was replaced by volunteers from R.M.L.I. at Deal).

R.M.L.I. Two crews for "Stokes" Trench Mortars. Lieut. D. Broadwood.
The Machine Gun Section was composed of :-
Captain C. B. Conybeare and 2nd Lieut. W. E. Sillitoe.
3 Sergeants, 3 Corporals and 52 Privates of all R.M.L.I. Divisions with 2 "Vickers" and 4 "Lewis" Guns.
Each platoon had one "Lewis" gun section.

It was of the highest importance that no rumour should get about as to the task for which the Battalion was designated; it was therefore given out that the Battalion was to be detached to the Royal Naval Division in France for a special raid. In order that training might be carried out as realistically as possible, this raid was described as "a mopping up of and consolidating the position occupied by an enemy advanced ammunition dump and store depot and holding the same during the time necessary for specially detailed Royal Engineers to prepare the various points for demolition; when the object is accomplished the battalion will be withdrawn." In order to reproduce the conditions that would probably be met with, the ground was supposed to be a canal bed, which had been drained, and in order

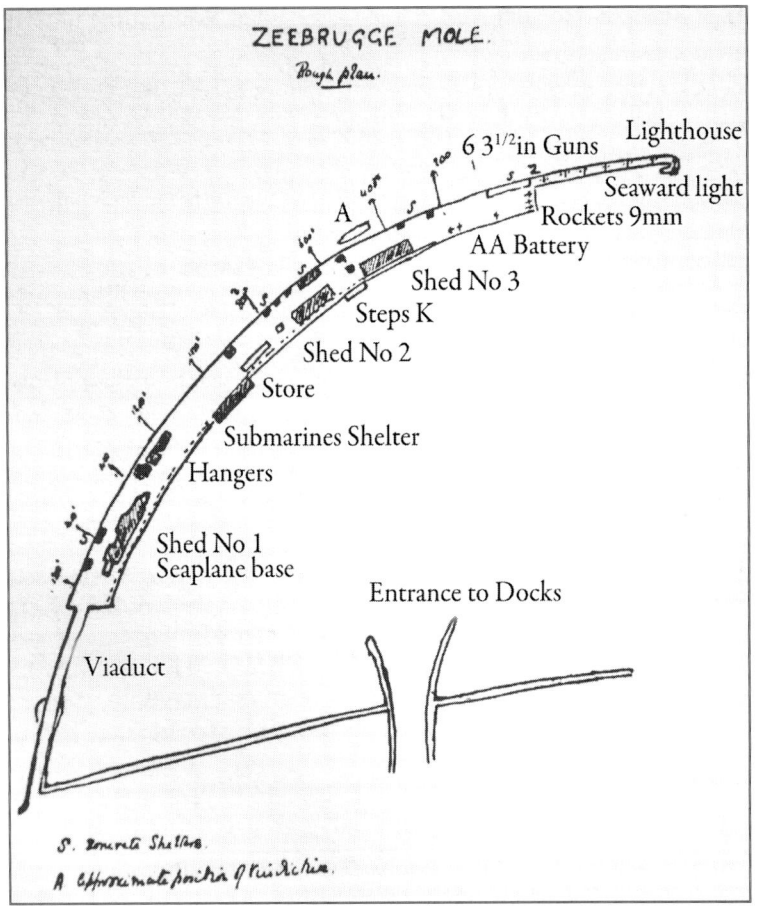

PLAN 11

to simulate the drop from the raised parapet of the Mole to the main platform, one of the canal banks was imagined to be cut down vertically for 15 feet. The ground was taped out on Freedown at Deal, as accurately as possible, from aerial photographs of the Zeebrugge Mole and the attack was rehearsed under every possible combination of circumstances.

As the ll-inch and 7.5-inch Howitzers were new weapons, the Royal Marine Artillery Officers and men, except those for the Stokes mortars, who were trained at Deal, were sent to Shoeburyness on 23rd February for instruction in their handling.

The machine gun section, which was formed at Gosport and trained for a few days at Browndown, arrived at Deal on 27th.

On 2nd March, the Battalion was inspected by the Adjutant-General Sir David Mercer, and on 7th March, H.M. the King inspected the Depot, Royal Marines at Deal, and the Battalion marched past him, but the actual secret of their destination was not even imparted to him.

On 1st April the Royal Marine Artillery Stokes mortars had a serious accident when at practice, as one gun burst, killing four men and wounding five, they were replaced by volunteers from the R.M.L.I. at Deal.

In order that the operations of the Royal Marine Battalion may be understood it is necessary to give an outline of the operations, the full details of which are so well described in the book of Captain Carpenter, V.C., R.N. who commanded the *Vindictive*.

The main object of the expedition was to block the harbours and canals at Zeebrugge and Ostend, which were being used by the Germans as sub-marine bases, by sinking blockships in the entrance to the locks; all the other operations were subsidiary to this main object and were directed to facilitate the task of the blockships. A further subsidiary object was to do as much damage to the Mole and shipping at Zeebrugge as the time available would allow,

The Mole was a long granite structure, with sheds and concrete shelters for aircraft, crews for the batteries, etc. On the seaward side the Mole rose to a height of about 30 feet above high water; on this side was a raised pathway, about 10 feet wide with a railing; from this pathway there was a drop of nearly 16 feet to the main platform of the Mole. At the seaward end was a battery of three 4.1 inch guns, from this end there also ran a continuation of the raised pathway, leading to the lighthouse, on which were mounted six 3'5-inch guns. The Mole was connected to the shore by a wooden viaduct, which was the point selected to be blown up by the submarine.

There were three large sheds on the Mole; No.1 the Base at the shore end, No.2 rather more than half-way along and No. 3 near the sea end; between No.3 and the battery was a battery of 1½ -inch anti-aircraft guns.

This is no place to describe all the wonderful and elaborate arrangements for the blockships and for covering the operations by monitors, destroyers, submarines, C.M.B.'s and motor launches, and all the myriad of small craft necessary for the successful conduct of the operation, planned by Sir Roger Keyes and his Staff; this record only attempts to deal with the action of the storming parties on the Mole.

In the operations other than those of the storming parties the Royal Marines were only engaged in the monitors, the *Erebus* and *Terror* bombarding Zeebrugge and the *Marshal Soult, Lord Clive, Prince Eugene* and *General Craufrod* bombarding Ostend; whilst the Harwich Force kept the ring to seaward. The Royal Marine Artillery Siege Guns covering Dunkirk also participated in the bombardment of Ostend.

The object of the storming parties was to destroy the batteries of guns on the seaward end of the Mole, so as to prevent their interfering with the blockships; they were then to advance along the Mole towards the shore and do as much damage as possible. The seamen party was also if possible, to show red flares by the lighthouse as a guide to the blockships H.M.S. *Thetis*, *Intrepid* and *Iphigenia*.

The storming parties were embarked in H.M.S. *Vindictive*, Captain A. F. B. Carpenter, H.M.S. *Iris*, Commander V. Gibbs, and *Daffodil* Lieut.-Commander S. H. Campbell; the *Vindictive* was one of the cruisers originally built by Lord Fisher as "Fleet Rams" and was armed with 6-inch guns; she had been specially prepared for her task; the boat deck was planked over and provided with broad ramps leading to the upper deck, in order that the storming parties could charge straight up, and on the boat deck 14 narrow brows had been hinged to her port side so as to enable the stormers to reach the top of the Mole. Her foretop had been strengthened and armed to enable the guns to fire over the Mole, and she had been sandbagged and strengthened as much as possible to fit her for her difficult task.

The *Iris* and *Daffodil* were two ferry boats that used to ply, and still do so, across the Mersey at Birkenhead, and had been similarly adapted for their task[22].

It was planned that the *Vindictive*, after towing the *Iris* and *Daffodil* across the Channel, should be secured against the Mole so that her stern was about 200 feet from the seaward end of the Mole at the broad part; she actually secured about the position marked "A" in the plan; the *Iris* was to pass ahead of her and secure to the Mole also; whilst the *Daffodil*, going ahead full speed, was to push the *Vindictive* broadside on the Mole and keep her there.

The *Vindictive* was to engage the Lighthouse battery with her 6-inch guns and the Mole with her howitzers, Stokes guns, Pom-poms, Lewis guns, etc., whilst the Stokes guns in the *Iris* and the Vickers guns were also to engage the Mole until landed.

In addition to the 4th Battalion Royal Marine storming party, there was also a seamen storming party under Captain F. C. Halahan, R.N., consisting of six Officers and 150 men, divided into three groups of 50 men each, two groups were in the *Vindictive* and one in the *Iris*; there was also a demolition party of 50 seamen under Lieutenant Dickenson, R.N., in the *Daffodil*, to which was attached a party of 22 N.C.O.s and men (Royal Marines) from the 4th Battalion.

The duties of the seamen storming parties were to work the additional Stokes guns in the ships, and to land them on the Mole if ordered; to place the gangways in the *Vindictive* and the scaling ladders in the *Iris*; and to help in securing the ships; to form the first flight on the Mole and fight their way out to the Lighthouse and light the flares at the end of the Mole as a guide to the blockships and finally to cover the retirement of the ships with smoke bombs from the Stokes guns.

In the *Vindictive* there were six Stokes guns on the forecastle, four manned by the seamen, and two by the Royal Marines; six Stokes guns on the boat deck were manned by the seamen until they joined the storming party. After getting ashore, three sections of seamen were to form for the attack on the 4.1-inch battery moving along the raised pathway, and the other section from the *Vindictive* was to assist the Iris group in securing that vessel and were then to form the reserve at headquarters.

The seamen demolition party, with the Royal Marines as carriers were also divided into three sections; one section was to act with the seamen party in destroying the guns when captured, and the others to work under Lieut.-Colonel Elliot in creating damage on the Mole.

The Orders for the Royal Marine Battalion were as follows :—

---

22. In commemoration of the part they played these two vessels are now called the Royal Iris and Royal Daffodil. and an inscription recording the fact has been placed on a bronze tablet in each vessel.

BATTALION ORDER No.2.

By LIEUTENANT-COLONEL B. N. ELLIOT, *Commanding 4th Battalion Royal Marines.*

H.M.S. *Hindustan*, 8th April, 1918.

1.-DISPOSITION.

    In *Vindictive*.   Battalion Headquarters.
                      " B " Portsmouth Company.
                      " C " Plymouth Company.
                      Lewis Guns Section of Machine Gun Section (Captain Conybeare)
                      R.M.A. Howitzers, Pom-poms and Stokes Guns.
                      (Captain Dallas-Brooks and Lieutenant Rigby).
    In the *Iris*.   " A " (Chatham) Company. (Major C. Eagles, D.S.O.).
                      Vickers Gun Section. (2nd Lieutenant Sillitoe).
                      2 Stokes Guns. (Lieutenant Broadwood).

2.- The position to be attacked and held by the Battalion in this operation is the Zeebrugge Mole. The object of the attack is the destruction of the guns on the seaward end of the Mole, and the causing of as much damage to the *materiel* on the Mole as practicable. A seamen demolition party under the command of Lieutenant Dickenson and Sub-Lieutenant Chevallier, R.N. has been organised for this purpose.

3.- The operation will be carried out as follows :-

"C" Company*[23] (Major Weller, D.S.C.), less two platoons, will carry out phase 1, and will disembark first and establish a *point-d'appui* by occupying and consolidating the Mole to the West (shore) end up to and including the No.3 shed and the A.A. battery, clearing up all points of resistance, as far as point 600. Nos. 11 and 12 Platoons under Captain Palmer will turn to the left and advance towards the battery and capture the guns.

"B" Company (Captain Bamford) will then disembark, and forming up under the cover of "C" Company attack along the Mole, securing the bomb ammunition dumps, shed and shelters as far as point 1200; the end of this sector is to be secured and held at all costs. The advance is to be covered by overhead fire from the 2 Vickers' guns of the Machine gun section operating along the raised pathway.

"A" Company (Major Eagles) when disembarked from *Iris* is to follow "B" Company and carry out the fourth phase, that is the occupation of the remainder of the Mole including the aeroplane base, and the attached quarters for aircraft personnel, actual length of sector is 650 yards. The advance is to be covered by the 4 Lewis guns of the Machine gun section operating from the raised pathway which are also to co-operate in the defence of the position; the two Stokes guns from the *Iris* are to be landed and act under orders of O.C. "A" Company.

The signal section is to establish a headquarters station and one station each with "A" and "B" Companies using the telephone.

4.- Officers commanding units are to imbue their commands with the idea of carrying the operation through with the bayonet; rifle fire, machine gun fire, and bomb throwing are only to be resorted to when necessary to break down enemy resistance.

5.- The position of the most advanced unit is to be marked by the firing of Red Very Lights. These will be the principal guide in the control of the covering fire afforded by the *Vindictive*.

---

23. The Companies had drawn lots to be the first to land and" C " Company had won.

6.- The seamen co-operating in the assault have orders to confine their movements to the raised pathway on the outer side of the Mole. They will endeavour to enfilade the three 4 inch guns from the footway. The success or failure of the attempt to silence these guns will affect the action to be taken by the units carrying out phase 1.

7.- It must be firmly impressed on all ranks that the capture of the fortified zone at the seaward end of the Mole is the first essential to ensure the success of the entire enterprise, but that the task allotted to the Battalion does not end there; every endeavour must be made to carry out the later phases of the operations; an elaborate scheme of demolition of material has been prepared; this scheme cannot be carried out unless the demolition parties are covered by the Battalion.

Nothing therefore except the strongest enemy opposition or the obvious lack of time must stop the advance along the Mole.

8.- A number of torpedo craft, submarines and other auxiliary craft including a Depot ship usually lie alongside the inner side of the Mole. It may be expected that the majority of these will get under way during the aerial attacks. Any craft found alongside must be cleared by units during their advance. Every assistance is to be given to the demolition party in dealing with these craft.

9.- The extent of the operation and the time at which it is to commence withdrawal will be regulated by the time for the *Vindictive* to leave the Mole, which varies on the different nights on which the operation may be carried out, and Officers will be notified.

10.-(*Refers to Instructions for Demolitions.*)

11.-The Battalion Quarter-Master will establish an ammunition and bomb dump on the Mole abreast of the ship; demands for ammunition and bombs should be sent to Battalion headquarters or to this dump.

12.-All wounded, both stretcher cases and walking, should be evacuated straight to the *Vindictive*. The Battalion Medical Officers will make the necessary arrangements for transporting from the Mole to the ship.

13.-Battalion headquarters will be established in a favourable position on the Mole abreast of the ship. Reports should be sent to this position which will be indicated by a white flag.

(Signed) A. R. CHATER, *Captain and Adjutant, R.M.L.I.*

The dress was to be drill order (khaki) with 60 rounds of ammunition, steel helmet, gas respirator in gas alert position, swimming belt, under tunic; Officers and men landing wore india-rubber soled gymnasia shoes to prevent slipping.

Each platoon was armed with a Lewis gun and a flame thrower; every man carried Mills hand grenades, and some had weighted clubs for close fighting. Each platoon carried two ladders and four ropes to enable them to get down off the raised pathway, and there were also heavy scaling ladders in charge of the Battalion Sergeant-Major to be placed from the pathway to the main platform of the Mole which were to be put in position by No.7 platoon.

Such were the orders, and their execution forms one of the stories which will live as long as Britain is a Nation.

The marching-out state of the Battalion shows :-

28 Officers, 1 Warrant Officer, 704 other ranks Royal Marines, with 2 Officers (medical) 6 other ranks Royal Marines.

ZEEBRUGGE

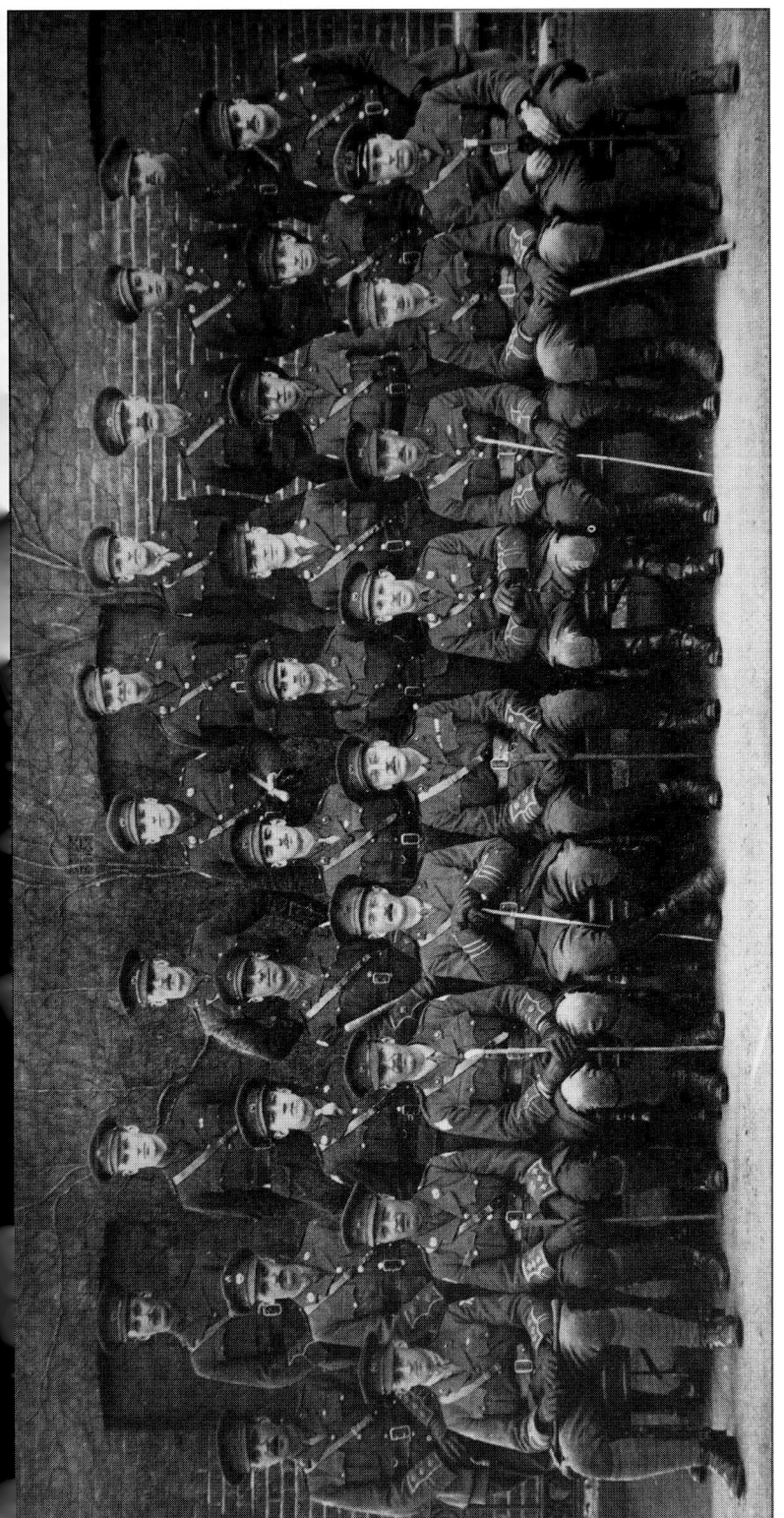

By permission of *Globe & Laurel*. [*Photograph by Sawyer, Deal.*]

OFFICERS OF THE 4TH BATTALION, ROYAL MARINES.

Back Row.-2nd Lt. H. B. LOVATT (wounded) Surgeon F. P. POCOCK, M.C., R.N. Lt. & Qr.-Mr. F. J. HORE (wounded). Lt. B. S. CLAUDET. Lt. D. BROADWOOD. Lt. R. G. O. STANTON (died of wounds). Lt. G. UNDERHILL. Lt. H. A. P. DE BERRY. Lt. S. H. E. INSKIP (killed).
Second Row.-Captain J. M. PALMER, D.S.C. (missing). Lt. C. R. W. LAMPLOUGH. Lt. J. JACKSON (killed). 2nd Lt. A. G. NORRIS. Lt. W. H. DOLLERY (killed). Lt. T. F. V. COOKE (wounded). Lt. W. E. SILLITOE (killed). 2nd Lt. W. C. BLOXSOM (wounded). 2nd Lt. W. H. BOXALL. Captain C. P. TUCKEY (missing).
Front Row.–Captain C. B. CONEYBEARE (wounded). Captain R. L. DEL STROTHER (wounded). Major C. E. C. EACLES. D.S.O. (killed). Major A.A. CORDNER (killed).
Lt.-Col. B. N. ELLIOT, D.S.O. (killed). Captain and Adjutant A. R. CHATER. Major B. G. WELLER. Captain E. BAMFORD, D.S.O. Surgeon H. ST.C.COLSON, R.N.
Note.-Lieutenants DALLAS-BROOKS and RIGBY, R.M.A. were at Shoeburyness.

The Officers of the Battalion who embarked were :-

Commanding Officer.	Lieut.-Colonel B. N. Elliot, D.S.O.
2nd in Command	Major A. A. Cordner.
Adjutant	Captain A. R. Chater.
Quarter-Master	Lieutenant F. J. Hore.
Signalling Officer	Lieutenant H. A. P. de Berry.
Trench Mortar Section	Captain R A. Dallas-Brooks, R.M.A.
	Lieutenant C. N. Rigby, R.M.A.
	Lieutenant D. Broadwood, R.M.L.I.
Machine Gun Section	Captain C. B. Conybeare.
	2nd Lieutenant W. E. Sillitoe.
Chatham Company.	Major C. E. C. Eagles, D.S.O.,
	Captain R L. del Strother.
	Lieutenants S. H. Inskip,
	J. Jackson,
	2nd Lieutenants H. B. Lovatt,
	W. H. Boxall.
Portsmouth Company.	Captain E. Bamford, D.S.O.;
	Captain C. P. Tuckey.
	Lieutenants T. V. F. Cooke,
	B. S. Claudet,[*24]
	2nd Lieutenants A. G. Norris,
	W. C. Bloxsom.
Plymouth Company.	Major B. G. Weller, D.S.C.;
	Captain J. M. Palmer, D.S.C.
	Lieutenants C. R W. Lamplough,
	G. Underhill,
	R G. Stanton;
	2nd Lieutenant W. H. Dollery.
	Sergt.-Major C. J. Thatcher.
Medical Officers	Surgeon-Lieutenants H. St. G. Colston, RN.,
	F. Pocock, RN.

The Battalion entrained at Deal at 7-45 a.m. on 6th April, for an unknown destination; actually they went to Dover and embarked in the transport *Royal Edward*, from which they transhipped to the *Daffodil* at the Mouse Lightship. From there they proceeded to the Swin (off the mouth of the Thames) and embarked in the *Hindustan* which was the Depot ship for the operation at 3-30 p.m. As there was not enough room on board "C" Company was sent to the *Vindictive*, Captain Dallas-Brooks with the Royal Marine Artillery party from Shoeburyness arrived on board at 11-30 p.m. that evening.

When they were all on board, Vice-Admiral R. Keyes at last informed them of the operation which was to be undertaken, and the following message was communicated to them the next day.

---

24. Lieut. Claudet was sent to Hospital after embarkation and was replaced by Lieut. de Berry.

VIEW OF UPPER DECK OF H.M.S. "VINDICTIVE" SHOWING THE BROWS.
The negative of this photograph was found in Lieut. Rigby's camera after his death and was developed by Lieut. Gardner, R.M.A.

"The object of the enterprise that we are about to undertake is the blocking of the entrances to Zeebrugge and Ostend. These ports are the bases of a number of torpedo craft and submarines, which are a constant and ever-increasing menace to the communications of our Army and to the trade and food supply of our Country.

"The complete achievement of our aims would have the most favourable and far-reaching effect on the Naval situation.

"I am very proud to command the force which has the great privilege of carrying out this enterprise.

"Drawn as this Force is from the Grand Fleet, the Harwich Force, the Dover Patrol, the three Depots, and the Royal Marine Artillery and Light Infantry, it is thoroughly representative of our service.

"I am very confident that the great traditions of our forefathers will be worthily maintained, and that all ranks will strive to emulate the heroic deeds of our brothers of the Sister Service in France and Flanders.

(Signed) ROGER KEYES, *Vice-Admiral, Dover Patrol.*"

To ensure the most absolute secrecy no communication with the shore was permitted; the 7th was Sunday and was observed as a day of rest. On Monday, 8th April, they prepared for the operation and were visited by the First Lord of the Admiralty and the First Sea Lord. The 9th was the first day and all stood by to leave, but the weather was unfavourable; on the 10th the troops again embarked in their ships, but as the weather was still unsuitable, they returned again to the *Hindustan*.

On 11th, Thursday, the third day, they left the *Hindustan* for the *Vindictive* at 1-30 p.m. and the squadron weighed and proceeded at 4.0 p.m.

The Squadron had reached within 16 miles of its destination, when it was found that the wind was no longer favourable for the smoke screens, etc. and the Vice-Admiral had to make his momentous decision that the operation must be cancelled for that day; the time was 12-45 a.m. By the marvellous skill of the Commanding Officers, the huge flotilla of small craft was safely out of sight of the shore before daylight, and the enemy had no inkling of what was in store for him; the Force arrived back in the Swin about 12-30 p.m. on 12th April and returned to the *Hindustan*.

On 13th, which was the fifth day, they left the *Hindustan* at 2.0 p.m., weighed and proceeded at 4.0 p.m., but at 6-30 p.m. the operation had again to be postponed and they returned to the Depot ship. The 14th was Sunday, and on the 15th and 16th bad weather made any movement impossible: H.M.S. *Dominion* arrived and "A" Company was transferred to her for accommodation on 17th, and "C" Company came to the *Hindustan*.

On this day in order to occupy the men, guns' crews were organised for the ships and gun drill was begun.

These disappointments and the strain of waiting were very trying to all ranks, and they were very grateful to Captain A. P. Davidson, D.S.O., the Rev. C. J. Peshall, Staff-Paymaster Baddeley, Chief Gunner Yendell and Ship's Steward Saunders of the Royal Navy for their great help in organising recreation and amusements, and for doing all in their power for their comfort. Games and exercises were started, and everything was done to keep all ranks fit, but of course no one could go ashore.

The Buglers, who in the Royal Marines normally carry no arms, demanded to be armed, revolvers were considered to be too dangerous (for their own side), rifles and bayonets too heavy for them, the matter was compromised by arming them with cutlasses !

The authorities were now beginning to get anxious, as there were very few days left, when the state and height of the tide would admit of the *Vindictive* being laid alongside the Mole, and allow her men to get up on to it; further the time she could remain alongside would also be curtailed; it was calculated that they should have about an hour and forty minutes alongside.

At last on 22nd April, the first day of the second period, they were warned to get ready at 10-45 a.m. and left the Depot ships for the last time, and embarked in the storming ships at 11-40 a.m. The Fleet sailed at 1-10 p.m. and proceeded to carry out the operation; this time the weather was favourable and everything went right; as the Battalion Diary puts it- "23rd April, St. George's Day; operation carried out; *Vindictive* reached Mole 12-5 a.m. ; left Mole about 1-0 a.m.; arrived Dover 8-15 a.m.; Battalion arrived Deal 10-30 a.m."

Fortunately we are able to fill in more details than the above bald statement.

The 23rd April was St. George's Day, and on the way over Admiral Keyes made the signal "St. George for England," and Captain Carpenter replied "May we give the dragon's tail a damned good twist."

The numerous units engaged in the operation proceeded in silence and darkness to carry out their various duties; marking channels, guarding against submarines, making smoke screens, etc.; the monitors took up their bombarding positions, and the aeroplanes prepared for attack, whilst the blockships and storming ships proceeded to their appointed stations.

At 11-0 p.m. the storming parties in *Vindictive*, *Iris* and *Daffodil* went to their "Action Stations" as they went to their places, the sea was beginning to get rough and the *Vindictive* was moving very slowly, whilst the Destroyers and Motor Launches went ahead to make their smoke screen.

The Portsmouth Company was in the port battery of *Vindictive*, the Plymouth Company in the starboard battery at the foot of the ramps leading to the boat deck; the seamen storming party were on the starboard side of the upper deck, between the screen bulkheads.

The four Lewis guns of the machine gun section, Royal Marines, were in sand-bagged positions on the superstructure; seamen Stokes guns crews on the port side of the boat deck with the four seamen and two Royal Marine crews on the forecastle; the 11-inch howitzer was on the poop, one 7.5 howitzer forward and the other amidships on the port side; these were under Captain Dallas-Brooks. Two pom-poms and several Lewis guns were in the foretop under Lieutenant Rigby; whilst the ship's company of the *Vindictive* manned her 6-inch guns. No.7 platoon was in charge of the scaling ladders. The Battalion headquarters were stationed on the port side of the signal bridge.

In the *Iris* the units were distributed as follows :-

Nos. 1 and 2 Platoons "A" Company forward on the main deck.

No.3 Platoon "A" Company on upper deck, starboard side aft.

No.4 Platoon "A" Company standing by the scaling ladders on port side of upper deck.

The Stokes mortar section was on the main deck, forward, one Vickers gun was mounted in the sandbagged position on the port bridge house, the other was in reserve on the upper deck.

The demolition parties were in the *Daffodil* and were to land across the *Vindictive*.

The aerial attack duly took place, and drove the enemy to their shelters, but as the ships approached the Mole, a shift of wind drifted the smoke screens and revealed them to the enemy. At 11-50 p.m. star shells began to fall around the ships showing that they had been seen, and a few minutes later they came under heavy shell fire. When 250 yards from the Mole, the two pom-poms and Lewis guns in the foretop opened fire, which was the pre-arranged signal for all guns to commence firing; the 6-inch guns and the pom-poms continued firing until the ship was within a few yards of the Mole, when they were obliged to cease firing; the Stokes guns continued firing until the ships were secured and the brows were lowered, when they too had to cease fire, unfortunately one gun burst causing several casualties. In order to cover the storming parties, orders were passed for fire to be opened by the howitzers, whose crews up to then had been keeping under cover; as no reply could be obtained from the foremost 7.5 inch howitzer, Captain Dallas-Brooks went forward and found that, whilst under cover, the whole crew had been killed or wounded by a shell; a volunteer crew of seamen from one of the 6-inch guns was then obtained and was in the act of getting the gun into action, when a shell burst amongst them, and all but two were killed or wounded. Captain Dallas-Brooks then went aft to the 11-inch howitzer and found them keeping up a steady rate of fire, which was maintained to the end, Sergeant F.J. Knill, R.M.A. who was in charge was in a semi-gassed condition, but stuck gallantly to his work. Gunner Hearn also distinguished himself.

At the midship 7. 5-inch howitzer a shell had damaged the lock, so that it was only brought into action as the ship was leaving the Mole.

The foretop, which could see over the Mole, was fiercely engaged, particularly by a destroyer lying alongside on the inner side of the Mole; the fire of the foretop was most valuable whilst coming alongside, but soon afterwards a shell hit the top killing Lieutenant Rigby and all the gun's crews except two who were wounded.; Sergeant N. A. Finch, Royal Marine Artillery, though wounded, most gallantly maintained his gun in action until the end.

As the ship approached the Mole a shell burst on the signal bridge and killed both Colonel Elliot and Major Cordner and knocked down the Adjutant, Captain Chater; the latter picked himself up at once and informed Major Weller, who handing over the command of his company to Captain Palmer, assumed command of the Battalion. Captain Halahan. Royal Navy, commanding the seamen storming party, was killed at the same time.

The shell fire caused many casualties and Nos.10 and 11 platoons of the Plymouth Company on the starboard side suffered severely. The heaviest casualties occurred as the *Vindictive* approached the Mole, both among the guns' crews and the storming parties drawn up on the upper deck waiting to storm.

Captain Carpenter placed his ship alongside at 12-5 a.m. in the position marked 'A' abreast of No.3 shed, instead of alongside the battery as originally intended; she was successfully secured and the *Daffodil* going ahead full speed kept her in position.

The brows were so damaged by shell fire that two only could be used, and these were sawing up and down with the motion of the ship, as one man puts it :- "in the anxiety to keep my balance on the see-saw of the gangway I forgot about the rain of lead, I really felt comfortable when I put my foot on the concrete."

Across them the remnants of the seamen storming party at once made their assault followed by the Royal Marines, and were received by a heavy fire from guns, rifles and machine guns; the seamen had now much further to go to reach the end of the Mole than was originally planned.

Owing to the position of the *Vindictive* and the casualties that had occurred while coming alongside, it was necessary to modify the scheme of attack, as it was obvious that a larger number of men would be required to go towards the seaward end of the Mole to attack and mop up the batteries.

Owing to the casualties in the Plymouth Company in going alongside No.5 Platoon of the Portsmouth Company under Lieutenant T. F. Cooke and Captain Bamford led the attack; this platoon proceeded to the right along the raised pathway and silenced a party of snipers who were near No.2 Shed and were firing into the units disembarking; this movement was initiated by Captain and Adjutant Chater, whose coolness and services throughout the action were invaluable. The platoon was led by Lieutenant Cooke with the greatest gallantry and dash though he was wounded very early. This platoon was immediately followed by No.9 .platoon of the Plymouth Company under the dashing and determined leadership of Lieutenant Lamplough together with the remnants of No. 10 platoon only 12 men out of 45; this party dropping ladders and ropes over the railing scrambled down to the main platform of the Mole, and proceeded at once to their duty of establishing a strong point at the shoreward end of Shed No.3, bombing the Germans who tried to stop them; they seized the shed and established themselves there to prevent hostile attacks up the Mole; they also engaged with Lewis guns and bomb; a torpedo boat destroyer which was lying alongside in the vicinity of the steps marked "K" and whose fire had been very destructive; they inflicted considerable damage on the boat and her personnel; the shed also was blown up before they re-embarked.

Units were now disembarking rapidly, No.7 platoon under Lieutenant de Berry got the heavy scaling ladders ashore and enabled the men to get down on to the platform of the Mole from the raised pathway; in this work Sergt.-Major Thatcher was largely instrumental in getting these ladders carried ashore assisted by Corporal B. Wells (Plymouth). No. 7 platoon then formed up in support of No.9 and 10 platoons. One man relates that when he got to the bottom of the ladder, there was a heap of bodies of Germans who had tried to knock down the ladders.

Information was shortly after received at the Battalion headquarters abreast of the ship, that the seamen storming party which was attacking the batteries along the raised pathway required reinforcement; Major Weller at once dispatched No.12 platoon, Lieutenant Underhill, together with the remnants of No. 11 to their assistance; this party advanced along the raised path and reached point "Z" where they were temporarily checked by machine-gun fire; at this point they found a gun about 3 ½ inches calibre that was still uncovered; which was a clear indication of the manner in which the enemy was surprised.

Captain Conybeare of the machine gun section had been wounded before landing, but the Lewis guns of the section were gallantly taken ashore by Sergeant W. Thompson (Chatham) and did most useful work on shore. Private W. Hopewell (Plymouth) specially distinguished himself, and was almost the last man to retire, bringing his gun out of action until it was rendered useless by a direct hit from a shell.

Meanwhile, No.5, 6 and 8 platoons of the Portsmouth Company under Captain Bamford, whose initiative and courage were a magnificent example to all, had formed up and launched their attack on the 4.1 inch Battery, but before it could be fully carried out the "General Recall" was sounded by the *Daffodil* as the *Vindictive*'s syren had been put out of action by a shell. However, Corporal Kingshott and Private A. G. Clarke of the Plymouth Company had ascertained that the battery at the end of the Mole was out of action; they had advanced and remained in observation till forced to retire by machine gun fire and this information was only acquired as the Battalion was on the point of leaving.

Their time had been considerably shortened, but in the wild hour on shore, the enemy's guns were silenced, the dumps and craft alongside destroyed and the wild uproar on the Mole drew the attention of all the 144 enemy batteries on shore and allowed the main object of the raid to be effected. The blockships steamed boldly in and were sunk by their crews with the utmost gallantry in the channel and the harbour was blocked.

The withdrawal had now to be commenced; in order to reach the raised path and so the gangways of the ship, the men had to climb up the scaling ladders carrying their wounded and their guns, and then cross the swaying brows to the ship. The enemy were shelling the Mole heavily; but the platoons, now reduced to very small numbers, came back in good order bringing their wounded with them. Lieutenant Cooke was again severely wounded in the head whilst carrying back a wounded man to the ladders; his batman Private J. D. L. Press (Portsmouth) who was acting as his runner remained with him and although himself wounded, eventually succeeded in carrying Lieutenant Cooke back on board the *Vindictive*. Private W. J. Wakefield (Portsmouth) also particularly distinguished himself in the work of getting the wounded up the ladders and Captain C. P. Tuckey, who was missing and later reported killed, when last seen was at the foot of the ladders helping men up.

Owing to the heavy casualties among the officers, several of the platoons were now commanded by Sergeants, who displayed the greatest gallantry and initiative. The final retirement was covered by No.9 platoon under Lieutenant Lamplough. Captain Palmer of the Plymouth Company, in supervising the retirement of his company, with two sergeants, one corporal and 10 privates, including two wounded, belonging to No.9 and 10 platoons who formed the rearguard, failed to reach the ship before she left the Mole and were captured by the enemy.

One man who fell between the Mole and the ship was rescued by Corporal G. J. Hewitt (Portsmouth) and a party with great gallantry. The *Vindictive* pushed off from the Mole about 1 a.m. with her main object and a good part of her secondary objects accomplished; whilst the heroic action of the submarine under Lieutenant Sandford, R.N. in blowing herself up under the wooden viaduct had completely cut off the Mole from the shore and caused heavy casualties to the enemy.

Turning to the *Iris*, when the *Vindictive* went alongside the Mole, Commander Gibbs placed his ship ahead of her and succeeded in getting alongside at 12-10 a.m. without any hits from hostile shell. It was then found that the grappling irons would not hold her in spite of the gallant and heroic efforts of Lieutenants Hawkins and Bradford, R.N. who clambered up on to the Mole to secure them and were both killed, and consequently the scaling ladders up which the men were to climb on to the Mole could not be placed in position. During these efforts the ship was subjected to heavy shell and rifle fire, Commander Gibbs was mortally wounded both legs being shot away and Lieutenant Spencer, R.N.R. took command. The machine guns replied to the fire, 2nd Lieutenant Sillitoe in charge of them was killed, but under Acting-Sergeant C. P. Budd (Portsmouth) the guns were kept in action; Private C. H. Martyn (Plymouth) on the port side of the bridge kept his gun going until it was put out of action, when he procured another and kept it in action until the bridge itself was shot away.

About 12.35 a.m. these attempts to land were abandoned by order of the Captain of the ship, who decided to take his ship. alongside the *Vindictive* and to land the Chatham Company across her. The *Iris* was brought alongside the *Vindictive* about 12-55 a.m., but before she could be secured the 'Urgent Recall' signal was made and the Iris was obliged therefore to cast off and commence to withdraw.

For the first few minutes of the withdrawal the *Iris* came under very heavy shell fire, and sustained many casualties; a small fire started on the upper deck, which was immediately taken in hand, and put out. Lance-Corporal (Bugler) C. Heffernan (Chatham), rendered the greatest assistance and removed the ammunition from the vicinity of the fire, being killed whilst doing this. A shell fell at this time among the officers killing Major C. E. Eagles, D.S.O. and killing or wounding all the officers of the Chatham company, except Lieutenant Broadwood ; the total casualties on board the *Iris* were eight Officers and 69 men killed and three Officers and 102 men wounded.

After the *Vindictive* pushed off, she sustained no further casualties, and in spite of her damaged funnels and the wounds and scars all over her, made good her way back to Dover at 17 knots together with the *Daffodil* and the host of small craft. At 5-0 a.m. Admiral Keyes in his flagship the *Warwick* passed them and signalled "Operation successful. Well done *Vindictive*," and both crews gave ringing cheers; as one who was there expresses it: "Never were cheers more heartfelt-for a great wave of affection was felt for our gallant Commander-in-Chief-as every one realised that his care and consideration and refusal to take unnecessary risks had brought them safely through the great adventure with their work accomplished."

They arrived at Dover at 8-15 a.m. and received a great reception, all the ships in harbour mustering crews on deck and cheering as they passed, a welcome accorded to each of the small vessels as they came in

H.M.S. "VINDICTIVE" AND "DAFFODIL" ALONGSIDE THE MOLE AT ZEEBRUGGE.
After the painting by Mr. De Lacy, in the Officers' Mess, Depot, Royal Marines, Deal.

[By kind permission of the Artist.]

after having so gallantly fulfilled their several tasks.

H.M.S. *Iris* however, was still missing and many anxious glances were cast to seawards, until she was eventually descried steaming slowly, reaching Dover safely a few hours later, after a most trying passage.

The Battalion disembarked at 9-30 a.m. and said good-bye to Captain Carpenter "the hero of the hour and no one can describe what he has done." Entraining at Dover station they arrived at Deal at 10-30 a.m. and marched through the town to the Barracks.

Probably never since medieval times in Britain has there been such a homecoming; the unit returned almost direct from the battlefield to its own home Depot, where with anxious hearts their relatives and friends were waiting to welcome them or to hear the dread news of their loss.

The Chatham company arrived later in the day and the next two days were spent in reorganising.

The success which came at such an opportune moment to lighten the darkness that was hanging over the Empire after the disasters on the Somme and the Lys in France, and to hearten the nation for the continuance of the struggle, was purchased at a heavy price by the Royal Navy and Royal Marines who lost large numbers of gallant Officers and men.

In the Royal Marines they were :-

	Killed.	Died of Wounds.	Wounded.	Missing.
Officers	9	1	6	1
R.M.A. Detachment	17	3		
Chatham Contingent	43	5		
Portsmouth Contingent	13	5	228	
Plymouth Contingent	19	5		
Total	101	18	234	13

The Officers were :-

Killed	Lieut.-Colonel B. N. Elliot, D.S.O.; Majors A. A. Cordner and C. E. Eagles, D.S.O.
	Captain C. P. Tuckey.
	Lieutenants C. N. Rigby, R.M.A., S. H. E. Inskip, W. E. S. Sillitoe, W. H. Dollery.
Died of Wounds	Lieutenant R G. Stanton.
Wounded Dangerously	Captain R L. del Strother.
	Lieutenant T. F. V. Cooke; 2nd Lieutenant H. B. Lovatt.
Wounded	Captain C. B. Conybeare.
	Lieutenant F. J. Hore (Q.M.) ; 2nd-Lieutenant W. C. Bloxsom.
Prisoner of War	Captain J. M. Palmer, D.S.C.

The surgeons of the Battalion, H. St. C. Colston and F. P. Pocock under Surgeon -Commander McCutcheon of the *Vindictive* were devoted in their attentions to the wounded, and had to work for many hours in gas fumes by the light of a torch.

Surgeon-Commander McCutcheon relates the following: "I found Lieutenant Stanton lying on the mess deck side by side with his servant; Stanton was unconscious due to a dangerous wound in the head, his servant, who was also severely wounded in the right arm and scalp, had his left arm round his master's neck and shoulders. He informed me that he was alright, but that Mr. Stanton was pretty bad and he was trying to keep the heat in him. This incident was, to my mind, typical of the loyalty and affection existing to such

[From Sketch by Col. C. Field, R.M.L.I.]

H.M.S. "IRIS" WITHDRAWING FROM THE MOLE.

a great extent in the Royal Marine Corps between officers and men."[25]

Admiral Sir Roger Keyes came over to Deal on the following day and addressed the Battalion, who had been paraded for his inspection; he thanked them for their services; words which coming from such a revered commander were praise indeed and valued accordingly.

Lieut.-Colonel Elliot was buried at Chatham, the funeral honours being paid by his own division.

The funeral of those whose bodies had been brought back to Dover, and whose relatives did not claim them for burial in their own home towns and villages, were buried on 27th April, two officers and 64 seamen and Marines in one large grave in the picturesque cemetery on the hillside at Dover, in the presence of Admiral Keyes and representatives of all His Majesty's Services, the chaplains of all denominations officiating.

H.M. the King conferred on the 4th Battalion Royal Marines the signal honour of the award of two Victoria Crosses under the provision of the Ninth Statute of the decoration.†

The ballot was duly held at Deal on 26th April, and the greatest number of votes were cast for Captain E. Bamford, D.S.O., R.M.L.I, the next being Sergeant N. A. Finch, Royal Marine Artillery, and they were duly recommended to His Majesty and received the Cross from his hands; it was also entered in the records of all those who formed the Battalion that they took part in the ballot for the award of the Cross.

The *London Gazette* in publishing the awards thus describes their actions :-

"Captain E. Bamford, R.M.L.I. for most conspicuous gallantry. This officer landed on the Mole from H.M.S. *Vindictive* with numbers 5, 7 and 8 platoons of the Marine storming force in the face of great difficulties. When on the Mole and under heavy fire he displayed the greatest initiative in the command of his company and. by his total disregard of danger showed a magnificent example to his men. He first established a strong point on the right of the disembarkation, and when satisfied that that was safe, led an assault on a battery to the left with the utmost coolness and valour."

"Sergeant N. A. Finch, Royal Marine Artillery, was second in command of the pom-poms and Lewis guns in the foretop of the *Vindictive* under Lieutenant C. N. Rigby. At one period H.M.S. *Vindictive* was being hit every few seconds, chiefly in the upper works, from which splinters caused many casualties. It was difficult to locate the guns which were doing the most damage, but Lieutenant Rigby, Sergeant Finch and the Marines in the foretop kept up a continuous fire, changing rapidly from one target to another and thus keeping the enemy's fire down to some considerable extent. Unfortunately two heavy shells made direct hits on the foretop which was completely exposed to enemy concentrations of fire. All in the top were killed or disabled except Sergeant Finch, who was however severely wounded, nevertheless he showed consummate bravery remaining in his battered and exposed position. He once more got a Lewis gun into action and kept up a continuous fire harassing the enemy on the Mole until the foretop received another direct hit; the remainder of the armament being then completely put out of action. Before the top was destroyed Sergeant Finch had done invaluable work and by his bravery undoubtedly saved many lives.

---

25. From an Account in the Globe and Laurel.

† "The Ninth Statute provides that in the event of any Unit of our Naval or . . . . . Forces consisting in the case of the Navy of a Squadron Flotilla or Ship's Company or of a detached body of Seamen or Marines . . . . . . having distinguished itself collectively by the performance of an act of heroic gallantry or daring in the presence of the enemy in such a way that the Admiral in command of the Forces to which the Unit belongs is unable to single out any individual as specially pre-eminent in gallantry or daring, then one or more of the Officers, Warrant Officers, Petty Officers, Non-commissioned Officers, Seamen, Marines, Private Soldiers, or Airmen in the ranks comprising the Unit shall be selected to be recommended to us for the award of the Victoria Cross in the following manner."

The selection to be by a secret ballot in such a manner as shall be determined, etc.

CAPTAIN AND BREVET MAJOR E. BAMFORD, V.C., D.S.O., R.M.L.I.

This very gallant Sergeant of the Royal Marine Artillery was selected by the 4th Battalion Royal Marines, who were mostly R.M.L.I., to receive the Victoria Cross."

It was also decided that in memory of their gallant exploit no other unit of the Royal Marines should bear the title of 4th Battalion Royal Marines, a name which would remain for ever as their lasting memorial.

Two Crosses were also awarded to Lieutenant A. L. Harrison, Royal Navy, who was killed and to Seaman McKenzie who was wounded of the Naval storming party in addition to the several Crosses awarded to individual officers and men of the Royal Navy for their special and gallant work, among whom to the delight of the Corps was Captain A. F. B. Carpenter, commanding the *Vindictive*.

In addition to the K.C.B. awarded to the gallant Commander-in-Chief, and those awarded to the officers and men of the Royal Navy the following honours were awarded to the Corps.

Major G. Weller who assumed command when Colonel Elliot was killed was given the C.B. and the Brevet of Lieut.-Colonel.

Captain A. R. Chater was given the D.S.O. and a Brevet Majority for the great share he contributed to the successes of the operation, in the planning of which he had also given great assistance to Colonel Elliot.

Captain R. A. Dallas-Brooks was given the D.S.O. and a Brevet Majority for his gallant work in command of the howitzers and the same reward was given to Lieutenant T. F. Cooke for his gallant actions described above, this officer was very severely wounded and was incapacitated for a very long time.

The D.S.C. was awarded to Lieutenant C. R. W. Lamplough who formed the strong point and covered the retirement; to Lieutenant G. Underhill who at a critical moment led forward the reinforcements for the attack on the battery with the greatest dash; to Sergeant-Major C. J. Thatcher who did such good work with the ladders and throughout the operation and also to Acting-Company-Sergeant-Major E. E. Kelly (Chatham Company).

The Conspicuous Gallantry Medal was given to Private W. Hopewell (Plymouth), Sergeant F. J. Knill (R.M.A.), Private J. D. L. Press (Portsmouth), for the actions which have been already described.

The Distinguished Service Medal was awarded to :-

Private C. H. Martyn (Plymouth).
Acting-Sergt. C. P. Budd (Portsmouth).
Private A. G. Clarke (Plymouth).
Corporal W. Kingshott (Plymouth).
Private A. V. Lee (Plymouth).
Private W. J. Wakefield (Portsmouth).
Gunner E. Hearn (R.M.A.)
Sergt. M. J. Thompson (Chatham).
Bugler L. F. Guttridge (Portsmouth).

Private J. W. Adam (Plymouth).
Sergt. R C. Burt (Portsmouth).
Acting-Sergt. J. Hewitt (Portsmouth).
Private L. I. Lane (Portsmouth).
Lance-Sergt. F. Radford (Plymouth).
Corporal B. Wells (Plymouth).
Gunner M.Ncl. McPhee (R.M.A.).
Private H. C. Proctor (Portsmouth).
Private W. Gillespie (Chatham).

The following were mentioned in Dispatches in addition to the above; Lieut.-Colonel B. N. Elliot, D.S.O., who had trained the Battalion and inspired it with his own dauntless spirit and who fell at the moment when his work was reaching fruition.

Majors A. A. Cordner, C. E. Eagles, D.S.O.
Lieutenants D. Broadwood, H. A. de Berry; 2nd-Lieutenant A. G. Norris.
C.S.M. C. J. Watts (Portsmouth), E. Taylor (Plymouth).
Colour-Sergt. E. E. Kirby (Chatham).   Gunner J. W. Arkill (R.M.A.).

Sergt. J. H. Bailey (Plymouth).	Sergt. W. J. Baker (Chatham).
Gunner W. Dance (R.M.A.).	Private J. Evans (Portsmouth).
Gunner J. H. Grady (R.M.A.).	Private G. W. Hall (Plymouth).
Private J. F. Hawkesworth (Plymouth).	Bugler C. Heffernan (Chatham), killed.
Private H. W. Hoath (Chatham).	Private N. S. Jeffery (Chatham).
Private A. B. Mann (Portsmouth).	Private F. W. Munday (Plymouth).
Sergt. H. J. Parker (Plymouth).	Gunner W. Ranson (R.M.A.).
Corporal N. Sharrock (Chatham).	Corporal W. Craig (Portsmouth).

Captain J. M. Palmer was awarded a bar to his D.S.C. and the D.S.M. was given to Sergeants H. Wright and W. H. Taylor (Plymouth), when released from Germany for their services in covering the withdrawal to the ship and whilst on the Mole[26].

His Majesty the King caused the following gracious letter to be sent to the Adjutant-General, Royal Marines.-

WINDSOR CASTLE,
28th April, 1918.

My Dear Adjutant-General.

By command of the King, I write to express through you to the Royal Marines, His Majesty's high appreciation of their gallant conduct during the recent operations undertaken at Zeebrugge and Ostend. It is a matter of special interest to the King to remember that the 4th Battalion, which took part in the fighting, was at Deal on the occasion of His Majesty's inspection on March 7th. As you are aware, the King has already sent a message to the Vice-Admiral at Dover, conveying His Majesty's congratulations on the success of the operations and appreciation of the conduct of all arms under his command, and as this comprises the Royal Marines you will understand that the King is not sending a special message to the Corps.

At the same time, I am to assure you of the King's deep sympathy with the relatives of those who have lost their lives, as well as His Majesty's solicitude for the progress of those who have been wounded, one and all having so valiantly maintained the splendid traditions of the Royal Marines.

Believe me, my dear Adjutant-General,

Yours sincerely,

(Signed) CROMER.

Maj.-General Sir David Mercer, K.C.B., A.G., R.M.

This letter was suitably acknowledged by the Adjutant-General.

The following telegram was also sent to the Officer Commanding the Battalion :-

---

26. *One of the captured N.C.O.s (Sergeant Wright), relates that when they were taken to Zeebrugge the next morning, there was a gap in the bridge where Lieut. Sandford's submarine was blown up, 30 yards long and they had to cross over two wires which had been planked over. The Kaiser himself also came to Zeebrugge that day, and interviewed Captain Palmer. It is interesting to note that the prisoners were closely questioned as to the whereabouts of the 3rd R.M. Battalion of which apparently the Germans were ignorant, and it shows that their intelligence was not very good as that Battalion had been for over 18 months in the Aegean, though they seemed to know about the 5th Battalion then forming. See Chapters 7 and 22.*

"I am directed by the First Sea Lord to convey to the Officers, N.C. Officers and Men of the 4th Battalion Royal Marines, his appreciation and thanks for the great gallantry displayed by them in the recent attack on Zeebrugge. The losses have been heavy, but the discipline and courage of the Battalion are worthy of the highest traditions of the Royal Marines. Please take steps to have this communicated to all ranks and to add the congratulations of the Adjutant-General, Royal Marines, on the fresh laurels they have added to the splendid records of the Corps."

The Battalion was dispersed to their own headquarters on Saturday, 27th April, after a. brief but very glorious existence.

(Photograph from painting by Major W. G. Sparrow, in the Mess at Portsmouth)

SERGEANT N. A. FINCH, V.C., R.M.A.

CHAPTER 13.

ROYAL MARINES IN NORTH RUSSIA.

H.M.S. Glory at Murmansk - H.M.S. *Cochrane* at Pechenga - Action with the White Finns - Operations in the White Sea -R.M. Field Force-Finnish Legion – Murmansk - Kem and Kandalaksha - Training on Skis -Action at Maselskaya - 6th R.M. Battalion - Action at Ussuna – Koikori.

AS stated in chapter 8 anxiety existed early in 1918 as to the position of affairs in North Russia, especially as regards the possible action of the Germans, who since the Russian Revolution, had penetrated into Finland and Russia and who were known to be pushing on towards the Murman Coast, where the Kola inlet, owing to the action of the Gulf Stream, provided an ice free port all the year round. Besides this the terminus of the railway which had been constructed in 1916 from the south was at Murmansk, a town which had only just sprung into existence. The houses were built entirely of wood and the place, which was controlled by the local soviets, was in a hopeless state of chaos and confusion and in an indescribably insanitary condition; it was full of refugees of all nationalities including every kind of undesirable. The railway was a single track line running from Petrosavodsk on the shores of Lake Onega, which had been built with the aid of German and Austrian prisoners of War; it was in a very bad state of repair and most inefficiently run until the British assumed control.

The ground was swampy; in the winter it is frozen hard and covered with snow, but its condition after the thaw is indescribable and movement becomes almost impossible. Roads, as usually understood, did not exist; in summer they were dusty sandy tracks, in the spring, swamps. The town, however, was lit by electricity and there were large storehouses; on three sides it was surrounded by mountain and swamps. Starvation was rife, as the Soviets ran the food supplies; communication with the south being practically cut off, most of the food had to be brought into the country by sea.

The political position was extraordinarily complicated and cannot be described in this place; it may be sufficient if it is stated, that in Finland the White Guard were acting in conjunction with the Germans and had driven the Red Guard, the Revolutionary Socialists, over the Frontier, and as the latter were opposed to the Germans, the Allies supported them. Among the Russians proper there were Bolsheviks and White Russians, and as at that time the Bolsheviks were supporting the Germans the Allies supported the White Russians. Bolshevism of course was everywhere and at that time their leaders were holding Archangel and were strong in Murmansk; it was not until July that the counter-revolution took place at Archangel.

Since the beginning of the War there had always been at least one of H.M. ships in these waters, to control the supply ships, sweep the sea for mines and perform all the numerous duties that fall to the Royal Navy at such places in time of War. At first it was H.M.S. *Jupiter*, later H.M.S. *Vindictive* and then H.M.S. *Glory*. The latter had spent the winter of 1917-18 as guardship at Murmansk and in the spring of 1918, in addition to the French *Admiral Aube* and the U.S.S. *Olympia* there was also the Russian ship *Askold* of whom more anon.

H.M.S. *Glory*, flagship of Rear-Admiral Kemp, was anchored opposite Murmansk, she carried a very large Royal Marine Detachment, about 176 N.C.O.s and men, a good many borne in lieu of seamen for the purpose of landing a strong detachment to quell any local disturbance; Major Fawcett, R.M.L.I. was the Royal Marine Officer. Special Lewis gun detachments of six N.C.O.s and 30 privates were sent out with Colonel Paterson's Force under 2nd Lieutenant A. G. Norris, R.M.L.I. to strengthen her detachment.

The duties of the detachment were unique, as they were divided into "Detachment" Marines and "Seamen" Marines, the latter carrying out all "part of the ship" duties as seamen. In May Captain C. T. Brown, Royal Marine Artillery relieved Major Fawcett who had been appointed to an Intelligence billet on shore; the latter was accidently killed somewhat later.

In March, 1918, H.M.S. *Cochrane* was detached from the Grand Fleet and joined the *Glory* at Kola on 7th March; on the 15th her Royal Marine detachment was landed, as the White Guard Finns and the Germans were reported to be advancing, whilst the seamen companies stood by and some 3-pr. guns were mounted in an armoured train and sent along the railway to the south; the ship herself was anchored to cover the railway between Kola and Murmansk. On 10th April the White Finns captured Kem on the White Sea, but were driven out by the Red Guards.

As it was necessary to secure the Pechenga Inlet, which lies close to the Norwegian Frontier, to prevent its being used as a submarine base, the *Cochrane* re-embarked her parties and left for that place on 2nd May, taking also 40 Russians and Red Guards.

The inlet was found to be full of ice, but the ship forced her way in as far as possible and landed 20 Royal Marines under Captain V. C. Brown, Royal Marine Artillery, also the Red Guards with two maxims to occupy three small villages at the head of the inlet. The villages consisted of some huts and the guest houses of the St. Tryphen Monastery, which is a great place for pilgrimages; the lower Monastery was about six or seven miles inland, and the upper Monastery, the real Monastery, was about 16 versts further.

Two roads led from the village, one due south to the upper Monastery and the other west, south-west to Chelmozero, 80 versts distant, and then across the Finland frontier to Kura.

The White Finns, about 1,000 strong, with machine guns, were reported to have occupied Chelmozero and to be pushing on to Pechenga. In Pechenga were 15 frontiersmen, expert rifle shots and skimen (these belonged to an old Russian Imperial Organisation), together with 40 Royal Marines, 40 Russians and 100 seamen, altogether a force of about 200. On the following day, the 5th, the remainder of the Royal Marines and the two seamen companies landed; the Russians were sent out to garrison the upper Monastery and the remainder marched to the lower Monastery, sledges drawn by reindeer provided the transport: here they were billeted in one of the largest hostels. On the 6th May, about 35 Royal Marines with five Lewis guns from H.M.S. *Glory* arrived, therefore, in order to make room 30 seamen returned in charge of the prisoners that had been taken.

On the 8th the Finns were reported to be 40 versts distant and a flying column of 30 Royal Marines with two Lewis guns and the frontiersmen was organised to attack them and endeavour to capture some prisoners.

It was soon after discovered that the Finns were using our telephone wires and by means of this their plans were discovered and their orders overheard. A naval 12-pr. field gun also arrived from the ship having been dragged over the ice, and was put into position on Observation Hill near the village.

On the forenoon of the 8th, Captain V. Brown and his party started off, two men on each sleigh and the frontiersmen on skis, and reached Lake Variema at 3 p.m.; in view of the information acquired on the telephone Captain Brown then started for the Gubernatorski River, Finn scouts retiring in front of them. The chase was continued till midnight and in the early morning, on approaching the river, the frontiersmen. advanced to the Rest House and fired at the door; a large number of Finns came out as did others concealed near the house; the Royal Marines left their sledges and advanced in open order, in two lines of 15 men each, at 10 paces interval, with a Lewis gun on each flank; the Ross rifles had frozen during the night and misfired continually, but the Lewis guns did great execution. The Finns who numbered about 200 advanced by rushes with covering fire and sent parties round the flank on skis and the Royal Marines were forced to retire; the reindeer drivers tried to bolt, but a corporal threatened to shoot them and kept them in hand; by the time the men had got into the sledges the Finns were only 100 yards off; the Royal Marines had one man wounded and one frontiersman was killed; the Finns did not attempt pursuit, having a wholesome respect for the Lewis guns; the party then returned towards the Monastery; on the receipt of the report of the fighting, the seamen companies and the remaining 40 Royal Marines started out to reinforce and met the returning party on the road, but in view of the fact that the Finns considerably outnumbered them, the whole party returned to the Monastery.

On the 10th a small party of Finns arrived in the village and declared that they had annexed it; it was at once decided to surround them, and with this object the Royal Marines marched across behind the village to cut the Kura road, whilst the seamen companies formed up below Observation Hill; before the British were formed up the Red Guards attacked the enemy and drove them out. Meanwhile a large hostile force appeared on Waterfall Hill to the southward and opened fire on the Royal Marines who facing half left attacked them; the field gun also opened fire; the Royal Marines encountered increasing opposition, so faced south and advanced parallel to the Chelmozero road till held up by a machine gun; one company of seamen came up on their right and the other on their left and a fire fight commenced. Captain Brown tried to stalk a machine gun but was shot in the shoulder when close enough to hear the crank handle going. A party of Finns in the meantime worked round to attack the camp, but were driven off by the field gun's crew; and as the 3rd seamen's company, principally stokers, under the Captain of the *Cochrane* appeared, the Finns retreated from in front of the Royal Marines and the other seamen companies. Pursuit could not be attempted as the men sank into the snow up to their knees. The ship however, fired a few rounds to register on the road, and it transpired later that one 9.2" shell fell within 200 yards of where the retreating Finns had halted, on which they bolted leaving all their gear, and Chelmozero was also evacuated.

Captain V. Brown, Royal Marine Artillery, was awarded the D.S.C. for his services on these occasions.

On 13th May a Finnish patrol appeared and was stalked by a seamen and Marine patrol, the latter laying an ambush, but the Finns were warned and escaped; the next day another party of 30 Royal Marines arrived from H.M.S. *Glory*. Information was obtained on 18th that the Finn losses on the 10th amounted to 10 killed, four missing and several wounded, whilst a number had deserted.

The time was now employed in entrenching the camp and training; the ice broke up so that the ship had to be communicated with by boat and finally broke on 31st July. As the Finns kept coming up to Waterfall Hill, a post of 15 Royal Marines with a Lewis gun was established. on the top of the hill; after three days the Finns re-appeared but were driven off by a patrol and did not come again. On the 8th June the Hill was occupied by the Royal Marines who built themselves turf huts on all the commanding positions. A small party of Finns tried to re-occupy Chelmozero, but were ambushed by the frontiersmen. On the 28th a Colonel of the Royal Engineers took over the command of the camp and 200 Serbian soldiers reinforced the garrison; the latter fraternised with the seamen and Marines, and proved themselves most excellent fellows.

On 17th July the *Glory's* Marines returned to Murmansk and in August some of the seamen returned to the ship to man part of the flotilla at Archangel.

On 29th September a few Finns having occupied Chelmozero, half a battalion of troops and a machine gun company were sent from Murmansk and the landing party of H.M.S. *Cochrane* returned to their ship; in October the Royal Marines from the armoured train also returned and the *Cochrane* returned to England.

Meanwhile the Royal Marine detachment of H.M.S. *Glory* had not been idle, as related above some had reinforced the *Cochrane's* at Pechenga, whilst on 13th June the transport offices and Russian barracks were burnt down by the Bolsheviks which was the beginning of the trouble. The arrival of the Allied troops was much resented by both the Russian parties.

To restrict the disturbances the Russian sailors from the battleship *Tchesma* and the cruiser *Askold* were forbidden to land under penalty of being fired upon; an order that led to one or two incidents, particularly on certain occasions when guards of Royal Marines having been sent to the ships they were fired on by the Army as they were returning although flying a large White Ensign. It was then decided to disarm the *Askold*; Captain C. T. Brown with 50 Royal Marines from the *Glory*, 50 French Marines and 50 Americans, accompanied by a number of Army Staff Officers carried out the work; the major part of the crew had been inveigled on shore and the Allies went on board as quickly as possible and put the remainder of the ship's company safely under lock and key. All the breechblocks and gunsights, etc. were removed and the work was completed in 21 hours very successfully, the Marines doing good work; after being cleaned the ship was commissioned as H.M.S. *Glory IV*.

On 25th March, 1919, the whole detachment of the *Glory* was dispatched on a curious mission under Captain C. T. Brown accompanying the Chief of the Army Staff and Lieutenant Stenhouse, Royal Navy. They were sent to a place called Knaja Ghuba on the Finnish border. Negotiations were in progress to repatriate the Finnish Red Guards and their ex-Prime Minister, M. Tochoi; the Red Guards were anxious to return home, but wanted to take their arms with them, as otherwise they had a shrewd suspicion that they would be murdered; to this the White Guards would not consent. Anyway as far as the detachment was concerned they travelled in cattle trucks for two days and then having pushed the train into a shunt line concealed themselves in a pine forest and awaited events. The snow was thick on the ground and the Finnish scouts on skis were all round them.

The Chief of the Staff and M. Tochoi were to have a conference and the latter was if possible to be induced to come to General Headquarters. The mission was successful and the detachment returned to their ship. Captain Brown was awarded the O.B.E. for his services in Russia and several of the N.C.O.s and men were decorated for the various actions in which they were engaged.

H.M.S. *Attentive* arrived to reinforce the squadron in 1918 and her doings in connection with the operations on the river Dwina are dealt with in Chapter 8; but before proceeding to this work, she was busy on the Murman coast and in the White Sea.

On 6th July it was reported .that the railway bridge at Skuia between Soroka and Kem had been burnt down and that Soroka, where the *Attentive* was lying was threatened; the landing party with machine guns and a 12-pr. gun was therefore sent ashore on the 7th. The Bolshevik Commissars had bolted off south, but it was found that they had made all preparations for burning the place and had indeed actually burnt the locomotive shed; with a small Royal Marine guard Captain Altham and the 1st-Lieutenant, who was an Interpreter in Russian, went to the railway station and after reading a proclamation collected all the arms they could find and quickly restored order.

The *Attentive* remained at Soroka for a week, trying to forward the refugees and feeding them as well.

Amongst those who sought their protection from the Bolsheviks, were the monks of the Solovetski Island Monastery; a small guard was sent to the island and put the W/T station out of action. Information having been received that the Bolsheviks were going to visit the monastery, the guard was reinforced by 18 Finns under Captain Heaton, R.M.L.I., from Kem and by forming themselves into a stage army, marching in and out, so impressed the delegates that they thought it desirable to leave at once.

2. THE ROYAL MARINE FIELD FORCE.
See Plan 3.

In May 1918, the Admiralty decided that as summer was coming on when Naval movements would become possible, there was a chance that the Germans might use the inlets as submarine bases, and that as the Army could not provide any troops, they would send out a small force of Royal Marines to hold Murmansk and by generally supporting the local forces to secure the railway and the White Sea ports when navigation opened.

For this purpose a small Royal Marine Field Force was formed consisting of:

Commanding Officer	Lieut.-Colonel R C. Paterson, R.M.A.
Field Battery	Four 12 pr. 8 cwt. Naval Field Guns.
	Lieutenant W. D. Craig; 2nd-Lieutenant S. Jervis;
	B.S.M. Bryan; 85 N.C.O.s and Men, R.M.A.
Company R.M.L.I.	Captain L. A. Drake-Brockman; Lieutenant C. R Lane.
	2nd-Lieutenants R C. Carvell, L. Merchant, H. W. Stephens and E. A. Heaton.
	(One Platoon each from Chatham, Portsmouth, Plymouth and Deal), 207 N.C.O.s and Men.
Machine Gun Section	2nd-Lieutenants S. Matts, H. McFarland, E. B. Harries;
	6 N.C.O.s. 54 Privates, RM.L.I., with 6 Lewis guns.

The force was fully equipped with both summer and winter clothing and took camp equipment.

The unit was formed on 5th May and left Eastney on 20th, embarking in the S.S. *Porto*, at Newcastle; it arrived at Murmansk on 29th after an uneventful journey. Lieutenant Lane was appointed Adjutant and during the voyage training was carried out.

They disembarked on 31st and took over a small wooden barracks previously occupied by a small detachment from H.M.S. *Glory* and later took over three large buildings with a number of storehouses and established the Royal Marine Barracks, which apparently became the hub of that small universe. The officers mess was for some time quartered in a railway car.

The unit was borne on the books of H.M.S. *Glory* and was known as *Glory III*. The Marines were soon scattered to their various jobs, which as usual were varied in their nature. Lieut.-Colonel Paterson took over charge of the town and the detachment provided guards, working parties and the multifarious duties required in a base of this nature. 2nd-Lieutenant Matts with a guard was sent down the line to Kandalaksha; whilst 2nd-Lieutenants Merchant and Harries with 60 N.C.O.s and men went to Kola for Probalaswa Post and 2nd-Lieutenant Mc.Farland was sent to Pechenga to teach the local militia how to handle the Lewis gun.

On 8th June, Lieutenant W. D. Craig, 2nd-Lieutenants Matts and Carvell with Sergeants Butler, R.M.A., Phillips and Jordan, R.M.L.I., Gunner Colgan, and Privates Young and Simonds, R.M.L.I., with three interpreters were sent to Knyajoya Gourba, south of Kandalaksha to take over and train the Finnish Red Guard.

Captain Drake-Brockman with 2nd-Lieutenants Norris and Heaton and 150 N.C.O.s and men with two 12-prs. were sent to Kem to investigate the activities of the bands of Finnish White Guards and restore order in that neighbourhood.

When Lieutenant Craig's party took over the Finnish Red Guard, they were received with suspicion and found these wretched men nearly starving, ill-clad, riddled with socialistic ideas and in a miserable condition, the three interpreters were not much use and the British knew no words of the language; however, local rank *without pay* being granted Lieutenant Craig became a Major; the 2nd-Lieutenants, Captains; and the Sergeants, 2nd-Lieutenants; and the party set to work to form the Finnish Legion. They had learned the phonetic rendering of a dozen words of command in Finnish and armed with these and the inimitable initiative of the Royal Marine they started to drill their levies. At first they only obtained 60 volunteers but among them was a youngster who had held a commission in the Russian Army; he proved invaluable as he understood some French, and by translating from various languages including English, French, German, Russian, Finnish and Swedish the "detail" was eventually transferred to the heads of the recruits. Needless to say, being Royal Marines, their first care was to see that the poor wretches were fed and clothed, and after struggles with authority (the Army having landed the "Syren" Force under Major-General Maynard at Murmansk in June), their requirements were met; after three weeks hard work they turned out 300 men in a passable condition for inspection by General Maynard; this was not done without troubles, one company mutinying, but the reduction of the leader to the rank of private, combined with firmness, brought them round and in six weeks time the Finnish Legion of 600 men was ready, clothed in khaki uniforms with a badge of a red triangle on their arms and with their own regimental flag; they rendered useful service as will be described later. A tribute to the N.C.O.s of the Corps.

The Field Force were responsible for 500 miles of railway; and until the "Syren" force arrived the only other troops available were a small battalion of Serbians and a few Finns; even when the Allied forces arrived, they were so few that these positions were really held by bluff; fortunately the Germans did not know the numbers and the bluff held.

One of the first duties of the force was to disarm the civil population because nearly everyone had a rifle or revolver; this duty entailed constant house to house searches and they were eventually successful in rounding them all up. As the troops commenced to arrive, the Royal Marines were fully employed landing their stores, ammunition and generally helping them to settle into their places. In addition to the "Syren" force the "Elope" force under Major-General Poole was sent out, the latter proceeded in July to Archangel, (see Chapter 8).

The Royal Marines had established examining posts at Kola, Kandalaksha, Kem and Soroka, who issued passes and regulated the traffic of refugees and deportees along the line, whilst guards were furnished for the bridge.

An attempt was made to raise a Slavo-British Legion at Murmansk, which at first was under the control of the Royal Marines; never very large, after four months it dwindled to a mere handful and was handed over to Russian control.

By the end of June, Colonel Paterson was performing the duties of Base Commandant at Murmansk, whilst Captain Lane looked after the Royal Marines. American seamen had replaced the Royal Marines who had gone south, and there were French and Serbian troops in the town. Lieutenant Merchant was Intelligence Officer at Kola and Lieutenant Jervis after discharging stores on the quay at Kola for the Army, was sent to teach gunnery to the Polish Contingent consisting of 60 officers and 90 other ranks, the armament comprised two 12 pounders, two French 75 m. and two Russian field guns, whilst Lieutenant Harries was instructing the contingent in infantry drill.

There were a few troops at Lopaskaya and there were some British and Serbian troops at Imandra on the shores of the lake of that name; Kandalaksha was the Headquarters of the Southern District where Colonel Marsh of the Army was in command, with a Royal Marine detachment and gun to protect the harbour and a few British troops and a Serbian battalion with some Finns.

Kem was the most southerly town actually occupied by the Allies at this time; the Royal Marine Detachment there had been reinforced by a company of Serbs, and Soroka, further south was controlled by an armoured train.

Kem was the recruiting centre for the Karelians; Captain Drake-Brockman had been appointed to command them with the local rank of Major, 2nd Lieutenant Heaton with the local rank of Captain was also attached, whilst 2nd Lieutenant Norris remained in command of the Royal Marines.

The Karelians were a fine body of men, who did good work, as were also their women kind of whom two were awarded the Military Medal for defending a boat-load of provisions of which they were in charge. Captain Drake-Brockman was eventually seconded for service with these men in November, 1918 and in May., 1919 was killed when leading a battalion of them.

The Army Staffs had now assumed charge of affairs on shore and Army officers were appointed to the Finnish Legion; they had also taken over command of the various stations in which the Royal Marine detachments were stationed. The detachment left at Murmansk provided parties for every description of work, guards, working parties, unloading transports, building quarters, laying down light railways, guarding food trains, building ammunition dumps, providing signallers to communicate between the Army and the Navy and guarding Russian prisoners of war.

On 17th July the Finnish Legion under Major Craig, R.M.A. sent out a party and got into touch with the White Finns about 60 miles from Knyajoya and about 10 miles from the frontier and after a skirmish killed four of the enemy and took some prisoners. It was then decided to occupy some posts near the Finland Frontier to cover Knyajoya; Riwa and L. Soukilla were occupied by Lieutenant Matts and 150 Finns, whilst Lieutenant Carvell was at Karasen on Lake Konda. Patrols were sent out and a watch kept on the White Guard movements; Major Craig and Sergeant Butler with 80 men were at Tumsa. On One patrol Lieutenant Matts was nearly cut off, escaping after a skirmish in which he lost some men. As the latter was suffering from an old leg wound he was shortly after invalided and Private Young, R.M.L.I. remained in charge, training his men and teaching them Lewis gun drill until relieved by Army Officers. Major Craig maintained these posts until the end of September when all the Royal Marines except Sergeant (T/2nd. Lieut) Jordan returned to Murmansk on relief by Army Officers.; Lieut. Carvell rejoining his company at Kem.

On 31st. July, H.M.S. *Attentive* was called to Archangel as described in Chapter 8, and the headquarters of the "Elope" Force proceeded with her. Lieutenants Merchant and Harries with 94 N.C.O.s and men of the Royal Marine Field Force accompanied this force as related and took part in the operations on the River Dwina, being transferred to the books of H.M. Monitor 25. Major Drake-Brockman and Captain Heaton with their Karelians accompanied a force under Colonel Woods towards the Finnish Frontier and after the sharpest fighting of the campaign defeated the White Finns.

At the end of October, Colonel Paterson was seconded for service with the Army and was appointed Base Commandant at Murmansk. Captain Lane took over the command of the Royal Marines with Lieutenants Jervis, McFarland, Norris and Craig who was appointed adjutant. Lieutenant Stephens was at Kola with a few men, Carvell at Kem, Merchant and Harries with their party at Archangel and Lieutenant Thirkell arrived as a reinforcement.

The Royal Marine detachment was now attached to the 236th Brigade instead of being directly under General Headquarters, but except for increasing circumlocution and delay this did not affect them much as they continued to do all the work as before.

On 17th December the Royal Marine Field Force from Murmansk was detailed to proceed to

Kandalaksha, where the detachment from Kem was to join up and go into training to become a mobile column. This upset all their arrangements for spending the winter at Murmansk.

Captain Lane with Lieutenants Thirkell and Stephens and 50 N.C.O.s and men left Murmansk on 31st December as an advanced party to prepare accommodation, travelling by train; at one place the officers got out and the train unexpectedly going on they had to march for seven hours over the frozen snow in face of a cutting wind till an engine picked them up. There was no accommodation at Kandalaksha and matters were rather chaotic, so the remainder of the Force remained at Murmansk until Captain Willes, R.M.A. arrived at end of January, 1919 to command *Glory III*.

The company detrained at a place called the "Dyke," eight miles south of Kandalaksha, where they were joined by the Royal Marines from Kem. The quarters were very poor and food supply rather difficult. Training was however, commenced and for the following account of the training I am indebted to Sergeant F. H. Jordan, R.M.L.I. Before leaving Murmansk each man was issued with an Arctic kit designed by Sir E. Shackleton consisting of four sets of Wolseley underclothing, One Burberry suit, one large woollen lined overcoat, 12 pairs of socks, one pair of Shackleton boots, one Arctic cap, special gloves, one pair blizzard goggles, one pair of skis and sticks, one Westinghouse rifle made in the U.S.A. The company also was equipped with small axes, sleighs as used in the Shackleton expedition to Antarctic, sleeping bags, Stockholm tar, and specially prepared food.

Captain Lane was in command and 2nd Lieutenant Stephens and Sergeant Jordan who had undergone a special course were appointed Ski-ing Instructors and training began.

After correct fitting of the skis and learning the use of the sticks, the first lesson was to learn how to move along in single file, the leading man being changed every ten minutes as it was very difficult and hard work to "beat track"; when fairly proficient they were taken for long runs through the woods with rifles slung. They were then instructed in "turnings on the move and at the halt" and the men gained confidence. Two or three pairs of snow shoes were always taken with the column in case a man should break his skis, as it was impossible to walk on the snow.

At the end of January Captain Willes relieved Captain Lane in command and he selected Popoff as a more suitable place to concentrate the force with better accommodation. Popoff was the Port of Kem on the White Sea. The remainder of the Force dribbled south as guards of food trains, etc. until the last party arrived on 10th March under Lieutenant McFarland; Lieutenant Craig was appointed Assistant Base Commandant at Murmansk and left the Force.

Training was now carried out on the White Sea which was easier than amongst the forests near Kandalaksha. The company was now able to form up as a company on parade with rifles slung and equipment worn over the Burberry suit; and they eventually mastered the difficult art of "turning together" and platoon drill was carried out exactly as on parade; they then went on to company and extended order drill in which they ultimately attained perfection. Having mastered the Close Order drill, they were instructed in musketry and were taught all the firing positions and also to use the ski sticks as a tripod, and the rifle was also fired whilst on the move down a slope. They were then instructed in the use of the sleighs and parties were sent out to camp and lived like the Eskimo. The temperature varied from 30 to 40 degrees below zero, but frostbites were comparatively few, and the health was very good. Approximately 200 men were trained and attained a high standard of proficiency.

During the first fortnight of April, owing to rumours of Bolshevik activity Captain Lane and 200 men were sent in to garrison Kem, Captain Willes remaining at Popoff where there were magazines and stores. The rising however, did not materialise and on 13th Captain Lane was appointed Assistant Base Commandant at Murmansk.

The winter now suddenly collapsed and the thaw came on so training came to an end and the column moved from Popoff to Kem where they were quartered in new Nissen huts and were employed on guards and fatigues.

About 27th April, Brigadier-General Pryce inspected the company and the company was organised for active operations with R.M.A., Chatham, Portsmouth, Plymouth platoons and a Lewis gun platoon; all the platoons being somewhat small.

On 29th April the company with 14 R.F.A. and a 65 m.m. gun left Kem in high spirits for a place called Urozeroy and detrained on 30th and were quartered in filthy huts lately vacated by the Bolsheviks. Colonel Lecky of the Army assumed command of the operations and an attack was planned for the following day in conjunction with one company of French Infantry and one company of the Slavo-British Legion (White Russians). 48 hours rations were taken.

At 2 p.m. 1st May, a train arrived with the other units and the company was crammed into the remaining carriages, the Headquarter Staff being left behind, and arrived as far as the train could go in about an hour where American bridge builders were repairing a bridge which had been blown up. Having detrained the advance commenced, the Russians leading followed by the other companies behind each other along a single line railway track; on both sides were thick forests and they had to march along the sleepers, a very risky but a necessary method of advance. At midnight an old siding was reached where a halt was made; 20 men had been told off to assist the R.F.A. to get their gun over the numerous blown up bridges and broken places in the line.

Fires were lit and rations eaten; starting again about 1-30 a.m. they pushed on and soon encountered a strong Bolshevik patrol, but as it was pitch dark the force retired and rested until daylight.

Advancing at daybreak the Plymouth Platoon was held up by a strong Bolshevik post until the arrival of the R.M.A. Platoon when they advanced and drove the enemy from his first position at 8 a.m. After re-organisation the advance was resumed and at 2 p.m. another post was encountered which was taken at 4 p.m., all the Royal Marine Platoons being engaged. As the troops were very exhausted from the marching on the sleepers, the force halted for the night and placed outposts. At this point they met an armoured train with machine guns which retired leaving four dead and the fireman severely wounded. The Allied Force lost two colonial sergeants killed in trying to bomb the engine.

At 4-30 a.m. next morning the advance was re-organised, the Russians, who were of little use, being placed in support, the French took the right flank and were eventually lost in the wood, the Royal Marines were in the centre and on the left. After advancing about five versts formation for attack was assumed and the gun took up a position on the right of the railway and opened fire over their heads. The armoured train came on to about 600 yards firing its machine guns but was forced to retire and all platoons advanced under rifle and machine gun fire until within sight of their objective. The forest was very thick on both sides, but the advance was made under cover until the clearing was reached when the force was held up. The enemy could be seen retiring, and a few minutes later a large engine shed was blown up and the troops marched into the place which was a large railway centre called Maselskaya about 11 a.m. on 3rd May, 1919. Rations were exhausted and they were badly off for food because twenty seven railway bridges had been blown up and supplies could only come up in small lots, biscuits coming up one day, bully beef the next and at last a small supply of tea and sugar came in on pack animals, but in four days the Americans who had worked day and night enabled the first train to get through with provisions.

Patrols were sent out, but the enemy retired for some distance, the General and Staff arrived and the company was inspected by General Maynard who congratulated them on their attack and said that he hoped to get them relieved shortly as they had now been out a year, but in the meantime they were to continue the attack; reinforcements of the Middlesex Regiment and K.R.R.C. and some foreign units arrived and were quartered in Maselskaya. During their stay here the quarters were destroyed by fire. About 14 days later the Royal Marines were ordered to advance again, and reached the next siding without meeting any resistance. Later they were reinforced by the K.R.R.C. And together they pushed on until they met the enemy holding a position at No. 12 siding, the enemy were quickly dislodged, but at the next siding, No. 11, strong resistance was encountered and the company was held up for 14 hours before the position was gained. Food supplies were still scanty and the men became very exhausted and were given 24 hours rest. The next morning the advance was continued under very trying conditions and during the day again met the armoured train, but the force were able to take cover in the forest. The 65 m.m. gun came into action and the enemy retired and the force arrived within attacking distance of a large village and railway station called Medvyeja Gora on the western edge of Lake Onega. After several hours fighting the Royal Marines alone took this position and held it; the retreating .enemy left dynamite in the fireplaces of many of the big buildings and also at the Railway Station and set the forest on fire. The enemy were very badly trained and led and there were no British casualties as the woods provided good cover. Whilst they remained here they were badly off for food and accommodation and were eventually relieved by army troops and returned to Kem.

Major L. Drake-Brockman had been killed in action on 10th May, whilst successfully resisting a counter attack at Karelian Maselska 12 miles west of the railway near Lake Onega, at the head of his Karelian battalion, by whom he was much beloved.

Leave and demobilisation were in the air, and those who got home on leave did not return: Lieutenant Jervis and Norris were the first to go and were demobilised, but at the end of March a draft of six officers and 24 N.C.O.s and men arrived and the strength of the Force was then about 300.

The force remained at Popoff until they returned home, after several vexatious delays, seven officers and 263 N.C.O.s and men finally embarking at Murmansk on 10th July.

The following rewards were awarded to this Force.

O.B.E	Lieut.-Colonel R C. Paterson, R.M.A.
	Lieutenant E. B. Harries, R.M.L.I.
D.S.M.	Private J. H. Metcalfs (Portsmouth) R.M.L.I.
	Acting-Bombr. A. W. Waltham, R.M.A.
	Private W. G. Geary (Portsmouth) R.M.L.I.
	Corporal C. Griffiths (Plymouth) R.M.L.I.
	Corporal W. J. Last, R.M.A.
	Sergt. A. Levett (Portsmouth) RM.L.I.
	Private W. E. Lewington (Portsmouth) R.M.L.I.
	Private W. G. Peters (Portsmouth) R.M.L.I.
	Sergt. E. C. White (Portsmouth) R.M.L.I.
M.S.M.	Colour-Sergt. C. Bryan, R.M.A.
	Q.M.S. H. R Underhay (Portsmouth) R.M.L.I.
Military Medal	Private E. T. Bolton (Portsmouth) R.M.L.I
	Private H. Gingell (Portsmouth) R.M.L.I.
	Private D. Welsh (Portsmouth) R.M.L.I.

3. 6ᵀᴴ ROYAL MARINE BATTALION.

(See Plan 12).

During the peace negotiations in 1919 it was decided that a plebiscite should be taken in Schleswig-Holstein as to whether the province should remain with Germany or return to Denmark from which it had been wrested in the war of 1864. A small Allied Force was to supervise the arrangements and prevent any disorder. The British contingent was to be provided by the Admiralty; Rear-Admiral Hon. A. D. H. Boyle, C.B., was appointed in charge with Brevet Lieut.-Colonel R. D. Ormsby as his Staff Officer. For the actual force to be employed a battalion of Royal Marines was raised consisting of one company R.M.A. and one each from Chatham, Portsmouth and Plymouth. They were concentrated at Bedenham near Gosport and placed under training in the middle of July.

The officers appointed- to the battalion were :-

Commanding Officer	Lieut.-Colonel A. de W. Kitcat, RM.L.I.
Second in Command	Major A. W. Ridings, R.M.A.
Adjutant	Captain R. Burton, D.S.C., R.M.L.I.
Quartermaster	Lieutenant A. C. Ackerman, R.M.L.I.
Sergt.-Major	Q.M.S.I. D. Board, R.M.L.I.
R.M.A. Company.	Captains W. R Boultbee, Ed. O. Walters.
	Lieutenants J. Franklyn, M.C., A. V. Hall, C. P. Sparrow, L. O. Jones.
Chatham Company	Major A. C. Barnby; Captain R. H. Watts.
	Lieutenants H. S. G. Eastman, P. R Smith-Hill, F. M. Bramall, G. W. Beasley.
Portsmouth Company.	Major R W. Laing; Captain E. J. Noyes.
	Lieutenants T. W. Wood, C. G. de B. Godfrey, W. J. Bisiker, R L. Harris.
Plymouth Company.	Major J. P. Nind; Captain D. B. Carter.
	Lieutenants W. A. N. Hanson, K. B. Previte, C. G. Luxmore, E. St. J. Brockman.
Surgeon-Commander	R A. Wilkinson, Surgeon Lieut-Commander E. C. Nicholls, R.N.
Chaplain	Rev. A. W. Briggs, RN.

Soon afterwards the Admiralty was asked to provide a Battalion of Royal Marines for Lord Rawlinson's force which was being sent out to relieve the North Russian garrison and the 6th Battalion Royal Marines was detailed for this duty, the Army troops were mostly volunteers. They were relieved for the Schleswig duty by the 7th Battalion Royal Marines formed of Royal Marines landed from the Grand Fleet under Major and Bt. Lieut.-Colonel F. J. Hudleston, R.M.A., but this Battalion was not required and the detachments re-embarked.

The 6th Battalion left Bedmenham on the night 31st July-1st August, 1919 and embarked at Tilbury in the S.S. *Czar* reaching Murmansk on 8th August, where they were surprised to find the sky and sea blue and the sun hot. The Portsmouth and Plymouth companies entrained that evening for Kem to relieve 1600 Army troops and the Chatham company followed the next day to Kandalaksha, after waiting eight hours their train managed to crawl 200 yards, but they eventually arrived on 10th.

The R.M.A. company was billeted at Murmansk and a portion were utilised as gun detachments for the armoured trains, the remainder being scattered up and down the line, the Company Headquarters moving later to Medvyeja Gora at the north west corner of Lake Onega. One train was engaged in the affair on, 17th August referred to later.

On arrival at Kem on 10th August, Battalion Headquarters and "C" (Portsmouth) Company proceeded to Kem town about two miles off. "D" (Plymouth) Company went into Nissen huts lately vacated by refugees, providing one platoon as a guard to General Headquarters and a section for police duties at Popoff.

On 14th "C" Company entrained for Medvyeja Gora which was Brigade Headquarters in the forward area; and on 20th "D" Company and Battalion Headquarters also left for the forward area. Whilst at Kem training was carried on with one day's field firing, but there was very little information as to the kind of fighting that was to be expected. The companies were composed of very young soldiers, mostly recruits and men who, after the necessarily shortened periods of training. had been embarked for duty afloat during the war years, whilst their training in England had been directed more to prepare them for the ceremonial parades in Schleswig-Holstein than for active service under very difficult conditions. Considerable numbers of men were taken by General Headquarters for batmen, clerks, checkers on the railway, etc. who were mostly old soldiers, so that the company strengths were much reduced, for example the Plymouth company was reduced to 140 men.

General Rawlinson on his arrival at Popoff was received by a guard from "D" Company and a guard from the same company accompanied him on his visit to the forward area.

It was not until 1st September that the Battalion learnt the object of the operations to be undertaken; the plan was to break the enemy resistance in order to enable the British troops to be withdrawn and the White Russian troops to take over whilst the Allied troops were evacuated.

On 17th August "C" Company in conjunction with an armoured train drove the enemy down the line so as to enable the outpost line to observe the railway culvert which was intact. On 21st "D" Company moved to Kapaselga Station in place of "C" Company who had taken over the outpost line.

On 23rd "D" Company took over the outpost line from "C" Company which moved on to Tivdia for operations against reported concentrations of the enemy at Koikori and Ussuna, places south west of Lake Pyalozero; Major Ridings took over command of the sector vice Colonel Kitcat who moved his headquarters forward with "C" Company.

It was now decided to move "C" Company and battalion headquarters across the lake to Snyatnavolok on the western shore as a more suitable jumping off place for the attack on Koikori. Lake Pyalozero had to be crossed in pulling boats six men to a boat manned by very indifferent Russian peasants, the crossing therefore took three hours and eventually "C" Company was assembled at Snyatnavolok; meanwhile on 26th "B" Company moved up to Medvyeja Gora.

On night 29/30th August "C" Company under Lieutenant-Colonel Kitcat left their camp for Koikori about 18 to 19 versts distant and advanced to 12 verst post where the roads to Koikori and Ussuna separated; touch was here gained with the enemy and the advance continued on Koikori, where fire was opened on them, the Bolshevik,; were well supplied with machine guns and the country was fairly open; "C" Company took up a position on the brow of a hill overlooking the village, but all attempts to advance were held up by machine gun fire, which the artillery failed to silence; attempts were made to outflank the enemy but this also failed; Colonel Kitcat was wounded and Maj. Ridings then took over command. As soon as it was dark the company, having lost three men killed and 18 wounded, fell back to Snyatnovolok where they arrived about 9 p.m. very exhausted as no food had been issued since mid-night the day before.

"B" and "D" Companies were then sent down to reinforce "C" Company; "B" Company marching from Medvyeja Gora on 1st September via Tivdia and the northern end of Lake Pyalozero. "D" Company were relieved of outpost duty on 28th; this company had not only held the outpost line watching the railway, but also the defence posts in Kapaselga village, which was the rail head for all stores for the main force; there was no company in reserve and in addition to being on outpost duty they were obliged to bring up all their own stores. When relieved, they proceeded to Tivdia, having handed over to two companies of the East Surrey Regiment at 11 a.m. All gear, kit bags, steel helmets, gas masks, etc. were left behind and they proceeded in full marching order carrying also two blankets and one waterproof sheet per man. Lewis guns and spare S.A.A. were carried in country carts; marching on to Lake Limozero (four miles) they embarked in a flotilla of pulling boats and rowed 10 miles across the Lake; it was impossible to steer a direct course owing to the islands; disembarking they marched to Tivdia where they went into billets, one half company taking over the outpost line at midnight from the Olonetz Regiment.

On 1st September a conference was held at Snyatnavolok and the forthcoming operations were explained by the Brigadier; it was really a flanking operation whilst the main force pushed down the line to Lijma station.

The plan was for "B" and "C" Companies under command of Major Williams of the Army with some artillery and Machine Gun Corps to attack Koikori, whilst "D" Company attacked Ussuna (at north east corner of Lake Sumozero). "B" Company was then to assist "D" Company and push on to Shuiski where the Russian troops would push through and take up the line.

They were to be at 9 verst post on the Snyatnavolok-Ussuna Road by 5th September and were to be withdrawn on 15th.

"B" Company left on 3rd for 10 versts post to hold it as a dump and put out an outpost line, which on 4th was in touch with the Bolsheviks, whilst aeroplanes bombed 12 verst post; after which some of the enemy came in saying they wanted to surrender, but when two sections went out they changed their minds and the patrol was fired on by a machine gun.

On the 5th a patrol under Lieutenant Smith-Hill found 12 verst post evacuated, and at noon half a company of "C" came up and occupied the post whilst the remainder relieved "B" Company who returned to Snyatnavolok.

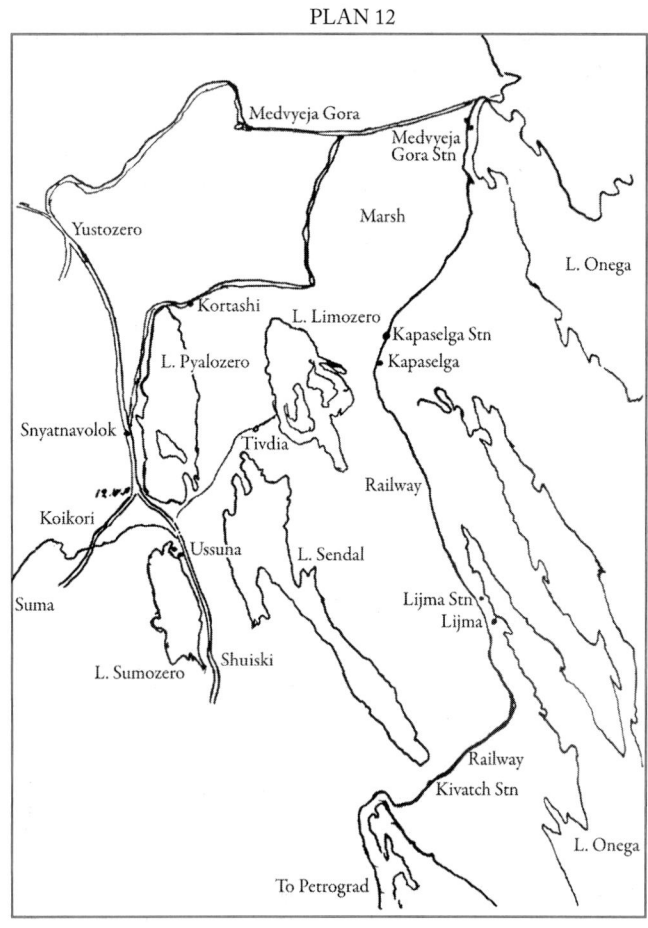

PLAN 12

"D" company meanwhile was to leave Tivdia and cross Lake Pyalozero (five miles wide) in two portions on nights 3/4 and 4/5th September; they were to be opposite Snyatnavolok by 10 p.m., and then under cover of the darkness to drop down southwards along the shore to a point where they could land and reach the road for the advance, keeping inside "C" Company's posts. Operations were delayed for two days, but as Major Nind and a half company had already started for the lake side he remained there, leaving Captain Carter and a half company to garrison Tivdia with the Russians.

The whole force was now under the command of Major Strover of the Army and Major Ridings was detailed for command of the Ussuna column. Platoons of "C" Company under Captain Noyes with a battery of R.F.A. and half a machine gun section were sent to place 12 verst post in a state of defence, which was carried out without interruption, and on the following morning one platoon escorted the battery forward to bombard the village of Koikori which was carried out successfully with one man wounded.

On the evening of the 6th "D" Company headquarters with one-and-a-half platoons in 17 boats crossed the lake, but the light at 9 verst post to guide them had gone out so after cruising up and down the night was spent in a bay to avoid drifting, and the search was continued at dawn, the pier being sighted at 6 a.m. on the 7th. Lieutenant Previte's platoon, which had crossed the day before, had a slight skirmish with the enemy on the 6th; one of their boats met company headquarters during the night but the remainder had gone off on some other errand.

Troops and stores were arriving during the afternoon of 7th; "B" Company relieved "C" Company at 12 verst post and took up a position at the Cross Roads. Lieutenant Previte with his platoon of "D" Company were sent on 5 versts on the Ussuna road to act as advanced guard the next day; and to make certain that there should be no mistake in directing Captain Carter's crossing that night Major Nind lit a bonfire on the pier. Captain Carter arrived at midnight having crossed to Snyatnavolok in a large sailing boat, but becoming becalmed there, he landed and seized some pulling boats and brought his half company in safety down the lake.

Dealing first with the Ussuna attack; the advance commenced at 6 a.m. on 8th. The Ussuna column was in front and picked up their advanced guard at 9 a.m. The advanced guard was fired on when nearing Ussuna, but the opposition was brushed aside and it was seen that the ground up to the village was fairly open with low scrub; the advanced guard then seized some fairly commanding ground with good cover; the remainder of the company (less one platoon in reserve and half platoon with battalion headquarters extended to the left in the hope of outflanking the defence.

Captain R. Burton with battalion headquarters and the half platoon of "D" Company was to try to get round the enemy's rear, but not before bombing operations by seaplanes at 10-30 a.m. were over.

The woods were now quite thick, and it was becoming difficult to keep touch; "D" Company was suddenly fired on from flank and rear, which proved to come from Captain Burton's party who had mistaken them for the enemy, this firing was pluckily stopped by two men from "D" Company.

By 1-30 p.m. a firing line was established at the edge of the wood ; it was found that the ground up to the village was intersected with hedges, haystacks etc. which had been cleverly made use of by the enemy; the company now opened a heavy fire supported by two 65 c.m. Russian guns and the Machine Gun Corps on their right rear; whilst Captain Burton's party was apparently firing with Lewis guns on the left. According to the "experts" in Bolshevist fighting this should have made the 'Bolos' run, but their M.G. fire was as active as ever; Sergeant Mumford with a patrol was then sent forward to ascertain the situation; in spite of a hot fire this N.C.O. got within 80 yards of the enemy trenches and found them to be excellent with barbed wire and well manned, the hand of the German was plainly evident (Sergeant Mumford was awarded the Military Medal). A message was now received from Lieutenant Brockman with Captain Burton's party that the latter had been killed and Sergeant-Major Board wounded and that he had taken up a position in prolongation of "D" Company's left flank. Lieutenant Hanson in working forward to make a reconnaissance was wounded at this time as were three men, he was awarded the Military Cross for his good reconnaissance work.

Their instructions from Army Headquarters were that "operations should be taken slowly, casualties can and should be avoided," so the Company Commander was ordered by the Commanding Officer of the Column to hold on during the night as it was no use risking an advance as casualties were not wanted; trenches were accordingly made as well as possible and water was brought up; they worried the enemy during the night, but only succeeded in drawing his fire and their hopes of finding the enemy trenches evacuated at dawn were disappointed; at daylight fire was opened on the right flank of the company by two field guns which had been brought up to the village in the dark and the right flank had to be withdrawn from the edge of the wood.

Meanwhile the attack on Koikori by "B" and "C" Companies had taken place. One platoon of Chatham company formed the advanced guard; "C" Company with two platoons of "B" Company was to make a frontal attack and to dig in one verst in front of the village, whilst "B" Company under Major Barnby less two platoons was to make a flank attack on the left, prior to assisting "D" Company at Ussuna. Major Williams (army) was in charge of the frontal attack which reached the position indicated but was ordered not to advance further. Koikori was strongly fortified with concrete machine-gun emplacements and Germans were assisting the Bolos. The headquarters and two platoons of "B" Company with two machine guns of the Machine Gun Corps turned off the road to the left at 151 verst post and advanced to a position from which Koikori church could be seen, but not the river as they had been told, (no one in these platoons was in possession of a map). The machine-guns were placed in position and opened fire and the platoons worked forward, but the Russian guide, who was found afterwards to be a Russian spy (Private Pyle saw him in their camp) had led them to the wrong point and into an ambush which was successful as most of the casualties were caused by fire from their rear, whilst the howitzers were unable to see the Very's lights fired by the company. Lieutenant Smith-Hill and Privates Jenkins and Pyle advanced to where they could reconnoitre the trenches and bomb them; in doing this Pyle was wounded and after two men had been killed in trying to rescue him he was captured and kept prisoner by the Bolsheviks for a year. Pyle was awarded the D.C.M. for his gallantry on this occasion and for the determination and loyalty displayed by him whilst a prisoner of war. Major Barnby was wounded at this time and as the machine guns could do no more, and the No.1 Platoon had used all its ammunition, they were ordered to fall back to 12 verst post and joined with "C" Company who had held on to their position till 5 p.m. and then retired to an outpost line at 7 verst post. Captain Noyes also was wounded, the losses being 10 killed and 23 wounded.

"D" Company remained in position in front of Ussuna on 9th and were informed that the Russian battalion was ready to relieve them in the afternoon. Heavy shelling recommenced at noon and in order to avoid casualties the company was slightly withdrawn to a reserve position during the afternoon; the enemy from across the river were very active, and as the situation had to be cleared up, the withdrawal was delayed till after dark and 12 verst post was not reached till midnight; one platoon being left on the Ussuna Road as protection to the general bivouac. The Russian Battalion and two machine-guns were left in observation of Ussuna. Many troops were passing through the cross roads; the British troops passing through on withdrawal and Russian troops passing up to the front.

On 10th September "D" Company less one platoon were ordered to Koikori to stand by to occupy the place if the strong patrol consisting of "X" Platoon (from "B" and "C" Companies) some R.F.A. and machine guns which had been sent out found it evacuated. They however, found that it was still held in strength by the enemy and in accordance with their orders retired on the supports. The country was very dense and difficult, and they occupied a very unsatisfactory line of outposts that night; one company of Serbians were ordered to relieve them on 11th but did not turn up till 12th when they and "X" platoon relieved "D" Company which marched back to Snyatnavolok 12 miles where they were billetted. On the 15th, Battalion headquarters and "B" and "C" Companies left for Medvyeja Gora by route march and "D" Company took over the outpost line. On 18th "D" Company's outposts were withdrawn and a column in charge of Major Nind consisting of "D" Company, "X" platoon, Machine Gun Corps and R.A.M.C. left Snyatnavolok, marching, via Yustozero. On 19th the weather broke and as no shelter could be obtained they pushed on through the night in awful mud and reached Medvyeja Gora village the next day; they arrived at the station on 21st where baths and a change of clothing were obtained, having had none for three weeks.

"D" Company left the station at 2 a.m. on 22nd arriving at Murmansk on 24th, during the journey there were many disquieting rumours that the Bolsheviks were raising their heads again as the British troops were leaving.

The Battalion reassembled at Murmansk and the men who had been left as employed and guards at Kem, etc. rejoined. On 8th October, they re-embarked ; General Lord Rawlinson travelling in the same transport and arrived at Glasgow on 13th October where they were dispersed to their several Divisions.

PART IV.

Ships' Detachment Landing Parties.

CHAPTER 14.

MEDITERRANEAN AND RED SEA.

1.-Coast of Syria – H.M.S. Doris, 1914-15. 2.-Long Island, Smyrna. 3. - Gulf of Akaba.

IN December, 1914 and January, 1915, H.M.S. *Doris* (Captain F. Larken) was operating on the coast of Syria and Asia Minor, with a view to interfering with the Turkish communications, in the event of an advance on Egypt, and this led to constant landings on the coast, for destruction of various points, and means of communication. The following is a short account of the several operations in which the Royal Marines were concerned.-

At Ascalon, on 15th December, after firing a few rounds of six-inch at a tent ashore, Captain Wilkinson, R.M.L.I, and 10 of his detachment with a party of seamen under Lieutenant Twigg, with a machine gun landed to investigate. The party came under fire, but effected their object without casualties. Again on 18th December, at Sidon, the seamen under Commander Brounger, destroyed two miles of telegraph and telephone wire; Captain Wilkinson and 15 R.M.L.I. acting as covering party, the work was carried out without opposition, and at dusk, another Naval party landed to cut the railway.

On 19th December, the *Doris* commenced the bombardment of the coast road and railway, leading out of Alexandretta to the northward, and then sent in an ultimatum, giving the Turks 18 hours in which to surrender all war materiel, or the town would be bombarded; two locomotives were ultimately surrendered for destruction.

On 21st December, Commander Brounger, with 39 seamen and Captain Wilkinson, with 24 Royal Marines, landed to demolish the railway bridge, near Dinort Yol station; the landing party came under rifle fire on landing, which was soon silenced by the ship's guns. The advance to the bridge, which was about one mile distant, was unopposed, the party successfully damaged the bridge and returned to their boats, bringing off the telegraph instruments from the station. Although a small party of the enemy was entrenched on the beach, they did not open fire on the boats.

On 5th January, 1915, Commander Brounger, with 100 seamen, and Captain Wilkinson, with 40 R.M.L.I., with a 12 pounder field gun and two machine guns, were sent in to destroy the railway bridge, which was three miles east of Messina, and two and a half miles inland. The boats left the ship at 3-30 a.m., to carry out the work before daylight, but on approaching the shore, they came under the fire of field guns and rifles of the enemy, and were recalled to the ship.

On 6th January, two parties were landed west of Alexandretta, one under Captain Wilkinson, the northern party, to cover a railway demolition, and the other to carry out a second demolition, each party consisted of 29 seamen, 5 stokers and 22 Royal Marines. The distance between the parties was about one and a half miles; the landings were unopposed, but the scouts were fired on by a party of Turks, who ran when the ship opened fire. All the demolition work was successfully carried out and the telegraph line was destroyed for some distance.

The Torpedo Lieutenant with 32 seamen, and Captain Wilkinson with eight Royal Marines, landed again on 7th January, four miles north of Alexandretta, to demolish a road bridge. The landing was opposed by snipers, and Corporal Warburton, (Portsmouth) was killed; Private Wallace (Portsmouth), was awarded the D.S.M., for assisting to carry the body back to the boat under fire. They re-embarked under fire and were lucky to escape with few casualties; three petty officers were also awarded the D.S.M.

That their operations had effected their object was shown by a report received from General Officer Commanding, Egypt, on 12th January, that the work of the *Doris* had prevented 40,000 Turks from marching towards the Suez Canal.

The Intelligence Officer with 25 seamen, and Captain Wilkinson with 15 Royal Marines landed again on 24th, four miles east of Alexandretta, to reconnoitre the ground, with a view to a landing in force by troops. They were fired at on landing, but carried out the examination of the ground as far as the railway line 200 yards away; having killed two of the enemy and wounded three, they re-embarked. The next day they were landed again under the Gunnery Lieutenant on a reconnoitring expedition, which pushed inland about three quarters of a mile, and the seamen destroyed more telegraph line without opposition.

On 27th, the same party with Captain Wilkinson and 15 Royal Marines landed one and a half miles west of Alexandretta, and the reconnaissance was pushed half a mile inland, but retired on sighting a party of the enemy, 22 strong, of whom they killed two and wounded four.

On 30th January, the Gunnery Lieutenant with 28 seamen and 1 N.C.O. and eight Royal Marines, landed at Jonah's Pillar (Alexandretta) to capture and destroy a railway trolley, which was used for repairing the telegraph line. They accomplished their purpose having killed one of the enemy, wounded two and brought off five as prisoners.

On 31st, Commander Brounger with 27 seamen, and Captain Wilkinson and 18 Royal Marines, landed again at the same place to carry out further destruction of the telegraph. The landing was opposed, but the enemy were silenced by six-inch shrapnel; 400 yards of telegraph wire were destroyed, and four prisoners brought off, the Royal Marines covered the landing and the re-embarkation, one seaman in the steam cutter being mortally wounded.

The *Doris* then left for the Suez Canal, where she served until she took part in the Dardanelles operations.

The foregoing operations are notable as an example of what can be accomplished by small parties, when skilfully handled and allotted suitable objectives.

Captain Larken was awarded the C.M.G., Commander Brounger the D.S.O., for this and the Dardanelles, whilst Captain Wilkinson received the Cross of Chevalier of the Legion of Honour, and the Italian Bronze Medal for military valour.

2. LONG ISLAND, SMYRNA.

After the evacuation of the Dardanelles, it was decided to occupy Long Island, at the entrance to the Gulf of Smyrna, as a kind of outpost to watch the port in the event of submarines making use of it. Captain L. S. Wilkinson, and 45 R.M.L.I. from H.M.S. *Doris*, in addition to Naval and Royal Naval Air Service ratings and 60 Greek Irregulars from Mitylene, were therefore landed there on 16th April, 1916, and remained in occupation till 27th May.

Sentry posts and patrols were established, connected by telephone with two centres, one at each end of the island, which is five miles long by two and a half broad.

The mainland was practically all round and at one point only 2000 yards distant, in consequence of which dug-outs were constructed to shelter the garrison from enemy shell fire, and two old field guns were sent from the ship for short range fire on the mainland.

Posts to observe the long range fire of the monitors were also established, which were manned at stated times by day and night.

The Turks, under German artillery officers, gradually erected gun and searchlight positions, all round the shores of the Gulf, and the island threatened to become untenable.

Reports showed that the object of the occupation was being achieved, but finally evacuation was ordered. The monitors, which at first used to lie in a small harbour at the north end of the island, were gradually driven further out to sea, by the enemy artillery, M 30 being sunk in the harbour. The garrison kept up communication with the squadron by means of drifters at night.

The evacuation was gradually carried out at night; the stores and live stock being first sent off in drifters and "K" lighters, and lastly the personnel. The withdrawal was successfully accomplished and no casualties were sustained during the occupation. The torpedo ratings, before they left, laid mines on likely beaches, which, from reports received later, appear to have been very successful, when the Turks at last visited the island.

After the evacuation, an officer's patrol visited the island nightly for about three weeks, and steps were taken to make the Turks believe that the place was still occupied. At the end of this time, the Turks subjected the island to an intense bombardment, which lasted off and on for 48 hours, and which set the island on fire from end to end, and it was not again visited by the British.

3. GULF OF AKABA.

Akaba is a small Arab town, at the head of the Gulf of that name, which assumed a certain amount of importance as being a place where touch could be obtained with the Arabs. The Turks had a small fort here, and it was a convenient depot for ammunition for troops in Arabia.

On 1st November, 1914, as soon as war with Turkey was declared, the *Savage*, and *Scourge*, torpedo-boat-destroyers, bombarded the fort and barracks, but the place had been evacuated by the Turkish troops. The destroyers then landed a small party and captured a lot of papers. At 4 p.m., H.M.S. *Minerva* (Captain Warleigh) arrived and opening fire finished off the place. On the 2nd, the Minerva landed 100 men to secure the fort, burn material, etc., and the next day a good deal of ammunition and some very important papers were discovered.

On the 4th, 200 men under the Commander with Maxims (the Royal Marine officer was Lieutenant A. G. Stacey, R.M.L.I.) proceeded inland for about five miles to the mouth of the valley Wadi-el-Ethem; one officer and six men went on half a mile further, and encountered a party of Arabs, who opened fire, which was returned; the main body coming up the Arabs made off, and the party returned to the ship. Touch was gained with the local sheikh but no satisfactory arrangements could be made.

At the end of 1914 H.M.S. *Diana* was sent to Akaba to see what Turkish concentration, if any, was taking place at Maan, a position on the Hedjaz railway, and secondly to see what facilities Akaba offered as a base of operations towards Palestine northwards up the Wadi Akaba or against Maan itself.

She took some seaplanes and personnel from the French squadron at Suez, but the planes were not powerful enough to cross over the mountains between Akaba and Maan, and were unable to carry out their second object. To carry out their first object, they had to survey the head of the Gulf; water was found in plenty and at the north west corner of the Gulf, a very suitable landing place, with a rapidly shelving beach which would have allowed even a ship's launch to come close in. The beach was several hundred yards long and several small nullahs ran into it. On the arrival of the ship the Royal Marine detachment under Captain J. W. Snepp, R.M.L.I. landed and went through the town without any opposition and a few days later an advance was made up the Wadi Akaba by a party of seamen and Marines; nothing was discovered, but on the way back a few shots were fired from the hills to the eastward of the Wadi.

On 31st December, Captain Snepp landed with a small escort to ascertain if the nullah opened out into a suitable camping ground; proceeding up the nullah, he left the escort spread out to his left and only went on accompanied by his orderly. The nullah opened on to a fine open space, but as he turned to come back, he found himself encircled by the Turks in a crescent. Firing commenced at once, the orderly was killed and Captain Snepp was severely wounded. Privates Keefe and Dean (Portsmouth) who formed the escort at once opened fire; though completely outnumbered, by their gallantry they kept off the Turks and Captain Snepp was rescued by the detachment, R.M.L.I. which landed at once, the occurrence having been seen from the ship; Keefe and Dean were awarded the D.S.M.

The incident is an illustration of the nature of the reconnaissances which may have to be made by Royal Marines afloat.

CHAPTER 15.

ROYAL MARINES IN GREECE.

Occupation of Lipso Island - Athens, 1st December, 1916.

FROM the commencement of the Salonica expedition, the attitude of the Greek Government towards the Allies had been very ambiguous; M. Venizelos, the Prime Minister, who was friendly to the Allies had fallen from power and the Greeks under their pro-German King and Queen had lost no opportunity of raising difficulties. In August, 1916, the situation had become critical and in consequence of strong rumours of an impending attack by Germans and Bulgarians and the belief that the King of Greece would not oppose an invasion by the German Forces, the French Naval Commander-in-Chief, Admiral Dartige du Tournet, formed a strong squadron at Milo for a demonstration in force at the Piraeus and Athens. On 28th August this squadron was formed consisting of seven battleships, three cruisers, three scouts, 16 torpedo-boat destroyers, monitors, sweepers, etc.; the British contingent was formed of the battleships *Exmouth* (flag of Rear-Admiral Hayes-Sadler) and *Duncan*, the scouts *Forward* and *Sentinel*, four torpedo-boat destroyers, three monitors and a sweeping flotilla. Major W. L. Huntingford, R.M.A. was the liaison officer on the French Admiral's staff.

The squadron having arrived in Salamis Bay on 1st September, anchored in Karatsini Bay, which is the southern sector of the harbour; the Greek Fleet were anchored in the inner or northern sector; 13 merchantmen, which were required by the Allies for transports were at once taken possession of and certain demands made on the Greek Government.

M. Venizelos left for Salonica where he established a Provisional Government and raised a Greek force to join the Allies.

On 10th October, the Greek Government were handed an ultimatum, to hand over to the French all the Greek light craft at Salamis. The *Kilkis* and *Lemnos* (battleships), and *Averoff* (armoured cruiser), to be disarmed and their complements reduced. All coastal batteries to be disarmed and Allied control over the Port of Piraeus, the police, and the railways, to be established. On the 11th the Greek Government yielded to the threat of force and handed over the light craft, and on that afternoon the Royal Marines of *Exmouth* and *Duncan*, under Major Harmar, R.M.L.I. landed and occupied Lipso Island (the main defence of Salamis Harbour). They were landed with all military precautions, under cover of the ships guns. As the island was found to be deserted, they took over two six-inch guns in concrete emplacements and several lighter guns and searchlights, which were all in good condition. A guard was mounted under Lieutenant Spicer, R.M.L.I., after arrangements had been made to fire on fixed points in Athens and the Piraeus, if necessary. The Royal Marines were relieved subsequently by French seamen. Major Huntingford was landed to take charge of the Port Control Office, at the Piraeus, and also in order to keep touch with the Embassies at Athens. On 16th October two companies of French seamen were sent to Athens for police duty.

Negotiations continued between the Greek and French Governments, but the situation gradually became worse, and possible action by the Greek forces against the rear of the Salonica Army became a pressing danger. At the same time the French were anxious to open up the Itea-Bralo route for reinforcements for the Salonica forces, by which troops would be able to cross from Taranto to Itea in the Gulf of Corinth, and then proceed overland by motor lorry and railway, via Bralo and Larissa, and so avoid the dangerous sea route round Cape Matapan.

Finally on 16th November, the French Government, through the Commander-in-Chief demanded that the Greek Government should hand over 16 field batteries, 16 mountain batteries, 40,000 Mannlicher rifles, 140 machine guns, and 30 motor lorries. The Greeks "backed and filled," and in order to enforce the demands, it was decided to land a force on 1st December, to make a "pacific demonstration" and that they should occupy certain points of military importance.

By this time the Greek Army and people were much excited, and everything was ripe for trouble; because the anti-Venezelist feeling was very strong, and the "Elustrati," a Greek reservist organisation, had been armed and were very turbulent.

In consequence of the negotiations that had been going on, the Greek General Staff knew both the plans of the Allies and the places that they intended to occupy, and were therefore able to place a superior force at each point.

In accordance with the orders, 3,000 seamen and marines of the Allies were landed at the Piraeus, at 3 a.m., 1st December. The British contingent, under the command of Major C. D'O. Harmar, R.M.L.I, consisted of two seamen companies, under Lieutenants Priestly and Palliser, Royal Navy, and a company of R.M.L.I., under Captain J. M. Palmer and Lieutenant M. H. Spicer, R.M.L.I., approximately 300 officers and men with two machine guns. The contingent included a small company of Italian seamen.

The brigadier was Capitaine de Vaisseau Pugliesi-Conte, of the French Navy. The Naval Brigade was organised into three battalions, with a special group for the occupation of the Piraeus, whilst a battalion of the 34th French Colonial Infantry (whose badge is an anchor), was to act as reserves.

The object of the operation was to occupy, by force if necessary, certain positions dominating Athens and certain buildings and military establishments. The main position to be occupied, included the hills Nymphes, Pnyx, and Philopapos about half a kilometre west of the Acropolis, whilst the military establishments to be seized were:-

Point *A*. A magazine on the Athens-Daphni Road, 4 kilometres north west of the Acropolis.

Point *B*. The Greek military engineering store at Rouf, two kilometres west of the Acropolis.

Point *C*. A cartridge factory and magazine, three kilometres south of the Zappeion, and three kilometres south west of the Acropolis.

The *Zappeion*. One kilometre, east of the Acropolis; this place consisted of the buildings of the Agricultural Exhibition, where the two French companies were quartered.

At the Piraeus, the special group were to occupy the naval magazine, on the north side of the dock and Castella Hill dominating Phalerum. Points A and B were to be seized by Nos. 1 and 2 French battalions, and Point C, by No.3 Battalion, which included the British contingent. If serious opposition was met, the force was to concentrate on the 2nd Battalion, on Nymphes Hill. Troops carried 96 rounds of ammunition, and two days provisions.

The Allied forces were to march on Athens by three parallel roads, whilst three French destroyers were sent to Phalerum Bay to cover the march, and the battleships were presumably held in readiness to bombard Athens if necessary, but adequate arrangements had not been made, and hence the delay in opening fire.

The British contingent and the French companies from the *Mirabeau* and *Vergniaud*, under Capitaine de Fregate Millot, formed the right flank column, and their route lay along the old coast road, through old Phalerum, and thence direct to the Zappeion.

The march commenced at 3-30 a.m., and was uneventful. Some Greek troops were met on the outskirts of the town, but they withdrew as soon as the column commenced to deploy. The *Zappeion* was reached at daybreak without further incident. The Commander-in-Chief arrived shortly afterwards, and at 9 a.m., ordered Major Harmar to seize Point *C*, the magazine and cartridge factory, in the south east suburbs.

The Royal Marine company and one from the *Vergniaud* were detailed for this duty, while the remaining companies under Lieutenant Priestly were left at the Zappeion, which became the headquarters of the Commander-in-Chief. By this time, Point A had been occupied, as well as Nymphes Hill, but Point B was found to be occupied by the Greeks in force, and there was a strong force of Greek troops with machine guns in the Acropolis.

The cartridge factory, which was to be seized by the Royal Marines, was situated at the foot of a sheer rocky hill from 300 to 400 feet high, which commanded an extensive view over the whole district. The magazine was about half a mile to the north of the factory, the intervening ground being occupied by scattered gardens and houses, which made visual communication impossible, except from the aforementioned hill (*See plan*.)

The magazine was built on a grassy knoll, bounded on the west and north by houses 200 to 400 yards distant, and on the east by a large cemetery, about 300 yards off. On the south side there was a gentle rock-covered slope, clear of houses or gardens for about 600 yards. A fifteen feet wall of stone enclosed the magazine with entrances on the east and west sides. Outside the magazine, it was possible to obtain an unrestricted view, over the roofs of the houses, of both the Zappeion and the main French position on Philopapos Hill; the former being 2,500 yards to the north and the latter 3,000 yards to the north west.

The two companies reached their destination unmolested, passing through the narrow streets. The French company was detailed to occupy the magazine, and the Royal Marines the cartridge factory; the latter was found unoccupied and after placing a guard in the building, the Royal Marines Company took up a position on the hill, to the south, commanding the approaches both to the factory and magazine, and established communication by signal with the Zappeion and the French on Philopapos Hill.

At the magazine, the French found a guard of Greek infantry, who refused to withdraw, and the Greek Commander formed up his men facing the French at a distance of 200 yards. On reporting this position of affairs to the French headquarters, orders were received for the Royal Marines to reinforce the French at the magazine. The Royal Marines were accordingly withdrawn from the cartridge factory and hill, and on arriving at the magazine about 10-30 a.m., took up a position on the south side of the building; the French who were facing the Greeks, were on the North side.

Columns of Greek infantry now commenced to arrive and were seen to be taking up positions completely surrounding the small force. A Greek colonel came up and informed Major Harmar, that he was in command of that section of the defences, and had received orders to place double the number of Greek troops vis-a-vis on any position occupied by the Allies, and at the same time pointed out how his force was disposed.

The movements of the Greeks had been reported to headquarters, and whilst Major Harmar was talking to the Greek colonel, he received orders that both companies were to withdraw to the Zappeion. On being informed that the Allies were about to withdraw, the Greek colonel replied that he also would withdraw his men after the Allies had left, and at the same time, sent his orderly to order a Greek company, which had come up on the south west side, to move further back. He appeared perfectly friendly, offered Major Harmar a cigarette, and remained talking for some time.

Meanwhile at Point *B*, the Greek attitude had become very threatening, the baggage of the 2nd Battalion had been cut off at 9-45 a.m., and when a French company tried to move it at 11 a.m., fire was opened on them from all sides by the Greek regular troops and armed civilians, and after another company had gone to their assistance, the French brigadier ordered the 1st and 2nd Battalions to fall back on Nymphes Hill and

Philopapos, which position was now being heavily fired on from the Greek troops, in the Acropolis.

Within a few minutes of the departure of the Greek colonel, and just as Major Harmar's two companies of the 3rd Battalion were forming up to march to the Zappeion, they observed the firing on Philopapos Hill, and a crowd could be seen running down the slopes away from the French position. It was at first thought that the French were firing blank to drive the crowd back, but the firing continued and seemed to spread like a wave over Athens.. At the same time, the Greeks in front of the French lay down and opened fire into the closed French ranks (the relative, positions are shown on the plan).The French company broke and came running into the midst of the Royal Marines on the opposite side of the magazine, and into this mass of men, British and French, rifle and machine gun fire was poured from the cemetery and surrounding houses.

The order was given to line a ledge of rocks, just below the crest of the hill (marked *A*), and about 90 men from the two companies fell back to this position, the rest remaining under the wall of the magazine. An attempt was made to get the machine guns into action, but the crews were immediately shot down. Lieutenant Deve, commanding the French company, attempted to work his gun himself, but was killed after firing a few rounds. This party, under Major Harmar, soon found that the position was untenable, as their rear was being fired into by the two Greek companies at the foot of the hill: a retirement was therefore ordered to the hill overlooking the cartridge factory. Major Harmar led his men through the gap between the Greeks, and in spite of being fired at from both flanks at very close range, reached the foot of the hill with few casualties; the inaccuracy of the Greek fire was no doubt attributable to their fear of hitting each other.

The hill was found to be occupied by Greek troops and on an attempt being made to seize it, the small party came under fire from the Greeks on the summit, and the two companies behind them. Major Harmar therefore decided to move round the hill to a ridge behind it and thus try to reach the French positions on Philopapos Hill; this ridge was also found to be occupied by the Greeks. It now became evident that to avoid being surrounded, the only course was to retire to the sea coast. Accordingly a temporary position was taken

PLAN 13

up to check the Greek advance, and to enable any stragglers to rejoin. The country was now undulating and open, well suited to rearguard fighting and after holding a succession of low ridges. the shore of Phalerum Bay was reached at a point near the Phalerum Zoo. During this retirement Sergeants Chapman and Tapsall, with nine Royal Marines and 15 Frenchmen lost touch with the main body, but eventually managed to shake themselves clear of the Greeks, and reached the shore, near the Greek Aviation School.

Communication was established with one of the French destroyers in the bay, and the men were embarked by means of a Greek fishing boat found on the beach.

The destroyer was unaware that fighting was in progress in Athens, but when informed of what had happened, the commander at once steamed to Old Phalerum Pier, where the party was landed with a view to assisting in the defence of the Piraeus, if necessary. A reserve company from the *Condorcet* was found here, but the commanding officer was quite ignorant of what was occurring, and in view of his orders, declined to agree to the suggestion that the two companies should try and reach the main French position.

It was now 3-30 p.m., and the men after practically 12 hours marching and fighting with only one hasty meal out of their haversacks, were very exhausted. Major Harmar therefore decided to march to the Piraeus with the *Condorcet's* company, where the men were left at the Port Control Office, under Lieutenant Spicer, whilst the Major went off to the *Provence*, the French flagship, to report.

Meanwhile at the magazine, Captain Palmer and the remnants of the two companies remained under the wall, sheltered by a slight depression from the Greek fire. After about 20 minutes, a party of Greeks, who had been inside the building, dashed out of the gate and down the slope. Captain Palmer and a few men headed by Private Cook pursued them for a short distance, and then taking advantage of the cessation of fire managed to reach the gate and to get inside the magazine. A hole was eventually dug under the wall, through which the rest of the men crawled; it was here that Private Short (Plymouth), by his gallant conduct gained the D.S.M., and the coveted Medaille Militaire. After two men had been shot while attempting to climb the wall, Private Short volunteered to try, and succeeded in getting over, and was mainly instrumental in digging the hole, which doubtless saved the lives of a number of men. A heavy fire was kept up on the two gateways by the Greeks, but they made no attempt to assault the position. At 4 p.m., firing ceased, and some Greek officers approached under a flag of truce, and offered to make arrangements for the Allies to return to the Piraeus with their arms, which offer was refused by Captain Palmer; a truce however, was agreed to and the Greeks collected the wounded and sent them to hospital. Surgeon-Lieutenant Milligan of the *Exmouth* continued to attend to the wounded on the crest of the hill all through the first period of the fighting, although fully exposed to the Greek fire, and was assisted by Sick Berth Attendant Grieve, who was wounded three times in the arm.

During these events, negotiations were in progress, and at noon, the Russian Ambassador arrived at the Zappeion, from the King, offering to hand over six mountain batteries, which offer was accepted by the French Commander-in-Chief, subject to confirmation by his Government, and in consequence fire was not opened by the battleships; but at 4-45 p.m., the *Mirabeau* and some destroyers opened fire on the Stadium Hill without much effect, but it had a steadying influence on the Greeks, and an armistice was declared. At 6-45, the Ministers arrived with the promise of the six batteries, and the ships ceased fire at 7 p.m.

At the magazine there was no further firing, and at 4 a.m. the next morning, a French officer arrived and informed Captain Palmer that he was to march back to the Piraeus.

The two seamen companies which had been left at the Zappeion with the *Mirabeau* company and two machine guns came under intermittent fire during the day, but were not directly attacked. One French officer and three seamen were wounded, but there were no other casualties. These companies also marched back to the Piraeus at 4 a.m., with the main body of the French forces.

At the Piraeus, at 2-30 p.m. on 1st, a report was received that the Greeks were marching on the Port. Major Huntingford was therefore sent on shore to take over the defences, because it was essential that they should be held for the re-embarkation of the Brigade. On his arrival only about 50 French and Italians were available, the Colonial Battalion having been sent along the Phalerum Road. He at once recalled all the troops to the line Castella Hill-Custom House and eventually collected about 1500 men on this line, being in the curious position of a British officer commanding a force, in which none of his own nation were serving. In the evening, a colonel of the French Regiment arrived and took over the duty.

The Allied casualties in this landing were 60 officers and men killed and 167 wounded, including 10 killed and 12 wounded in the Royal Marine Company. The wounded were taken to the hospital in Athens by the Greeks, the killed were brought down to the Piraeus and buried in a special part of the cemetery.

The Greek Government was obliged to make public atonement for their treacherous attack on the Allies.

Amongst other reparations, the troops of the 1st Greek Army Corps, that formed the garrison of Athens at the time, had to perform the humiliating duty of saluting the Allied colours.

This took place on the large gravel promenade in front of the Zappeion, where Athens society were accustomed to assemble. The Greek troops in review order, were formed up in mass facing the buildings. At a given signal, the doors were opened and the French, British, Russian and Italian colour parties advanced down the wide steps and took up a position in line opposite the Greeks, whilst the Colour Guards of 100 seamen from each of the four nations, moved out from behind the building and were drawn up on either flank of the line of colours. The British Colour Party consisted of Lieutenant Spicer, R.M.L.I. and six N.C.O.s and men, Royal Marines, who had been given the Croix de Guerre for their services.

The Ministers with their staffs accompanied by the senior Naval and Military officers of the Allied Nations were present at the head of the steps.

At the sound of a bugle, the Greek troops advanced in review order, halted and saluted the Allied Colours, while their bands played the National Anthems of the Allies; the Greek colours were lowered to the salute and those of the Allies remained at the "Carry" throughout. The Greeks then marched past and again saluted, Prince Andrew of Greece leading the cavalry past the saluting point.

Major Harmar was awarded the D.S.O., the Legion of Honour and the Croix de Guerre, and Captain Palmer the D.S.C. as well as the French decorations.

The D.S.M. was awarded to Cr.-Sergeant P. J. Strachan (Chatham), Corporal T. H. Wedge (Plymouth), Privates J. A. Short (Plymouth), J. Cook (Chatham), J. Jones (Chatham), T. M. Symons (Plymouth), whilst the above and Privates F. T. Gorman (Plymouth), A. Whittle (Plymouth), G. T. James (Plymouth), received the Croix de Guerre. Cr.-Sergeant Strachan, Corporal Wedge, and Privates Short and James were awarded the Medaille Militaire.

CHAPTER 16.

RED SEA - ACTION AT SALIF.

THROUGHOUT the War, the Navy blockaded the coast of Arabia in the Red Sea, and at the end of 1916, there was great activity to prevent arms reaching the Turkish troops, who were besieging Aden, and operations were directed also to help King Hussein of the Hedjaz and the Arabs who were in revolt against the Turks. The British were in occupation of the island of Kamaran, opposite Salif on the mainland of Yemen. The island of Kamaran was a quarantine station for pilgrims on their way to Mecca, and at Salif there were large rock salt works belonging to the Turkish Government. Work to improve the pier there was in hand when war broke out, and a lot of valuable plant had been left by the contractors, Sir John Jackson and Company.

The Naval Commander-in-Chief learnt that the garrison was only 100 men, and asked that a company of Indian troops might be lent to assist in recovering the contractors plant, but the request was refused by the Indian Government. He therefore decided to make the attempt with his own resources. The detachment of H.M.S. *Exmouth* were to have taken part in the operation, but the ship left the station before the arrangements were completed, and the Commander-in-Chief decided to carry out the work with the ships at his disposal.

The orders to Captain Boyle, the Senior Naval Officer, were that he was to hold the enemy whilst the plant was being removed or destroyed, and that he was to be guided by circumstances as to the capture of the garrison.

The squadron consisting of the *Northbrook* (R.I.M.), *Topaze*, *Odin*, *Espiegle*, and *Minto* (R.I.M.) left Aden on 10th January, 1917.

Salif lies on a peninsula, the north end of which is a mud flat covered at high tide by the sea. On the east side of the village is a hill with a hollow depression in its face, in which the garrison took up their position, when the ships approached at dawn on 12th; here they were well screened from the fire of the ships. The *Espiegle* entered the inlet between the peninsula and the mainland, so as to bring a cross fire on the place. The *Northbrook* went close inshore at the south end of the peninsula, *Minto*, *Topaze* and *Odin* made a line to the north of her, as near the shore as possible. The *Topaze* and *Odin* ran in so close that the enemy could not depress their guns sufficiently to reach them. The Turks had two Krupp mountain guns and three one-inch Nordenfeldts; their shells did no harm as they had to be laid so that their line of fire would clear the crater.

The *Northbrook's* men landed at the south end of the peninsula, and took up a position on the right of the town, the others all landed at the pier and extended behind a ridge, which was flanked by a salt mine on the south, and by houses on the north. The Royal Marines were in the centre of the line. The Odin's seamen entered the village and took possession of the condensing plant and the telegraph office.

Commander A. R. Woods, D.S.O., R.N. of the *Topaze*, was in command, with Commander Salmond second in command, there was no Royal Marine officer present. By means of an excellent system of signals, the ships' guns fired a barrage on the hill, and under cover of this the parties advanced and gained the foot of the hill. The attack was directed against three sides, the fourth being closed by the *Espiegle*. At a given signal, the hill. was rushed and they completely surrounded the Turks, who had made a good fight; the affair being over in three hours. Sergeant J. F. McLoughlin (Portsmouth R.M.L.I.), encountered 12 Turkish soldiers and went for them single-handed, luckily P.O. Beadon, Royal Navy, was close behind him, and between the pair they shot one, took seven prisoners and the rest bolted; both were awarded the Conspicuous Gallantry Medal, which was also given to Private H. Bartlett (Portsmouth R.M.L.I.), who approached a hut and putting his head inside discovered three Turks and three Arabs all fully armed, and made the lot prisoners. Commander Woods was awarded a bar to his D.S.O.

The *Espiegle* remained behind to clear up all the plant, and destroy what they could not move, and a company of Indian troops moved over from Kamaran to garrison the place, which, however was not permanently retained.

Among the casualties, Private Read; R.M.L.I., was killed.

PLAN 14.

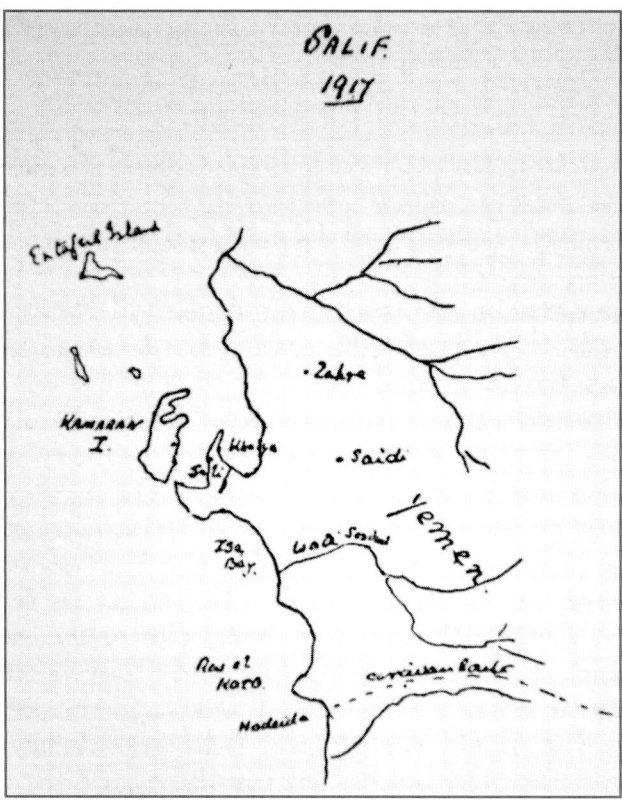

CHAPTER 17.

PERSIAN GULF.

1. - Landing at Fao. 2. -Dilwar, 1915. 3. - Bushire.

1. LANDING AT FAO.

WHEN hostilities were declared against Turkey, it became necessary to protect the Anglo-Persian oil fields at Ahwaz (on the borders of Mesopotamia), which provided such a large proportion of the oil fuel of the Navy. Consequently an expeditionary force of an Indian Brigade under General Delamain was despatched from India to seize in the first instance the mouth of the Shatt-el-Arab River, which forms the estuary of the Euphrates and Tigris rivers, and which was the boundary line between Turkish territory and Persia.

The force was escorted by H.M.S. *Ocean* and *Odin*; owing to the shoal water the ships had to lie 11 miles away. At the mouth of the river was a small Turkish fort on the west bank together with a battery of light guns. The Sheikh Mohammerah on the Persian bank, however, was friendly. Fao, a few miles up the river was the landing place of the cable to India.

The object of the landing was to capture the fort, in order to obtain command of the entrance to the river and re-establish cable communication with India.

It was decided to land at Fao, nine miles up the river, as the ground round the fort was marshy and unsuitable for landing.

The troops detailed to act as covering force consisted of the Dorset Regiment, 20th Native Infantry, Royal Marine detachment H.M.S. *Ocean*, under Major R. C. Temple, R.M.A., and Lieutenant C. Crick, R.M.L.I., machine gun detachment of seamen, one section Pack Battery, R.F.A., and medical detachment.

The Royal Marine detachment with stokers, Royal Navy to carry ammunition for two maxim guns, stretcher party, etc. was about 120 strong. Another native infantry battalion was to be landed later to garrison Fao, whilst the covering force moved south to round up the fort, and to capture the battery.

On 7th November, H.M.S. *Odin*, preceded by two armed launches sweeping for mines, entered the river to engage and silence the battery; she was followed by two transports, towing on the starboard side (the disengaged one), the boats in which the covering force were to land. On the port side, mountain guns and machine guns, protected by sandbags, coal, etc., so as to form additional cover, had been mounted to deal with any fire from the shore, whilst proceeding up the river. The Turkish battery opened fire and held them up for some time, and there was considerable sniping as the transports moved up the river. The troops transferred to the boats on getting into the river, and as soon as the transports anchored off Fao, the boats cast off and made for the shore; the Royal Marines on the right, 20th Native Infantry in centre, and the Dorset Regiment on the left.

The landing was effected at 2 p.m. without opposition, and the village was found to be deserted. After ascertaining that it was not an ambush, and forming up, the force moved beyond the date groves about half to one mile in depth, to an open mud-flat; it was really a small peninsula formed by the delta of the river.

The advance was over soft sand which created a lot of difficulty for the guns, mules and machine guns. The Royal Marines formed the rearguard and helped the machine gun section along by frequent reliefs, so that the main body was not delayed. They had not advanced many miles before dark, when they bivouacked for the night; but they experienced the usual trouble about water. There had been no opportunity to refill the water bottles, for the water in the transports was brackish, while the pools and ditches on shore were forbidden; the corned beef also had turned sour, so that they only had biscuits for their meal. To add to their discomforts, it was bitterly cold, and the heat in their bodies drew pools of water from the sand.

At daybreak on 8th, the advance was continued to the fort, and on arriving within striking distance, the force formed for attack. As there was no reply to the fire from the mountain guns, they advanced on the objective, which was found to have been hurriedly evacuated. The cable instruments, which had been removed from Fao were recovered here, and also some water tanks full of good water were found.

The General Officer Commanding and a party of Royal Marines then proceeded to search for the battery which had delayed the advance up the river. It was found about a mile or so away, and consisted of Krupp guns of about four-inch calibre, which had evidently been hastily abandoned. The breech blocks had been withdrawn and thrown into the mud; two were discovered in the reeds and after some improvising were secured and taken away with them.

The force returned to Fao, marching back by the shorter route through the palm groves, which proved however to be a steeplechase over the small canals. On reaching Fao, they obtained some water and dates; as soon as they arrived, the troops re-embarked in the transports, in order to proceed up the river after the retiring enemy, but the Royal Marine detachment was recalled to the *Ocean*, as they were required to man the guns of the ship, in consequence of the continuous reports of the approach of the *Emden*. The detachment was taken back in an armed launch, but did not reach the Ocean until the next day; as they were held up by the low tide. Although the detachment saw no actual fighting on shore, they gained some valuable experience about water and other matters.

2. DILWAR, 1915

On 9th July, 1915, H.M.S. *Juno*, which had been on Atlantic patrol since the beginning of the war, completed her refit at Queenstown, and on 11th started to tow a monitor to Gibraltar, which task being completed, she turned back for England, but was recalled to Gibraltar, and ordered to proceed at full speed to Port Said, and then on to Bombay. On arrival, she completed with stores and was ordered to proceed to Bushire in the Persian Gulf, to co-operate with the troops against the Tangistani Tribe.

The town of Bushire stands on what would be an island, were it not for a low-lying strip of sand which joins it to the mainland. This causeway is known as the Mahsilah, it is five to seven miles across, and is occasionally inundated at high tide; at all times the area of firm sand is narrow.

Ships prevented the enemy from approaching by sea, so that the Mahsilah was the only line of advance, moreover it was devoid of cover. Round the edge of the island on the Mahsilah side, is a line of low cliffs forming a rampart, with numerous gullies; at the top are some rocks, and at the bottom a belt of palm trees, where the enemy could find cover.

The Tangistanis on the mainland, who had been incited by Herr Wassmuss, the ex-German Consul at Bushire, had on 12th July raided the town, two British officers being killed and several sepoys killed and wounded.

As the Persian Government were quite unable, even if willing, to make any reparation, it had been decided by the British Government that operations should be commenced against the tribe.

The following squadron and troops were concentrated at Bushire, on 6th August. H.M.S. *Juno*, Captain D. St. A. Wake, with Captain G. Carpenter, R.M.L.I. as his Marine officer, *Pyramus*, *Lawrence* (R.I.M.)

Dalhousie (R.I.M.), with 300 officers and men of the 96th Berar Native Infantry. The force sailed for Dilwar, the principal village of the tribe about 30 miles from Bushire to the southward. The village lay about two miles inland; owing to unfavourable weather the landing was postponed until 11 a.m. on 12th August.

The general plan of operations was to establish and fortify a base camp on the first day, and to attack and destroy the walled village of Dilwar on the second day; then to re-embark and return to Bushire on the third day.

The force was divided into two parts, the covering force (commanded by Captain Carpenter) and the main body.

The covering force, 250 all ranks was composed of :-

R.M.L.I. - H.M.S. *Juno*	Captain Carpenter, 50 N.C.O.s and men, 1 machine gun.	
H.M.S. *Pyramus*		9 men.
Royal Navy -H.M.S. *Juno*, machine gun section	11 P.O.s and men, 1 machine gun.	
demolition party	1 warrant officer, 20 men.	
Signallers	4 men.	
Medical and stretchers	1 officer, 10 men.	
Seedie Boys, ammunition and machine gun carriers	24.	
Berar N.I.,	2 officers, 120 men.	

The landing was effected with considerable difficulty, owing 'to the poor towing powers of the steamboats, and the action of a strong inshore current, so that the landing took place nearly a mile away from the point selected, also the boats had to be slipped some 400 yards from the beach and then pulled in under a heavy fire from the enemy trenches on the foreshore.

Until the boats were slipped, H.M.S. *Juno* bombarded the foreshore at a range of about 8000 yards with her six-inch guns, but with little material effect. While pulling ashore there were several casualties, in the *Juno's* pinnace there were four killed and seven wounded; but as soon as the covering force commenced landing, the enemy evacuated their trenches and retired inland, the disembarkation was then carried out without further opposition. Camp was formed and entrenched, stores landed and the surrounding country reconnoitred.

At 3 a.m. the next morning, the force commenced the advance on Dilwar; the leading troops being the R.M.L.I., and one company of the Beraris. The intention was to concentrate the force in a palm grove, which the map showed as 500 yards in front of the village, and then attack at dawn.

PLAN 15.

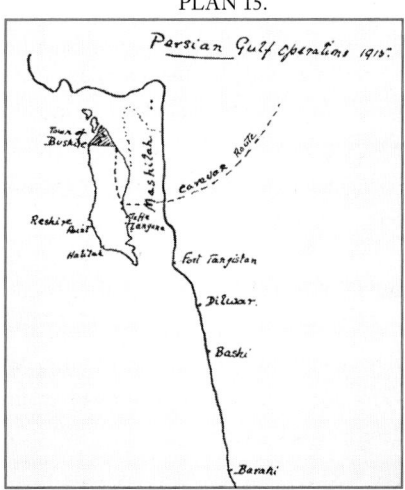

About 40 to 50 of the enemy were encountered in the grove, and were at once driven out by a bayonet charge. At daybreak, however, it was discovered that the village was actually one mile north east of the grove, and that only the ruins of an old village were in the place marked on the map. The enemy were found to be holding an entrenched position along a line of small sandhills, between the new village and the grove. The officer Commanding (Major Wintle, 96th Berar N.I.) assembled the officers to issue instructions for attack; but enemy reinforcements were now approaching from the village of Madamari, about five miles away on the right, which threatened to envelop the force; also about this time a salvo of five 6-inch lyddite shells from H.M.S. *Juno* fell into the grove and caused several casualties, which considerably shook the morale of the troops; this mishap combined with the increasing heat and the lateness of the hour, decided the Commanding Officer to withdraw behind the grove to a position where he could re-organise and then fall back to the camp with a view to carrying out the attack next day. The retirement was successfully effected, the R.M.L.I. forming the rearguard; the enemy following up until they came under machine gun fire from the camp, when they withdrew to their village.

When a fresh advance was made the next day the enemy's resistance was much weaker and the village was taken and destroyed without much opposition.

The force re-embarked on 15th and the Squadron returned to Bushire; considering the active part taken by the Royal Marines their casualties were very small, one killed and six wounded, but they suffered considerably from the heat, especially as they had so recently come from northern latitudes. The Commander and 1st Lieutenant of the *Juno* were among the casualties.

3. BUSHIRE.

On 8th September, 1915 a party from H.M.S. *Pyramus* consisting of 35 officers and men R.N. with the Royal Marine detachment of a sergeant, one corporal and seven privates and three machine guns were landed under Captain Carpenter, R.M.L.I. of the *Juno* for a week's training at Bushire. On the following morning when the party were returning from drill at about 7-0 a.m. a message was received from the General Officer Commanding, Bushire, directing the Naval machine guns to move to the Reserve Camp at Imam Zada; on arrival there, they learnt that the enemy were attacking across the Mahsilah and that the machine guns were to proceed further east to a tower near the village of Zangena and then to take up the best position they could find to command the two gullies leading down to the Mahsilah at that point, the Rajputs and Ghurkhas were holding a line of outposts along the edge of the Mahsilah, and then west across the island excluding the village of Halilah. It was found that the British batteries were engaged whilst the Rajputs were holding on grimly; the *Pyramus* company, when they were 800 yards from their proposed position, came under heavy fire at 300 yards; advancing by rushes they got to the tower and mounted a gun (maxim) there, with another on the left, but the right gun could get no cover. Captain Carpenter called for volunteers to get it into action and Lieutenant-Commander Dorman and yeoman of signals Wood went forward to it. Wood was mortally wounded and Carpenter ordered Dorman back. For two hours the machine guns hung on to their exposed position, covering a gap between two of the outpost companies. The small detachment of R.M.L.I. under Sergeant Wall (Plymouth) rendered most excellent service in covering the left flank of the machine gun position, and keeping a party of the enemy, who had worked round by a nullah to about 200 yards from the guns, pinned to the ground until the troops arrived from the general reserve and drove the enemy back across the Mahsilah about 10 o'clock. The Naval party moved forward with the machine guns to hold the gullies and the cavalry got into the flying enemy, who were also caught by the guns; and so ended the coup which Herr Wassmuss had been planning.

Captain Carpenter was awarded the D.S.C. and Sergeant H. G. Wall (Plymouth) the D.S.M. for their services in these operations.

For their services in the operations in the Gulf, Privates F. W. Rayner (Chatham), A. Ramsey (Chatham) and G. Yates (Plymouth) were also awarded the D.S.M.

The detachment of H.M.S. *Juno* were landed on three other occasions during the next ten months in view of impending attacks on Bushire, but they never materialised into anything serious up to November, 1916: part of the detachment however, finally landed in 1918 and took part in the Caspian operations as described in Chapter 23.

CHAPTER 18.

THE CAMEROONS, 1914-1916.

H.M.S. *Cumberland* at Victoria - Base at Suellaba Point - Dwarf and Nachtigal - Surrender of Duala - Action at Japoma Bridge - Edea Expedition - Buea Operations - Nyong River Operations - Campo River - Kribi - Nyong and Campo Rivers, 1915-1916.

AT the end of August, 1914, Togoland having surrendered to the Allies, preparations were made for an Allied expedition to the German Cameroons to capture the shipping and settlements. For this purpose the *Cumberland* (Captain Fuller), arrived at Fernando Po on 31st August and after coaling was joined by the Dwarf. The *Cumberland* carried a detachment of 60 R.M.L.I. under Captain J. Goldsmith and the *Dwarf* one corporal and seven privates.

On 4th September the *Cumberland* and *Dwarf* were off Victoria and the Royal Marines were landed on Mendolah Island to look for cables of observation mines, but drew blank.

At 5-15 p.m. Captain Goldsmith and 52 R.M.L.I. with a Lieutenant, R.N. and 25 seamen, were sent to Victoria to destroy gear, telegraph and post offices, and to collect food and any steamers and lighters that they could find. The Germans tried to delay them by talking but the work was carried out and they returned to the *Dwarf*. In the meantime the Commander of the *Dwarf* had discovered a large food store at Bota, on the opposite side of the bay. The Royal Marines were therefore landed again to occupy it; by some misunderstanding part went to Victoria and the rest to Bota. During the night Captain Goldsmith became aware that something was in the wind, but could not ascertain what it was; leaving Sergeant Wells and 20 men with the Surgeon at Victoria he went with the remainder to Bota to destroy the store there.

The Germans then came down to the Surgeon, and told him to clear out, as the place would be attacked shortly. Sergeant Wells in the meantime, had placed his men to cover the pier, and had also collected three of the principal inhabitants, who had now put on military uniforms, as hostages. He incidentally relieved them of their field glasses, for the use of his N.C.O.s. Sergeant Wells then informed them that they would be the first to be shot, if any attack was made. Fortunately the Lieutenant, Royal Navy, in his search for lighters arrived and took the party off to the *Dwarf*. Captain Goldsmith and his party were re-embarked at 10 a.m., and the store at Bota was destroyed by fire from the ship. It was discovered that strong German forces were collecting outside the town and were preparing to attack the small isolated parties.

The Nigerian yacht, *Ivy* joined the other ships and on the night 6/7th September, an old time cutting out expedition secured and brought off six valuable lighters, though the enemy were in the trenches twenty-five yards off, expecting a party to land.

On 9th September, *Cumberland*, *Dwarf*, and *Ivy*, bombarded Suellaba Point, at the entrance to the estuary leading to Duala, which was followed by a reconnaisance by Royal Marines landed from the *Dwarf* and *Ivy* at Cape Cameroon and Suellaba Point, 25 at each place; they captured some Europeans and the enemy signal station at Cape Cameroon. Later in the day the *Dwarf* had a spirited engagement with the *Herzogin Elizabeth*, which resulted in the latter retiring up the river; on 10th, the *Cumberland* anchored north of Suellaba Point.

An advanced base for the expedition was now established here, for the mine-sweeping and auxiliary craft, which were necessary to clear away the mines and obstructions that had been laid in the river; for the enemy had sunk several ships to form a barrier across the river.

The base was also required for the troops who were shortly to arrive. Major General J. F. Daniell, Royal Marines, the General Officer Commanding at Sierra Leone, had been very active in the preparations for the expedition.

On 11th September, the *Dwarf*, while covering the mine sweepers, had an engagement with an enemy battery at Joss Point, which she silenced, having five wounded, among them Private L. H. Sands (Chatham), who after being wounded gallantly remained at his voice pipe which was in an exposed position, and was mentioned in dispatches.

The barrier was attacked with explosives, and every means taken to clear a way through; the Germans made attempts to torpedo the *Dwarf*, which was covering the operations. On 16th, the *Dwarf* proceeded up the Bimbia Creek and anchored; soon after it was dark a ship came down, which proved to be the *Nachtigal*, and tried to ram her. The *Dwarf* slipped her cable and came into action at point blank range, the *Nachtigal* crashed into her, and then swung round. The two ships lay alongside, pounding each other, the *Nachtigal*'s gun was blown overboard, and she burst into flames; when the *Dwarf* got clear the German ship drifted ashore and then blew up.

On 23rd September an advanced base was established at Bwape Sand, and the *Dwarf* tried again to draw the Joss Battery. On this day H.M.S. *Challenger*, Captain Beatty-Pownall, arrived with six transports, conveying West African Frontier Force troops. The Royal Marine officer of this ship was Captain C. L. Hall, R.M.L.I., and she carried a detachment of about 40 R.M.L.I. The General Officer Commanding was Major-General C. M. Dobell, and among his staff officers was Captain J. Brough, Royal Marine Artillery.

Steps were at once taken to lighten the *Challenger*, so. as to enable her to pass over the barrier, which had been partially cleared; on the 25th, five French transports also arrived. On this day, the *Challenger* passed through the barrier and anchored at Bwape Sand, within range of Duala, and on the morning of 26th September she fired a few rounds of six-inch into the town, and also prevented anyone crossing the river to Bonaberi, the terminus of the Northern Railway. At the same time, 1,200 troops went up the Dibamba River, to land at Mbonjo, so as to prevent any retirement towards Edea, but owing to swamps and bush they had to abandon the attempt. Two armed tugs were sent at the same time to threaten the Japoma Bridge.

However, the threat coupled with the bombardment was sufficient, and at 9-30 a.m., 27th, after blowing up the wireless telegraphy station, and the magazine, the Germans hoisted the white flag, and Duala and Bonaberi were surrendered unconditionally. Captain Fuller, the General Officer Commanding, and the French Commander with a guard of Royal Marines under Captain Hall, landed and made a ceremonial taking over of the place, and precautions were taken to preserve order until the troops could come up from Suellaba. Lieutenant-Commander Sneyd did the same at Bonaberi with a party of seamen. These detachments were relieved on 28th by 150 West African Frontier Forces, and on the next night, as a French transport had stuck in the mud, the Royal Marines were sent out to hold a section of the outpost line until relieved by 150 Sengalese.

The minefields were now cleared, and a channel buoyed up to Duala, so that the *Cumberland* was able to get up and arrived there on 2nd October. From 3rd-5th October, reconnoitring parties were sent up the Mungo river, and came into touch with enemy at Mbonjo.

By 2nd October, the French had driven the enemy over the Japoma Bridge, which was destroyed in two places, and they requested assistance to capture the place. Two field guns from *Challenger* and *Cumberland* under Lieutenant Hamilton, Royal Navy, were sent and some armed craft with the Royal Marines of the *Cumberland* under Captain Goldsmith co-operated from the Dibamba River below the bridge.

PLAN 16.

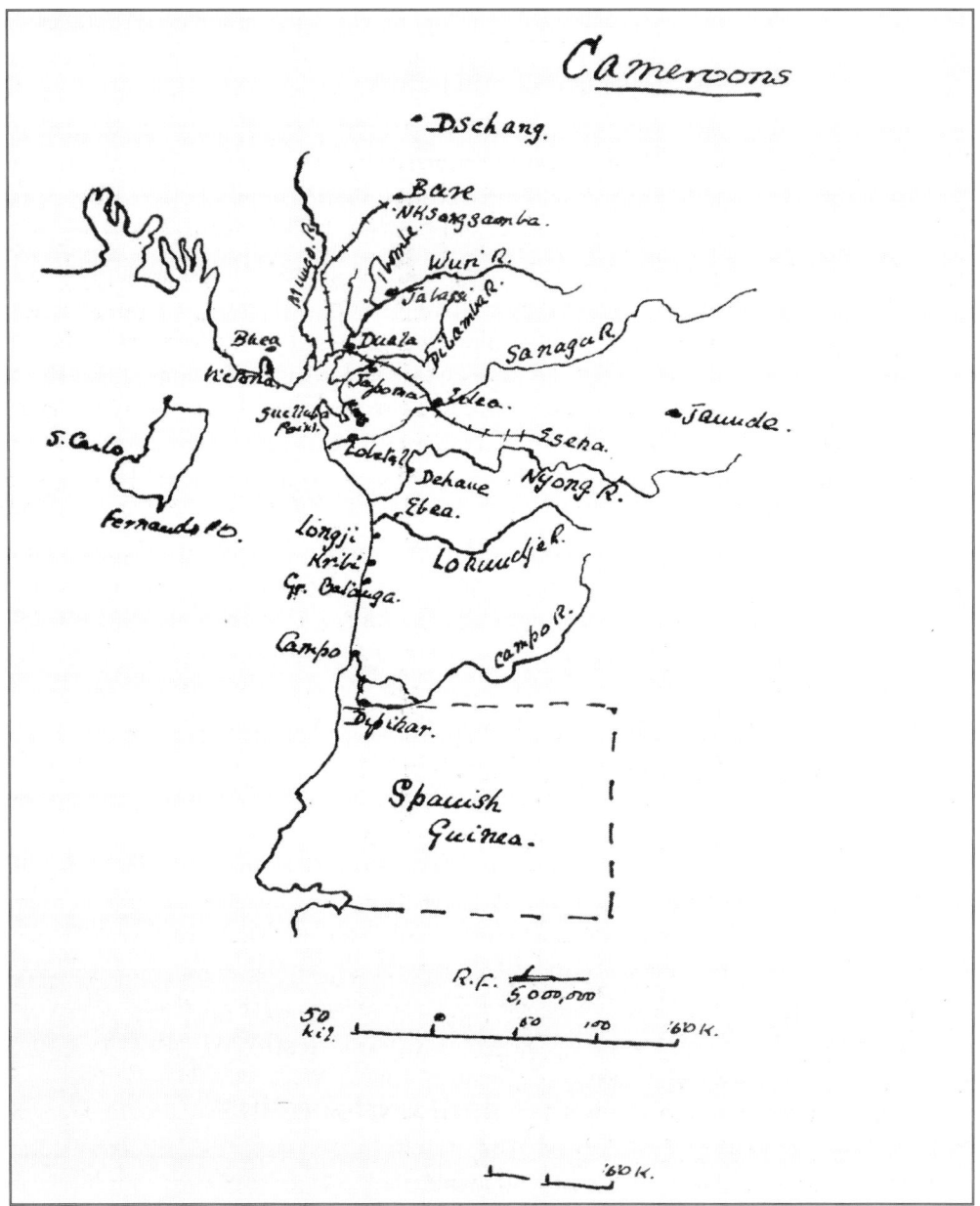

THE CAMEROONS, 1914-1916.

The Germans were presumed to have a well defended position in the vicinity of the bridge, and it was decided to send a reconnoitring patrol up the river, and if the Germans had not already crossed to blow up the bridge. Captain Goldsmith with 30 R.M.L.I. and 16 native soldiers with two British officers were embarked in a tug armed with 12 pounders. They disembarked about 500 yards below the presumed position, and advanced so silently that one man actually looked into the trenches before being discovered. The enemy opened a very heavy fire, under which it was necessary to withdraw; which was successfully carried out in spite of barbed wire, steep banks and swamps; one man was mortally wounded. After they had returned on board, the tug steamed up almost opposite the position and was fired on, being hit in several places, without material damage. She replied with shrapnel and rifle fire, and it was ascertained that the enemy's strength was about 200, who were posted in a good position commanding the river. At dawn the next day, the tug passed the position at full speed without being fired on, and two miles further on came to a large clearing with trenches, which however were unoccupied, but a strong boom defence had been placed in the river, through which, however, the tug forced its way. On reaching the bridge it was found that it had already been blown up, but it was impossible to determine whether the enemy had yet crossed or not, because owing to the shallow water, the tug was obliged to anchor 1400 yards from the bridge. Captain Goldsmith therefore took a surf boat with five natives as crew and a patrol of eight Royal Marines to ascertain the position of affairs. On reaching the bank near the bridge one corporal and two privates were landed as scouts, and soon gained the top of the bank. On their reporting "All Clear" the boat was made fast and the remainder landed; when half way up the bank, a heavy fire was opened from the other side of the river, which was about 200 yards wide, evidently from a strong force concealed in the bushes. The patrol retired to the boat, where they found that the native crew had jumped overboard. All the patrol got back safely except the scouts, from whom they could get no reply; as one native was mortally wounded, and one Marine, it was decided to return to the tug and obtain reinforcements. They retired under heavy fire for 600 yards, the tug covering them with her guns.

More men were obtained and with Marines to form the boat's crew they pulled back under fire, not only from the position but from snipers in the swamp, to which they replied by shooting from the boat at some Germans on the bridge. They picked up one of the native boat's crew and one of the scouts swimming in the river and about 100 yards further up another scout was found on the bank, both were very exhausted and one was wounded.

As soon as they had withdrawn out of range, two volunteers were landed to look for the third scout, whilst the boat returned with the wounded. The third man could not be found; it transpired that he remained on the bank until it was dark, and then decided to try and make his way to Duala. Fortunately he met a French patrol, who took him into the headquarters of the Allied Forces, who were moving forward to attack the bridge, and to whom he was able to furnish some useful information as to the positions.

He rejoined his party 24 hours later when they assisted the French to attack the German outpost, before proceeding to capture the position at Japoma.

The Allied casualties were slight compared with the Germans, who suffered heavily from the fire of the field guns and that of the tug.

The scouts were Corporal J. Cridland (afterwards awarded the D.S.M. for service in the armoured train in Siberia and Russia), with Privates Rogers and Saxton, all of the Plymouth Division.

On 6th October, the French carried the bridge and established themselves on the left bank of the river. On this day, the troops made an advance on Jabassi, 50 miles up the Wuri River, assisted by a flotilla from the Navy, with lighters mounting six-inch guns, and a mixed company of seamen, Marines and stokers. The numbers of the Royal Marines were very few, owing to malaria, and the absence of guards taking prisoners to Lagos. The troops landed, but the bush was too dense for them to see what they were firing at, and as they became very exhausted with the heat, they were re-embarked and returned to Duala. On 14th another attempt was made, and this time was successful, as they entered Jabassi with very little opposition.

Edea Expedition 20th-26th October, 1914. The plan was to attack from three sides, one by the Sanaga River, secondly by the Nyong River to Dehane and thence overland, and thirdly by the Midland Railway from Japoma. In the first column, the flotilla was under Commander Braithwaite of *Cumberland*, one part proceeding by Kwa - Kwa Creek, the other entering the Sanaga River from the sea; all craft assembled at Suellaba on 20th October. These two parties after encountering opposition and considerable navigational difficulties reached Lobetal and concentrated on 24th. On 25th, Captain Braithwaite in the *Remus* landed the troops, but they had to be re-embarked owing to the bush, and on 26th the flotilla, after bombarding the place, steamed past Edea to the delight of the natives, the Germans having evacuated the place.

For the Nyong column, H.M.S. *Cumberland, Dwarf, Surprise* (French), and six transports with French troops, followed by the *Ivy* and smaller craft went to the Nyong River. In crossing the bar on 21st, Captain Fuller, the Senior Naval Officer, with the Director of the Nigerian Marine and other officers, was capsized in the whaler, Captain Fuller was rescued with great difficulty, the other officers being drowned. That evening the flotilla proceeded to Dehane and captured it, and the next day the French troops marched on Edea, leaving a British guard at Dehane. They reached Edea on 26th, and informed the Sanaga River party that the place was evacuated. The flotilla left Edea on 27th and reached Duala on 31st, to which place the ships and transports had returned on 23rd, after the troops had landed.

The third column, provided by the French, was accompanied by a Naval 12 pounder; they had fighting on 25th, 26th, and 27th, when they reached Edea and then returned to Duala.

Buea operation 12th-18th November, 1914. Buea was the German seat of Government and a health resort on the slopes of Cameroon Mountain. The plan of attack comprised four columns:-

(1) Demonstration at Bibundi by the *Dwarf* with a small transport as if to land. Krooboys were landed in surf boats, and then withdrawn, but it made the necessary impression.

(2) A force consisting of the *Ivy* and two armed tugs escorted all the available Royal Marines about 80 under Captains Hall and Goldsmith, the French cruiser *Bruix* remaining in the offing. The force arrived at Victoria on 13th November, and Commander Hughes, Royal Naval Reserve (*Ivy*), demanded the surrender of the place, which was refused. A bombardment was opened on Victoria and the neighbouring village of Bota, and the Royal Marines landed at Bota and marched on Victoria. Within a few hours the enemy were driven out of Victoria, and the town was occupied at 11-30 a.m. The enemy did not even stop to destroy the light railway, running inland from Bota, which was captured by the Royal Marines in good condition, with the rolling stock intact. All non-combatant Germans were sent to Duala, and the Royal Marines were relieved shortly after by native troops, and returned to the base.

(3) The main force was composed of native troops and proceeded to Tiko. The flotilla under Captain Beatty-Pownall in the *Remus* escorted six river transports each towing a lighter full of troops and an armed tug towing a lighter in which a six-inch gun had been mounted; a party of. seamen under Lieutenant Hamilton were with the *Cumberland* and *Challenger* field guns. The force reached Tiko at daylight on 13th November, and disembarked at the pier, whilst a lighter went up the creek west of Tiko to cover the advance; it there came under machine gun and rifle fire, which was soon silenced, and Tiko was occupied without further opposition. The advance on Buea was begun the next day; the column reached Bole Famba with

slight opposition and halted for the night, reaching the capital and occupying it without opposition on 15th.

(4) The column for the Mungo River with flotilla under Lieutenant-Commander Sneyd, consisted of two boats from *Cumberland*, the sternwheel gunboat *Sakata* and three armed launches. They reached Mbonjo on 12th, and on 13th Mpundu, where the enemy was found in a strong position, but the guns of the boats soon drove him out and the village was occupied; from here the troops moved on Buea. The combined effect of all these columns cleared the enemy out of Buea without opposition.

The rivers and creeks were patrolled, and operations took place on the Nyong and Lokundji rivers, and at Kribi from 18th November to 1st December. It having been ascertained by the *Ivy* and a small flotilla that vessels could still reach Dehane, it was decided to clear the Dehane - Kribi district of the enemy. So on 27th November 450 French troops were landed at Longji. Another French force was to march from Edea to Dehane, which party was then to be transported across the Nyong River, and to co-operate with the force from Longji in the attack on Ebea on the Lokundji River. The Edea column met with considerable opposition and never reached Dehane, and the date for the advance on Longji was postponed. The flotilla under Commander Braithwaite with the Royal Marines of the *Challenger* and *Cumberland* under Captains Hall and Goldsmith left on 26th November for the Lokundji River to co-operate in this attack, but owing to its delay and final abandonment by the French, the naval force could only make a small reconnaissance towards Ebea, whilst waiting for the French troops; they therefore occupied Kribi on the coast on 1st December and landed the Royal Marines, and the force then returned to Duala.

Operations were then undertaken by the troops along the Northern Railway, which resulted in the capture of Dschang. Railhead at Nkongsamba was occupied on 10th December, and Barea on 11th, Dschang being finally captured on 2nd January, in which the *Challenger's* field guns took part.

On 4th December, the *Cumberland* left for England, but Captain Fuller, the Senior Naval Officer and 45 R.M.L.I. transferred to the *Challenger*, thus bringing her detachment up to 91.

Captains Hall and Goldsmith[27] with Sergeant E. Wells, Lance-Sergeant F. J. Oakes, Corporals H. Wright, J. P. Cridland, and Privates C. R. Hall, G. P. Branston, A. L. Rogers, E. Saxton, W. C. Lea, R. Aitken (all Plymouth), and A. Richter (Chatham) were all favourably noted for these operations.

During November and December, the naval flotillas were accomplishing effective work in the various rivers, being in constant contact with the enemy.

On 19th December, the spit at the entrance of the Nyong River was occupied by the Royal Marines, and an armed flotilla was established on the Lokundji River. As soon as the Nyong depot had been made secure, the Royal Marines were transported southwards for operations against Campo (another example of a small advanced base force).

On 23rd December, H.M.S. *Margaret Elizabeth* (late *Herzogin Elizabeth*), Commander Sneyd with two other armed vessels and a transport with all available Royal Marines under Captain Hall proceeded to Campo River and occupied Campo on 24th after a short fight, and the flotilla proceeded up stream until stopped by the Dipikar waterfalls.

The Royal Marines carried out several reconnaissances in the Campo hinterland, marching from village to

---

27. *Captain C. Hall died after his return to England from the effects of service, and Captain Goldsmith died of wounds received in the battle of Arleux. (see chapter 26).*

NOTE.-*In order to remove the large number of German Prisoners of War H.M.S. Laurentic (A.M.C.) was sent out on 25th December to bring them to England, she (was given a guard of Royal Marines under Major W. N. E. Smith, R.M.L.I. (retired) and as personnel was short it was composed of recruits who had not completed their drills.*

village for the next fortnight; also at various places on the coast between Campo and Great Batanga. Owing to the dense bush, they were unable to gain contact with the enemy, though much useful work in the destruction of enemy look-out stations, camps and means of communication, etc., was carried out on the coast before returning to Duala on 2nd January, 1915.

A strong defended base was established at Campo by the flotilla, and a redoubt constructed at Dipikar, with an advanced post a few miles up the river. On 14th January, the enemy made an attack on Campo, which was repulsed, and in the following week, all available Royal Marines returned to Campo and a vigorous offensive was undertaken, but in spite of strenuous efforts, the enemy favoured by the bush could not be brought to action, and on 29th the Royal Marines proceeded to Kribi to relieve two companies of British Native troops, who were required for operations on the Northern Railway. They garrisoned that place with the French, whilst the flotilla at Campo continued the operations there and at Dipikar with what force they had available.

In February, 1915, as the French desired to withdraw their men from Kribi, and as the garrison had been suffering from dysentery, the place was evacuated on 27th, and the Royal Marines returned to their ships. As Captain Hall put it "Here we stopped as part of the outpost line for a month, our main occupations being covering the front with wire, loopholing blockhouses, and going down with dysentery and malaria."

In March, it was decided that an advance should be made on Jaunde, the seat of Government since September, 1914. A British Force, and French Columns, therefore, advanced on the place, encountering considerable opposition, the enemy disputing every yard of the way, which lay through very difficult country; but when within 50 miles of the place it was learnt that the French Force from the south was not advancing further owing to sickness. As the Allied columns were much depleted the advance was abandoned, and the column returned to the Kele River. In connection with this operation, all available Royal Marines under Captain Hall were employed in the *Margaret Elizabeth, Ivy* and *Fullah*, in demonstrations against Kribi Plantation and Longji, from the 11th to 13th April, and the Royal Marines subsequently carried out a reconnaissance up the Nyong River.

On 30th April, 1915, H.M.S. *Astraea* relieved the *Challenger* as Senior Officer's ship, Captain Tootell, R.M.L.I., being the Royal Marine officer of this ship. H.M.S. *Sirius* and *Rinaldo* also joined the squadron in June; whilst the *Challenger* proceeded to the Cape and then to East Africa, where she took part in the campaign on that coast.

On the Nyong River, on 5th July, two companies of the West African Frontier Forces co-operated with the flotilla against the stockade at Ebea, which was captured on 8th July, Etima was occupied on 9th, and fortified camps at Mamaong and Dehane were captured and burnt on 10th, after considerable opposition and loss on the British side. Reinforcements of British and French from Edea arrived on 13th, and Etjahi was captured on 14th after slight opposition, when the troops returned. Throughout August, September and October, the Nyong flotilla was in frequent contact with the enemy in the Dehane district, to which the enemy had returned when the troops were withdrawn for other work.

On the Campo River, a column of the Gold Coast Regiment with a small naval party and some native levies, left Dipikar on 12th July and proceeded to Bipa and thence to Ngat, which was occupied after slight resistance on 14th. The force then occupied Afan, after some resistance on 15th, and Akak on 16th. Bitanda and Ebabomwode were found evacuated, and the column returned to Dipikar, leaving garrisons at Akak, Bitanda, and Moloko. At the same time, an armed party from the *Sirius* occupied Bodge on the coast road, and a section of the Gold Coast Regiment was posted at the junction of Bitanda and Mbula Moloko Road to cut off the enemy's retreat. In the course of these operations, the enemy were hunted out of exceptionally strong positions with loss.

On 28th July, the force at Campo was reinforced by two more companies of the Gold Coast Regiment, with a Naval maxim gun detachment, and other naval units. On the 2nd August, the naval and military force was concentrated at Ngat, for an advance on Njabesan, which was a depot for German convoys. On 7th and 8th, the enemy were encountered in force in a strong position five miles east of Manimanji; after three hours fighting, our force retired to Manimanji and returned to Ngat on 11th, leaving an advanced force at Bitum.

On 11th September, Commander Hughes, Royal Naval Reserve, was placed in command of the Naval and Military forces, who were ashore at Campo. Headquarters were at Dipikar with a base at Campo, and outposts at Ebabomwode, Bongola, and Moloko. During September, enemy activity increased. and they re-occupied Akak on 20th September. As no troops were available, 50 R.M.L.I. (Captain Tootell), were landed on 26th September, and proceeded to strengthen the outposts, and the British patrols were in touch with the enemy throughout the month; on 28th, the enemy approached within three miles of the camp.

On 6th October, Moloko, which was a Naval post on the Campo River, was attacked in force, but after two and a half hours fighting at close range, the enemy retired. Private J. Hammond (Chatham) of the *Astraea* was wounded, and was awarded the D.S.M., for having with 10 native levies delayed the advance of a superior force of the enemy until other outlying parties had had time to reinforce the post, and subsequently when retiring to the post he was wounded but continued to direct the retirement of his party. The position was fairly quiet for the rest of the month, but on 20th a patrol from Moloko forded the Nipe River and had a successful engagement with a large hostile patrol, which it put to flight.

On 5th November, a French column advanced from Campo along the Ngat road, the British protecting their communications and transport; the French marched to Njabesan in order to gain touch with Colonel Meillour at Amban. The naval force of seamen and Marines at Moloko was reinforced by some British troops and made a demonstration along the Bipe Road. They engaged a hostile force at Mbula on 5th and occupied the place on the following day; on this day they occupied the enemy's camp at Metum after slight opposition and then returned to Moloko.

Corporal F. W. Hemmings (Chatham), and Lance-Corporal A. C. Rutland (Chatham), were awarded the D.S.M. for their conduct, when the small force of native troops and Royal Marines captured Mbula and Metum.

An officer's patrol visited Metum several times during November, and on 29th there was a sharp engagement near Bipe, the enemy being put to flight. On 7th December, the French relieved the British at Ebabomwode, and the latter occupied Bipe. On 12th, the French also relieved the post at Moloko, the British troops being withdrawn to take part in the advance on Jaunde, and the Naval forces left for Dipikar.

The second advance on Jaunde from Duala commenced at the end of October, 1915, General Cunliffe from Nigeria and the French from the east and north. Jaunde fell on 1st January, 1916 to the British forces from Duala, and by the middle of February the whole of the country was in the hands of the Allies, and the Germans were retiring into Spanish Guinea. In January, 1916, 900 Europeans and 40,000 natives were counted crossing the frontier.

The evacuation of the British troops in the Campo district commenced in March, 1916, the French taking over the country, including the Naval posts at Dipikar and Campo. By the end of the month the evacuation was completed and on 1st April, Duala was also transferred to the French and the British portion of the campaign was finished.

CHAPTER 19.

COASTAL OPERATIONS IN EAST AFRICA.

Tanga - Bweni Bluff – Sadani – Bagamoyo - Coastal operations August to September, 1916- Lindi, etc. 1917-18 - Quilimane.

IN the first six months of 1916, the campaign on shore in East Africa had made considerable progress, and by June the British forces had advanced as far as Kondea Irangi, whilst another German force had been driven from the hills on the east side of the Ruwu River to the Pangani River. It was therefore necessary to open up communication to the coast, and to establish new bases for the troops.

Tanga, Pangani, Sadani, and Dar-es-Salaam on the coast of German East Africa, were still in the hands of the Germans, whilst the Navy were blockading the coast. Further there was the danger that the enemy on the coast might strike westward and make a flank attack on the British forces working south. The Navy were therefore asked to assist the Army in the capture of these towns.

On 7th June, 1916, under cover of the fire of H.M.S. *Talbot* and *Severn*, with the *Vengeance* (Flag of Rear-Admiral Charlton, the Commander-in-Chief), and the kite balloon ship *Manica* standing by, the Army occupied Tanga, the scene of the disastrous reverse in the early days of the war. Captain F. H. Thomas, D.S.C., R.M.L.I., and his detachment with two machine guns landed from the *Talbot* at Ulenge Island, which he held whilst the troops landed at Kwale Island and marched on Tanga. After the occupation, the *Talbot's* detachment was landed daily up to 21st July, in case of emergencies.

On 21st July, as reports had been received that the enemy had mounted a gun at the mouth of the Pangani River, the *Talbot* (Captain R. Lambert) arrived off the Pangani just before dark on 22nd, and bombarded the Bweni Bluff. At daylight the next morning white flags were seen to be flying and Captain Thomas was sent in under a flag of truce, and was informed by the natives that the Germans had evacuated the place at 3 a.m. Seamen and Marines were then landed; the Royal Marines occupying the hill on the south side of the river to hold the abandoned defensive position, whilst the seamen took over the town. The 57th Native Infantry, who had thus been enabled to cross the river, marched in from the north side, and the Royal Marines were embarked the next day. On 25th the R.M.L.I. took over the town until the 57th Native Infantry had crossed to the south bank and ascertained that the enemy had left the immediate vicinity. The *Talbot* proceeded 20 miles down the coast to Kipombwe, and shelled the village and a few of the enemy who were seen, and again on 26th the *Talbot* shelled Mkwadja, and the *Mersey* shelled Sadani.

It became evident that the Germans from Tanga and Pangani were moving on Sadani, therefore on 27th July, as there was no satisfactory report from Mkwadja seamen and Marines from the *Talbot* were landed under Captain Thomas to take the village. The *Thistle* arrived at the same time and took up a position to cover the landing, which was effected without opposition. Shortly after the village was occupied, about 50 of the enemy were reported to be about a mile outside. Captain Thomas at once advanced with the Royal Marines detachment and engaged the enemy who retired into the bush. He then cut the Pangani - Sadani telegraph line and withdrew again to the village. The Royal Marines were re-embarked on 29th July. Captain Thomas, Lance-Sergeant Perry and Privates W. Cooper and F. Galloway (all Plymouth R.M.L.I.), were brought to notice for these operations.

On 1st August, the squadron occupied Sadani, the place was important as a base of supplies for Andeni and Morogoro. The town was secured by a force of 250 seamen and Marines (the Marines being under Major

C. Hall of the *Challenger*), with 50 Zanzibar Rifles, after a very feeble opposition. The Naval party held it until relieved by the Army on 7th August. Major Hall, and Captain Thomas and Colour-Sergeant P. E. Smith (Plymouth), were noted for good service.

CAPTURE OF BAGAMOYO, 15th AUGUST, 1916.

On 13th August, Lieutenant-Colonel Price, commanding at Sadani, asked the Naval Commander-in-Chief if he would take and occupy Bagamoyo, because it was essential that it should be occupied at the earliest possible moment, and all the available Military forces were engaged at Mandera; the Army, however, would relieve the Navy at Bagamoyo as soon as the Mandera operations were completed.

The Commander-in-Chief replied "This will be arranged." He also asked that the R.M.L.I. detachment of the *Talbot* under Captain Thomas, which had been left at Sadani to supplement the Army garrison, together with a detachment of the Zanzibar Rifles might be sent to him.

At Bagamoyo, therefore, the Navy acted alone, and it was here that the stiffest fight was experienced.

The Intelligence Officer had reported that it was held by only 10 whites and 400 Askaris, but as a matter of fact they were stronger than the landing party, being composed of 60 whites and 350 Askaris. The Askari is a good soldier and a great bayonet fighter but an indifferent shot.

On 15th August, the *Vengeance, Challenger, Mersey* and *Severn*, with the kite balloon ship *Manica*, and the tug *Helmuth* anchored off Bagamoyo, at 3-30 a.m. At 4-30 a.m., the landing party went ashore in bright moonlight, the surprise was therefore not complete; the boats proceeded in a straight course towards the Governor's house, and then turned six points to port and steered a zig-zag course, so that the Germans were deceived as to the actual landing place, and kept their men in the wrong place.

The boats actually ran ashore where a thick belt of trees ran down the slope almost to the water's edge. At the top of the slope, the Germans had mounted a 4.1-inch gun, which however, could not be depressed sufficiently to fire into the boats, but engaged the *Mersey* and *Severn*, which had closed in to bombard. The boats, however, came under fire from machine guns, rifles and pom-poms, on their starboard side. The *Helmuth* and a picket boat with a three-pounder gun closed in and plastered the 4.1-inch gun at 500 yards range. Sub-Lieutenant Manning, Royal Naval Reserve, with a machine gun section rushed and captured the gun. The kite balloon and aeroplanes which were observing the fire reported at 6-30 that the Germans were abandoning their trenches, and falling back towards the French Mission buildings, behind the town. The enemy tried to take advantage of the natural reluctance to shell the Mission buildings and the Catholic Cathedral, by taking shelter there, but the French Fathers objected and the Germans did not actually enter the buildings; unfortunately the buildings were hit by a 12-inch shell from the *Vengeance*.

In the meantime, the Royal Marines of the *Talbot, Vengeance,* and *Challenger* (60 all told), under Captain Thomas to whom were attached the Lewis gun parties of the *Mersey* and *Severn*, landed in the motor boats of the monitors, directed by Lieutenant Chapman, Royal Navy, under a heavy fire from pom-poms, machine guns and rifles. They then advanced and captured the Governor's house, and being joined by a party of the Zanzibar Rifles, advanced in a westerly direction. Parties of the enemy had concealed themselves in the long grass, and the Royal Marines came under a heavy fire.

Then gallantly led by Captain Thomas, they proceeded to clear the grass in front of the house, and came under fire from cleverly concealed trenches and dug-outs, during which movement Captain Thomas was killed, Private Dennis, his servant, immediately bayonetted the man who had fired the shot. His death was a great loss to the Corps as he had shown himself both at the Dardanelles and in Africa, as a most gallant and skilful officer.

COASTAL OPERATIONS IN EAST AFRICA

PLAN 17

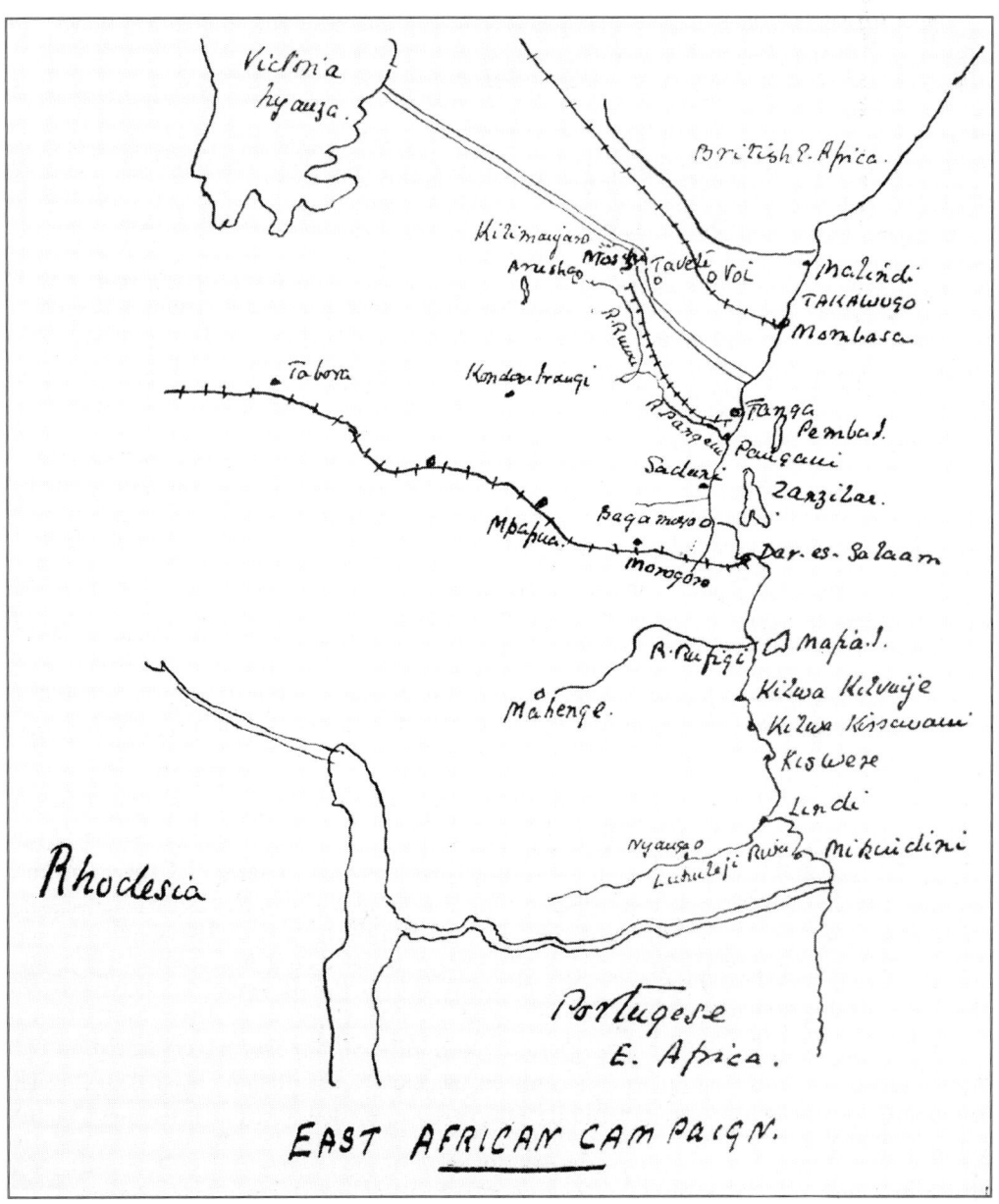

EAST AFRICAN CAMPAIGN.

The seamen had simultaneously pressed forward, and charging across the front of the Boma, captured the enemy trenches, whilst another party worked round the Governor's house, cutting the line of retreat. This charge was ordered on information brought by Lance-Corporal E. V. Deane (Plymouth R.M.L.I.), who very bravely rushed across to the Commanding Officer, under heavy fire, to point out the situation, and then opened fire himself to cover the seamen's advance; for this service he was awarded the Conspicuous Gallantry Medal.

The enemy fled in confusion, and lost maxims and two light guns, whilst the two German officers were killed and many of the enemy were captured in the dug-outs.

Arrangements were then made to meet a counter-attack; picquets were posted and defences strengthened. Commander Watson, Royal Navy, being placed in charge.

There was another strongly fortified post at Mtoni Ferry, about six miles up the Kigaki River, but the enemy were badly shaken and a large number of Askari deserters came in.

Bagamoyo was regarded by the natives as a place of importance, as it was formerly the terminus of the slave caravans. Owing to Commander Watson's tact and diplomacy, the natives became friendly and gave useful information, and the capture of the place greatly enhanced the British prestige. The Germans had, among other things, forbidden the natives to fish, permission to do so was at once restored, which made them very contented, and many other similar acts were done. There was no doubt that the natives were greatly struck by the difference between the British and German methods of treating them.

On 18th August, the troops from Sadani arrived and took over on 19th.

Acting Company-Sergeant-Major P. E. Smith, Lance-Corporal W. Bradley, and Private W. Dennis (all Plymouth), were awarded the D.S.M., whilst Captain Thomas, Colour-Sergeant W. J. Fouracre (Plymouth), and Sergeant Harry Carter (Portsmouth), were mentioned in dispatches.

On 20th August, the Royal Marines of the *Vengeance*, *Challenger*, and *Talbot*, were re-embarked and replaced by Lieutenant T. F. Connew and 24 Royal Marine Artillery, but this party returned to the *Vengeance* on 26th.*[28]

On 21st August, the Naval squadron commenced the bombardment of Dar es salaam, which was the principal enemy port, and on 29th, Lieutenant Connew and the Royal Marines of the ships present were sent to the *Trent* to organise for coastal landings.

On 2nd September, the Royal Marines under Lieutenant Connew landed at Kondechi, north of Dar es Salaam, and the next day the troops from Bagamoyo approached and the bombardment was resumed. On the 4th the *Challenger* was sent in with a flag of truce to demand the surrender of the town. The German Governor surrendered on that day, and the place was occupied. Lieutenant Connew and his detachment returned to the *Trent* on 5th.

On 7th September, the Royal Marines were again landed at Kilwa Kivinte, which surrendered to the *Vengeance*, and Kilwa Kisiwane to the *Talbot* and *Challenger*.

On 9th September, the Royal Marines Force embarked in H.M.S. *Himalaya*, and landed on 13th September, with the Army troops at Mikindani, without opposition, and on 16th the troops occupied Sudi. The squadron proceeded to Lindi and found the place deserted, the Royal Marine force landed, but re-embarked on 17th.

---

28. This Officer and 24 R.M.A. (Short Service Gunners) had been sent out to reinforce the Batteries (Chapter 27), but as they were not at that moment required by the Army they were utilised by the Commander-in-Chief to replace the detachment of the Vengeance which had been landed in February for service with the Batteries. A second draft under 2nd Lieutenant H. Gardner of the same strength arrived on 30th September and were embarked similarly in the Challenger.

PLAN 18

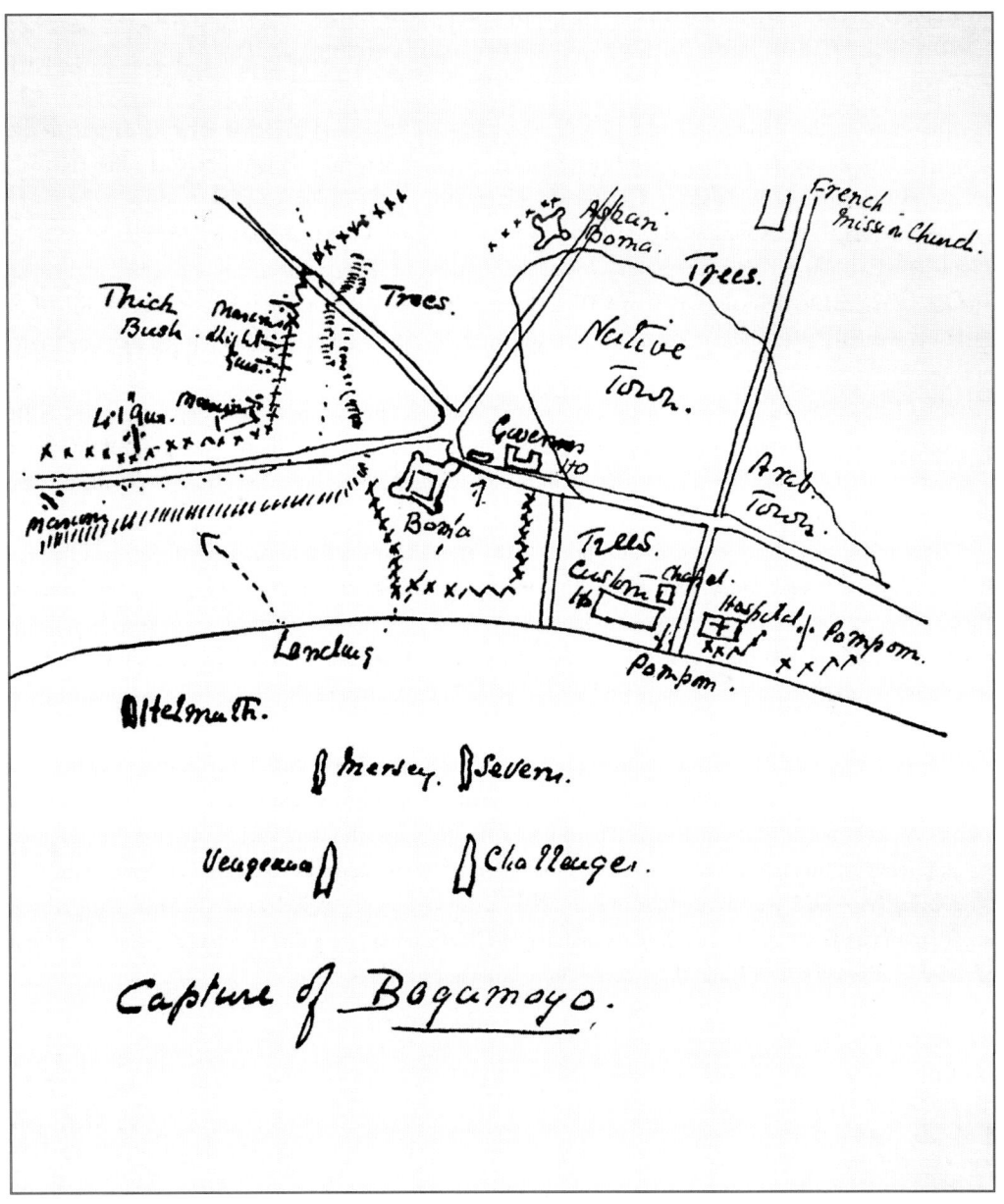

On 18th, the *Challenger* and a transport were sent to occupy Kiswere. The whole coast was now in British hands, so on 27th, the *Vengeance* left the station for Bombay, and returned home shortly after, Lieutenant Connew and his party returning with her.

Following on these successes and to shorten the lines of communication, the base of the Expeditionary Force was first moved to Tanga from Mombasa, in July, 1916. In September, it was moved to Dar es Salaam, and in October, it was proposed to move to Kilwa, but in January, 1917, the base was moved to Lindi.

On 5th January, Lieutenant Gardner and his Royal Marine Artillery were landed from the *Challenger* and joined the batteries, being replaced afloat by Lieutenant Weir, and a full R.M.L.I. detachment from England.

The ships on the station *Hyacinth*, (Flag), *Minerva*, *Challenger*, and *Talbot* with *Rinaldo*, and *Thistle* sloops, and two monitors, with an armed merchant cruiser, were now fully occupied in blockading the coast and preventing stores being landed for the German Forces.

In June-July, 1917, a portion of Von Lettow's forces were reported to be making for Port Amelia, in Portuguese East Africa, where there was a considerable supply of stores and ammunition, quite unguarded. The *Talbot* embarked two companies of a West African Regiment, and these together with 40 R.M.L.I. and three machine guns under Captain A. P. Dawson, R.M.L.I., were landed and put the town in a state of defence.

The Germans approached within three miles of the place, but fearing a trap, they turned back. The British forces was too weak to pursue, so the enemy escaped. After six weeks ashore, the Royal Marines were relieved by a battalion of the King's African Rifles, and a Baluchi Battalion; this place afterwards became one of the British bases.

Patrol of the coast was resumed until June, 1918, by which time *Minerva*, and *Rinaldo* had left the station. The *Talbot*, and *Thistle* were ordered in June to Quilimane, at one of the mouths of the Zambesi River. Every available man was ordered to land, seamen, stokers, and Royal Marines, to put the town in a state of defence against the Germans, who were advancing. About 180 men were landed (80 seamen, 60 stokers, 40 Royal Marines), under Captain Dawson, R.M.L.I.; there were also about 200 Portuguese troops in the town, who were doing nothing.

The force was ordered not to go more than five miles from the town, they therefore dug trenches, and put houses into a state of defence. The enemy approached one morning at daylight, and came into contact with the patrols, but after a few shots had been fired, the Germans who were about 500 strong retired, two Askaris being captured. The force was ashore for about three weeks and was not again interfered with.

During 1917-1918, patrols from the ships were landed at various places such as Lindi, Mikindani, Kilwa, etc., to round up Germans, but as the Commander-in-Chief's orders were that they were to remain in sight of the ship, only occasionally did they succeed in making any captures.

COASTAL OPERATIONS IN EAST AFRICA

PART V.

Advanced Bases.

CHAPTER 20.

THE SCOTTISH BASES.

Cromarty – Aultbea - Inverness Firth - Kyles of Loch Alsh - Corpach.

CROMARTY had been fixed as one of the principal bases for a war, which would have the North Sea as one of its main theatres, and the matter having been thrashed out between the Admiralty and War Office, the former eventually decided to fortify it themselves, and to man the fortress with Royal Marines. Plans were accordingly drawn up, and the work carried out by the Admiralty. The 9.2-inch guns, and the anti-torpedo craft batteries of four-inch guns with the searchlights had been mounted prior to the war, and the nucleus Royal Marine garrison had taken over the works in the spring of 1914; the garrison being accommodated in huts. The place was therefore in going order on the declaration of war.

Lieut.-Colonel L. Conway-Gordon, R.M.A., was in command, with Captain J. W. Hudleston, R.M.A., as Staff officer and gunnery instructor, and the garrison was provided by R.M.A. and R.M.L.I. in the usual proportions. The garrison was borne on the books of the depot ship at Rosyth for pay and discipline, and was under the command of Naval Commander-in-Chief of the coast of Scotland.

When war was imminent, the garrison was completed with active service officers and men and shortly afterwards Captain D. J. Munro, the King's Harbour Master, devised a most effective boom, which was one of the first placed in position. Cromarty was one of the best protected of all the anchorages of the Grand Fleet, and grew into a most important base, with floating docks, workshops, etc., and was greatly used by the squadrons for rest and recreation after the strain of Scapa Flow. The defences were further strengthened by observation mine fields, and a detachment of the Royal Marine Submarine Miners was added to the garrison to man them. The land defence was provided by a Territorial Infantry Brigade under an Army Commander; Colonel Conway-Gordon was the fortress Commander, with the fire Commanders, North and South Sutors, under him.

It was soon obvious that so many active service officers and men should not be locked up in garrison duties of this sort, and they were gradually replaced by officers promoted from the ranks, and temporary officers, together with reservists and officers and men who had been wounded or invalided from overseas.

The garrison was drawn on to a certain extent to provide officers and men for Scapa Flow as the defences of that place expanded, and also for the various mining bases described later. In addition to R.M.A. officers, officers of the R.M.L.I. were trained in coast artillery, and took their places in command of batteries after being invalided from the Fleet or Expeditionary Forces.

Although submarines were constantly reported off the port, they were careful not to come within reach of the defences, and in common with all the other fixed defences, except Hartlepool and Dover, they had not to resist any enemy attacks.

Lieutenant-Colonel Conway-Gordon was awarded the C.B., and Major Hudleston the brevet of Lieutenant-Colonel for their services, and in 1918, Major G. Rutledge, R.M.A., relieved Lieutenant-Colonel Hudleston as Staff Officer.

2. AULTBEA.

In the early days of the war, it was found necessary to establish a small base on the west coast of Scotland for various purposes; Aultbea being selected. H.M.S. *Illustrious* landed her Royal Marine officer Captain C. H. Regnart, R.M.L.I. (retd.), with two N.C.O.s, one gunner, R.M.A., and eight privates, R.M.L.I. (reservists), and some 12-pounder guns, to form a small battery to guard the entrance to the loch.

When H.M.S. *Illustrious* left, a reinforcement of two N.C.O.s and 19 privates from Chatham were sent up and the battery was properly organised. This small party maintained their lonely and monotonous duties throughout the war, gradually improving their organisation and accommodation. The battery was under the control of the Senior Naval Officer as it was required for Naval purposes, and had to be organised quickly as an "Advanced Base."

3. INVERNESS FIRTH-KYLES OF LOCH ALSH-CORPACH.

Consequent on the entry of the United States into the war, and the more active mining policy then adopted, it became necessary to increase the number of bases for small craft, etc., and to guard them against the possible enterprises of the submarines.

For this purpose it was decided to arm the above mentioned places with some guns and searchlights, and the Royal Marines were called on to provide the necessary garrisons.

The general principle was adopted of detailing the R.M.A. to the guns, and the R.M.L.I. to the searchlights, but the provision of these garrisons was rather a drain on the manning resources. Endeavours were made to send only men in medical categories B and C, or who had been invalided; where this was impossible recruits under age for overseas were sent. The provision of officers presented difficulties, but this was met by drawing on those who had had experience at Scapa Flow and Cromarty, and completing those places with more junior officers.

In April, 1918, Major C. Williams, R.M.L.I., from Cromarty and Lieutenant H. Gardner from East Africa were sent to the Kyles of Loch Alsh, and Captain G. H. Knott, R.M.A., from Scapa Flow, with 2nd Lieutenant F. M. Gibson, R.M.L.I. from France to Corpach.

Major W. A. Jolly, R.M.A., from Cromarty had taken over Inverness Firth in March. These places all worked in close touch with the local Senior Naval Officer, and were borne for pay and discipline on the books of the depot ship.

The detachments were accommodated in buildings close to the defences and were employed in the construction of the batteries and the mounting of the guns. These bases were quickly organised and fulfilled the requirements very efficiently.

CHAPTER 21.

ORKNEYS AND SHETLANDS.
1. SCAPA FLOW.

As Lord Jellicoe has related, Scapa Flow had been selected before the war as the main base of the Grand Fleet, in the event of a war in the North Sea, but owing to financial stringency, nothing had been done, either to equip or fortify it.

A Committee, of which Lieutenant-Colonel D. Mercer, R.M.L.I., A.A.G., R.M., was a member, had gone into the requirements for strengthening and defending the base, and during the manoeuvres of 1913, a small Royal Marine Force under Lieutenant-Colonel Poole, R.M.A., had carried out some experimental work, which proved of great value. The proposed organisation and equipment of the "flying column" Royal Marines (see chapter 9), had been based on the probable requirements of such a base, but no action had been taken on the Committee's recommendations.

The Royal Marine Brigade had been equipped in August, 1914, with 12-pounder guns, and stores had been collected as far as possible, but the Brigade was diverted to other purposes, and though after the Ostend expedition, the R.M.A. Battalion was available, they were in process of being organised for the Howitzer and Anti-Aircraft Brigades for service in France.

There were three main entrances to be defended, Hoxa Sound, Switha Sound, and Hoy Sound, with some smaller and more tortuous channels at Holm Sound, etc. The principal channel to be protected was Hoxa, and to guard it the Fleet had landed some 12 and 3 pounder guns, and also some guns at Switha and Holm, but there were no searchlights available. The main defence, therefore, depended on the light cruisers and destroyers, who guarded the entrances whenever the Fleet were in the Flow, there were also picket boat patrols. This, however, did not give the rest and feeling of security that were so necessary for the well being of the Fleet. Captain G. L. Raikes, R.M.A., with a few pensioner Royal Marine Artillery, were sent up in September to man the guns, and portable searchlights were provided as soon as possible.

Batteries were then constructed at Hoxa and Stanger Heads, and to cover Switha and Holm Sounds; the guns surrendered by the Brigade, with their special mountings and platforms, also became available.

Pending the construction of the batteries, and their improved armament, H.M.S. *Magnificent* and *Hannibal* were stationed at the entrances at Hoxa and Hoy, later relieved by the *Royal Arthur* and *Crescent*, when these vessels were no longer required for the 10th Cruiser Squadron; the other entrances being blocked by sinking merchantmen.

On 17th November, 1914, Lieutenant-Colonel G. N. A. Harris, R.M.A. was appointed to command the defences, and Q.M.S. G. Harrington, R.M.A. was given a temporary commission as quartermaster for supplies and stores; the headquarters were fixed at Kirkwall.

Captain A. F. Simson, R.M.A. (retd.), was appointed Fire-Commander of the Southern Defences, and with Captain H. L. Twiss, R.M.A. (retd.), commanded the batteries at Hoxa and Stanger. Through the efforts of these two officers, the batteries were brought to a state of efficiency, whilst they kept their personnel, consisting mostly of old men in a fit and efficient condition throughout the trying winter of 1914-15. The men were for a long time in tents on the boggy ground without even bottom boards, for the winter was well advanced before the huts were built; this was a high test of the stamina, discipline and courage of the Royal Marine Reservist, which triumphed over all difficulties and even over his rheumatism.

In the Orkneys, there was a Territorial unit, the Orkney Royal Garrison Artillery, which was placed at the disposal of the Admiralty and formed a welcome reinforcement to the personnel.

Guns were obtained from America, and as they became available the armament of the existing batteries was increased, and a number of new batteries were also added. The portable searchlights were replaced by powerful lights with petrol engines which were run by the Royal Marine crews, who had been trained in the torpedo schools.

By 29th December, 1914, the first line of booms was in place in the Hoxa channel, and the nets were continually being improved, whilst the boom at Hoy was completed on 19th February, 1915.

Early in 1915 it was decided to increase the number of batteries and searchlights in order to release the cruisers, which were guarding the entrances, and during the summer of 1915 these were erected. This entailed an increase in the Royal Marine garrison which, fortunately for the manning situation, were not required until the following October. This arrangement entailed an increase of nearly 400 officers and men, and in order to provide them the numbers were equally divided between the Divisions. They were composed as far as possible of reserves, and men invalided from the various fronts, and were completed with recruits, and this arrangement was maintained throughout.

The personnel of the defences were borne on the books of the depot ship, which was responsible for their feeding and pay.

Admiral Sir Stanley Colville was appointed Admiral of the Orkneys and Shetlands, and Rear-Admiral F. S. Miller was Senior Naval Officer of the base. These two officers, as soon as protection had been provided, rapidly developed the equipment and facilities of the place, and it was soon fully equipped with repair ships, etc., to supply the requirements of the Fleet.

As soon as the defences of Hoy Sound had been completed they .were constituted into a separate Fire Command, known as the Western Defences, under Lieutenant-Colonel C. L Brooke, R.M.A., from Cromarty. When this officer was appointed D.A.A.G., Royal Marines, in December, 1916, he was replaced by Major A. F. Binney, R.M.A. Captain Simson remained Fire Commander of the Southern Defences throughout.

Lord Jellicoe had insisted that the batteries, as far as possible, should be commanded by Royal Marine officers owing to their acquaintance with the Fleet, and in consequence considerable difficulty was experienced in 1915 in providing officers, as there were very few Royal Marine Artillery officers available. Some of the R.M.A. Warrant and N.C. officers who had been promoted to commissions, were appointed to the batteries, and two Royal Marine gunners S. W. Bucknall (R.M.L.I.), and G. H. Knott (R.M.A.), were also commissioned for these batteries; later some R.M.L.I. officers (Major R. Cator and Captain Knight), were drafted in as were some temporary officers.

In 1917, the War Office wished to withdraw all the men of the Orkney R.G.A. (T) fit for service overseas, and as this meant a considerable alteration in the manning of the batteries, the opportunity was taken to replace them by Royal Marines. Though this necessarily caused rather a drain on the Divisional resources it was successfully effected, but the provision of officers was more difficult; this was solved by transferring six officers of the Orkney unit, who had served in the batteries since the beginning, to the Royal Marines with temporary commissions. The officers so transferred being Major J. White, Captain J. D. Dennison, C. E. Swanney, Lieutenants F. M. McKay, J. M. Shearer, and 2nd Lieutenant S. Stanger: the necessary numbers. of N.C.O.s and men being completed by wounded and invalided men, as well as officers of whom more were now available.

[Photo by Capt. Whale, R.M.A.]

SCAPA FLOW, HOLM BATTERY IN WINTER.

[Photo by CapT. Whale, R.M.A.]

4-INCH GUN AT ALEXANDRIA.

(See Chapter 31).

When the Royal Marine Submarine Miners were formed, observation mines were laid at Hoxa and Hoy, and it was one of these fields, under Lieutenant A. Innes, Royal Marine Submarine Miners, that destroyed a submarine towards the end of the war.

In view of the range of the Zeppelins, and the eventual establishment of an aerodrome in the Orkneys, an anti-aircraft battery was mounted at Burray Island, and another at Carness and manned by Royal Marines.

The garrison was quartered in huts, and in time the accommodation and other conditions were greatly improved, rifle ranges were erected by the Fleet, and the facilities for recreation were increased.

Among the incidents recorded in the diaries was the loss of H.M.S. *Hampshire* on 5th June, 1916, which was last seen by the signal station of the Western Defences. Rescue parties were provided by the Hoy batteries, but only a few survivors were rescued from rafts; they, however, found the body of Captain C. S. Hazeon, R.M.L.I., the Marine officer, on a raft.

Nothing could relieve the monotony and isolation of the batteries, and the long and dreary months of waiting and watching for an enemy who never came; whilst the long hours of darkness in the winter months made the strain of watching more trying than at the southern ports. They were at last rewarded by seeing the German High Seas Fleet led captive by the First Battle Squadron to its last resting place in the Flow.

Lieutenant-Colonel G. N. Harris was awarded the Brevet of Colonel, and the Order of the C.B.E., for his work in organising and commanding so successfully the defences. Major Simson, who bore the heavy responsibilities of the Southern defences throughout, was promoted to Major and awarded the O.B.E., Lieutenant and Quartermaster Harrington receiving the M.B.E., as well as Lieutenant (Acting Captain) H. J. Burrage, R.M.A.

In addition to the headquarters, the following officers commanded batteries at various times.

Western Defences:-

		Southern Defences:-	
Major G. Y. Russell, R.M.A.	1915	Captain J. Lambert, D.C.M., R.M.A.	1914-1919
Major R Cator, R.M.L.I.	1915-16	Captain J. W. Hills, R.M.A.	1915-1919
Major F. Knight, R.M.L.I.	1916-19	Captain H. L. Twiss, R.M.A.	1914-1915
Captain J. Jones, R.M.A.	1915-1917	Captain Van der Kiste, R.M.A.	1914-1915
Captain S. W. Bucknall, R.M.L.I.	1915-1919	Captain C. M. Durrant, R.M.A.	1915
Captain P. R. Simon, R.M.A.	1917-1919	Major B. G. Warder, R.M.A.	1915
Major McKay, R.M.	1915-1919	Captain G. H. Knott, R.M.A.	1915-1918
Major J. White, R.M.	1916-1919		
Captain Dennison, R.M.	1916-1919		

2. SHETLANDS

There were no fixed defences in these islands, but Major H. C. Evans, R.M.L.I., had organised a service of look-out posts, and small defence patrols from the local Naval Reserve men, which was at once put in force under his command, and fulfilled all requirements. Major Evans was relieved later by Lieutenant-Colonel F. T. Phillips, R.M.L.I., who remained in command until April, 1918, when he was in turn relieved by Colonel C. E. Collard, C.B., R.M.L.I. (retd.) The Royal Naval Volunteer Reserve officers were withdrawn at the same time for sea service, and replaced by N.C.O.s, Royal Marines, who were granted temporary commissions as Lieutenants, Royal Naval Volunteer Reserve, the N.C.O.s so promoted being Colour-Sergeants D. T. Moore (Chatham), C. T. Piper (Portsmouth) and R. F. Rogers (Plymouth).

Lerwick was the base of the 10th Cruiser Squadron, to which all the intercepted shipping was sent for examination. Up to the end of 1917, old cruisers had been detailed to guard the anchorage, etc., but owing to the submarine menace, and the importance of protecting the port, added to the necessity of economising manpower, some guns had been landed to cover the entrances, which were manned by Royal Naval Reserve men under three acting warrant officers, Royal Marines, and the ships were withdrawn. As it was decided in 1918 to increase and improve the armament, Royal Marine Gunner Uren and a party from the Chatham Division, R.M.L.I., were sent up, which in April was considerably reinforced by drafts from all Divisions. The several batteries were commanded by acting warrant officers, Royal Marines, who had had gunnery experience, some of whom were later granted commissions, as the importance of the batteries increased (e.g. Lieutenant Tildesley, R.M.L.I., and F. J. Chivers, R.M.A.)

The organisation gradually grew into quite a large system of defences, under the command of Colonel Collard, who was relieved at the Armistice by Lieutenant-Colonel F. C. Edwards, R.M.L.I.

CHAPTER 22.

ADVANCED BASES ABROAD.

The Aegean Islands -Lemnos – Imbros – Tenedos -3rd R.M. Battalion - The West Indies - St. Helena - Ascension.

As soon as the Naval attack on the Dardanelles was decided on it became necessary to find a base, where the colliers, store and ammunition ships, etc., could lie and where the battleships and other craft could coal, water, and provision as necessary. Malta was too distant, but the three islands Lemnos, Imbros, and Tenedos were most conveniently situated, and Mudros the principal harbour in Lemnos was a magnificent anchorage, where the largest fleet could lie protected from the weather.

The islands had belonged to Turkey, but during the Balkan Wars of 1912-13 had been seized by Greece. The treaty of peace had never been ratified and as they were therefore nominally Turkish, they were occupied by the Allies, though the Greek authorities remained in charge of the Civil Government, police, taxes, etc. Admiral Lord Wester Wemyss has wittily described in his book on the Dardanelles the difficulties and absurdities created by this extraordinary state of affairs and the onerous duties thrown on him in his capacity as Senior Naval Officer, acting as Military Governor. However, Lieutenant Luckach, Royal Naval Volunteer Reserve, was appointed Government Secretary, and with a staff of officers appointed to the several islands from gentlemen with a knowledge of those parts, soon produced a satisfactory working arrangement.

The Greeks had mounted some guns and searchlights to protect Port Mudros; two four-inch guns being mounted in a battery on each side of the entrance to the inner harbour, the batteries being known as Buda and Lemni; whilst some good searchlights had also been mounted at these places, as well as near the lighthouse at Kombi. An anti-submarine net, a port war signal station and an examination service rendered the place a tolerably safe anchorage. The guns and lights were manned by the Royal Marine Artillery from H.M.S. *Inflexible* in April as their ship was being repaired at Malta, but when the *Triumph* was sunk on 26th of May, her Royal Marines under Captain J. G. Home, R.M.L.I., took over the batteries and the *Inflexibles* returned to their ship. Later the batteries were taken over by some of the Royal Naval Division, who were relieved by Royal Garrison Artillery and Royal Engineers when the former went to France, and this arrangement was maintained until the 3rd Royal Marine Battalion took over the islands.

In view of the large number of trawlers, drifters, and other subsidiary craft, another harbour was necessary where they would be independent of the larger ships. This was found in Port Kondia, to the westward of Mudros, the head of the harbour, being only about half-a-mile overland from Mudros Harbour. Here H.M.S. *Osiris*, the depot ship, and all the small craft were based under Captain Rombulow-Pearse, Royal Navy. There was also an anchorage at Purnea Bay, on the north side of the island, which was useful for submarines. Although the anchorage was invaluable, among its other defects Mudros is subject to a constant succession of strong winds blowing from the north across the harbour, which on many days makes it impossible for small boats to communicate, except in the few billets under the lee of the land.

There were no harbour facilities, only one small wooden pier at the village of East Mudros, and as the principal depots of the British troops were placed at West Mudros, piers had to be built there. There were no cranes or other facilities for loading or unloading ships, but most serious of all the water supply was totally inadequate, even for the local inhabitants, whereas water was required not only for the troops in Lemnos, but also for the ships and the troops at Gallipoli. In addition to distilling ships, a distillery, which had been intended for the east was commandeered and erected at West Mudros, where, worked by the Royal Navy, it rendered good service till 1920 when it was practically worn out. The islands produced nothing but a certain amount of barley, melons and tomatoes, so could not be drawn on for supplies, but there seemed to be an inexhaustible supply of Raki, a vile description of "firewater" which was retailed to the troops at exorbitant prices. Labour also was unobtainable in any quantity; besides the labour corps, which were raised in Egypt, etc., only refugees from Asia Minor were available.

In spite of the defects, the place was converted into a tolerably well equipped advanced base, with repair ships, store ships, hospital, etc., to meet the needs of a large fleet and army. It was also equipped with a most excellent aerodrome and seaplane base, and was so utilised until the end of the war.

Imbros, a mountainous and roadless island, was very conveniently placed, only about seven miles from the Peninsula. The harbour at Kephalo, was converted into a convenient advanced harbour by sinking two of the "dummy" dreadnoughts to form a breakwater, and with a net ships were able to lie safe from submarines. As the peninsula could be seen clearly with glasses, this place became the headquarters of Sir Ian Hamilton, whilst an aerodrome was established between Kephalo and Aliki Bay. Later after the evacuation, when the Turks mounted eight-inch guns at Cape Helles, which were able to shell Kephalo, the aerodrome was moved to the north side of the island to Gliki, whilst only trawlers and drifters were able to use Kephalo, the enemy shelling destroyers, or any larger ships using the Harbour. Look-out posts were established at Blake's Post (north-east of the island), above Kusu Bay, which was used as an anchorage by the monitors, until after the *Raglan* was sunk by the *Goeben*; Pyrgos on the south side of the island, where the Royal Marine signallers were stationed to communicate with the patrolling destroyers, and at Skinudi in the centre of the island, where the telephone cable necessitated an exchange.

Tenedos, lying only four miles off the Asiatic shore was of importance, because it controlled the channel past Gadaro Lighthouse, leading to the Dardanelles. In Dimitri Bay, on the west side of the island, the ships were able to rest and shelter from the forts after bombarding. During the early days, an aerodrome .was established on the island.

Mavro or Rabbit Island, a small island not much more than a rock, was useful as a station for the monitors bombarding the Peninsula, and after the evacuation was occupied as a convenient look-out station, which could watch the entrance to the Straits, and give early information as to vessels leaving them; it was constantly bombed by the Turks, so that the garrison lived in dugouts, on the west side of the cliff, and were relieved every three months.

After March 18th, 1915, the Royal Marine detachments of H.M.S. *Ocean* and *Irresistible* garrisoned Tenedos and Mavro, under the command of Major Temple, R.M.A., who was appointed governor of the island, until he became Intelligence Officer at Mudros, and was succeeded by Lieut.-Colonel G. J. Mullins, R.M.L.I., from H.M.S. *Lord Nelson* for a short time until he joined the Royal Naval Division.

3rd ROYAL MARINE BATTALION.

After the evacuation of the Dardanelles, though no longer required as a base by the Army, Lemnos, Imbros, and Tenedos were still essential to the Navy, for the Dardanelles patrol and the control of the communications to Salonica, and in consequence it was decided to retain the islands. The Royal Naval Division was detailed at first as a garrison, and on their removal to France in May, 1916, the islands were taken over by the Army, who stationed there a Brigade of garrison troops, with some artillery, engineers, and details.

In the following November, however, the Army were again anxious to remove their troops. This proposal could not be agreed to by the Admiralty, for whose operations the islands were essential; consequently, the Admiralty agreed to provide a Battalion of Royal Marines to replace the artillery and infantry part of the garrison. The 3rd Royal Marine Battalion, 1000 strong was raised under the command of Lieut.-Colonel F. D. Bridges, R.M.L.I., with Major J. A. M. A. Clark, R.M.L.I., second in command, Captain W. de T. L. Clarke, R.M.L.I. as adjutant, and Lieutenant A. Jameson, as quartermaster. One company R.M.A. (Captain Hamer), Chatham Company (Captain R. N. White), Portsmouth Company (Captain M. H. Marshman), Plymouth Company (Captain E. H. Bockett-Pugh).

They proceeded overland to Marseilles, and embarked in the *Royal George* on 17th November. On arrival at the island on 24th, after a very stormy passage, headquarters and the Portsmouth Company were stationed at West Mudros, with a detachment at East Mudros. The Chatham Company went to Tenedos, with a detachment of one officer and a platoon at Mavro Island, and a detachment at Thaso Island to guard the aerodrome. The Plymouth Company was sent to Kephalo, Imbros under Major Clark, who also supervised Tenedos. The R.M.A. took over the four guns at Buda and Lemni in Mudros, and the A.A. battery at Beacon Hill, also the A.A. batteries of two six-pounder Q.F. at Tenedos Hill and in Imbros two Bulgarian guns and some three pounders at Kephalos.

The Senior Naval Officer at Mudros continued to act as Military Governor, and the Army Brigadier General and his staff were in command of the troops. There was apparently a Naval Officer in charge of the gun defences, though eventually Captain Hamer was appointed in charge of anti-aircraft defences.

There were a considerable number of look-out posts, and in addition to those already mentioned, there were Aliki Bay and Kephalo Lighthouse in. Imbros, the Hill, Dimitri Bay, and Cable Post in Tenedos, and Cape Ponente in Lemnos. These were in addition to the numerous posts of six to twelve men posted to watch the possible landing places, or to guard particular points. Officers and men were much scattered in small detachments throughout the three islands, and it speaks well for their discipline and conduct that there were no complaints and no serious offences.

These posts required a considerably larger number of signallers than the battalion establishment provided, and to increase the number it was necessary to start classes not only for Army signalling but also for Naval, in order to be able to communicate with the ships. The officers and men were mostly those who had been invalided after wounds or sickness from the various fronts or recruits too young for service in a theatre of war.

During the next two years, Mudros, Imbros, Tenedos, and Mavro, were subject to constant air attacks, and the anti-aircraft guns were considerably increased in number. They were constantly in action, and drove the enemy off. Imbros and Tenedos in 1917 were also constantly shelled from the mainland of Gallipoli Peninsula and the Asiatic shore by 8.2 and 5.9-inch guns, but without sustaining any serious damage, although the shells fell around the camps, etc., but in consequence of the shelling and damage to the castle at Tenedos, the company moved to Paraskevi, on the other side of the island, where hutments were erected.

In November, 1917, as the War Office insisted on withdrawing all their troops, the Royal Marine garrison was expanded and took over all the duties; thus becoming an advanced base with Royal Marines in charge. Colonel E. J. Stroud, C.M.G., R.M.L.I., was appointed Brigadier-General to command, with Major R. D. Ormsby as D.A.Q.M.G., who took over their duties from the Army Brigade staff on 1st December. A transport section was formed under Captain L. Malcolm, of the Divisional Train, Royal Marines, and Lieutenant Jameson took over the supply duties, with a small section to relieve the Army Service Corps, and also the Ordnance section. Some R.M.L.I. trained at the school of Military Engineering, Chatham, took over the searchlights and engines. The Royal Naval Medical Officers of the battalion under Surgeon-Commander T. W. Myles, Royal Navy, took charge of the hospital. The signal section presented the principal difficulty as there were miles of telegraph and telephone wires to be maintained. The Army consented to leave the Royal Engineer Officer, and a small expert staff of telegraph operators to work the Eastern Telegraph Company's cable and the Royal Marines took over all the other work. After the Armistice, the Royal Marines under Lieutenant Guest took over everything, which included not only the telegraph exchanges, but also the large number of telephones.

On 20th January, 1918, the *Goeben* and *Breslau* made their celebrated sortie. Owing to fog and mist, they were not observed at first from Mavro Island on coming out of the Dardanelles, and shells falling on the camps at Kephalo were one of the first intimations of their appearance, as related in Chapter 5. The *Breslau*, was sunk through striking a mine off Cable Post in Aliki Bay, and the *Goeben* was also injured, but in spite of the gallant attacks by the British torpedo-boat-destroyers, she managed to crawl back into the Dardanelles, and grounded at Nagara Point, where she was attacked by aircraft from Mudros.

In the early part of 1918, proposals were made by the Naval Commander-in-Chief, Sir Sidney Fremantle, for raids on the adjoining Turkish coast line, and to provide the requisite troops a number of the outlying posts, including Thaso, where the detachment had suffered much from malaria, were called in and a small mobile force collected, but before any action could be taken, the call for reinforcements for France consequent on the German offensive in March, supervened and in accordance with orders from England, Lieutenant Flower, C.G.M., and 100 R.M.L.I., were at once dispatched to join the battalions in France. Captain Pearson and Lieutenant Clanchy with a further 50 men were, however, hung up at Itea in the Gulf of Patras, and went eventually to Corfu, as described later.

When Rear-Admiral C. F. Lambert assumed command of the Aegean Squadron in February, 1918, he found the many difficulties caused by the retention by the Senior Naval Officer of the duties of Military Governor. He therefore appointed Brigadier-General Stroud to be Military Governor, and the staff of the Government secretary with the intelligence officers, except Colonel Temple, came under his command; also the civil guards, raised from Greek refugees who performed police duties. The Greek Civil Government were responsible for the collection of taxes, education, post office and police; the Sub Governor was Mr. Michaelopoulos who had been educated in England, and at Oxford. In June, 1918, General Stroud was appointed Commandant at Plymouth and was relieved by Colonel H. E. Blumberg, C.B., R.M.L.I. with the temporary rank of Brigadier-General.

At the same time, Major J. G. Horne, R.M.L.I., was sent from England to command the Royal Marine Guard at Corfu, which was detailed to relieve the troops from Salonica as part of the International Force. The French Commander-in-Chief was in command of Corfu, and on his staff as liaison officer was Major W. L. Huntingford, who had charge of most of the arrangements on shore. The guard was formed of Lieutenant Clanchy's detachment of the 3rd Royal Marines and was reinforced by a party from England under Lieutenant H. Jones, R.M.L.I. They were nominally under the command of the General Officer Commanding Aegean at Mudros, but communication was practically impossible. The guard was quartered with the Allies in the fort at Corfu, and Major Horne by the display of great tact and the good behaviour of his men maintained the British prestige under very difficult circumstances; after the Armistice the guard was sent to Mudros arriving there just before Xmas, 1918.

During 1917-18, the anti-aircraft defences in the islands were much increased and a battery of two 3-inch guns at Beacon Battery, was mounted at West Mudros, whilst the guns in the battery at One Tree

MUDROS HARBOUR FROM FRENCH HOSPITAL ABOVE BUDA POINT.

[By permission of the Imperial War Museum.]

Well, guarding the aerodrome at East Mudros were increased to six. Another battery of two 3-inch guns was mounted at Gliki Aerodrome in Imbros. The work of mounting these guns was carried out by the Royal Marines, the concrete foundations being constructed by the Royal Marine Works Department, under Captain E. Nottingham Palmer, R.M.L.I., who was also responsible for the maintenance of the piers, roads and buildings, and also the construction of the railway at East Mudros for the Air Force.

In August, 1918, the Royal Marines took over charge of the Turkish prisoners of war, Lieutenant D'Arcy Bunyan, R.M.L.I., being appointed to command with the temporary rank of Major, and Lieutenant W. H. Rogers, R.M.A. was appointed Assistant Commandant. There were 700 of these prisoners, who were principally employed in coaling the ships.

Civil labour was one of the greatest difficulties of the port, as the numbers required for the railway and other works of the Air Force were very large, in addition to the various Naval service.

The Royal Marine garrison during 1918 was raised to a total strength of about 1400, and as anti-aircraft batteries absorbed a considerable number, both R.M.A. and R.M.L.I., were employed on these duties. The anti-aircraft gunnery was new to all ranks, but by study and application with the presence of some temporary R.M.A. officers, who had had experience in France, the officers and men soon acquired a satisfactory knowledge of their duties. In the middle of September, 1918, Major Woodcock, R.M.A., relieved Captain Hamer, who had been invalided at the beginning of July, as artillery commander.

The French Admiral Amet, the Commander-in-Chief of the Aegean, and the French Command were rather anxious about the defences of the harbours in which their squadron of battleships was lying, especially as the defences except for anti-aircraft guns and aircraft were practically non-existent, whilst Imbros was only seven miles and Tenedos four from the mainland. Proposals were therefore made to mount 9. 2-inch and 6-inch guns and a commission of Artillery and Engineer officers arrived from England, in September, 1918. An interesting month was spent in reconnoitring for possible gun positions, etc., but fortunately the Armistice put a stop to what would have been a great waste of money. The garrison was, however, supplied with a number of machine guns, and sections of two guns were formed and trained to guard possible landing places, and a defence scheme was drawn up to reinforce these with mobile forces, but as is generally the case in such places, the action of the land forces could only deal with raiding parties and cause delay, whilst the Naval forces afloat prevent any reinforcements being landed or attack from the sea.

During the latter half of 1918, several air raids took place on the British Aerodrome, and caused a good deal of destruction of material, but the Royal Air Force under Colonel Gordon (late R.M.L.I.), retaliated with constant attacks on Constantinople, which did a great deal of damage[29].

After the repatriation of the Turkish prisoners, labour difficulties increased, and a Greek Labour Corps of 600 men was raised, recruited mostly in Smyrna by Lieutenant Georgiadas, R.N.V.R., but they were not satisfactory, and after a few months were disbanded; some members of the corps, however, gained some valuable experience in dealing with such an organisation.

After the occupation of Smyrna by the Greeks, the garrison of the islands was gradually reduced. The anti-aircraft batteries were dismantled, the guns and stores being returned to Malta; the Naval stores, etc., were also returned and H.M.S. *Europa*, the depot ship proceeded to Smyrna in October, 1919, while the Royal Air Force were also evacuated. The disposal of the stores, Air, Naval and Army with no adequate transport and an impoverished population presented many problems.

---

29. For the taking over of the Dardanelles Forts see chapter 35.

The brigade and battalion staffs were amalgamated, and the garrison was reduced to a minimum. General Blumberg returned to England on 3rd November, on promotion to the command of the Portsmouth Division, and Major F. H. H. Hall, D.A.Q.M.G. returned with him. Brigadier-General Finlaison was appointed to succeed him as the retention of the islands was still considered desirable.

After the collapse of General Denikin's army in South Russia, in March, 1920, some of the wounded and refugees, about 4000 men, women and children were sent to Lemnos. They arrived without any warning, and had to be landed as soon as possible, owing to typhus and other epidemics in the transports. The much reduced garrison were called on to improvise accommodation, and under the guidance of Lieutenant W. Willey, R.M.L.I., the Royal Marine Works Officer, camps were erected, and within a short time all the refugees were landed and under canvas, whilst Surgeon-Commander Myles and his staff grappled with the problem of the sick. The shortage of water problem was solved by Lieutenant-Commander Ponsford, R.N.V.R., the Government Secretary, who found water at Agrionis across the lagoon at West Mudros, to replace the old distillery, which was at last giving out. The Engineer-Commander, and the Royal Marines of the *Emperor of India*, under Major Snepp rendered most useful service in laying this pipe line. Army personnel and Red Cross units were sent down from Constantinople, for work in connection with the camp, and Captain S. J. Bassett, R.M.L.I., was seconded to the Army as Staff Captain and liaison officer, between the Military Governor and the Army, later on being sent to Constantinople and attached to General Wrangel's Army. The camp ran very smoothly, and was tactfully and efficiently policed by Royal Marines under Lieutenant R. Gumm. It was. however, considered that as the majority of the refugees were women and children, a winter camp under canvas was out of the question, and arrangements were made with the Serbian Government to take the whole camp into Serbia. The transfer of the refugees in batches of 500 in October to Salonica was supervised by Captain Rymer, Royal Navy, of the *Dublin*, and Captain H. E. Beere, R.M.L.I., escorted the first batch. The refugees eventually settled in Serbian towns and villages.

The garrison was reduced in November to eight officers and 186 N.C.O.s and men.

Later when Wrangel's army of nearly 15,000 men, after their defeat in South Russia, were brought to Mudros on 20th November[30], the French assumed control, and after handing over their huts and stores on 7th December, General Finlaison removed his headquarters and the remnant of the garrison to Kastro, the town on the west side of the island, and the seat of the Greek Civil Government; the small British garrisons, however, remained in Imbros and Tenedos.

On 25th June, 1921, the three islands were formally handed over by the Military Governor, General Finlaison, to the Greek authorities, and the British flag was hauled down. The last of the garrison embarked in H.M.S. *Bryony*; after an occupation of six years, of which the Royal Marines had been in charge for nearly four years.

2. WEST INDIES.

In May, 1917, orders were issued for a party to be detailed for a duty which surely was as strange as any ever allotted to the Royal Marines.

The enemy submarines were going further afield and as they were now armed with guns were attempting to bombard defenceless places; also surface raiders were known to be at large, and where they would appear was uncertain. As attempts might be made on the West Indian Islands, a party consisting of 10 N.C.O.s and

---

30. This was not the first time that Russians had been accommodated in Lemnos, because one of the villages was called Roussopoul, the town of the Russians.

40 men under Major and Brevet-Lieutenant-Colonel J. R. H. Homfray, R.M.A., was ordered to be sent out together with the necessary 4.7-inch guns and mountings. The N.C.O.s and men were drawn equally from all the Divisions. Each party was allotted one gun and consisted of one N.C.O. and four men, one of whom was to be a gunlayer, and if possible each party was to include a gunnery instructor; the parties were to be self-contained and equipped with camp equipment and the necessary stores.

They left Liverpool in the *Olympic* on 12th May, 1917, taking with them six of the guns, the other four were sent by another ship, which was sunk, causing considerable delay until they could be replaced. On the passage over the Royal Marines manned the six-inch defensive guns and landing at Halifax were taken to Bermuda in H.M.S. *Drake*, the guns following by Royal Mail. Arriving at Bermuda on 22nd, there was a delay of two weeks, which was utilised by Colonel Homfray in making a rough selection from the charts of probable places for mounting the guns. Embarking in the Royal Mail ship, they arrived at St. Kitts on 10th June; remaining in the ship, they in turn visited Antigua, Montserrat, Dominica, St. Lucia, Barbadoes, St. Vincent, and Grenada, arriving at Trinidad on 14th. At each place a preliminary survey was made with the local authorities, and it was found that practically all the positions provisionally fixed on were suitable; everywhere they were received with the most unstinted help from the Governors and their staffs.

Arriving at Trinidad, all the men and stores were disembarked and were accommodated in the grand stand of the racecourse. After consultation with Commodore Simpson and the Governor as to sites and allotment of guns, the orders were issued and the detachments told off.

They were allotted as follows :

Gun.	Detacht.	Place	Officer in charge	Crew completed by
"A"	R.M.A.	Trinidad	2nd Lieut. Hamilton, (Trinidad Garr. Art. Volunteers)	11 Natives.
"B"	R.M.A.	Trinidad	2nd Lieut. Hamilton (Trinidad Garr. Art. Volunteers)	11 Natives.
"C"	Chatham	Barbadoes	2nd Lieut. V. Henschell, Volunteers	12 Natives.
"D"	Chatham	Barbadoes	2nd Lieut. Da Costa, Volunteers	12 Natives.
"E"	Portsmouth	Grenada	Major G Smith, K.O.S.B.	12 White Volunteers.
"F"	R.M.A.	Antigua	Captain Downing	12 Natives
"G"	Plymouth	Dominica	Captain H. Walker, Defence Force	12 Natives
"H"	Plymouth	St. Kitts	Lieut. Skinner, Cadet Corps	12 Natives
"I"	R.M.A.	Nassau		12 Natives
"K"	Portsmouth	St. Vincent	Major Osment, Police	12 Natives {Trinidad}
"L & M"	R.M.A.*	{Oil Fields}	Mr. Ibbet, C.E.	12 Natives

* Mounted later to protect the oil fields.

The ordnance stores, etc. were divided up, Sergeant Marlow, R.M.A., performing excellent work, so that the detachments were able to move with their material and stores complete.

The sites to cover the harbour at Port of Spain, Trinidad having been settled and the work put in hand, Colonel Homfray left on 1st July in H.M.S. *Eileen* (lately Mr. Joel's yacht), for the other islands, taking with him the base plates, bolts and plans for the emplacements. The party went first to Grenada, where the work was at once put in hand, and going on to Barbadoes, the emplacements were started and the pedestals which had arrived were sent to the sites. Gentlemen in the islands rendered invaluable assistance by lending their ox teams, carts, engines and trucks to move the gear up. At Barbadoes the guns were landed in Trafalgar

Square, under the statue of Nelson, and going up to the site the weight of the pedestal burst the water mains.

Colonel Homfray returned to Trinidad and the work was pressed on so that by the 27th August the first gun was fired for test; the second was not ready until 4th October. The detachments for Barbadoes, Grenada, and Antigua were dispatched to their stations on 14th July. By 18th August the Grenada gun had reported that they were ready to fire, and fired their test rounds before Colonel Homfray arrived. The gun had been mounted on the Morne, 573 feet above sea level, and as the oxen would not pull, the whole populace, men, women, and children turned out and man-handled the gun up a precipitous, but good road, in one day.

The guns at Barbadoes, which were mounted to cover Bridgetown were, ready by 13th September; by the 17th of that month the guns had arrived and been landed at Nassau, St. Kitts, Dominica, St. Vincent, and the detachments for those guns who had been employed in mounting the guns for the oil fields in Trinidad which had arrived on 20th August were dispatched to their stations, on 5th October, to mount their guns. At Dominica, the gun and pedestal had been landed by the Civil Engineer, Mr. Noble, and the local troops under Captain H. Walker, at great personal risk on a raft made of two barges lashed together and towed by row boats, and were then pulled to a position 350 feet above sea level.

The guns were now quickly reporting ready for service, and headquarters were established at Barbadoes. At Antigua, where the gun was mounted to protect St. John's Harbour, it was ready on 10th October. At Dominica, the gun, which was mounted to cover Roseau Roads, was ready on 17th, and at St. Kitts to cover Basseterre on 25th. In St. Vincent, where the delay in the arrival of the gun had delayed matters, the gun at Kingstown was ready on 15th November, and that at Nassau on 21st November.

The work of constructing the battery emplacements was done by the Public Works department of the several islands, and the enthusiasm and skill of the local authorities surmounted the numerous difficulties. The Governor of Trinidad, Sir J. Chancellor, was an old Royal Engineer Officer, whose advice was of the greatest assistance to Colonel Homfray.

The guns were mounted by their own detachments, in some cases under the supervision of Colonel Homfray, in others by their own N.C.O.s.

The officers were selected from gentlemen in the islands belonging to the local forces, who were too old or who had been medically rejected for service with the British West India Regiments; most of them served without pay and combined the work with their own other duties. They soon became efficient in their gunnery, and took the greatest care of the comfort of their men and the islands vied with each other in the excellent arrangements made for their men's accommodation.

All gunners and privates, Royal Marines, were made acting bombardiers or lance-corporals, to give them command over the natives, and the way in which they, on their own initiative, drilled and trained the natives, was beyond praise. The N.C.O.s, Royal. Marines at each place spent a great deal of time drilling the negroes at squad drill, and physical training, and it was wonderful how the negroes improved in soldierly bearing, and were even able to turn out guards for the Governors. The natives were selected from those who had been medically rejected for service with the British West India Regiments.

The detachments made gardens and grew vegetables; at one island the effort to combine camouflage and gardening proved disastrous and the first round fired resulted in a shower of squashed melons and tomatoes. The life of the men was particularly lonely in some positions, but they went through it without any complaint and made themselves very popular with the negro population. The men were usually quartered in huts or houses close to the emplacements and every provision possible for their health and comfort was made. The health remained very good and there were only a few cases of malaria and dysentery; one gunner died of apoplexy at Barbadoes. When possible, exchange of station was carried out to relieve the monotony. Colonel Homfray visited each island himself and calibrated the guns and made the necessary arrangements for fire control and rangefinding; in contrast to other Marine units they had been given rangefinders and instructional practices were fired.

They were not called on to fire a shot in anger, but valuable experience was gained, and their presence probably had the desired effect and prevented submarines and raiders from making any attempt on the islands.

The ammunition, which had in most cases to be carried up to the positions by hand, was carried up by the negroes and negresses on their heads; for fear that they should drop them and break the points of the A.P. shell, they were told that if they let them fall a fearful explosion would result; all went well until one negress dropped one, on which she fled with a loud wail into the bush and was not seen again!

After the Armistice nothing happened for three months and then orders were received to dismantle everything, which was done by the Royal Marine detachments with the help of the natives. The party left Trinidad on 13th February, 1919 and picked up the detachments in succession. At each place the Governors bade adieus to the detachments and expressed their admiration of their behaviour, whilst the populations turned out to wish them "God speed" and the whole party returned to Bermuda.

They returned home via St. John's, New Brunswick, where they had to drill for the Governor and came through as the Royal Marines always do, though they had not seen each other for 18 months; and after five days embarked for Liverpool; during the passage having to turn out and quieten some 100 German prisoners of war who were returning in the same ship.

As a reward for his services, Colonel Homfray was made a C.B.E.

3. ST. HELENA.

Before the war the Admiralty had taken over the garrison of this coaling station, and there was a small care and maintenance party of R.M.A. of about 12 men under Major G. Matthew, R.M.A.

On the outbreak of war the War Office sent out from England a siege battery to garrison the island. In September, when the urgent need of Heavy Artillery in France began to be recognised the Admiralty agreed to take over the garrison in order to release the siege battery; the R.M.A. party who were on the point of returning to England were ordered to stand fast and a reinforcing draft of R.M.A. and R.M.L.I. under Lieutenant-Colonel S. Gaitskell, R.M.A. was sent out with Captain F. J. Brett, R.M.L.I. and two temporary R.M.A. Officers, Lieutenants Webb-Bowen and Ogston.

The details of the R.E. and R.A.M.C. were left by the War Office and the batteries were organised and held in readiness for action; and to provide the land defence a company of volunteer infantry was raised from the local inhabitants to assist the R.M.L.I. under Captain Brett.

Until all the German raiders and Von Spee's squadron were disposed of the garrison were kept very much on the qui vive and in fact until the Armistice there was always a possibility of a visit from one of the raiders, who however, studiously avoided the place.

Owing to the absence of the Governor, Lieutenant-Colonel Gaitskell, Officer Commanding Troops became Acting Governor and carried out the civil as well as the military duties.

In the latter part of 1917 he was relieved by Major W. Dixon, R.M.A. who was appointed Governor of the island in addition to his military duties. Major Dixon who remained in command till after the Armistice was awarded the C.M.G. and promoted to Lieutenant-Colonel for his services. The original officers who were fit for service were gradually relieved by officers who had been wounded and invalided and the N.C.O.'s and men were similarly relieved as opportunity offered. Every effort was made to relieve the monotony of the long watching and waiting by organising cricket, theatricals and rifle shooting and other amusements and a great deal of talent was discovered, and the ships of the local squadron often visited the island.

4. ASCENSION.

This island which had always been a naval base, garrisoned by Royal Marines, was at once put on a war footing under the Commanding Officer, Major H. C. Benett, R.M.L.I. with Lieutenant Boultbee, R.M.A.

A reinforcing draft under Captains C. G. Billing and P. W. Malcolm of N.C.O.'s and men from the Chatham Division was at once dispatched. The island which is an important cable station was of great value as a centre of intelligence and it was selected as one of the first places for the erection of a wireless station, which was put up and organised by Major C. H. Malden, R.M.L.I.

Captain Billing was relieved early in 1915, (he was killed in June in Gallipoli), and Captain Malcolm was relieved later and proceeding to the Persian Gulf took part in the Caspian operations (see Chapter 23).

Major Benett was awarded the C.M.G. and owing to the difficulties of relief completed nearly seven years as Commandant; he was relieved in 1918 by Captain and Brevet Major H. Grant.

In spite of its importance as a cable station and its antiquated armament the German cruisers and raiders made no attempts against the island, and except for the constant watch, the ordinary peace routine was observed. This island had always been unique because the Royal Marines in addition to their garrison duties had always been responsible for the works services and for working the farm which supplied the garrison, and for some years the Commandant, who was formerly a Captain, Royal Navy, had been replaced by a Major of Marines and the naval officers had been withdrawn.

After garrisoning the island for more than 100 years the Royal Marines were finally withdrawn in 1922.

CHAPTER 23.

THE CASPIAN NAVAL FORCE.

THE work carried out by this force is very little known and it has been difficult to collect particulars. In consequence of the Russian revolution and the spread of Bolshevism the Russian army that had been facing the Turks in the South Caucasus, and which was in touch with the British on the Persian-Mesopotamia Frontier, had gradually melted away, and there was nothing to prevent the Turks from advancing from Erzeroum on Georgia and all the rich country they had coveted.

It was thought that the Georgians and Armenians could be roused to defend their homes; so as it was impossible to send troops the eight hundred miles from Baghdad to Baku, Major-General Dunsterville and his "Dunster" Force of two officers and 41 men were sent to see what could be done, and in the miraculous way described in the General's book contrived to fill the gap of 300 miles in North Persia. To assist him it was decided to place a small Naval force on the Caspian Sea in order to prevent the war spreading into Transcaspia.

The Caspian Sea is 630 miles long and varies from 125 to 300 miles wide, the northern end is shallow and freezes from January to April; there was considerable shipping on the Sea, consisting of 244 steam vessels and 570 sailing ships besides large barges.

On 27th July the first Naval party under Commodore Norris from the East Indian Squadron left Baghdad, and arrived at Enzeli on the south shore of the Sea on 6th August, having made the journey in motor lorries.

On 11th August, another party of 88 P.O.s and seamen with two sergeants Colour Sergeants Brookes and Wyld (Chatham) three buglers and six privates who were waiting passage home left Basra, where they had been fitted with khaki, etc. in P. 55 and during the passage up the river Tigris training was carried out; they disembarked at Baghdad and went to Hiniadi, the rest camp, on 16th where they were joined on 1st September by Major P. W. Malcolm, R.M.L.I. with one sergeant and 19 privates from H.M.S. *Juno* who had come up from Colombo, and one sergeant and 20 privates from H.M.S. *Diana* who had been picked up at Karachi.

Meanwhile the first party had left Enzeli and embarking in the S.S. *Kruger* and *Kursk* had gone to Baku where they took part in the siege from 26th August to 15th September and were present at the evacuation.

The party now officially belonged to the "Dunster" Force and an advanced party of 60 naval and Marine details under Lieutenant-Commander Charsley, R.N. left by train for Ruz and detraining there, loaded up their gear in lorries, Sergeant Wyld and four privates remaining behind to guard the 4.7, 4-in. and 12 pr. guns and ammunition which were being sent up to arm the ships on the Sea.

Leaving Ruz on 5th September in a convoy of motor lorries they reached Hamadan on 18th and remained there training for a few days and during this time some of the 4-in. and 4.7 in. guns arrived and were sent on. An advance party of one gunner R.N., one P.O. and 14 men marched from Hamadan to Kasvin, a distance of 150 miles, doing 22 miles each day.

On 19th September, Major Malcolm with Sergeant Hipkiss and 26 privates, three naval officers and three A.B.s left Hiniadi. Leaving Ruz on 21st September they arrived at Hamadan on 27th a distance of 340 miles by motor lorry. At the nightly halts preparations had to be made against the Turkoman raiders. Each man had his rifle tied to his body to prevent its being stolen whilst asleep.

About this time they heard of the evacuation of Baku, because the first party had come back to Enzeli on

15th September. Colour-Sergeant Brooks was therefore sent on with ammunition lorries, arriving at Enzeli on 26th September; the distance from Hamadan to Enzeli is about 250 miles; the main party left Hamadan on 28th September for Kasvin.

At Enzeli the *Kursk* manned by seamen from H.M.S. *Moth* and *Mantis* was the depot ship and the flagship the *Kruger*, flying the pennant of Commodore D. T. Norris, was the only armed ship, she having been armed with the guns of the 8th Field Battery, R.F.A.

On 3rd October, Major Malcolm with one N.C.O. and 26 privates arrived with two 12 pounders and one 4-inch gun at Enzeli and on 8th October, Commander Guy, V.C. with 200 seamen and stokers and two sergeants (Payne and Heard) and 49 privates, R.M.L.I. from the *Fox* and *Venus* also arrived at the same place.

The force was now called the "Norper" Force (the North Persian Force).

The men and guns now arriving were utilised to commission other ships, the first to be completed being the *Venture* which commissioned on 8th October, 1918, her Royal Marine Detachment consisting of one sergeant (Hipkiss) and 11 privates.

On 9th October the ratings from the *Fox* with Sergeant Payne and 12 privates R.M.L.I. sailed for Krasnovodsk to commission the *Emile Nobel*. On 20th the *Alla Verdi* commissioned, her Royal Marine detachment being Sergeant Heard and 12 privates and a little later the *Slava* with one corporal and eight privates. On 20th November the *Bibi Abat* commissioned with one corporal and 15 privates followed. by the *Zoroaster* and *Asia*; owing to the shortage of Royal Marines only W.R.O.s were sent to these ships.

The ships were merchant ships plying on the Caspian that were seized and converted into men-of-war temporarily; they flew the Russian Naval Ensign and it was not until March 2nd, 1919 that the White Ensign was hoisted for the first time.

On 5th November, *Kruger* (Captain Washington), *Asia* and *Alla Verdi*, including Major Malcolm and his party, *Venture* and *Emile Nobel* left for Petrovsk arriving there on 6th. Fighting was going on here between. the Russians under Bicharakov and the Azerbaijan troops and Turks; so after communicating with the shore they returned to Enzeli.

On 8th December *Zoroaster* and *Alla Verdi* were surprised by and had an engagement with three armed Bolshevist ships, the *Zoroaster* having a few casualties including one Royal Marine wounded. The Royal Marines relate that the snow was falling and they had several misfires and had to resort to percussion firing, incidentally having "pinched" the lock of the seamen's gun.

At this time the strength of the Royal Marines was one major, four sergeants, two corporals and 120 privates, who had all come up through Persia. On 29th December, *Venture, Slava, Bibi Abat* and *Asia* bombarded and burnt the Bolshevik base at Star-Tchernaya.

Soon after the Armistice in November, 1918, the armed ships under the command of Captain Washington and a convoy of 12 ships with troops and stores made a triumphal entry into Baku; Major Malcolm remaining as Resident Naval Officer at Enzeli with Colour-Sergeant Brooks and four privates. In January, 1919, the Royal Naval Barracks at Baku were put into commission by Commander Parnell, D.S.O. On 8th February the base at Enzeli was closed and Major Malcolm and his party embarking in the *Kruger* with Commodore Norris, who had returned from hospital after being wounded, on 15th went to Petrovsk, reaching there on 21st, where the advanced sub-depot was commissioned by Major Malcolm as S.O., R.M. and resident naval officer. The billets were placed in a state of defence: two six-inch guns Q.F. which had been taken from a monitor at Mudros and sent across the Black Sea and on by rail from Batoum and then by sea from Baku, were mounted to defend the place by the Royal Marines of the *Alla Verdi* (about eight) and some Ghurkas. The guns were dragged up 100 feet through the snow on a steep gradient by means of an R.A.F. lorry and an ancient chassis dragged by mules; they were mounted in concrete emplacements, blasted out and constructed by the Royal Marines themselves with the help of the Ghurkas and the guns were fired as soon as the concrete was set; Magazines and quarters were also constructed. The guns were sited to command the town, railway and anchorage, and were manned by the Royal Marines of the sub-depot.

At Petrovsk the small garrison had some lively times with the Hill tribes, who with the Bolsheviks were all round the place. The position of the wireless station was a constant source of anxiety, because quite a lot of street fighting went on. By the end of March the total of the Royal Marines in the force had risen to 160. The Depot became an important place where the Russian ships were fitted out and all repairs to the armed ships were undertaken. It was also a base for the coastal motor boats.

On 19th April the *Asia* had a long-range duel with two enemy torpedo boat destroyers and on the 25th another action took place between the *Zoroaster* and *Venture* and the enemy torpedo boat destroyers. The R.A.F. from the Aegean were now on the Sea and made their first air raid on the Bolshevik Fleet bases near Astrakhan on 21st April.

On 21st May the squadron made a reconnaissance of Fort Alexandrovsk H.M.S. *Kruger* (Commodore Norris) with *Venture, Asia, Windsor Castle* and *Emile Nobel* steaming up the harbour containing a partially hidden enemy of unknown strength and also an unlocated battery. The Commodore made the signal "we are going up to Ramoth Gilead." They came under the fire of a battery of 12 pounders as well as from two armed merchant cruisers, some armed barges, three torpedo boat destroyers, motor launches, etc. and succeeded in sinking about nine craft and this combined with some air raids cleared the enemy out of the harbour.

On 28th the *Kruger, Venture* and *Sergie* (C. M. B. carrier-Commander Robinson, V.C., and Lieutenant Robertson) visited Fort Alexandrovsk again to see what damage they had done and found they had sunk one barge with two 6-inch guns, one torpedo boat destroyer, one armed minelayer, one submarine depot ship, one ammunition carrier and four smaller craft, besides the ice breaker damaged; they torpedoed three more barges and the place surrendered. The enemy ships retired to the mouth of the Volga where the commander was relieved, whilst the command of the motor launches was taken over by the new commander's wife!

On 8th August H.M.S. *Bibi Abat* and *Orlionock* (seaplane carrier) captured the Russian gunboats *Chasavry* and the steamships *Van* and *Elburz* with 200 prisoners at Ashurada.

Commencing on 28th July the Caspian Flotilla was gradually turned over to the White Russians and on 2nd September, 1919 the last details of the Caspian Naval Force left Petrovsk for Novorossisk where they were dispersed, Major Malcolm going to Malta to close the accounts of the ships and stores.

Among the rewards for this campaign were the following :-

O.B.E. Major P. W. Malcolm.
D.S.M. Private A. E. Crafts (Plymouth).
Mentioned in Dispatches.

Corporal H. Hansler (Portsmouth).	Private F. Barraclough (Chatham).
Lance-Sergeant A. H. Hull (Plymouth).	Private F. Firth (Chatham).
Colour-Sergeant H. Brook (Chatham).	Corporal A. J. Regan (Portsmouth).

PART VI.

Units attached to the Army.

CHAPTER 24.

THE HOWITZER BRIGADE, ROYAL MARINE ARTILLERY

6-inch B.L. Batteries - Formation of Howitzer Brigade - Description of Howitzer and Mounting - Technical details - Personnel - Table of Battles and Actions in which Brigade was engaged - List of Commanding Officers - Summary of Diaries - Honours and Rewards
Services of Brigadier - General F. W. Lumsden, V.C., C.B., D.S.O. and three Bars, R.M.A.

AFTER the R.M.A. Battalion was withdrawn from the Royal Marine Brigade on its return from Ostend, there was an interval whilst a decision was being taken as to the use to be made of it, during which Captain G. L Raikes and a few R.F.R. men were sent up to Scapa Flow to man the naval guns landed from the Fleet.

The first suggestion was that the R.M.A. should form three field artillery brigades and one howitzer brigade on the Army model to provide the Divisional artillery of the Royal Naval Division, but this proposal was rejected. The Admiralty and War Office however proposed that the R.M.A. should man three batteries of 6-inch (MK. VII.) guns mounted on field carriages and drawn by tractors; the Director of Naval Ordnance provided the guns and mountings with ammunition and the War Office the transport and equipments; the guns and mountings were actually delivered at Eastney and drill commenced under Major and Brevet Lieut.-Colonel G. R. Poole, who had had great experience of heavy artillery in Canada.

Other influences however were at work and the guns and mountings were withdrawn from Eastney and, manned by R.G.A. Rendered valuable service at the first Battle of Ypres in 1914; it was unfortunate that the R.M.A. were deprived of the opportunity of rendering such valuable service to the Army, a service for which they were peculiarly fitted.

In their place instructions were issued that the following units were to be formed :-

    (a) A Howitzer brigade.   (b) An Anti-aircraft brigade.

In October, however, the Antwerp expedition took place, and after the R.N. Brigades of the R.N. Division had been sent to reinforce the R.M.L.I. Brigade, further reinforcements of Royal Marines were ordered to proceed to Dunkirk; and details as described in Chapter 10 were sent over. When the R.M.A. Battery returned to England their lorries were transferred to the Royal Marine Motor Transport; Company (see Chapter 28).

HOWITZER BRIGADE.

After the invasion of Belgium by the Germans, reports poured in as to the great effect of the large Austrian howitzers on the armoured forts of Liege, Namur, etc. The Coventry Ordnance Works, of which Rear-Admiral Bacon was manager, had designed a 15-inch howitzer which could be mounted in the field on a platform and which was comparatively mobile owing to its construction in several portions, which could be taken apart and transported separately. The First Lord of the Admiralty ordered 12 of these howitzers, which were at once put in hand; and Admiral Bacon was promised that he should himself take them into action, for which purpose he was given a commission as Colonel 2nd Commandant R.M. Artillery.

The numbers of the R.M.A. personnel available were now definitely divided into the details for the Howitzer brigade and those for the Anti-Aircraft Brigade (see Chapter 25). The former were placed under the command of Lieut-Colonel Poole for training.

An Admiralty Committee, of which Lieut-Colonel C. F. Osmaston and Major E. W. Harding, R.M.A. were members was appointed to superintend the design and mountings, and arrange for the transport, etc. Also to make out the organisation and equipment for the brigades; both of which were new departures and there was no previous experience to go upon.

The howitzer itself and mounting consisted of six parts :-

1.-Inner Tube known as the barrel.   4.-Carriage.
2.-Jacket and breech fittings.   5.-Pivot.
3.-Cradle with recoil buffers, and at   6.-Racer.
   first running-out springs;

The platform was composed of steel girders bolted together, with fore and aft girders, cross girders and base plates and the greatest difficulties experienced with the weapon were caused by these platforms.

The projectile weighed 1,400 lbs. and as this was a new nature in the service (the 15-inch gun having only recently been introduced into the Navy), not only was the supply limited at first, but until its idiosyncrasies were discovered it caused a great deal of trouble. Only high explosive shell were used and the maximum range was 10,800 yards. At first there were many failures owing to the fuses, etc., but eventually these difficulties were overcome and the last pattern fuse proved most satisfactory.

Special motor tractors of 100 horse power were built by Messrs. Foster of Lincoln, of which each howitzer had five, and the parts of the howitzer platforms, spare stores, etc. were carried on special trucks of which each howitzer had 11[31].

With so much motor transport, workshops were also provided of which there were five, one for each pair of guns. Also a spare tractor to each pair of guns.

In order to deal with this transport it was necessary to enter drivers and mechanics from civilian life on short service engagements; men who were already skilled motor mechanics and artisans were enlisted; they were at first trained at Messrs. Foster's works, but later were trained at Eastney at the Brigade Depot. A welcome reinforcement was received when the Royal Marine Transport Company was disbanded.

Officers who were skilled motor or mechanical engineers were also entered for charge of the transport and workshops, one being allowed for each howitzer and one for each workshop.

---

31. The trucks were allocated as follows:-

No. 1 Truck	carried		Base Plate of Platform
No. 2	"	"	Fore and Aft Girders
No. 3	"	"	Cross Girders
No. 4	"	"	Pivot
No. 5	"	"	Racer and Sheer legs for erecting.
No. 6	"	"	Carriage
No. 7	"	"	Cradle, including Recoil Buffers and gear
No. 8	"	"	Jacket and Breech Fittings
No. 9	"	"	Inner Tube or Barrel
No. 10	"	"	11 Rounds Ammunition
No. 11	"	"	11 Rounds Ammunition .

Each tractor pulled two trucks, but one had to pull three.
A spare tractor and platform on three trucks was allowed for each pair of guns.
The tractors were provided with drums for winding in a wire hawser, which proved invaluable in mounting and dismounting the piece.

The Howitzer Brigade, Royal Marine Artillery

[Photo by Russell & Sons, Southsea.]

LIEUT.-COLONEL G. R. POOLE, C.M.G., D.S.O., R.M.A.

Commanded R.M.A. Howitzer Brigade, 1914-1919; Colonel Commandant, R.M.A., 1921-22
Created C. B.. 1922; Major-General, 1922; Lieut.-General, 1924.

The detachment allowed for each howitzer consisted of:-

1 commanding officer, (captain or major).	1 battery sergeant-major.
1 gun officer.	1 battery quartermaster-sergeant.
2 observing officers.	55 N.C.O.s and men.
1 motor transport officer.	25 drivers.
1 artificer.	

Armourers and sick berth attendants were lent from the Royal Navy and there were three staff surgeons and surgeons, Royal Navy attached to the Brigade. Although originally organised with a brigade headquarters and arrangements made that each pair of howitzers should form a battery, this organisation was not retained in France; Colonel Poole remained in command of the Brigade throughout the war after August, 1915 but, in May 1916, was appointed to command the 26th Heavy Artillery Group and only dealt with the howitzers administratively. The battery organisation was abandoned immediately and the howitzers were used singly throughout and were known on the Western Front as "Grandmother".

The first howitzer completed was sent to Shoeburyness for proof, which proved satisfactory, and was retained there for experiments, construction of range tables, etc. and the detachments under training at Eastney were sent there for drill at the howitzer. Beyond the fire control and training of observers the method of mounting involved a very great knowledge of Repository work, and the diaries are filled with the difficulties encountered in mounting and dismounting in wet and boggy ground, which only the great ingenuity of all concerned and the wonderful capacity of the tractors and their drivers enabled them to overcome .

The diaries record a few instances of the tube and jacket becoming so locked after firing that only after the greatest labour for two or three days were they able to be separated, but the howitzers themselves, until they become worn from constant firing, gave little trouble; numbers 1 and 2 Howitzers fired about 3200 rounds with various charges. Nor did the mounting, after the first few months prove unsatisfactory, but it was soon found that the running-out springs would not return the piece to the firing position and were constantly breaking, thus putting the piece out of action; consequently number 5 Howitzer was fitted with pneumatic recuperators before proceeding to France, as were all the later howitzers, whilst Nos. 1,2,3 and 4 were fitted with them during the winter of 1915-16 and no further trouble was experienced.

But the platforms seem to have been a constant source of trouble; when firing they would slip back on the muddy ground and a more serious defect, slue round, so that the piece was taken off its target; numerous methods were devised to counteract this movement, one gun relates how the tractors were used to tow it bodily round back to its original line; in other cases rounds were fired at another target, which had the effect of slueing it back; one howitzer developed a method of anchoring which seemed fairly satisfactory. Also the girders became bent and sometimes the bolts could not be taken out except by drilling them out; this work had generally to be carried out at night and often under shell fire. It was found generally to be necessary to dig a new gunpit and shift the mounting and platform after being in action a certain time, often after as few as 50 rounds. This work, combined with the constant digging to construct magazines, dug-outs, shelters, etc. and the heavy transport of ammunition, imposed a great strain on the guns' crews and they were frequently complimented by the authorities on their work.

Owing to the great weight of the shell, ammunition was brought to the guns whenever possible by Decauville light railways, but it had often to be transported in lorries.

Considering the length of time the Brigade was at the front, 3½ years in the case of some batteries and about 2 ½ years in others, the casualties both to personnel and material were comparatively slight; three officers, Captain M. Williams and Lieutenants Warman and W. D. Hart were killed, Lieutenant Boissier was accidentally drowned by the upsetting of a motor car, whilst 10 were wounded (Lieutenants H. N. Elphick, E. Dashwood, G. E. Burnside, L. H. Harries, 2nd Lieutenant O. H. Armstrong, Captain H. M. Leaf, Lieutenants S. H. Wood, C. A. Blunt, E. A. Taylor and W. D. Hart), Captain W. W. Ward, Lieutenants S. H. Wood and E. Flaye were gassed; of the N.C.O.s and men approximately 35 were killed, 97 wounded and 69 gassed. Most of the casualties occurred during the Passchendaele operations in October and November, 1917, when No. 11 and 12 Howitzers suffered very heavily.

As regards the material No.8 gun was put out of action in July, 1916, during the battle of the Somme for four months owing to damage to the recoiling gear due to the premature bursting of a shell of No.2 Howitzer which damaged No.8 close by, and on 3rd November, 1917 near Dunkirk, No.2 received a hit on the carriage which put it out of action until the middle of December. Except for temporary accidents and an occasional hit on the platforms the only actual losses were No.1 gun during the retreat on Albert in March, 1918, though the breech, tube and jacket were very gallantly got away, the train conveying the remainder of the gear became bogged in a side road (see Table "C" for account of incident). Spare parts were obtained from England and after a time the howitzer became again fit for service. In April, 1918 during the retreats round Ypres No.5 Howitzer after the breech had been salved had to be blown up and abandoned (see Table "C"). On 14th July the premature burst of a shell tore all the rifling out of No.4 which was replaced by a new gun from England (probably No.9) as only 10 howitzers were actually maintained in the field.

Owing to these losses and as several of the howitzers were condemned for scoring in the bore, they were replaced in the autumn of 1918 by the Army 12-inch howitzer; and Nos. 1 and 2 Siege Batteries, R.M.A. were formed from Nos. 5 and 6 Howitzers and 11 and 12 Howitzers respectively. When the Allied offensive was launched in August, 1918, the rapid advance of the British armies and the collapse of the Germans, after the Hindenburg Lines and the St. Quentin Canal were broken, soon carried the infantry beyond the range of the howitzers and owing to the congested state of the roads and their condition these heavy howitzers could not be brought up; though the personnel of No.1 Siege Battery armed with captured German howitzers did excellent work as long as the ammunition lasted, being christened the "A" Hun battery (see Table "C").

There was a certain amount of discussion as to the respective merits of the Army 12-inch and the R.M.A. 15-inch Howitzer; the value of the heavier guns against field entrenchments was always doubtful and they were not employed against the targets for which they were designed, viz. concrete permanent fortifications and were consequently principally employed in destructive shoots on observation posts, towers, villages, etc. with occasional counter-battery work; owing to the area of effect of the blast of the shell they had to be used with circumspection in support of the infantry; one of the main objections to them was the comparative shortness of the range, about 11,000 yards, which caused them often to be pushed further forward than was desirable with such big weapons.

It has not been possible in this account to give an analysis of the shooting of the Brigade, but on the whole the officers were satisfied with its accuracy, and excellent work was done by the observers, once the principle was established of two observing posts to each howitzer. The earlier howitzers to proceed to the front each took a nucleus of the detachments of those that were to come later, so that these officers and men could obtain practical instruction in their duties, and were able to bring the newer guns into action as soon as they arrived.

The first howitzer was fired at Locre on 6th March, 1915, but it has not been possible to give an account

[By permission 01 the Imperial War Museum.]
15-INCH HOWITZER PREPARING TO FIRE.

[By permission of the Imperial War Museum.]
15-INCH HOWITZER IN ACTION.

of their tactical employment as they were firing only on certain occasions. Consequently the list of actions in which they took part are given in Table "A," and extracts from the diaries for each month giving the most interesting items are given in Table "C" at the end of the chapter.

The howitzers were employed entirely on the Western Front with the exception of No. 3 under Captain Ledgard (late Lieutenant-Commander, R.N.). This howitzer had no sooner arrived in France than the Admiralty ordered it to the Dardanelles, and it was hurriedly entrained for Marseilles where it embarked on 12th April, 1915 and though ammunition was very short, it was supplied with some rounds. It never appears to have occurred to anyone in authority that it would probably be impossible to hoist out and land these heavy weights on the open beaches of Gallipoli and after arriving at Gallipoli, the ship was sent to Mudros where it lay for many months with the personnel eating their hearts out in inactivity until they were sent to Egypt in the summer and landed at Alexandria where it was not employed. Eventually they left Alexandria on 6th March, 1916. and returned to France in time to take their part in the Battle of the Somme.

Rear-Admiral R. H. Bacon, C.V.O., D.S.O. was given a commission in the R.M. as mentioned before, dated 16th Jan., 1915; he proceeded to France with Nos. 1 and 2 Howitzers on 15th February. He conducted the preliminary operations and satisfied himself that the initial technical difficulties were in course of being overcome; on 10th April he was appointed Admiral of the Dover Patrol and was succeeded in command of the R.M.A. Howitzer Brigade in France by Major F. W. Lumsden, R.M.A. (for the later gallant exploits of this officer see Appendix to this Chapter). On 27th July Major Lumsden was appointed G.S.O. 3 of the First Army and Lieutenant-Colonel Poole arrived to take command of the Brigade which he assumed in France on 14th August, 1915.

A list of the honours gained by the Brigade is given in Table "D," the names of Commanding officers of batteries in Table "B" at the end of this chapter.

After the conclusion of the Armistice the batteries were gradually moved back until by January, 1919, Nos. 1 and 2 Siege Batteries were at St. Cecilie Plage, No.1 Howitzer at Samer (Pas de Calais) No.2 at Questrecques (Boulogne), No.3 at Hesdin L'Abbe, No.4 at Hesdineul, No.8 at Arras, No. 10 at Wirwignies (Pas de Calais).

They were demobilised under Army arrangements and the batteries were reduced to cadre strength by June, 1919; when all the howitzers and stores were handed in to the Ordnance and on 14th all the detachments left Havre in S.S. *Lydia* and arrived at Eastney at 3 p.m. on 15th, where the Brigade was finally dispersed.

THE HOWITZER BRIGADE, ROYAL MARINE ARTILLERY
TABLE "A."
LIST OF BATTLES IN WHICH THE HOWITZERS WERE ENGAGED.

Date.		Actions, etc	Howitzers engaged.
10th-13th March	1915.	BATTLE OF NEUVE CHAPELLE	No. 2
8th-13th May		BATTLE OF FREZENBERG RIDGE	No. 2
9th May		BATTLE OF AUBERS RIDGE	Nos. 1 and 4.
15th-25th May		BATTLE OF F'ESTUBERT	Nos. 1 and 4.
25th September-8th October		BATTLE OF LOOS	Nos. 1, 2 and 4.
21st May 1916		GERMAN ATTACK ON VIMY RIDGE	No. 2
		BATTLE OF THE SOMME.	
1st-13th July		BATTLE OF ALBERT	Nos. 1, 2, 3, 4, 5, 6, 8, 10.
14th-17th July		BATTLE OF BAZENTIN RIDGE	Nos. 1, 2, 3 and 10
15th July-3rd September		BATTLE OF DELVILLE WOOD	No. 3
23rd July-3rd September		BATTLE OF POZIERES RIDGE	Nos. 1, 2 and 10.
3rd-6th September		BATTLE OF GUILLEMONT	Nos. 3 and 10.
9th September		BATTLE OF GINCHY	Nos. 3 and 10.
15th-22nd September		BATTLE OF FLERS-COURCELLETTE	Nos. 2 and 10
25th-28th September		BATTLE OF MORVAL	Nos. 1 and 2.
26th-28th September		BATTLE OF THIEPVAL RIDGE	Nos. 1, 2 and 5
1st-18th October		BATTLE OF TRANSLOY RIDGES	No. 3.
1st October-11th November		BATTLE OF ANCRE HEIGHTS	Nos. I, 2 and 10.
13th-18th November		BATTLE OF THE ANCRE	Nos. I, 2, 4, 5, 10, 12.
9th-14th April	1917.	BATTLE OF VIMY RIDGE	Nos. 1, 11, 12.
9th-14th April		FIRST BATTLE OF THE SCARPE	Nos. 3, 4, 6, 10.
23rd-24th April		SECOND BATTLE OF THE SCARPE	No. 11.
28th-29th April		BATTLE OF ARLEUX	Nos. 10 and 11.
3rd-4th May		THIRD BATTLE OF THE SCARPE	Nos. 1, 3, 4, 10, 11.
11th April-16th June		Round Bullecourt	No. 11.
28th June		Capture of Oppy Wood	No. 12
		FIRST ATTACK ON BULLECOURT	No. 11.
3rd-17th May		BATTLE OF BULLECOURT	Nos. 5 and 6.
29th May-16th June		ACTION IN HINDENBURG LINE	Nos. 3, 4, 6.
3rd-25th June		SOUCHEZ RIVER	Nos. 1 and 11
26th-29th June		CAPTURE OF AVION	Nos. 1 and 11.
15th-25th August		BATTLE OF HILL 70	Nos. 1
		FLANDERS OFFENSIVE.	
7th June		BATTLE OF MESSINES	Nos. 2, 5, 8
10th-11th July		GERMAN ATTACK ON NIEUPORT	Nos. 2 and 5.
31st July-2nd August		BATTLE OF PILCKEM RIDGE	Nos. 4, 6, 11, 12
16th-18th August		BATTLE OF LANGEMARCK	Nos. 4, 6, 11, 12.
20th-25th September		BATTLE OF MENIN ROAD	Nos. 4, 6, 8, 11, 12.
4th October		BATTLE OF BROODSEINDE	Nos. 4, 6, 8, 11 and 12.
9th October		BATTLE OF POELCAPELLE	Nos. 4, 6, 8, 11, 12.
12th October		FIRST BATTLE OF PASSCHENDAELE	Nos. 4, 6, 11, 12
26th October-10th November		SECOND BATTLE OF PASSCHENDAELE	Nos. 4, 6, 8, 11, 12
30th November-3rd December		BATTLE OF CAMBRAI	Nos. 1 and 10.
		GERMAN OFFENSIVE IN PICARDY.	
21st-23rd March	1918	BATTLE OF ST. QUENTIN	Nos. 1, 3, 6, 10.
10th-11th April		BATTLE OF MESSINES	Nos. 4 and 5.
29th April		BATTLE OF SCHEPENBERG	No. 12.
		ADVANCE IN FLANDERS.	
18th August		Action of Outersteen Ridge	No. 4.
		SECOND BATTLE OF THE SOMME.	
21st-23rd August		BATTLE OF ALBERT	Nos. 3 and 10.
31st August-3rd September		SECOND BATTLE OF BAPAUME	No. 3.
		BREAKING OF HINDENBURG LINE.	
26th-30th August		BATTLE OF SCARPE	No. 8.
12th September		BATTLE OF HAVRINCOURT	No. 3.
18th September		BATTLE OF EPEHY	No. 3.
27th September-1st October		BATTLE OF CANAL DU NORD	
		CAPTURE OF BOURLON WOOD	Nos. 1, 3, and 8.
29th September-2nd October		BATTLE OF ST. QUENTIN CANAL	No. 1 R.M.A. Siege Batt No. 5 and 6 howitzers.
8th-9th October		BATTLE OF CAMBRAI	No. 8
28th September-2nd October		BATTLE OF YPRES	No. 12
17th-25th October		BATTLE OF THE SELLE	"A" Hun Battery.

The Howitzer Brigade, Royal Marine Artillery

COMMANDING OFFICERS.
TABLE "B."

Colonel (Rear-Admiral) R. H. BACON, C.B., 15th February to 19th April, 1915
Major F. W. LUMSDEN, R.M.A., 19th April to 27th July, 1915.
Lieut-Colonel G. R. POOLE, R.M.A., 14th August, 1915 to 14th June, 1919.
                (also in Command of 26th Heavy Artillery Group from May, 1916).

BATTERY COMMANDERS.

No. I.	Major F. W. LUMSDEN, 15th February, 1915 to 17th April, 1915	
	Captain M. WILLIAMS, 15th February, 1915 to 22nd August, 1916	Killed in action.
	Captain A. D. GODFRAY, 23rd August, 1916 to 9th September, 1916	To Ordnance Inspection
	Brevet-Lieut-Col. A. G. TROUP, 9th September, 1916 to 29th December, 1916	Invalided.
	Invalided Captain L. L. FOSTER, 1st February, 1917 to February, 1919	Demobilised
	Captain W. H. BEBGIE, to 14th June, 1919	Demobilised.
NO.2.	Major G. L. RAIKES, 15th February, 1915 to 14th December, 1915	To No.6
	Major H. WORTHINGTON, 22nd December, 1915 to 6th May, 1916	To No. 12
	Captain C. MICKLEM, 6th May, 1916 to 12th February, 1919	Demobilised.
	Lieut. E. K JOHNSON, to 14th June, 1919	To Eastney.
No.3.	Captain W. R. LEDGARD, 26th March, 1915 to 18th June, 1917	Invalided and died.
	Captain J. H. PERCY, 1st July, 1917 to February, 1919	Demobilised
	Lieut. H. H. JARMAN, February to June, 1919	Demobilised
No.4.	Major A. P. LISTON FOULIS, 14th March, 1915 to 1st January, 1917	To command R.G.A. group; killed in action 30th November, 1917.
	Captain T. CUMING, 1st April, 1917 to 22nd April, 1919	Demobilised
	Captain E. K. ALEXANDER to June,1919	Demobilised
No.5.	Lieut. H. BOFFEY, 13th December, 1915 to 31st March, 1918	Invalided
	Captain C. CRAVEN, 1st April, 1918 to 7th August, 1918	
No.6.	Major G. L. RAIKES, 14th December, 1915 to 7th August, 1918	
	Note.-Nos. 5 and 6 formed into No. I Siege Battery, 8th August, 1918.	
No.7.	Retained at Shoeburyness for proof, etc.	
No.8.	Captain A. D. B. GODFRAY, 22nd April, 1916 to 22nd August, 1916	To No. 1
	Lieut. W. WELLINGTON, 23rd August, 1916 to 14th September, 1916	
	Major G. MATTHEW, 15th September, 1916 to January, 1919.	To Eastney.
	Lieut. FRANKLYN, until June, 1919	
No. 9.	Drill Gun at Eastney.	
No. 10.	Major G. C. WOODCOCK, 20th May, 1916 to July, 1917	To No. 12.
	Captain C. CARUS-WILSON, 18th July, 1917 to 14th June, 1919.	Demobilised.
No. 11.	Captain R. C. MORRISON-SCOTT, 3rd July, 1916 to July, 1918	To Siege Train.
	Lieut. M. H. COLLET, 8th August, 1918 to 8th October, 1918.	
No.12.	Brevet-Lieut.-Col. H. WORTHINGTON, 10th September, 1916 to 6th March, 1917	To England.
	Major G. C. WOODCOCK, July 1917 to 15th September, 1917	Invalided
	Captain W. WARD, 31st March, 1917 to 14th July, 1917 (Gassed) 16th September, 1917 to 8th October, 1918.	
	Nos. 11 and 12 combined to form No. 2 Siege Battery.	
No.1.	Siege Battery, R.M.A.,11th August 1918 - Major G. L.RAIKES	
No.2.	Siege Battery, R.M.A. 8th October 1918 - Captain W. W. WARD	
No. "A"	Hun Battery (1.5.9 inch howitzer, 2.4.2. inch howitzer, Howitzers, 1.77 m.m.) Captains CRAVEN and BURNSIDE, 7th-October, 1918 to 26th October, 1918.	

Royal Marines in the War of 1914-1919

EXTRACTS FROM BATTERY DIARIES.
TABLE "C."

No. of Howitzer.	Place	
	1915	
		FEBRUARY,
Nos. 1 & 2		Embarked Southampton 15th. Total personnel 14 officers, one W.O., 141 N.C.O.'s and men. Col. Bacon, T/Hon. Major C.D. Bridge, Capt. G.L. Raikes, T/Hon. Lieut. W. T. Webley, Assistant Paymaster E. C. Oliver, Surgeon J. C. Russell -Cargill, R.N., Major F. W. Lumsden, Captain M. Williams, Lieutenants H. Boffey, C. H. Hazell, F. L. Robinson, W. W. Ward, G. L. Wilkes (M.T.) G. M. Boissier (M.T.). Proceeded to St. Omer and mounted the first howitzer at Locre.
		MARCH.
No.1.	LOCRE	Fired successfully on 6th.
No.2.	NEUVE CHAPELLE	Battle of Neuve Chapelle.
No.3		Embarked Southampton 26th, Captain Ledgard, three officers, 200 N.C.O.'s and men.
		APRIL.
Nos. 1 & 2		Experimenting.
No.3		Left General Headquarters, embarked Marseilles 12th to join Dardanelles Force. Captain Ledgard, Lieutenants Craven Webley, Barrington-Ward and Rigby.
No.4		Arrived France 14th, Major A. P. Liston-Foulis in command.
		MAY.
Nos. 1 & 4		Battle of Aubers Ridge on 9th and again at Battle of Festubert, 5-12th.
		JUNE.
		In this month the Establishment was fixed as follows :- Two Batteries of four howitzers each to form the Brigade, but this organisation was never adopted; the personnel remained about the same and was as follows; Headquarters, 2 officers, 1 W.O. 17 other ranks. Batteries, 32 officers, 472 other ranks. Transport and Workshops, 8 officers, 238 other ranks. Each howitzer was allowed- 4 officers, 2 sergeants, 1 artificer, 55, rank and file, R.M.A. 1officer (M.T.) 25 drivers and mechanics, R.M.A.
		The Diaries prior to August, 1915 are not available. NOTE.-In these extracts the following terms are employed:- "No Firing" means that gun was in position ready to fire but did not fire. "Gun Parked." Gun and transport parked, and personnel resting or training. "Standing By" means that howitzer was in position and fired occasionally for special objects.
		AUGUST.
No. 1	N. E. OF BETHUNE	No Firing. Gun remounted in 3 ½ hours plus 2 ½ hours for platform.
No. 2	VLAMERTINGHE	Standing by. Moved to La Bourse. Lieutenant Robinson awarded the M.C. and Corporal R. E. Payne, the D.C.M.
No. 4	BOUVIGNY	No Firing.
		SEPTEMBER.
No.1.	N.E. OF BETHUNE	⎫
No.2.	LA BOURSE	⎬ Battle of Loos.
No.4.	BOUYIGNY	⎭
		OCTOBER
No.1.	N.E. OF BETHUNE	⎫
No.2.	LA BOURSE	⎬ Battle of Loos to 8th October, afterwards no firing.
No.4.	BOUYIGNY	⎭
		NOVEMBER.
No.1.	LE HAMEL	Standing by.
No.2.	LA BOURSE	Overhauling gun and gear.
No.4.	BOUYIGNY	Moved to Raincheval on 14th and Parked.
		DECEMBER
No.1.	LE HAMEL	Fitting Recuperators.
No.2.	LA BOURSE	Fitting Recuperators.
No.4.	RAINCHEVAL	Parked

The Howitzer Brigade, Royal Marine Artillery

No.5.	PUCHEVILLERS	Arrived in France 13th; Marched to Puchevillers and Parked.
No.6.	PUCHEVILLERS	Arrived in France 13th; Marched to Puchevillers and Parked.
	1916	JANUARY
No.1.	LE HAMEL	Registering and Testing.
No.2.	LA BOURSE	Fitting Recuperators.
No.4.	RAINCHEVAL	Gun Parked.
No.5.	PUCHEVILLERS	Gun Parked.
No.6.	PUCHEVILLERS	Gun Parked.
		FEBRUARY
No.1.	LE HAMEL	Standing by; moved to La Clytte on 18th and stood by.
No.2	LA BOURSE	Moved to Dickebusche on 22nd; mounted in a snow storm and went into action on 25th.
No.4	RAINCHEVAL	Gun Parked.
No.5	PUCHEVILLERS	Gun Parked.
No.6	PUCHEVILLERS	No firing.
		No. 1 Howitzer was congratulated by the "V" Corps Commander on the way they had got their gun into action, and on the good work of Nos. 1 and 2 in supporting the operations.
		MARCH
No.1.	DICKEBUSCH	After firing at Wytschaete marched to Barlin and parked on 7th.
No.2.	DICKEBUSCH	Dismounted under great difficulties owing to shifting of Platform; marched to Barlin on 7th; Mounted at Bois de La Haie on 29th.
No.3.	ALEXANDRIA	Embarked on 6th; disembarked Marseilles 16th; arrived Talmas 21st.
No.4.	BEA UMETZ	Mounted gun on 11th-13th.
No.5.	ENGELBELMER	Training
No.6.	DAINVILLE	Mounted at Dainville on 20th.
		APRIL
No.1.	BARLIN	Parked
No.2.	BOIS DB LA HAIE	No firing
No.3.	SAILLY AU BOIS	Mounted on 22
No.4.	BEAUMETZ	No firing
No.5.	ENGELBELMER	No firing
No.6.	DAINVILLE	Registering
No.8.	MAILLY MAILLET	Disembarked Boulogne 22nd, marched to Mailly Maillet.
		MAY.
No.1.	MAZINGARBE	Mounted on 9th.
No.2.	BOIS DE LA HAIE	Standing by; fired in support of operations on 23rd and 24th.
No.3.	SAILLY AU BOIS	Training.
No.4.	SIMENCOURT	Reconnoitring for position.
No.5.	ENGELBELME	Training.
No.6.	DAINVILLE	Standing by.
No.8.	MAILL Y MAILLET	Preparing position.
No.10.	LA HOUSSA YE	Disembarked Boulogne 19th, moved to La Houssaye. *The question of allowing two O.P.s for each of these howitzers which had been at first refused was decided and approved.*
		JUNE
		Commencing on 26th all howitzers took part in preliminary bombardment prior to Battle of the Somme.
No.1.	MAZINGARBE	Moved to Mailly Maillet on 9-12th and mounted.
No.2.	BOIS DE LA HAIE	Supporting attack on Vimy on 2nd, moved to Mailly Maillet on 5th and mounted. Premature burst of shell on 27th caused casualties (2) and put No.8 out of action.
No.3.	SAILLY AU BOIS	Fired 133 rounds
No.4.	SOUASTRE	Mounted on 1st.
No.5.	ENGELBELMER	Target, Beaumont Hamel.
No.6.	SOUASTRE	Mounted on 4th. Target, Gommecourt.
No.8.	MAILL Y MAILLET	Put out of action on 27th see above, several casualties; personnel relieving No. 2.
No.10.	ALBERT	Mounted 16th-17th, Target Pozieres.

		JULY
No.1.	MAILLY MAILLET	Battle of the Somme. Targets, Beaucourt and Grandcourt. On 6th remounted; Targets, Thiepval and Pozieres.
No.2.	MAILLY MAILLET	Targets, Thiepval and St. Pierre Divion, Remounted on 6th;Targets Ovillers and La Boisselle. Remounted 8th; Targets Pozieres.
No.3.	SAILLY AU BOIS	Battle of Somme, Remounted gun at Billon Wood on 10th Targets Longueval, Guillemont and Delville Wood.
No.4.	SOUASTRE ENGEBELMER	Fired on 1st and 2nd but ceased fire as attack on Gommecourt failed. No. 5
No.6.	SOUASTRE	Fired on 1st and 2nd but ceased fire as attack on Gommecourt failed. No. 5
No.8.	MAILLY MAILLET	Gun out of action.
No.10.	ALBERT	Target Mametz Wood; Remounted to shift centre line; Target Contalmaison, Bazentin; destroyed Contalmaison and 97 Germans on 8th; in continuous action; Target Courcellette.
No.11.	CAESTRE	Disembarked Boulogne 2nd; moved to Caestre near Hazebrouck
		AUGUST
No.1.	MARTINSART	Captain M. Williams killed and Staff Surgeon Nunn wounded by a shell which fell near gun as they were dismounting on night of 22/23, but gun remounted before the morning.
No.2.	MAILLY MAILLET	Targets, Mouquet Farm, Thiepval and St. Pierre Divion.
No.3.	BILLON WOOD	Target. Guillemont.
No.4.	SOUASTRE	Moved to Fricourt Wood on 8th Target Martinpuich. Majors Foulis and Woodcock exchanged commands temporarily
No.5.	ENGELBELMER	Targets. St. Pierre Divion and Bridges over the Ancre.
No.6.	SOUASTRE	No Firing.
No.8.	MAILLY MAILLET	Out of Action.
No.10.	BECOURT	Barrel out of action on 2nd; Personnel of Nos. 10 and 4 exchanged guns on 6th and No.10 moved to Bailleulmont where new barrel was received.
No.11.		Near Hazebrouck drawing stores and preparing gun.
		SEPTEMBER
No.1.	MARTINSART	Target, Thiepval; on 22nd shifted Target to Miraumont and Schwaben Redoubt.
No.2.	MAILLY MAILLET	Target, St. Pierre Divion and Thiepval; by 26th of the month had fired 874 rounds since 24th June
No.3.	BILLON WOOD	Ceased firing on 16th as Targets out of range. Up to this time from 18th July, 573 rounds had been fired from the same pit, as this gun had their own method of anchoring the platform.
No.4.	BAILLEULMONT	Mounted at Silly on 13/14 and standing by.
No.5.	ENGELBELMER	Standing by.
No.6.	SOUASTRE	No Firing.
No.8.	HEDAUVILLE	Under repair.
No.10.	FRICOURT	Standing by, moved to Mametz Wood on 27/28th and then standing by.
No.11.	Near HAZEBROUCK	No firing, preparing position.
No.12.	MAMETZ WOOD	Arrived Boulogne 10th mounted in .Mametz. Wood on 20th. Registering and standing by.
		OCTOBER
No.1.		Mounted at Engelbelmer on 7th. Targets Grandcourt.
No.2.	MAILL Y MAILLET	Targets, Grandcourt, Beaumont Hamel, Baillescourt Farm.
No.3.	BILLON WOOD	Moved to Trones Wood on 3rd; Targets Le Transloy.
No.4.	SAILLY AU BOIS	Standing by.
No.5.	ENGELBELMER	Standing by; H.R.H. the Duke of Connaught visited the position on 31st and three rounds were fired in nine minutes, and the target a windmill, destroyed with the second round.
No.6.	SOUASTRE	No firing.
No.8.	WARLOY	Under repair till end of month.
No.10.	MAMETZ WOOD	Standing by.
No.11.	ERQUINGHEM	Mounted on 11th; No firing.
No.12.	LA BOISSELLE	In action till 14th; then moved to Engelbelmer and remounted: Target, Beaumont Hamel.
		NOVEMBER.
No.1.	ENGELBELMER	Targets Miraumont and the River Crossings.
No.2.	ENGELBELMER	Targets St. Pierre Divion and Baillescourt Farm. Both ceased firing on 18th.

The Howitzer Brigade, Royal Marine Artillery

No.3.	TRONES WOOD	Gun dismounted for repair.
No.4.	SAILLY AU BOIS	Gun dismounted for repair.
No.5.	ENGELBELMER	Supporting attack on 13th; afterwards no firing.
No.6.	SOUASTRE	No firing.
No.8.	MAILL Y MAILLET	Supporting attack on 13th; then running out gear failed to act and gun was out of action.
No.10.	MAMETZ WOOD	Standing by.
No.11.	ERQUINGHEM	Standing by.
No.12.	ENGELBELMER	Standing by.
		DECEMBER
No.1.	ENGELBELMER	Target Miraumont Crossings till 4th; no firing;
No.2.	ENGELBELMER	Moving to new position close by.
No.3.	VILLE SUE ANCRE	Under Repair.
No.4.	ARRAS	Remounted and no firing.
No.5.	ENGELBELMER	No firing.
No.6.	SOUASTRE	Standing by.
No.8.	MAILL Y MAILLET	Under Repair.
No.10.	MAMETZ WOOD	Standing by.
No.11.	NEUVE EGLISE	No firing. On 20th Sir D. Haig visited the camp and told the Commanding Officer. to tell the men how very highly the services of the R.M.A. throughout the war were appreciated at G.H.Q. and also to let the men know how gratified he was with everything he had seen during his visit.
No.12.	ENGELBELMER	Standing by.
	1917	JANUARY.
No.1.	ENGELBELMER	Overhaul.
No.2.	MAILL Y MAILLET	No firing.
No.3.	VILLE SUER CORBI	Gun in workshop. Major Ledgard awarded D.S.O. Bombr. Pike the D.C.M. and Lieut. Rigby mentioned in dispatches in New Years Honours List.
No.4.	ARRAS	No firing.
No.5.	ENGELBELMER	No firing.
No.6.	SOUASTRE	No firing.
No.8.	MAILL Y MAILLET	Out of action.
No.10.	MAMETZ WOOD	No firing.
No.11.	NEUVE EGLISE	Drill and training.
No.12.	ENGELBELMER	No firing.
		FEBRUARY
No.1.	ENGELBELMER	Marched to Bois de la Haie on 18th; prepared position.
No.2.	MAILL Y MAILLET	No firing.
No.3.	BERNEVILLE	Arrived 15th and prepared position.
No.4.	ARRAS	No firing.
No.5.	ENGELBELMER	Training.
No.6.	SOUASTRE	No firing; shifted position under great difficulty owing to frozen mud
No.8.	MAILL Y MAILLET	Under repair.
No.10.	ANZIN ST.AUBIN	Shifted position on 4-6th; very difficult owing to frost.
No.11.	BOIS DE LA HAIE	Marched to Bois de la Haie on 9th, arriving on 14th and prepared position.
No.12.	BOIS DE LA HAIE	Arrived on 15th; preparing position.
		MARCH
No.1.	BOIS DE LA HAIE	Preparing position.
No.2.	AVELUY WOOD	Working Parties.
No.3.	BERNEVILLE	Reconnoitring; Mounted at Agny on 31st.
No.4.	ARRAS	No firing.
No.5.	ENGELBELMER	No firing.
No.6.	SOUASTRE	Moved to Dainville and mounted on 22nd.
No.8.	MAILL Y MAILLET	Gun Parked.

No.10.	ANZIN ST. AUBIN	Working Parties.
No.11.	BOIS DE LA HAIE	Mounting completed 18th; Standing by.
No.12.	BOIS DE LA HAIE	Mounting completed 18th; Standing by.
	APRIL	
No.1.	BOIS DE LA HAIE	Commenced on 2nd preliminary firing for Battle of Vimy Ridge. Moved to Souchez on 30th.
No.2.	AVELUY WOOD	Under repair. Moved to Dunkirk.
No.3.	DAINVILLE	Targets Hindenburg Line, Heninel and Wancourt for Battle of Arras.
No.4.	ARRAS	Remounted at Dainville on 3rd; Battle of Arras, Fired 136 rounds. Targets Thilloy village and Feuchy village. Captured 4.2 German howitzer got into action and fired 350 rounds into Pelves.
No.5.	HAMELINCOURT	No Firing.
No.6.	DAINVILLE	Battle of Arras; Gun parked after 9th.
No.8.	MAILLY MAILLET	Gun parked; personnel supplied ammunition to other batteries; in 10 days they supplied 22,000 shells, weight 1,260 tons with equivalent charges, in several cases by hand across country roads.
No.10.	ANZIN ST. AUBIN	Mounted by 4th; Battle of Arras, Target Fampoux moved to St. Laurent Blangy on 25th, and remounted
No.11.	BOIS DE LA HAIE	Battle of Vimy Ridge, remounted near Roclincourt and fired in Battle of Arleux.
No.12.	BOIS DE LA HAIE	From 2-9th fired 147 rounds on Givenchy, the British advance then took enemy out of range.
	MAY	
No.1.	SOUCHEZ	Destroyed Avion Church (O.P.). Gun was pulled back to proper line by tractors. Counter battery work.
No.2.	LA CLYTTE	Marched to La Clytte, mounted gun in a very exposed position opposite Wytschaete Prepared position.
No.3.	ST. LEGER CROISJLLES	Mounted 1/2nd; Standing by.
No.4.	BOIS DE BOEUFS	Standing by.
No.5.	BULLECOURT SECTOR	Fired 134 rounds between 1st and 14th; marched to Woeteren mounted 23rd and came into action.
No.6.	DAINVILLE	Parked till 7th; mounted at Boiry Becquerelles on 9th and stood by.
No.8.	NEUVE EGLISE	Marched to position near Dranoutre and mounted night 21/22nd.
No.10.	ST. LAURENT BLANGY	Targets, Roeux and Plouvain; on 15th Cradle required repair.
No.11.	S. of THELUS	Target, Oppy village. Mounted in the new position on 6th; Standing by.
No.12.	THELUS ROCLINCOURT	Mounted in new position on 20th; Standing by.
	JUNE	
No.1.	SOUCHEZ	Standing by.
No.2.	LA CLYTTE	Supporting attack on Wytschaete Ridge. Ordered to go to Wytschaete Ridge, but roads were impracticable for 15-inch transport. Owing to firmness and initiative of Captain Micklem the Corps Artillery over-ruled the Group H.Q. and gun was mounted on Kemmel-Wytschaete Road by 22nd; Fire opened 24th. Arrived Coxyde, Dunkirk on 29th.
No.3.	ST. LEGER CROISILLES	Standing by.
No.4.	BOIS DE BOEUFS	Standing by.
No.5.	NEAR KEMMEL	Supporting attack on Wytschaete Ridge. Remount on 16th and fire continued till 26th.
No.6.	BOISLEUX AU MONT	Standing by.
No.8.	NEUVE EGLISE	Bombarding Messines 2-7th; Targets in Warneton Area, till 18th.
No.10.	St. LAURENT BLANGY	Standing by.
No.11.	S. OF THELUS	Standing by.
No.12.	THELUS-ROCLINCOURT	Standing by.
	JULY	
No.1.	SOUCHEZ	Out of action after firing 14 rounds on 2nd due to shearing of bolt; remounted again 24th.
No.2.	OOSTE DUNKERQUE	Opened on Lombartzyde on 10th; used same O.P.s as Heavy Siege Train. The tractors also helped the train in mounting 7.5 and 9.2 inch guns.
No.3.	OOSTE DUNKERQUE	Arrived here on 7th. Target Westende.
No.4.	NEAR YPRES	Arrived 13th; Supporting attacks by 2nd Corps.
No.5.	OOST DUNKERQUE	Standing by.
No.6.	N.E. OF POPERINGHE	Mounted by 12th and supported attacks on Langemarck firing 657 rounds.

The Howitzer Brigade, Royal Marine Artillery

No.8.	NEUVE EGLISE		Bombarding Warneton Area.
No.10.	BLANGY ST. LAURENT		Standing by; remounted 17/18 between Thilloy and Wancourt.
No.11.			Mounted in four hours near Steenvorde. Support attacks on St. Julien.
No.12.	YPRES		10th July, position selected in Ypres; mounting interfered with by shell fire, causing several casualties. Work had to be abandoned owing to damage to Tractors. C.O. and many gassed and battery out of action. Major Woodcock took command on 29th, gun was mounted outside the town on 24th and fire opened.

The state of the Brigade in July 1917 was :-

	Establishment	Actual Strength.
Officers	59	64
Other Ranks	972	1015
Howitzers	10	10
Tractors	60	58
Lorries	50	50
Workshop Lorries	5	5
Store Lorries	5	5
Trucks	145	151
Motor Cycles	25	25

AUGUST

No.1.	SOUCHEZ	Standing by; silenced enemy battery on 13th. Supported Canadian attack on Hill 70. Then under repair and remounted at Angres on 25th.
No.2.	OOSTE DUNKERQUE	Standing by; averaging 10 to 12 rounds a day. Tractors assisting Heavy Siege Train.
No.3.	OOSTE DUNKERQUE	Standing by; Target, Westende. In continuous action.
No.4.	YPRES	Standing by; supported attack on 16th.
No.5.	OOSTE DUNKERQUE	Counter battery work Nieuport with. very good results.
No.6.	WOESTEN	Standing by. Target, Langemarck area. On 15th destroyed enemy strong point at Wijoen Drift. Supported infantry attack on 16th and congratulated by Corps Commander. Remounted S. of Boesinghe on 27th.
No.8.	NEUVE EGLISE	Difficult dismount owing to mud; completed on 17th after herculean efforts by half detachment of 46 men due to leave and sickness. Remount on 18th; Target Warneton.
No.10.	BLANGY ST. LAURENT	Standing by.
No.11.	YPRES	Target, Poelcapelle area, several moves to new pits.
No.12.	W. OF YPRES	Standing by; Sergeant McLeish and Corporal Blundell brought to notice for good work done when lent to Gun 12 at Ypres, on the occasion of the gun being moved from Ypres and remounted in new position; awarded the Military Medal. Fired 498 rounds during the month.

SEPTEMBER

No.1.	ANGRES	Standing by.
No.2.	OOSTE DUNKERQUE	Standing by.
No.3.	OOSTE DUNKERQUE	Standing by. Platform hit by shell on 23rd. Gun and gear sent for repair.
No.4.	YPRES	Standing by. dismounted on 8th when Tube and Jacket could not be separated, so both put on Jacket waggon. Remounted E. of Ypres.
No.5.	OOSTE DUNKERQUE	Standing by.
No.6.	NEAR BOESINGHE	Standing by; Supporting Infantry Attack.
No.8.	VORMEZEELE	Standing by.
No.10.	Between WANCOURT and TILLOY	Standing by.
No.11.	W. of YPRES	Standing by; heavy casualties; 9 killed, Lieut. Harries and 13 wounded
No.12.	YPRES	Standing by; moved to position N.E. of Ypres by 14th. Note.-During this month several of the howitzers were engaged in the opening of the Passchendaele Battles encountering great difficulties in moving whenever a change of position was necessary. Also in order to get within range as the infantry advanced, it was necessary to push forward over impossible roads and bring the guns into action in places very far advanced for such large weapons.

Royal Marines in the War of 1914-1919

		OCTOBER
No.1.	ANGRES	Standing by.
No.2.	OOSTE DUNKERQUE	Standing by; Destroyed dam across the Yser River with 53 rounds and received congratulations from Corps Commander and all authorities.
No.3.	OOSTE DUNKERQUE	Mounted at Pervyse on IS/16 and then stood by.
No.4.	MENIN ROAD	On 4th supported Australian attack on Passchendaele when all objectives gained. Dismounted and remounted at Outpost Farm on 19th. Hit by shell and temporarily out of action, ready again on 20th; 7 casualties; on 28th another direct hit by a 4.2 howitzer, only loading tray damaged.
No.5.	OOST KERKE	Remounted on 15th and then standing by. On 31st hit by shell and loading derrick, circuits and loading tray damaged.
No.6.	Near BOESINGHE	Preparing attacks Q.M.S. Avery and 1 gunner died of wounds and 7 wounded on 6th.
No.8.	LA CHAPELL	On 2nd a 4.2 shell hit platform and did a certain amount of damage also a direct hit on ammunition recess ignited two charges. Bombr. Brighten ran from shelter and extinguished them and was awarded the Military Medal. Preparing the infantry attacks, Targets Becelaere and Gheluvelt.
No.10.	WANCOURT-TILLOY	Standing by.
No.11.	MENIN ROAD	Fired 443 Rounds.
No.12.	N.E. Of YPRES	Standing by and shifting position under great difficulties.
		NOVEMBER
No.1.	GOUZEAUCOURT WOOD	Moved to Gouzeaucourt on 14th, supported attack on 20th. Targets Banteux and Vauyelles. On 30th information received that the enemy were advancing and had taken Gonnelieu and later in the day Gouzeaucourt. Transport sent back and gun ordered to continue firing as long as possible and then to remove breech block; breech block removed at 1p.m. and put into a lorry which stuck in the mud. After having taken the breech block 300 yards ready to put into lorry again, orders received to remount it and continue fire, as the Guards Division had been successful in their counter-attack; breech block in place by 4 p.m. but fire could not be opened as air pressure had been lost. Enemy came within 1000 yards of the gun.
No.2.	OOST DUNKERQUE	On 3rd direct hit on carriage put gun out of action and it was removed to Hazebrouck for repair.
No.3.	PERVYSE	Standing by; removed on 16th to Hazebrouck for overhaul.
No.4.	POPERINGHE	Removed to Tractor Park on 17th.
No.5.	OOST KERKE	Out of action owing to shell fire on 6th and 7th. Dismounted 8/9th one officer and six other ranks killed and 11 wounded. Gun taken to workshop at Hazebrouck.
No.6.	Near BOESINGHE	Standing by.
No.8.	LA CHAPELLE	Standing by; Target, Gheluveldt area.
No.10.	WANCOURT_TILLOY	Moved to position Neuville Bourjeval. Standing by; Targets Havrincourt, Flesquieres and Graincourt. Moved on 30th to position near Beaumetz.
No.11.	N.E. YPRES	Standing by.
No.12.	N.E. YPRES	Supporting attacks till Passchendaele captured on 6th, then standing by.
		DECEMBER
No.1.	GOUZEAUCOURT	Standing by.
No.2.	HAZEBROUCK	Under repair.
No.3.	HERAMVILLE	Arrived Hermaville on 25th and parked.
No.4.	POPERINGHE	Overhaul.
No.5.	HAZEBROUCK	Overhaul.
No.6.	HAZEBROUCK	Moved to Hazebrouck for overhaul. Lieut. Taylor wounded on 15th.
No.8.	LA CHAPELLE	Standing by; Target Gheluveldt.
No.10.	HAVRINCOURT WOOD	Moved to position in Wood on 19th and stood by.
No.11.	MENIN ROAD	Standing by.
No.12.	N.E. YPRES	Standing by, then overhaul for 14 days.
	1918	JANUARY.
No.1.	GOUZEAUCOURT	Prevented by state of ground, frost and then thaw, from moving. From April to December, 1917 this howitzer fired 1117 rounds.
No.2.	LILLERS	Gun parked.
No.3.	HERMAVILLE	Gun parked.
No.4.	PEPERINGHE	Gun parked. Mounted on 11th at Outpost Farm.
No.5.	NEUVE EGLISE	Gun parked.

No.6.	HAZEBROUCK	Overhaul. Remounted Boesinghe on 29th.
No.8.	LA CHAPELLE	No firing.
No.10.	HAVRINCOURT WOOD	Standing by; Target Marcoing area.
No.11.	YPRES	Partial overhaul.
No.12.	YPRES	Standing by.

FEBRUARY

No.1.	W. OF METZ	Standing by.
No.2.	LILLERS	Gun Parked
No.3.	VAUX VRAUCOURT	Gun moved to Judas Farm near St. Leger on 25th.
No.4.	OUTPOST FARM, MENIN ROAD	Standing by.
No.5.	NEAR KEMMEL	Standing by.
No.6.	BOESINGHE	Marched on 6th with 4 other siege batteries to Arras. Mounted Neuville Vitasse on 13th.
No.8.	ROBECQ	Reached Robecq on 17th; gun overhauled at Merville.
No.10.	HAVRINCOURT WOOD	Standing by.
No.11.	YPRES	Overhaul.
No.12.	YPRES	No firing.

MARCH

No.1.	W. of METZ	On 21St the German offensive was launched and No. 1 came into action. Fired their last round at 11-55 a.m. on 22nd and prepared to move to Moislains. At 3 p.m. the breech block was got away in a lorry; at 9-30 p.m. the tube and jacket; the dismount, except the platform, was finished at 1.0 a.m. on 23rd; they were told they could not go through Fins as it was occupied by the enemy; therefore moved by Metz Equancourt Road, which after the first mile was only a track; Enemy in Fins and Neuville; about half way the front tractor became hopelessly bogged, and the train had to be abandoned; Proceeded to Equancourt, here a party of infantry informed them that there was no one between them and the enemy and they marched to Moislains arriving 5-30 a.m. on 23rd. Leaving at 7 a.m. they went to Combles: eventually picked up tractor and lorry with breech block and jacket at Bray and marched to Corbie and so to Amiens. Lieutenant Foster awarded M.C. for his gallant attempt to save gun.
No.2.	MAROEUIL	Gun parked.
No.3.	ST. LEGER	On 21st Firing till 7 p.m. Dismounted and on 22nd retired to Moyenneville and Douchy. Mounted on 24th, but had to dismount in evening and proceeded to Arras and on 26th to Habarcq.
No.4.	OUTPOST FARM	Standing by.
No.5.	NEAR KEMMEL	Target Warneton, destroyed tower, and German O.P. on 6th
No.6.	NEUVILLE VITASSE	Firing 21st and 22nd. Dismounted ,at night, when infantry had withdrawn to a line 1500 yards from gun. Remounted at Beaurains; Salved most of their gear in 24 hours on which they were complimented. On 26th when firing they were ordered to dismount immediately and proceed to Savy; whilst loading up were heavily shelled and after four loads had been got away, a shell burst near crew killing four, died of wounds 2 and wounded 13. Worked after dark but continually shelled and eventually got away,about 10 a.m. Sergt. Inman and Bombr. Morris were awarded the Military Medal for exceptionally good work. Moved to Savy.
No.8.	ROBECQ	Gun Parked.
No.10.	HAVRINCOURT WOOD	In action till 21st. Heavily engaged all 21st and prepared to dismount at 4-45 p.m. One tractor was bogged, one broke its steering chain and they were deficient of one, leaving only two available; by 6-30 a.m. on 22nd the breech block, tube and jacket were dismounted after most strenuous exertions under heavy shell fire; on 22nd the bogged tractor was got away with the breech block and tube. During the afternoon stores were got away in lorries; the dismount resumed at 5-30 p.m. and completed at midnight; by this time enemy were very close and Fins was in their hands. Left the wood at 12-30 a.m. 23rd and proceeded to Barastre ; The men had worked magnificently and deserved every praise; the party proceeded through Albert to Villers Bocage arriving on 25th where they parked.
No.11.	YPRES	Standing by.
No.12.	YPRES	No firing.

APRIL

Note.- in this month the German offensive on the Lys took place.

No.1.	ST. VALERY	Awaiting Spare gun.
No.2.	ECOEUVRES	No firing.
No.3.	HABARCQ	Mounted at Bailleulmont. No firing.

No.4.	LA CHAPPELLE	Counter battery till 10th; on 13th enemy launched heavy attack. Dismounted under heavy shell fire and withdrew to Poperinghe on 16th and Lederzeele on 18th.
No.5.	NEAR KEMMEL	Counter battery till 10th; then ordered to remove breech block and retire at 4-30 p.m. Retired at 5 p.m. with breech block, one tractor and barrel waggon. On 11th Captain Craven reconnoitred the gun position with a view to recovery of gun but on 12th was ordered to demolish gun if possible which was done; and detachment retired to Locre at 2 p.m. The personnel assisted other siege batteries R.G.A. and event- ually moved to Abeele and then to Audruicq.
No.6.	ARRAS	Moved to N.W. Corner of Arras on 17th and stood by; Men billetted in Citadel.
No.8.	MAZINGHEM	Moved to Aire on 10th; and parked at Mazinghem.
No.10.	ABEELE	Arrived Abbeville on 7th.
No.11.	WORMHOUDT	Arrived on 12th and parked.
No.12.	ESQUELBECQ	Marched to Wormhoudt and parked at Esquelbecq then took up position at Abeele on 27th coming into action on 29th and 30th in support of French counterattacks at Bailleul and Dranoutre.
	MAY.	
	ST. VALERY	Reorganising.
	MAZINGARBE	Mounted on 11th; then counterbattery work.
	BAILLEULMONT	No firing.
	LEDERZEELE	Resting
	AUDRUICQ	Reorganising.
	ARRAS	Counterbattery work.
	DIEVAL	Arrived 29th, gun parked.
	ABBEVILLE	Reorganising; Mounted at Contay on 8th.
	MILLAIN-SCHIPSTAAT	Resting
	ABEELE	Supporting the French till 7th then parked.
	JUNE	
No.1.	ABBEVILLE	Reorganising
No.2.	MAZINGARBE	Counterbattery till 25th; when enemy shell struck some projectiles which exploded, killed 1 officer (Lieut. Hart) and 2 men, 8 wounded and nearly every piece of the gun damaged. Gun sent to workshop.
No.3.	AGNY	Standing by.
No.4.	W. OF YPRES	Mounted in 1 hour 50 minutes on 11th and then stood by.
No.5.	AUDRUICQ	Waiting rearmament.
No.6.	ARRAS	Standing by.
No.8.	FLEURY	Resting; moving to Arras on 29th.
No.10.	WARLOY-HEDAUVILLE ROAD	Standing by; Target Aveluy area.
No.11.	W. OF YPRE	Mounted and stood by.
No.12.	BULESCAMPS	Resting.
	JULY	
No.1.	AUTHIE	No. 7 gun arrived on 5th from England. Arrived on 12th at Authie; Mounted and standing by, Target Pusieux.
No.2.	MAZINGARBE	No firing.
No.3.	AGNY	Standing by.
No.4.	NEAR POPERINGHE	Standing by till 13th when at 12th round a shell burst prematurely, all the rifling was torn and the howitzer was condemned and dismounted.
No.5.	AUDRUICQ	Parked
No.6.	FLEURY	Overhaul
No.8.	ARRAS	Counterbattery. The record of the accuracy of 15-inch howitzer whilst on Canadian Corps front showed that out of 105 observed rounds there were 14 O.K.'s 39 Y's, 17 Z's, 26 A's, 7 B's, 1 C and 1 D
No.10.	WARLOY-HEADUVILLE	Standing by.
No.11.	NEAR POPERINGHE	Standing by; Target Kemmel.

The Howitzer Brigade, Royal Marine Artillery

No.12.	ABEELE	Mounted at Abeele on 8th. On l0th a shell fell on a barn where the men were at dinner and killed five, eight died of wounds and seven wounded. Counterbattery work.
		AUGUST
No.1.	AUTHIE	Lieut. Warman killed and Corpl. Woodard wounded while in O.P. Standing by till 17th then Parked as enemy were retiring.
No.2.	MAZINGARBE	Counterbattery; Target Cite St. Elie; Gun had now fired 3400 rounds, Total equivalent full charges 1769. Weight of shell approximately 2,000 tons
No.3.	BLAIREVILLE	Standing by till 23rd. Remounted at Ervillers on 28/29th then standing by.
No.4.	BEIRA FARM near YPRES	Mounted new gun on 7th Standing by. Target Kemmel area.
No.5.	AUDRUICQ	Returned l5-inch howitzer equipment on 7th. On 10th drew one 12-inch Mark IV. howitzer from Calais and took it to Audruicq.
No.6.	AUDRUICQ	Parked on 17th. *Note.–No. 5 and 6 were now combined to form No. I R.M.A. Siege Battery armed with 12-inch howitzers, Major G. L. Raikes in command. Capts. Craven and G. E. Burnside, Lieuts. T. W. Lewis,]. G. Lang, H. H. Jarman, A. J. Hope, A. J. Beere (M.T.), W. Price, (M.T,) Capt. F. M. Burnside (Workshop).*
No.8.	ARRAS	Counterbattery shoots till 22nd, then moved to St. Laurent Blangy, and came into action.
No.10.	WARLOY-HEADUVILLE	On 6th moved to a position in front of Forceville. Standing by ; dismounted 27/3Ist.
No.11.	NEAR POPERINGHE	Standing by Lieut. Blunt wounded at O.P. on 8th. On 24th Gun condemned for scoring and sent to Park.
No.12.	ABEELE	Standing by till Kemmel evacuated by enemy on 31st.
		SEPTEMBER
No.1. Siege Batty.	AUDRUICQ	Drill and training. Moved 23rd to Villecholles; mounted and came into action on 26th. Fired 80 rounds a day supporting infantry attacks, mostly without observation.
No.1.	AUTHIE	On 5th, Major Foster tried to salve the train lost in March at Equancourt, but enemy still holding the place. On 22/23 gun mounted at Hermies and supported attacks on Hindenburg line on 27th; by 28th enemy out of range.
No.2.	MAZINGARBE	Counterbattery work.
No.3.	ERVILLERS	Mounted at Beaumetz on 10th; supported operations against Flesquieres, Havrincourt, etc. Firing daily and supported attacks on 27th.
No.4.	LA CLYTTE	Remounted on 3rd; Standing by till enemy out of range on 29th
No.8.	BLANGY ST. LAURENT	Mounted at Dury by 22nd; Supported attacks on crossings of Canal du Nord 27th.
No.10.	FORCEVILLE	Parked; Mounted on 23rd near Hermies. on 27th supported attacks on Hindenburg Line.
No.11.	STEEVNORDE	Gun in workshop. Personnel assisting other batteries on 14th a party under Lieut. Collet salved a battery of 6.75 m.m. French guns recaptured by the British after the fall of Kemmel.
No.12.	ABEELE	Towards end of month supported Belgian attacks till enemy was out of range at 8 p.m. on 28th.
		OCTOBER
No.1. Siege Batty.	VILLECHOLLES	Parked on 2nd; personnel formed "A" Hun Battery.
"A" Hun Battery	LIHAUCOURT	On 7th a battery consisting of one 5.9" howitzer, two 4.2" howitzers Battery and one 77 m.m. captured guns, was formed under Captains Craven and Burnside working in four day reliefs: on 8th they exchanged the 5.9" howitzer for another 4.2" making three. On that day advanced to a position on the Leverges -Ramicourt Road and bombarded Fresnoy le Grand. Then moved on to the East of Sequehart and next day to Fresnoy le Grand; fired on the cross roads, remaining at Fresnoy le Grand on 11th (one gunner killed, two wounded). Moved to Bohane in evening, here they remained firing on Bois de Ricqueval with gas and H.E. shell until 17th, firing 1,100 rounds on 14th; on 17th advanced to Vallee-Hassard, from here they were firing a barrage on Wassigny; advanced on 18th to Audigny les Fermes; on 19th to Wassigny; on 21st in action against Fresny; advanced on 22nd to a position on Wassigny-Ribeauville Road and took part in the barrage from 1.20 a.m. to 8 a.m. on 23rd, firing 1250 rounds. From this position they fired 150 rounds on 24th, 1200 rounds on 25th and finished their ammunition on 26th: turned the howitzers over to 214th Siege Battery and rejoined their own battery at Villecholles on 27th. They fired altogether about 7500 rounds of German ammunition; the ranges table were translated by Major Raikes and prisoners stated that the enemy suffered heavily from the Gas bombardment.
No.1.	LEALVILLERS	Received congratulations for their work on 27th; Moved to Lealvillers on 3rd and Parked.
No.2.	LOOS	Gun Parked
No.3.	FREMICOURT	Gun Parked on 4th.
No.4.	YPRES	Gun Parked.

No.8.	DURY	Counterbattery till 12th when enemy retired East of Canal. On 15th moved to White Chateau at Bourlon and gun overhauled.
No.10.	HERMIES	Moved to Forceville on 3rd and Parked.
No.11.	AUDRUICQ	1 gunner killed, marched to Audruicq and parked.
No.12.	AUDRUICQ	Parked. *Note.-* On 8th Nos. 11 and 12 howitzers and No. 5 workshop formed into 2nd R.M.A. Siege Battery armed with two 12" howitzers Mark 11. The 15" howitzers were returned to Calais and new guns drawn on 17th. Captain Ward in command. Training and Organising.

NOVEMBER

The position of the Howitzers at the signing of the Armistice on November 11th was as follows:

No.1. Siege Batty.	Vaux Audigny. Parked.
No. 2 Siege Batty.	Arrived Poperinghe night 10th; and on morning of 11th moved to Siege Batty Bisseghem.
No.1.	Lealvillers; Parked.
No.2.	Orchies; Parked.
No.3.	Acheux; Parked.
No.4.	Beira Farm; moved on 11th to Menin.
No.8.	Bourlon; parked.
No.10.	Forceville; parked.

TABLE "D"
HONOURS AND REWARDS AWARDED TO THE R.M.A. HOWITZER BRIGADE.

C.M.G. Lieutenant-Colonel G. R. Poole 1/1/17

D.S.O. Lieutenant-Colonel G. R. Poole 30/5/19	Captain T. S. Dick 1/6/17
Major R. C. Morrison-Scott 1/1/18	Major C. Micklem 1/1/19
Captain W. R. Ledgard 1/1/17	Captain G. L. Wills, (attached Tank [Corps)
D.S.C. Major G. L. Raikes	Captain T. C. Cuming
Lieutenant F. L. Robinson	

Military Cross

| Lieutenant H. N. Elphick | Lieutenant J. Franklyn |

For laying wires across the open at the Battle of the Somme, being cut off on one occasion for nine hours under heavy shell fire. Lieutenant Franklyn also carried out some hazardous reconnaissances in search of observation posts.

Lieutenant S. H. Wood

Gallantry in establishing a forward observation post, and establishing communication when others had failed. He pushed forward to a very advanced position, where he was severely wounded in two places, but remained at his post mending wires throughout the night and then brought his party back to the gun position.

Lieutenant A. E. Holton

On two consecutive nights, he brought his gun into action under heavy fire; has managed the ammunition supply, his management and keenness have kept the gun in close touch with the advance.

| Lieutenant M. H. Collet | Captain C. C. Carus-Wilson |
| Lieutenant T. A. Ryder | Captain L. L. Foster |

For making a bold effort to extricate No. 1 howitzer and equipment, after the enemy had penetrated the battle zone on 23rd March, 1918. He saved the howitzer and part of the mounting by taking a bye lane after the enemy had got across the main road, in rear of them.

D.C.M. Bombardier W. Pike

Showing marked courage and determination as part of the gun's crew under arduous and trying circumstances.

Corporal R. E. Payne
Staff-Sergeant Mechanic H. Williams

Performed continuous good work, until wounded whilst repairing a tank.

Corporal F. Cross

Repeatedly repairing wires to the observation posts, and setting an excellent example to his party.

Sergeant E. C. Tye
Sergeant A. C. Woodhouse

For two and a half years has shown gallantry and devotion to duty under fire; on one occasion when casualties were heavy he showed extreme devotion to duty in helping wounded and dispatching them to the dressing station.

B.S.M. C. Dadd

On many occasions has rescued wounded men under fire, particularly on 27th July, 1918, when he carried six men out of a farm, which was being shelled and again on 2nd August, when he dug out two civilians, who had been wounded and buried by a shell in a farm house.

Corporal T. Forsyth

The Howitzer Brigade, Royal Marine Artillery

TABLE "D"

Military Medal

- Gunner A. S. Butchers
- Bombardier E. J. Redman
- Sergeant E. A. Vinnell
- Gunner H. H. Jarman
- Gunner E. A. Bevan
- Gunner W. Wright
- Driver C. A. Gamble
- Gunner J. Halden
- Bombardier E. J. Goff
- Sergeant A. Chatfield
- Gunner W. Frew
- Gunner F. H. Parkes
- Corporal N. F. Brown
- Bombardier L. Hinchliffe
- Gunner A. Hutchison
- Gunner R. Fulton
- Sergeant J. Heaton
- Bombardier S. Hooper
- Gunner S. E. Pearce
- Bombardier A. Shepherdson
- Bombardier F. J. Brighten
- Gunner J. Howarth
- Bombardier S. M. Curtis
- Sergeant H. Tarbottom
- Driver W. Wheeler
- Corporal G. E. Wood
- Sergeant C. Inman
- Bombardier J. Morris
- Corporal H. Bland
- Sergeant T. J. Lee
- Gunner G. L. Willis
- Gunner W. G. Blundell
- Corporal S. Berry
- Corporal T. C. Lockley
- Driver W. Barnes
- Bombardier W. S. C. Jeffery
- Gunner T. H. Woodrow

Mentioned in Dispatches.

- Major G. L. Raikes (twice)
- Captain T. C. Cuming (twice)
- Lieutenant F. L. Robinson
- Major F. W. Lumsden
- Captain M. Williams
- Lieutenant A. H. Brownrigg
- Lieutenant-Colonel G. R. Poole (3 times)
- Captain W. R. Ledgard
- Captain L. L. Foster
- Lieutenant C. N. Rigby
- Sergeant E. A. Vinnell
- Mechanic H. M. Avery
- Major A. P. Liston Foulis
- Lieutenant H. Boffey (twice)
- Captain C. Micklem (twice)
- Captain R. Morrison-Scott (twice)
- Lieutenant W. T. Webley
- Colour-Sergeant C. J. Miller
- Sergeant A. C. Milson
- Lieutenant G. E. M. Burnsside
- Lieutenant T. G. Atkinson
- Captain W. W. Ward
- Lieutenant G. Wilson (twice)
- Driver E. W. Gellatly
- Gunner A. Jennings
- Driver J. C. Lowe
- Bombardier E. Parish
- Gunner E. Bennett
- Gunner T. C. Englefield
- Lieutenant T. W. Lewis
- Major G. Matthew
- Major G. C. Woodcock
- Driver Baverstock
- Corporal W. T. Robins
- Gunner E. H. Roxby
- Captain J. H. Percy (twice)
- Lieutenant C. A. Stock
- Lieutenant W. D. Hart
- Captain H. Vincent
- Lieutenant T. G. Wright
- Colour-Sergeant W. Chave
- Driver G. Johnston
- Sergeant W. H. Ruffle
- Driver A. B. Turner

APPENDIX TO CHAPTER 24.

BRIGADIER-GENERAL F. W. LUMSDEN, V.C., C.B., D.S.O.

MAJOR LUMSDEN, who was a graduate of the Staff College, left the R.M.A. howitzers on 27th July, 1915, on appointment as G.S.O. (3), on the First Army Staff. He became staff officer of Canadian Corps troops on 27th November, 1915. On 27th January, 1916, he was appointed G.S.O. (2), on staff of "V." Army Corps, and then G.S.O. (2), of the 32nd-Division. It was with this Division, first on the staff, and then as brigadier, commanding one of its brigades, that he won such undying fame.

He was awarded the D.S.O. on 1st January, 1917, and then received what must have been an unique honour, as he was awarded two bars to his D.S.O. in the same Gazette of 11th May, 1917. The first for reconnoitring the enemy's position, moving over open ground under very heavy fire and bringing back most valuable information, rendering invaluable service in the subsequent operations. When he won the second bar he went out in charge of a strong reconnaissance party, and carried out his task with conspicuous success and withdrew his party with great skill at a critical moment, and by his conduct, rapid decision, and good judgment, saved many casualties.

In order to qualify for the command of an infantry brigade, he gave up his appointment on the staff, and was appointed to command the 17th Highland Light Infantry on 6th April, 1917, he only held the command for six days, when he was appointed to command the 14th Brigade of 32nd Division, but in that period he had gained the honour most coveted by all soldiers.

AWARD OF THE VICTORIA CROSS.

Six enemy field guns had been captured, but as the enemy kept them under heavy fire, it was necessary to leave them in dug-in positions, 300 yards in advance of the position held by our troops. Major Lumsden then undertook to bring these guns into the British Lines. To do this, he personally led four artillery teams and a party of infantry through the hostile barrage. As one of the teams sustained casualties, he left the remaining teams in a covered position, and under a very heavy rifle, machine gun and shrapnel fire he led the infantry to the guns. By force of example, and inspiring energy he succeeded in sending back two teams with guns, going through the barrage with the team of the third gun. He then returned to the remaining guns to await further teams, and these he succeeded in attaching to two of the three remaining guns, despite rifle fire, which had become intense at short range, and removed the guns to safety. By this time, the enemy in considerable strength had driven through the infantry covering posts, and blown up the breech of the remaining gun. Major Lumsden then returned, drove off the enemy, attached a team to the gun and got it away.

Whilst in command of the 14th Brigade, he was wounded on 2nd August, but returned very soon to duty. He commanded the Brigade with his usual skill, gallantry and daring and in the Gazette of 22nd April, 1918, he was awarded a third bar to his D.S.O. When his Brigade formed the left of an attack in a raid on the enemy's lines, he first of all superintended the assembly in the advanced trenches, and then advanced to each successive objective encouraging the men. At the final objective where there was some slight hesitation owing to the heavy machine gun and rifle fire added to the exhaustion of the troops, he led the assault on a group of seven 'pill-boxes' and after their capture made a valuable reconnaissance of the enemy's position. He

The Howitzer Brigade, Royal Marine Artillery

[Photo by Russell & Sons, Southsea, of Picture by A. Durrant Smyth, in Officers' Mess, Eastney.]

MAJOR (TEMPORARY BRIGADIER-GENERAL) F. W. LUMSDEN, V.C., C.B., D.S.O. (with three Bars). Promoted Lieutenant-Colonel, R.M.A., 1917; Served with R.M.A. Howitzer Brigade and on Staff in France; Commanded 14th Infantry Brigade, 1917-1918; Killed 3rd June, 1918.

then supervised the withdrawal, forming the covering party, with which he himself withdrew, being the last to leave the position. As the Gazette says :- "Such coolness, determination to succeed and absolute disregard of danger, not only ensured the success of the operation, but afforded a magnificent example to all ranks, the value of which can hardly be exaggerated."

On 25th October, 1917, he was promoted Lieutenant-Colonel in the Corps for his distinguished service, and was awarded the C.B. on the King's Birthday, 1918, an honour of which he probably never knew.

At last he fell a victim to his own daring; on the night of 3rd June, 1918, he was up in the front line trenches, when an alarm of an attack took place. He at once in his fearless manner walked up to see for himself where the trouble was, and exposed himself. He was shot through the head by a rifle bullet, and was killed instantly.

The country and the Corps were the poorer by the loss of one of the finest officers that ever wore His Majesty's uniform; as an officer of the 32nd Division said "His Brigade became the finest in the Division, solely owing to his fine influence and example."

CHAPTER 25.

ANTI-AIRCRAFT BRIGADE, ROYAL MARINE ARTILLERY.

Formation of Brigade – Equipment - Arrival at Dunkirk – Ypres - Formation of additional Batteries - "C" Battery attached to Third Army - "B" Battery at Nieuport - Disbandment of Brigade - "B" Battery at Dunkirk - Formation of Special Battery.

THE Anti-Aircraft brigade was formed at Eastney during November and December, 1914, by Lieutenant-Colonel C. A. Osmaston. This officer was not only the Commanding Officer, but also the technical expert, who designed and prepared all the equipments and transport and more particularly the fuses, which he greatly developed.

The anti-aircraft organisation was at that time non-existent, very little was known about that special form of gunnery, and as far as the R.M.A. were concerned, everything had to begin from the beginning.

The gun adopted was the two-pounder pompom, which Colonel Osmaston adapted for the purpose. The guns were mounted on special motor lorries, which were armoured and carried the guns, crews and ammunition; the mounting, which was of the high-angle type, admitted of all round training and the guns were fitted with special sights. There were other lorries for personnel, baggage and stores, both armoured and unarmoured the officers had small Stellite cars or motor cycles, so that the unit was completely mobile.

Each Battery was supplied with four guns, the details of the guns, personnel, and transport are given later, as they varied as experience was gained.

In addition to training gunners and observing officers, it was necessary to train drivers for the mechanical transport and temporary officers with engineering experience rendered invaluable service in developing and utilising the equipments. The brigade was retained under Admiralty control, though they were entirely at the disposal of the Army; but as a matter of fact they occupied a very independent position.

The brigade remained at Eastney till March, 1915, training, collecting equipment, and carrying out experiments with the material.

At 10 p.m., 23rd April, 1915, the Brigade Headquarters, the personnel of "B" Battery and part of that of "C" with the ammunition column arrived at Dunkirk from Dover.

Brigade Headquarters were composed of :- Lieutenant-Colonel C. A. F. Osmaston, Captain A. L. Forster, Adjutant, Major P. W. North, Royal Berks Regiment, attached. "B" Battery:- Captain E. H. Barr, Captain F. S. Richards (Commanding Officer of "A" Battery), Lieutenants H. R. Lambert, B. O. March, S. C. Knight, G. F. Hazard. "C" Battery :- Captain D. L. Aman, Lieutenants M. D. Quill, E. Walters, V. H. Cartwright, R. H. Fox, and G. Evans.

On 24th, the guns and lorries of "B" battery arrived, and the brigade was billetted at a factory in the suburbs at Coudekerque branch.

The Commanding Officer reported to Brigadier-General, the Earl of Athlone, the head of the British Mission with the Belgian Army, under whom they were to work, and received orders to assist the French troops in the neighbourhood of Dunkirk with one battery. On 26th, the remainder of "C" battery, under Captain Aman, with the guns and stores and. some of the vehicles of that battery arrived.

On 28th April, "B" battery fired their first shells in the afternoon at an aeroplane passing over the town.

That evening the battery moved to a position near Nieuport, in which neighbourhood they were to spend the next three and a half years.

On the 29th "C" battery moved to Malo, and also came into action for the first time.

Some of the officers and personnel of "A" and "D" batteries, the equipment of which was not yet ready, accompanied the other batteries for instruction and to gain practical experience. The batteries generally worked by sections of two guns; the sections were usually posted apart from each other, which necessitated rather a high percentage of officers for observation duties.

On 30th, Lieutenant J. Berrington brought over the remainder of the personnel and vehicles of "B" and "C" batteries, and on that day, "B" battery claimed to have brought down its first aeroplane.

The state of the brigade at this date was:- 27 officers, seven warrant officers, five staff sergeants, 36 N.C.O.s, 64 .gunners, four armourers, 122 drivers, 17 mechanics, four S.B. staff, Total 280.

On 2nd May, Lieutenant-Colonel Osmaston and his staff proceeded to Abeele and reported to the Commander Royal Artillery, "V." Corps, and reconnoitred for positions in and around Ypres. In the afternoon, "C" battery, Captain Aman with four guns, six armoured cars, two store lorries, and two ammunition lorries with 500 rounds per gun reached Poperinghe; the strength was six officers, two warrant officers, 50 N.C.O.s and men. This battery was attached to the 28th Division "V." Corps and came under the orders of the Corps; it was posted with one section on the canal bank at Ypres, and the second section, north of the town.

On 5th May, the second section of "B" battery moved to Lampernisse, near Dunkirk and came under the orders of the Belgian Army. The first section of "C" battery was now at Potijze, and the second section, which was temporarily commanded by Captain and Adjutant Forster, was north-west of Ypres and claimed to have brought down another aeroplane; headquarters and base details remained at Coudekerque.

During the month, "B" battery had one section at Nieuport with the French, and one with the Belgians in the neighbourhood of Lampernisse and Forthem. "C" battery was moved to various positions in and around Ypres, under the orders of the Corps; they were continually in action and took part in the Battle of Frezenberg Ridge 8th-13th May.

This was in the very early days of anti-aircraft defence, when everything was in an experimental stage; but experience was being rapidly gained and the moral effect of the guns was very great. Owing to the short range of the gun, or rather of the fuze, it was necessary to place the batteries as far forward as possible to prevent hostile aeroplanes from crossing our lines. The gun proved that it was able to develop a very high rate of fire, which was found most effective in turning aeroplanes back from their objective if they came within range. At this time, owing to the great shortage of anti-aircraft guns, the enemy planes were flying at low altitudes. The shell was a common shell, and so lacked hitting power at such objects and was only effective if actually burst on a vital part of an aeroplane.

The R.M.A. gunners, however, being used to firing at rapidly moving objects, were able to make good shooting in spite of many mechanical difficulties with the guns due to jambs and defective cartridges. It also became evident that concealment of guns and personnel was most essential, as they drew the enemy fire of shrapnel and high explosive whenever they came into action.

On 17th May, the first section "C" battery proceeded to Bethune and was attached to 47th Division; in the middle of the month it became necessary to return some of the guns to Dunkirk for overhaul; they were replaced temporarily by guns from "B" battery. On 24th May, the day of the gas attack, Captain Richards, temporarily with "C" battery with B 4 gun and its detachment were overwhelmed with gas near Potijze. The gun and ammunition were saved by the drivers and brought into Vlamertinghe; the drivers of the two cars, Rudd and Kemp behaved with great gallantry though themselves gassed, as did Motor Cyclist Everill, who brought in two men on his cycle. C 7 car under Lieutenant March did good work in trying to recover the gear and in going back to search the gun position and bringing back gassed and wounded men of all units.

In June the longer fuse with two rings became available, and its effect was to keep the aeroplanes about 1000 yards further off; the guns were also provided with sight strips marked in degrees instead of ranges, which facilitated the putting on of vertical deflection, as well as elevation for range.

On 16th June, Captain A. L. Forster and Corporal W. L. Stone displayed the greatest gallantry in bringing in wounded men of the King's Shropshire Light Infantry, under very heavy shell fire near Tuileries (Ypres). Captain Forster was awarded the D.S.O. and Corporal Stone the D.C.M. This incident occurred during the first battle of Bellewarde.

The whole of "C" battery, Captains Cartwright and Evans, section commanders, was concentrated in the Ypres Salient at the end of the month. Captain Evans' section brought down a plane in which was a German colonel of Artillery as observer and shortly afterwards another was brought down by the section under Lieutenant Quill; 230 rounds being fired in four minutes.

At this time more new sights were issued, which enabled the vertical deflection to be put on independent of the elevation due to range and also enabled a "rate of change" to be worked.

"B" battery carried out very effective work at Nieuport in protecting the French artillery and repeatedly gained the recognition of the French commanders. Determined efforts were made by the German gunners to knock it out ; the guns were hit and put out of action three times. On 16th July, Lieutenant S. C. Knight was mortally wounded in a gallant action against hostile aeroplanes; whilst the section was being shelled Lieutenant Knight remained in an exposed position observing for the fire of his section, and in spite of heavy shelling kept his guns in action until he was hit. On 26th July, one section of "B" battery moved to St. Pol (Dunkirk), to protect the aerodrome there and henceforth to the end of the war there was always at least one gun guarding this aerodrome; the pom-poms being replaced by the three-inch 20 cwt. guns, when they became available.

During these months, the guns were continually in action, and within the limits of the gun, were very successful in their shooting.

On 8th August, two more guns arrived, and the formation of "A" battery, under Captain Richards was commenced; new drafts arrived from England and training classes were formed at St. Pol.

In August the establishment was fixed as follows :-

Headquarters :- 4 officers, 1 warrant officer, and 18 other ranks.

Four Batteries :- 28 officers, 8 warrant officers, 4 staff sergeants, 24 sergeants, 8 armourers, 8 mechanics, 180 rank and file, 120 drivers.

Ammunition Column and Workshop :- 3 officers, 1 staff sergeant, 1 sergeant, 20 mechanics and drivers, 5 rank and file.

Medical details :- 2 officers, 2 drivers, 18 rank and file, total 22.

Base Details :- 1 lieutenant and quartermaster, 1 quartermaster sergeant, 3 gunners, total of 490.

Each battery consisted of the following:-

4 guns.

4 armoured five-ton lorries, for guns and equipment

2 armoured lorries, for ammunition

1 unarmoured lorry, for ammunition

2 unarmoured lorries, for baggage and stores

2 six-cwt. lorries, for baggage and stores.

1 motor car, for personnel

1 motor cycle, for personnel

2 dispatch cars, for personnel

4 motor cycles, for personnel.

The workshop consisted of:-

1 motor car	2 workshop lorries
1 dispatch car	8 armoured lorries
2 motor cycles	4 unarmoured lorries.

Headquarters :-

1 motor car	2 motor cycles
1 dispatch car	2 lorries for baggage and stores.

This establishment came into force on 21st August; one section of "B" battery was transferred to !A" battery, and "B" battery was reformed.

On 22nd, "A" battery took over a sector at Nieuport, and on 24th, one gun of "C" battery at Ypres was hit by a 5.9-inch shell, and completely destroyed beyond repair; fortunately, the crew had taken cover and so escaped injury. About this time eight Ford eight-cwt. lorries were received, two for each battery. On 26th, "B" battery, having. been completed, resumed its duties at Nieuport.

On 27th August, two 18-pounder field guns and a Belgian 75 m.m. gun were added to "C" battery; one 18-pounder was placed east of Dickebusch, the 75 m.m. was mounted on a cartwheel pivoted on the ground to give a large arc of training, but it was not sufficiently accurate; at this time "C" Battery was protecting the artillery area of the "V" Corps.

The positions on 1st September were:-

"A" Battery	one section	St. Pol.
"B" Battery	first section	Nieuport Railway Station.
	second section	Lampernisse-Oestkerke Road.
"C" Battery	first section	North-west of Ypres.
	second section	Menin Road.

On 5th September, they received the first consignment of the two ring fuzes, giving a range of 4900 yards, an increase of 200 yards; and on 13th, the first section of "A" battery, Captain Cartwright, marched to Ypres and came into action on the canal bank, outside the ramparts, whilst the second section of "C" battery was dispatched to Dunkirk to form the nucleus of "D" battery, under Captain G. Evans.

From the 18th onwards, there was great enemy activity over Ypres, so that "C" battery and the section of "A" were heavily engaged. From 26th-28th, "C" battery took part in the second attack on Bellewarde. On 28th September, "D" battery was completed, and the 1st section under Lieutenant M. D. Quill moved to Ypres, and took up a position near "C" battery; whilst on 29th, the headquarters and 2nd section under Lieutenant D Berrington relieved "C" battery, which returned to Dunkirk to rest and train new personnel.

The new long fuze had greatly increased the efficiency of the guns and enabled them to keep hostile observing planes from approaching near enough to obtain accurate observation of artillery positions.

During the summer, Colonel Osmaston had visited England several times, in order to consult with the Director of Naval Ordnance, and Woolwich authorities on improvements in fuzes, guns, etc., and it was due to his efforts that the great improvements in fuzes and sighting arrangements had been made.

On 1st October, the positions were as follows :-

"A" Battery	1st section	St. Pol Aerodrome
"B" Battery	1st section	near Oost kerke
	2nd section	Nieuport
"C" Battery	re-forming at St. Pol.	
"D" Battery	in position at Ypres, but on 2nd one gun went to Abeele to protect the aerodrome there.	

On 7th October, anti-aircraft sections of artillery were placed under command of the Army headquarters, instead of forming part of the Corps artillery as hitherto, and under this organisation, the "D" battery came under the Second Army headquarters, in the Ypres Salient.

By 18th October, "A" and "C" batteries were complete in personnel, but "A" still had only two guns.

On 21st October, orders having been received that "C" battery was to be attached to the Third Army in the south, Lieutenant-Colonel Osmaston, and Captain Aman (Battery Commander), with Captains Forster and Fox proceeded to VII. Corps area and arranged for battery headquarters to be at Louvencourt; they were to protect the Corps area in conjunction with two sections of 13-pounder anti-aircraft guns; accordingly on 22nd the battery marched via Cassel – Aire - St. Pol - Doullens; the strength being seven officers, 88 other ranks, four guns, 11 lorries, three motor cars, and a motor cycle. On 23rd October, Captain Richards with headquarters "A" battery and one section, Lieutenant Shadwell, proceeded to join the Second Army and took up a position at Petit Pont, one mile west of Ploegstreet, and on 26th brought down an Aviatik plane and captured the observer. One gun of "A" battery remained at St. Pol guarding the aerodrome, being joined by one gun from "B" battery.

On 30th, the 2nd section of "A" battery, which had now arrived, moved to La Clytte, south of Dickebusch.

The batteries were still suffering from the effects of the careless manufacture of fuzes, but the rapid rate of fire of the pom-poms, four rounds a second, which put such a large number of shells in the sky, was proving to have a great moral effect on the enemy's aviators, as was shown by their actions. Also the enemy's artillery always retaliated by shelling the anti-aircraft guns positions heavily when they could locate them. Fortunately at Nieuport, where concealment was practically impossible, they were fairly safe in an excellent bomb-proof constructed behind the railway embankment.

Colonel Osmaston and Lieutenant Dunkley were at this time carrying out experimental firing at Dunkirk to determine variations of burning of fuze, and the range at various settings of the fuze, with different angles of sight, of which up to then there were no data.

By the end of October, eight of the guns were working singly, which brought extra work on the officers, and at this time Lieutenants Walters, H. R. Lambert who had been awarded the D.S.C. for work at Nieuport, and Quill, were withdrawn for sea service.

The workshop section under Lieutenant Barnes, which had carried out the repairs was also now in good working order in the building, where it remained till the end of the war rendering assistance not only to the anti-aircraft batteries, but also to the siege guns.

On 1st November, the positions were as follows :-

"A" Battery	1st section	north-east of La Clytte (Petit Pont)
		one gun at St. Pol Aerodrome
"B" Battery	1st section	Nieuport with the French
	2nd section	Oostkerke with VI. Belgian Division
"C" Battery	1st section	Fonquevillers to south-east of Sailly aux Bois
	2nd section	Hamel-Bouzincourt
		one 13-pr. No. 10 north of Bienvillers to Fonquevillers
		one 13-pr. No. 25 from Sailly to Hamel
	The guns returned to Louvencourt every evening for rest.	
"D" Battery	1st section	south-west corner of Ypres
	2nd section	Belge Farm
	one gun of No. 1 at Abeele Aerodrome	

On the 7th, one section of "C" battery moved to Marieux, to protect the aerodrome there, and one section to near Mailly.

On the 9th, the "A" battery gun from St. Pol went to Nieppe to act under the Second Army, being relieved by a gun from "B." On 16th, one gun left La Clytte for a position close to Kemmel, where the guns of the section were 1700 yards apart. "A" battery was now completed by the arrival of the last gun, but on 28th, they were heavily shelled and badly knocked about, one gun was hit, one gunner killed and another wounded. Battery Sergeant-Major F. Merckel and Motor Drivers Baker and Thompson, displayed great gallantry in getting the section out of action, for which they were awarded the D.S.M. Lieutenant W. G. A. Shadwell by his prompt action and judgment saved the gun and removed the wounded to safety, and was able to bring the gun into action the following day, for which he was awarded the D.S.C.

At Nieuport, "B" battery, owing to the heavy shelling adopted the plan of having alternative positions, and keeping constantly moving from one to the other; they also adopted four field platforms in various positions, one gun being moved at night to one or other of them, the other remaining in the armoured car.

On 8th December, 1915, a hostile aeroplane endeavouring to cross the lines was engaged by a section of "B" battery, commanded by Lieutenant G. F. Haszard; as soon as the section opened fire, they were subjected to a very heavy shelling with shrapnel and high explosive; the aeroplane repeated the attempt, but was again turned back, in spite of the enemy shelling; this action continued for an hour and a half; Lieutenant Haszard keeping his guns in action with great skill and judgment, and was awarded the D.S.C. for his gallant work. A similar duel took place on the 25th December, but the enemy fire was so accurate and heavy that Captain Barr ceased fire, except with one gun, which he kept in action himself with a volunteer crew. The hostile planes were turned back, and in retaliation tried to bomb the battery. Captain Barr was awarded the D.S.O. for his work at Nieuport, and B.S.M. W. T. Clarke and Gunners J. H. Messum and R. G. McCurrack the D.S.M.

During January, 1916, there was considerable difficulty in obtaining sufficient ammunition, and on 19th, the car of one gun was severely damaged by shell fire, but fortunately the gun escaped serious damage. During this month, also the enemy aircraft were very active, particularly on 25th, on all the battery fronts. February was also a very busy month.

On 7th February, Lieutenant-Colonel Osmaston was appointed to the Ordnance Committee in England, and relinquished the command, being awarded the C.B., for his services. Major E. H. Barr succeeded him in the command, but was invalided to England on 28th February, and Captain Forster remained in command.

By March, 1916, all the guns required repair and overhaul, and great difficulty was experienced in obtaining the necessary spare parts, but the supply of ammunition was improving.

On 1st March, the positions were as follows :-

"A" Battery	one gun	La Clytte
	one gun	Kemmel
	one gun	Drauwecht on a field platform
	one gun	Petite Pont
"B" Battery		around Dunkirk
"C" Battery	one section	Marieux, moved to Albert on 8th
	one section	Flemelles
"D" Battery	one section	Dickebusch
	one section	Poperinghe

On 17th March, Second Lieutenant Abigail was killed, whilst examining an unexploded shell, which fell on the gun position. On 18th, Captain Cartwright assumed command of "B" battery, which he retained until January, 1918. This battery remained under the British Mission with the Belgians, and continued there until the Armistice in November, 1918, and when the R.N. and R.M.A. siege guns were mounted, as described in chapter 34, "B" battery afforded them the necessary protection against aircraft.

The other batteries were gradually absorbed by the Army, so that the need to retain the brigade headquarters ceased, and it returned to England in June, 1916. The workshop and base details, however, remained at Dunkirk under Lieutenant and Quartermaster Littleton and Lieutenant Barnes.

"A," "C," and "D" batteries gradually lost their identity as R.M.A. batteries, and were merged in the R.G.A. Captain Aman, however, remained in charge, and served under the orders of the Army, until the last details returned to Eastney in June, 1917. He was awarded the D .S.C., for his services in command of "C" battery at Ypres as was Captain G. Evans the commanding officer of "D" battery. Sergeant McNeil was awarded the D.S.M., for attending to wounded men in a barn and getting them clear before the barn was destroyed.

In July and August, 1916, one section of "B" battery at Nieuport was very active, the number of rounds fired per week averaging 1000. Three hostile machines were shot down and two others were damaged, and seen to land behind their own lines. A continual shift of position was necessary to avoid the enemy shell fire. It was during this period that Lieutenant Sawyer was wounded. The section in the Belgian area was continuously employed, but its guns were retained in the armoured cars; one plane was shot down and others damaged.

It was becoming evident even at this time, that the pom-poms, although serviceable up to 6000 feet, were not sufficiently powerful to deal effectively with the new German machines, which were increasing their ceiling in bounds at this time. Steps were therefore taken for the re-arming of the batteries. This led first to the attachment of 13 and 18-pounders to "C" battery and later to three inch 20 cwt. guns specially mounted for anti-aircraft work.

In September and October, 1916, both sections of "B" battery were sent to Adinkerke to protect the 12-inch mark X. Naval gun, which had been mounted at Dominion Farm (see chapter 34). The battery was very busy, driving off the aeroplanes which were sent over to locate the 12-inch, and also later on, when others came to spot for the ll-inch German guns in the Tirpitz battery. On one occasion, a plane was shot down on the beach at La Panne.

From November, 1916, to February 1917. At the request of the French Corps Commander, in the coastal section, and the Commandant Superieur de la Marine du front de Mer de Nieuport, one section was sent back to Nieuport. This section took over its old positions, and did much good work. Two enemy planes were shot down during this period, and the battery was congratulated by the French Commander on its work. The section at Adinkerke moved to a better position at Cabour, and was kept very busy, chiefly on account of the night flying of the enemy, which was very frequent at this time. On one occasion the crews manning the guns for 16 hours out of the 24. Satisfactory methods for dealing with the night bombers were evolved, and two machines were claimed by this section to have been shot down at night.

From March, 1917 to the Armistice. After strenuous efforts by Major Cartwright R.M.A., the Admiralty approved of the supply of four three-inch 20 cwt. guns and platforms. When these guns arrived, two were mounted at Cabour; a very marked effect was soon noticeable, as the enemy machines, were obliged to fly at a far greater height. This section remained at Cabour till the Armistice.

The amount of firing may be judged from the fact that four new guns were supplied during this period. In consequence of the shortage in the supply of guns, firing was always continued until pieces of the "A" tube broke away.

At the date of the Armistice, this section had been responsible for the destruction of ten enemy machines. It was commanded by Captain W. Russell, and his voice communication at the guns was the pride of the district, in which they were stationed.

The other two guns were mounted in concrete pits close to Nieuport Bains. These pits took six weeks to build, all the work being done by the R.M.A. themselves who proved themselves quite capable of doing work, which up to that time had been thought to be the job of the Royal Engineers. These two guns also saw much service and had six enemy machines to their credit. In one week 2000 rounds were fired and in return, the enemy sent over the same number of six inch shell. The dugouts on this occasion stood up to direct hits by ll-inch shells, giving the builders considerable satisfaction. This section had to spend many hours daily digging itself out from masses of sand sent into the pits and dugouts by the bombardment. On 10th July, 1917, the day of the German Offensive in this sector, the enemy commenced the lavish use of mustard gas, and so added to the trials of an already sorely tried section.

On 31st July, a large ammunition dump was blown up within a few yards of the guns causing a crater of an acre in extent. The complete detonation of this dump was caused by a bombardment of six-inch howitzers. Very good work was done in rescuing wounded under fire by Lieutenant Haszard and Gunners Bristow and Walker. Lieutenant Haszard was awarded a bar to his D.S.C., and Gunner Bristow was awarded the D.S.M. Gunner Walker unfortunately died of wounds. Later the same day, Corporal Grantham did good work in rescuing soldiers from a three-inch ammunition dump which caught fire. During August and September, this section was heavily engaged and one of the new German Gothas was shot down. On 9th of September, one of their guns was smashed to pieces by two direct hits with six-inch shell, and the other severely damaged. This position was then abandoned, and the remains of the guns removed. One new gun and mounting was sent out from England and the other was repaired at Calais. A new position was chosen on the Oost - Dunkerque - Oost Dunkerque Bains road, and was occupied without incident.

Major Cartwright established his headquarters with the forward section at Nieuport until 20th September, 1917, when they were transferred to La Panne. He was awarded the D.S.O., for his good services in command of this battery; this officer who had .been the captain of the English Rugby Fifteen, joined the corps on the outbreak of war, his commission being dated 20th September, 1914. Lieutenant Haszard was awarded the O.B.E., for his valuable services with the Brigade since its formation, and also received the bronze medal of the Royal Humane Society, for the gallant rescue of some American seamen from a coastal motor boat, which he effected in conjunction with Surgeon Bigger, R.N., also of the Brigade.

At the end of 1917, Major L. D. Briscoe, R.M.A., raised another battery of anti-aircraft- guns at Eastney for special service. This battery was also armed with three-inch guns; the service for which the battery had been designated did not materialise, and it was sent to Chatham, where they became part of the anti-aircraft defences, and was engaged with enemy planes on several occasions.

On 30th December, 1917, Major Briscoe and Major Cartwright exchanged commands.

When the Germans commenced their Offensive in March, 1918, the aerial activity increased, and "B" battery in the forward area at Dunkirk was in action every day, on which flying was possible; it was also subjected to long range heavy artillery fire from the large calibre batteries at Ostend.

In June, 1918, Major Cartwright, D.S.O., brought over the battery from Chatham, which was stationed on the outskirts of Dunkirk.

On the night of 16th September, a bomb fell on the base depot, destroying a lot of stores and all the mechanical transport spares and tyres of the batteries. Driver Glass received the D.S.M., for his conduct on this occasions, and Quartermaster-Sergeant Saunders the M.S.M.

"B" battery fired its last shot on 10th October, when the Germans were retreating and at once prepared to move forward to Ostend, but owing to the enemy's rapid retirement, and the difficulties of supply and transport, the move was abandoned. There was very little to do after the Armistice, but the batteries maintained their good reputation for conduct and efficiency, during that trying period.

The chief of the British Military Mission wrote :- "It has been a great pleasure to me and to the officers of the mission, to have been associated with such an efficient battery. Having come across the R.M.A. before, it was not a surprise to me to find that they were so good, but with these long weary years of stability and little to relieve the monotony, I must congratulate you on the manner in which you kept them in form, and very good form at that. This to my mind is the test of well disciplined troops, and I therefore congratulate both officers and especially the N.C.O.s on their success. Many regrets at not seeing you to thank you personally."

The battery left for England in 16th January, 1919, and was demobilised at Eastney.

The following honours were awarded to the unit :-

C.B.	Lieut.-Colonel C. A. F. Osmaston, R.M.A.	
O.B.E.	Lieutenant G. F. Haszard, D.S.C.	
D.S.O.	Major E. H. Barr	Capt. & Brevet-Major A. L. Forster
	Major V. H. Cartwright	
D.S.C.	Captain D. L. Aman	Lieutenant H. R Lambert
	Captain G. Evans	Lieutenant G. F. Haszard, with Bar
	Captain W. G. A. Shadwell.	
M.C.	Lieutenant W. Russell	Lieutenant R H. Sawyer
D.C.M.	Corporal W. J. Stone.	
D.S.M.	Acting Sergeant-Major W. T. Clarke	Sergeant E. S. Lewis
	Acting Sergeant-Major F. Merckel	Sergeant W . H. Rogers
	Gunner J. H. Messum	Sergeant A. J. E. Thorburn
	Gunner R G. McCurrack	Gunner A. H. Bristow
	Driver F. Baker	Gunner E. G. Chamberlain

Driver J. E. Thompson Corporal H. C. B. Callaway
Sergeant S. Bull Corporal L. H. Tomlin
Sergeant F. S. Chapman Battery-Sergeant-Major C. Bryan
Driver Glass
M.M.   Colour-Sergeant J. D. Ottignon

Mentioned in Dispatches.

Lieutenant J. Pordage Gunner J. Beresford
Sergeant A. E. Howard Driver Puttock

R.M.L.I. Battalions In France

CHAPTER 26.

R.M.L.I. BATTALIONS IN FRANCE, 1916-1919.

Arrival in France – Reorganisation - Souchez Area Trench Routine - Preparations for Beaumont Hamel - Wounding of General Paris - Battle of the Ancre - Operations on the Ancre, 11th January to 13th March, 1917 – Grandcourt – Miraumont - Battle of Arras - Second Battle of the Scarpe - Capture of Gavrelle - Battle of Arleux - Capture of Gavrelle Windmill - The Gavrelle Sector, 1917-Machine Gun Company - Trench Mortar Battery - Battles of Ypres, 1917 - Second Battle of Passchendaele - Welch Ridge - Flesquieres Salient - March Retreat - First Battle of the Somme - Battle of St. Quentin - First Battle of Bapaume - Rearguard at Bertincourt - Crossing of the Ancre - Aveluy Wood, April - Amalgamation of Battalions – Training - Second Battles of the Somme - Battle of Albert - Logeast Wood - Loupart Wood and Le Barque - Second Battles of Arras - Battle of Drocourt - Queant Line -Attacks on the Canal du Nord - Battle of the Canal du Nord – Anneux – Cambrai - Battle of Cambrai – Niergnies - The Pursuit to Mons - The Armistice - Official Entry into Mons – Demobilization - Return to England - Speech of H.R.H. the Prince of Wales – Dispersal - List of Honours.

AT 3 p.m. on 7th May, 1916, the 2nd R.M.L.I. at Mudros received the order to embark for France and were on board the S.S. *Briton* by 4-30 p.m. and sailing at once arrived at Marseilles at 5 a.m. on 12th May and on disembarkation marched to La Valentine Camp, about seven miles out and left on 14th for Longpré. The 1st R.M.L.I. strength 25 officers (including medical officers and chaplain) and 1021 other ranks embarked in S.S, *Aragon* on 14th and disembarked at Marseilles on 19th. The Cyclist Company and other Royal Marine units of the Royal Naval Division were also transferred to France at the same time.

They proceeded by rail to Pont Remy and on detraining there, marched to Longpré in the training area of the IV. Corps. Here they were re-equipped and re-organised, and the first line transport was reformed. The 2nd Royal Naval Brigade under General Trotman became the 1st Brigade and Lieut.-Colonel Stroud resumed command of the 1st R.M.L.I. Major Cartwright was second in command, Captain A. K. Evans, Adjutant, and Captain T. H. Burton, Quartermaster. Lieut.-Colonel. A. R. H. Hutchison was in command of 2nd R.M.L.I. with Major C. E. Eagles as second in command, Captain C. G. Farquharson Adjutant and Lieutenant F. J. Hore, Quartermaster.

Major-General Sir A. Paris resumed command of the Division with Lieut.-Colonel C. F. Aspinall, Royal Munster Fusiliers as G.S.O.1, Major Sketchley, R.M.L.I. as G.S.O. 2; Captain A. K. Evans became G.S.O. 3 in August; Lieut.-Colonel R. F. Foster, R.M.A. from headquarters in England became A.A. and Q.M.G. and Captain Lough, D.S.O., R.M.L.I, D.A.A. and Q.M.G.

At first General Trotman remained in command of the 1st Brigade with Major M. C. Festing as Brigade Major and Captain E. J. Tagg as Staff Captain, but on 16th July when the numbers of the Brigades were changed, Brig.-General G. E. Prentice, H.L.I., assumed command of the 188th Brigade and General Trotman took command of the newly formed 190th Brigade consisting of the 7th Royal Fusiliers, 4th Bedfords, 1st H.A.C. and 10th Royal Dublin Fusiliers with Major C. F. Jerram, R.M.L.I. as Brigade Major.

Meanwhile a fierce controversy had been raging in England over the control of the Royal Naval Division; the Admiralty desirous of being rid of their responsibility and the War Office wishing to mould it on the lines of one of the New Army Divisions, and to destroy its distinctive naval characteristics; with the powerful aid of the First Lord, at that time Sir Edward Carson, this was prevented. The War Office assumed responsibility for its recruitment, maintenance, training and discipline; the Admiralty retaining the appointment of officers to commissions, pay, allowances, etc.; the Royal Marines however remained on their usual footing. The Division retained its distinctive naval ranks and ratings, and the Admiralty kept its records in their own hands. Recruiting was removed from the Crystal Palace, and the recruits were sent to Blandford where Reserve Battalions were formed to feed the Battalions in the Field. The R.M.L.I. recruits, however, continued to be trained at Deal and were then sent to the First Reserve Battalion R.M.L.I. for completion of training and draft (see Chapter 42).

In France the Divisional Train, Royal Marines was reformed under Lieut.-Colonel A. Liddell, R.A.S.C., many of the drivers being recovered from Salonika, where they had been sent as part of the 28th Divisional Train.

On the 20th July the name of the Division was changed to 63rd (Royal Naval) Division, the 1st Brigade became the 188th, the 2nd the 189th, and the Army Brigade under General Trotman the 190th.

In May, Machine Gun Companies had been formed for each Brigade; for the R.M.L.I. the Company was formed by drafts from the three Headquarter Divisions, under Captain E. Bastin, T/Captain T. R. Mcready, T/Lieutenants Goldingham, Northrop, Abelson and Watson and later Lieutenant R. S. Wilkie. On arrival in France, after training at the Machine-gun Centre in England it was attached to the 190th Brigade, and renumbered the 190th Company. Another company was raised from the R.N.V.R. at Blandford for the 189th Brigade. Light Trench Mortar Batteries were also formed for each Brigade the 188th being under the command of Lieutenant Alan Campbell, R.N.V.R. formed of men drawn from the Battalions and throughout officers, R.M.L.I. were attached to this battery.

The Divisional Engineers were renumbered as the 63rd Division Signal Company and the Field Companies became the 247, 248 and 249 Field Companies. T /Major G. H. Harrison became C.R.E. of the Division, till appointed Director of Light Railways in France.

The Field Ambulances of the Medical Unit, Royal Marines, became Nos. 148, 149 and 150 and Fleet Surgeon E. Finch, R.N. succeeded Fleet Surgeon Gaskell, C.B., as A.D.M.S. of the Division.

The Cyclist Company was finally disbanded on 24th June.

For the first time the Division obtained its own Divisional Artillery; Brig.-General de Rougemont, R.A. becoming C.R.A. with the 223 and 317 Brigades R.F.A. (these were Territorial Brigades) and a Divisional Ammunition Column. It was also supplied with the other units such as mobile veterinary, sanitary section, etc.

In the Naval Battalions, Captain A. S. Tetley, R.M.L.I. from 2nd R.M.L.I. became C.O. of the Drake; Major F. J. Saunders, D.S.O., R.M.L.I. from Brigade-Major to C.O. of the Anson; Brevet-Lieut.-Colonel N. O. Burge, R.M.L.I. and Lieut.-Colonel L. Wilson, D.S.O., R.M.L.I. retained command of the Nelson and Hawke respectively, whilst Major A. H. French, D.S.O. assumed command of the Howe until appointed to the Signal Staff in France.

The 190th Brigade did not join until the middle of July. An Infantry Base Depot, numbered 63rd, was established at Calais under command of Lieut.-Colonel G. J. H. Mullins, R.M.L.I. which also became the depot for the R.M.A. units in France (see end of chapter).

The Battalions remained at Longpré, training and equipping (they now received their Lewis guns and surrendered their Maxims) until the end of the month. On 1st June, General Trotman went on leave and Colonel Stroud assumed command. On that day they left Longpré and entrained at Pont Remy for Badin and from there marched to Hersin, arriving at 12-15 a.m. on 2nd; on the 3rd the 1/R.M.L.I. and Anson were inspected by the G.O.C. 1st Army at Maisnil.

From this time until the 13th June the companies were sent in turn to the 47th Division for training in the French trench routine returning to billets at Hersin. They were now operating in the Angres - Souchez Sector of the IV. Corps Line from Lens - Vimy Ridge.

After this they were employed working on the Bajolles - Maistre Line of Defence whilst companies were sent for training to Frevillers, to which place the whole of the 1/R.M.L.I. removed on 26th June and went into Battalion training until 12th July, when they returned to Hersin. On 13th July, 1/R.M.L.I. marched to Fosse 10 via Hermin - Fremicourt - Hersin and took over the front line trenches on 14th from the 24th London Regiment in the Angres II. sub-sector. Lieutenant W. C. A. Elliott went out on patrol that night; he was wounded and died on the night 15/16; several of his men remaining with him and not returning to the line till 18th. Private L. J. Elliott, Chatham R.M.L.I. was awarded the D.C.M. for his gallant conduct in trying to bring in Lieutenant Elliott, he persisted in his efforts for 48 hours and only gave up when the officer died; he was between the lines for four days without food.

On 16th Lieut.-Colonel Stroud resumed command of 1/R.M.L.I. and on 29th this Battalion was relieved by 2/R.M.L.I. and moved into support.

On 17th July General Paris took over command of the Angres – Souchez Sector on a two brigade front (the R.M.L.I. Battalions were in the Angres II. sub-sector on the left); on the 29th the Division artillery come into the line and on 30th August the 190th Brigade came up into the Callonne sub-sector on the left of the 188th Brigade. This section of the line lay in front of the heights of Notre Dame de Lorette, which had been captured by the French in 1915. At this time the old system of holding the front line and support lines in strength had been given up; artillery fire was the dominating feature, and under the new system the front and support lines became in effect a line of sentry groups and a line of pickets; there was still lateral communication by means of a continuous trench, but in 1916 a line of posts became the normal first line; the support line was the line for delaying action and holding up local attack; the third line was generally the main line of resistance, which was held by two companies on a battalion front of 600-800 yards with dug-out protection, machine gun and trench mortar emplacements.

From 14th July to 20th September the two R.M.L.I. Battalions relieved each other in the front line of this sub-sector, the usual routine being to spend four days in the front line, moving then to Reserve, when the companies were placed two in Fosse 10, and two at Bully Grenay; after three days in reserve they moved up into support and the next day took over the line; when in support, two companies were at Bully Grenay, one company in Mechanics Trench and one at Cordon D'Oix and Cap de Pont. The usual trench routine in the line, with training and recreation when out of it, was carried out.

The trenches were swarming with rats and great rat hunts were instituted; water was brought up from the support lines by parties of two or three men, each man taking his turn; the water was carried in petrol tins which were very useful, although sometimes too much petrol had been left in them. The trenches were very muddy and wet in August and they had a lot of trench mortar duels using the "rum jars" or "toffee apples." The 2/R.M.L.I. note that they used test boxes made from empty bomb boxes at the corner of the trenches for locating breaks in the telephone wires, these had not been used before, and were found very useful.

On 11th August, Lieut.-Colonel Stroud, when going round the trenches broke his ankle and was invalided to England; Major Cartwright was appointed to the command of 1/R.M.L.I., with the temporary rank of Lieut.-Colonel, on the 12th. On the 17/18 August, Captain St. Clair Morford, of the 2/R.M.L.I. carried out a daring reconnaissance in the neighbourhood of Thompson's crater, which was a point of dispute between the lines, during which he was severely wounded in the ankle and was awarded the Military Cross.

On 16th September Lieut.-Colonel Hutchison assumed command of the 190th Brigade, vice General Trotman to the sick list, Major Eagles taking command of the 2/R.M.L.I. On 20th September 2/R.M.L.I. left the line on relief by the 37th Division and marched to Beguin where they were training till 27th; on the same day 1/R.M.L.I. marched from Hersin to Dieval where they also were training till the end of the month; 2/R.M.L.I. moved on 27th to Monchy Bretton. It is noted that during the training here the transport sergeant found a bed of watercress, when watering his horses, which was much appreciated. Both Battalions took part in a route march of the whole Division on the 30th.

On 2nd October Major H. Ozanne and Captain C. L. Muntz joined the 1st R.M.L.I., and Major L. W. Miller the 2nd R.M.L.I., from England, and Lieut.-Colonel Hutchison resumed command of the 2nd R.M.L.I.

On 4th October both Battalions marched to Ligny St. Flockel and entrained for Acheux; on arrival on 5th I/R.M.L.I. marched to Mailly Maillet and went under canvas in Mailly Wood, the 2/R.M.L.I. marching to billets in Engelbelmer, the places which they were to know so well during the next two years; Lieut.-Colonel Hutchison again taking over 190th Brigade on 6th and Major Eagles succeeding to the Battalion.

They had now to prepare to take their part in the Battle of the Somme that had been raging since July, and which had now reached an acute stage.

By 25th September the German Third Line, Courcelette – Martinpuich – High Wood – Flers - Delville Wood, was in British hands; Thiepval was taken on 30th. By the 3rd of October it had become clear that either the battle must be allowed to die down or else the base of the salient in which the army was advancing must be widened by attacking the flanks.

It therefore became necessary, in order to continue the battle and maintain the pressure, to attack north and south of the river Ancre against the line Serre - Beaumont Hamel – Beaucourt - St. Pierre Divion. The attack was to be made by the 5th Army, the "V" Corps on the north and the "11" corps on the south of the river. The R.N.D. were attached to the "V." Corps on 4th October and were warned to prepare for attack. The 190th Brigade took over the sector from Serre to Beaumont Hamel. On 7th October 2nd R.M.L.I. marched to Forceville and on 8th 1/R.M.L.I. marched to Varennes, proceeding to Forceville on 9th, the 2/R.M.L.I. moving on to Hedauville. They now went into intensive training, the Battalion staffs and company officers reconnoitring the trenches and area east of Colincamps; whilst fatigue parties carried up ammunition at night, and during the day the companies were employed in training and sweeping the mud off the roads. They remained in these places till the 18th.

On 13th October whilst visiting the 190th Brigade in the trenches General Paris was most dangerously wounded and Major Sketchley killed by a 5.9 shell, which burst between them as they were going up the communication trench; fortunately Lieutenant B. Nicholson, R.N.V.R., A.D.C. was only knocked down by the concussion and quickly rendered aid to General Paris, who was very seriously wounded in the left leg (which had to be amputated) and also in the shoulder and back.

This was a grievous loss to the Division which he had commanded since Antwerp and both educated and fathered so well; his patience and sympathy, combined with high professional skill, had been invaluable to such a novel formation. Major Sketchley, joining the Brigade as Adjutant of the Portsmouth Battalion and becoming Brigade Major at Ostend and later joining the Divisional Staff, had on many occasions displayed his great gallantry and devotion to duty, and had been staff officer to General Paris, to whom he was much devoted since Antwerp days. The 1/R.M.L.I. provided the firing party of 200 for Major Sketchley's funeral.

General Paris was succeeded by Major-General C. D. Shute, C.M.G., D.S.O. a very able soldier, but at first matters did not go altogether smoothly, as the methods of the R.N.D. were peculiar to themselves and somewhat puzzling to newcomers.

On 18th October, Colonel Hutchison resumed command of 2/R.M.L.I. and General Trotman, being recalled to England to command the Portsmouth Division was relieved in command of 190th Brigade by General Heneker.

Owing to the mud, bad drainage, and generally unhealthy conditions of the camps many men were taken seriously ill and removed on stretchers and unless the bearers could keep on the single plank they sank knee deep in the mud; this affected the strength of the Battalions considerably.

It was now decided that the 63rd Division should attack in the Hamel sector, and on 17th 1/R.M.L.I. marched to Hedauville, and on 20th to Engelbelmer; 2/R.M.L.I. proceeding to the latter place on 21st. Bivouacs were made of cross sticks at each end with a stick on top in the forks, covered with canvas painted all colours; there was plenty of rain and they had no coats as they were purely in battle order, and water for washing was very scarce and mostly obtained by breaking the ice at the bottom of the shell holes; many availed themselves of the old Marine privilege and grew beards. "The rum issue was very welcome, but some one in authority had a brain wave and issued pea flour every alternate night instead of the rum, much to the disgust of the 'Royals.'" Occasionally they succeeded in killing a hare which with a few carrots and turnips made a pleasant addition to the rations, and on November 7th it is noted that an issue of cardigans was made which were very welcome.

Reconnaissances were made in the Hamel sector and training continued.

On 22nd 1/R.M.L.I. relieved the Howe in the left section of the front line, remaining there until 25th, when they were again relieved by the Howe, and returned to Engelbelmer, relieving the Howe again on 27th.

On 28th Sir Douglas Haig inspected the 2/R.M.L.I.

On the same date Captain C. L. Muntz was confirmed in his appointment as Adjutant of 1/R.M.L.I., which Battalion was relieved in the front line on 30th October by the 4/Bedfords and returned to Engelbelmer, whence they marched on 1st November to Varennes where they remained until 5th. They then marched to Puchevillers. The 2nd R.M.L.I. who had been employed on working parties, went on the same day to Puchevillers, moving on to Hedauville on 7th.

On 6th November 1/R.M.L.I. relieved the 10th Royal Dublin Fusiliers in the line, remaining there till 8th when they returned to Engelbelmer proceeding to Varennes on 9th. 2/R.M.L.I. returned to Engelbelmer on 11th and went into bivouacs. 1/R.M.L.I. returning to the front line, relieved the Nelson in the left sector. The 12th was "Y" day and both Battalions were preparing for the attack. At 2 p.m. on that day 2/R.M.L.I. moved into their battle stations. 1/R.M.L.I. being in the line had Captain Clarke wounded and 30 other ranks killed or wounded; the trenches in the sector were very bad, and the weather was very wet, so that the strain on the troops during the interval of preparation had been very heavy. Assembly trenches had been dug on the slopes leading down to the river Ancre, because the front line bent back sharply there.

In consequence of the heavy losses that occurred in all the set attacks, and the consequent difficulties of reorganising the Battalions, it was now the rule for the 2nd in command with a proportion of the company officers and two of the company sergeant majors with a proportion of the N.C.O.'s and others to remain at the transport lines whence they could be called up to replace casualties if required, and were also available for the reorganisation when the battalion was relieved.

BATTLE OF THE ANCRE, 1916 (BEAUMONT HAMEL). (See Map 6.)

The plan of the attack was as follows: the line Serre - Beaumont Hamel – Beaucourt - St. Pierre Divion was to be attacked by the 2nd Division of "XIII." Corps, 3rd, 51st, 63rd Division "V" Corps, and 31st Division "11" Corps in this order from left to right. The length of front allotted to the 63rd Division was 1200 yards, their right being on the north bank of the river Ancre which ran due east to Beaucourt.

Their objective was Beaucourt and the intervening positions; the trenches from which they were to advance ran north to south.

The German front line, which was from 180-250 yards distant, consisted of three lines. The 3rd, known as the "Dotted Green Line," was the first objective; behind this line was a valley through which ran the Beaucourt Station Road. Beyond this road was a ridge running from Beaumont Hamel to Beaucourt Station; this ridge which was strongly fortified, was known as the "Green Line" and formed the second objective; beyond the ridge there was no outstanding features except on the right front where the ground sloped up to the hill immediately in front of Beaucourt; this hill covered the enemy's communications. On the western face of this hill was a trench parallel to the British Front, and extending to the north across more level ground. This was the third objective and was known as the "Yellow Line." The final objective was the "Red Line" a position beyond Beaucourt, which was to be taken up and consolidated.

A section of the Machine Gun Company was attached to each Battalion, and the Trench Mortars were to follow; the 190th Brigade was in Divisional Reserve.

The attack was to be covered by a creeping barrage and the tactics of the time were that each wave mopped up the trench allotted to it.

On the morning of the 12th the line was held by the Hood, Hawke, Howe with 1/R.M.L.I. on left next the 51st Division; 2/R.M.L.I. were in the open behind the 1/R.M.L.I.

The Dotted Green Line (first objective) and the Yellow Line (third objective) were to be attacked by 1/R.M.L.I., Howe, Hawke and Hood in this order from the left each advancing in four waves. The Green Line (second objective) and Red Line (final objective) by 2/R.M.L.I., Anson, Nelson and Drake. The first battalions were to rest on the Dotted Green Line (German third line) and reorganise, whilst the other four battalions passed through and captured the Station Road (Green Line) here the latter were to rest, whilst the first battalions passed through to the Yellow Line, the final assault on the Red Line was to be made by 2/R.M.L.I., Anson, Nelson, and Drake.

The two R.M. Battalion Headquarters spent the night in the headquarters dug-out and the well-known Cook-Sergeant, Jerry Dunn, of the 2nd Battalion saw to it, with his yarns, that they passed a cheerful night, and gave them hot cocoa before they started for the attack in the morning.

The 1/R.M.L.I. moved in four waves, in touch with 1/7 Gordon Highlanders on left, with one platoon of each company in each wave. Certain platoons crawled out into No Man's Land and got close up to the Germans while waiting for zero. The following officers took part in the attack :-

Lieut.-Colonel Cartwright, Captain C. L. Muntz, adjutant (*died of wounds*), Captain H. Hoare (*wounded*), Major V. D. Loxley (*killed*), Captains M. C. Browne, D.S.C. (*killed*), G. H. Sulivan (*killed*), J. M. Pound (*killed*), Lieutenants F. J. Hanson (*killed*), A. G. Kyle (*wounded*), C. Watkins (*wounded*), A. C. Donne (*wounded*), E. Cohen (*wounded*), N. B. Walker (*wounded*), H. B. Van Praagh, W. M. Hodding (*wounded*), P. Dewar (*wounded*), Second Lieutenants F. Goldie (*wounded*) E. L. Platts (*wounded*), C. W. Martin (*killed*), J. W. Richards (*missing*), H. E. Upham (*killed*), Surgeon E. B. Eykyn (*wounded*).

The 2nd R.M.L.I. left their bivouacs at 9-30 p.m. and arrived in position in the dark, the following officers taking part:-

R.M.L.I. Battalions In France

Lieut.-Colonel Hutchison, Captain C. E. Eagles, Captain and Adjutant C. G. Farquharson (*wounded*), Captain T. Edwards (*wounded*), Staughton (*died of wounds*), Goldring (*wounded*), O. Bisset (*wounded*), Lieutenants Thorold (*wounded*), J. T. Thomas (*wounded*), R. West, Second-Lieutenants Stokes (*killed*), Welman (*killed*), L. J. Dewar (*killed*), Holloway (*wounded*), Grayson (*wounded*), Wrangham (*wounded*), Garnett (*wounded*), Surgeon J. McBean-Ross (*wounded*).

Machine Gun Company-

Captain E. Bastin (*killed*), Lieutenants T. R. McCready, Abelson, (*killed*), Northrop, Goldingham, and Watson.

There was a thick mist in the morning and it was very dark when the first wave moved off at 5-45 a.m.; in seven minutes the whole of the Battalion had moved out; the enemy barrage did not do much damage to the right and right centre battalions but fell heavily on the 1/R.M.L.I. and 2/R.M.L.I. as they started. Every company commander in 1/R.M.L.I. was killed before crossing the first German line, and both adjutants were wounded; the ground to be crossed by the Royal Marine Battalions was also particularly muddy rendering advance difficult; the enemy trenches were practically obliterated by our artillery fire, and the ground as far as the slope down to the Station Road was pitted with shell holes; the enemy kept up a heavy machine-gun barrage and it was estimated that 50 per cent. of the casualties occurred in No Man's Land before reaching the German first line.

The attack of the Hood on the right supported by the Drake was very successful; keeping well up to the barrage and covered by the slope of the river valley, they were soon in the Dotted Green Line, here Colonel Freyberg, commanding the Hood, displayed his great initiative and gallantry, and without waiting for the Drake to pass through he pushed on and seized the Green Line, where he was joined by the remnants of the Drake who had lost heavily in the barrage, including their commanding officer, Lieutenant-Colonel A. S. Tetley, R.M.L.I., who was killed.

The Hawke, next to them, were not so fortunate; both they and the Howe on their left came up against a strong point, a redoubt between the 1st and 2nd line of the enemy, that had been missed by the Artillery; a few of the Hawkes reached the Dotted Green Line, but the commanding officer, Lieutenant-Colonel L. Wilson, R.M.L.I. was seriously wounded. The Nelson pushing on to pass though the Hawke came against the same redoubt; the majority of the battalion including their Commanding Officer, Lieutenant-Colonel N. O. Burge, R.M.L.I, fell around the redoubt, and only isolated parties struggled through to the Green Line. The right flank of the Howe was uncovered by the failure of the Hawke and Nelson to get past the redoubt, but they seized the 1st and 2nd German lines and after a severe fight a portion established themselves in the German third line. Parties of the Anson passed through them and fought their way on to the Green Line, a fact which was unknown to the Divisional Headquarters and even to the Hood on their right. The Anson also lost their commanding officer, Lieut.-Colonel F. Saunders, D.S.O., R.M.L.I., who was killed.

The 3rd and 4th waves of the 1/R.M.L.I., in spite of their losses, established themselves in the 1st and 2nd German lines, but only isolated parties of the 1st and 2nd waves got into the 3rd line.

The 2/R.M.L.I., who had crossed the line dribbling a football (now in the possession of the Portsmouth Division), on passing through the 1/R.M.L.I. became involved in hand-to-hand fighting in the 3rd line, but parties got through and joined the Anson on the Green Line across the station road and at 11 a.m. another party reported being in touch with 51st Division west of the station road.

At 7-30 a.m. Lieut.-Colonels Hutchison and Cartwright went forward with their headquarters to the 2nd line to superintend the further advance; at which time the redoubt was still holding up the supporting Brigade, the 190th.

LIEUT.-COLONEL A. R H. HUTCHISON, C.B., C.M.G., D.S.O., RM.L.I.
D.A.A.G., Royal Marines, 1914-15; Commandant, 2nd Battalion R.M.L.I., 1915-17; Appointed Temp-Brigadier-General commanding 190th Infantry Brigade, 1917-18; A.A.G., Royal Marines, 1918-21; Colonel-Commandant. Chatham Division, 1921-24; Adjutant-General, Royal Marines, 1924.

R.M.L.I. Battalions In France

The advance to the Yellow Line was timed to begin at 7-30 a.m. and the barrage commenced at that time; Hood and Drake advanced at once and seized the trench in front of Beaucourt, where they established themselves; parties of the Anson under Lieut.-Commander Gilliland with details of the 1st and 2nd R.M.L.I. also advanced to the Yellow Line, isolated parties of the 1st following the barrage to that line; on the left the 51st Division did not capture Beaumont till after a fine attack in the afternoon, so that the flank of the Royal Marines was uncovered till then and had to be closed.

The Headquarters of both Royal Marine Battalions which were together, were in touch with their Brigade Headquarters as Colonel Hutchison had run a telephone wire up to the 3rd German line.

The following account of this move is given by the 2nd Battalion Signal Sergeant, Meatyard (Plymouth): "Receiving a certain code word, the C.O., Adjutant and our headquarter staff went over amidst not many shells but plenty of spitting bullets and arrived at a German trench which under previous arrangements was now the advanced telephone station. From here I received orders to lay a wire to a certain position ahead and with Private Peach proceeded to lay the wire forward, unreeling as we went along. Almost everything had been hit with shell and it was one continual mass of debris and mud, and pools, some half filled with water and many badly wounded men lying helpless. Eventually reaching the position I connected up and got through to headquarters (Brigade) Many around me were getting sniped and as the Commanding Officer came along I gave him the tip to keep very low, which he did. The Adjutant, Captain Farquharson, was wounded here, and was wounded again whilst going back; Captain Muntz, Adjutant of 1/R.M.L.I. was also sniped here, being shot in the head (from which he afterwards died). The German trench we were now in was in a chronic state, once you took a step you had a job to get your leg out, the mud being so deep and sticky. Wounded Germans and our own men were lying about all over the place; what had been dug-outs were now partly closed by the muddy landslides that had taken place as the result of our gun fire and choked the entrances. The telephone was working well and I was in communication with Brigade. German prisoners were now coming in in large numbers holding up their hands and saying 'Finny.'"

At 9-15 a.m. Colonel Freyberg was anxious to advance to the Red Line, but General Shute decided not to advance until 188th and 190th Brigades had cleared up the position on the left; so the attack was therefore postponed. The Hood attack was one of the earliest examples of the "soft spot tactics," where the initiative and resolution of the leader on the spot gained such a signal success.

Lieut.-Colonel Freyberg was awarded the Victoria Cross for his gallantry on this day.

At 9-30 a.m. General Prentice ordered all battalions of the 188th Brigade to advance to the Green Line, and a ten minute barrage was put down by the artillery, under which Colonels Hutchison and Cartwright with the men of the R.M.L.I. Battalions advanced. In spite of the flanking fire from the still untaken strong point on their right and the German dug-outs on their left (in front of the 51st Division) they seized a line west of the Station Road, making a block on the right against the strong point with a party of the Ansons under Captain Gowney, R.M.L.I., Adjutant of that Battalion. Lieutenant-Colonel Cartwright who had gone forward to the front line, re-organised and supervised the mixed parties of men of different units, and pushed forward to this line; he was awarded the D.S.O. for gallantry and good leadership[32].

The following is an account of the attack of the 2/R.M.L.I.: "the C.O. waving his cap shouted 'come

---

32. The strong point on the right was firing at them with machine guns, and the commanding officer asked the liaison officer (artillery), to open up a barrage on the next trench, but the guns about 12-20 p.m. opened on them instead; the artillery officer could not get the batteries to understand, and as the position was desperate the signal sergeant asked to be allowed to send the message and as he was more used to it he succeeded in stopping the guns and a message was sent to lengthen the range.

on Royal Marines' and over they went to the next trench. The signallers joined on another reel of wire and ran forward and dropping into shell holes worked their way forward and connected up the wire in the new trench, the sergeant who was a crack shot had just before dropped three enemy snipers who were interfering with the telephone men. Private C. O. Turner, a short service recruit, always ready for work, had brought up the aeroplane shutter which was awkward and heavy to carry. Arrived in the trench Sergeant Love, the orderly room sergeant, saw to the consolidating whilst Sergeant Meatyard got the telephone through. During the evening touch was gained with the 4th Gordons on the left."

During the night the Battalions fought their way forward and by 4 a.m. on 14th Colonels Hutchison and Cartwright with the remnants of the Royal Marine Battalions and Captain Gowney with a party of the Anson dug in in two lines east of the Station Road on the Green Line. Colonel Hutchison, when the attack was checked, rallied and re-organised the line and led it forward, and then most ably supervised the consolidation for which he was awarded the D.S.O.

Another account says "at dawn they advanced over the sunken road and established communication with the trench they had just left by visual from whence it was passed on to brigade by telephone. When the contact plane came out early on 14th they were addressed by red flares and the foremost station had the battalion sign laid out and by means of the aeroplane shutter were able to signal to the plane; the signallers were very pleased as this battalion was the only one to communicate with the plane by means of the shutter." Sergeant Meatyard who was seriously wounded whilst taking in a visual signal was awarded the Military Medal.

During the morning of the 14th, Tanks came forward and took the strong point and so enabled the Howe Battalion to come up and extend the line; the parties that had reached the Yellow Line were not sufficiently strong to close the gap between the H.A.C. of the Reserve Brigade who had come up in the right centre and the Battalions on the left and by this time these parties had come back to the Green Line, where they consolidated; the scattered parties were collected and received some reinforcements from the transport lines.

Colonel Hutchison only had one officer fit for duty, Lieutenant J. Campbell, all the rest having become casualties; whilst the 1st Battalion in addition to Colonel Cartwright only had Lieutenant Van Praagh and Captain Nourse (who had come up as reinforcement) unwounded. The Battalions remained on this line under heavy shell fire till relieved on 15th by the 37th Division, 2/R.M.L.I. being relieved at 12 noon, and 1/R.M.L.I. at 2 p.m., when they marched to Hedauville via Engelbelmer.

On 16th they were moved in motor lorries to Puchevillers. 1/R.M.L.I. who had gone into action 400 strong in spite of reinforcements returned with 138, having had 47 killed, 210 wounded and 85 missing. Of the 23 officers, six were killed, 12 wounded and three missing. The missing were all killed.

On 17th they moved, 1/R.M.L.I. to Morlay and Ponthoise and 2/R.M.L.I. to Romaine arriving on 24th, having marched via Bernaville (where they rested three days to clean up) – Cramant – Froyelles – Brailly - Le Titre - Forest L'Abbaye. Here they remained training and assimilating reinforcements till 12th December, when 2/R.M.L.I. moved to Rue and 1/R.M.L.I. to Vron. On 14th 1st Bn. received Captain E. J. Huskisson, appointed Adjutant and 11 subaltern officers, and 2/R.M.L.I. Capt. H. B. Inman and 14 subalterns as reinforcements.

The 2/R.M.L.I. moved to Vron on 19th, Surgeon Ross rejoining on 20th. The Battalions remained here till 13th January, 1917 when 1/R.M.L.I. moved to Sailly Bray and 2/R.M.L.I. to Le Titre. They now marched back to Engelbelmer, the transport having a very bad time owing to the ice and snow; The

2/R.M.L.I. relieved the 7/Sherwood Foresters in the St. Pierre Divion Sector on 19th; the 1/R.M.L.I. remaining at Beauquesne and moving to Engelbelmer by 'bus on 20th and on 25th relieved the 2/R.M.L.I. in the line; the left of the line was on the south bank of the Ancre, about 100 yards west of Grandcourt.

OPERATIONS ON THE ANCRE (11th January-13th March. 1917). (See Map 6.)

The German line ran through Serre to Puisieux and thence through Beauregard Dovecote to Miraumont and Pys with an outpost at Grandcourt. On the night of 18/19th January the 188th Brigade was south of the river in the St. Pierre Divion Sector, and the 189th Brigade on the north bank was opposite Beaucourt.

They were now in the area Engelbelmer – Martinsart - Aveluy which was to be the scene of so many of their later exploits. On 22nd Lieutenant Spinney of the Intelligence Corps and two of the 2/R.M.L.I. scouts captured an enemy outpost of four men about noon. On the 24th Lieutenant Spinney with Lieutenant Wrenn and a small party of 2/R.M.L.I. repeated the raid, but they found the enemy on the alert and were received with bombs; one of the enemy was killed but unfortunately Lieutenant Spinney was mortally wounded, and Lieutenant Wrenn slightly wounded.

When in support the Battalions occupied the St. Pierre Divion Tunnel, or else the German dug-outs in Thiepval. The tunnel was about 3,000 yards behind the front line, and was a wonderful piece of engineering; it was 200 yards long, bored through the side of the hill, and about 50 feet inside. the hill; it consisted of a main passage with rooms leading off it; passages led to officers' quarters and hospital. There were passages and rooms above, but owing to the dirty habits of the Germans these were blocked up when the British occupied the place. On the top of the hill were deep dug outs which could not be occupied owing to the yellowish fumes which were continually coming up; they were connected with the tunnel below. At this time the weather was bitterly cold.

On night of 3rd February, the 189th Brigade attacked Puisieux and the River Trench, the 2/R.M.L.I. co-operated from the south side of the river by Lewis gun fire against the enemy trenches in their front immediately south of Grand court; on the morning of the 4th the 2/R.M.L.I. could see that the enemy were counter-attacking the 189th very heavily, but the situation was well in hand and the latter maintained its hold on the spur in front of Miraumont.

On 5th February 2/R.M.L.I. (Major Miller being in temporary command) reported a fire in the German trench named O.G. 1, which ran in front of Grandcourt; the fire lasted for four hours and at midnight an officer's patrol under Capt. Inman found the trench deserted as far down as the river; it was occupied at 3 p.m. on 6th by a platoon and a Lewis gun, which was reinforced by another platoon at 4-15 p.m. Officers' patrols reconnoitred Grandcourt and entered it during the night, where they were fired on. One. patrol however, moved east round the south of Grandcourt and reached the cemetery without opposition. In the early morning of 7th the patrols worked east through the village also without opposition and "B" Company, Captain Inman, and "C" Company, Captain Cutcher, occupied Grandcourt and dug in on a line round the eastern edge of the village as far as the cemetery, which was about two miles in front of our old line; one company was in support on a north and south line through Grandcourt and the reserve was in the old British line. The fact of the retirement of the enemy was established and the German retreat to the Hindenburg line had begun; Captain Inman was awarded the Military Cross.

On 5th February the Divisional Labour Company was formed of N.C.O.'s and men from the battalions who were medically unfit for the trenches.

On 8th February 1/R.M.L.I. Relieved 2/R.M.L.1. in Grandcourt but were themselves relieved on 9/10th by 12/Middlesex and marched to Martinsart.

ACTIONS OF MIRAUMONT 17th and 18th February, 1917. (See Map 6.)

On 14/15 February, 1/R.M.L.I. relieved the 10/R.D.F. in the river Ancre sector north of the river, and just abreast of Grandcourt. "B" and "D"Companies in Puisieux Trench, headquarters in Puisieux sunken road north of Beaucourt. On 16th Battalion Headquarters moved forward to Puisieux trench and the Battalion lined up for attack at 10 p.m. The 188th Brigade had been ordered to complete the capture of the spur in front of Miraumont, which the 189th had seized on 3rd February.

The objective was the sunken road running north from Baillescourt Farm, about half a mile in front of the British front line; it included two strong points one known as "The Pimple." Posts were to be established 50 yards beyond the road; the trenches from which they were to attack were a line of shell holes joined in some places, but the trench system which had been battered out of all recognition lay on a large round topped hill with no landmarks of any kind, and during the days preceding the attack, ration parties, orderlies and patrols were constantly losing themselves.

The officers of the battalion in the attack were :-

Lieut.-Colonel Cartwright, Major H. Ozanne "D" Company (*wounded*), Major F. Wellesley*. (*wounded*), Captains E. Huskisson (*wounded*), J. Pearson, Lieutenant H. W. Hall, A. C. Donne (*wounded*), L. W. Robinson (*killed*), Second-Lieutenants A. A. O'Kell (*killed*), F. Savage (*killed*), E. Sanderson (*wounded*), C. R. Burton (*killed*), W. C. Girdlestone (*wounded*), E. G. Coulson (*killed*), C. W. Rugg (*wounded*), R. E. Champness, F. W. A. Perry (*killed*), H. C. Brown (*killed*), Surgeon Unthank.

The 188th Brigade were to attack, the Howe on the right, 1/R.M.L.I. on the left; two companies of 2/R.M.L.I. were lent to the first Battalion to form a defensive flank on left.

The thaw had set in and the ground was in a terrible state. Zero hour was fixed for 5-45 a.m. on 17th; the Battalions advanced at that hour and gained their objectives; the Howe easily, the 1/R.M.L.I. encountered more formidable opposition, but had gained the sunken road and the "Pimple" by 6-40 a.m. The hill from which they advanced had been shelled continuously for over seven months, and it is probable that the iron affected the compasses, because the R.E. officer, who laid out the tape for jumping off, advanced the left of the line so that instead of advancing straight to the front "A" Company (Captain Pearson) and "B" Company (Major Wellesley) started in a diagonal direction to the right, with the result that by the time they were in the neighbourhood of the "Pimple" they had closed in on to "C" and "D" Companies, leaving the left of the objective untouched. This affected 2/R.M.L.I. who had told off seven parties of one N.C.O. and 10 privates each from "B" Company as consolidating parties, to move in file behind the second attacking wave of the 1st Battalion and on reaching a certain point which was marked, they were to march along a tape line running north-east and dig posts at 80 yards interval, No.7 occupying the marked point. They were covered by battle patrols from "A" Company who were to be withdrawn at dark; owing to the deflection of 1/R.M.L.I. touch was not gained till dark, and considerable anxiety existed as it was known that the 1/R.M.L.I. had gained the sunken road.

The mistake of "A" and "B" Companies was in a way fortunate, as there was a great deal of wire in front of "A's"objective and none in front of "C." "A" and "B" Companies were reorganised and attacking from right to left took the strong point in rear with hardly any casualties.

During this advance Captain Pearson commanding "A" Company, looking to his left saw an enemy machine-gun being got up out of its hole and brought into action; he picked off one man with his rifle and shot another, he was then joined by Lieutenant Sanderson and between them they picked off five men and the enemy gave up the attempt; if the gun had been brought into action it would have swept the sunken road, which was packed with men as they were reorganising and would have turned a great success in to a dreadful failure. Captain Pearson was awarded the Military Cross. When "A" and "B" Companies made the attack to their left they captured about 60 prisoners.

Major Ozanne, "D" Company, captured the "Pimple" at 6-40 a.m. Sergeant W. G. Scott (Plymouth) organising a party of bombers and attacking it from the rear where the entrance was situated, he was awarded the D.C.M. Headquarters were established in the road, the four companies who were holding the objective had been reduced to 200 men on a front of 1000 yards, and touch was still being sought with 2/R.M.L.I. At dusk two platoons of the Hood came up and formed a support west of the sunken road.

At 7-30 a.m. on 18th the enemy put down a barrage on the road, but did not attack, the atmosphere being very misty. At 10-30 a.m. as the mist was clearing Captain Pearson reported that a German counter-attack was less than 300 yards away but fortunately at this moment the signalmen, who had maintained communication under the greatest difficulties, reported that the line was working to Battalion headquarters and the S.O.S. signal was answered in two minutes by a magnificent barrage from the guns; the strength of the enemy was estimated at two battalions; the one on the left turned and fled and was soon followed by the battalion on the right.

This led to an amusing incident, Major Ozanne in reporting to Battalion Headquarters added "Boche bolting like rabbits" the commanding officer in passing on the report thinking he was speaking to the signal officer, repeated the addition; horrified to realise that the Brigadier was at the other end he reported "Enemy retiring hastily Sir, helped by our fire." However "Boche bolting like rabbits" went through to Corps and Army Headquarters and was well received. The rest of the day was marked by heavy shelling and the thaw increasing. On night 18/19 1/R.M.L.I. were relieved by 2/R.M.L.I. who had themselves been relieved by a battalion of the 190th Brigade. The 2/R.M.L.I. took over the line of their own flanking posts, and the strong points, in the sunken road. Owing to mud the first company did not get up till 4 a.m. and the last company did not arrive till after dawn, fortunately there was a mist and the reliefs were successfully carried out. The 2/R.M.L.I. occupied the road with "C" Company (Captain Cutcher), the line consisting of four strong points each of half a platoon with a Lewis gun, the remainder of the platoons were in three posts about 30 yards in front of the old enemy strong points. During the relief the S.O.S. signal had to be made again and the enemy's threatened counter-attack was soon crushed. The 1/R.M.L.I were not molested in their return to rest, the enemy having definitely retreated.

The Commander-in-Chief, departing from his usual practice sent his congratulatory message direct to Brigadier-General Prentice: "Warmest congratulations on success of your operations on 17th." Major Ozanne was awarded the D.S.O. for directing the consolidation of the position with marked ability and to his courage and determination was largely due the holding of the position against enemy counter attacks. Twelve N.C.O.s and men were awarded the Military Medal (see end of chapter).

In addition to the officers named above the 2/R.M.L.I. casualties included Lieutenant H. E. Bennie, died of wounds and 2nd Lieutenants C. C. Palmer, Captain H. B. Inman and Lieutenants H. A. Taplin, J. S. Lee, P. R. Hardy and R. J. Williams wounded; of the 16 officers and 500 men of the 1/R.M.L.I. who commenced the attack, only three officers and 100 men remained fit for duty. The Adjutant (Captain Huskisson) buried as many as possible of those in the line of the attack, erecting crosses with the dead man's number and name written on a piece of paper and placed in a bottle at the foot of each cross, later zinc plates stamped with the names were put on the crosses; this was officially known as the Royal Marine Cemetery.

On 22nd 1/R.M.L.I. on relief by 10/R.D.F. marched to Engelbelmer, being met at Martinsart by the band of the Depot from Deal which played them in to billets; from then till the end of the month both Battalions were occupied in re-organising and in providing working parties on the roads; they remained at Engelbelmer and near Aveluy till 19th March working and training, on which date they marched to Labourse (see Map 7) arriving on 30th having marched via Gezaincourt – Bouret – Croisette – Sains - les Pernes – Erquedecques - Calonne sur la Lys - Hesdigneul, here they remained till 7th April. These marches were very exhausting as they experienced bitter northerly head winds, and the men's kit, etc., weighed about 96 lbs.

The 1/R.M.L.I. then moved into the front line in the Angres sector in their old neighbourhood, three companies in front line and one company in Mechanics Trench; during their tour in these trenches the Canadians captured the Vimy Ridge about five miles to their right. (The Battalion was in the area recognised as participating in the battle).

The Battle of Arras (1917) was commencing and the Royal Naval Division had been moved up to take their share in it. On 10th April Captain V. H. Jones took over command of "D" Company and Captain J. Goldsmith of "C" Company 1/R.M.L.I. On the 13th this Battalion was ordered to send out patrols in the evening to ascertain if the enemy had vacated his trenches; the patrols went through the northern part of Angres and the right patrol passed through Bois de Rollencourt and Rollencourt village; the left patrol moved along the communication trenches to Cite de Cornailles and the southern edge of Lievin and found all deserted; a third patrol under Captain Huskisson captured three Germans and obtained some useful information; by 9 p.m. posts were established in the German lines, the old German 1st line forming their Reserve line; that night they were relieved by 3/Rifle Brigade and returned to Bully Grenay, moving on 15th to Maroeuil; on 21st Captain Huskisson took over "B" Company, Lieutenant Van Praagh becoming Adjutant; on the 24th the 1/R.M.L.I. rejoined ,the remainder of the Division which had been resting at Arras.

CAPTURE OF GAVRELLE (23-24th April). (See Map 7 and Plan 19.)

The remainder of the Royal Naval Division were now called on to take part in the Second Battle of the Scarpe and to attack; the 189th and 190th Brigades were detailed to capture the Gavrelle spur which they successfully accomplished after a very fine attack, on 24th and 25th April the 188th Brigade being in reserve. On 24th "B" Company 1/R.M.L.I. were ordered to proceed at 8 p.m. with about 250 men to a point east of Bailleul, opposite Oppy, and remove a large dump of ammunition, barbed wire, bombs, etc. to a position on the western edge of Gavrelle village (just captured), the way lay along a ravine running along the south side of Bailleul, across which large trees were lying, making progress very slow, especially on the return journey when the men were laden with rolls of wire and ammunition; they reached the dump and started back for Gavrelle about a mile away and Captain Huskisson tried to cut across the ravine, but was warned by troops waiting to attack and had to go back through it, and then moved across the Arras - Gavrelle road and down an old German communication trench, successfully completing their job at 4 a.m. in spite of heavy shell fire.

On 26th the 188th Brigade relieved the 189th, 1/R.M.L.1. holding the left of the line, then 1/H.A.C., the 2/R.M.L.I. next, and the Ansons on the right.

BATTLE OF ARLEUX (28th and 29th April) CAPTURE OF GAVRELLE WINDMILL.

On 28th the 1st and 2nd Battalions Royal Marines were ordered to attack; the objectives of 1/R.M.L.I. being the German trenches in their front, and of the 2/R.M.L.I. the Gavrelle Windmill and the German trenches to the south of it; The Ansons were to form a defensive flank on the right of 2/R.M.L.I. as the Army on the right was not to advance. 1/R.M.L.I. were to attack the line that ran from Oppy to Mericourt, and endeavour to come up into line with the 2nd Battalion, but as zero hour was fixed at the same time for both Battalions, it was obvious that the 2nd Battalion would have both flanks in the air at the commencement of the attack.

Dealing first with 1/R.M.L.I. "B" Company Major Huskisson had been sent on night 26/27 April to occupy a small isolated trench about midway between Oppy and Gavrelle (C-D on plan), which was done at 3 a.m. 27th; when the enemy's wire was reconnoitred it was found to be very strong and uncut, and the two runners with this information were unable to get through during the 27th owing to the heavy shelling; rations also were very short. The tape had been laid out for the attack of the Essex Regiment on their left, but that for 1/R.M.L.I. was not laid out by the R.E., consequently on the night of the attack Major Huskisson extended his company on the jumping off line for the Battalion to form on in prolongation of the Essex Regiment's tape; the objectives of the several companies are shown on plan 19, "B" Company having to pass through the others to attack the furthest objective. The company commanders were "A" Company, Lieutenant N. Lion (killed), "C" Company, Captain Goldsmith (died of wounds), "D" Company, Captain V. H. Jones (died of wounds), "B" Company Major Huskisson; C.S.M. Rogers (Chatham) rendered very good service with the guides in bringing up both the Essex Regiment and the 1/R.M.L.I. to the jumping off line and was awarded the Military Medal.

Zero hour was 4-30 a.m. 28th, the Windmill to be attacked by the 2nd Battalion stood out very conspicuously on the sky line. The enemy were evidently expecting an attack as their guns replied immediately to the barrage. Our artillery had failed to cut the wire and when the Battalion advanced they found the wire absolutely impenetrable and were forced to consolidate in shell holes in front of it; one officer and about 30 men apparently did force their way through and when their ammunition was expended they were made prisoners; the Essex Regiment also had failed to penetrate the wire as did the Battalions detailed to attack the following night. Lieut.-Colonel Cartwright, soon after the attack commenced, in getting out of the trench to redirect a Lewis gun section, was shot in the stomach and died of his wounds on 30th April; a very great loss to the Battalion and Corps where his splendid character was highly appreciated. The enemy constantly counter-attacked the 1/R.M.L.I. who maintained their position though unable to make any further progress in spite of the assistance of the very gallant bombing attacks by the H.A.C. from the flank. Major Huskisson was awarded the Military Cross for his gallantry in reconnoitring the position, and for his good work in organising the guides and aligning his company as a mark which enabled the Battalion to be formed up for the assault; the attack failed owing to several causes: the enemy were aware of the intention to attack, there was inadequate artillery preparation, and the jumping off place was on a forward slope so that all movements were visible against the sky line.

Meanwhile on the right, the 2/R.M.L.I. attacked the Windmill and trenches to the south of it. The Battalion advanced on its objective under the barrage, but the Anson company which was to form the defensive flank came under heavy fire and owing to their serious casualties were unable to connect up and a reserve company was sent up. The 2/R.M.L.I. had already passed on and at 7-45 a.m. Colonel Hutchison reported that the first objective had been taken and that the troops were going well to the second line.

Machine-gun fire and sniping from both flanks made it almost impossible for information to get back. The Commanding Officer reported later that the Battalion had gone on to its objective, but that the enemy had closed in on the flanks; as a matter of fact the barrage was bad and the wire was only cut in one place,

PLAN 19

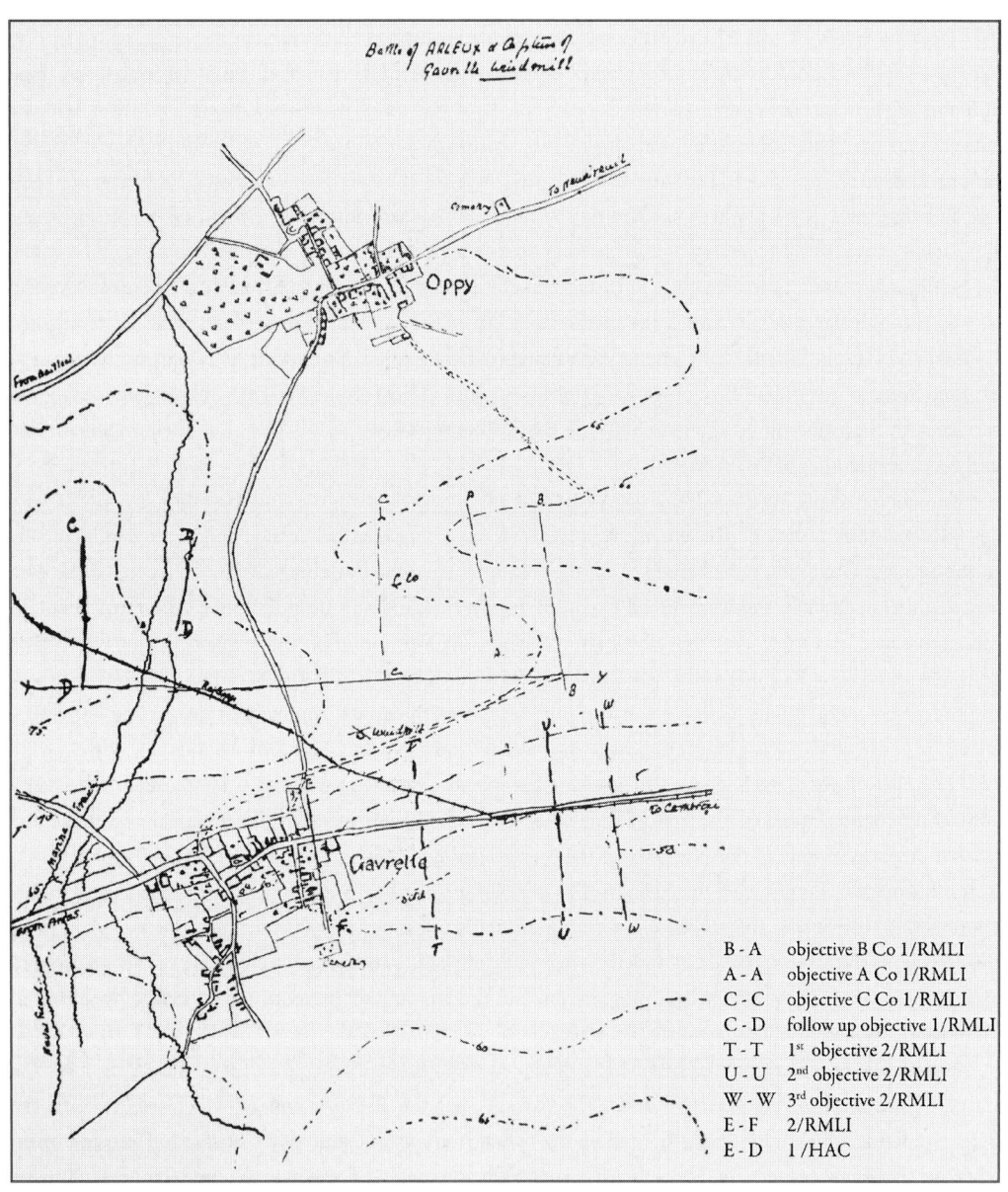

B - A objective B Co 1/RMLI
A - A objective A Co 1/RMLI
C - C objective C Co 1/RMLI
C - D follow up objective 1/RMLI
T - T 1st objective 2/RMLI
U - U 2nd objective 2/RMLI
W - W 3rd objective 2/RMLI
E - F 2/RMLI
E - D 1/HAC

"A" "C" and "D" Companies streamed through and reached their objective but they had overlooked a trench immediately behind the wire and were cut off; after very heavy losses the remnants were captured by the enemy.

In the meantime Lieutenant Newling with his platoon of Major Eagle's company advanced and captured the Windmill with about 100 prisoners, whom they sent back without escort; he then most gallantly held the Windmill all day against violent counter-attacks; the other three platoons of "B" Company had followed the other companies but were held up by machine-gun fire and dug in. For many hours the old front line was held by the orderly room sergeant (Sergeant W. Love, Portsmouth) and two privates who patrolled it.

During the day, one of the headquarter runners (Private London) went out four times to the Windmill with messages, and Colonel Hutchison also visited the post to make what arrangements were possible; "B" Company had seized and were holding the German front line and during the night 28/29 they reinforced Lieutenant Newling at the Windmill; Lieutenant Newling was awarded the Military Cross for his gallantry and determination.

At one time the attacks on the l/R.M.L.I. were so threatening that Colonel Hutchison took his headquarters (signallers, cooks, etc.) and reinforced the left of the H.A.C. to help repel the attacks. The counter-attacks were all beaten off and the Windmill position was consolidated and held; the Howe Battalion was sent up at night to hold the front line and the R.M. Battalions were relieved on night of 29/30th.

The 190th Machine Gun Company had participated in the attack and rendered most valuable service, suffering heavy casualties.

The capture of the Windmill position rendered this portion of the line secure for many months.

In addition to Lieutenant Newling, 2nd Lieutenant E. A. Godfrey was awarded the Military Cross for working the guns of the trench mortar battery with great skill and gallantry for 60 hours without a rest, under heavy enemy fire against an enemy strong point which eventually surrendered, whilst Lance-Corporal T. Salt (Chatham) was awarded the D.C.M. for crawling backwards and forwards for three hours under heavy high explosive barrage to signal the effect of the Stokes mortar fire and Private Glyndwyer Davies (Plymouth) was also awarded the D.C.M. for advancing alone to a strong point, demanding its surrender and singlehanded bringing in 50 prisoners, a considerable number of Military Medals were also awarded (see end of chapter). The D.C.M. was awarded to Acting Corporal W. A. Watts (Plymouth) of the T.M. battery who kept command of his detachment though wounded, and continued to fire his gun for four hours until again severely wounded, when he had to be carried away.

In l/R.M.L.I. in addition to Colonel Cartwright and Captains Goldsmith and Jones, Lieutenants Lion and Fielding were killed and Captain Pearson, M.C., and Lieutenants Atkinson, Evans, Roberts, Kenny, Perry, and J. W. Thomas were wounded.

In 2/R.M.L.I. Captains Burton-Fanning and J. Campbell, Lieutenants Kearney, W. A. Lake, P. R. Hardy, D. H. Walker, H. E. Markham were missing and later reported killed and Lieutenant R. H. Marsland, A. E. Hughes and Lieutenant R. S. Wilkie (machine gun company) wounded.

A man named Powell 1/R.M.L.I. is reported to have had a very terrifying experience; a shell exploded and buried him up to his neck, and he remained buried for two days, when he was discovered by passing troops, who dug him out; although he was asked if he wanted to go back for a rest, he at once volunteered for company runner.

Among those taken prisoner was Company Sergeant-Major Chapman, who was wounded and died of his wounds in Germany; he joined the Brigade at the outset as a bugler and after serving throughout Gallipoli, rose to the rank of Company Sergeant Major; he was a very fine non commissioned officer, who like so many others, commenced his career in the Drums.

[By permission Of the Imperial War Museum.]
TROOPS RESTING PRIOR TO AN ATTACK.

[By permission Of the Imperial War Museum.]
TROOPS RETURNING FROM FRONT LINES IN YPRES SALIENT, 1917.

The Division after a rest and re-organisation remained in this area. Lieutenant-Colonel Hutchison was promoted to command the 190th Brigade with rank of Brigadier-General and was succeeded in command by Major (T/Lieut.-Colonel) L. W. Miller. Capt. C. G. Farquharson who had recovered from his wounds, resumed duty as Adjutant. Major (T/Lieut.-Colonel) H. Ozanne became Commanding Officer of 1/R.M.L.I. vice Cartwright.

During the period of rest the Divisional Horse Show was held on 14th June; the 1/R.M.L.I. won the prize for battalion transport having to show one water cart, one cooker, one limbered wagon with pair of horses, one limbered wagon with pair of mules and two pack animals under a mounted non-commissioned officer. They also gained a prize in a special competition for the best limbered wagon.

The Royal Naval Division carried out the preparatory work for an attack by the 5th and 31st Divisions on the front Oppy - Gavrelle on 28th June which was successful.

Whilst in the Oppy - Gavrelle sector the R.M.L.I. Battalions were inspected by Admiral Lord Charles Beresford, who had been appointed Honorary Colonel of the Royal Marine Brigade when it joined the Royal Naval Division in 1914.

On 24th June Major E. K. Fletcher and G. C. Wainwright joined the 1st and 2nd Battalions respectively as second in command.

On 4/5th July the Division took over the old sector at Gavrelle and the Brigade sector on the left of it. On the right the 188th Brigade held Gavrelle with two Battalions and on the left the 189th had three Battalions in the line.

On 12th July the additional Brigade sector was given over, and on 14-15th a new front line was dug in Oppy Wood by the Hawke and Hood and another in front of the Windmill by the 2/R.M.L.I. Reliefs were arranged triangularly in order that the 188th Brigade should always hold the Windmill sector. The two Royal Marine Battalions were in the Gavrelle right sub-sector, from the right of the Windmill to the junction of Cairo Alley and Cadorna Trench, with the Battalion Headquarters in Marine trench; on 4th July this front was extended to the right southwards to Thames Alley and Chico Trench. From now on till the end of September they remained in this sector, the two Battalions relieving each other in front line, the usual procedure being four days in front line, three in support then another spell in front line and then to reserve; when in reserve they were at Maison Blanche or else Beverley Camp, Roclincourt.

The normal trench routine of working, watching and repairing trenches with its daily toll of casualties went on, with training whilst in support and reserve; officers and men being sent to the various Army and Corps schools of instruction.

In July, Colonel Ozanne was in hospital for a short time, Major Fletcher being in command, and on 18th July 1/R.M.L.I. commenced a new trench in front of the Windmill from a point in Cecil Trench, north-east of the Windmill to the northern end of Chico Trench, which was completed on 21st and the Divisional Commander expressed his satisfaction at the work done by the Battalion. The weather in August was very wet and the trenches required a great deal of attention; Major Fletcher also went to hospital on 9th August. On the 16th whilst going round the trenches Lieut.-Colonel Miller fell and broke his ankle, and was relieved in command of 2/R.M.L.I. by Major Wainwright. On 17th 2/R.M.L.I. were relieved by Hood Battalion and moved to Frevillers for training, Major G. L. Parry who had joined from England being temporarily in command; here they remained till 2nd October. On 22nd 1/R.M.L.I. moved to Bailleul aux Cornailles for training; the Battalions received reinforcements from the Base, and were warned that they would shortly be transferred from XIII. Corps to the XVIII. Corps in the North to take part in the battle then going on north and east of Ypres. During the training one diary recalls the practice known as "lorry jumping" a practice well-known to regimental officers and men, who when they wanted to visit a village to get stores or to go to dentist, etc., used to jump on to a lorry going roughly in the direction they wanted and then jumping off, and boarding another when the first diverged, until eventually their destination was reached.

The following letter dated 17/9/17 was received from Captain J. S. Campbell, R.F.A., the 63rd Division Trench Mortar Officer and is interesting as illustrating the work of the R.M.L.I. Trench Mortar Battery during 1916 and 1917 :-

"Having had the honour of commanding a small section of the Corps for the last fifteen months, namely the trench mortars of the Division in France, I thought it may be of interest to know that this little unit composed of R.M.L.I., and numbering only about 60 of all ranks, has won for itself a reputation worthy of the Regiment. In the last fifteen months, one D.C.M., and 10 Military Medals, including one Bar have been awarded to the R.M.L.I. personnel, for gallantry in the field. In addition the unit has been specially commended by the Army Corps, and Divisions, that we have been serving under from time to time.

"The conduct and bearing of these men at all times, their steadiness under fire, and cheerfulness under the most adverse conditions have won for them the admiration of all who have met them. For instance, once, during a bombardment by trench mortars prior to an attack, the Boche was retaliating rather heavily, one of the gun's crew though hit absolutely refused to leave his gun. He was again hit soon afterwards, rendered unconscious, and placed "on one side to await a stretcher: in the meantime he regained consciousness and attempted to stagger back to his gun."

During this period of training the Divisional Commander, General Lawrie presented four silver bugles to be competed for in cross country running, boxing, football, and bayonet combat by the units of the Division. The 1/R.M.L.I., won those for cross-country running, boxing and football, the 1/H.A.C. winning that for the bayonet combat. The bugles are now at Chatham, Plymouth and Deal Headquarters.

BATTLES OF YPRES, 1917.

SECOND BATTLE OF PASSCHENDAELE (26th October-10th November). (*See Map 5.*)

On the night of the 2nd October the Battalions marched to Tinques and entrained there for the north, 1/R.M.L.I. going to Poperinghe, and 2/R.M.L.I. to Houpoutre. The Division was now transferred to the XVIII. Corps and were to be prepared to take their part in the Passchendaele struggle that had been raging for some time.

On 5th October both Battalions embussed for Le Nouveau Monde near Wormhoudt and from then until 22nd were under intensive training for the attack to take place on 26th; in fact some considered that the training was rather overdone and that the men became stale.

The 188th Brigade were to carry out the attack on 26th, and the 190th on the 30th; therefore the 189th took over the line. The ground was in a terrible state and the Flanders mud was at its worst; owing to the delays caused by the change of plans in the winter 1916-17, which led to the abortive French attacks in Champagne; the British attack in Flanders had been postponed and only reached its culmination in the autumn weather, when the rain and mud combined with the enemy to render attacks almost impracticable.

The enemy had now also adopted the plan of placing their strong points in concrete shelters resembling pill boxes, and continuous trenches were non-existent; the attackers clung precariously to muddy shell holes, and worked forward as best they could; communications were practically impossible, men who wandered from the recognised paths were liable to be drowned in the mud, which also choked the barrels of the rifles and Lewis guns, further the mud also rendered it very difficult for the infantry to keep up with the barrage. Objectives were almost unrecognisable, and once an attack was launched, everything depended on the initiative of the platoon leaders and their N.C.O.'s.

In these conditions the attack was commenced, and to increase their difficulties rain commenced to fall at midnight on 25th, and continued steadily throughout the 26th.

On 23rd October 1/R.M:L.I. went to the Canal Bank, 1000 yards north of Ypres, and on 24th relieved the 11/Royal Scots of 9th Division in the front line on the line Inch Houses - Burns House - Oxford Houses, south-east of Poelcapelle, which was merely a line of shell holes. The 2/R.M.L.I. went to the Canal Bank, and on 24th marched to Irish Farm relieving 9th Division troops in the support line. The operations that follow took place south of the Poelcapelle – Spriet Road (map 5)

The plan of the attack was as follows: the Royal Naval Division with the 8th Brigade, 3rd Canadian Division on their right and a Brigade of the 58th Division on the left were to attack the enemy's position in front. The attack was to be made by the 188th Brigade with the Hood battalion as counter-attack battalion and the Hawke in Brigade reserve.

The northern boundary of the Brigade was the Lekkerboterbeek Stream, whilst the Paddebeek, a muddy stream, ran across the front of the Brigade making the ground still more difficult.

Two objectives were assigned to the Brigade, the first objective (AA on plan) comprised the following enemy strong points on the near side of the Paddebeek. Berks Houses, Bray Farm, Banff House, Varlet

PLAN 20.

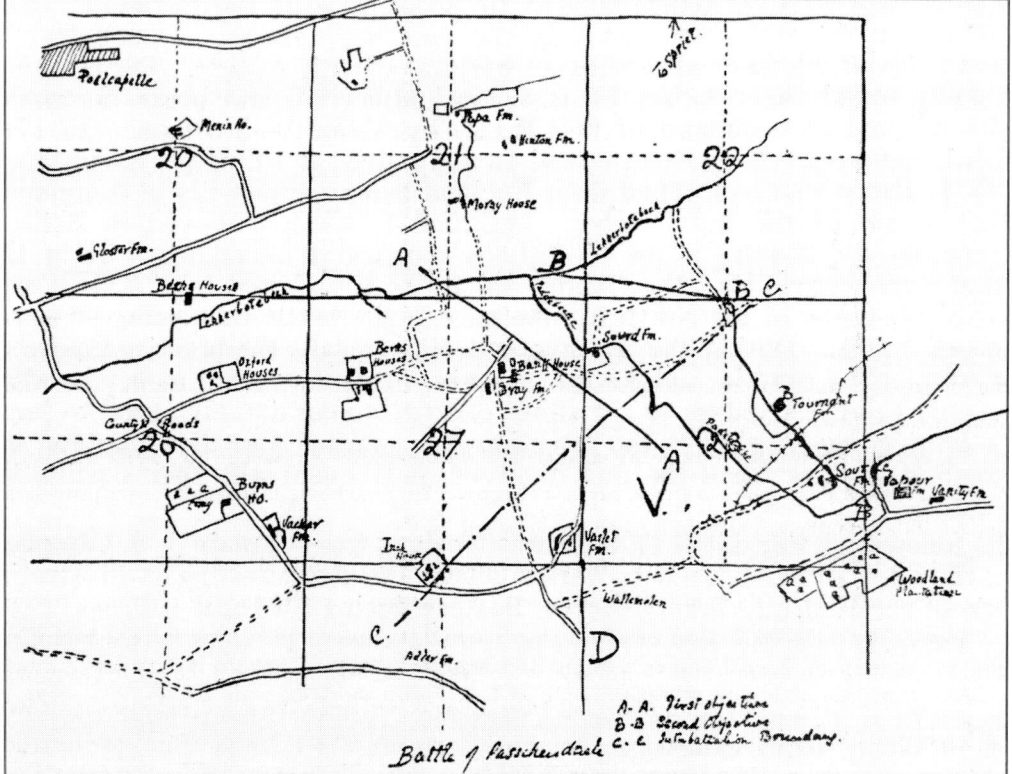

BATTLE OF PASSCHENDAELE 26 OCTOBER, 1917.

Farm. and on the right, near the Canadians, Source Trench. The furthest limit of the second objective (B B on plan) was across the Paddebeek and from left to right extended from point V. 21, d. 8. 8.-north end of house at V. 22, c. 9. O.-east end of Source Farm. The dividing line (C.C. on plan) between Battalions of the 188th Brigade was for the first advance a line from Inch Houses to V. 28 a. 2.3., for the Second from this point to the Paddebeek stream V. 28 a. 5.5. thence by the south side of the dotted track to V. 28 b. 0.9.

The Anson on the right and 1/R.M.L.I. on left were to attack the first objective, the Howe on right and 2/R.M.L.I. on left were to pass through and attack the second. The frontage of the Brigade was 1500 yards and that of 1/R.M.L.I. was 900 yards, the strength of the Battalion was only 16 officers and 597 other ranks.

The line was taken over by 188th Brigade on night 24/25th, the time was too short for proper reconnaissance, but the troops could not be kept longer in the line owing to the weather conditions.

1/R.M.L.I. commenced to line out on the tape at 8 p.m. on 25th and all battalions were in position by 2 a.m. on 26th.

In 1/R.M.L.I. the following officers took part :-

Lieut.-Colonel Ozanne, Captain Van Praagh (adjutant), Lieutenants J. M. Woods, F. C. How, Surgeon Morgan (*wounded*).

"A" Company-Second-Lieutenant Trotman (*wounded*), H. J. Jones, F. C. Balcombe (*killed*)

"B" Company-Captain B. G. Evanson (*wounded*), Second-Lieutenants W. C. Williamson (*wounded*). B. C. Pippet, and S. S. Easterbrook.

"C" Company-Captain D. A. Pipe (*killed*), Lieutenant J. E. Cornish, C. E. Mennell (*wounded*), E. C. Bonnett (*died of wounds*)

"D" Company-Lieutenant D. J. Aldridge (*killed*), Second-Lieutenant McKeand (*wounded*).

The attacking formation was three lines of skirmishers, or small columns of platoons or sections, according to the objective assigned to each. At 5-40 a.m. the barrage opened and the battalions advanced with great difficulty but 1/R.M.L.I. managed to keep well up to the barrage and gained all their objectives, including Berks Houses, Banff House and Bray Farm and reached the further limit of their objective; they suffered heavy casualties from enfilade fire on their left because the Brigade on that flank was unable to advance; Captain Van Praagh, the Adjutant, during an enemy counter-attack led a small party forward through an intense barrage to garrison one of the positions captured, and also made a useful reconnaissance, whilst 2nd Lieutenant W. C. Williamson, although wounded, led a platoon forward and captured one of the strong points which he organised under heavy fire till severely wounded a second time; they were both awarded the Military Cross.

The Anson also advanced and gained a good many of their objectives but failed to get Varlet Farm. Each platoon was given a fixed point to attack, but the defence was fluid and it was not possible for any platoon to find out if those on their right and left had been successful.

The orders for the 2/R.M.L.I. stated that passing through the 1/R.M.L.I. they were to attack with two companies in front, "A" on the right and "C" on the left, "B" Company in reserve, and "D" company carrying; the frontage allotted was 800 yards; their greatest strength was to be opposite the concreted positions at V. 28 a. 9. 9. No one was to cross to the north side of the Lekkerboterbeek stream, but the left company was to cover that area with Lewis gun fire. The following strong points were to be seized and garrisoned; five organised shell holes at V. 27, b. 7. 6; eight organised shell holes at V. 27, b. 6. 7; Sourd Farm and a concrete position at V. 28 a. 9. 9. The Battalion was directed to assemble on a line 150 yards east of Burns House - Vacher Farm Road. At 6-30 a.m. they were to pass through 1/R.M.L.I. and form for attack behind the stationary barrage at the limit of the first objective, and move forward with the barrage at 7-36 a.m.

"A" and "C" companies were to drop parties to consolidate as they went forward. The Battalion duly passed through 1/R.M.L.I. but it was only on the flanks that they were able to make any headway; "A" Company gallantly led by Lieut. P. Ligertwood, who had connected his men together with spun yarn to prevent their leaving the narrow tracks through the mud, crossed the Paddebeek and made good his position there. He had provided each platoon with a small red flag, which in the absence of regimental colours, had been blessed by the Battalion chaplain, and these were carried forward and served as rallying points for the platoons; three of these flags now rest at the Chatham, Portsmouth and Plymouth Divisions, the bearer of the fourth was killed and it was lost in the Flanders mud. Lieutenant (acting Captain) Ligertwood, although three times wounded, maintained his position, but when wounded for the fourth time and compelled to go to the rear, he pointed out the further objective and ordered his men to go forward; this very gallant officer died of his wounds[33]. The Adjutant, Captain Newling, had also been severely wounded and Lieutenant Balcombe who was killed did most gallant work, fighting personally with the bayonet.

Meanwhile the Howe on the right had no better success, and two companies of the Hood were ordered up by Commander Asquith to assist; he himself made a most wonderful reconnaissance and discovered that the Howe were not in touch with the Canadians on the right. The 2/R.M.L.I. on the left considered that they were on their objective but it was very difficult to recognise the positions; the enemy counter-attacked heavily in the afternoon and "C" Company of the Hood had also to be brought into the line. The Machine Gun Companies did excellent work, one group of batteries under Lieutenant Goldingham, R.M.L.I. was brought into action after this officer had personally reconnoitred the position for each gun, and when one of the batteries suffered heavy casualties, he reconnoitred a fresh position under heavy fire and brought it into action there, and also maintained a complicated machine-gun barrage with great effect; whilst Lieutenant Westby who was in charge of four mobile machine-guns, after making a reconnaissance under heavy fire, disposed them with such skill that he achieved his task with negligible casualties; both these officers were awarded the Military Cross.

At dusk "A" Company 2/R.M.L.I. had been forced back behind the Paddebeek and "C" Company of the Hawke had also come up into the line; by this time all positions on the near side of the Paddebeek had been consolidated, and at 5 p.m. next day, 27th, the two Battalions, R.M. were relieved by the Hawke and were withdrawn to Irish Farm. The line was in the end composed of five strong posts and represented an advance of 300-400 yards; the Army Commander, General Gough sent a message: "Please convey to all ranks engaged in to-day's operations my very great appreciation of their gallant efforts; they have my sincere sympathy, as no troops could have had to face worse conditions of mud than they had to face owing to the sudden downfall of rain this morning. No troops could have done more than our men did to-day, and given a fair chance, I have every confidence in their complete success every time."

In addition to the awards before mentioned, Surgeon McB.- Ross was awarded a bar to his Military Cross and Sergeant Priestley, Chatham R.M.L.I. was awarded the D.C.M. for leading his platoon, after his officer was a casualty, against a party of the enemy who were assembling on a flank, killing or capturing the whole party.

The 2/R.M.L.I. in addition to Captain Ligertwood lost Captain Trevor Edwards (killed), he had been with the Battalions since the very earliest days and 2nd Lieutenant T. W. Brogan and Lieutenant G. W.

---

33 Lieutenant Ligertwood, who was one of the crack shots of the Corps, was commissioned in 1916, and had proved himself a most valuable and gallant officer.

Denman-Dean were also killed. Captain Newling and Lieutenants E. D'A Barnard and R. F. Orfeur and Surgeon Ross were wounded; the Battalion also sustained a great loss in C.S.M. W.W. Love, Portsmouth R.M.L.I. who had been its orderly room sergeant since Gallipoli days and had recently been promoted to Company Sergeant Major. The 1/R.M.L.I. in addition to the officers named, suffered 270 casualties and 2/R.M.L.I. 391.

From Irish Farm the Battalions went to Danube Camp near Poperinghe to refit and re-organise, where they remained until 4th November. On 30th October Major G. L. Parry relieved Lieut.-Colonel Wainwright in command of 2/R.M.L.I. and Captain Burton resumed the duties of Adjutant vice Newling wounded; on 4th November Colonel Ozanne was sent to hospital and as he was invalided to England, Lieutenant-Colonel Bromfield, Leicester Regiment, temporarily attached, took command of 1/R.M.L.I. till 19th when Major C. G. Farquharson was appointed Commanding Officer.

On 4/5 November 2/R.M.L.I. returned to the line to relieve the Drake; "Y" Company of 1/R.M.L.I. (both Battalions had been re-organised into two companies until drafts could be provided) being attached to them, but on 7th they were relieved by 2/K.R.R.C. and returned to Irish Camp; on 8th both Battalions moved by rail to School Camp, Poperinghe, where they rested for five days; then 1/R.M.L.I. marched to Ledringham arriving there on 13th; 2/R.M.L.I. to Steenbrugge; 1/R.M.L.I. moved to Brielen and 2/R.M.L.I. to Reifersberg on 23rd. Working parties and training filled their time till the end of the month.

During this time Brig.-General J. F. Coleridge (Indian Army) had relieved General Prentice in command of the 188th Brigade. General Coleridge who commanded the Brigade so successfully till the end of the war had very close associations with the Corps; his father who was Adjutant of the Plymouth Division R.M.L.I. was killed on the Brickfields whilst on duty.

ACTION OF WELCH RIDGE.

At the end of November was fought the successful battle of Cambrai, in which the British had obtained considerable gains and had created the Flesquieres Salient which included about four miles of the front and support lines of the Hindenburg Defences in that area. On 30th November the Germans had counter-attacked and broken through at Gouzeaucourt where they were counter-attacked and stopped by the Guards Division. For adventures of the R.M.A. Howitzers see chapter 24.

A defensive flank had been made running south-west along Welch Ridge, which ran at right angles to the Hindenburg sector and was important for it commanded the approaches to Masnieres and Marcoing. The Royal Naval Division relieved the 31st and 62nd Divisions on 15-20th November. The frontage taken over was 6000 yards and included the north slopes of Welch Ridge and the whole length of the eastern face. On the right where it overhung the British Line the slope fell down steeply to the valley. This point was the Army, Army Corps and Divisional Boundary; on the left was the 19th Division and the 9th was on the right.

Before the arrival of the Royal Naval Division in this sector a German document was captured, saying that the 63rd Division would arrive shortly and that a determined resistance must be expected!

The line was very thinly held by small posts, with no reserve trenches and until 30th December the troops were occupied in improving the trenches and making the defences possible in order to settle down for the winter.

The Royal Naval Division were holding the line with two battalions of each Brigade in the line, 190th on the left, 189th in the centre, and 188th on the right: of the 188th the Howe and 1/R.M.L.I. were in the line, with 2/R.M.L.I. in support; the 1/R.M.L.I. were the right battalion.

R.M.L.I. Battalions In France

At dawn on 30th December the enemy, dressed in white suits as the ground was covered with snow, delivered a strong attack along practically the whole front of the Division, which at first met with considerable success, for the defences were penetrated at certain points, and the enemy actually gained Welch Support ; counter-attacks were delivered in the afternoon and drove the enemy out of the positions; the 1/R.M.L.I. had defeated the attack and stood fast, but the Howe on their left were driven back; the Anson temporarily commanded by Lieutenant-Commander Buckle made a fine counter-attack at night and drove the enemy out of Welch Support; Lieut.-Commander Buckle was awarded the D.S.O. The enemy, however, retained the front line and thereby deprived the British of the observation which they had hitherto enjoyed, and further the enemy were now able to observe the British rear defences. The attack was renewed on the morning of 31st in the vicinity of the centre, but was repulsed after heavy fighting. The Trench mortars rendered most valuable aid on 30th and 31st, but unfortunately Lieutenant Alan Campbell, R.N.V.R., who had commanded the R.M.L.I. Trench Mortar Battery was killed, a great loss to the Division. On these two days the defeat of the enemy attacks was largely due to the co-operation of the machine-guns, both by direct and indirect fire. Lieutenant Westby, M.C., R.M.L.I. of the Machine Gun Company and Lieutenant Gayner, 1/R.M.L.I. were killed.

1918.

During January there were no considerable activities, as the weather rendered operations impossible, whilst heavy snowfalls, followed by the thaw, made the trenches in a terrible state.

On 2nd the front was reduced to that of two Brigades, the 190th moving into reserve.

In February the 2/R.M.L.I. lost yet another Commanding Officer, Lieut.-Colonel G. L. Parry when going his rounds was hit by a sniper, when passing over an open bit of trench and died of his wounds on 2nd February, much regretted by all ranks to whom he was affectionately known as "Old Bill." Major C. G. Farquharson, who had transferred back from 1/R.M.L.I. on 8th, assumed command on 18th and Captain C. H. Coode became second in command.

On 22/23rd the Division was relieved by the 2nd Division; 190th moving to Beaulencourt, 189th to Metz and Equancourt and on 23rd the 188th moved back to these places, the 189th moving on to Barastre; on 24th the Brigade moved by rail to Rocquigny.

On 30th January Major N. S. Clutterbuck took over command of 2/R.M.L.I. temporarily; Lieut.-Colonel E. K. Fletcher had assumed command of 1/R.M.L.I. on 9th January, Major Huskisson, who had been second in command, having left the Battalion, and Captain R. A. Poland joined the 1/R.M.L.I. from service afloat.

In February the reorganisation of the Brigades of the Expeditionary Forces into three battalions instead of four commenced, and in the 188th the Howe was broken up and the R.M.L.I. Battalions received drafts from that battalion; by the 14th the reorganisation was complete and on 14/15th the R.N.D. relieved the 19th Division in the Couillet sector; on 15th February, Major Clutterbuck joined 1/R.M.L.I. as second in command, the appointment of Major Farquharson M.C., with temporary rank of Lieutenant-Colonel to command the 2/R.M.L.I. having been confirmed.

The 190th Brigade held the left sector and the 189th the right; on 24th they took over the sector of the 47th Division on their left, being relieved of part of their own front by the 2nd Division; the Brigades making a side step to the left and the 188th becoming the left Brigade on 24th. On 28th Surgeon Pearce-Gould joined 2/R.M.L.I. as medical officer.

The left boundary of the Royal Naval Division was the Flesquieres - Graincourt Road; as the positions they were now in were maintained up to the 21st March it may be as well to explain the positions of 188th Brigade and the method of holding them, remembering that the two R.M.L.I. Battalions and Anson relieved each other at regular intervals. The Division was on a three-Brigade front, the 188th on left; the 188th Brigade front included the Flesquieres heights, which ran up from the Grand Ravine, culminating at the point where the village stands; the possession of these heights was of vital importance to the defence of the remainder of the front system as it gave extensive observation in a southerly direction. The front line ran round the east and north sides of the village, the Flesquieres - Graincourt Road being the boundary. The front system consisted of a front, support and reserve line. (See Map 6).

The Intermediate Line was originally the main Hindenburg Line, but in the area of 188th Brigade a new trench was constructed to run in continuation of the remainder of the line with its left resting on Havrincourt; the Chapel Wood - Bilhem Switch line was in front of this and ran southwards to 2nd system north-east of Trescault.

The 2nd System ran east of Trescault across the Grand Ravine and up west of Havrincourt. In rear of this was the Metz switch, which ran due south across the Metz - Trescault road east of Metz.

The Third System ran east of Neuville and Ruyaulcourt.

The method of holding the line in 188th Brigade was as follows: one battalion with one company of the counter-attack battalion was in the front system; one battalion less one company (the counter-attack battalion) was in the Chapel Wood Switch and Intermediate Line and one battalion in reserve in East Wood Camp behind Havrincourt Wood.

There were 12 machine-guns of the Machine Gun Battalion in the Intermediate Line.

On 1st March the Machine Gun Battalion came officially into existence, under command of Lieut.-Colonel T. R. McCready, R.M.L.I. On 9th March 2/R.M.L.I. carried out a trench raid to secure indentification, the raid was successful in its object, but 2nd Lieutenant Fielden and two other ranks were killed; Lieutenant E. W. Collier was awarded the Military Cross for his gallant leadership in this raid, but was killed during the bombardment of the 22nd before the award was published.

On 15th Captain R. Burton the adjutant of 2/R.M.L.I. went to hospital and was succeeded by 2nd Lieutenant J. C. Lee, another raid was made on 18th, without result but 2nd Lieutenant Saunders was wounded and on the same day Major C. H. Coode was dangerously wounded. Lieut.-Colonel Fletcher, commanding 1/R.M.L.I., was also sent to hospital, and Major Clutterbuck assumed command temporarily. On 19th 1/R.M.L.I. relieved 2/R.M.L.I. in the front line, so that the position on 20th was: 1/R.M.L.I. in front line, 2/R.M.L.I. in support and counter-attack and Anson in reserve.

There had been many signs and warnings that the Germans were contemplating an offensive, but there were no clear indications to show on what part of the line it would fall. For some days the lines had been subjected to a heavy gas bombardment and the Division had suffered severe casualties[34], amounting to approximately 2,800, which had fallen heaviest on Drake and Hawke Battalions. It was estimated on morning of 22nd that the trench strengths were Hawke 150, and the remainder about 500 apiece.

On 21st March the storm broke on the 5th Army and aided by the fog the enemy gained a considerable area of ground and seriously threatened the right of the 3rd Army of which the "V" Corps to which the Royal Marines belonged was the right unit.

At 4-45 a.m. the weather was fine but misty and at that hour the bombardment fell on the flank

---

34. Captain C. L. McKheand, Lieutenant C. F. Yeldham, 2nd-Lieutenant A. H. Pettman, of the R.M,L.I.

divisions of the Corps, evidently with the intention of making an effort to pinch out the positions of the Royal Naval Division.

FIRST BATTLES OF THE SOMME, 1918.
BATTLE OF ST. QUENTIN.
(Map 6.)

At 6 a.m. the Machine Gun Battalion sent up four guns to the Intermediate Line, and at 9-15 the Divisional Reserves were ordered up to the second system, together with the remainder of the Machine Gun Battalion.

At 9-40 a.m. the enemy had taken that part of the 189th line which ran from Premy Switch southwards; the battalions counter-attacked, but by 2 p.m. the enemy had occupied our old line north east of Ribecourt. So far the R.M.L.I. Battalions had maintained their trenches, but by 4 p.m. the Corps on the right of the "V" Corps had fallen back and the one on the left of the 188th Brigade had been also pressed back, at one point as far as Beaumetz.

The Royal Naval Division were therefore informed by Corps headquarters that if the counter-attack did not restore the position they were to fall back to the Intermediate Line that night. The counter-attack was not successful, and owing to the further progress made by the enemy on the right flank, orders to withdraw were issued at 9-45 p.m. 1/R.M.L.I. passing through the 2/R.M.L.I. which then became the front battalion. The move was completed without opposition to the Chapel Wood Switch during the night of 21/22nd, the enemy having failed to follow up. At about 3-30 a.m. on the morning of 22nd, the enemy, who had by then discovered that the original defences had been evacuated, endeavoured to close. His action was preceded by a heavy bombardment with H.E. and Lachrymatory shell; the difficulties of the situation were increased owing to the thick fog, which rendered communication between the headquarters and the two forward companies of 2/R.M.L.I. almost impossible. Owing to the obscurity of the situation Lieut.-Colonel Farquharson ordered one of the two support companies, which were being held in reserve in the Grand Ravine, to occupy the portion of the Chapel Wood Switch immediately to the North, in order to assist the two forward companies. While leading this company to its position Colonel Farquharson was seriously wounded by a shell and died later. This officer was a great loss to the Battalion, with which he had served since Gallipoli days; he had been adjutant at the evacuation and until wounded at Beaumont Hamel; and later became second in command. As there was no second in command, Major Coode having been wounded, Lieut.-Commander Coote of the Anson assumed command. Lieutenant Collier was killed and Captain Wrangham wounded at this time.

About 3-30 p.m. on 22nd there was a heavy attack on Havrincourt, which was beaten off; the "V."Corps however, ordered a withdrawal to the second system to be carried out when dark, but later orders were received to withdraw to the Metz switch; the rearguards to move back at 2-30 a.m. and the move to be completed by 3-30 a.m. on 23rd, the 189th to move straight on to the third system into reserve, the other two Brigades manning the Metz switch; this move was successfully carried out, the backward movement due to the enemy's outflanking movements on the right having been so rapid that contact was temporarily broken.

At 10 p.m. 22nd, stragglers reported that Fins to the right rear of the Division was in the hands of the enemy, which was confirmed by the Corps Headquarters (see also Chapter 24) and Divisional Headquarters moved to Beaulencourt at 2-30 a.m. on 23rd.

At 7 a.m. 23rd, instructions were issued that 188th and 190th Brigades were to thin out their troops in the Metz Switch and move back to the Green Line, (This line which ran east of Ytres and Bertincourt was about 6000 yards long) leaving rearguards behind, whilst the 189th was at once to man the Third System with strong posts within the Divisional boundaries. The two Royal Marine Battalions which had made a temporary halt under cover of the northern portion of Havrincourt Wood, proceeded in a direct westerly line crossing the Canal du Nord arriving in the Green Line about mid-day. The rearguards withdrew at 1 p.m. and the 189th withdrew their posts when the rearguards had passed through. The 47th Division on the right and 17th on left conformed to their movements; the 17th, after having fought a very fine rearguard action, passing through the Green Line and the 2nd Division coming in on the left.

The defences of the Green Line, which were incomplete and broken at frequent intervals, ran north and south some 200 yards to the east of the high railway embankment in front of Bertincourt. The strips of fire trench were short and about three feet in depth, there was a complete absence of wire entanglements.

This semi-prepared line afforded very little protection, whereas it clearly indicated to the enemy the position that had been taken up; the Germans were consequently able to put down a successful "box barrage" on the following day. During the afternoon the two Royal Marine Battalions worked feverishly to strengthen their position on the new line. Two companies of each Battalion were placed in the front line immediately east of the embankment, while the remaining companies were disposed in support on the western side, with their forward sections on top of the embankment. The headquarters of each Battalion were placed on the eastern side of the village; ammunition and supplies were dumped on the position in order not to retain the transport in the forward area because the situation on both flanks of the position was grave.

The 190th were on the Green Line at 2 p.m. and 189th in the centre reported at 10-15 p.m. that they were in touch with both the other Brigades and by 10 p.m. the Battalions were in line from left to right: Oxford and Bucks Light Infantry, (2nd Division), 1/R.M.L.I., 2/R.M.L.I., Hood, Drake, 4/Beds., 1/Artists. In reserve 7/Royal Fusiliers about Lechelle, Hawke about Bus, Anson at Bertincourt - Bus road. The 188th Brigade Headquarters were at Barastre, and the others at Rocquigny. The Divisional Headquarters were at Les Boeufs.

Throughout the afternoon the enemy appeared to be pressing heavily from the north-east, but no movement was observed on the left of the Royal Naval Division front. At about 4 p.m. however, the enemy who had probably observed the working on the new line, commenced to shell the line of the embankment with field guns; and during this period Captain Gibbons was killed by a shell. He was one of the long service Non-Commissioned Officers who had been given a temporary commission and his loss was very keenly felt in the Battalion where his cheery and courageous spirit was largely responsible for the high morale and fighting qualities of his company. As darkness came on the result of the demolitions of huts and stores became apparent; large fires could be seen over the ground which had been evacuated[35]. The important ammunition dumps at Ytres had been fired and they continued to burn furiously for some hours. The country round was lit up for miles and shells and S.A.A. continued to explode till the following morning.

---

35. *Lieutenant T. Buckley, 2nd R.M.L.I., had been entrusted with the work of demolishing stores during the withdrawal, he blew up large ammunition dumps at great personal risk and fired stores and buildings. He accomplished this work under heavy fire, being among the last to leave the ground on each occasion: he was awarded the Military Cross.*

FIRST BATTLE OF BAPAUME.

At about 11.30 p.m. it was discovered that units of the 47th Division on the right were withdrawing, thus necessitating the formation of a defensive flank which was done with one company of the Anson. By this time battalions were out of touch with Brigade Headquarters and it was not till two hours afterwards that the situation could be reported. Reports were coming in to Divisional Headquarters at midnight 23rd that the enemy were in Bus and Lechelle, but that they were being held by the Hawke and 7/Royal Fusiliers who were holding the exits of those villages and that the position of 190th Brigade was very serious. The Royal Naval Division was informed by Corps Headquarters that a counter-attack would be made by the 17th Division in the morning and that a fresh Division would attack towards Sailly Saillesel, but these attacks did not materialise and touch was lost with 47th Division till that Division reported at 4-30 a.m. 24th that they were holding a line practically along the Divisional boundary, but with a gap.

At 4-53 a.m. 24th a heavy barrage was opened by the enemy on the whole front and a box barrage of H.E. shrapnel and smoke shell was put down by the enemy on the village of Bertincourt, the infantry simultaneously advancing to the attack against the forward companies of the Royal Marine Battalions.

A desperate hand-to-hand encounter ensued, during which numbers of the enemy were killed; the enemy's "infiltration" tactics had partially succeeded on the right, and it was soon evident that that flank would become dangerously exposed; accordingly units from the right support company of 2/R.M.L.I. were placed so as to stop any attempted enemy advance from that direction.

At 5 a.m. a message arrived with orders that the battalions of the 188th in conjunction with the rest of the Division were to withdraw to the Red Line (Rocquigny - Barastre) in front of Villers au Flos and Rocquigny, Divisional Headquarters moving towards Bazentin Le Grand.

In the short space of time available, vain attempts were made to extricate the two forward companies of each battalion and to break off the fight in which they had now become heavily involved; owing to the dense fog inter-communication and measures for reinforcement were rendered almost impossible and what remained of the forward units were eventually surrounded and taken prisoners. The supporting companies of each battalion managed, after severe fighting, to clear the village of Bertincourt , having suffered heavy casualties from shell fire.

The enemy had by now penetrated to a depth of some two miles on the immediate right flank and when the battalions got clear of the village they realised the seriousness of the situation.

The 2nd Division had also commenced to fall back and the withdrawal was now in progress along the whole front. The enemy in front of the Royal Marine Battalions had now become cautious, and though he was slow to follow up his success, he subjected the troops to a heavy machine-gun fire from the right flank which fortunately mostly passed over their heads and caused few casualties.

Throughout this action the Divisional Artillery and Machine Gunners had greatly assisted in stemming the enemy's advance and in covering the withdrawal from Bertincourt their mobility and close liaison with the infantry enabled them to give most effective support.

On arrival at the line of the Rocquigny - Villers au Flos Road, the Royal Marine Battalions were re-organised under the direction of Major Clutterbuck. The Divisional machine-gun officer Lieut.-Colonel McCready, R.M.L.I. brought up 12 machine guns under Lieutenant Anderson, R.N.V.R., and placed them south-west of Les Boeufs, where they did most valuable work in checking the enemy, and by 1-30 p.m. the Division appeared to be holding its own in this line. Here a number of Tanks, led by staff officers, passed through the lines and going on towards the enemy drove him back as far as Bus and Lechelle creating great havoc among his troops, and their timely arrival did much to stabilise the position and steady the troops, but owing to the difficulties of petrol supply few of these Tanks returned. A Brigade of the 17th Division also counter-attacked towards Bus and a fresh Division towards Sailly Saillesel, but at 2 p.m. the Divisional Headquarters having arrived at Beaulencourt, as also the Brigade Staffs, the General Officer Commanding decided that, as they were out of touch with Corps Headquarters and the Divisions on their right and left, he would withdraw to the line Martinpuich - Bazentin Le Petit, which was six miles behind.

Orders to this effect were given at 2-30 p.m. The march began at 3 p.m. in three parallel columns, each Brigade with its own artillery accompanying its column; the 190th and 188th providing strong flank guards; the march occupied three hours passing over the old battle grounds, through Guedecourt and just north of Flers.

Throughout this retirement the use made by the Germans of coloured lights indicating the position of their forward troops was most noticeable.

At 5 p.m. orders were issued for the Royal Naval Division to fall back on to a line east of High Wood. The 189th arrived there at 6-15 p.m. and were ordered to take up a position, the 188th on their left did not receive the orders and moved to a position in front of Martinpuich. The converging roads in the area to the south-east of Martinpuich proved a trap, for the columns of transport withdrawing became involved in a block with the result that at dusk the enemy attacked and occupied the east corner of High Wood and ground to the north, firing on the gun teams and transport. In the hand-to-hand fighting which ensued some guns were lost. Throughout the move the attacks of low flying aircraft had harassed the troops, whilst the 190th under Brig.-General Hutchison, R.M.L.I. had fought a fine rearguard action.

By 9 p.m. the 189th had established an outpost line and the 188th receiving their orders later, moved up in the early morning into line; with Anson in the line 1/R.M.L.I. in support, 2/R.M.L.I. and Hood carrying parties. 190th were at Courcellette and Divisional Headquarters at Albert.

Captain F. G. Eliot and Lieutenant J. W. Middleton, the transport officers, had displayed great gallantry throughout the withdrawal, Captain Eliot had always delivered the supplies of food, ammunition, water and stores in the immediate presence of the enemy, extricating his vehicles in the midst of confusion and congestion with the utmost skill and courage, whilst Lieutenant Middleton had rendered similar service for 1/R.M.L.I., they were both awarded the Military Cross.

At 5-30 a.m. on 25th the 47th Division on the right flank fell back and at 8-20 a.m. the enemy attacked from Flers; the 190th Brigade, who were now only 500 strong, were placed at the disposal of the 188th and were called up to Martinpuich; by 11 a.m. the attack was developing, the enemy employing "infiltration" tactics and their machine-guns coming on in rushes; the Royal Naval Division extended both flanks, but could not get into touch with the Division on their right. At 2-40 p.m. the 189th Brigade withdrew and at 3-15 p.m. were holding the Pozieres Road south-east of Courcellette, 190th were on the Courcellette – Pozieres Road, the 188th were still in front of this line.

The 188th then fought a rearguard action back to Thiepval where they established themselves in a strong outpost position for the night with the object of securing the bridges over the river Ancre, preparatory to effecting a crossing the next day. General Coleridge held a conference of his Commanding Officers and Adjutants on top of Thiepval Ridge, and it was here that the Brigade-Major, Major Thompson, was wounded by a H.E. shell. At this time Lieut.-Colonel Kirkpatrick, commanding the Anson, who had done splendid work during the retreat, was killed.

Whilst the enemy continued to press on the northern and southern extremities of the valley, the 188th passed a quiet night after five days of almost incessant fighting and marching.

R.M.L.I. Battalions In France

At dusk the Royal Naval Division were holding a general line in front Ovillers - La Boisselle – Thiepval.

At 12-45 a.m. on 26th orders were issued for the Royal Naval Division to withdraw across the river Ancre during the early hours of the morning; the 188th with 1/R.M.L.I. acting as rearguard were across without incident by 6 a.m., most of the small foot-bridges were destroyed by the Divisional Engineers after the last troops had crossed.

Shortly after the withdrawal from Thiepval Ridge to behind the Arras-Albert Railway the Germans who throughout followed closely, attacked the 1/R.M.L.I. and succeeded in gaining a footing in the position. A successful counter-attack led by Lieutenant G. J. Wharf and Captain and Adjutant R. H. West drove the Germans out and re-established the line; Lieutenant Wharf was killed, he was awarded the Military Cross posthumously; although gassed he set a fine example to his men and engaged the enemy with skill and determination; he had been one of the old long service non-commissioned officers of the Corps and had distinguished himself by his gallantry and efficiency.

Captain R. H. P. West, the Adjutant, who had been badly gassed, carried out his duties with great gallantry and ability and it was largely due to him that the Battalion had been able to withdraw when ordered, he also was awarded the Military Cross.

The Division had now arrived on ground with which it was familiar, for they were again in the neighbourhood of their great fight at Beaumont Hamel.

The position to be taken up was of great natural strength; the river Ancre with its pools served as a valuable obstacle, while the line of the Arras-Albert railway which consisted of a low but formidable embankment, provided a strong defensive position to the east of Aveluy Wood; the trees of the wood were very close and there was an unusually thick undergrowth.

The Royal Naval Division was in position from the south point of Aveluy Wood to Hamel facing the Thiepval Ridge with the 47th Division on the right, and 2nd Division on the left. The 1/R.M.L.I. was in position some 300 yards to the east of Mesnil, while the 2/R.M.L.I. were in support in rear of that village. The 190th were on the right of the Division and 189th on left. The troops had fought continuously and heavily for six days and the march over the old Somme Battlefield had severely tested their endurance. Many were now weary and footsore for the weather had been hot, the roads dusty, and full marching order was carried, and to add to their discomfort there was a shortage of water. Yet the spirit of the Battalions never fell and their conduct throughout, not only upheld the great traditions of the Corps, but indicated from time to time their ability to stand a hard knock as well as to give one.

It was immediately after the crossing of the Ancre that the Division were told "that they must check the enemy's advance north of the Bouzincourt - Albert Road facing south east." A German officer was captured during the afternoon, while carrying out a reconnaissance in front of 2/R.M.L.I. position; orders and maps taken from him stated that the Engelbelmer Ridge must be captured at all costs in order to command the approaches to Amiens.

Lieut.-Colonel Fletcher resumed. command of the 1/R.M.L.I. and Major Clutterbuck took over the 2/R.M.L.I. in place of Lieut.-Commander Coote, R.N.V.R. The enemy attacked that day south and north of the Royal Naval Division with a view of cutting off the Royal Naval Division by cutting up north-west from Albert but they were driven off by the 17th Division and the line was held. The 12th Division had now arrived in rear of the Royal Naval Division and during the afternoon the 190th were relieved by the 53rd Brigade, and withdrew to Engelbelmer. The 188th and 189th were also relieved at 7 p.m. The 1/R.M.L.I. were relieved by a battalion of the Queen's and moved to Martinsart; the 2/R.M.L.I. by a battalion of the Buffs and moved to

Engelbelmer, but owing to the uncertainty of the situation and the importance of retaining a strong force to stop any further attempt of the enemy to advance towards the Engelbelmer Ridge, 2/R.M.L.I. moved to Martinsart, where the 188th Brigade were now assembled complete in billets. The 189th had gone to Engelbelmer, but at 8-15 p.m. the 190th were ordered to Bouzincourt and the 188th and 189th were placed at the disposal of the 12th Division, which was holding the general line of the high ground Hamel - Mesnil thence south-east and along the railway embankment. The enemy had made contact along the whole line of the Ancre valley, but the rapidity of his advance had not only tired his troops, but also rendered the provision of ammunition and supplies exceedingly difficult for him.

No time was lost in reorganising the Royal Marine Battalions and in replenishing them with supplies as far as possible. There was a great shortage of ammunition and an almost complete absence of Field Artillery. The Commander-in Chief's famous order "Backs to the Wall!" had just been received and instructions issued that on no account was any more ground to be ceded.

Preparations had been made by Battalion Commanders to occupy a defensive line east of Martinsart, and lines of counter-attack had been arranged. At about 8 p.m. rations were being issued when the enemy began to shell the village; the transport was quickly evacuated and the troops took cover in the cellars, the shelling ceased at about 11 p.m.

At midnight 26th a sudden outburst of fire was heard and troops of the 12th Division began to fall back through the village of Martinsart. Simultaneously reports were received that the enemy had broken through, and that strong patrols had penetrated the line at Mesnil and the centre of Aveluy Wood. Battalion and company commanders at once made a forward reconnaissance and discovered that the enemy had in places penetrated as far as the western edge of Aveluy Wood. Machine gun fire was now coming from both flanks, and the situation was very obscure. The Brigade Commander, General Coleridge, whose headquarters were in the Chateau at Martinsart, ordered the Anson, 1st and 2nd R.M.L.I. to clear the wood and endeavour to restore the line with all speed. The three Battalions at once formed a continuous line and swept through the Aveluy Wood with great dash and gallantry; large numbers of the enemy were killed and 50 prisoners with four machine-guns were captured. By 3-30 a.m. 27th the original line was restored and handing over again to the 12th Division they returned to Martinsart.

At 7-30 a.m. on 27th the 190th attacked and drove the enemy back over the railway embankment down the Ancre Valley and by 1 p.m. were holding the western outskirts of Albert.

At 2-10 p.m. the line ran from Sailly le Sec – Mericourt - West along the Ancre to Hamel - Beaumont Hamel.

In the evening the 188th and 189th Brigades were to be relieved by 2nd Division and proceed to Mailly Maillet, the 190th were to follow later on relief by 17th Division, but at 7 p.m. the 188th Brigade had to take up a position of readiness to support the 12th Division (2/R.M.L.I. were just outside Aveluy Wood) and at 7.-30 p.m. assisted in defeating a strong enemy attack, whilst at 8 p.m. the Hawke assisted the 37th Brigade in repulsing an encircling movement from the south on Martinsart; they were back in their billets by 3-30 a.m. on 28th.

The two R.M.L.I. Battalions proceeded on the morning of 28th to Mailly Maillet and later in the day to billets at Forceville. The 29th was spent reorganising and cleaning up; on 30th they were inspected by the General Officer Commanding 188th Brigade and on 31st rested and had church parade.

The losses as recorded in the diaries of the two Battalions on the 28th inst. as having occurred during the retreat were :-

R.M.L.I. Battalions In France

Killed.	*Wounded.*	*Missing.*
1st RM.L.I.-1 officer, 20 other ranks.	5 officers, 78 other ranks.	7 officers, 337 other ranks.
2nd RM.L.I.-3 officers, 13 other ranks.	6 officers, 83 other ranks.	4 officers, 213 other ranks.

Of the missing approximately 270 were reported as Prisoners of War of whom many were wounded; whilst the total wounded reported in hospital was about 200.

The officer casualties included-,

	1st R.M.L.I.		2nd R.M.L.I.
Killed -	Lieutenant G. J. Wharf	*Killed -*	Captain C. Gibbons
Wounded -	Captain B. C. Pippet		Lieutenant E. W. Collier, M.C.
	Lieutenant D. W. R Hall		Second-Lieutenant S. N. Witting
	(*died of wounds*)	*Wounded -*	Lieut.-Colonel C. G. Farquharson. M.C.
	2nd-Lieutenant C. H. Lawrence		(*died of wounds*)
	2nd Lieutenant M. K. Gilbert		Captain L. H. Wrangham
	2nd-Lieutenant W. H. Hughes		Lieutenant A. S. Perry
Missing -	Lieutenant W. C. Gwynne		2nd-Lieutenant C. V. Egan
	2nd-Lieutenant S. E. Cailes		2nd-Lieutenant J. A. Smith
	2nd-Lieutenant H. J. Irwin (*killed*)		(*died of wounds*)
	2nd-Lieutenant W. G. Stuart		2nd-Lieutenant A. H. Mitchell
	2nd-Lieutenant M. E. Taylor	*Missing -*	Captain R J. Williams
	2nd-Lieutenant R Blackburn		Lieutenant P. S. Watts
			2nd-Lieutenant F. Deaton
			2nd-Lieutenant F. Gray (*killed*)

AVELUY WOOD.

The Battalions remained at Forceville on 1st April, marching next day to Toutencourt and returning to Engelbelmer on 3rd, where they bivouacked round the village and were subjected to intermittent shelling. On the 4th reinforcements of officers were received, consisting of one R.M.L.I. and five Middlesex Regiment for the 1/R.M.L.I. and of two Royal West Kent Regiment for 2/R.M.L.I.

On 2nd April, Captain Vibart, M.C., R.E., was appointed Brigade Major of the 188th Brigade vice Major Thompson and Lieutenant R. A. Neville. R.M.L.I. replaced him as G.S.O. 3, on the Divisional Staff.

On night 3/4th April the 190th Brigade relieved the 2nd Division in the front line with the 188th in support and the 189th in reserve at Forceville.

The front line which was east of Aveluy Wood was very irregular; it followed the line of the railway, but was withdrawn on both flanks to the upper western slopes of the valley, part of the line was formed by existing trenches and in other parts there were merely posts. Owing to the close proximity of the enemy, it had not been possible to construct an immediate support line. On 5th April Engelbelmer was heavily shelled and drenched with gas and at 9 a.m. the 7/Royal Fusiliers were attacked and minor breaks occurred, which were at once restored by counter-attacks. At 1-30 p.m. the 1/R.M.L.I. were placed at the disposal of the General Officer Commanding 190th Brigade and "A" Company, Captain Campbell, moved up in support of the 7/Royal Fusiliers, followed at 3 p.m. by Battalion Headquarters and "B" Company. The situation in the wood was obscure, but by 7 p.m. patrols of the 1/R.M.L.I. had discovered two gaps in the line; Lieut.-Colonel Fletcher also made a personal reconnaissance which proved to be of great value, as he discovered a gap that had been made on the right flank of his Battalion and dealt with the situation promptly; a defensive flank being formed by "A" Company, linking with the left of the 24th London Regiment, Captain Campbell commanding the company was awarded the Military Cross. The two gaps in the line were closed after mixed fighting in which Lieutenant Proffitt distinguished himself and was awarded the Military Cross. Lieutenant C. H. Bailey also won a Military Cross by clearing up a most difficult situation under heavy machine-gun fire; 2nd Lieutenants Perry, R.M.L.I. and Shimold (Middlesex Regiment) were wounded.

In the early morning of 6th April the 2/R.M.L.I. moved into a position of readiness north-west of Aveluy Wood.. At 2-30 a.m. on 6th the line was intact, but later the position became more obscure and at 7-45 a.m. 2/R.M.L.I. came up in support of 1/R.M.L.I. About 9-30 a.m. the two Battalion commanders, Lieut.-Colonel Fletcher and Major Clutterbuck organised a counter-attack which was most successful in re-establishing the line. Captain G. A. Newling who was 2nd in command of 2/R.M.L.I. made a bold and valuable reconnaissance under heavy fire prior to the attack. He personally established touch with the 4/Bedfords on the left, and then finding that the counter-attack, which had already commenced, was checked, he dashed forward and followed by men of the right company, assaulted a nest of machine-guns which was holding up the attack; the personal example and great bravery of this officer contributed largely to the success of this operation, during which 55 prisoners and 10 machine-guns were captured. Captain Newling was awarded a bar to the Military Cross which he had won so gallantly at Gavrelle Windmill. The line was consolidated under heavy shell fire, and both Battalions re-organised with 1/R.M.L.I. on right and 2nd on left.

Lieutenant-Colonel Fletcher was awarded the D.S.O. for his gallant and successful leadership in the fighting and counter-attack in Aveluy Wood, as was also Major Clutterbuck for his share in the successful counter-attack. The Military Medal was awarded to many N.C.O.'s and men (see list at end of chapter).

2nd Lieutenants Spragon (Middlesex Regiment) and H. R. Smith (Royal West Kents) attached were also awarded the Military Cross. The two Brigadier-Generals A. R. H. Hutchison and J. F. Coleridge were awarded the C.B. for their skilful leadership during the last month's strenuous fighting.

The remaining details of the 7th Royal Fusiliers were withdrawn after dark, and the two Royal Marine Battalions remained in the line until the afternoon of the 7th when they were relieved by the Anson and returned to billets at Forceville on 8th.

1/R.M.L.I. lost 2nd Lieutenants Tregedga, Berger and Spragon (Middlesex) Dark (Royal West Kent's) wounded and 2/R.M.L.I. Lieutenants Proffitt, Braid, Greenwood, 2nd Lieutenant Bing and Sub.-Lieutenant Oldham, R.N.V.R. wounded with 15 killed, 55 wounded and 26 missing of the N.C.O.s and men.

Captain Poland became second in command of 1/R.M.L.I. and reinforcements of 10 officers and 265 other ranks of Middlesex Regiment and 75 R.M.L.I. were received; the companies were now commanded as follows "A" Company Captain Walter (Middlesex Regiment), "B" Company Captain Campbell, R.M.L.I. "C" Company 2nd Lieutenant Horne, R.M.L.I. And "D" Company Lieutenant Hotham, R.M.L.I.; 2/R.M.L.I. received Captain E. L. Andrews and 65 R.M.L.I.

The Army Commander, Sir J. Byng visited the two R.M.L.I. Battalions with the Divisional Commander and congratulated them on their successful counter-attack on the 6th.

On 9th April, 1/R.M.L.I. relieved the Anson in Aveluy Wood and 2/R.M.L.I. relieved the Hood in the front line. They were relieved on night 11/12th and returned to Forceville where they were resting and refitting until 14th when they marched to Arqueves.

Training, reorganising and provision of working parties now filled their time. Major P. Sandilands joined 2/R.M.L.I. as second in command and Major F. B. A. Lawrie joined 1/R.M.L.I. in a similar capacity.

R.M.L.I. Battalions In France

RE-ORGANISATION.

The remainder of April was spent in training and manning the Reserve Line about Talmas and Toutencourt.

The question now arose of bringing the Battalions up to strength again; there were insufficient recruits in the Reserve battalion and depot; the Fourth Battalion had absorbed the greater part of the "floating population" at the R.M.L.I. Headquarters and the personnel lent to the R.G.A. to complete the 525,526,527 and 528 Siege Batteries had still further depleted the Corps resources. All that were available were sent from Headquarters and 150 men were withdrawn from 3rd Battalion in the Aegean under Lieutenant Flower, C.G.M. but of these 50 were diverted to Corfu for Naval Services.

In these circumstances orders were reluctantly given to amalgamate the First and Second Battalions into the 1/R.M.L.I., the Second ceasing to exist, after a service of nearly three years.

The First Battalion R.M.L.I. was now formed as follows :-

Commanding Officer - Lieut.-Col. E. K. Fletcher, D.S.O. *Intelligence Officer*-Lieutenant R W. Spraggett
Second in Command-Major F. B. A. Lawrie *Signals Officer*-2nd-Lieutenant Dean
Adjutant-Captain R H. P. West, M.C. *Transport Officer*-Lieutenant Lewis
Assistant-Adjutant-Lieutenant J. C. Lee *Captains of Companies*-Captains E. L. Andrews
(late adjutant 2nd R.M.L.I.) F. G. Eliot, M.C., B. G. Andrews,
 T. Buckley, M.C.

Quartermaster-Captain T. H. Burton, M.C. *Sergeant-Major*-Sergeant-Major F; R Graham

The surplus officers were sent to the Divisional Wing, The Quartermaster of 2/R.M.L.I. (Lieutenant Monk) was detailed for the Record Office at the Base and the Sergeant-Major Spry returned to England. The 2nd Royal Irish Regiment arrived on 23rd to replace the 2/R.M.L.I. and the amalgamation took effect from 29th April. It is interesting to recall that this Battalion of the Royal Irish served in the same Brigade with the R.M.L.I. in the Egyptian War of 1882.

The 188th Brigade was training until 7th May when it took over the left sector of the line in front of Hamel, the 1/R.M.L.I. relieving the 2/R.I. in support on the night 7/8th May, and the Anson Battalion in the front line on 13/14th. The Division was now disposed on a three Brigade front with the 188th on the left. On the night 18/19th "C" Company (four platoons under Lieutenants Prunell, Wolstenholme, Boucher and Hollamby) in conjunction with the Hawke Battalion on the right attacked and raided the enemy outposts in the Hamel Sector under cover of a heavy artillery and trench mortar barrage. The enemy were found to have evacuated their posts and consequently the raiding parties continued to advance until stopped by machine-gun fire from the railway embankment;they failed to obtain any identifications, but caused considerable damage to the enemy trenches and dug-outs which were fired and burnt furiously for several hours. The raiding parties returned just after midnight, having Lieutenants Boucher and Hollamby slightly wounded.

On the afternoon of the 19th whilst standing outside the Battalion Aid Post, Surgeon-Lieutenant Pearce-Gould, R.N., was killed by a fragment of shell. The loss of this officer was much felt in the Battalion, for he had rendered most valuable aid all through the heavy and prolonged fighting from Flesquieres back to Ancre; he had tended the wounded with utter disregard of his personal safety and his interest and care for the Battalion had been appreciated by all.

On night 19/20th May 1/R.M.L.I. was relieved in the line by 2/R.I. and moved to Forceville less one company which remained in the Engelbelmer Support Line.

On night 24/25th the Division carried out an extensive raid along practically the whole front of the Ancre Valley. Commencing at 11-10 p.m. and assisted by artillery, mortars and machine-guns, raiding parties on the whole of the Divisional front gained contact with the enemy. The Anson Battalion distinguished itself by penetrating as far as the railway embankment, killing numbers of the Germans and capturing one officer, 22 other ranks and seven machine-guns; before leaving they planted some home-made "death's heads" in conspicuous places along the embankment, which could be clearly seen from our trenches the following day. The Hood Battalion met with strong resistance before reaching the objective, but in desperate hand-to-hand fighting they killed many of the enemy; the 4/Bedfordshires also inflicted heavy casualties; the Royal Naval Division sustained casualties amounting to 18 Officers and 210 other ranks.

After training the Battalion returned to the line in front of Hamel on 25th May, moving into support on 1st June and being relieved on 5/6th June. They were encamped at Hedauville on 8th and for the next week were deployed in digging on the defence line at Varennes, marching on 15th to Herissart. Here they were bombed by aircraft during the night of 16th June, Lieutenant-Colonel Fletcher and Captain R. H. West were slightly wounded; Major Lawrie took over command temporarily and Captain Poland did duty as Adjutant, Colonel Fletcher however rejoined on 26th. Training continued at Herissart until 22nd when they moved up again into reserve to the Beaumont - Hamel Sector near Auchonvillers. On 24th Major Sandilands was appointed 2nd i/c and Captain Campbell was attached to 188th Brigade Headquarters for duty as Acting Brigade Major.

On 10th June Brigadier-General A. R. Hutchison left the Division on appointment as A.A.G., Royal Marines at the Admiralty and so severed one of the last links with the Gallipoli days; Brigadier-General Leslie took over command of the 190th Brigade. During their training the R.N.D. were attached to XXII. Corps, but reverted to V. Corps on 21st June.

On 6th July the Battalion took over the advanced forward line at Auchonvillers, moving into support to the Beaumont - Hamel Sector on 13th. On 25th they returned to Arqueves and were training until the end of the month, when they moved to Authie where they remained until 4th August when they moved to Vauchelles and Acheux, and were employed working on the defensive line until 8th of August, the day of the commencement of the Great Offensive, when they were sent to Contay to continue their training until 19th August.

A great change had come over the training and the attitude of all towards the War; in place of digging rear defences the Division now passed to intensive training for open warfare.

Foch had commenced his great offensive with Mangin's victory near Soissons in July and this had been followed by his second victory between the Ourcq and Soissons whilst the German attacks near Rheims had definitely failed and they were again withdrawing across the Marne.

The spirit of keenness and confidence of success were confirmed by the staggering victory of the Fourth British Army in front of Amiens on 8th August, the failure of the Germans in Champagne and the deadly blows struck at the Austrians on the Piave.

The impending operations marked the beginning of a fresh phase in the history of the Royal Naval Division, and in the next three and a half months they passed from one victory to another. The heavy losses of the March Retreat had been made good, and the reinforcements had been trained, to which work Colonel Fletcher had devoted himself unsparingly and the Division went forward sure of their superiority to their enemy.

SECOND BATTLES OF THE SOMME. BATTLE OF ALBERT (21st-23rd August, 1918). LOGEAST WOOD (21st and 22nd August).
(Map 6).

The Battalion left Henu for Souastre on 19th August, proceeding to the Chateau de la Haie Switch of the Red Line Defences the same evening where it remained until the following day. On the morning of 20th preparations were made for the coming battle and Colonel Fletcher and his Battalion Staff carried out a forward reconnaissance as far as Hebuterne where fighting was in progress. It was the intention that the Third Army should press in north of the Ancre towards Bapaume, whilst the Fourth Army advanced astride the Somme on Peronne. The IV. and V. Corps therefore received orders to capture by means of a surprise attack Bucquoy and Ablainzeville and the Ablainzeville - Moyenneville Spur, the dividing line between these Corps being in this area.

The operation, which was a manoeuvre for position, was entrusted to the 37th Division of the IV. Corps. If the 37th were successful, the 5th and 63rd Divisions were to pass through the 37th and push forward to a line passing through Irles – Bihucourt - Gomiecourt and thence following the Achiet le Grand - Arras Railway. While the V. Corps on the right of the 5th Division were to continue the attack by forcing the passage of the Ancre in a south-easterly direction towards Pozieres. On the left of the Royal Naval Division the 3rd Division of VI. Corps was holding the line.

The plan of attack for the Royal Naval Division involved the employment of the three Brigades, the 190th were detailed to exploit the success of the other two. The 188th on left and 189th on right were ordered to capture the first objective, the Brown Line, which ran along the eastern edge of Logeast Wood in a north-east-south-west direction from Achiet le Petit. The 189th were to be just north-east of that village. The objective having been taken, both Brigades were to continue the advance to the second objective, the Red Line, which was the line of the railway passing through Achiet le Grand. The 190th were then to pass through and capture the final objective Bihucourt - Irles. 16 Tanks were sent to assist the Division in the attack on the Brown Line and more to assist in that on the Red Line. One company of the Divisional Machine Gun Battalion was attached to each Brigade.

For the attack on the first objective, which was to be covered by an artillery barrage the following units from left to right, were allotted :-

1/R.M.L.I. and two companies Anson, Hood Battalion and two companies Drake.

For that on 2nd objective which was to be covered by Tanks :-

2/R.I. and two companies Anson, Hood Battalion and two companies Drake.

During the night of 20/21st August 1/R.M.L.I. carried out an approach march from bivouacs in the Chateau de la Haie Switch to their assembly position in Top Trench, situated some 1,500 yards to the west of Ablainzeville. Lieut.-Colonel Fletcher, realising that he would have to cross over the trenches taken and held by 37th Division was anxious as to possible loss of direction in case the morning should be foggy. He therefore sent his intelligence officer to the quartermaster, Captain Burton, with orders that he was to provide forthwith 1000 yards of white tape and as usual in this Battalion they were at once forthcoming (from somewhere); armed with these, Lieutenant Spraggett proceeded to No Man's Land and laid out the direction by compass on each flank to guide the flank companies and thanks to these precautions, although the morning was foggy, the Battalion arrived on the jumping off line exactly in its place.

The morning was fine but the thick fog did not lift until noon; the 37th Division, which was holding the front line advanced under the artillery barrage and quickly gained their objective, the line Bucquoy - Ablainzeville, and at 4-55 a.m. the Royal Naval Division supported by a creeping barrage passed through to the attack. 1/R.M.L.I.

accompanied by Tanks successfully assaulted the enemy advanced posts, but at 5-40 a.m. the two right companies encountered obstinate resistance from enemy machine-guns firing from huts on the road at north-west corner of Logeast Wood. To deal with these "C" Company and two platoons of "D" Company moved to their right and energetically attacked the position which was quickly cleared of the enemy; Lieutenant T. G. Stewart, D.C.M., and Lieutenant J. P. Curran displayed great gallantry; the "D" Company platoons resumed their advance, and met the remainder of the Battalion at the south-east edge of the Wood; the Wood was cleared and Colonel Fletcher reported at 8 a.m. that they had captured their objective, Logeast Wood north of the Central Road; the Battalion had captured a 5.9 inch gun, 250 prisoners, six trench mortars and much war materiel. The 189th reported that their first objective was gained at 9-45 a.m. and the second by 11-57 a.m., but that they were held by strong resistance. In the 188th Sector the 2/R.I. and Ansons commenced the advance on the second objective, but the former lost direction owing to the fog. At 9 a.m. as the Mark V. and Whippet Tanks were advancing, Major Poland, who was forward, at once led "C" and "D" Companies to the attack on the second objective in a very gallant manner. The attack started well but met with very severe opposition from machine-guns in huts and field guns in the cemetery in front of the railway. Nearly all the Tanks were knocked out and set on fire, Major Poland and Captain B. G. Andrews were killed and Captain Campbell and Lieutenant Barber wounded.

The party was forced back with the exception of a small force under Lieutenant Stewart who hung on till about 3 p.m. when the enemy started to envelop their flanks and permission was given them to withdraw; they were extricated with casualties, as it had been found impossible to help them owing to the direct fire of field guns; Lieutenant Stewart was awarded the Military Cross for his gallantry and Sergeant Hastings (Plymouth) was awarded the D.C.M. for organizing a local counter-attack which drove off the enemy and in which he displayed great gallantry and conspicuous powers of leadership.

The Drake Battalion was also held up and by 1-15 p.m on 21st the Division was holding a line running north-east and south-west about 500 yards in front of Logeast Wood. During the day the 1/R.M.L.I. were subjected to three strong counter-attacks which were repulsed with heavy loss to the enemy. Captain Buckley was mentioned for the manner in which he had led his company forward in the face of heavy machine-gun and rifle fire; on reaching his objective he had consolidated with initiative and ability, and repelled the counter-attack which was launched shortly afterwards; it was due to his example that the line he had gained was maintained intact. Captain R. H. Vance, who was severely wounded, his arm being blown off, was also awarded the M.C. for his gallantry in repelling the counter-attacks. Sergeant Hill (Plymouth) displayed great gallantry in moving forward with a Lewis gun with which he did great execution and although wounded he remained at duty till ordered to the aid post. He was awarded the D.C.M. At 4-35 p.m. the 190th Brigade were ordered to consolidate the position east of Logeast Wood, whilst the 188th and 189th Brigade were ordered to push on to the railway line which they were to hold and consolidate. At 5-30 p.m. the Anson's and 2/R.I. made a fresh attack, in which they advanced at some points, but were forced to withdraw and eventually the line was consolidated on a line running north-east and south-west from the cross roads north-east of Achiet le Petit to the west of Achiet - le - grand Cemetery and thence due north. By the evening of this day however the success of the Commander-in-Chiefs plan was assured and the line of the Arras-Albert Railway had been gained.

At 1-15 a.m. on 22nd Colonel Fletcher reported that information gained from a prisoner showed that the enemy were going to attack at dawn; he also reported that he had only 200 men left in his companies and that he had put his Battalion Headquarters into the line to fill a gap, and therefore requested that all detached men might be returned to him.

Except for active patrolling the night 21/22nd passed comparatively quietly, but during the early hours of the morning the line was subjected to intermittent shelling. At 4-45 a.m. a heavy enemy barrage was put down along the whole front and at 5 a.m. isolated groups of the enemy attempted to advance on 1/R.M.L.I. but were driven back. At 11 a.m. supported by machine-gun fire the enemy made a further attempt to attack, but was repulsed with heavy loss by rifle and Lewis gun fire; a further counter-attack on 189th Brigade was also broken. Captain West, the Adjutant had been taken ill on 21st just before the attack started (he however rejoined on 24th and performed the duties of Adjutant for remainder of the war) and Lieutenant Spragget was detailed for the duty. About 1-30 p.m. on 22nd the left flank of the Division consisting of the 7/Royal Fusiliers and Ansons were forced back slightly and at 3 p.m. the enemy made a determined counter-attack against the centre of the Division driving in the posts of the battalion on the immediate right of the 1/R.M.L.I. and units began to fall back through the centre of Logeast Wood. Immediately realising the seriousness of the situation Lieut.-Colonel Fletcher and his Adjutant, Lieutenant Spraggett, got together the greater part of the Battalion Headquarters and having assisted in rallying the withdrawing troops, they led them forward in the face of heavy fire and restored the line. While displaying the utmost gallantry and utter disregard for his own safety Lieut.-Colonel Fletcher was severely wounded in the leg, but refused to be carried away until he was able to report that the situation had been restored and the right flank of his Battalion was secure. He was awarded a Bar to his D.S.O. and Lieutenant Spraggett was given the Military Cross.

Sergeant H. J. Trigg (Plymouth) moved his platoon forward and attacked the enemy with such determination that the counter-attack was completely broken up; he killed many of the enemy with a Lewis gun and displayed fine qualities of leadership. He was awarded the D.C.M. 2nd Lieutenant A. G. Stone was also awarded the M.C. for dispersing the enemy with heavy loss, manning a Lewis gun himself, after its team had become casualties and his gallant example completely restored a critical position.

Sergeant A. Paterson (Plymouth) who had displayed the greatest gallantry and devotion to duty and initiative in taking charge owing to the loss of all his company officers was also awarded the D.C.M.; though wounded he continued to lead his men forward and even when wounded a second time refused to leave his men and was wounded a third time, but he did not retire to have his wounds dressed till the objective was taken and consolidated when he was ordered to the aid post. (For awards of Military Medals see table at end of chapter).

The following extracts from letters of Colonel Fletcher[36] are interesting and instructive-

"I found that the formations, general principles, etc., laid down in my notes, on the advance
"and attack were absolutely sound and require no alteration. Immediate re-organisation after
"an attack acquired by daily drill, is imperative. Without it you lose all power of manoeuvre
"and the battalion ceases to exist as a battalion." And again "I wrote you a book on
"re-organisation; the lesson I learnt was that it was far more important than anything else. It
"should be taught as a drill every day for a week. Without it you lose all control of the men,
"once they are committed to battle. Personally I should in future always hold back specially
"detailed N.C.O.s and men for the job, to follow say 400 yards in rear, and on no account to
"allow themselves to be drawn into the battle, until the objective has been gained" and he concludes
"Will you please convey to all ranks my utmost admiration for the dashing advance
"and fine fighting qualities displayed by everyone in the battalion. No commanding officer
"could have been better served; my only trouble was to do justice to them."

---

36. Colonel Fletcher died at Deal in 1922, from the effects of his wounds, and the gassing and hardships he had undergone.
† The unnamed wood S.W. of Grevillers on Map 6.

The Division was ordered to be relieved that night; it had captured 19 officers and 500 prisoners, though they had not gained all their objectives. 1/R.M.L.I. were relieved at 5-30 a.m. on 23rd August by a battalion of the Rifle Brigade, and proceeded to a position in the line east of Bucquoy - Ablainzeville, south-east of the latter place.

They had sustained a great loss in their Commanding Officer, Lieut.-Colonel Fletcher, who had trained and led them so successfully and gallantly since January. In Major Poland the Corps lost a very fine officer and good soldier, he had been senior subaltern afloat at the Battle of Jutland serving in the *Warspite*, and since his arrival in France he had endeared himself to the officers and men of the Battalion and had gained their love and respect for his great qualities; during the attack in which he was killed he had displayed bravery of a very high order.

By the loss of Captain B. G. Andrews another link with the Gallipoli days was broken, he as a Lieutenant, having commanded the rear party at the evacuation.

Major P. Sandilands took over command of the Battalion and Major Clutterbuck became second in command.

† LOUPART WOOD AND LE BARQUE. (*Map 6*).

As the 37th Division were to continue the attack on the line Irles - Bihucourt, the Royal Naval Division replaced them in the Bucquoy - Ablainzeville Lines. On 23rd Achiet le Grand was captured by the 37th, 5th and N.Z. Divisions, and the enemy retired to a line Grevillers - Loupart Wood - Warlencourt, and on 24th the N.Z. and 37th Divisions renewed the attack against Loupart Wood, but a mist in the evening of 24th, when the Royal Naval Division were to have advanced, stopped the attack. Another attack was ordered for 25th and the orders to the Royal Naval Division stated that the N.Z. Division had captured Grevillers and was advancing on Biefvillers and towards Bapaume; that the 37th Division were pressing eastwards to a line Favreuil - St. Aubin, the 5th Division holding Loupart Wood; the 42nd Division on the right were to envelop Miraumont and push on to Pys, with the objective Warlencourt. The Royal Naval Division which had been in reserve, moved forward soon after mid-day on 24th to their assembly positions, the 188th Brigade some 800 yards to the west of Grevillers, 189th immediately north-west of Loupart Wood, with 190th in rear.

The 188th was to advance on the left, keeping in touch with the N.Z. Division, with its right refused; the 189th in echelon on right, ready to cover its right flank; the 190th was to move by bounds in support, and be prepared to protect the right of the 189th and maintain touch with the 5th Division. The dividing line between the New Zealanders and the 188th Brigade was the Grevillers - Thilloy Road; six Tanks were allotted to the 188th and two to the 189th Brigades.

In the 188th Brigade the Anson were on the left at Grevillers and 1/R.M.L.I. on the right, their right boundary was the north-east edge of Loupart Wood inclusive, with the 2/R.I. in reserve. The Brigade was in position by 7-30 p.m. on 24th.

The first objective of the R.M.L.I. was a line of trench, known as Grevillers Trench, between Grevillers and Loupart Wood, the next objective another line of trench about 1000 yards south-west of this, running north-east and south-west; and their final objective was the eastern edge of the village of Le Barque. The 1/R.M.L.I. gained their first objective at 5-40 a.m. When the early stages of the advance were impeded by fire from a machine gun, Private W. Brindley (Chatham) went forward and single handed captured the gun, taking its whole team prisoners, for which he was awarded the D.C.M. Captain Buckley, M.C. also rendered good service.

By 6-10 a.m. 25th all troops were reported to be through the intermediate objective on the south side of Loupart Wood; the 1/R.M.L.I. reached the final objective, the east side of Le Barque at 6-30 a.m. and immediately consolidated the south part of that village; the Anson consolidated the northern part and were astride the Albert - Bapaume Road by 7.45 a.m. The R.M.L.I. had captured 150 prisoners, two trench mortars and six machine-guns.

At 9 a.m. the fog which had been very thick at 5 a.m. was lifting, and the remainder of the Division found themselves hung up on the outskirts of Thilloy and Ligny Thilloy, the latter village stood on higher ground and was strongly held by enemy machine-guns; the line of the Royal Naval Division now ran roughly north and south on the western outskirts of Thilloy, the 190th forming a defensive flank to the southward. The Brigades were ordered to consolidate the line on which they were, whilst Thilloy was bombarded; the Hawke and Hood who had suffered heavy loss from the south-west corner of the Loupart Wood, were on the right on the southern outskirts of Le Barque, the Hood on the right, whilst the Drake formed a flank with the right drawn back. The Royal Irish were on the left of the Anson. At 1 p.m. the position on the flanks was confused, but they had been secured by 3-40 p.m. As soon as the 1/R.M.L.I. had gained Le Barque, the enemy made attempts to counter-attack, but were repulsed with heavy loss; and throughout the day all attempts of the enemy to mass were broken by rifle and Lewis gun fire and the line was intact at the close of the day. Lieutenant Buckley was awarded a Bar to his Military Cross for his work in repelling these attacks. C.S.M. F. Windybank (Portsmouth) displayed great initiative, when his company officers had become casualties in organising the company and consolidating until another officer was detailed to take command and was awarded the D.C.M.; he had already displayed great courage at Logeast Wood and later he was again noted for good work at Drocourt - Queant Line (he had only joined the Corps on the outbreak of war as a short service recruit and risen to the rank of Company Sergeant-Major).

It is noted that there was great difficulty in bringing up rifle ammunition, so boxes were dropped by the contact aeroplanes.

The attack had isolated the enemy in Bapaume from the south-west with very important results. Enemy forces were now being forced due east and his troops and transport were generally converging on the town of Bapaume, with its important backward lines of communication. Among other results it had the effect of bringing the retiring troops of the German Naval Division in a diagonal direction across the front of the British Naval Division which was making its thrust in a south-easterly direction, and was the first occasion on which the two Divisions had encountered each other since the Antwerp days. This converging movement was mainly responsible for the large number of prisoners and machine-guns, captured by the Royal Naval Division on 25th during the advance to the Albert - Bapaume Road.

During the 26th the 188th and 189th Brigades tried to advance by infiltration, but were stopped by fire from Thilloy, which was strongly held. The capture of Thilloy had been ordered, but this involved a frontal assault, which the Divisional Headquarters did not consider practicable, owing to the fact that the N.Z. Division was not to advance further; the General Officer Commanding therefore decided to contain the village and try to pinch it out by "infiltration"; strong patrols were therefore active all day seeking to penetrate into the place, but during the night orders were received that the 190th Brigade was to attack and capture Thilloy, zero hour to be 11 a.m. on 27th. The 188th and 189th Brigades were to support the attack, but not to get mixed up with 190th. At 11 a.m. the attack was launched with great energy and two companies entered Thilloy, the flanks however were held up and the two companies had eventually to fall back with very heavy casualties. In spite of repeated most gallant efforts, the attack had definitely failed by 9 p.m. and the position was as before, the 190th digging in about 200 yards in advance of the 188th.

The Division was relieved on night of 27/28th August by the 42nd Division, their old comrades of Gallipoli; the 1/R.M.L.I. were relieved by the 8th Manchesters and proceeded to Miraumont to reorganise and rest. This period of fighting from 21st to 28th had cost the Battalion heavy casualties.

Killed- 5 officers, 46 N.C.O.s and men

Wounded- 10 officers, 260 N.C.O.s and men

Missing- 31 N.C.O.s and men

The killed included the following officers :-

Major R. A. Poland	2nd-Lieutenant C. A. Barber
Captain B. G. Andrews	2nd-Lieutenant W. Matthews (died of wounds)
Wounded- Lieut.-Colonel E. K. Fletcher	Lieutenant D. M. Smith
Captain R. H. Campbell	Lieutenant A. E. Creed
Captain R. H. Vance	Lieutenant J. E. Flower
Lieutenant H. L. Hardisty	2nd-Lieutenant J. D. A. Steele

In the advance on Le Barque Captain E. L. Andrews was killed, the second of two brothers, the younger having been killed in Gallipoli on 11th May, 1915. Captain Newling, M.C., who had been attached to 188th Brigade Headquarters was also wounded on afternoon of 25th, as was 2nd Lieutenant Robus.

On 30th August, the Royal Naval Division was transferred to XVII. Corps under Sir Charles Fergusson, with which they were to add so greatly to their honours and marched to Boiry St. Rietrilde and rested on 31st.

The Company Commanders during the coming great events were:-

"A" Company-Lieutenant H. Hardisty, "C" Company-Lieutenant Stewart, M.C., D.C.M.

"B" Company-Lieutenant J. P. Curran, M.C. , "D" Company-Lieutenant A. G. Stone, M.C.

later T. Buckley, M.C.

Major-General C. E. Lawrie, C.B., D.S.O., R.A., who had commanded them with such success since December, 1916, was relieved by Major General C. A. Blacklock, C.M.G., D.S.O., K.R.R.C. on 30th and Lieut.-Colonel J. H. Mackenzie, Royal Scots, became G.S.O.1 in place of Lieut.-Colonel Soutry invalided.

Lieut.-Colonel R. F. Foster, R.M.A., the A.A. and Q.M.G. was appointed A.Q.M.G. of a Corps Headquarters and was relieved by Bt.-Lieut.-Colonel R. R. Smythe (Army).

On 31st August they marched to Boiry St. Rietrude in readiness for the next move and the days were spent in reconnaissances by Battalion and Company Commanders.

THE SECOND BATTLE OF ARRAS, 1918.
26th August-3rd September, 1918.

On August 26th the Canadians and 57th Division had captured Monchy le Preux, east of Arras, and the First Army had followed up the success by driving the enemy into the northern extension of the Hindenburg Line known as the Drocourt - Queant Switch and the object of the forthcoming operations was to seize this system. A success here would force a wedge between the Lys Salient and the line to which the enemy was being driven back on the Somme; this would cause him to evacuate the Lys Salient and fall back on the lines of the Canal du Nord and the Canal de St. Quentin.

The Canadian Corps formed the right of the First Army, the XVII. Corps the left of the Third Army; the XVII. Corps comprised the 52nd, 57th and 63rd Division.

The plan for this attack in which the Royal Naval Division was to take part was as follows: the First Army were to attack the Drocourt - Queant Line, south of the River Scarpe. The XVII. Corps was to co-operate with the Canadians on their left, and by pushing their left forward gain a position to attack Queant from the north. The VI. Corps on their right were to capture Morchies and Lagnicourt and push forward to Beaumetz – les – Cambrai.

The objectives of the XVII. Corps were as follows (See Plan 21):-

First, The Blue Line, a line running east of Hendecourt and Riencourt.

Second, the Red Line, a line about 1,000 yards in front of the first on the far side of the Drocourt - Queant Switch.

Third, the Green Line, a line encircling Queant on the north, west and south.

The Blue Line was to be captured by the 52nd Division on the right and the 57th on the left. The 52nd were to keep touch with the left of the VI. Corps and the 57th were not to make a frontal attack on the Drocourt - Queant Line, but if the Canadian Division on their left was successful in breaking through, the 57th were to follow passing through the enemy position, the Drocourt Line, N.E. of Riencourt; then turning south-east gain the Red Line, mopping up the southern portion of the line, the junction with the Hindenburg Line, from the north. The attack on the Green Line was to go on as soon as possible.

If the 57th Division reached the Red Line, i.e. if the Drocourt - Queant Line was broken, the Royal Naval Division were to pass through their left to exploit the success; the general line of their advance to be along the high ground north of Queant to Inchy en Artois.

As the movements of the Royal Naval Division were dependent on the success of the 57th Division, they were divided into three phases; in the 2nd phase the 188th Brigade were to move up to the west of Hendecourt and 189th to south east of Fontaine, this phase was calculated at 2 hours 15 minutes after zero; in the 3rd phase the 188th were to deliver the attack, the 189th to move up to the Drocourt - Queant Line, north-east of Riencourt and 190th to south-east of Fontaine, the last two Brigades to be in Divisional control.

The 3rd phase was to be contingent on the Canadian Corps reaching their first objective and the 57th reaching the Red Line, the objective given to the 188th Brigade was the Railway Line.

The assembly positions which were behind the front held by the 57th Division, Bullecourt - Hendecourt, were allotted the 188th Brigade in the valley of Sensee River between Croisilles and Fontaine the remainder on Henin Hill. From the assembly positions, moving south of Hendecourt and through Riencourt, the 2/Royal Irish were directed on the railway; 1/R.M.L.I. after passing the junction of the Drocourt - Queant Switch with the Hindenburg Support Line were to swing to their right and attack the Hindenburg Support Line on a front from the Queant - Cagnicourt Road to the Queant - Buissy Road inclusive facing south towards Queant Village; the Ansons were to fill the gap between the two Battalions.

The 189th were ordered to support, moving north of Hendecourt to the southern limits of the Bois de Bouche, where one Battalion, the Drake, was to move south of the Wood and then in rear of the Royal Irish on the railway, the Hood moving through the Bois de Bouche to the north-east corner in touch with the Canadians, the Hawke was in Brigade Reserve. There would be no regular barrage after 9-30 a.m., but artillery would be moved forward to support, and three companies of the Machine Gun Battalion were to support the attack of the 188th Brigade.

At 5-40 a.m. on 1st September 1/R.M.L.I. left Boiry St. Rietrude and arrived at 9 p.m. in a trench north-west of Croisilles - Fontaine Road between Cherisy and Fontaine and on the morning of 2nd moved up to their position north-west of Hendecourt; 1/R.M.L.I. were on right, 2/Royal Irish on the left, the Ansons in support.

The approach march of the Division entailed a march of 17,000 yards over broken and difficult country in the dark.

Zero hour was at 5 a.m.; the day broke fair with some rain. The attack of the 57th Division started with the barrage and went very well; at 6-40 a.m. the 172nd Brigade reported that all was going well and the troops of this Brigade were seen on their objective at 7-5 a.m.; at 7-15 a .m. the Canadian Division Headquarters reported that escorts could be seen bringing back prisoners from east of the Drocourt - Queant Line and that there was no doubt that the 1st Canadian Division had reached their first objective, where there would be a pause of one hour.

Therefore in accordance with the discretionary power, which had been accorded to the Royal Naval Division Commander to advance if the information was favourable, orders were issued at 7-20 a.m. for the 188th and 189th Brigades to "Move."

1/R.M.L.I. advanced at 7-45 a.m. in artillery formation, with the 2/Royal Irish on their left; they passed through Riencourt and then through the 57th Division and attacked the 3rd Objective, the Green Line; at 10 a.m. the Canadians had captured Cagnicurt; at 11-45 a.m. it was reported that the troops were going well ahead to their objectives, and at that time the 1/R.M.L.I. were astride and beyond the last line of the Drocourt system and were wheeling to their right; the Royal Irish were to the east of them, but the ridge on the near side of the railway was still strongly held by the enemy. General Coleridge, who was in charge of the attack, had been impressed with the necessity of pressing on and the troops were responding well. At 1 p.m. the Drake were ordered to prolong the left and move through the Bois de Bouche and thence southward to turn the position from the north, but their Commander had already taken action.

At 1-20 p.m. the Germans were observed to be retreating over the railway line closely followed by the British and harassed by machine-gun fire, and at 3-45 p.m. the Royal Irish were on the railway, the 1/R.M.L.I. in the Hindenburg support line on an east and west line between the Queant - Cagnicourt Road and the Queant - Buissy Road, facing towards Queant, the Ansons in position connecting the two Battalions; at 4-50 p.m. the Germans were retiring from Pronville and Queant. The Drake under the inspiring leadership of Commander Beak, passing the left of the R.M.L.I. had made a most gallant and unexpected advance to the south-east and had gained the Pronville - Inchy Road, capturing many prisoners and much war materiel, in fact the success of the Royal Naval Division on this day was largely due to the action of the Commanding Officer of the Drake.

At 6 p.m. the 57th Division was ordered to hold Queant and Pronville and the Royal Naval Division to push on and capture Inchy, for which duty the Hawke Battalion was detailed; the Hood had, however, already pushed on and at 6-30 p.m. they reported that they expected to reach the junction of the Hindenburg Support and the Buissy Switch at 11-45 p.m. The Hood and Hawke were however held up in front of Inchy and in spite of hard fighting in the dark did not make any further progress, but by 2 a.m. on 3rd the Drake had established themselves east of Pronville, thus clearing the way for the 52nd Division.

The 1/R.M.L.I. had suffered a great loss in the death of the Regimental Sergeant-Major F. G. Weight, who was killed on this day when bringing up S.A.A. to the front line; he was a fine and gallant soldier, who had done good work at Logeast Wood and his loss was keenly felt. He had succeeded Sergeant-Major F. R. Graham (Colour-Sergeant, Plymouth), who had died of wounds and was himself succeeded by Sergeant-Major S. J. March, also of Plymouth.

The weather was fine on the 3rd and at 9 a.m. a message of congratulation was received by the Division from the Commander-in-Chief on the great success attained by the XVII. Corps.

At 9-50 a.m. the Drake were ordered to take Tadpole Copse, west of Moeuvres, and the Hawke and Hood to continue their attack on Inchy, whilst the Field Artillery were to push forward to block the Cambrai Road west of Moeuvres. The 188th Brigade were re-organising on the railway, the 1/R.M.L.I. being in an assembly position just west of the railway, ready to move at short notice.

The Hood Battalion entered Inchy at noon on 3rd and was ordered to seize the crossings over the Canal du Nord east of that place; and by 1.30 p.m. the Hawke, who had reached the western edge of Inchy, were endeavouring to seize the crossings south-east of the village and the Hood were advancing through Inchy apparently unopposed. By noon also the Drake had occupied Tadpole Copse without difficulty, and two companies of cyclists had been dispatched, one to assist the seizing of the crossings east of Moeuvres and the other to assist the Hoods, but the former was involved in the fighting at Inchy and never reached Moeuvres.

The Royal Naval Division were now ordered to hold the whole Corps front with the 52nd in support and 57th in reserve. The enemy resistance was stiffening and the attacks on the crossings were held up by machine-gun fire and made no headway.

At 7 p.m. 1/R.M.L.I. were ordered to proceed to a support position at the junction of the Buissy Switch and Hindenburg Support Lines, just west of Inchy and were placed at the disposal of the 189th Brigade and reached this position at 9 p.m.; at this time the attacks on the crossings north and south of Inchy were in progress.

In the evening the following congratulatory message was received from the First Lord of the Admiralty :-
"On behalf of my colleagues on the Board of Admiralty and myself, I congratulate you
"and the troops of the Royal Naval Division under your command most warmly, on your share
"in the brilliant success, which was achieved in storming the junction of the Drocourt - Queant
"and Hindenburg lines yesterday. The praise bestowed on you by the F.M. Commander-in
"Chief will be most gratifying to all ranks and ratings of the Royal Navy and Royal Marines.
"(Signed) ERIC GEDDES."

At 9 p.m. orders were issued for the 189th Brigade to gain a footing on the east side of the Canal, so as to secure the crossings for an advance over the Canal at daylight by the 190th Brigade.

The crossings had not been secured by 11 p.m. and at 1 a.m. on 4th, "D" Company, Lieutenant Buckley, M.C., 1/R.M.L.I. was sent to assist the Hawke in their attack on the bridge-head south-east of Inchy, and at 5 a.m. "A" Company, Lieutenant Hardisty, went forward to assist the Hood in the attack on the bridgehead, north east of the village. Lieutenant Buckley led a bombing attack up a trench to the bridge-head at the lock and gained a footing there at 8-30 a.m. which he maintained until reinforced, he displayed the greatest gallantry under heavy machine-gun fire from flanks and rear and was awarded a second bar to his Military Cross, "A" Company also did good work. The Division was now held up on the western bank of the Canal and could make but little headway as the Canadians on the left and the Guards Division on the right were not yet as far forward as the Royal Naval Division.

The Division was ordered not to make any more big attacks on the 4th, but to rest the troops and be ready to move at short notice, and meanwhile to try and advance by "infiltration." At 10-30 a.m. the Drake advanced on Moeuvres which they gained and held, though it was not really in the Royal Naval Division boundaries. At 1-30 p.m. the Hood and Hawke made a further attack on the bridge-heads, but had to withdraw under heavy fire and by 5 p.m. the line ran east of Inchy and through Moeuvres; the Royal Fusiliers were sent up to relieve the Drake in Moeuvres, whilst the latter helped the Guards to clear the area south of that place.

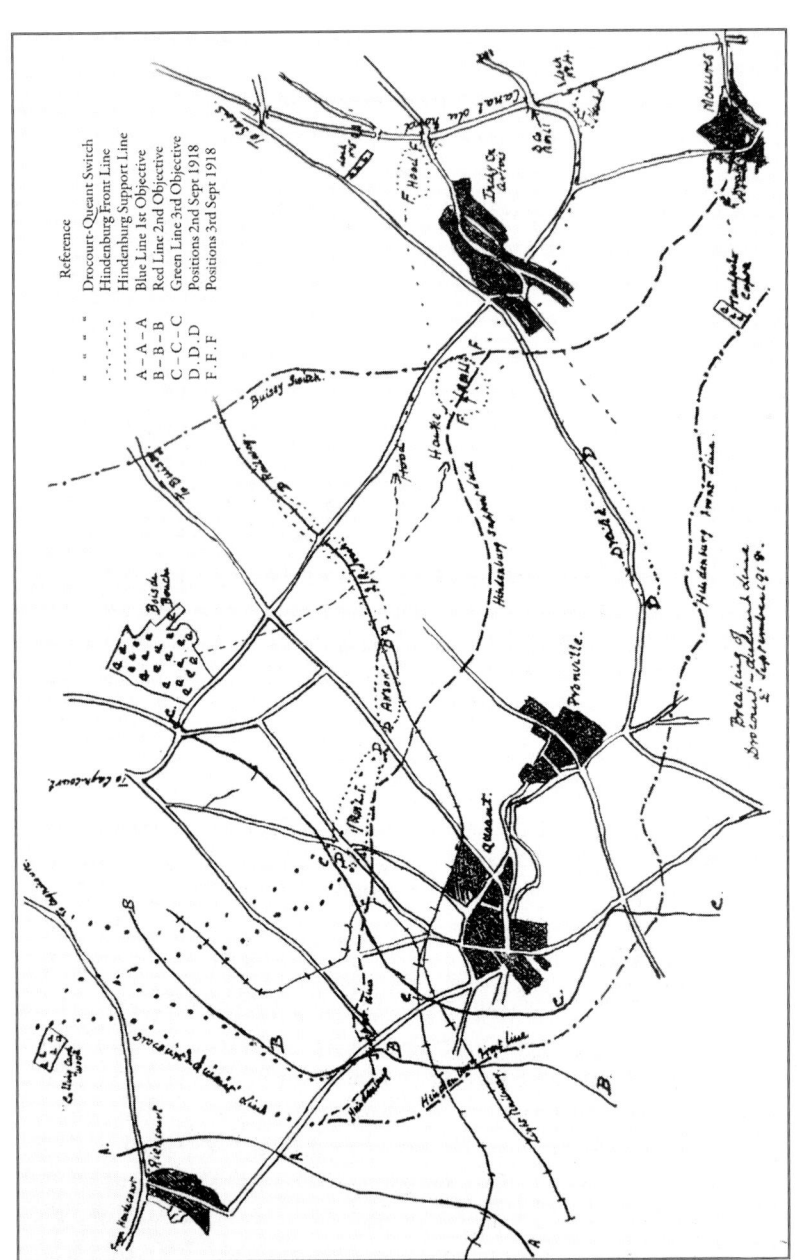

PLAN 21 BREAKING OF DROCOURT-QUEANT LINE, 2ND SEPTEMBER, AND ATTACKS ON CANAL Du NORD, 3RD & 4TH SEPTEMBER.

At 6-40 p.m. a heavy bombardment was opened by the enemy on Inchy and Moeuvres and the German infantry attacked the troops north of the former village; the Hood were forced to withdraw from the north-east end of the village, owing to shortage of ammunition; but a machine-gun post did excellent work in repulsing the Germans; at 7 p.m. the Hood and "A" Company 1/R.M.L.I. counter-attacked and the original line was completely restored between 9-30 and 11 p.m. Lieutenant Hardisty led his company forward in a most fearless manner under heavy machine-gun fire, and established the original line on the east side of the village, and afterwards maintained the position until relieved by another unit, he was awarded the Military Cross.

At 10-40 p.m. the 190th Brigade relieved the 189th, the 4th Bedfordshire Regiment taking over north of Inchy, 1/1Artists part of Inchy, and the 7/Fusiliers Moeuvres; 1/R.M.L.I. remained in Buissy Switch in support being subjected to heavy shell fire during the 5th. There were heavy showers of rain that day and at 11-30 a.m. the Guards relieved the Fusiliers in Moeuvres.

Fighting to gain possession of the Canal Bank continued throughout the 5th, 6th and 7th, but the Germans facing the Royal Naval Division were still on the west bank of Canal on 7th. On the night of 7/8th the Royal Naval Division was relieved by the 57th Division, and 11 p.m. 1/R.M.L.I. the last to be relieved, moved via Bullecourt to a position south-west of Boyelles and entrained for Labeliere whence they marched to Gouy en Artois for rest and training.

For the great results attained the casualties were few: the Division having 11 officers and 107 other ranks killed, 23 officers and 707 other ranks wounded and one officer and 135 other ranks missing, of which the 1/R.M.L.I. had one officer (Lieutenant J. R. Bates) and 21 killed, four Officers (Lieutenants A. C. McAdam, died of wounds, D'A. Barnard, Captain T. Buckley, 2nd Lieutenant H. Baker) and 130 wounded and 17 other ranks missing of whom 15 were afterwards reported killed. (For the awards of the Military Medal see table at end of the chapter).

The following message was received from Lieutenant-General Sir C. Fergusson commanding XVII. Corps:-

> "I wish to express to all officers and men of the XVII. Corps my congratulations on their
> "achievements in the recent fighting.
> "The task which fell to the corps was difficult, and was only accomplished by the gallantry,
> "devotion, and co-operation of everyone in the line and behind it, in his own particular sphere
> "of duty. The success gained in the culminating operation of 2nd September to which all
> "previous work had led up, had considerable effect on the situation outside the corps front.
> "I thank all from the bottom of my heart for their loyal support, and am proud and delighted
> "that their good work has been recognised.
>
> "(Signed) CHARLES FERGUSSON.
> "4th September, 1918"
> "Lieut.-General, commanding XVII. Corps."

On 12th September the Americans broke the St. Mihiel Salient, and the preliminary offensives of Marshal Foch were now completed and he was preparing for his final knock-out blow.

The goal of the advance was the great Railway, Metz – Sedan – Mezieres – Maubeuge – Mons - Brussels which formed the spinal cord of the German communications.

The Americans were to advance between the Meuse and Argonne on Sedan; the French Army under General Gouraud between the Argonne and Rheims on Mezieres.

The First French Army with the First, Third and Fourth British Armies were to attack between the rivers Scarpe and Oise and to be directed through St. Quentin and Cambrai on Maubeuge; whilst the Belgians, some French troops, and the Second and Fifth British Armies were to advance in Flanders and clearing the Belgian coast drive towards the north of the Ardennes.

The Americans commenced their attack on 26th September as did General Gouraud and were very successful; the Germans to their surprise were now confronted with a very serious crisis. The British attacks were timed to begin on 27th September, on which day the Third Army and First Army commenced their attacks on the Cambrai Front. The attack on the Flanders Front commenced on 28th September and the weakened German Lines there fell quickly before the attack, and on 29th September the Fourth Army attacked the heart of the Hindenburg Line on a front of 12 miles.

Our record is concerned with the events on the front of the Third Army.

Before commencing this work the Royal Naval Division had a period of rest, during which a very successful race meeting was held and performances given by the Divisional Follies.

BATTLE OF THE CANAL DU NORD.
27th September-1st October, 1918.

The Division remained training at Gouy en Artois until the 17th September when it moved into support; the 188th Brigade were sent to the Blaireville area, moving into the St. Leger area near Croisilles the next day. Training was continued until the 23rd, when the Royal Naval Division was warned that it was to take part in the attack on the Canal du Nord, with the further objectives of Anneux and Cantaing; the next few days were spent in preparations and the Division gradually moved up on 26th.

The general idea of the attack was for the Canadian Corps of the First Army to attack north of the Cambrai - Bourlon Road with a view to capturing Bourlon Wood and the Canal de la Sensee; the XVII. Corps of the Third Army (to which the Royal Naval Division belonged) was to attack from the neighbourhood of Moeuvres to turn the Hindenburg Support Line from the north and establish itself first on a general line – Graincourt - Anneux; the VI. Corps to attack the Hindenburg Support Line frontally and thence to the Flesquieres Ridge; the turning movement of the XVII. Corps was designed to make the frontal attack of VI. Corps practicable.

The final objective of the attack was the Canal and River de L'Escaut south-west of Cambrai. The Guards Division was to be on the right of the XVII. Corps and the 4th Canadian Division on their left. In the XVII. Corps area, the 52nd Division was to be on the right, 63rd (R.N.) on the left and the 57th in Reserve.

The operation was divided into three phases; the first was the capture of the Canal du Nord, and the spur running south-west from Bourlon Wood.

The second was the turning of the Hindenburg Support Line from the north as far as the Corps Southern Boundary, which involved a right wheel.

In the first phase the 190th Brigade was to cross the Canal du Nord and secure the spur running south-west from Bourlon Wood, with the 188th Brigade and Machine Gun Companies following in rear. On arrival on this line (the Red Line), the second phase would commence in which the 188th were to leap-frog over the 190th and capture Graincourt - Anneux Spur (the Brown Line), the 1/R.M.L.I. were detailed to capture Anneux, whilst two battalions (of the 190th) mopped up the Hindenburg Support Line; the 189th were to be prepared to assist or take over these tasks. (*See Map 6).*

In the third phase the 57th Division was to leap-frog over the Royal Naval Division on the Brown Line and capture the Third Objective, the high ground east of the Canal and River de L'Escaut; but as will be seen later the Royal Naval Division took a large share in this phase also.

For the first phase the 190th moved up on 26th to Moeuvres, one Battalion south-east of the town in touch with the 52nd Division, the second west of the Railway line north-west of Moeuvres, and the third in rear of No.2 in touch with the 10th Canadian Brigade. The 188th Brigade with two Machine Gun Companies were in the Hindenburg Front Line west of Moeuvres with the 189th in the area south of them. 1/R.M.L.I. were in Tadpole Copse. The approach march was rendered difficult by rain and darkness, but the morning was fine with a slight mist and at 5-5 a.m. on 27th the barrage opened.

The 190th started off well, and crossed the Canal du Nord successfully; the 4/Bedfords had stiff fighting on the banks of the Canal and captured a number of prisoners with six field guns; the 7/Royal Fusiliers kept touch with the Canadians while the 1/1Artists, mopping up as they went forward, caught up the barrage as it pivotted and reached their objective the Red Line.

At 5-30 a.m. the 188th moved from their assembly positions to the jumping off line and by 7 a.m. were over the Canal, which was dry and crossed without difficulty. By 6-50 a.m. British troops were over the Canal east of Moeuvres and prisoners were coming in freely and the 52nd Division had reached the Bapaume - Cambrai Road.

1/R.M.L.I. after crossing the Canal and the Sains - Havrincourt Road wheeled to their right to the south-east to reach their jumping off line, and gained the high ground west of Bourlon Wood before meeting enemy opposition. In getting up to their line the 188th Brigade were frequently checked by machine-gun fire, and the nests of machine gunners had to be mopped up, which however, was done without difficulty. At 7-58 a.m. the advance of the 188th Brigade began, and at 8-40 a.m. the 189th moved off to support the 188th and by 10 a.m. were in close support on the right.

At 9-45 a.m. the 190th had gained their objective and the 188th passed to the attack; the Ansons on the right were directed on Graincourt and the high ground south-east of it via the factory on the main road, the left Battalion (1/R.M.L.I.) were directed on Anneux, the 2/Royal Irish in reserve to the north of the sugar factory.

1/R.M.L.I. attacked on a three company front, "A," "B," and "C" with "D" company in immediate support.

The mopping up battalions of the 190th had been held up by machine-gun fire as had the units of the 52nd Division; therefore as soon as the Ansons passed through the 190th they came under heavy machine-gun fire, especially from the Factory; an attempt was made to outflank and capture it, but after a hand-to-hand struggle in the Factory itself the party of the Anson, which had entered, was forced to withdraw; 1/R.M.L.I. pressed forward until the fire from the Factory and Anneux checked their advance, whilst both Battalions were reinforced by the Royal Irish. Captain Eliot, M.C., Lieutenants McBryde, Albury and Hollamby were all killed here in gallant attempts to advance.

The Drake and Hawke of the 189th were therefore ordered to attack, one to capture the Hindenburg Support Line on a front from west of the Sugar Factory to west of Graincourt, the other to attack the Factory. This attack failed so a heavy barrage was put down on the Sugar Factory from 1-15 to 2-15 p.m. and two Tanks were sent up; the attack was then gallantly renewed and the factory captured; the three battalions, Anson, Drake and Hawke continued their advance rapidly and captured Graincourt and the Brown Line. Meanwhile the Canadians had gained Bourlon Wood and the 1/R.M.L.I. as soon as the Factory fell, captured the village of Anneux after hard fighting, and the Graincourt - Anneux Spur assisted by the Hawke. In the village they captured two heavy howitzers and nine field guns. The village, which was

[By permission Of the Imperial War Museum.]
TROOPS RESTING IN A SUPPORT TRENCH.

[By permission Of the Imperial War Museum.]
TROOPS WAITING TO ATTACK IN THE CANAL DU NORD.

in their hands by 2-30 p.m. was at once consolidated. The final objective the Brown Line was secured by about 4 p.m. when orders were issued for the Brigades to reorganise.

Corporal J. W. Coulthard (Plymouth) was awarded the D.C.M. for great gallantry north-west of Anneux; when his company was held up by strong resistance from the Quarry, he led his section towards the village in the face of a heavy artillery fire, and eventually succeeded in outflanking the quarry and getting enfilade fire to bear on it, with the result that the enemy were forced to retire.

At 6-45 p.m. the enemy made a strong counter-attack which was repulsed with heavy loss and by 7-30 p.m. all was quiet and food and ammunition were pushed up. Lieutenant Buckley had again handled his company most ably and his skilful siting of his Lewis guns on the north-east outskirts of Anneux did great work in repelling the counter-attack.

The casualties among the officers of the Battalion had been very heavy during the attack, so that Lieut.-Colonel Sandilands went forward himself under heavy machine-gun fire and supervised the organisation of the defence and ensured touch with the units on the flanks; Acting Captain L. H. Wrangham, who had displayed great dash and courage in the attack on the village, was also most prominent in repelling the counter-attack, for he supervised the company on his right, all of whose officers had become casualties, as well as his own, and though wounded in the arm he restored the original alignment until ordered by the medical officer to go to the aid post, he was awarded the Military Cross.

For the awards of D.C.M. and Military Medal see table at end of chapter.

The Battalion also received a message from the Brigadier.

"I am very pleased the R.M.L.I. can add Anneux to their laurels with a dozen guns and many prisoners. Our, role to-night is to hold our gains thus.

R.M.L.I. IN ANNEUX.   ANSON IN GRAINCOURT.
ROYAL IRISH IN CEMETERY BETWEEN THE VILLAGES.

XVII. Corps Commander sent the following message: "Well done. Reported that German Naval Division*[37] is waiting for you on Canal de L'Escaut. When Greek meets Greek."

To which the Divisional Commander added: "A division has seldom been set a harder task than you were to-day. After 10 hours hard fighting, you completely accomplished it. A real fine soldierly performance." and to the Drake added "Well done again Drake."

The 57th Division were then ordered to capture the crossings over the Canal de L'Escaut. Zero hour was fixed for 5-15 a.m. on 28th. As a result of the operations of the 27th September the Hindenburg Support Line had been pierced and the way opened for the advance on Cambrai.

CROSSING OF THE CANAL DE L'ESCAUT AND CAMBRAI.

The morning of 28th was spent in reorganising on the Brown Line; the role allotted to the Royal Naval Division for 28th was to move through the 57th Division after it had secured the high grounds east of the Canal and encircle Cambrai from the south to seize the eastern exits and commanding ground east of Cambrai.

The 189th Brigade, two Companies, Machine Gun Battalion with the New Zealand and 93rd Army Brigades, R.F.A. were detailed as Advanced Guard, and moved off 10-15 a.m., but as the 57th had not yet

---

37. *Actually the 3rd Marine Division.*

secured the crossings, the move was stopped in the Cantaing area; the 188th Brigade on the Graincourt - Anneux Spur and the 190th on the Bapaume - Cambrai Road at the Factory.

At 3 p.m. the 189th Brigade were ordered to establish themselves on the high ground east of the Canal, as it was found that the 57th had succeeded in passing only a few men over the Canal, and it was therefore necessary to attack all along the front. The 1/R.M.L.I. were moved to a trench between Fontaine and Cantaing, west of La Folie Wood in support.

Most gallant attacks were made by the Drake Battalion, supported by the Machine Gun Companies, but they failed to capture the lock opposite La Marliere in daylight; whilst the Hood and Hawke were trying to pass opposite La Folie Wood. The attacks were continued during the night and the Divisional Engineers, with most intrepid daring threw pontoon bridges (two) across the Canal during the night under heavy fire, these were the Royal Marine Divisional Engineer Companies who had been transferred to the Royal Engineers in 1917.

By dawn next morning two companies of the Drake had forced themselves across and later a third succeeded in crossing.

At 7 p.m. on 28th the 188th Brigade had been concentrated in rear of La Folie Wood.

The Machine Gun Companies had been assisting the attempts to cross and an effort during the early hours of 29th by the Hawke to cross by the pontoon bridges failed in face of heavy fire. By 8 a.m. little progress had been made, but an artillery bombardment of the Marcoing Front and La Marliere Farm enabled the Drake and Hawke to capture Cantigneul Mill, where much assistance was rendered by the Machine Gun Companies, who had been personally placed by Lieut.-Colonel McCready, R.M.L.I. who was awarded the D.S.O.

By 10 a.m. the resistance began to weaken, and the Drake was firmly established in La Marliere Farm, whilst the Hood and Hawke enlarged the bridge-head towards the east and north-west.

At noon the 189th Brigade having established itself east of the Marliere Farm the 188th were ordered to cross the Canal de L'Escaut, leapfrog over the 189th and attack the high ground between Proville and the Faubourg de Paris (Cambrai).

The 2/Royal Irish advanced on the right, 1/R.M.L.I. on left, the Anson in reserve to follow the 2/Royal Irish; two companies of the Machine Gun Battalion also advanced and caught the enemy as he was retreating. 1/R.M.L.I. moved through La Folie Wood and had crossed the Canal by 1-30 p.m. and by 2-15 p.m. the Ansons were also across. In face of considerable opposition 2/Royal Irish established themselves 500 yards in advance of the 189th being checked by machine-gun fire from the Faubourg de Paris.

The R.M.L.I. advanced until checked at 3-30 p.m. by enfilade fire from Proville on a line about 600 yards south-west of that place, but in touch with Royal Irish on right and Hood on the left. Ansons were in support just east of La Marliere; the Drake and Hawke were collected into reserve. The enemy were still holding the suburbs of Cambrai in strength and machine-guns were in position on the roofs of the houses, which caused heavy loss and the R.M.L.I. had 3 officers wounded, 16 N.C.O.s and men killed, and 112 wounded. Colonel Sandilands by his influence and determination had worked his Battalion forward in the face of strong opposition and in spite of the casualties, and for this and his work at Anneux he was awarded the D.S.O.

After dark the 190th Brigade crossed the Canal and at 7-30 a.m. on 30th attacked the southern outskirts of the Faubourg de Paris endeavouring to seize the Cambrai - Masnieres Road, but were hung up by machine-gun fire though a few of the 7/Royal Fusiliers got over the road.

At 10-40 a.m. the 188th Brigade were ordered to renew the attack at 1 p.m. against a trench system extending from Proville to south of the Faubourg de Paris, whilst the 190th attacked the railway line east of the main road; the 190th attack failed again, but the 188th gained their objective by 4-15 p.m.

At 10-30 p.m. "D" Company, R.M.L.I and one company of the Ansons attacked the strong point in the trench system on the southwestern outskirts of the Faubourg and consolidated portions of it, but at 6-10 a.m. the following morning (1st October) the enemy counter-attacked heavily and "D" Company was forced to withdraw slightly further back, where they were isolated, and as no assistance could be sent to them they had to remain for the rest of the day; the fighting on 30th had been remarkable for the persistent efforts of the 190th and 188th Brigades to make progress eastwards in the face of heavy machine-gun fire, particularly from the Faubourg.

In the afternoon of the 1st the 52nd Division advanced under a heavy barrage, in order to push on as far as possible and so automatically relieve the Royal Naval Division, and at 5-40 p.m. a battalion of Royal Scots Fusiliers passed through the R.M.L.I. and consolidated a line 200 yards in front of them.

At 8-20 p.m.1st October the 1/R.M.L.I. formed up on the road at the southern entrance to Preville, and moved to bivouacs on the hill, north-east of Annuex.

For awards of D.C.M. and Military Medal see table.

The casualties during these operations from 27th September to 1st October amounted for the Division to 21 officers killed and 326 other ranks; wounded 83 officers and 1978 other ranks; missing two officers and 407 other ranks.

The losses of the R.M.L.I. being :-Killed, five officers (Captain F. G. Eliot, Lieutenants L. F. Albury, J. McBride, A. W. Gregory, G. R. B. Hollamby), 60 N.C.O.s and men; wounded, 10 officers (Captain L. H. Wrangham, Lieutenant, T. J. Walsh, C. W. Watson, A. G. Bareham, H. E. Chater, H. Tulley, F. Gordon, C. E. Eves, E. A. Brindley, W. E. Vincent), 258 N.C.O.s and men; missing, 56 N.C.O.s and men.

The strength of the Battalion was now only 200, only two company officers with seven Headquarter Wing remaining fit for duty. The Chaplain at this time was the Rev. Martyn-Jones, whose extraordinary coolness and disregard of danger in the front line made him the admiration of all ranks.

On 1st October St. Quentin fell into the hands of the French and on 3rd October the Fourth Army had broken through the Beaurevoir Line and by the 5th the whole line of the St. Quentin Canal and the Hindenburg defences were in the British hands[38].

The Germans were now withdrawing to their positions in rear of the Selle, and the Third and Fourth Armies were making arrangements to continue their attack which culminated in the big attack on a front of 17 miles at dawn on 8th October when the Fourth Army made important progress in the direction of Le Cateau, whilst the Third Army completed the encirclement of Cambrai from the south and in this movement the Royal Naval Division was destined to take a large part.

BATTLE OF CAMBRAI. 1918.
Capture of Niergnies, 8-9th October.

After relief on night 1/2nd October, the Royal Naval Division moved back to bivouacs in their former area near Annuex - Graincourt; 1/R.M.L.I. were between Annuex and Cantaing. On 4th October they

---

38. On 29th September the 46th Division (North Midland Territorials), of which Division Lieut.-Colonel C. F. Jerram, R.M.L.I. was G.S.O.1, equipped with lifebelts from the Channel steamboats and with mats and rafts had crossed the St. Quentin Canal at Bellenglise, by swimming across and storming the German trenches on the far side.

were under orders to entrain for a rest area under the First Army and leave was being granted, the Divisional Commander had actually started, when at 6-30 p.m. on, the 4th, XVII. Corps Headquarters informed them that the orders were cancelled, and that they were required for further operations; the Divisional Commander was recalled and on 6th they were given the orders for the attack on Niergnies, south of Cambrai and the ground between that place and Rumilly, which would entail an advance of nearly 5,000 yards. The operations were however postponed for twenty-four hours.

The attack of the Third and Fourth Armies in the Battle of the Beaurevoir Line was continuing, with the result that the enemy was retiring on the front of the IV. and V. Corps, there was therefore a possibility that the retirement might extend northwards opposite the fronts of the VI. and XVII. Corps which were immediately south of Cambrai.

The objectives of the VI. Corps were to be Forenville - Wambaix, and of the XVII. Corps, Niergnies and the main road running from Rue St. Ladre to Esnes; the 2nd Division on their right was the left Division of the VI. Corps, whilst on the front of XVII. Corps the Royal Naval Division were to be the attacking force, and were also responsible for the protection of the left flank from the Railway eastwards against attacks from Cambrai; the 57th Division were responsible to the west of the Railway.

Owing to the restricted front and the necessity of crossing the bridges, it was necessary for the Royal Naval Division to pass through the 2nd Division to reach their jumping off place. The attack was to be covered by a large number of batteries of Field and Heavy Artillery (see Chap. 29) and the 24th Division was to follow in support to exploit the success.

The jumping off line was marked out from the Rumilly - Seranvillers Road to the Rumilly - Fbg de Paris Road about 1000 yards north-east of Rumilly.

The 188th Brigade were on the right and the 189th on left, the 190th to move in support of the 188th. As the 188th were to advance on a one battalion front, the 2/R.I. were detailed to capture the first objective a trench on the road running from south-west corner of Cambrai to Seranvillers, this line passed along the western outskirts of Niergnies. The 1/R.M.L.I. were to pass through the Royal Irish and attack the second objective, the main road Rue St. Ladre to Esnes from La Belle Etoile to a point just south of Mon Neuve; with the 2nd Division on their right; the Ansons, following in rear were to encircle Niergnies from the south-east. In the 189th Brigade the Drake were to advance on the left of the Royal Irish with the Hawke on their left again, the latter was to form a defensive flank from the railway to the left of the Drake (this Brigade was on a two battalion front); the Hood moving astride of the Brigade boundary was to take Niergnies from the south in conjunction with the Anson and swinging to the north-east under the barrage establish a defensive flank north of the Village between the Hawke's and the. left of the R.M.L.I.

The 190th Brigade was to move in support of 188th; the Machine Gun Battalion and two companies of the 52nd Machine Gun Battalion were to fire an overhead barrage to cover the advance on the first objective, and then, less two companies, to cover the advance to the second objective; whilst the two companies and two companies of 57th Machine Gun Battalion covered the left flank of the advance.

As Niergnies was the last general action fought by the Battalion the Battalion Order is given in full.

1st BATTALION ROYAL MARINES.
OPERATION ORDER No.9.

Reference Maps. 57 C.   N.E. 57 B. N.W. 1/20,000

Bn. Headquarters, 7/10/18.

INFORMATION-The 63rd (R.N.) Division in conjunction with troops attacking to the south, is being called upon to capture Niergnies, and the high ground to the north-east and east of it.

The 188th and 189th Brigades will carry out the attack within the Divisional boundaries and the 190th Infantry Brigade will be in reserve.

INTENTION-The 188th Infantry Brigade will attack at zero from the trench line G. 17a. 30. 50.-G. 10.d. 30. 60. The 2nd Bn. The Royal Irish Regiment leading followed successively by 1st Bn. Royal Marines and the Anson Bn. The 2nd Bn. The Royal Irish Regiment, will capture the first objective-the trench line running G. 12b. 55. 70-G. 6c. 70. 80. within the Brigade Boundary. On this objective being gained the 1st Royal Marines Battalion with "A" and "B" Companies in the leading wave, followed by "C" and "D" Companies in the rear wave, "A" on the right and "C" on the right of their respective waves, pass through the 2nd Bn. The Royal Irish Regiment, and attack the second objective-the road running H.1.c. 85. 90.-A 30d. 9.9. the Battalion will move in echelon in rear of the 2nd Bn. The Royal Irish Regiment, and as far as possible hug the right flank, shaking out into attack formation immediately in rear of the first objective.

BOUNDARIES-Right Boundary G. 16 d. 00. 70.-G. 12 a. 70. 00-H. 1 c. 90. 85.

Left Boundary G. 10 a. 40. 00-G. 6 b. 45. 30-A. 30 d. 90. 95

Inter company boundaries after first objective a straight line from G. 6 d. 10.45 to H. 1 a. 40. 65.

BARRAGE- The barrage opens at zero and dwells on a line G.17a.8.8.-G.4.C.4.3. for ten minutes. The barrage then pauses for 30 minutes east of the first objective and hereafter will move at the rate of 100 yards in four minutes. On lifting off the first objective, the barrage pivots on A 29, central and swings so as to form a protective barrage round the second objective and the left flank.

TANKS-Three Tanks will co-operate with the attack by this Battalion moving along the left boundary and generally assisting the Battalion against heavy machine-gun fire and any other unforeseen circumstances.

CONTACT AEROPLANES - Contact aeroplanes will call for flares at the following hours; zero plus three hours, zero plus three and a half hours, zero plus four and a half hours. This is to be very carefully explained, and even though some doubt may exist in the mind of the troops, on the Klaxon Horn being sounded, one flare per man will be immediately lit. Counter-attack plane will be up from zero onwards.

BATTLE HEADQUARTERS-Battalion Headquarters will move from the present location to a house in G 20. b. 70. 85. and will probably move to G. 16. c 00. 90.

RUNNERS-Each company will detail one runner to report to Battalion Headquarters immediately their respective companies have reached the assembly area.

This runner will remain with Battalion headquarters, to within a few minutes of zero, after which he will be dispatched to rejoin his company.

COMMUNICATIONS - Communications will be by runner and visual. After zero a report centre will be established in the house at G. 16. c 00, 90

Administrative Instructions will be issued later.
(Signed) R. H. P. WEST,
Captain and Adjutant.

Administrative - Instructions issued in conjunction with Operation Order No.9.

Battalion Headquarters, 7/10/18.

Reference Maps-57 C. N.E.; 57 B. N.W.

1. Men proceeding into action, will carry the following :-Fighting Order equipment, including haversack and waterproof sheet, 170 rounds S.A.A., two No. 36 grenades, two ground flares. In addition the following will be carried five picks and 15 shovels per company (the quarter-master will dispatch these forthwith), 50 Very lights per company, one S.O.S., will be carried by each officer and four sets will be maintained in reserve at each company headquarters, and 10 at Battalion Headquarters. Each Lewis gun will carry 16 filled drums.

2. TRANSPORT-All pack animals, Lewis gun limbers, and cookers will accompany the Battalion to the assembly position. A hot meal will be served at this point and the Lewis guns and Lewis gun ammunition issued.

3. GREAT COATS-Great coats will be taken as far as the assembly position and before the Battalion moves up they will be rolled up in bundles of 10, clearly marked and dumped in the sunken road.

   Lieutenant Lewis will arrange for these to be collected and returned to quartermaster stores by the Lewis gun limbers. Cookers and pack animals will remain at this point.

4. OFFICERS' VALISES-will be dumped at quartermaster stores by 3 p.m. to-day. Quartermaster will report completion.

5. PRISONERS OF WAR CAGE-will be situated at L. 11 b. 6. 6.; all prisoners captured by the Battalion will be sent through the cage and receipts obtained for them. Company commanders are reminded that escorts are responsible that prisoners do not destroy papers, maps, etc., which are likely to be considered of military value. Further the practice of giving prisoners of war cigarettes and other comforts is forbidden.

6. AMMUNITION-Demands for ammunition will be sent to Battalion Headquarters as required. The Regimental Sergt.-Major, will be responsible for its distribution after it leaves the pack animals.

   Medical arrangements will be issued later.

(Signed) R. H. P. WEST,
Captain and Adjutant.
Issued to all recipients of Operation Order No.9.

Eight Tanks were allotted to the Division, three of which were to co-operate with the R.M.L.I., one with Royal Irish and the remainder with the 189th Brigade.

At 4-0 a.m. on 7th the 188th Brigade moving south of Cantaing through Noyelles, assembled on the Canal west of Mon sur L'Oeuvre, crossing the Scheldt by No.5 Bridge and the Canal de St. Quentin by No. 12 arriving in their assembly area by 6-50 p.m. The 189th Brigade moved north of Noyelles and assembled north of the 188th, reaching their position at 8 p.m.; one pontoon bridge was destroyed by shell fire after the troops had crossed, but it was soon repaired.

After a hot meal the 1/R.M.L.I. fell in at 7-30 p.m. on the Rumilly Road, passing the starting point at 1.10 a.m. and reached the jumping off line about 3-30 a.m. and lined out at 4 a.m.

Niergnies, which had been bombarded with incendiary shell was burning at 10-15 p.m. and gave a good mark for the troops to march on, and the march was uninterrupted.

They were now informed that if a break through occurred, the 24th Division would pass through them and exploit the success towards Awoignt and advance towards Cauroir - Cagnarolles; the Royal Naval Division would then form a defensive flank towards Cambrai.

During the night two more pontoon bridges were constructed by the Engineers.

Zero hour was fixed at 4-30 a.m. 8th October and at that hour the attack was launched; though the enemy were in strength, there was little resistance and the first objective was gained by the Royal Irish as well as by the Drake at 6-10 a.m.

The 1/R.M.L.I. had followed immediately in rear of the Royal Irish in two waves; "A" Company on right, "B" Company on left of first wave, "C" Company on right, and "D" Company on left of the second wave.

They moved in artillery formation, covering the Brigade front; on reaching the trench in rear of the 1st objective they shook out into attack formation; at 6-44 a.m. the protective barrage lifted and went on and the R.M.L.I. passing through the Royal Irish, advanced to the attack which progressed rapidly and with few casualties until the south edge of the village of Niergnies and the cemetery on the road leading south-east from the village to the main road were reached. At these points heavy fighting occurred, and severe casualties were inflicted on the enemy, who were holding the cemetery with numerous machine-guns. Tanks materially assisted in the clearing of this cemetery and the attack was continued to the second objective, the main road, which with the exception of La Belle Etoile was gained at 8-10 a.m.; the first frontal attack on La Belle Etoile having failed, "D" Company immediately attacked on left and "B" Company on the right and succeeded in encircling the position and assisted by some of the Ansons the post was captured with four machine-guns and 30 prisoners; the whole objective was in the hands of the Battalion by 8-40 a.m. and touch was established with the K.R.R.C. of the 2nd Division on the right and the Hood on the left.

Lance-Corporal T. W. Child (Plymouth) displayed conspicuous gallantry and skill in handling his Lewis gun section; after the objective had been gained he pushed forward his section to an advanced post, advancing under covering fire by short rushes; later he engaged an enemy Tank, during the counter-attack described presently, and when it was knocked out and the crew were attempting to take out the machine-guns to engage our position he forced them to retire, he was awarded the D.C.M.

Meanwhile the Hawke had established the defensive flank to the north of Beurre Mill for the 2/Royal Irish and were also in touch with the 57th Division as ordered; and portions of the Anson and Hood were fighting their way up through the village of Niergnies at 8-27 a.m. Acting-Sergeant W. S. Carey (Chatham) R.M.L.I. attached to the Hood Battalion, led his platoon against a strong enemy position and captured one officer and 60 other ranks, he then pushed on alone and successfully captured a machine-gun, then returning to his platoon, he again led them forward setting a splendid example of courage to his men; he was awarded the D.C.M. At 8-5 a.m. the S.O.S. had gone up from the troops to the south-west of the village and the enemy were seen to be issuing from it, but were driven back. About 9 a.m. the Germans counter-attacked on the village making use of British Tanks that had been captured; this was the first experience the Division had had of the terrifying effect of these monsters. Seven Tanks emerged from the Sunken Road north-east of Niergnies and encountering one of our. Tanks near La Belle Etoile which had run out of ammunition, forced a withdrawal. Lieut-Commander Buckle commanding the Anson, knocked out one with an Anti-Tank Rifle (German) and was awarded a third bar to his D.S.O., another was knocked out by the Officer Commanding Hood Battalion using a captured German gun (parties had been organised in the Division to man captured guns), one was knocked out by the Machine Gun Company as described below, one by the Artillery and one by the Artillery also using a captured gun, and only two escaped towards Wambaix.

Acting-Sergeant L. Insley, M.M. (Chatham) R.M.L.I. attached to the Machine Gun Company, showed great gallantry, leadership and devotion to duty when in charge of two machine-guns. During the enemy attack he kept his guns in action against shell and machine-gun fire from the Tanks, finally putting one of them out of action when 100 yards from his gun position. He then re-formed and took command of a large party of infantry and led them forward to their position. He was awarded the D.C.M. being already in possession of the Military Medal and bar.

Efforts were made by the 1/R.M.L.I. to form a defensive flank, but the forward posts were driven back for 200 yards; the troops were however immediately reorganised, and, assisted by the barrage, recaptured all the objectives by 10 a.m. When the Tanks attacked, the posts on the right and left of Lieutenant Bareham's post were driven back and this allowed the Tanks to get in rear of his company; Lieutenant Bareham immediately rallied all available men, including some of other units and with great dash succeeded in forming a defensive flank to the left. He inflicted heavy casualties on the enemy and later succeeded in re-establishing the whole line and taking up the original positions. He was awarded the Military Cross, but was unfortunately killed later; he was one of the old Long Service N.C.O.s of the Corps (Portsmouth Division) who had been commissioned in 1916.

By 9.55 a.m. the village of Niergnies was again in possession of the Division, and the Hood had established a defensive flank between the Hawke and 1/R.M.L.I., whilst the Ansons were holding the village.

At 1 p.m. the 2nd Division were driven back on their first objective and were bombarding Forenville, preparatory to another attack on the main road at 3 p.m.; this attack also unfortunately failed and preparations were made to renew it at 6 p.m. During the afternoon the enemy were gathering for counter-attack between Wambaix, Cattinieres and Estormel and a battery was sent up to Niergnies to deal with any hostile Tanks. About 4 p.m. the enemy opened a heavy bombardment and at 4-30 p.m. attacked heavily at the junction of the Royal Naval Division and 2nd Division, principally against the latter. At this time a battalion of the East Surrey Regiment had arrived to relieve the R.M.L.I., but the relief was postponed until the situation was cleared up. By 5-30 p.m. the counterattack was checked, but our troops had been driven back to a line about 200 yards west of the 2nd objective; the Ansons had been able to catch the enemy in enfilade and check their attack. The East Surreys were then instructed to push forward and take over this line and the Royal Naval Division to withdraw when this was done. By 9-30 p.m. the 2nd Division had captured Forenville and the relief of the Royal Naval Division by the 24th Division was begun. At 6 p.m. the Divisional Engineers had replaced the pontoon bridges east of Noyelles by trestle bridges.

The 1/R.M.L.I. were withdrawn at 1 a.m. on 9th and marched back to bivouac near Anneux. Their casualties having been: killed, two officers (Lieutenants A. G. Bareham and A. Wallis) and nine N.C.O.s and men; wounded four officers (Lieutenants A. G. Stone, M.C., W. H. Ford, W. G. Elmes, 2nd Lieutenant R. James) and 116 N.C.O.s and men and 14 missing.

The Divisional casualties amounted to 12 officers killed and 61 other ranks, 27 officers and 363 other ranks wounded, and 40 missing.

The Battalion captured two field guns, 12 machine-guns and approximately 1,000 prisoners.

In this action a bugle was captured from a German Marine by a Sergeant of the Portsmouth Division and is now treasured by that Division.

CONGRATULATORY MESSAGES RECEIVED.

From XVII. Corps Commander.

"Warmest congratulations to you and the Division on their success to-day. I told the
"Army Commander they would not fail, and my confidence has been amply justified. It is
" a fine finish to the exploits of the Division, while with the XVII. Corps."

From the Divisional Commander to all Units.

"The Divisional Commander wishes to convey to all ranks of the Royal Naval Division

"his great appreciation of the whole hearted way in which they performed their task yesterday.
"Without the Division taking part, the Third Army would have been unable to have participated
"in the general battle all along the line; Niergnies being the key to the position.
"The splendid success which the Division attained shows the highest standard of leadership
"and a whole hearted discipline and willingness on the part of the men. No better award could
"be asked for than the news published in this morning's communique."

(Signed) R. R. SMYTHE, Lieut.-Colonel, A.A. & Q.M.G.

From General Officer Commanding Third Army.
"I cannot allow the 63rd (Royal Naval) Division to leave the Third Army, without expressing
"my sincerest appreciation of their gallant behaviour during the Battle of Cambrai.
"In every operation success has crowned its efforts. This was brought about by sound
"preparation on the part of its staffs, by skilful tactical handling by all leaders and by a
"determined resolve on the part of all ranks to beat the enemy.
"The Third Army's record of ground gained and prisoners and guns captured is a splendid
"one and I owe my deepest thanks to all ranks of the 63rd (Royal Naval) Division for their
"fine share in this achievement."

(Signed) J. BYNG, General

From XVII. Corps Commander.
"I wish to express to all ranks of the Royal Naval Division my appreciation of and sincere
"thanks for the splendid work, which they have done since joining the Corps on 31st August.
"The Division has always been in the front of any fight and has never failed to get its
"objectives, however difficult the task; its final performance, the capture of Niergnies with
"1000 prisoners, could only have been effected by troops imbued with determination and soldierly
"spirit. I congratulate all ranks and wish them good luck and success in the future. It will
"always be a matter of pride to me to have been associated with the Royal Naval Division
"during this eventful period of the war."

(Signed) CHARLES FERGUSSON, Lieut-.General.

Cambrai was occupied on 9th by the Canadians and the 57th Division and the Third and Fourth Armies took up the pursuit to the Selle river which was forced on 20th October.

On 9th October the 1/R.M.L.I. left their bivouacs at 11-30 a.m. and marched to Morchies arriving there at 4-30 p.m.; they spent the next day in bivouacs and on 11th entrained at Vaulx Vraucourt for St. Pol, where they arrived at midnight the next day and marched to billets at Pierremont; here they remained training and resting till 21st. On 22nd they marched via St. Pol to Ambrines where they remained till 31st October.

THE PURSUIT TO MONS.

The Battle of Valenciennes had been fought on 1st and 2nd November, which was followed by the Battle of the Sambre on the 4th, when the enemy were being driven back towards Mons.

On 1st November the 1/R.M.L.I. moved by omnibus convoy to Evin – Mal - maison (five miles north-west of Douai) and they spent from 2nd to 4th training; they were now back in the area where the Royal Marines had commenced their career in the far off days of Dunkirk, but during their days with the Naval Division, it was a new area for them, because, except for the Passchendaele Battle, they had always been employed in the Arras – Albert - Cambrai area.

On 5th November the Division was ordered to join the XXII. Corps, the 189th Brigade moved to Douchy, the 188th group to Haulchin (on the railway between Denain and Valenciennes), 190th group to Thiant; the Machine Gun Battalion and Pioneers to Farmars. The movement was made by 'bus convoy, the 189th reaching Aulnoy on 5th.

The 11th and 56th Divisions were to continue the advance on Mons - Aulnois Railway on 6th November and the Royal Naval Division were to take over the XXII. Corps front north of the 56th Division on 7th. On 6th, 189th Brigade was placed temporarily under the 56th Division and with two. companies of Machine Gun Battalion moved to Sebourgquiaux; the 190th advanced to Saultain and the 188th to Aulnoy. On 7th the 189th relieved the 168th Brigade at 5 a.m. and in conjunction with the 56th Division on their right and the 2nd Canadians on their left, attacked at 9 a.m. Their first objective was the Montignies - Quievrain Road and the second a line running along the east edge of the Bois de Rampemont and the Bois d' Audregnies; five Field Artillery Brigades were to cover the front. The weather was very bad and the night was very dark but the relief was carried out by 7 a.m. and the Brigade advanced, Hawke on the right, Hood on the left, and Drake in reserve. When the first objective was gained, Drake was to leap frog over the Hood and then Hood was to outflank the Bois d'Audregnies from the north. By 11 a.m. Hood and Hawke had gained the 1st, objective, and the 56th Division had also captured Onmezies. The left company of the Drake reached the 2nd objective at 12-30 and maintained themselves, but the enemy counter-attacked the right company of the Drake and the Hood; the enemy were driven off and the advance continued until checked by machine-gun fire east of Witheries, the area was then bombarded and at dusk the line ran along the railway north-west of the Bois d'Audregnies to Witheries - Baisieux Road; the Germans were, however still holding the Wood, the 189th Brigade then took a share in the battle of the Sambre. During the day the 190th and 188th Brigades moved on; 1/R.M.L.I. marched to Saultain, halted there for four hours and then went on to Sebourgquiaux where they were billetted.

It was becoming clear that the main difficulties to be overcome would be the state of the roads and country, broken up by the enemy and churned into mud by the traffic and rain.

On 8th November the 189th continued their advance to the Mons - Aulnois railway; by 9 a.m. the Drake and Hawke were on their objective, Witheries was apparently evacuated and by 11-30 a.m. the 189th were on the road running north from Equennes to Dour, and still pushing on.

At 2 p.m. the 190th Brigade passed through the 189th and by 4 p.m. had passed through Offignies and were still advancing being met by a slight machine-gun fire. 188th moved up to Angre where they halted for two hours and then marched on to Audregnies for the night.

The advance was resumed at 7-30 a.m. on 9th with the 190th leading; the first objective was the western edge of the Bois de Montreuil, the 2nd objective the Sars La Bruyere - Eugies Road; the first objective was gained without opposition and the second with only slight opposition to the cavalry patrols and the advance was continued to the Maubeuge - Mons Road, which was reached at 10 p.m. The 188th and two companies of Machine Gun Battalion moving to Offignies and Blangies; 1/R.M.L.I. went to Blangies and then after a four hours' halt marched on to Sars la Bruyere.

The advance was continued at 7 a.m. on 10th; the 190th to occupy Harveng - Nouvelles Road by 11 a.m.

when 188th were to pass through them, and then move north-east as the Advanced Guard of the XXII. Corps, forming part of the encircling movement on Mons. At 9-15 a.m. the 190th captured Asquillies and reached the Harveng - Nouvelles Road at 9-40 a.m.

The 188th Brigade then commenced their advance to the line Harmignies - Malplaquet and the villages of Villers St. Ghislain and St. Symphorien; the line to be established east of these villages.

The Ansons on right, 2/Royal Irish on left, each with a Brigade of Field Artillery and one machine-gun company. The 1/R.M.L.I. in Brigade Reserve.

1/R.M.L.I. left Sars la Bruyere at 6 a.m. and proceeded to Bourgnies; during the march verbal orders were issued for the attack. They arrived at Bourgnies at 10 a.m. and Asquillies at 11-15 a.m. The Royal Irish moved by Asquillies - Nouvelles Road and the Anson to a sunken road east of the village. Before the 1/R.M.L.I. cleared Asquillies the enemy opened a concentrated bombardment inflicting a few casualties; the Battalion then moved into the sunken road vacated by the Ansons. The Ansons also had suffered casualties from the bombardment; the advance was however continued, passing through the 190th at 12-30 p.m. until checked by heavy cross machine-gun fire from the Chateau de Bourgnies (on outskirts of Harmignies) and the cliffs to the north-west of that village above the railway; they were also hampered by the swamps at the foot of the cliffs. after three unsuccessful attempts the Ansons and Royal Irish established themselves in the Chateau and along the railway line. The R.M.L.I. moved to Nouvelles on the left flank in artillery formation, suffering a few casualties. Second Lieutenant S. Goodwin being killed and Lieutenant-Colonel P. Sandilands, D.S.O., and Lieutenant H. L. Hardisty, M.C., wounded. Captain R. H. P. West, the Adjutant, assumed command. At dusk the Ansons and Royal Irish were able to advance and establish the line east of Spiennes and Harmignies at 3-30 a.m. on 11th.

THE ARMISTICE

At 5 a.m. on 11th the 1/R.M.L.I. were ordered to attack and establish a line east of Harmignies and Villers St. Ghislain, but at 7 a.m. information was received that hostilities would cease at 11 a.m. and orders were received that the Battalion was to push on to the line ordered if possible, but not to incur any casualties.

The advance was resumed at 8 a.m. "C" Company on right, "B" Company on the left, "D" Company in support of "C" and "A" Company in support of "B"; progress was rapid with no opposition. By 10-45 a.m. the Battalion had passed through the Anson and Royal Irish and consolidated its objective.

At 8-30 a.m. the following message was signalled to the units of the Division.

G. 419 11th November.

"Hostilities will cease at 1100 hours, November 11th. All troops will stand fast on line reached
"at that hour, which will be reported to Divisional Headquarters. All defensive precautions
"will be maintained and an outpost line established. There will be no parleying with the enemy
"who if he attempts to come over, will be sent back by an officer.
" Addressed to all concerned," -(Signed) C. A. BLACKLOCK,
"Major-General, Commanding 63rd Royal Naval Division,"

On hostilities ceasing an outpost line was put out by "B" and "C" Companies running approximately north and south about half a mile east of Villers St. Ghislain, "A" and "D" Companies in that village. The 189th Brigade were on their right and the Canadians on their left.

In the evening Major Lawrie rejoined to take command, but as he had been appointed to command a Battalion in North Russia, he left immediately and Major Clutterbuck, D.S.O. arrived from the Divisional

Wing to assume command; Captain West becoming second in command and Captain Spraggett, Adjutant. Captain T. H. Burton, M.C. was the only officer who had served continuously from the outbreak of war, beginning as Quartermaster of the Deal Battalion and then joining the 1st Battalion on its formation in Gallipoli and serving with it in Gallipoli, Macedonia and France; he remained as Quartermaster, in the position in which he had done so much for the Battalion in all its weary wanderings and whose comfort was ever his first aim. The Sergeant-Major was S. J. March (Colour-Sergeant, Plymouth) and the Company officers were :-

"A" Company, Lieutenant H. L. Hardisty, M.C. "C" Company, Lieutenant J. P. Curran, M.C.

"B" Company, Lieutenant T.G. Stewart, M.C., D.C.M. "D" Company, Captain T. Buckley, M.C.

The casualties during these operations had been :-Killed one officer (Second Lieutenant S. Goodwin), and four N.C.O.s and men; wounded two officers (Lieut.-Colonel Sandilands, Lieutenant Hardisty), 23 N.C.O.s and men.

On 15th November six officers and 200 N.C.O.s and men of the Battalion took part in the official entry into Mons under the command of Captain T. H. Burton, M.C.; they were stationed near the beginning of the Boulevard Folez in two ranks on either side of the road; each unit of the Division was represented by a certain number of officers and men under command of Brigadier-General Leslie. The Bands of the Hood and the 7/Royal Fusiliers accompanied them. The dress was Fighting Order with steel helmets.

They were sent to St. Symphorien on 20th, but returned to Villers Ghislain where they remained until

PLAN 22

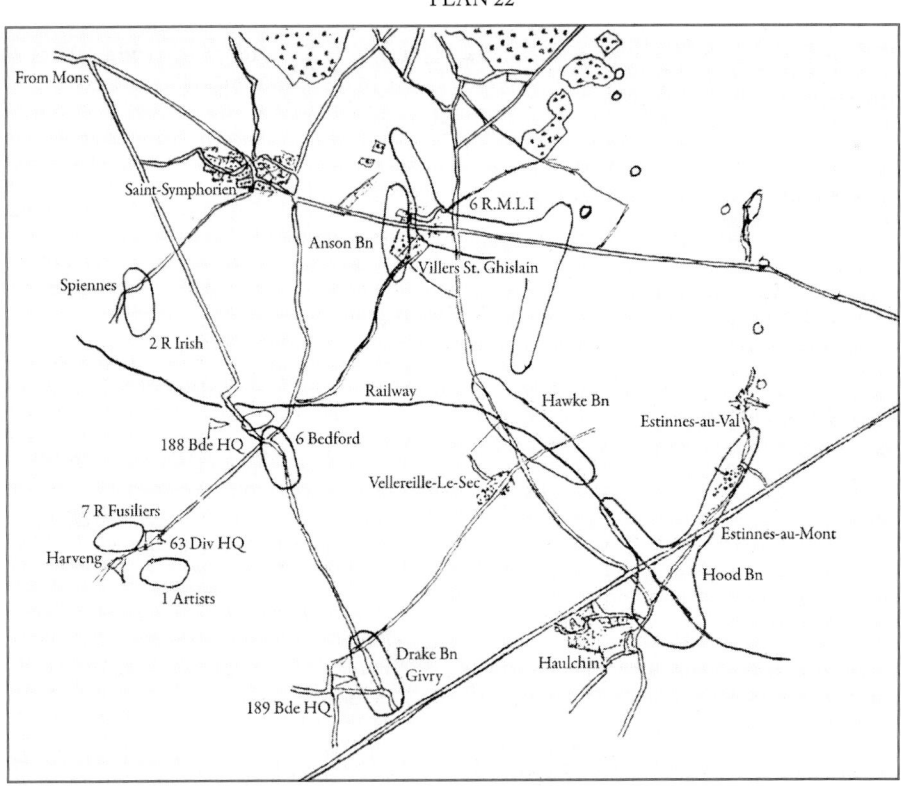

THE POSITION AT THE ARMISTICE.

26th carrying on training, etc. They then marched via Harmignies – Harveng – Noirchain - Genly to Eugies and La Bouverie in which two villages they were billetted till they returned to England.

The Battalion was reorganised, and all the men who had been scattered in courses, employments, etc. rejoined and the strength rose to approximately 1100. The Colours of the Chatham Division R.M.L.I. were sent to them and they spent the long months of the Peace Negotiations in training, recreation, etc. Educational training was gone into, and every step taken to make the anxious months of demobilisation to pass quickly.

They were demobilised under Army arrangements and at last at the end of May when reduced to cadre strength, the units of the Division proceeded to Antwerp where they embarked for Dover, so leaving the Continent at the place where they had had their first experience of Modem War.

They returned to London and were billetted in South Kensington, and on 6th June were inspected by H.R.H. the Prince of Wales who addressed them as follows :-

> "It is a great pleasure to me to see you all here to-day, and it is a privilege to inspect you
> "on parade. More than four years have passed since the King at Blandford Camp inspected
> "the Royal Naval Division, on the occasion of your departure for the Dardanelles. Since then
> "the story of the war has unfolded itself, and after many vicissitudes and disappointments,
> "strange turns and changes of fortune, the complete victory of our arms, and of our cause, has
> "in every quarter of the World been attained. In all this you have borne a part which bears
> "comparison with the record of any Division in the Armies of the British Empire. In every
> "theatre of war, your military conduct has been exemplary. Whether on the slopes of Achi
> "Baba, or on the Somme, or in the valley of the Ancre, or down to the very end, at the storming
> "of the Hindenburg Line, your achievements have been worthy of the best traditions both
> "of the Royal Navy and the British Army.
> "There are few here to-day of those to whom the King bade farewell in February, 1915.
> "Some who were lieutenants have risen to be generals, and have gained the highest honours
> "for valour and skill. The memories of those who have fallen will be enduringly preserved
> "by the record of the Royal Naval Division and of the Royal Marines. They did not die
> "in vain. I am proud to have been deputed by the King to welcome you back, after many
> "perils and losses to your native land, for which you have fought so well."

They were then dispersed to their respective Divisions and the Battalions after an existence of nearly five years ceased to exist.

Rewards earned by the Battalions and Staff Officers, R.M. of Royal Naval Division in France, 1916-18.
ALL R.M.L.I. EXCEPT WHEN OTHERWISE STATED.

C.B.-   Brigadier-General A. R H. Hutchison, C.M.G., D.S.C. (March Retreat).

C.M.G.- Major C. F. Jerram, D.S.O. (Staff). (Crossing of Canal de S. Quentin).

         Major & Bt.-Lieutenant-Colonel R C. Foster, R.M.A. (Staff).

O.B.E.- Major A. K. Evans, M.C. (Staff).

         Major R H. D. Lough, D.S.C. (Staff).

D.S.O.-

         Lieut.-Colonel A. R H. Hutchison, C.M.G. (Beaumont Hamel).

         Lieut.-Colonel F. J. W. Cartwright. (Beaumont Hamel).

         Major H. Ozanne. (Miraumont).

         Major C. E. Eagles.

         Major M. C. Festing, Brigade Major. (Staff).

         Captain E. J. B. Tagg. (Staff).

         Bt.-Lieut.-Colonel R F. Foster, R.M.A. (A.A. & Q.M.G.). (Staff).

         Major C. F. Jerram, Brigade Major. (Staff).

         Major N. S. Clutterbuck. (Aveluy Wood, 5-6th April, 1918).

         Major E. K. Fletcher. (Aveluy Wood, 5-6th April, and Bar, Logeast Wood).

         Lieut.-Colonel T. R McCready, M.C., M.G. Battalion. (Canal de L' Escaut).

         Major P. Sandilands. (Anneux and Cambrai).

Military Cross.-

         Lieut.-Colonel A. St. C. Morford. (Souchez Area).

         Lieutenant B. C. V. Weeks, (Souchez).

         Lieutenant H. V. Scott-Willcox, T.M. Battery. (Beaumont Hamel).

         Captain H. B. Inman. (Grandcourt).

         Captain J. Pearson. (Miraumont).

         Captain A. K. Evans. (Staff).

         2nd-Lieutenant E. A. Godfrey, T.M. Battery. (Gavrelle).

         Captain E. J. Huskisson. (Arleux Oppy).

         2nd-Lieutenant G. A. Newling (Gavrelle Windmill and Bar. Aveluy Wood)

         Lieutenant G. R. Goldringham (Passchendaele and Bar). M.G. Company. (Welch Ridge).

         Captain H. B. Van Praagh. (Passchendaele)

         Lieutenant G. Westby. M.G. Company. (Passchendaele).

         2nd-Lieutenant W. A. Williamson. (Passchendaele).

         Captain T. H. Burton.

         Major C. G. Farquharson.

         Captain T. R McCready, M.G. Company.

         2nd-Lieutenant E. W. Collier. (Flesquieres Ridge).

         2nd-Lieutenant C. H. Bailey. (Aveluy Wood).

         Lieutenant Theo. Buckley and 2 Bars. (Aveluy Wood, Le Barque, Inchy and Canal Crossings).

         Captain R H. Campbell, (Aveluy Wood).

Captain F. G. Eliot. (March Retreat).
Lieutenant J. W. Middleton. (March Retreat).
Lieutenant F. A. Proffitt.. (Aveluy Wood).
Captain R. H. P. West. (Martinsart and March Retreat).
Lieutenant G. J. Wharf. (March Retreat).
Captain R. H. Vance. (Logeast Wood).
Lieutenant J. C. P. Curran Logeast Wood).
Lieutenant H. L. Hardisty. (Le Barque).
Lieutenant R. W. Spraggett. (Logeast Wood).
Lieutenant T. G. Stewart. (Logeast Wood).
2nd-Lieutenant A. G. Stone. (Logeast Wood).
2nd-Lieutenant H. C. Smith (Staff).
Lieutenant A. G. Bareham. (Niergnies).
Lieutenant L. H. Wrangham. (Anneux).
Surgeon J. McBean-Ross and Bar, R.N. (Passchendaele).

Distinguished Conduct Medal.-
Corporal W. A. Watts (Plymouth). T.M. Battery. (Souchez).
Private L. J. Elliott (Chatham). (Souchez).
Sergt-Major A. J. Banks (Hawke Battn.) (Plymouth).
Sergeant W. G. Scott (Plymouth). (Miraumont).
Private Glyndwyr Davies (Plymouth). (Gavrelle).
Lance-Corporal T. Salt (Chatham). (Gavrelle).
Sergeant G. A. Priestley (Chatham). (Passchendaele).
Coy.-Sergt.-Major A. H. Sands (Plymouth).
Lance-Corporal A. Sadd (Portsmouth). (Aveluy Wood).
Sergeant G. W. Woodward (Portsmouth). (Loupart Wood).
Private W. Brindley (Chatham). (Grevillers).
Sergeant G. H. Hastings (Plymouth). (Logeast Wood).
Lance-Sergeant A. L. Hill (Plymouth). (Logeast Wood).
Sergeant A. Paterson (Plymouth). (Logeast Wood).
Sergeant H. J. Trigg (Plymouth). (Logeast Wood).
Coy.-Sergt.-Major F. Windybank (Portsmouth). (Le Barque).
Sergeant W. S. Carey (Chatham). (Niergnies).
Lance-Corporal T. W. Childs (Portsmouth) (Niergnies).
Corporal J. W. Coulthard (Plymouth). (Annuex).
Sergeant L. Insley, M.M. (Chatham). (Niergnies).
Corporal T. W. Smith (Plymouth).

Military Medal.-

SOUCHEZ.

Private R. J. Hulme (Plymouth).	Private D. J. James (Plymouth) and Bar.
Private G. H. W. Duckling (Portsmouth).	Sergeant W. O. Knight (Portsmouth).

BEAUMONT HAMEL.

Private D. Dutton (Portsmouth).	Sergeant W. W. Love (Portsmouth).

Corporal G. W. Gannon (Chatham).
Private E. Gill (Chatham).
Private H. Godfrey (Portsmouth).
Corporal A. W. Heselton (Chatham).
Private J. Smith (Plymouth).
Corporal A. G. South (Plymouth).
Lance-Sergt. H. D. Thompson (Chatham).

Sergeant W. H. Meatyard (Plymouth).
Corporal G. Pidduck (Chatham).
Sergeant C. S. Riman (Chatham).
Sergeant J. M. Sanders (Plymouth).
Sergeant L. B. Wagner (Plymouth).
Private P. J. Willett (Portsmouth).
Private A. W. Wyatt (Chatham).

MIRAUMONT.

Sergeant W. N. Bennett (Plymouth).
Private E. Berry (Plymouth).
Private W. H. Bullen (Plymouth).
Private J. Collinson (Portsmouth).
Private W. J. Duke (Chatham).
Private G. W. Elliott (Plymouth) and Bar.
Private C. F. Gilbert (Chatham).
Private R. Hancock (Plymouth).
Private J. E. Hubbard (Chatham).
Corporal J. A. Innes (Portsmouth).

Private A. E. Janes (Chatham).
Corporal J. S. Marston (Plymouth).
Private J. K Matthews (Portsmouth).
Coy.-Sergt.-Major R. Milne (Portsmouth).
Sergeant F. A. Pearce (Plymouth).
Private J. Postin (Portsmouth).
Private K. Robson (Chatham).
Private E. Scott (Plymouth).
Private G. H. Warren (Chatham).
Private J. Sherman (Chatham).

GAVRELLE.

Private J. Baird (Plymouth).
Private E. Booth (Chatham).
Sergt.-Major J. Bushnell (Chatham).
Private H. Castley (Portsmouth).
Private P. Coyne (Plymouth).
Corporal C. F. Cumiskey (Portsmouth).
Private J. Donkin (Portsmouth).
Sergeant A. T. Eaves (Plymouth).

Private A. F. Hutton (Plymouth).
Private S. Jackson (Portsmouth).
Sergeant A. J. Kearslake (Plymouth).
Sergeant E. R. Ludbrooke (Portsmouth).
Private D. Mackenzie (Portsmouth).
Private W. Rodger (Plymouth).
Colour-Sergt. R. C. Rogers (Chatham).

GAVRELLE AREA.

Private A. E. Crook (Plymouth).
Corporal W. H. Watts (Chatham).

Private A. Wormold (Plymouth).
Lance-Corporal W. Marsden (Portsmouth).

P ASSCHENDAELE.

Private H. W. Nash (Chatham).
Lance-Corporal W. E. J. Sully (Plymouth).
Corporal T. Salt, D.C.M. (Chatham).

Private R. W. Booth (Portsmouth).
Lance-Corporal F. H. Dobson (Portsmouth).
Private A. E. Barker (Portsmouth).

WELCH RIDGE.

Lance-Sergeant J. B. Bamber (Plymouth).
Sergeant L. Insley (Chatham) and Bar.
Sergeant W. J. Lock (Portsmouth).
Private J. Lyson (Chatham).
Private F. A. Morris (Chatham).
Private T. Urquhart (Plymouth).
Private H. H. Waite (Plymouth).

Lance-Corporal J. H. Bolan (Chatham).
Private A. James (Plymouth).
Sergeant C. Scott (Portsmouth).
Corporal G. K. Stanton (Plymouth).
Sergeant W. T. Todd (Portsmouth).
Sergeant G. Wetton (Plymouth).

MARCH RETREAT AND AVELUY WOOD.

Corporal F. Shuttleworth (Chatham).
Private J. Tomlinson (Portsmouth).
Private E. Smith (Plymouth).
Lance-Corporal J. Meese (Portsmouth) and Bar.
Private F. Cooper (Portsmouth).
Sergeant J. H. Carter (Plymouth).
Coy.-Sergt.-Major T. W. Read (Plymouth).
Private E. Martin (Plymouth).
Sergeant G. Smith (Portsmouth).
Private J. Grimshaw (Plymouth).
Private E. V. Holden (Portsmouth)
Private F. G. Penny (Portsmouth).
Corporal G. Ingram (Portsmouth).
Private J. Partridge (Portsmouth).
Private F. B. Wilson (Portsmouth).
Coy.-Sergt.-Major W. J. Waters (Portsmouth)
Lance-Sergt. G. W. Parkes (Chatham).
Sergeant G. H. Hastings (Plymouth).

AVELUY WOOD.

Corporal W. H. Gardner (Plymouth).
Private W. Artis (Portsmouth).
Private E. T. Bell (Chatham).
Private G. W. Bell (Plymouth).
Sergeant W. D. Croke (Plymouth).
Corporal E. Beresford (Portsmouth).
Private A. S. Green (Portsmouth).
Lance-Corporal E. Holway (Plymouth).
Sergeant J. Hissock (Plymouth).
Corporal J. Larter (Plymouth).
Corporal G. J. McCormack (Plymouth). and Bar.
Sergeant W. S. McCullough (Plymouth).
Sergeant H. Trusler (Portsmouth), and Bar.
Sergeant D. O. West (Plymouth).
Private P. Marshall (Portsmouth).
Private T. Jones (Plymouth).
Sergeant J. C. Robson (Portsmouth).

LOGEAST WOOD.

Coy.-Sergt.-Major F. T. Collins (Portsmouth)
Sergeant E. G. Copland (Portsmouth).
Corporal E. Dixon (Plymouth).
Corporal D. Partington (Plymouth).
Corporal G. W. Simpson (Portsmouth).
Corporal W. Tildesley (Portsmouth).
Private F. Blythe (Chatham).
Private W. E. Clarke (Plymouth).
Lance-Corporal G. H. Ellis (Chatham).
Private C. Fletcher (Portsmouth).
Private E. Jefferey, (Portsmouth).
Private F. Jones (Plymouth).
Private J. Keating (Plymouth).
Private C. Kibbler (Portsmouth).
Corporal A. Morrison (Portsmouth).
Corporal V. G. Smeethe (Portsmouth).
Private J. Sumner (Portsmouth).

DROCOURT-QUEANT LINE.

Private J. Lock (Portsmouth).
Corporal E. E. Burnett (Portsmouth).
Private W. C. Beer (Chatham).
Private A. E. Bell (Chatham).
Sergeant H. L. Evans (Plymouth).
Sergeant H. J. Smith (Portsmouth).
Private W. C. Arnold (Chatham).

CANAL DU NORD AND CAMBRAI.

Private S. H. Feltham (Chatham).
Private W. Hann (Portsmouth).
Private G. B. Jones (Plymouth).
Private C. A. Lock (Chatham).
Lance-Corporal W. Mills (Plymouth).
Private W. G. Phillips (Chatham).
Private G. W. Williams (Chatham).
Private W. Wood (Plymouth).
Private D. L. Grant (Portsmouth)

St. Ghislain.

Meritorious Service Medal.

Superintending Clerk F. Cook (Chatham). Cr.-Sergeant J. Amos (Portsmouth).
Cr.-Sergeant B. G. Tomkins (Chatham). Private (Acting-Sergt.-Major) J. Edwards (Chatham).
Qr.-Master-Sergeant S. Jones (Plymouth).
Cr.-Sergeant F.R. Graham (Plymouth) acting Bn. Sergt.-Major (killed).
Sergeant A. J. Spry (Plymouth) as Bn. Sergeant- Major.
Private A. E. Howe (Portsmouth).
Quartermaster - Sergt. A. M. Butler (Plymouth).
Private J. Moore (Portsmouth). Sergeant R Dewhurst (Portsmouth).
Private F. A. Morris (Chatham). Quartermaster - Sergt. E. Diggle (Portsmouth)
Private B. Ortlieb (Chatham). Private A. H. Dowding (Portsmouth).
Quartermaster - Sergt. F. G. Wright (Chatham) Private H. B. Spencer (Portsmouth).
Coy.-Sergt.-Major W. White (Chatham). Private A. N. Waters (Chatham)
Sergeant A. Sharp (Portsmouth).

Mentioned in Dispatches.-
(ALL R.M.L.I. UNLESS OTHERWISE MENTIONED.).

Major-General Sir A. Paris, K.C.B., R.M.A. 2nd-Lieutenant F. W. Goldie.
Brig.-General C. N. Trotman, C.B. 2nd-Lieutenant J. W. Middleton, M.C.
Major F. J. Saunders, D.S.O. Private R Foster (Chatham).
Major E. F. P. Sketchley, D.S.O. Lt.-Colonel A. R Hutchison, C.B., C.M.G., *D.S.O.*
Major C. F. Jerram, C.M.G., D.S.O. (4 times). (twice).
Major C. E. Eagles, D.S.O. Lieutenant W. M. Curtis.
Captain E. J. B. Tagg, D.S.O. (3 times). 2nd-Lieutenant B. G. Andrews.
Lieut.-Colonel J. A. Tupman. Major M. C. Festing, D.S.O. (3 times).
Lieutenant W. A. Pinkerton. Lieut.-Colonel R F. C. Foster, C.M.G.,
 D.S.O.(4 times). R.M.A.
Sergeant G. W. Rayner. Major L. W. Miller.
Major R H. D. Lough, D.S.O., O.B.E.
Lieut.-Colonel A. S. Tetley. (3 times).
Captain G. E. Cutcher. Quartermaster - Sergt. S. Jones (Plymouth).
Lieutenant R H. Marsland (twice). Lieutenant F. G. Eliot, M.C.
Lance-Corporal J. Downie (Plymouth). 2nd-Lieutenant J. Fielding.
Lieut.-Colonel F. J. Cartwright, D.S.O. Lieutenant G. R Goldingham, M.C.
Major H. Ozanne, D.S.O. (twice). Lieutenant T. Westby, M.C.
Lieutenant A. G. Kyle. Corporal F. E. Donovan (Chatham).
Corporal A. M. Butler (Plymouth), M.S.M. (twice)
Private W. T. Osborne (Portsmouth).
Private G. H. Page (Portsmouth).
Private A. W. Dowding (Portsmouth). Major N. S. Clutterbuck, D.S.O.
Sergt.-Major E. C. Gardner (Plymouth). Major E. K. Fletcher, D.S.O.
Corporal I. Moore (Plymouth). Lieutenant J. C. Lee.
Sergeant J. J. Russell (Chatham). Major P. Sandilands, D.S.O. (twice).

Cr.-Sergeant J. Turnbull (Chatham).
Brig.-General G. E. Matthews, C.B., C.M.G.
2nd-Lieutenant J. V. Lord.
Lieut.-Colonel T. R McCready, D.S.O., M.C. (twice).
Major A. K. Evans, M.C., O.B.E.
Captain R A. Neville.
Captain G. A. Newling, M.C.
Lance-Corporal C. Cox (Portsmouth).
Private F. Craig (Chatham).
Corporal A. R Ford (Chatham).
Corporal H. R. S. Frankland (Plymouth).
Private H. D. Gorringe (Chatham).

2nd-Lieutenant H. C. Smith, M.C.
Private A. Cooper (Portsmouth).
Private F. J. Webb.

Captain G. T. Monk.
Sergt.-Major S. J. March.
Quartermaster - Sergt. J. Milne (Chatham).
Coy.-Sergt.-Major P. E. A. Smith.
Private J. T. Todd.

63RD ROYAL NAVAL DIVISION INFANTRY BASE DEPOT.

On arrival in France the reinforcement camp, which had been at Malta under Lieut.-Colonel Mullins, was formed into the Infantry Base Depot on the Army model to receive and train reinforcements, convalescents, etc. The Depot differed from the Army to a certain extent in that it received men and officers for all units of the Division, and it also dealt with the reinforcements for the Royal Marine Artillery units in France.

The Depot was at first stationed at Etaples from 10th June to 31st October, 1916 and then was moved to Beaumarais at Calais from 1st November, 1916, to 31st December, 1917.

Later the system of having depots for each Division was abandoned, and larger depots were formed, but the 63rd (R.N.) Division in common with the Guards and Dominions Divisions enjoyed the very great advantage of always being reinforced by the men of their own regiments, and in the case of the Royal Naval Division as far as possible by men of their own Battalions.

Lieut.-Colonel G. J. Mullins, R.M.L.I. was in command, graded as a D.A.A.G., from 10th June, 1916 to 15th December, 1917. The adjutants in succession told off temporarily were Lieutenant J. O. Curtis (Cyclist Company); G. H. Littleton (R.M.A.) ; Captain D. J. Gowney, R.M.L.I.; R. H. P. West, R.M.L.I.; and Sub.- Lieutenant A. Hobbs, R.N.V.R.; the Quartermasters being Lieutenants R. Bell and J. G. W. Gillman, both R.M.L.I.

As an illustration of the wastage in units the following statement of the reinforcements supplied during the period 10th June, 1916 to 15th December, 1917 shows that-

1/R.M.L.I. received	114 Officers	2651 N.C.O.s and men.
2/R.M.L.I. "	96 "	2249 "
R.M.A. Units "	47 "	766 "

CHAPTER 27.

ROYAL MARINE BATTERIES IN EAST AFRICA.

Formation of the Batteries - Action at Salaita - Latema – Reata - Advance down Pangani River - No.15 Battery to Morogoro - The Rufigi River - No.16 Battery in Myanna Column – Four-inch gun at Lindi-Actions at Tandamuti Hill and at Narunyu - Advance on Nyangao - Honours and Rewards. (See Plan17).

No units of the Corps were employed in the land campaign in East Africa until early in 1916, when it was decided to send out General Sir H. Smith-Dorrien to clear up the campaign. There were, however, some representatives with the local forces, as several officers and men who had settled in the country were retained for service with the local units. They included Major N. A. W. Scott, Captains E. H. Pardoe, A. J. H. Smith and Lieutenants R. M. Bradshaw and L. J. Innes all of the R.M.L.I., some of whom rose to the command of Battalions of the King's African Rifles.

Early in 1916 as there was a shortage of heavy artillery, the Admiralty agreed to send out four 4-inch Mark VII. B.L. and four 12-pounder 18 cwt. guns on field mountings. Major and Brevet Lieut.-Colonel P. Phillipps, M.V.O., Captain G. Y. Russell, Lieutenants J. C. Guy, E. Morres and Act. Sergeant-Major W. H. C. Rogers, all R.M.A. Embarked in S.S. *Saxon* for passage, whilst Major F. J. French, Captain H. R. Purser, 2nd Lieutenants B. S. Hawes and C. A. Stock with 19 specialist N.C.O.s and men, R.M.A. with the 12 pounders took passage in the *Durham Castle*.

At the same time H.M.S. *Vengeance* was commissioned to join the station with a detachment composed of 50 per cent. R.M.A. and 50 per cent. R.M.L.I.

On 31st January, 1916, Colonel Phillipps and his staff landed at Kilindini and on 14th February the Royal Marine Detachments of the East African Squadron were landed to form the Batteries.

The numbers landed were :-

H.M.S. *Vengeance*-Captain H. C. Atkinson; Lieutenant J. F. Ellison, D.C.M., R.M.L.I.
    2 sergts. 1 bugler - corpls. 27 gunners, R.M.A.
    4 sergts.   -   3 corpls. 31 privates, R.M.L.I.

H.M.S. *Hyacinth*-Captain R. C. A. Glunicke, R.M.L.I.
    2 sergts. 1 bugler   – corpls. 23 privates, R.M.L.I.

H.M.S. *Challenger*   -   -   2 corpls. 24 privates, RM.L.I.

H.M.S. *Armadale Castle*   1 sergt.   - corpls. 7 privates, R.M.L.I.

H.M.S. *Orbita*   -   -   1 corpl. 10 privates, R.M.L.I.

H.M.S. *Lanconia* }
H.M.S. *Mersey*   }   -   -   2 corpls. 20 privates, R.M.L.I.
H.M.S. *Severn*   }

On 3rd March Battery S.M. J. Bach, six N.C.O.s and 11 gunners, R.M.A., three privates, R.M.L.I. and the 4-inch guns were landed from the *Armadale Castle*.

Khaki clothing, etc. had been sent out from England in the S.S. *Trent* so that the men could be equipped.

On 14th February, Colonel Phillipps and the personnel with the 12-pounder guns entrained for the base camp at Maktau, which was an entrenched camp with a shelter trench all round, outside of which was a deep belt of cut thorn bushes called a 'Boma.'

Captain Glunicke was appointed Adjutant and the Brigade was organised as follows. The 12-pounders were formed into No.9 Battery under Captain Russell with Lieutenants Ellison, Guy and Morres and Lieutenant Helyar, R.F.A. attached, B.S.M. V. C. Willcox. The 4-inch guns which arrived on 8th March were formed into a battery under Major French with Captains Atkinson and Purser, 2nd Lieutenants Hawes and Stock and B.S.M. Bach - this battery had no number. Surgeon Wollaston, R.N. was medical officer and served throughout with one or the other of the Royal Marine units with whom he was most popular.

Except the R.M.A. specialists most of the men were quite untrained in land artillery, especially as there was such a large proportion of R.M.L.I.; training was therefore commenced at once and made good progress.

With the force was another battery of two 4-inch Naval guns from H.M.S. *Pegasus* (chapter 2), numbered No. 10 manned by seamen and Marines drawn from the Fleet on 10th February and commanded by Captain Orde-Browne, late Royal Artillery; this battery was christened "H.M.S. Peggy" and the guns were drawn by lorries. Nos. 9 and 10 Batteries were brigaded under Colonel Phillipps and attached to Army Troops.

There were also two Naval 12-pounder 8-cwt. guns manned by men of the 1st Bn. Loyal North Lancashire, Regiment.

The guns of the 4-inch Battery weighed 4 ½ tons on their carriages and had to be provided with wheels suitable to the country before they were fit to operate in the field; the original wheels sent out were not adapted to the dust and mud of the bush tracks and the battery was finally not formed until May, when it was numbered No.15.

The General Officer Commanding, Royal Artillery (General Crowe) in his book gives an interesting description of the heterogeneous collection of guns provided; except the Mountain Batteries from India and the Field Batteries from South Africa, there was nothing but out-of-date guns. Colonel Phillipps relates that though he picked up a few directors and other instruments he was never given a range-finder.

No.9 Battery (12-pounders) was at once provided with oxen as transport animals and put through a course of instruction in land artillery warfare and gunnery practice.

General Sir H. Smith-Dorrien having been invalided, General Sir J. C. Smuts assumed command and carried out a most successful campaign.

When the advance commenced, the advanced guard was furnished by the 2nd Division (Gen. Malleson), touch was soon gained with the enemy who were in position at Salaita and on 8th March a reconnaissance was made of the position. With other batteries No. 10 Battery was in position behind a low ridge to the south of the road about eight miles east of the drift over the Ngoro River; with some field batteries No.9 Battery was to the north of the road in a position screened by bush: fire was kept up all day, but at dusk the guns returned to Serengeti Camp, and an infantry screen remained in position. On the 9th the force again advanced, No.10 Battery to its previous position, No.9 to the north of the road under cover of a low ridge about one mile west of Ngoro Drift; the guns kept up a heavy bombardment and at 2 p.m. the infantry advanced and by 4 p.m. they had occupied the position.

On 10th March the force advanced to Taveta, an important post and township, where information was obtained that the enemy had retired to the position of Latema-Reata, two hills connected by a nek, to the south-east of the town. No. 10 Battery had been left behind and Colonel Phillipps and his staff accompanied No.9. The 2nd Division was detached to attack the position, and on 11th March at 4-30 p.m. No.9 Battery crossed the river and was brought into action on the south side of the village and was joined by the 5th S.A. Field Battery and 2nd S.A. Infantry Brigade from Chala. Parties of the 2nd Rhodesians and King's African Rifles gained a footing on Latema Hill where they held on all night, but the attack on Reata was not successful; the attack was renewed on the morning of the 12th when information was received that the enemy were retiring on Kahe; No. 9 Battery and No. 5 S.A. Field Artillery were then pushed up to the nek, the Commander-in-Chief accompanying them. No.9 opened fire on the enemy column, and from the disappearance of the dust clouds the enemy had evidently dispersed into the bush. The Battery was then ordered back to Taveta.

On 17/18th March, the advance was continued southwards and at 8-30 a.m. on the 18th the 1st East African Brigade supported by No.9 Battery from Latema Nek was ordered to co-operate in the attack on Unterer Himo on the River Himo ; the East African Brigade advanced and occupied the hills which lie behind Unterer Himo and Mokinni and No.9 Battery returned to Latema; but later in the day it was brought forward to the river arriving about 5 p.m.; the result of the day's fighting was very satisfactory. On 19th an attack was made on the Rasthaus position, covering the River Ruwu, from Unterer Himo and Euphorbien Hill; the attack failed and under cover of the guns the infantry withdrew, but the 21st Indian Cavalry swam the river and reached Kahe Hill, and in spite of counter-attacks held on so that General Deventer was able to occupy the station during the night; the Germans blew up their 4.1 inch gun and withdrew from the Rasthaus position leaving the waggon bridge over the River Ruwu intact; this action gave the force a hold on the railway, also on Moschi and all the country north of the River Ruwu. Posts were established along the river from L. Jippe to Kahe.

On 17th March, Colonel Phillipps and his staff were sent to Maktau to train the 4-inch battery, but on 23rd as no transport animals were available for the Battery the guns were returned to the Ordnance Store at Voi and the personnel were employed on outpost duty at Maktau for about six weeks. Whilst entraining these guns Colonel Phillipps got sunstroke and was sent to hospital in Nairobi whence he was invalided home. Major French and Sergeant-Major Rogers were also returned to England in April, 1916 and Captain Atkinson, R.M.L.I. to H.M.S. *Hyacinth.* The R.M.A. Brigade staff was broken up and on 11th April Captain Glunicke became Adjutant of the 3rd Division Artillery Group, taking with him seven of the Royal Marine Headquarter details; Colonel Forestier- Walker, R.A. was in command of this group.

When the column advanced down the Pangani River, as all the oxen were required for supply duties, No.9 Battery was left behind at Himo at the foot of Kilimanjaro and later moved to Mbyuni near Taveta. At the same time the right flank column under General Deventer also advanced to Kondoa Irangi.

On May 9th the enemy made four determined assaults on Deventer's Force, which were beaten off and the enemy withdrew; fighting on this flank was then confined to long range artillery and General Deventer was reinforced by No. 10 Battery.

Captain Glunicke and his detachment accompanied the 3rd Division from Mbyuni on 17th June in the advance down the Pangani; they were attached to a mounted brigade and known as the "Horse Marines" in the Division, with which they underwent great hardships. They also accompanied the advance of the troops through the Nguru Hills to Morogoro and suffered greatly from fever, want of water and food added to the difficulties of transport, but earned the respect of the troops for the way in which they stuck to their unaccustomed duties and they shared in all the actions during the advance. Owing to the want of transport animals this column had no heavy artillery to reply to the German 4.1 inch guns near the Nguru Hills.

On 12th September, 1916, Captain Glunicke was appointed Staff Captain to Brigadier-General Crowe, commanding R.A. at General Headquarters, taking Bombr. Lawson and his attendant with him; as there was no brigade major he combined the two duties until he was invalided on 30th June, 1917.

At the beginning of May the 4-inch Battery was ordered to be re-formed as No. 15. Captain Purser was appointed to command with 2nd Lieutenants Hawes and Stock and B.S.M. Bach. Only two of the guns were taken into use, the guns and stores were drawn from store and training commenced afresh; a lot of the men had been drafted off to other units and the best had to be made of what remained; although nominally an R.M.A. Battery most of the men were R.M.L.I. who had had no previous training in land artillery. In 10 days time they were licked into shape by their most efficient B.S.M. Bach sufficiently to be complimented on their smartness and the efficiency of the specialists by the Colonel Commanding the R.A. (Forestier-Walker) when he came to see the Battery shoot.

No. 15 Battery moved forward to Mbyuni, there to complete their training in readiness to move off with one of the mounted brigades, but still no transport was available. Eventually they were moved forward by rail as far as possible and arrived at rail-head 220 miles distant without mishap; the railway running alongside the Pangani river for some distance amidst typical African scenery. The Battery was then completed with transport, the guns being drawn by powerful motors and the waggons by oxen. Roads were deep in sand and the men had a lot of hard work, hauling the guns through particularly bad places; water was very scarce, whilst the country was infested with the tsetse fly which killed a number of the oxen; the men also suffered greatly from fever.

After a week's hard trekking the Battery arrived at the advanced base at Msiha on 11th August in time for the advance to Morogoro. General Smuts inspected the Battery and they then advanced south with the main column, the enemy retreating rapidly; eventually the Battery reached the Central Railway. They found that the Germans had evacuated Morogoro, after destroying the bridges, ammunition and stores and had left the place to the mercy of the British who occupied the town on 26th August.

Here the Battery remained halted until December; this trek was over 215 miles of bad roads, but all kept remarkably well and cheerful despite the fact that they were on half rations for some time.

In September, 1916, No.9 Battery had been sent by rail to Tanga where the 12-pounder 18-cwt. guns were returned to store; Major Russell, Captain Ellison, Lieutenant Guy and B.S.M. Willcox with the personnel proceeded by sea to Dar-es-Salaam, and the Battery was re-armed with the 12-pounder Horse Artillery guns, formerly belonging to the Calcutta battery and was renumbered No. 16 Battery. Mules were supplied for transport and leaving Dar-es-Salaam on 2nd December, it took part in the advance on the Rufigi River; it formed part of the Myanna Column under Colonel Burne, South African Forces, and it was in action several times. On 21st January, Major Russell went sick and Captain Ellison took command. On the commencement of the rains it returned to Dar-es-Salaam, arriving there on 1st March, 1917 and returned its guns to store.

Meanwhile a reinforcing draft consisting of Lieutenant Connew and 25 R.M.A. which had arrived at the Base Camp but was not required for the Batteries, was appropriated by the Naval Commander-in-Chief in August, 1916 as a detachment for H.M.S. *Vengeance* whose Royal Marines had been landed in February and was utilised for the Coastal Operations subsequent to the Capture of Bagamoyo (see Chapter 19) and returned to England in the *Vengeance* in October, 1916. A second reinforcement consisting of 2nd Lieutenant H. Gardner and 25 R.M.A. who arrived in September, were also embarked in the *Challenger* to replace the detachment, where they remained until relieved by R.M.L.I. from England, when they were sent to the Base Detail Camp on 5th January, 1917 for instruction in order to form the nucleus of a Stokes Mortar Battery at Dar-es-Salaam; at this place they suffered a good deal from fever and eventually joined No. 16 Battery on 1st March.

No. 15 Battery took part in the advance to the Rufigi River and left Morogoro on 21st December, 1916 and crossed the Uluguru Mountains by way of "Shepherd's Pass" and reached Duthumi on 24th after a very

[Photograph by Sergt.-Major J. Bach, Royal Marines.
4-INCH GUNS IN ACTION IN EAST AFRICA.

[Photograph by Sergt.-Major J. Bach, Royal Marines.
No. 15 BATTERY CROSSING THE RUFIGI RIVER IN EAST AFRICA.

exhausting four days march, first over mountain tracks and then through low and swampy country in the Rufigi River Valley. Kitoho was occupied as an artillery observation post and the map was marked out in squares. The Battery took part in the action on January 1st and 2nd in support of the attack by the Nigerian Brigade from Mkessas on Mgeta, and on 8th January advanced to the Rufigi; on 10th January the Battery reached Kimbambwe after another very trying march; (on one day, marching from 6.,0 a.m. to 7-0 p.m., they only covered three miles). This Battery was in action on the 12th to 15th and 20th January, 1917.

As the heavy rains were now imminent, half the personnel under Lieutenant Hawes were sent to Msiha (the highest point in the Uluguru Mountains) whilst Captain Purser, B.S.M. Bach and the other half remained in the Rufigi Valley, which is most unhealthy; Lieutenant Stock had already been invalided. The party on the return to Msiha had a very difficult march owing to the rains, most of the men were sent to hospital by the way; they were therefore sent on to Morogoro where all the artillery were concentrated during the rainy season. No. 15 Battery, now consisting of Captain Purser, B.S.M. Bach and 13 other ranks with two guns, was the only unit remaining at Kimbambwe Crossing, all other troops having gone to New Crossing about five miles up stream. Captain Purser was taken ill[39], and on 23rd February was sent to hospital by Surgeon Wollaston; on the 28th he was sent on to Morogoro where he died on 17th March, 1917. He was buried there, and the graves of several Marines are close together, among them Private "Jock" White, the well-known footballer of the Forton Division and Gunner Bolton, R.M.A. The 26th Squadron R.A.F. made a wrought iron cross for each grave.

On 28th February, General Beves ordered Sergeant-Major Bach to move No. 15 Battery, which had now moved to New Crossing, across the Rufigi river and to take part in the advance to the south. The river, which here is twice as wide as the Thames at London Bridge, was crossed on a pontoon made by the Indian Sappers and Miners. Only one gun was taken across, as the only men available were Sergeant-Major Bach, one Acting Sergeant (a Private of Plymouth Division) one Acting Bombardier, and six men with about 300 Native Porters to haul the gun and carry ammunition.

The native gun porters are a semi-military force, and not to be confused with ordinary carriers.

The objective was Niakasika, a fairly strong German position on the farm of Pretorious, who held the rank of Major as he was the Chief Scout of the British Expeditionary Force with which he gained the D.S.O. and the M.C. The gun could only be brought to an escarpment which was 15,000 yards from the objective. Trees were felled to make a platform and to clear an arc of fire, and a wire was run out to the F.O.O. (Captain Floyd, R.A.) this advance of 14 miles had been made through dense bush in two days. No sooner were they ready for action than the enemy evacuated their position and the gun was moved back to the south bank of the river; practically every one was sent to hospital.

Owing to the rains the river was now rising rapidly so that the gun and party only just managed to recross in time; the Nigerian Brigade being the only troops left on the south bank. The guns and remnants of the personnel remained at the New Crossing Camp until August, 1917, and like Marines made the best of things in spite of the rains; they lived in 'Bandas,' large airy huts made of grass, and were constantly improving their arrangements. The native gun porters were trained as gunners and the Marines all became specialists, and quite expert at using the slide rule, etc. Game of all sorts abounded and as rations were short, shooting parties went out daily to augment them; unfortunately there was no shot gun so that they were not

---

39. Captain Purser, who joined the Corps as a temporary officer in September; 1914, had seen a great deal of active service, having served in the Matabele War, and the South African War. He served with the R.M.A. contingent in German South-West Africa, and on his return to England, was appointed to the Royal Marine batteries in East Africa.

able to get any game birds; as soon as the rains ceased, road gangs set to work and on 21st July, 1917, Major Russell arrived with the motor transport and after an arduous march across the Uluguru Mountains they returned to Morogoro.

Meanwhile all the other Royal Marines had been collected into one Battery at Dar-es-Salaam which was organised in four sub-sections, each capable of acting independently. Some reinforcements had been sent to Lindi to receive one of the 4-inch guns which was sent there from Voi, and on 10th April, 1917 Captain Ellison and Lieutenant Guy with one sub-section and equipment left Dar-es-Salaam to join them. On their arrival they found that the gun had been fired with the tampeon in, the muzzle was blown away and one man badly wounded. Ellison with great initiative got four inches cut off the muzzle and .brought the gun into action and the German 4.1 inch gun was silenced as soon as the British gun opened fire. This gun was fitted with narrow wheels, but Captain Ellison told the General Officer Commanding that he had seen two wheels at Zanzibar which would be very useful and these when brought over in H.M.S. *Thistle* and fitted proved invaluable for the work.

Meanwhile Major Russell and the remainder of the Battery proceeded to Morogoro on 11th April, where they remained until it was possible to bring in B.S.M. Bach and the details of No. 15 Battery as related above in August.

OPERATIONS IN THE KILWA AND LINDI AREAS.

On 1st July Lieutenant Gardner and a small draft left for Lindi to take over the damaged gun, arriving there on 18th.

From 26th April until the advance on Mingoyo on 11th June, Ellison's gun had been constantly in action against Mingoyo village, Schaeffer Farm, and the adjoining German Camps. Lieutenant Guy carrying out the duties of observer on Kitulo Hill.

When the push began, it was decided to leave the gun behind, Ellison was therefore made acting Major to command the 25th Royal Fusiliers, whilst Colonel O' was away; Lieutenants Guy and Gardner with the remainder of the personnel were sent to form a section of a new Stokes mortar battery. With a couple of Stokes mortars, they were in action on 3rd August on Tandamuti Hill, a very hot fight; the Germans were strongly dug in with machine-guns and the Stokes guns fired 70 rounds into them without much effect. The British Force, consisting principally of new levies was forced to retreat, and in retirement bumped into a German raiding party under Krant; the porters stampeded and there was a good deal of confusion. The Battery remained at Ziwami until the next move.

The Germans who were very strongly entrenched at Narunyu with their 4.1" gun at Mtua now realised that the British had no long range artillery so that their 4.1 inch gun became rather a nuisance. As the force was to remain stationary for some time in order to give the Kilwa column time to act, the 4 inch gun was ordered to be brought up from Lindi; Lieutenant Guy was sent on with a small party; the remainder to follow as soon as they could be relieved with the Stokes guns; in the meantime Lieutenant Gardner and his party was sent to man the right post of the strong point, established close in front of the German positions at Narunyu, where they remained for three days without fires, lights or talking above a whisper after dark, and so were present at the affair of Narunyu on 18th August.

On 25th August the reliefs arrived and also the information that Lieutenant Guy was very seriously ill after bringing the new gun by raft as far as Mingoyo. Lieutenant Gardner therefore returned to Mingoyo and secured some strong trolleys and mounted the gun on two of them and with the help of native porters pushed the gun along the trolley line until it was abreast of Tandamuti Hill, and there prepared a position and camp. From that day the German gun never fired again by night. From August 29th they were almost daily in action, with aeroplane observation, though on two occasions Lieutenant Gardner observed from neighbouring hills. They were employed bombarding the area about Mtua; information as to vulnerable points was obtained from the natives, and the aeroplanes would then try and locate them, a very difficult task in that bush country. The Germans generally replied with a few rounds always aimed at the British gun and one day it was nearly hit, the shell dropping within 16 paces. The range was 14,000 yards and the Royal Marines made use of observation posts on both flanks. and obtained their revenge two days afterwards; the Germans did not reply and moved their gun out of range. Sergeant Allman, R.M.A. died of malaria about this time, he had kept at duty when unfit which was probably the cause of his final illness.

On 24th September, General O'Grady resumed the advance and on 29th the gun was moved by trolleys to Mtua, the end of the line in British hands.

The gun was then mounted on a carriage with the big wheels and moved to a position between Nambalika and Nyenged. Captain Ellison resumed command on 2nd October and various targets in the Mtama area were bombarded; the infantry occupying Mtama on the 15th. On 17th and 18th the Battery heard in the distance the firing at Nyangao, the fiercest fight in the whole campaign where there were 1700 British casualties, but the Royal Marine gun was out of range.

On 23rd October they started with 500 porters and marched all night; spending the day at Mtama they left again in the evening, reaching Nynagao at midnight marching over a sandy road. There was very little firing from this position; Lieutenant Gardner on November 6th accompanied General O'Grady in case long range artillery co-operation was required, and though there was sharp fighting at Hatia the gun was not required.

On 17th November, Major Russell arrived with Battery Headquarters and Captain Ellison was sent to hospital. The Germans had now run out of 4.1 inch ammunition and therefore took their gun to pieces and buried it, but it was all disinterred except the sliding breech block.

On 3rd December the Battery left for the coast, towing the gun behind F.W.D. lorries, two and sometimes three lorries being required to move it. Reaching the coast on 5th they went by water on 16th from Mingoyo to Lindi and thence to Dar-es-Salaam. The following embarked for Durban on 4th January, 1918 ; Major Russell, Captain Ellison, Lieutenant Gardner and 41 N.C.O.s and men and left for England on the 21st January.

The personnel of the batteries had suffered very much from fever and privations and though none were killed or wounded, one officer and 22 N.C.O.'s and men died of disease whilst considerable numbers were invalided.

Total originally landed 199, reinforcements 22	221
Invalided or rejoined the ships	177
Embarked for home	44

It is interesting to recall that Colonel Von Lettow-Vorbeck the German Commanding Officer, who as every one agrees conducted his campaign in a very brilliant manner was also a sea soldier, being a member of the German Marine Corps.

The following rewards were gazetted for service in this unit during the campaign.

Military Cross. Captain J. F. Ellison, D.C.M., R.M.L.I. Lieutenant J. C. Guy, R.M.A.

Meritorious Service Medal. Battery Sergeant-Major V. C. Willcox, R.M.A.

Acting-Corporal W. O. Croft, R.M.A. Corporal J. W. Lawson, R.M.A.

Legion of Honour (French). Captain R. C. A. Glunicke, R.M.L.I.

Mentioned in Dispatches.-

Captain R. C. A. Glunicke, R.M.L.I.
Battery Sergt-Major J. Bach, R.M.A.
Bombardier A. Simms, R.M.A. (twice)
Bombardier J. W. Lawson, R.M.A.
Private W. G. Mann (Portsmouth R.M.L.I.)
Captain J. F. Ellison, R.M.L.I.
Captain H. R Purser, R.M.A. (died)
Corporal G. P. Branston (Ply. R.M.L.I.)
Sergeant J. Clark, R.M.A. (twice)
Bombardier W. O. Croft, R.M.A.

Sergeant K. McK. Johnson (Ply.) R.M.L.I.
Gunner T. C. Westall, R.M.A.
B.S.M. V. C. Willcox, R.M.A.
Lieutenant J. C. Guy, R.M.A.
Sergeant F. Allman, R.M.A. (died)
Private J.W. Fields (Portsmouth R.M.L.I.)
Sergeant W. H. Mills, R.M.A.
Lieutenant H. Gardner, R.M.A.
Gunner F. Ellis, R.M.A.
Sergeant M. Powers, R.M.A.

CHAPTER 28.

ROYAL MARINE MOTOR TRANSPORT COMPANY.

Formation – Antwerp - St. Omer – Ypres – Inventions – Disbandment - Honours and Rewards.

ABOUT the time that the Royal Marine Brigade was dispatched to Dunkirk in September, 1914, it was realised by the Administrative Staff of the Royal Naval Division that some form of transport was necessary, whilst at the same time they appear to have been contemplating some sort of guerilla campaign, moving the infantry by automobiles, etc. Therefore under the orders of the First Lord of the Admiralty 90 of the 'buses of the "B" type of the London General Omnibus Company were purchased (it transpired later that these were the Army Reserve vehicles) and dispatched to Dunkirk. At the same time their drivers were enrolled and sent to the Royal Naval Recruiting Office where they were attested as Marines; they then drove their vehicles down to Dover or Southampton, stopping en route at Chatham or Eastney, where they were given a suit of uniform and a few articles of kit and then on to Dunkirk.

Captain Dumble, Reserve of Officers, R.E. had been sent over to Dunkirk with a temporary commission as Lieutenant-Colonel, Royal Marines to organise the transport.

About the same time the Royal Naval Division Administrative Staff had also arranged with the Royal Automobile Club to obtain the services of 50 gentlemen, who were to bring their own cars and place them at the disposal of the Admiralty; they were granted commissions as Honorary Second Lieutenants, Royal Marines with pay £1 a day with free petrol and tyres, and these were also dispatched to Dunkirk; among them was the Lawn Tennis Champion, Lieutenant Wilding, who was unfortunately killed; incidentally the invitation had been broadcast and one of the first duties of the Adjutant General, Royal Marines on assuming control, was to limit the numbers to those authorised and return the remainder to their homes. These cars and their drivers proved very useful for transport of ammunition and wounded at Antwerp, though the bill for compensation to the large limousine and other luxury cars involved was a heavy one. Many of the drivers attached themselves and their cars to the 7th Division and 3rd Cavalry Division at Ostend, and it was some time before they were all rounded up and returned to England by Sir John French's Staff after the return of the Royal Naval Division to England. Two of these gentlemen were afterwards well-known in the Division, Lieutenant B. Nicholson R.N.V.R. and the Hon. R. Westenra, who served as orderly officers to General Mercer in Gallipoli and afterwards as A.D.C. to General Paris and General Lawrie, when commanding the Division in France.

Lieutenant-Colonel Dumble obtained a garage at Dunkirk and from among the Hon. 2nd Lieutenants appointed Mr. F. Summers as his Adjutant, and he was given a commission in the Corps. The convoy officers were Captains Hon. Geoffrey Howard, H. M. Leaf and Lieutenant Churchyard who were all commissioned in the Corps.

On 1st October, 35 'buses under Captain Leaf and Lieutenant Churchyard went to Cassel, the then Headquarters of the Royal Marine Brigade; and manoeuvres with parties of the Royal Marine battalions were carried out at Steenvorde to test the best methods of handling the vehicles under the directions of the General Staff. Two days later the orders to proceed to Antwerp having been received, they assisted the Brigade to entrain at the Railway Station, and on this day they proceeded themselves to the aerodrome at Dunkirk, where they formed a convoy of 75 vehicles under Commander Samson, transporting the machine-gun party (see Chapter 10) to Antwerp reaching Bruges at 11 p.m.; and leaving at 7 a.m. on 4th they arrived at Antwerp and encamped on the Aviation ground. They were then detailed for transport and supply work and also as ambulances for the Brigade and the R.N.A.S. units and did most valuable work under fire.

Before starting for Antwerp there had been very little time to organise the 'bus companies properly, and it was impossible to control a long convoy of 80 'buses through the traffic of Dunkerque on its way to Antwerp, Fortunately Captain Leaf was an old hand who had only recently given up the command of the London Electrical Engineers (Territorials). So hurried had been the departure that the actual number of 'buses and other vehicles was never known to the officers in charge of the convoys, nor had a complete list of the names of the men been given to them. On arrival at Bruges it was quite dark, and as they started again early in the morning it was impossible to organise anything. Immediately on arrival every vehicle was told off for all kinds of services.

The journey through the villages on the way to Antwerp resembled a Lord Mayor's procession-all the inhabitants turned out to greet them and showered sweetmeats and fruit on the drivers. The buses with their flaming advertisements, just as they had left the London streets, and the drivers with a mixture of civilian and military uniform made an impression never to be forgotten. Their driving was magnificent, the men were among the pick of the L.G.O.C. drivers and during the whole expedition there was no trouble from a disciplinary point of view and only one driver got over the Border and was interned in Holland with the Naval Brigade.

On 6th October they were ordered to the Linoleum Factory within the inner circle of Forts, the move being effected at night. Just before leaving Antwerp billets had been secured for the men in a girls' school; all the beds were excellent and clean, and washing arrangements perfect, Captain Leaf had hoped to stay there many days, but they were shelled out on the morning of the 8th October.

The work continued on 7th and 8th, but on Saturday they received the orders to evacuate and having loaded up they left by the Bridge nearest the coast, transporting the sick and wounded who could be moved. Captain Leaf's convoy, passing the Tete de Flandre and St. Nicholas, arrived at St. Gillaes Waes in the early hours of 9th October, from here they were ordered to Selzaete for petrol and orders, but on arrival found that the communications were cut and that no petrol had arrived; six 'buses had to be left for want of petrol, whilst others had dropped out by the way owing to mechanical defects. The rest went on to Bruges and parked just inside the town about 8-30 p.m. Here petrol was obtained and they proceeded to Ostend via Blankenberghe. At Ostend, Captain Leaf joined up with Lieutenant Churchyard and a portion of the convoy which had left Selzaete ahead of them.

After one night at Ostend the convoy returned to Dunkirk. The services rendered by this company were invaluable and without them the rationing and supply of the Naval and Marine Brigades in Antwerp could not have been carried out and the evacuation of their stores and sick would have been impossible.

After their return to Dunkirk they appeared to be "nobody's children" (not an unusual event for a Royal Marine Unit) as the Royal Naval Division had returned to England; but the Army had recognised their value and by arrangement between Captain Howard and Mr. Churchill they were lent to the Army and proceeded to St. Omer which was now the General Headquarters of the Expeditionary Force arriving there on 15th October with 46 'buses and 23 lorries and were placed under the orders of the Director of Transport, General Gilpin, R.A.S.C.

On 17th October 50 lorries that had accompanied the R.M.A. reinforcements and Field Battery to Dunkirk (see Chapter 10) were sent to join the company at St. Omer).

On 25th October, Colonel Dumble returned to England for the organisation of the transport of the R.M.A. Howitzer Brigade and Captain Hon. G. Howard assumed command. The other officers of the company were now: Lieutenant F. Summers, Adjutant; Captain H. M. Leaf in charge of the Garage; Lieutenant Hon. Lionel Guest, R.N.V.R.; Lieutenant Churchyard, 2nd Lieutenant Hon. H. Mulholland (invalided in November), Sergeant-Major J. Murfitt (later Lieutenant).

A garage was secured in St. Omer and here most useful work was performed under Captain Leaf and it also became the home of the unit.

The R.N.D. Staff had made no arrangements for the pay, records or upkeep of the unit, so that on the Adjutant General assuming administrative control one of the first duties was to organise this unit. With some difficulty nominal lists of the officers and men were obtained and they were affiliated to Eastney, being allotted R.M.A. numbers and being placed for pay on the Home Base Ledger of that Division. The officers except Lieutenant Guest were given commissions in the Royal Marines.

Arrangements were made for the supply of uniforms and clothing and at first the Royal Marines had to supply the spare parts and other technical equipment, a difficult task for officers and men totally unacquainted with motor equipment, but this responsibility was finally taken over by the Army.

The Unit continued to give most efficient service, and the skill of the drivers was noted throughout France; but difficulties arose with the Army over the rates of pay, the Royal Marine Drivers being paid ten shillings a day, whilst the Army rate was six shillings; but competent observers reported that the Royal Marine drivers were fully worth the extra pay.

They were employed in transporting troops in every direction as the great move to cover the Channel ports was taking place, and they rendered valuable service during the long drawn out struggle of the first battle of Ypres in October and November, 1914.

From now on they were continuously and busily employed in the work of transporting troops, leave parties and the numerous services that such a unit is capable of rendering. The work was very hard on the drivers and frequently they went to sleep on their seats, and sometimes a 'bus was overturned, but fortunately no serious damage was ever done. The work of keeping the buses in running order entailed a very great deal of hard work.

By the end of the year other 'bus companies were formed by the A.S.C. and co-operated in their work.

In January, 1915, Lieutenant L. Guest invented and had made an articulated steel band for machine guns, a very clever invention which was later developed most successfully, and replaced the ammunition bands made of webbing for the maxim guns which were so unsatisfactory under the varying conditions of weather and temperature.

On 12th January, the 'buses were used for the first time in transporting Indian Troops.

On 16th February, 1915, Captain Howard was recalled to his Parliamentary duties (he was the Chief Liberal Whip) and Captain Leaf assumed command.

On the 17th the first R.M.A. Howitzer arrived at Boulogne and six 'buses were used to carry the personnel about 100 to G.H.Q.

On- 6th March, the first R.M.A. Howitzer was fired at Locre.

On 2nd April the diary notes that they went to Bailleul to bring the Artist Rifles to St. Omer there to become an Officers' Training Corps and General Headquarters Guard until they joined the R.N. Division in 1918. On 14th 2nd Lieut. J. Gilliat, Royal Marines, was appointed to the Company[40].

---

40. This officer was transferred to the Life Guards and was killed later.

During the second battle of Ypres they were very active, all 'buses under Lieutenant Guest being ordered to Steenvorde and were there employed under fire between Hazebrouck and Vlamertinghe; on 29th April they note that they brought back 800 wounded and refugees. Again in the battle of Aubers Ridge and Festubert they had much to do.

In June improvements were made in the sights of maxim guns in their garage for Major Baker-Carr and they were much used for work with the machine-gun school at Wisques. Captain Leaf was mentioned in dispatches in June; owing to his great engineering knowledge Captain Leaf was much consulted as to the provision of electric light for the trenches, pumping, etc. and rendered valuable assistance to the Royal Engineers.

At last in August, 1915, after much discussion it was decided that the Army were to take over the unit and incorporate it with the A.S.C., the Royal Marine unit being disbanded. The N.C.O.'s and men were given the option of discharge or transfer to the A.S.C. at the lower rates of pay; very few so transferred, but a considerable number became drivers with the R.M.A. Howitzer and A.A. Brigades and continued their services as Royal Marines.

Captain Leaf became one of the transport officers of the R.M.A. Howitzer Brigade with which he served till the end of hostilities, being wounded; Lieutenant Guest reverted to the R.N.A.S., whilst Captain F. Summers became an officer of the Tank Corps and was one of the first Lieutenant-Colonels commanding a Tank Battalion being awarded a D.S.O.

In the *London Gazette* of January, 1916, for their services with this unit Captain Leaf was awarded the D.S.O., Captain Summers the D.S.C., and Sergeant (Road Inspector) A. Chouffot received the D.S.M.

CHAPTER 29.

ROYAL MARINES ATTACHED TO ROYAL GARRISON ARTILLERY.

AFTER the German Offensive in France in March, 1918, the question of reinforcements for the Army arose in an acute form, and the Admiralty offered what assistance they could to replace the losses; after consultation four steps affecting the Corps were decided on.

(1) The suspension of Royal Marine recruiting for a month to allow of recruits being sent to the Army.

(2) The provision of 400 N.C.O.s and men R.M.A. and R.M.L.I. to reinforce the Royal Garrison Artillery in the form of heavy batteries.

(3) Further reinforcements for the R.M.L.I. Battalions in France as described in chapter 26.

(4) The release of Category A. men of the R.G.A. in certain coast defences by the provision of Royal Marine recruits too young for service overseas, but qualified in naval gunnery.

This chapter deals with the men in the second and fourth categories.

The Army were very desirous of replacing the heavy batteries that had been lost in the retreat; but though the armament was available the personnel were not ready. There were four siege batteries to be armed with 6-inch Mark XI. guns forming at Lydd. The officers and specialists were available and they were only waiting for the guns' crews. The Admiralty therefore offered four officers and 400 R.M.A. and R.M.L.I. The R.M.L.I. were practically all trained long service Royal Marines qualified in Naval Gunnery; the R.M.A. were about one third long service and two thirds short service. They were provided as follows:

From R.M.A. Eastney,	4 officers, 3 sergeants, 11 corporals and 146 gunners.
From Chatham, R.M.L.I.	4 sergeants, 4 corporals, 72 privates
From Portsmouth, R.M.L.I.	2 " 4 " 74 "
From Plymouth, R.M.L.I.	3 " 1 " 65 "

These details were sent to Lydd on 3rd April, 1918 and were posted by the School of Gunnery authorities as follows:-

525 Siege Battery, R.G.A.,	Lieut. O. S. Smith	80 Chatham	20 Plymouth
526 Siege Battery, R.G.A.,	Lieut. F. H. Durham	80 Portsmouth	20 Plymouth
527 Siege Battery, R.G.A.,	Lieut. C. W. Stiles	80 R.M.A.	20 Plymouth
528 Siege Battery, R.G.A.	Lieut. W. J. Backhouse	80 R.M.A.	20 Plymouth

The above officers were long service R.M.A. who had recently been given temporary commissions. The Commanding and other officers belonged to the Royal Artillery. The personnel of each battery was about 150 of whom two thirds were Royal Marines.

After about a month at Lydd, shaking down, learning the new weapons, etc. they proceeded to Hilsea and other camps to be mobilised and supplied with their equipment. N.C.O.'s and men were selected for layers in each battery and paid as gunlayers in the Royal Navy; the Army authorities made all arrangements to preserve their identity as Royal Marines as far as possible; they were eligible for promotion to acting rank in their own batteries and even in others if required.

They were mobilised in the following order.

No. 527 Battery on 3rd May, 525 on 7th May, 526 on 9th May and 528 on 10th May and proceeded overseas to France at the end of the month.

No. 525 Battery, formed of Chatham and Plymouth Marines, was commanded by Major Gaskill, R.G.A.

(T) and commenced their training at Lydd where four privates were trained as gunlayers and did all the work in France. The Battery had motor and tractor transport; they finished their mobilisation at Codford camp in Wiltshire and embarked for France on 1st June, 1918 disembarking at Havre, from whence they proceeded to the Arras Front (Saulty le Bret) and two guns came into action at Monchy and two at Berles au Bois; during this time they were only shaking down and did not do much firing. They were then sent to a position near Villers. Bretonneux (Blangy) and took part in the bombardment prior to the advance on August 8th. Owing to the success of the attacks and the rapidity of the advance they were rarely able to bring their guns into action on the specially prepared platforms, and generally they were firing with the wheels scotched with huge wooden wedges; they advanced via Mericourt - Rosieres and Vrielly; at the latter place they put down the platforms, and owing to the great range of these guns were employed in harrasing fire on the enemy's lines of communications. One gun had a premature burst of a shell which wrecked it, but fortunately without causing casualties to the detachments. They were then sent to the Arras Front at Bienvillers, moving forward to St. Leger Wood, Croisilles and Queant supporting the attacks on the Hindenburg line and close to their comrades of the Royal Naval Division. They took part in the attacks on the Canal du Nord, Cambrai and Niergnies, moving forward in succession to Pronville, Bourlon Wood, Anneux, Cantaing and Niergnies, all names familiar to the 1st R.M.L.I. vide chapter 26. During this time they were often heavily bombed, as the enemy were looking for them; on one occasion a bomb intended for them seriously injured a number of the transport horses of the 1st R.M.L.I. This Battery was often pushed up in line with the R.F.A. with whom they were not very popular, as it was said that they attracted too much of the enemy's attention by their firing, but the Battery itself was fortunate as regards casualties. They then moved through Cambrai and reached St. Martin near Valenciennes on Armistice Day; they then moved back by stages to Neuvalette where they were demobilised, the N.C.O.s and men returning to Headquarters.

No. 526 Battery commanded by Major Oliver, R.G.A. and formed of Portsmouth and Plymouth men disembarked at Havre at the end of May, and after a week in Rest Camp went to Poperinghe. They came into a silent gun position at Roam Farm on the Albertinghe - Vlamertinghe Road and came into action in the left sector at Ypres on 4th July. Here they remained till 23rd September, moving forward to a position on northern outskirts of Ypres on 26th; they were then supporting the offensive of the Second Army and took part in their advance, taking up positions at Zonnebeke, Dadizeele, eastern outskirts of Courtrai, St. Leger area, and Tournai, reaching the western outskirts of Enghien on Armistice Day. They then went to Bierghes and were demobilised, the cadre returning to England on 19th April, 1919. Sergeant H. Walton (Portsmouth) of this Battery was awarded the Military Medal.

No. 527 Battery commanded by Major Moore, M.C., R.G.A. with Battery Sergeant Major Robinson, R.A. and formed of R.M.A. and Plymouth men arrived in France on 22nd May. They were supplied with limbers, caterpillars and an A.S.C. Section for ammunition column of 16 lorries, one car and four motor cycles. After five days they went to Bruay marching thence to Gouay Servins opposite Lens; gun positions were prepared at Lievin about 4,000 yards west of Lens and when the guns arrived from Calais they went into action on 6th June, remaining here for two months firing on the areas Carvin – Seclin - Henin. During the latter part of the time they had heavy casualties from mustard gas. On 15th August they moved to the Arras front to take part in the great battle and came into action at Villers Cagnicourt on 30th, and subsequently took part in the breaking of the Drocourt - Queant Line on 2nd September when the R.N. Division so distinguished itself. They crossed the Canal du Nord on 7th September and came into action about 800 yards east of Marquion; whilst here on 10th September one of the ammunition lorries was hit by a German 11-inch shell and an officer R.G.A. and 14 N.C.O.s and men were wounded. On 11th they moved forward to Raillemont coming into action 1500 yards east of that village, and so taking part in the battle of Cambrai. After crossing the Canal de L'Escaut they came into action against Douchy Thiant and Maing; passing through Valenciennes and Saultain they reached Sebourg where they were in position at the Armistice. Gunner R. Watson of this Battery was awarded the Military Medal.

No. 528 Battery, Major Ryan, R.G.A. in command with Colour-Sergeant Fell Plymouth R.M.L.I. as Battery Sergeant-Major and composed of R.M.A. and Plymouth men proceeded to France and were employed in the Ypres sector[41].

2. COAST DEFENCES, R.G.A.

At the same time that the foregoing Batteries were formed 300 Royal Marine recruits were lent to the R.G.A. to release category "A" men in the coast defences in England and Scotland.

They were posted as follows:-

2 N.C.O.s and 120 R.M.A. to the Portsmouth Defences.

2 N.C.O.s and 60 Portsmouth, R.M.L.I., to Portland Defences.

2 N.C.O.s and 60 Chatham, R.M.L.I., to Forth Defences.

2 N.C.O.s and 60 Plymouth, R.M.L.I. to Plymouth Defences.

The recruits were to be under 19 years of age (the age for draft overseas) and they were to have completed or partially so their course of Naval Gunnery; the N.C.O.s were naval gunnery instructors who would continue the training of the recruits. The arrangement was that the men were to be relieved every three months by fresh recruits so that they could take their turn for ordinary draft to sea. The Army were very grateful for this arrangement as it enabled them to mobilise three or four batteries of heavy artillery and these recruits though the conditions were not altogether desirable for such young lads, felt that they also were pulling their pound in the country's emergency. This arrangement continued throughout 1918 and they were finally relieved in December, 1918.

---

41. It is regretted that no details of this Battery could be obtained.-Ed.

ROYAL MARINES IN THE WAR OF 1914-1919

PART VII.

Miscellaneous.

CHAPTER 30.

THE ROYAL MARINES IN SERBIA.

Arrival in Serbia – Distribution - Battle of Belgrade - Retreat to Salonica - Retreat to San Giovanni di Medua - Honours and Rewards.

FROM the commencement of the war, the Austrian monitors on the Rivers Danube and Sava had been a continual menace to the Serbians, and the Serbian light guns were unable to do anything against them. In October, 1914, French and Russian naval detachments had arrived, together with a commander and a warrant officer of the British Royal Navy to help in an advisory capacity. Later an application was made for a British force and Major B. N. Elliot, R.M.L.I. with a party of Seamen and Marines from H.M.S. *Egmont* at Malta were put under orders to proceed to Serbia, but the news of the first evacuation of Belgrade caused these orders to be cancelled.

On 25th December, however, orders were issued by the Admiralty for this party to start, and they left Malta on 27th December, arriving at Nish on 4th January, 1915; after two days they went on to Belgrade, as the Austrians had been driven back across the Danube, and Belgrade had been re-occupied by the Serbians. A big railway viaduct having been blown up, all their materiel had to be left at Ralia. The party eventually arrived in Belgrade on 7th January and got to work the next day.

Rear-Admiral Troubridge arrived to take command on 22nd February, and the other officers were Lieutenant-Commander C. A. Ker and Paymaster-Lieutenant Fitch; the Naval Commander returned to England. On 5th February Sergeant C. A. Pearce, Corporal A. H. Turner and six gunners, R.M.A. left England with another party of seamen and joined the mission in the first week of March; they brought with them eight 4.7 inch guns on field mountings and 4,000 rounds of ammunition. The mission also had a picket boat, which did gallant work on the rivers, together with a supply of mining gear and torpedoes. On 1st May a unit of the Scottish Women's Hospitals was attached to them.

Major Elliot and his party of R.M.L.I. from the *Egmont* were employed with the torpedoes and mines, on which they had been working since they arrived; the R.M.A. were assigned to the guns. The guns were divided into four batteries of two guns each, under the general command of Lieutenant Ker. The R.M.A. formed No.1 Battery, the others being manned by seamen; three British were allotted to each gun and the remainder of the gun's crew and the magazine parties were Serbians, of whom Sergeant Pearce said he could not speak too highly. T/Lieutenant G. Bullock, R.M.L.I., an English gentleman, who had attached himself to the Serbian Army, was assigned to Major Elliot's party and given a temporary commission in the Corps and served with them throughout and later with the Corps in other spheres.

On 21st April the picket boat under Lieutenant Ker made a most gallant attack with torpedoes on the Austrian monitors lying above Semlin, which was not successful, but on the next night he tried again and sank one of the monitors and then made good his escape to Belgrade, for which he was awarded the D.S.O.

The guns were mounted to protect the town and vicinity, not as part of the town defences, but for action against the monitors and munition ships in the rivers and to prevent their bombarding the Serbian trenches and making use of the river as they pleased.

The mining section of Seamen and Marines laid minefields, both in the Danube and Sava rivers and also constructed some floating batteries of torpedoes, and these measures effectually put an end to the activities of the Austrian vessels. These minefields were laid in the rivers under fire and the greatest gallantry was displayed by all concerned: Major Elliot was awarded the D.S.O. for his services in laying the mines and in charge of the minefields in the rivers for several months; which work was carried out many times under fire from the enemy's patrols and always with a fine courage and much skill in organisation.

By the end of September the British batteries were in position as follows :-

No.1 R.M.A. on a hill Veliki Vracher, S.E. of the city.

No.2 Seamen - Ostrujnitza on River Sava 12 miles from Belgrade.

No.3 Seamen - Teholin Grob on Danube 10 miles from Belgrade.

No.4 Seamen - Grotoka on Danube 20 miles from Belgrade.

During September, owing to the threatening attitude of the Bulgarians, the bulk of the Serbian Army had been withdrawn to guard the Eastern frontier. The only Serbian guns left were two 12 c.m. howitzers on Topchider Hill where there were also two 14 c.m. French guns, the Russians had two 14 c.m. and one 65 m.m. quick-firing guns in the fortress. The Serbian infantry were holding the trenches along the river banks.

BATTLE OF BELGRADE.

On 3rd October the great bombardment of the city began; a plan was found on an Austrian officer which showed clearly the position of the mining and torpedo stations and these came in for the greater share of the bombardment, but they stuck to their posts until all the connecting wires of the observation mines had been shot away and only the torpedoes remained. They showed great gallantry and resource in extricating themselves from their dangerous positions. Sergeant Bolton (Plymouth), R.M.L.I. was killed whilst going to the river to blow up torpedoes.

The bombardment was terrific, 42,000 shells from 12-inch downwards fell into the town in the first twenty-four hours, being directed by aeroplanes; the city was soon in a blaze and the townspeople were fleeing for refuge.

The Austrians had massed troops on the islands in the river below Belgrade for the crossing and particularly on the island of Semendria. By 6th October during the battle of Semendria the mechanism of the torpedoes in the station opposite Semendria had been so badly damaged by the bombardment that it was found at first impossible to fire them. After the enemy had crossed the river Lieutenant Bullock, fearing that the Austrians might make use of the torpedoes and having placed his men in safety, ran down himself to the river bank and succeeded in firing one, but before he could make the other work the Austrian infantry were within a few hundred yards, and he had to run back under a heavy fire of shrapnel and bullets; he then marched his men away to the south. For this gallant action he was awarded the Serbian Gold Medal for bravery and gallant conduct.

The section at the railway bridge over the Sava fired their two torpedoes before retiring, which they did not do until the enemy had crossed and landed troops in all directions.

Turning to the guns, No.1 Battery remained quiet during the first two days of the bombardment, but they were located by aeroplanes on 5th October and on that day and the next were heavily shelled, but still remained quietly waiting until the enemy should begin crossing. On 7th they opened fire with lyddite and shrapnel on the enemy batteries at Kazora about 6-0 a.m. and also engaged the guns in their immediate front, as there were 24 guns in sight. The enemy soon found the range and Gunners Carter and Davis were slightly wounded; the enemy then concentrated on the Battery and the dug-outs were blown in, so that the Battery had to be temporarily abandoned; after dark the debris was cleared away and the guns brought into action against the boats off Kazora, but a heavy shell entered No.1 gun casemate and smashed the sight telescope bar and bracket putting the gun out of action. An attempt was made to lay the gun by clinometer, but it was found impracticable, so the ammunition was transferred to No.2 gun which was dug in about 100 yards off. The guns were really mobile guns with field carriages and were intended to be drawn by bullocks.

On the 8th, No.2 gun opened fire on the enemy monitors in the river, and hit one badly amidships, whilst another ship was believed to have been also hit; the monitors withdrew for a short time but returned and opened fire with such accuracy on No.2 gun which was now the only gun left in action that three men were wounded and the remainder of the crew were compelled to retire under cover. Owing to the heavy fire the detachments were obliged to strip the breech blocks and carriers and later under cover of darkness the gun detachment retired to a small village a few miles from Belgrade.

The casualties in the gun's crews were two killed and 14 wounded, this number includes Serbians, no R.M.A. were killed. No.4 Battery was transferred on 7th to Sanovo Hill, south-west of Belgrade, but was too late to take any part in the defence.

When Belgrade fell the British detachments fell back with the Serbian Army, Nos. 2, 3, and 4 Seamen Batteries had effected their retirement with their guns and were joined by the R.M.A. of No.1 Battery. The batteries took part in the retreat of the Serbian army to Durazzo, whilst Major Elliot's party retired to Monastir and Salonica.

The mining sections left the city on Friday morning, 8th October, and marched by a circuitous route to Torlak, whence they proceeded to Tchupria where the whole force except the guns was assembled on 10th; they waited here for a fortnight and on 24th commenced their retreat. With Major Elliot were Lieutenant Bullock and 26 men, four Serbian officers and six Scottish nurses; they retired partly by rail and partly on foot. Finding their way blocked by the Bulgarians, they were obliged to cross the frontier into Albania and marched down through that difficult country by goat paths, with only four horses to carry provisions for the party. The ladies also marched all the way with them, fortunately they were able to house the ladies in sheds every night as the weather was bitter with snow through the mountains. They recrossed the frontier into Serbia at Dibra, and the Salonica force had sent out lorries which brought them into Monastir as the Bulgarians were approaching that town. The party caught the last train on November 28th (the day of the blizzard) and reached Salonika, where they were received on board H.M.S. *Exmouth* and sent on to Malta, where they rejoined the *Egmont* after nearly a year's absence.

The guns meanwhile received orders on 2nd November to proceed to Stalatch railway station and to entrain for Nish; the R.M.A. had been attached to No.2 Battery and this battery reached Nish at 4 a.m. on 3rd November; the battery then marched to Akeaxandrovitz. From that date to 11th November they remained halted, occasionally opening fire. On 12th orders were received to march to Procupia, but the road was quite unfit for guns and waggons and one gun sank below the axles in a bog and could not be extricated, so that after being dismantled it was abandoned. From 12th to 18th they were retiring under great difficulties over the mountains, snow falling on the 17th to add to their miseries.

On 18th they reached Pristina, where they were ordered to halt beyond the town because 500 rounds of ammunition had been found at Mitrovitza; they remained quietly here until the 21st and resumed the retreat on 22nd, but in crossing a river they lost two more guns, so pushed on with the limbers and spare parts. The retreat continued over difficult paths covered with snow until 30th, being directed towards Pech in Montenegro; orders were now received to march to Scutari. Remaining halted from 1st to 3rd December waiting for No.4 Battery, they resumed the retreat on 4th; the thaw had now set in which turned the country into a quagmire. The road to Pech was knee deep in mud and was crossed by deep streams; the roads were strewn with the debris of the Army, broken limbers, damaged guns, rifles, ammunition, bombs and dead animals; after passing Pech the going improved and that night there was plenty of wood, water and food.

On 5th December they were informed that waggons could not pass, so these were emptied and destroyed, and the party went on with pack transport; they only had three horses, one of which was ridden by the sick petty officer. On that day too they met some of the Red Cross ladies leading a few horses packed with their belongings. On the 7th the batteries arrived at the Pass, blocked with transport, thousands of horses, oxen, and their drivers waiting to get through. The animals were dying of hunger as it was impossible to get food for them. Fortunately the magic word "English" enabled the party to get ahead of other transport and they kept on marching all night. It was a nightmare march, as the roads were slippery with ice and snow, Rosia being reached the next morning; moving on again in the afternoon it was rumoured that the Germans from the north were likely to cut them off, on which they pressed on until 3-30 a.m. The road now improved and the gradients became easier as it had been built by the Italians; it was also possible to purchase food at a price. The party which now numbered 26 reached Podgavitza on 13th.

Leaving there in a motor waggon on 15th for Plovnitza on the shores of Lake Scutari they reached the lake after an hour's drive; here an ancient sailing boat took them across the lake to the town; the crossing took 5 ½ hours, during which an enemy aeroplane flew over the lake but did not drop any bombs. On arrival they were met by Admiral Troubridge, who had reached Scutari by another route. After a rest and a wash they left for San Giovanni di Medua with pack animals and a cart on 18th; the cart had soon to be abandoned, as the road was very difficult and dangerous; Medua was reached on 19th where they remained until the 27th; new clothes were issued on Xmas day, and the party embarked in H.M.S. *Dartmouth* on 27th. Sergeant (afterwards Lieutenant) Pearce was ill with dysentery, but the remainder of the party were fairly fit and proceeded to England.

For their services in this campaign the following rewards were given :-

D.S.O.

    Major B. N. Elliott, R.M.L.I. also received the 2nd Class of Order of the Sava and 4th Class of the White Eagle.

Serbian Gold Medal/or Bravery.

    Lieutenant G. Bullock, R.M.L.I. also 3rd Class of Order of Sava.

D.S.M.

    Sergeant C.A. Pearce, R.M.A.   Private A. G. May (Chatham), R.M.L.I.
    Corporal A. H. Turner, R.M.A.

Serbian Gold Medal/or Bravery (Battle of Belgrade)

    Sergeant C. A. Pearce, R.M.A.   Corporal A. H. Turner, R.M.A.

Silver Medal for Bravery (Battle of Belgrade)

    Gunner S. E. Davies, R.M.A.   Gunner H. J. Carter, R.M.A.
    Gunner D. Wass, R.M.A.   Gunner H. T. H. Fish, R.M.A.

Gold Medal for Zealous Service (Devotion to duty in action at Belgrave and subsequent operations).

    Gunner P. H. Oates, R.M.A.   Private F. Fry (Portsmouth). R.M.L.I.
    Gunner J. R Ransome, R.M.A.   Private F. Turner (Plymouth), R.M.L.I.
    Sergeant H. Bolton (Plymouth), R.M.L.I.

Silver Medal for Zealous Service.
    Corporal A. H. Turner, R.M.A.
    Gunner D. Wass, R.M.A.
    Gunner A. T. H. Fish, R.M.A.
    Gunner S. E. Davies, R.M.A.
    Gunner H. J. Carter, R.M.A.
    Gunner R H. Oates, R.M.A.

Gunner J. R Ransome, R.M.A.
Private F. Fry (Portsmouth), R.M.L.I.
Private F. Turner (Plymouth), R.M.L.I.
Private C. E. Bird (Plymouth). R.M.L.I.
Private A. E. Joyner (Chatham). R.M.L.I.

Gold Medal for Military Virtue.
    Sergeant C. A. Pearce, R.M.A.

CHAPTER 31.

ROYAL MARINE ARTILLERY BATTERY IN EGYPT, 1915-16.

Alexandria - Mersa Matruh - Sollum.

WHEN the news of the fall of Belgrade and the loss of the naval guns reached England, the Admiralty were anxious to replace them as soon as possible. In consequence orders were given for a Battery of four 4-inch guns on field carriages to be sent out; for which Major E. W. Harding, R.M.A. in command; Captain H. R. Twiss, Lieutenants F. Russell, H. L. Whale, R. F. D. Baker, W. H. Begbie and 40 N.C.O.s and men R.M.A. were detailed.

The personnel left Eastney on 15th October, with a certain proportion of battery stores, camp equipment, etc. and spent the night at the Royal Marine Barracks, Plymouth, embarking the next day in the S.S. *Minnewaska* in which the guns and ammunition had already been shipped by the naval authorities for passage to Salonica. On arrival at Malta further stores were obtained, including a rangefinder (4 ft. 6-in.) and two of the guns were mounted for antisubmarine defence in the ship. Here they were diverted to Alexandria, to which base the troops for the forthcoming expedition to Salonica were being sent.

On arrival at Alexandria on 30th October, they were sent to camp at Gabbari, where the 15-inch howitzer (No.3) under Captain Ledgard had spent the summer, as it had been unable to land in Gallipoli. The howitzer tractors and transport conveyed the battery guns and stores to camp. Major Harding at once put his battery under training for mobile work, and obtained horses, mules, and transport from the Army authorities; as he had not sufficient men with a knowledge of horses, and mechanical transport was not available, he obtained the loan of some of the Royal Marine Drivers of the Divisional Train of the Royal Naval Division for transport duties; when the R.N. Division left for France in May, 1916, these men were replaced by R.A. Drivers.

The Battery had not been included in the establishment of the Salonica force and in spite of Major Harding's efforts they were kept at Alexandria. In November the General Officer Commanding inspected the Alexandria Coast Defences with Major Harding, with a view to defence against submarines and light craft, though the commanding officer pointed out the unsuitability of his guns and mountings for this purpose. However, early in December, Major Harding was instructed to take over the Coast Defences of Alexandria and to incorporate his guns in them; Major-General R. C. Boyle was now General Officer Commanding and under his orders Major Harding was appointed Officer Commanding Coast Defences and two of his guns were placed at Sil Silleh and two at Mustapha. The Headquarters were fixed at Sil Silleh.

A few days later two modern 6-inch B.L. guns on naval mountings with semi-permanent platforms were discovered in the stores and permission was obtained to make use of them. They were mounted at Chatby with the aid of the howitzer tractors under Captain Ledgard, and the work was carried out by the personnel of that howitzer under Lieutenant Webley; the first trial round was fired before the end of January, 1916, and the second gun was mounted by the middle of February; when mounted they were manned by the Royal Garrison Artillery.

All necessary steps to organise the defences were taken, telephones were installed, squared charts prepared and the fire commands organised, etc. H.M.S. *Hannibal*, the port guardship, was included in the defence scheme. It was decided to use the naval system of fire control as preferable to the R.G.A. methods for such improvised defences, Major Harding assisted by Lieutenant V. C. Brown devised the necessary rate of change instruments, etc.

Captain Whale was placed in command at Sil Silleh and Captain Russell at Mustapha; the extent of the defences was nine miles, so that considerable work was entailed in supervision and supply.

On 18th December, two of the 4-inch guns were detached under the command of Captain Twiss for service on the Western Front of Egypt at Mersa Matruh, in connection with the Senussi Campaign; the object being to protect the anchorage and camp and also to assist the inland defence and if transport could be obtained, to take part in any local field operations. Captain Twiss, Lieutenant Baker and 20 N.C.O.s and men embarked on 25th December and disembarked at Matruh on 26th. The guns were hauled by double teams provided by the Australian Mounted Troops into a position where they were able to fire both to sea and inland, and the Battery also took over two 9 c.m. Krupp guns that had been captured from the Senussi, which were manned by troops trained locally. In January, Captain Russell was sent to Matruh also and on 16th Captain Twiss and one gun went by sea to Sollum, which had been captured by the armoured cars. The gun was mounted to fire both to sea and inland; when Captain Twiss was recalled to England, Captain Russell took over command at Sollum and Matruh, Lieutenant Baker remaining in charge at Matruh.

After this detachment left, the R.M.A. remaining at Alexandria were concentrated at Sil Silleh and the R.G.A. took over Mustapha, and in March a detachment of the Royal Malta Artillery consisting of one major, one lieutenant and 20 other ranks was attached. In Maya reinforcement of two officers (Lieutenants V. C. Brown and Fawcett) and 40 N.C.O.'s and men, R.M.A. was received from England; the two officers were sent to Mersa Matruh and Sollum with another R.A. officer. The detachments at Mersa Matruh and Sollum did very good work which was much appreciated by the local commanders, as considerable fighting took place outside these places.

The defence of Alexandria presented some very interesting technical problems which were successfully solved; though actual contact with the enemy was only established on one occasion when a round was fired at a suspicious "feather" in the water, which at once disappeared, independent observers reported that it was a submarine.

Target practice was fired quarterly; and the detachments were instructed in infantry drill and riding; the smartness and efficiency of the detachments were commented on by all inspecting officers. Every step possible was taken to vary the dull monotonous routine of the coast defence batteries. As the work they were performing belonged properly to the Army, they were recalled to England-by the Admiralty in the autumn of 1916 for Royal Marine duties.

CHAPTER 32.

SOUTH AFRICAN HEAVY ARTILLERY, R.M.A. CONTINGENT.

Organisation - Campaign in German South - West Africa - Formation of the South African Heavy Brigade- Services in France.
NOTE :-The personnel of this unit were enlisted in South Africa, and as it formed part of the South African Forces, this record only deals with the R.M.A. nucleus of Officers and other ranks, who were lent with the 4-inch and 12-pounder 18-cwt. guns by the Admiralty to organise the unit.

COLONEL J. Markham Rose, Major W. H. L. Tripp, Lieutenants A. E. Rann and H. R. Purser with 50 N.C.O.s and men, R.M. Artillery left England on 21st October, 1914 in S.S. *Saxon* taking with them four 4-inch and four 12 pr. 18 cwt. guns on field carriages to assist the South African Forces in their campaign against German S.W. Africa. They arrived at Capetown on 19th November and encamped at Groot Schuur. After arrival Sergeant-Majors Jenvey and Reynolds were granted commissions in the Union Defence Forces, the latter as quartermaster; they were later transferred to commissions in the Corps.

The batteries were organised as follows :-
In command of Brigade-Major W. H. L. Tripp.
C. 1. battery, two 4-inch guns-Lieutenant Rann.
C. 11. battery, two 4-inch guns-Lieutenant Purser.
1 battery, two 5-inch howitzers.
1 battery, four 12 pounders.
1 A.A. battery, one 15 pounder gun on special mounting.

The detachments were formed of Cape Garrison Artillery and officers and men drawn from the South African Forces, together with new recruits. Each battery had a small nucleus of R.M.A. The batteries were trained and equipped by Colonel Rose and his staff.

On 24th November after testing the guns in the sand, it was found necessary to replace the mules by oxen in the 4-inch batteries and also to replace the wheels by large steel wheels made at the Salt River Works at Capetown.

On 1st December C. 11. battery under Lieutenant Purser embarked for Luderitzbucht, being attached to the Central Force and took part in the investment of Aus.

After the Falkland Island Battle on 8th December as a temporary protection, Captain Rann with Sergeant-Major Jenvey and a detachment manned an armoured train with a six-inch gun at Fishhoek to assist the forts in case of an attack on Simon's Town by the escaping cruisers.

On 25th December, C. 1. battery (Captain Rann) with a 5-inch howitzer and the 12-pounders landed at Walfisch Bay. Infantry with machine-guns were landed to cover the main landing and they were taken ashore in boats manned by Royal Marines. The landing was covered by the *Hyacinth* and *Albion* (see chapter 2) and as soon as the troops landed positions were taken up in the sand dunes.

On 19th January the 5-inch howitzer was sent up to Swakopmund where the South African Forces had also landed.

On 25th February Nonidas and Goaknontes were attacked and captured, Major Tripp was in command of the artillery and the 5-inch and 12-pounders were in support, but the Germans retired very quickly.

South African Heavy Artillery, R.M.A. Contingent

Another draft of 25 R.M.A. under Major Peacock and Captain H. C. Harrison arrived in February to reinforce the contingent. On 18th March, C. 1. battery under Captain Rann moved up to Swakopmund and Nonidas; and on 20th Riet and Jakalswater were taken by the South African Forces after a sharp fight, Major Tripp was in charge of the artillery; C. 1. battery was then moved up to Riet.

On 23rd April, 1915, the northern force was split into three columns; the 5-inch howitzer and a section of the 12-pounders were attached to the right column, Colonel Albert; C.1. battery to the central column, Colonel Wylie, which marched via Jakalswater - Kubas, where the wells were found to have been blown in and poisoned. The A.A. 15-pounder accompanied the left column, this gun had one R.M. gunlayer and took part in the attack on Trekkopjies on 26th, being the only gun there and it assisted to drive off the attack of two German light batteries.

C. 11. battery which was now commanded by Captain Harrison, was hurried up by train to the central column as Aus had now been evacuated, but arrived too late; C. 1. battery accompanied the column to Karibib, C. 11. arriving a little later; C. 1. and 11. were now merged into one battery under Captain Harrison with Captain Rann as second in command.

Karibib was occupied on 5th May and on 10th Windkoek, the principal town was occupied by General Mackenzie; on 20th an armistice for eight days was concluded, and as the main resistance was broken a good many troops were sent home.

The further trek northwards commenced on 16th June, the troops travelling light with only six days rations; on the 22nd. the enemy were reported by aeroplanes to be holding a strong position at Kalkfeldt. "C" Battery and the 5-inch howitzer came into action and the Germans retreated; the troops following them up reached Otavifontein where the Germans unconditionally surrendered. Colonel Rose had been on General Botha's staff. The batteries returned to Capetown arriving at the end of July, 1915, where all troops were paid off and discharged.

During this campaign there was practically very little fighting for the artillery, the Germans retreating and blowing up railway lines and wells and poisoning the latter. Troops and animals however, suffered very much from the long marches over sand and from the shortage of food and water.

Colonel Rose then set to work to organise the South African Heavy Artillery for service in France; it consisted of five batteries recruited: No.1 in Western Cape Province, No.2 in Eastern Cape Province, No.3 in the Transvaal, No.4 in the Kimberley district, No. 5 in the Province of Natal. The Brigade left South Africa for England in the *Kildonan Castle* on 28th August, numbering approximately 650 officers and men.

For their services in South Africa Colonel Rose was awarded the D.S.O., Major Tripp the M.C., Captain J. E. Reynolds the D.S.C., whilst Captain Harrison and Sergeant-Major Flaye were mentioned in dispatches. Sergeant-Majors Flaye and Jenvey were given commissions in the Corps.

On arrival at Bexhill the Brigade was incorporated with the R.G.A. Siege Batteries, but retained their South African cap badge. They were re-armed with the 6-inch 26 cwt. howitzers and were sent to Lydd for training. Colonel Rose with Lieutenant Jenvey was appointed to command the Depot; Major Peacock and Lieutenant Purser returned to Corps duty and the other Royal Marine Officers were allotted to :-

    71st Siege Battery (Transvaal)-Major Harrison, Captain Rann, Battery-Sergeant-Major Dacombe.
    73rd Siege Battery (Cape)-B.S.M. Guest, R.M.A.
    74th Siege Battery (Eastern Province)-B.S.M. Davis, R.M.A.
    75th Siege Battery (Natal)-Major W. H. L. Tripp, B.S.M. Usborne.

There was still a nucleus of R.M.A. in the Batteries but. they were gradually withdrawn; the Batteries however served throughout the war in France.

Captain Harrison was awarded the D.S.O. and a Brevet Majority for his gallantry in command of 71st Battery, especially for his reconnaissances at the battle of Pozieres; he was gassed on 1st August, 1916, and was succeeded by Captain Rann; resuming command on 25th September he was finally invalided on 22nd December, 1916. Captain Rann who succeeded him remained in command till 20th July, 1917 when he was wounded, having been awarded the M.C. for his services as observing officer at Bazentin on 9th November, 1916; he was made first a member, and then an officer of the British Empire Order for his services with the Brigade. B.S.M. Dacombe was awarded the D.C.M. for his services at Ypres during a Canadian counter-attack in June, 1916 when he showed great gallantry and determination in rescuing three wounded men in the open. Corporal Naitby, R.M.A. of this Battery was awarded the Military Medal for services at Ypres in September, 1917, and Sergeant H. Mann, R.M.A. the Medaille Militaire and M.S.M. for general services in the field. Sergeant Backhouse was also granted a temporary commission in the Corps and served with No. 528 Battery later.

In the 75th Battery, Major Tripp was awarded the D.S.O. for his services and appointed to command a group of heavy artillery with the temporary rank of Lieutenant-Colonel. B.S.M. Usborne was awarded the D.C.M.

In the 73rd Battery, B.S.M. Guest was awarded the D.C.M. for showing courage and determination throughout and setting a fine example under fire.

In 74th B.S.M. Davis was also awarded the D.C.M. for performing good work throughout and setting a fine example under fire; he was later appointed Regimental Sergeant-Major of the Reserve Brigade at Plymouth, having commenced the war as a mobilised gunner in the R.F.R.

CHAPTER 33.

ROYAL MARINE BATTALION IN IRELAND, APRIL-MAY, 1916.

ON 27th April, 1916, late in the evening, telegraphic orders were received at the several Royal Marine Headquarters for a Battalion to be detailed for a service which was not specified. The various companies left by special trains during the night and arrived at Pembroke Dock the following afternoon; they were accommodated for the night in Army hutments and hospitably entertained by the Reserve Battalions quartered there. It was then found that the Battalion was formed as follow:- and that owing to the Easter Rebellion in Ireland the destination was Queenstown.

Commanding Officer: Lieutenant-Colonel H. E. Blumberg, C.B., R.M.L.I.
Second in Command: Brevet Lieutenant-Colonel J. B. Finlaison, R.M.L.I.
Adjutant: Captain H. C. Pope, R.M.L.I.
Machine Gun Officer: Lieutenant G. P. Lathbury, D.S.O., R.M.L.I.
Quartermaster: Lieutenant F. E. Benham, R.M.L.I.
R.M.A.: two 12-pounder Field Guns: Captain Van der Kiste, Lieutenants Mead and Lyne.
Chatham Company: Captain C. Shelton, Lieutenants J. Cheetham, D.S.C., G. Rutherford, L. F. Tayler, S. H. Inskip, C. Watson.
Portsmouth Company: Captain C. H. Coode, Lieutenants J. Harris, A. Bareham, L. Wrangham, B. G. Andrews.
Plymouth Company "C": Major L. Norcock, Lieutenants A. N. Williams, C. P. Tuckey, F. C. Law, D.S.C., S. Tracey, A. Boyle.
Plymouth Company "D": Captain M. R Yeo, Lieutenants G. M. Crick, W. J. Stuart, G. Underhill, H. Bennie, E. L. Platts.

A detachment of A.S.C. of two officers with waggons and horses came from Woolwich and a large number of machine-guns together with the necessary camp equipment had also been picked up en route by the Chatham train.

That night, the 28th, Lieutenants Crick and Law with 100 N.C.O.s and men of the Plymouth Companies left in the *Iris* for Kingstown. On the following morning the Battalion embarked in the S.S. *Archangel* with all its stores; the A.S.C. and their horses embarking in the *Innisfallen*.

It was then found that the Plymouth companies were 100 over strength; this was due to; men joining up in the dark in their eagerness to proceed on an unknown adventure; though the ship was very crowded it was decided to retain them and it was not until some days later, when the whereabouts of the Battalion became known at the Headquarters, that piteous appeals for their return were received from the Drafting Officer; in the ship matters were made worse by the arrival, just as the ship was sailing of a company of the Queen's Westminster Rifles.

The ship left Pembroke after dark and after a good passage arrived at Queenstown on Sunday morning 30th April, and the Commanding Officer reported to the Commander-in-Chief, Admiral Sir Lewis Bayly.

A company of the Portsmouth Division R.M.L.I. under Major J. A. M. A. Clark with Captain Bell, Lieutenants Dowding, Parvin and Ligertwood had left Forton on 25/26th April and embarking at Pembroke on 26th had arrived at Queenstown on the 27th. Major Clark had at once taken over the guarding of Haulbowline Dockyard and Admiralty House, whilst Captain Bell and 100 N.C.O.s and men had proceeded to guard the naval establishments at Galway.

The rebellion was now in full swing, but more particularly in the east and round Dublin; the measures adopted by Admiral Bayly had been effective in preventing any general rising in the south and west.

Immediately on the arrival of the Battalion Major Clark and the remainder of his company embarked for Galway; Lieutenant Mead and one gun's crew with one 12-pounder accompanying them.

Major Norcock's company took over the guard of the Dockyard and Admiralty House and were quartered in one of the storehouses. As large numbers of the workmen in the yard were Sinn Feiners and rebels this work was of a very anxious nature. The remainder of the Battalion were temporarily transferred to H.M.S. *Albion* for accommodation, the A.S.C. being quartered in the Army Camp at Queenstown.

In the afternoon Captain Yeo, Lieutenants Underhill and Bennie with two platoons and two machine-guns embarked in H.M.S. *Primrose* and were landed at Fenit near Tralee, which they placed in a state of defence to protect the Naval Base there.

Lieutenants Stuart and Platts with one platoon and one machine-gun also left in H.M.S. *Iris* for the signal station at Sybil Head which they placed in a state of defence. In the evening, headquarters were established in the Isolation Hospital in the Dockyard and the remaining platoon of "D" Company and the rest of the R.M.A. encamped in the Dockyard. Late in the evening Lieutenant Rutherford and one platoon of "A" Company with one machine-gun proceeded in H.M.S. *Bluebell* to Cahirmore near Berehaven and garrisoned the signal station on 1st May.

On the evening of 1st May Lieutenant Stuart's post at Sybil Head was attacked by the rebels and three men were wounded (one seriously), the assailants, though met with heavy fire escaped.

Major Clark arrived at Galway on 1st May and took over the duties of Officer Commanding troops. This company after occupying the place, made raids in conjunction with the Police, and during the next few days rounded up about 300 prisoners, who were handed over to the Army to be taken to Dublin; they also raided some of the islands in the bay and secured further prisoners.

Owing to the inconvenience of the companies being quartered in H.M.S. *Albion* camps were arranged in the Dockyard and on 2nd May the remainder of the Battalion were disembarked and placed under canvas where they quickly made themselves comfortable, receiving the most kindly assistance from all the dockyard officials.

On 3rd May, as the post at Fenit was too large for the garrison allotted, Lieutenant Boyle with the remaining platoon of "D" Company and Lieutenant Tayler with one platoon "A" Company were sent to reinforce Captain Yeo, and on the same day Lieutenants Crick and Law with the detachment from Kingstown rejoined the Battalion; they had not been landed to take part in the fighting which was going on in Dublin, but were kept at short notice to protect the naval establishments ashore.

The Battalion and transport were then organised as a mobile force to move as directed by the Commander-in-Chief (Sir Lewis Bayly), wherever their services might be required; the S.S. *Great Southern* being kept ready with steam up to move at short notice. No one was allowed to leave Haulbowline Island; the object of the Battalion was to protect all the Naval establishments round the coast.

The Battalion then went into training in the Dockyard, a miniature range and bayonet range being constructed, whilst crews were trained to man additional 12-pounder 8 cwt. and 18 cwt. guns, arrangements being made to fit limbered waggons to draw them by mules.

Whilst they were at Queenstown divers recovered from the German ship that had been sunk at the entrance specimens of the arms that Sir Roger Casement was bringing over for the rebels, and it was interesting to note that they were Russian arms that had been captured by the Germans. 7th May, being a Sunday, service was held in the Dockyard chapel, but mindful of Indian mutiny experience the church parties carried their arms during the service. On 8th May, Lieutenant Inskip and a half platoon "A" Company proceeded to Berehaven to guard the Naval centre at Castletown.

As the rebellion in the south was now well in hand Sir Lewis Bayly decided that he could dispense with the Battalion; the company at Galway was therefore withdrawn on 11th May, and orders were issued on 12th that the Battalion was to return to England, leaving guards of 25 men at Fenit, Cahirmore and Sybil Point with 130 N.C.O.'s and men under Lieutenants Crick and Tracey for duty at Haulbowline and Admiralty House. Little did they imagine that these posts would be held by the Corps for the next six years, being reinforced in 1920 by the 8th Royal Marine Battalion; it was not till 1922 that the posts were finally withdrawn.

On 13th May Major Clark's company with Captain Yeo's, together with the R.M.A. and their guns returned to England in S.S. *Great Southern* under the command of Lieut.-Colonel Finlaison, whilst Lieutenant Stuart's platoon proceeded in H.M.S. *Iris*.

On 15th May the Commander-in-Chief, who had been most kind and helpful to the Battalion, inspected the camps of the remaining portion, and in the evening they embarked in S.S. *Connaught*; after a most unpleasant voyage due to fog and delays on the part of the ship, they disembarked at Neyland (Milford Haven) and were dispersed to their respective headquarters.

CHAPTER 34.

ROYAL MARINE ARTILLERY, HEAVY SIEGE TRAIN AT DUNKIRK.

WHEN the First Lord of the Admiralty promised assistance to the Belgians in the defence of Antwerp, among the units sent out were some 9.2-inch and other guns. These were manned by a small party of seamen under Lieutenant Littlejohns, R.N.; they failed to get into Antwerp in time, but their commanding officer mounted them in a train and they were a very valuable aid to the Belgians, when they established themselves on the Yser. The Germans after occupying Ostende, had mounted several heavy batteries, principal among which was one of four 28 c.m. (11-inch) guns in the south-west suburbs of Ostende, known as T4 or Tirpitz, which was a thorn in the side of the ships operating off the Belgian coast, because these guns had a range of 30,000 yards.

The bombardment of the docks at Ostende in September, 1915, by the Monitors made it clear that no further results could be gained by these methods of attack, so long as Tirpitz battery was active and unhampered.

Admiral Bacon now commanding the Dover Patrol, therefore decided to land four 9.2-inch guns from the ships and one 12-inch with a special land mounting to deal with them; the 9.2-inch guns were manned by naval personnel. In order to relieve a naval officer, Captain H. Peck, R.M.A., was sent over in December, 1915, for duty with these guns as adjutant, and served with them till 1918.

The 12-inch gun was on a special land mounting, with a girder platform, similar to those of the 15-inch howitzers, and was placed at St. Joseph's Farm, near Adinkerke, and to hide it from aeroplanes, a skeleton barn was built over it, similar to those in use in that country. The gun was mounted with the aid of some Canadian railway troops, in compliment to whom it was named "Dominion;" Captain W. P. Dyer (retired), R.M.A. and 16 N.C.O.s and men who had received a special training at the Coventry Ordnance Works, were sent over in April, 1916, and were billetted in the farm. In June, Captain H. Peck relieved Captain Dyer and remained in command till the formation of the R.M.A. Siege Train, when he became adjutant in February, 1917.

The four 9.2-inch guns were mounted well forward near Nieuport Bains; two of them known as "Eastney" and "Barbara," were mounted in concrete gun pits near Groenendijk; two known as the "Carnac" battery were about 400 yards in rear of the others. "Eastney" was manned by a R.M. detachment, who had constructed the emplacements, the work having to be carried out at night, Captain J. H. Hollingsworth, R.M.A., being in charge, the others were manned by seamen.

These four 9.2-inch guns with two 6-inch guns, and a 9.2-inch, on a railway mounting formed the unit known as the Royal Naval Siege Guns, under Captain Halahan, R.N. (killed later at Zeebrugge). The French, who were in command in this sector, could call on this unit for assistance, but the Admiral retained the control of the 12-inch gun, under himself. Captain V. C. Brown, R.M.A., was for a short time in command of the six-inch guns.

In view of the operations which were to be undertaken in Flanders in 1917, two more 12-inch and three more 9.2-inch guns, as well as later eight 7.5-inch guns (ex - *Swiftsure*), were sent out early in 1917. The 12-inch and one 9.2-inch were mounted in structures of timber and canvas, intended to represent the numerous barns in the vicinity; the other two 9.2-inch were mounted in concrete emplacements, east of the Coxyde - Coxyde Bains Road. These guns together with "Dominion" became in February, 1917, the

R.M.A. Heavy Siege Train under Major R. E. Kilvert, with Captain H. Peck as adjutant, and Lieutenant Littleton as quartermaster, and were manned by R.M.A., so that there were now two units under the Admiral of the Dover Patrol, the Royal Naval Siege Guns and the R.M.A. Heavy Siege Train. They were all borne on the books of the *Attentive II*.

One of the 12-inch guns "Nameless" (Captain Bishop), was mounted near "Dominion" at Adinkerke, and the other "Jutland" under Captain Connew, six miles in rear at Leffrinckhouke. Two of the 9.2-inch guns, were as stated before at Coxyde, the third at a farm called "Henri" near the "Dominion" gun. This battery was under Major Chancellor, with Captain Stewart at "Henri" and Captain Mathieson at Coxyde. Captain Webb-Bowen, R.M.A. and C. F. Woolley, R.M.L.I., were attached as observers; Captain Hollingsworth was transferred from "Eastney" to the new unit, where his mathematical knowledge was invaluable. The headquarters were fixed at Dominion Camp.

The moving of these guns without a hitch or accident, using only skidding, jacks and tractors was very wonderful. Captain R. F. Reynolds was chiefly responsible, his skill and coolness were remarkable, whilst Commander Bickford, R.N. (son of the late Colonel Bickford, R.M.A.), was indefatigable in the help afforded.

Great assistance was also received from the tractors and transport staffs of No.2 and 3 Howitzers of the R.M.A. Howitzer Brigade, who were operating from Oost - Dunkerque during July and August, 1917.

The eight 7. 5-inch guns were also added in the late summer and autumn to the forward guns under the Royal Naval Siege Guns. During 1917, these batteries were engaging the German heavy guns, to assist the French and Belgian artillery, as well as to assist the monitors bombarding the sea defences. In June, 1917, the British having taken over the sector in preparation for the Offensive, the Fourth British Army took over both the R.N. Siege Guns and R.M.A. Heavy Siege Train[42]. In June the German 15-inch gun, known as "Leugenboom" bombarded the town of Dunkirk; this gun was their great opponent in this sector and many duels were fought between it and the 12-inch guns, but the end of the war found both sides still in action.

On 10th and 11th July, 1917, the Germans made their big attack on Nieuport and Lombartzyde (in this action the Howitzers and Siege Train shared the same observation posts and did very useful work). The Germans established themselves so close that "Eastney" and "Barbara" batteries became untenable, working parties being several times compelled to cease work owing to machine-gun fire ; "Carnac" remained in action till the end.

In November, 1917, the French relieved the Fourth British Army in control of the sector, and French gunners relieved the Royal Artillery personnel. Both the French staff and later the Belgians were most anxious to retain the naval heavy guns, as they fully realised the great value of these heavy pieces in replying to the German heavy guns.

The Admiralty, however, were anxious to withdraw the naval personnel and arrangements were accordingly made. In December, 1917, Major Iremonger, R.M.A., relieved Lieut-Commander Brewill, D.S.C., R.N., as gunnery lieutenant of the Royal Naval Siege Guns. As the mounting of the guns was now approaching completion, and an increase of personnel was required, it was decided to withdraw all the naval personnel and replace them entirely by R.M.A., and to amalgamate the two units into one as the R.M.A. Siege Guns.

---

42. *Two of the 9. 2-inch guns and the 7 .5-inch guns of the R.N. Siege Gun Unit, were manned by Royal Artillery personnel.*

Major R. E. Kilvert, who was awarded the D.S.O., for his services in commanding and organising the unit in the Gazette of 1st January, 1918, was appointed Brigade-Major at Eastney, and was relieved in January by Major and Brevet-Lieut.-Colonel R. T. Ford.

In January, 1918, the 6th Belgian Division took over the sector and the Siege Guns henceforth worked in conjunction with them.

The establishment of the unit was finally fixed in May, 1918, as follows :-

31 officers, 2 warrant officers, class 1., 427 N.C.O.s and men, R.M.A.

3 officers (medical)	23 armourers, carpenters, etc., RN.
1 officer	8 signallers, R.E. and R.G.A.
1 officer	120.R. Canadian railway troops (for construction work)

Owing to the increase of the personnel, the command was raised to that of a Lieut.-Colonel, and Lieut.-Colonel P. Peacock, was appointed to command in March, 1918.

The guns were organised into three groups:-

"A" Group (Lieut-Colonel Ford), and when he was appointed D.A.A.G., RM.,

    Major A. W. Ridings, until invalided, and relieved by Major Morrison-Scott, D.S.O.

    The three 12-inch guns "Dominion," "Nameless" and "Jutland."

    One 9 .2-inch "Henri"

    Two 9 .2-inch "Stella" (the battery near Coxyde).

"B" Group (Major J. B. Chancellor).

    Two 9 .2-inch "Carnac"

    Two 9 .2inch "Terrible" (near Coxyde).

    One 9 .2-inch on a railway mounting.

"C" Group (Major H. E. Iremonger).

    Two 7. 5-inch guns "Saskatoon" (in the sand dunes, north-east of Oost- Dunkerque).

    Two 7. 5 guns "Diana"

    Two 7 .5-inch guns "Langley."

The guns were on ships' mountings with girders and concrete platforms.

The ground west of Furnes and south of Adinkerke was waterlogged three inches below the surface, so that it was impossible to make efficient dug-outs; the personnel lived in adjacent farms, with splinter proof huts for the cordite and the shell were laid out in the open.

Among the sand dunes the garrison were in concrete pits covered with sand, and by constant work it was possible to keep enough sand on top of the emplacements to keep out even an 11-inch shell.

The mounting of all the guns was completed by March, 1918. In this work, most valuable work was done by the R.M.A. tractor drivers, under the motor transport officers, R.M.A. The Siege Train had also the advantage of the use of the workshop of the Anti-Aircraft Brigade, under Lieutenant Barnes, which had been established at Dunkirk since 1915. The unit included its own motor transport officers, Captain Primrose and Lieutenant Ruffles. As in the case of the Howitzer Brigade, the work of the tractor drivers in mounting and dismounting the guns, generally at night, was beyond praise, and the final dismounting and conveyance of the guns and mountings to Dunkirk without accident is a convincing proof of their skill.

A base depot of supplies and reinforcements was established at Dunkirk, which also supplied the Anti-Aircraft Brigade; this was organised by Lieutenant and Quartermaster Littleton, and when he was appointed to the staff of the Director of National Service in England, he was relieved by Lieutenant and Quartermaster W. Holloway.

The role of the Siege Guns was to act in conjunction with the Senior Naval Officer, Dunkirk, for any services required for H.M. Fleet, and generally entailed engaging the coast batteries, from Ostende to Raversyde, which harrassed the monitors and other craft; secondly to co-operate with the Belgian artillery, in counter-battery work and to carry out shoots on distant tactical points.

The German artillery was very powerful, ranging from 38 c.m. guns in Jacobnissen battery to 10.5 c.m. at Antwerpen. Their mountings had all round training and could therefore fire at points behind the lines, such as Nieuport dock gates, Fumes, La Panne, etc., as well as seawards.

Their lines Slype - Keyen and Leffringhe - Zande were bristling with howitzers of 28 c.m. and below, also high velocity guns of 17 c.m. and below, added to which were some guns on railway mountings. The best known enemy guns in 1918, were "Leugenboom" a 38 c.m. gun, which bombarded Dunkirk from a range of 27-28 miles, and "Tirpitz"; other well known batteries were "Hindenburg," "Antwerpen," "Aachen," "Cecilie," (7-inch guns), "Baeseler," "Jacobnissen," and "Mariakerk."

It is interesting to note that these batteries were manned by the German Marine Artillery. This corps seems to have been unpopular with the German army, as Captain Carpenter ("Zeebrugge") quotes a German officer as saying "that he would like to shake the hand of officer in charge of the British siege guns on the coast, and that of the officer commanding the attack on Zeebrugge, because these two officers had 'put it across' that section of the German navy which had charge of the Flanders coast defence."

The firing on both sides was carried out with meticulous care, and the most careful calculation and ranging, and in spite of the extreme range (the British guns firing at ranges up to 30,000 yards), with very creditable results. Captain Hollingsworth, a mathematical expert, did most valuable work in ranging the guns, and was awarded the D.S.C.

In March, 1918, the Germans bombarded Dunkirk, even more aggressively than usual, and the 12-inch guns were called on to retaliate. On one occasion, they opened fire at 32,000 yards after very careful calculations. Suddenly the officer commanding realised that one of the range sheets had been so made out that one gun would be dropping 200 yards short ; visions of damage to cathedrals and churches in Ostend (the British fire was much restricted so as not to damage the town), flashed across his mind, and seizing his map to ascertain where the shells would be dropping if the gun was shooting true, he was much relieved to find that they should just about drop on the officers' mess of the German Marine Corps.

On 18th March, an enemy shell hit the right gun pit of "Carnac" battery, and dismounted a gun, causing a fire. Lieutenant B Baseby, who had been gassed the previous evening and was still on the sick list, at once proceeded to the gunpit, and by his example and personal efforts, extinguished the fire, which might otherwise have reached the ammunition in the ready magazine; he was awarded the D.S.C. for his gallantry.

A little later in the month, a shell buried a good many of the crew and damaged the gunpit of the same battery. Lieutenant D. Harding, after extricating himself, did most valuable work in extinguishing the fire and attending to the wounded; he also was awarded the D.S.C. In June Captain Peck was awarded the D.S.C., for his services with the guns since 1915.

In the Zeebrugge - Ostend operation, 22nd-23rd April, the Siege Guns bombarded the batteries west of Ostend, in conjunction with the monitors, and the aerial attacks. Similar bombardments had been carried out on the previous night in order to give the enemy no reason to anticipate anything unusual on this occasion. Firing was continued from 11-10 p.m. to 11-25 p.m. and again from 11-35 p.m. to midnight. The targets being "Tirpitz," "Hindenburg," "Antwerpen," "Aachen," "Cecilie," "Baeseler." Twenty rounds

[Photos lent by Lieut.-Colonel P. Peacock, C.M.G., R.M.A.]
MOUNTING HEAVY SIEGE GUNS.

of 12-inch, 78 of 9.2 and 80 of 7.5 were fired; the enemy replied with 15 c.m. and 10 c.m. guns, but the shooting was very wild and did very little damage. The dispatches stated that the shooting of the monitors and Siege Guns was undoubtedly useful as a blind, and kept down the fire of the shore batteries.

In the further attack on Ostend on 9th -10th May, fire was opened by monitors, Siege Guns, and air squadron, by order of the Commodore, and their fire undoubtedly gave the enemy a warm time; "the Siege Guns maintained a valuable fire on the enemy heavy coast batteries," They were in action for about an hour, against the same targets as on 22nd - 23rd April, and fired thirty-one rounds of 12-inch, 126 of 9.2, and 142 of 7.5.

Lieut.-Colonel Peacock was mentioned in dispatches, and received the C.M.G.

Dunkirk was the objective of many of the enemy's air raids, and the Siege Guns came in for their full share of the enemy's attentions. In September and October, the Siege Guns took their share in the offensive operations, which were now being launched against the staggering German forces. On 28th September, the beginning of the Offensive, whilst the monitors were bombarding the coast, the Siege Guns engaged the batteries with a view to keeping the enemy in doubt as to whether a landing was to be attempted, and so prevent his moving troops elsewhere; the Siege Guns fired 37 rounds of 12-inch, 81 of 9.2, and 75 of 7.5-inch. Throughout the day, they were continually in action firing bursts of fire of three to four minutes duration at long range points, such as Ostend - Bruges railway, and the Ostend - Thourout railway, and important road junctions, varied occasionally by counter-battery shoots, expending 160 ton of shell in 24 hours, this continued with less intensity on 29th, and again on 1st October, 142 rounds were fired.

Opportunity was taken of a pause in the operations to replace both the 9.2 guns at "Stella" and one 7.5 at "Saskatoon" which were worn out.

In October, the Germans opened fire on "Stella" with 15-inch guns. The detachment at first could not realise what the explosion was, and thought it must be a premature from one of the monitors, but the third burst right under the muzzle of "Q" gun, luckily doing no damage, but filling the muzzle with sand; the Germans were firing with great accuracy at 31,000 yards, and their greatest error was 400 yards. Great delight was caused among the crews of the 9.2, when they were able to reply to this battery ("Jacobnissen"); the new guns had just been mounted, the wind was slightly in their favour, and with 45 degrees of elevation, representing 32,900 yards range, they gave "Jacobnissen" twenty rounds.

The 9.2-inch on the railway mounting under Lieutenant Bryant was detached to a special group of Belgian and French heavy guns. A position was selected on the railway between Fortem and Gronies, and on night 28th-29th September it came into action and fired all night from 2-30 a.m. to 9 a.m., under extremely difficult conditions due to the perfect blackness of the night, and torrents of rain; it was almost impossible to stand, and the gun ran back 30 to 40 feet after each round; the crew behaved magnificently, and in spite of the conditions, set up a record by increasing the number of rounds per hour from 10 to 23.

On 14th October, the offensive was resumed; the Siege Guns being placed at the disposal of the General Officer commanding Belgian artillery, with the proviso that the 12 and 9.2-inch should be available to assist the monitors if required.

At 5-30 a.m., the 7.5 guns were ordered to neutralise six selected batteries and gave them 132 rounds, and during the day all guns fired on a pre-arranged programme at distant tactical points; at 2-15 p.m. as the enemy coast batteries opened fire on a monitor, that had closed in, two of the 12-inch and two of the 9.2-inch were switched on "Tirpitz" and the remaining guns on to the other batteries. The railway gun was also in action at Gronies, and fired 87 rounds.

On 15th and 16th, the enemy artillery was very active, firing on the back areas and evidently getting rid of their ammunition; on these days, the Siege Guns had their final shoots on "Tirpitz," "Leugenboom," "Jacobnissen," etc., because on the evening of 16th, a large number of fires were seen and explosions reported in the German Lines, and the enemy evacuated their batteries during the night.

The batteries at once started dismounting guns in case there should be an opportunity of moving forward for further employment.

Major Iremonger, who had organised and commanded the 7.5-inch batteries, and who had maintained such happy relations with the Belgian Army, was awarded the D.S.O., and promoted to Lieut-Colonel.

The following rewards were also gained by this unit :-[43]

Lieut.-Colonel R Ford, was awarded the C.B.E.

Surgeon-Lieutenant W. G. Bigger, was awarded the D.S.C.

D.S.M - Colour-Sergeant W. R. Bryan   Gunner W. Jackman
Colour-Sergeant W. J. Coen   Gunner W. A. Sewell
Sergeant B. P. Beale   Gunner J. A. Taylor
Sergeant L. R. Jacobs   Drivers G. W. Stanton
Sergeant E. C. Sessions   Drivers F. D. K. Newman
Corporal J. E. Kersey   Chief S.B.S. T. Young, R.N.
Gunner H. J. Brookes   S.B. Attendant J. Layland, R.N.
Gunner W. R. Ash   S.B. Attendant F. E. Morse, R.N.
Gunner A. Campbell.

Meritorious Service Medal.
C.S.M. E. E. Edwards   Corporal Driver C. Sutton
Q.M.S. W. J. Saunders   Driver A. Hicks

Mentioned in Dispatches.
Lieut-Col. P. Peacock, C.M.G.   Gunner A. H. Mason
Major J. B. Chancellor   Sergeant W.H. Rann
Captain F. T. Connew   Gunner E. W. Rayson
Captain D. Primrose   Sergeant A. J. E. Thorburn
C.S.M. G. Barton   Lance-Bomb. R. L. Turner
Gunner W. Howells   Gunner W. A. Underwood
Corporal W. Hutchins   Staff-Sergt. H. Williams, D.C.M.
Driver J. Baker   Staff-Mechanic L. C. Freemen.
Gunner E. J. Marshall.

Fortunately the casualty list was small; in 1917, Lieutenants Hamilton-Cox and T. E. Hulme were killed, and two N.C.O.s and men died of wounds. In 1918, Lieutenant Hunt was killed and Lieutenants Cope and Baseby were wounded; six N.C.O.s and men were killed and 14 wounded.

After the Armistice, the guns were dismounted and guns, stores and shell were returned to England, much hampered by the congestion on the railways, and it was not until March, 1919, that the last of the unit returned to Eastney.

---

43. Owing to the number of different small units of R.M.A. in France, it has been difficult to identify the recipients of honours and it is hoped that this list is fairly accurate. A large number of French and Belgian decorations were awarded to the unit, vide Appendix.

The relations with the Belgian Army were always most cordial, and the R.M.A. Siege Guns furnished guards of honour when H.R.H. the Duke of Connaught presented decorations to the Belgian officers on 2nd July, 1918, and again on Belgian Independence Day, on 21st July, for which they received the thanks of the Belgian General Officer Commanding, and after the Armistice on 21st November, five officers and 50 N.C.O.s and men, on the invitation of the Belgian General Staff, were present at King Albert's ceremonial entry into Brussels.

The following farewell order of General Didier, General Officer Commanding, 6th Division Artillery, was published to the Siege Guns.

"Au moment de quitter Nieuport je me fais un devoir d'addresser a tous, officiers,
> grades, et soldats de l'artillerie de la zone, mes remerciements pour le concours eclaire et devoue qu'ils m'ont prete dans l'accomplissement de ma mission.
>
> Pendant ces six mois d'activite incessant, les artilleries francaises, britanniques, et belges, de la zone ont rivalise d'entrain et de bonne volonte affirmant chaque jour le moral eleve qui les anime.
>
> J'addresse un dernier hommage aux officers et soldats morts au champs d'honneur; leur souvenir vivra dans nos coeurs.
>
>   Le General Major Commandant.

4th August, 1918.
(signed) F. Didier.

CHAPTER 35.

VARIOUS INCIDENTS.

Dardanelles - Bosphorus, 1918 - Sevastopol, 1918 - Buda Pesth, etc.

1. DARDANELLES AND BOSPHORUS.

As soon as the Armistice with Turkey was signed at Mudros on 31st October, 1918, Colonel R. Temple, R.M.A., having proceeded to the Dardanelles and obtained a chart of the mines and forts from the Turks, arrangements were made by Admiral Culme-Seymour and his staff (including Major Hunton, R.M.L.I.) to take over the forts in conjunction with the Salonica Army. The 28th Division was detailed to take over the Gallipoli and Asiatic shores in conjunction with the French; this Division only had six battalions available and no artillery, so a force of 500 all ranks from 3rd Battalion, Royal Marines was collected at Imbros on 3rd November from the garrisons of Lemnos, Imbros and Tenedos. Lieut.-Colonel. Bridges, C.M.G., R.M.L.I. was in command; 300 of this force was organised into six platoons, one platoon being attached to each battalion of the 28th Division. Embarking in trawlers on 11th November they proceeded to their destinations, viz.: Headquarters and one platoon to Chanak, with a platoon each at Sedd-ul-Bahr, Suan Dere, Kilid Bahr, In Tepe, and Kum Kale.

Their duties were to take over the guns and ammunition from the Turkish authorities; two batteries at the entrance to the Straits were prepared as anti submarine batteries as the whereabouts of the German submarines were uncertain. Guns not required for defensive purposes were dismantled, breech blocks being stripped and dismounted. As in some places this meant dealing with 14-inch guns with but improvised appliances, considerable ingenuity was required.

Major Woodcock, R.M.A. with Lieutenant H.M. Jones, R.M.L.I. and a special party of armourers entered all forts in turn, scheduling the guns and seeing that all were properly dismantled.

On the 12th the Allied Fleet passed through the Dardanelles, headed by the *Superb*, the Flagship of Admiral Sir S. Gough-Calthrop. The Royal Marines provided guards at their forts and saluted as the Fleet passed up, as did the 28th Division, and the guards were an epitome of Empire comprising as they did British and Native Troops. The Fleet went on to Constantinople and anchored in triumph off the Golden Horn. Conditions for the Royal Marines at the Straits were hard, accommodation being very poor, and considerable difficulty was experienced in obtaining rations, particularly in Gallipoli where the French had relieved the 28th Division.

On 13th November, Lieut.-Colonel J. A. Clark, R.M.L.I. with four officers and 200 men proceeded to the Bosphorus Forts and took them over from the Turks. Half of these were on the European shore and half on the Asiatic. Certain forts were placed in readiness and manned for action by the Royal Marines in case of any movement by the Russian Black Sea Fleet, the condition and possible action of which was uncertain, and also as a protection against submarines; Major Woodcock arrived on 18th and continued his work.

Incidentally the party at Chanak discovered the hidden howitzer battery near Erenkeui that used to shell the troops at Gallipoli so heavily.

The details were settling down and expecting to spend Christmas there when orders were suddenly issued for them to proceed to Sevastopol.

2. SEVASTOPOL.

The Allied authorities were very anxious to evacuate the 11,000 German troops who were in Sevastopol, but the French troops, who were to take over the town were not yet available; the Naval Commander-in-Chief, Sir S. Gough-Calthorp, who was also High Commissioner at Constantinople, therefore ordered the duty to be performed temporarily by the 3rd Royal Marine Battalion, and all available troops were ordered to be sent from the Aegean Islands. Owing to the influenza epidemic and other causes it was only possible to send the Mavro garrison and a few from Imbros to reinforce those already in the Dardanelles and Bosphorus, but this party of about 50 took with them 18 machine-guns. They embarked in H.M.A.S. *Brisbane* which calling the next day, 8th December, at Chanak embarked Colonel Bridges and his 300 men and proceeded direct to Sevastopol; Colonel Clark with the Bosphorus detachment, less Major Woodcock's party, had also sailed on 8th December in the destroyers *Hope* and *Warrego* direct to the same place.

Meanwhile the Royal Marine detachment of the *Temeraire* under Captain C. Atwood, R.M.L.I., three officers, 30 men and four Lewis guns, had landed at 8 a.m. on 1st December to take over the railway station, and loading wharves at Sevastopol from the Germans, and had a lively time settling the disputes between Germans and Russians, regulating the station and incidentally cleaning it; on 3rd the strength of the guard was raised to 60 men and took over the magazine to the east of the station and the pioneer park, etc. This step was necessary because the Bolsheviks were very anxious to get hold of the bombs stored there. On 4th some Bolsheviks tried to raid and break into the magazine but the sentries got one fair in the back with a hand grenade, and only his boots could be found the next morning and they were not troubled again. On the 8th 200 Russians and Germans attacked the station, but were driven off by rifle and Lewis gun fire with casualties and on 10th the *Superb* landed one Royal Marine Gunner and 10 men to take charge of the loading wharf on the west side of the Bay, and they had some incidents with would-be looters.

Colonel Clark and his party about 150 arrived on 9th and took over the Naval Barracks on the west side of the harbour. On the 10th Colonel Bridges with the Headquarters and the remainder of the Battalion disembarked on the town side at the Mining wharf, but moved to the Russian Army Headquarters. On this day a raiding party attacked the provision store but were driven off. The Germans were very pleased to be relieved and to be free from the Bolsheviks, but they were not looking forward to their long journey through Besserabia.

The detachment of the *Superb* was relieved, but the *Temeraire's* detachment remained at the railway station until the 14th, when they also were relieved by the 3rd Royal Marine Battalion.

The Battalion took short and sharp measures with the Bolsheviks and order was soon restored; the Russian officers even putting on their uniforms which they had not dared to wear for months. Day and night patrols were sent out and the 3,000 Bolsheviks were for a time quite cowed. There were many warnings of proposed riots, particularly on 22nd, 23rd and 24th December, but strong patrols were sent out each night and nothing out of the ordinary disturbances took place.

Captain Atwood, Royal Marine Gunner H. Boffey and 44 N.C.O.s and men landed again from the *Temeraire* as a reinforcement on 16th.

The Royal Marines were thus the first British Troops to set foot in Sevastopol since the Crimean war and officers and men took the opportunity of visiting all the places rendered famous by the great siege; route marches were arranged to afford everyone an opportunity of seeing them.

On 26th December 3,500 French troops arrived and on 27th French guards relieved the Royal Marines, the *Temeraire* detachment returning to their ship.

The 3rd Battalion embarked on 30th in one of the French transports and returned to Mudros, dropping 170 officers and men at Biyuk Dere in the Bosphorus to man the forts at the entrance, under Major Woodcock.

It is interesting to recall that the French troops were driven out of Sevastopol by the Bolsheviks about six weeks later.

Major Woodcock's party remained in charge of the Forts in the Bosphorus till 4th November, 1919, when they were evacuated to England. The detachment had a pleasant time in spite of the heat. Major Woodcock was appointed Officer Commanding Defences under the Army of the Black Sea with his Headquarters at Therapia. Lieutenant Unwin, R.M.A. was awarded the Royal Humane Society's Bronze Medal for a very gallant rescue of a gunner, R.M.A., who had fallen overboard from a launch in the swift current of the Bosphorus. Major Woodcock was awarded the O.B.E. for his services.

3. BUDA PESTH.

The 3rd Royal Marine Battalion furnished another party for yet another side show. Some British troops were required in October, 1919, to assist the British Mission of Control at Buda Pesth. Captain Fawckner, R.M.A. with Lieutenant Caffyn, R.M.L.I. and 20 N.C.O.'s and men had been sent from H.M.S. *Ajax* at Constantinople, but the Commander-in-Chief was anxious that they should rejoin their ship; Lieutenant (Temporary Major) D' Arcy Bunyan, R.M.L.I. and Lieutenant W. R. Rogers, R.M.A. (who had been in charge of the Turkish Prisoners of War Camp at Mudros) with 20 N.C.O.s and men of 3rd Battalion were sent from Mudros on 24th October; they travelled via Malta and Trieste and joined the *Ajax's* detachment in Buda.

Their duty was to provide guards, escorts, etc. for the Military Mission and for control of the Danube, but their most interesting job was to supervise the departure of the Roumanian Army and the arrival of the White Hungarian Army. For this work they were also lent a party of 50 seamen from the gunboats in the river. Major Bunyan thus describes the scene: "Our object was to prevent any collision between the White Army's advanced guard and the Roumanian rear guard (R.N. 50, R.M. 40 all told!) I had Marines on the bridge across the Danube between Buda and Pesth to prevent the White Troops from crossing before the stated hour. Rogers was in charge of Pesth, Caffyn in charge of Buda, Fawckner was responsible for the detraining of the White Army and I was standing by with my forces to go where necessary (N.B.-These towns have 900,000 inhabitants). The Roumanians got rather 'windy' and vanished during the night before they were all expected to be clear. I was on the bridge when the advanced guard troops of the White Army entered; the cavalry gave us a smart salute."

The *Ajax* detachment returned to their ship, but the 3rd Battalion detachment remained on till January. They had very cold and severe weather and were employed on various isolated jobs in charge of trains containing supplies of food, munitions etc., until they returned to England.

4. SINGAPORE.

On 15th February, 1915, a mutiny occurred in the Native Infantry Regiment at Singapore, and as the British Battalion had already left for service in France, the Naval details in the place were called on and rose to the occasion, as always happens. The Commander-in-Chief, Admiral Jerram, was in the place and the Naval General Staff Officer was Major C. B. Mullins, R.M.L.I., the only ship available being the sloop *Cadmus* with a small complement of 113 including 11 Marines and the Admiral's four orderlies.

A few of the white officers escaped and telephoned to the Admiral's office where Mr. Cross (late Barrack

Sergeant, R.M.L.I., Chatham) was on duty. The latter immediately informed all the Naval and Military authorities and also took on himself to order the *Cadmus* to "land every available man" and by his initiative and promptitude relieved a serious situation. He was awarded the M.B.E. Prompt measures were taken by the Admiral. The Malay States Volunteers, who had just completed their training, held the Colonel's bungalow which was a stout building in the Alexandra Barracks. Major Mullins was dispatched to bring in all the women and children to the town and then assisted to place guards on the main hotels, etc. There was also a small force of R.G.A. and R.E. available in addition to the Naval party because the other native troops were unreliable. Allied Russian, French and Japanese seamen were also landed until British reinforcements could arrive from Rangoon. The mutineers divided into two parties, one went to Tanglin Barracks and released the German prisoners of war who, however, made off without assisting them and the other came towards Singapore but were met by a party from the *Cadmus* under Lieutenant Sloan, R.N. in a motor lorry with a Maxim and driven off.

On night 16/17 February the *Cadmus* party, the R.G.A., and R.E. under Colonel Brownlow, who was accompanied by Major Mullins advanced to the Alexandra Barracks to relieve the M.S.V.R. who were holding the Colonel's bungalow and at dawn carried out a frontal attack and raised the siege; the resistance was rather half hearted as the mutineers lacked a leader; the Royal Marines under Lieut. Sloan, R.N. formed the right flank of the attack; the Sergeant-Major behaved very pluckily in breaking into the huts and arresting the mutineers in hiding in order to clear the rear of the force. Colonel Brownlow re-occupied the mutineers' barracks on 17th. The Navy and Marines were then employed until about 25th February rounding up the mutineers in the jungle which was very exhausting work and the *Cadmus*' boats were manned and armed to search the creeks. The mutineers who were captured were tried by court-martial of which Major Mullins was a member, being temporarily disembarked to enable him to sit as there were not enough Army officers for the Court.

Among the reinforcements were the Johore Forces of which Captain Cullimore, late R.M.A., was Adjutant; he was killed during the fighting.

5. NEW GUINEA.

At the outbreak of War, Major General E. A. Wylde, R.M.L.I. happened to be staying with his daughter in German New Guinea, and was of course at once interned. As the last idea that could arise was that a British Expedition would arrive in this out of the way spot he was placed on parole. A few days later however, the Australian Expeditionary Force appeared on the horizon, and General Wylde was at once placed under a guard, from which he was released by the landing of the British Force. The colony was annexed to the Empire and all the Germans made prisoners. The knotty problem to decide whether the fact of his being placed under the guard released his parole or not gave occupation to certain international lawyers for the next few years and covered reams of paper, but it never seems to have been decided before the war was over.

PART VIII

Special Units.

CHAPTER 36.

ROYAL MARINE SUBMARINE MINERS.

TOWARDS the end of 1914 the realisation of the possibilities of the submarines in their attack on merchant shipping, and the potential activities of "raiders" made the Admiralty anxious to prevent access to certain ports on the east coast of England and Scotland, which could not be protected by booms or where additional protection to the booms was needed.

For this purpose proposals were made to revive the old observation mines, which had been abolished by Lord Fisher, when submarines were first introduced. Now as First Sea Lord he directed that they should be resuscitated and laid in certain places. Captain Fraser, R.N. (retired) who was one of the few naval officers remaining that had any knowledge of the work, was put in charge with the title of Captain of Defensive Mining, and he collected a staff of retired Naval Officers and pensioners to lay the mines. The question then arose of their watching and firing when required; the Royal Engineer Submarine Miners, Regular, Militia and Volunteer no longer existed, nor were the R.M.A. details who had manned the submarine mines at Esquimalt in the 1890's available, but it was essential that the personnel to fire them should be part of the Fortress Defence Troops.

In these circumstances it was decided that a small force of Royal Marines should be raised for the purpose and the offer of Colonel F. G. Scott commanding the Tyne Electrical Engineers, an old submarine miner, to raise the unit was accepted.

He was given a temporary commission in the Corps as Colonel Second Commandant, Royal Marines, and brought with him a nucleus of officers and men of the Tyne E.E. (T) who were the successors of the Tyne Submarine Miners, and who had had experience of the work.

They were transferred to the Royal Marines on 5th February, 1915, the officers being given temporary commissions in the Corps, and the unit was known as "The Royal Marine Submarine Miners."

Though enlisted into the Corps for short service they were paid at Royal Engineer rates of pay with submarine mining pay; recruiting was opened for the duration of the war and officers were entered who had experience of the sea, or were local yachtsmen with knowledge of the harbours; some were expert electrical engineers, of whom more anon.

The unit was affiliated to the Chatham Division, R.M.L.I. and given Chatham register numbers, but departing from the usual custom of the Corps, the Headquarters of the unit was stationed at Newcastle-on-Tyne, with its own staff and pay office where the recruits were approved and trained and other administration except clothing carried out. Sergeant Major J. Long, R.M.L.I. was attached for duty as Superintending Clerk and Sergeant-Major; Lieut.-Colonel J. Martin, an old officer of the Royal Engineer Submarine Miners, was appointed second in command.

The stations were quickly established and were soon in working order; watch being kept in huts and the men billetted near or quartered in barracks where possible, the old Army Barracks at Tynemouth being used as the Depot. Detachments were also stationed at Cromarty and Scapa Flow as part of the Royal Marine garrisons.

The station at Felixstowe under Captain Cramer was largely used as an experimental station and during 1917 considerable developments and new inventions came into existence; the value of the work was much increased by the development of the hydrophone, in the use of which officers and men were trained in the Naval Schools.

At the end of 1917 as it was considered desirable that the Headquarters of the unit should be more directly under the Commandant of the Division, the Headquarters were moved to Chatham; Lieut.-Colonel J. Martin was appointed to command vice Colonel Scott and Sergeant-Major Long was given a commission as Lieutenant and Adjutant.

Consequent on the new inventions, which had been elaborated by Captain Fraser and his staff, assisted by Captain Cramer, R.M.S.M., a considerable number of new stations were opened, and the numbers of the officers and men were increased in order to man them. Several successes against submarines were claimed, notably one attempting to pass into Scapa Flow for which Captain Innes was awarded the O.B.E. As time went on officers and men from other Royal Marine units who had been invalided from the fighting fronts were drafted into the unit. It was, however not until near the end of the war that it was realised what an important part this form of mining was capable of playing in the defence of a port and further the desirability of the personnel to man the stations being trained Royal Marines.

The R.M.S.M. were trained in repairing cables, laying mines, etc., but as this work was in the hands of the Navy their services were not utilised except towards the end when the new inventions came into use, when the officers and men of the unit erected and fitted out the stations themselves and the organisation was considerably expanded under Rear-Admiral C. F. Dampier, Admiral of Controlled Minefields.

In the autumn of 1918 their work became merged in that of the 5th Royal Marine Battalion (see Chapter 7) but the unit remained distinct and was demobilised at the end of the War and their knowledge and experience was dissipated.

The following Officers were rewarded for their services in this unit.

    O.B.E. - Captain J. H. Morgan for services i/c of a controlled Minefield.
            Major P. A. Smith for services in Defensive Mining.
            Captain A. Innes for services in Defensive Mining.
            Captain F. T. Blumberg for services on the Staff of the Rear-Admiral of the Controlled Minefields.

CHAPTER 37.

ROYAL MARINE UNITS IN THE ROYAL NAVAL DIVISION.

Divisional Engineers - Divisional Train - Medical Unit.

AFTER the Antwerp expedition, when the Royal Naval Division was formed on the lines of an Army Division, it became necessary to raise all the auxiliary units that form part of that organisation. It was decided not to provide Artillery and as is well known the Division was without Divisional Artillery in Gallipoli; but on arrival in France in 1916, it was equipped with Brigades of Territorial Artillery, R.F.A. under the command of Brig.-General C. H. de Rougemont, R.A.

However, the services of other units were a necessity if the Division was to exist at all, and the first unit formed was a small Ordnance Section. Major Lord Bangor (late R.A.) was given a temporary commission in the Corps, as was Lieutenant J. Morsley, R.A. These officers were sent to Deal to grapple with the mass of stores that were beginning to pour in for the Naval Battalions and other units. Their office was established in the old guard room in the South Barracks and by great exertions they produced order out of chaos; Lord Bangor served throughout as D.A.D.O.S., on the Divisional Staff, with Lieutenant W. J. Taylor as his assistant, whilst Lieutenant Morsley organised the small Ordnance Company established at Blandford, formed of R.M.L.I. pensioners and R.N.V.R. not fit for general service, with several pensioner N.C.O.s, R.M. in the responsible positions. Two gentlemen who were medically rejected by the doctors, Lieutenant Hon. L. Montague and Lieutenant H. B. Wallis were told off for these duties and given temporary commissions in the Corps, but evading the doctors the former served with the Hood Battalion in France and won the D.S.O. being severely wounded and the latter was also wounded with one of the fighting units in France.

DIVISIONAL ENGINEERS.

The first unit to come into existence was the Divisional Engineers. Major A. B. Carey, R.E. was appointed C.R.E. of the Division with a temporary commission as Lieut.-Colonel Royal Marines and raised the unit. Lieutenant G. H. Harrison was appointed Adjutant. Preparations were made to raise two Field Companies and a Divisional Signal Company with the Army Establishments. Recruiting was undertaken by the Institute of Civil Engineers in London, and a most splendid body of men was obtained, in fact at first it was almost an Officers' Training Corps, for a very large percentage received commissions in the Royal Engineers and other Corps. At the beginning nothing was settled as to the status of the Corps, so Colonel Carey to make sure, had his men enrolled as R.N.V.R. and also attested as Royal Marines, and in the first instance they were clothed as seamen in blue. However, when the Adjutant-General Royal Marines assumed the control of the Administration of the Division at the beginning of October 1914, the questions of pay, conditions of services, etc., were settled and it was decided that the men should be enlisted as Royal Marines and serve under all the conditions of that Corps, but that they should receive pay at Army rates for Royal Engineers, for which a special Order in Council was obtained. The unit was affiliated for records and administrations to Deal, being allotted Deal register numbers, but they had their own pay office and staff, additional clerks being added to the Depot Office for records. The officers in command of companies were:

Divisional Signal Company	Major G. H. Spittle, RM.
No.1 Field Company	Major A. T. Chivers, RM.
No.2 Field Company	Major S. R Adams, RM.

The officers were all trained engineers and also many of them were railway engineers of great experience with an intimate knowledge of the sources of supply of engineering material combined with abounding energy; the unit was therefore very quickly equipped with its technical material and became most efficient, especially as proposals for equipping it entirely on a motor basis were nipped in the bud.

They were quartered under canvas at Freedown near Walmer, and constructed their own rifle range (miniature) and made the best of the terribly wet conditions of that autumn, and as soon as possible were moved to the hutments at Blandford, which became henceforth their recruit depot for training and for preparation of reinforcements. None of this unit went over to Antwerp with the Royal Naval Division, where a small detachment of Royal Engineers under Captain Rooke, Royal Engineers accompanied the Division.

The first party to proceed on service was the 3rd Brigade Signal Section which accompanied the Royal Marine Brigade to the Dardanelles in February, 1915; the remainder of the unit accompanied the Division to Gallipoli on 1st March.

Meanwhile the Army having added a 3rd Field Company to the Divisional organisation, No.3 Company was raised by Major Aveling, which accompanied the Benbow, Hawke and Collingwood Battalions to Gallipoli at the end of May,1915.

The unit was clothed as Royal Marines and wore the badge of the Globe and Laurel. No.1 Field Company and the 3rd Brigade Signal Section landed with the Chatham and Portsmouth Battalions at Anzac on 28th April, and No. 2 Field Company and the Signal Sections landed at Cape Helles with the remainder of the Division.

It is impossible to separate the work of the Engineer Unit from that of the Division, but they took their full share of all the operations described in Chapter 11 and in addition did most valuable work in the construction and maintenance of the piers on the Peninsula, where their special knowledge was particularly useful, and in all the preparations for the evacuation they had a very large share. Their casualties were heavy and a considerable number of officers and men earned recognition for their gallantry.

The 3rd Field Company and Signal Section accompanied the 2nd Brigade to Stavros and served there with them till April, when in common with the other units they were withdrawn for service in France, arriving at Marseilles in May, 1916.

Lieut.-Colonel Carey left the Division at this time on receiving another appointment and Major G. H. Harrison became C.R.E. of the Division.

The following rewards for service in Gallipoli were gazetted-

C.M.G.-Lieutenant-Colonel A. B. Carey.

D.S.C.-Lieutenant T. N. Riley, F. H. Lamb, R. H. Roe.

D.S.M.-Sapper W. Bottomley, Company-Sergeant-Major C. Thornton.
Sergeant H. S. Smith, Corporal F. R. Smith.
Sapper J. H. Murray, Corporal J. B. Fathers.

Mentioned in Dispatches.-
Lieutenant-Colonel A. B. Carey. Major J. W. Teale.
Captain J. S. Marshall. Major G. H. Harrison.
Captain J. W. Revell. Lieutenant A. B. Stewart.
Lieutenant A. M. Oakden Quarter-Master-Sergeant J. Lintott.
(died of wounds). Sergeant S. B. Andrews.
Lieutenant C. F. Edwin. Sergeant S. Ainsworth.

Captain R. Grierson.
Captain J. H. Lawson.
Captain L. H. Rugg.
Lieutenant R. H. Roe.
Lieutenant E. H. Lamb.
Lieutenant G. F. Hilditch.
Lieutenant T. N. Riley.

Sergeant G. A. Burn (twice).
Sergeant R. O. C. Thompson.
Sergeant A. B. L. Dutton.
Sergeant F. P. Widdington.
Sergeant W. F. Garnham.
Corporal C. S. Blake.
Lance-Corporal A. D. Kerr.

Signal Company.-
Major G. H. Spittle.
Lieutenant C. Bollam.
Sergeant A. C. Branch.
Sergeant W. H. Jayne.
Sergeant J. H. Turner.
Corporal W. J. Smith.
Sapper J. H. P. Burchell.

Sapper W. E. Curtis.
Sapper L. F. Summers.
Sapper R. S. Norrie.
Sapper E. L. Damant.
Sapper E. Best.
Sapper J. H. Murray.
Sapper J. Paton.

On arrival in France the units received new designations, becoming the 63rd Divisional Signal Company, and the Field Companies being numbered 247, 248, and 249.

As in Gallipoli their doings are inseparably bound up with those of the Brigades with which they were working and are described in chapter 26; but exception must be made to the most gallant and effective service rendered by these Companies after their transfer to the Royal Engineers at the bridging of the Canal de L'Escaut at end of September, 1918.

Towards the end of 1916 the War Office, who were now responsible for the maintenance of the Division were desirous of amalgamating the Divisional units with the corresponding Corps of the Army; although this was much resented by the officers and men, backed up by the Admiralty, it was finally decided to transfer the Divisional Engineers to the Royal Engineers, as they were on a purely Army basis as regards pay and allowances (in the case of the other units, pay and administrative arrangements prevented any transfer) and the Engineers were accordingly transferred to the Army in 1917; but the personnel and numbers of the companies remained unchanged, except for the necessary replacements due to casualties and promotions. Lieut.-Colonel G. H. Harrison eventually became Director of Light Railways in France, receiving the C.M.G. and D.S.O.

In the *London Gazette* of 1st January, 1917, which was the last issued whilst they were serving as Royal Marines, the following were mentioned in dispatches-

Lieutenant-Colonel T. C. Aveling.
Lieutenant J. E. Adam.
Sergeant-Major C. J. Feeny.

Lieutenant-Colonel G. H. Harrison
Lieutenant W. Beloe.

2. THE DIVISIONAL TRAIN. ROYAL MARINES.

In raising the Divisional Train the Royal Marines were confronted with a new problem, as hitherto their dealings with horses and mules had been confined to very small limits; they now had to raise a Train, on the Army Service Corps model.

However they rose to the occasion, Major F. D. Bridges, R.M.L.I. was sent to the Crystal Palace, the

Depot of the R.N.V.R. to raise the unit. Volunteers were called for from both R.N.V.R. and R.M.L.I. and a proportion of steady old R.F.R., R.M.L.I. were obtained who became a valuable nucleus. Major E. C. Chaytor of the New Zealand Forces was appointed to command with the temporary rank of Lieut.-Colonel Royal Marines, Captain W. R. Liddington of the Oxfordshire Hussars first became Adjutant and then Officer Commanding Depot at Blandford.

Like the Divisional Engineers they were affiliated to Deal for records, pay, etc., but following the idiosyncrasies of the Royal Marine Service they were nominally borne on the books of H.M.S. *Victory* so that their pay and accounts were kept in the Royal Naval Division offices.

Officers and men were paid at the corresponding rates of the Army Service Corps and the various A.S.C. ranks such as wheeler, farrier, driver, etc., were introduced, but they received allowances such as separation, field allowances, etc. on Naval scales.

On 26th November, 1914, the Establishment was fixed as follows :-

Headquarters	2 Officers,	10 N.C.O.s and Men.	Ammunition Column	8 Officers,	254 N.C.O.s & Men	
H.Q. Company	5 "	101 "	Medical Officer	1 "	-	"
Nos. 2,3 & 4 Cos	12 "	234 "	1st Reinforcement	2 "	74	"

Total. 30 Officers, 673 N.C.O.s and Men.

To which were added the details required for the transport of the Medical Unit, which comprised-

For Field Ambulances 132 N.C.O.s and Men   Reserve 26 N.C.O.s & Men
    (including 42 Motor Drivers). Workshop: 1 Officer 17

Total.1 Officer, 175 N.C.O.s and Men.

The horses and mules numbered 378 with 142 carts and waggons; and in addition there were 16 horses or mules, 23 vehicles and 21 motor ambulances for the Medical Unit.

The numbers included all the supply details as well as those required for transport.

The Depot was established at Blandford and the companies were raised and trained there; officers and N.C.O.'s being sent to the Army Service Corps School of Instruction at Aldershot for technical instruction.

Major Bridges, having been appointed to the Benbow Battalion and the unit being on a firm footing, left the Train in December, 1914.

By the end of January, 1915, the unit was ready for its vehicles and animals which were supplied by the War Office; though they had been carrying out the duties of supply and transport for the Division with a few vehicles, etc. since November.

The senior supply officer of the Division was Major F. Holmes and all the Division testifies to the excellence of their supply arrangements in Gallipoli. Lieutenant Lovatt accompanied the Royal Marine Brigade in February as supply officer and was wounded at Anzac soon after landing. The remainder of the unit embarked on 1st March with the Royal Naval Division, many are the tales that could be told of the entraining of the raw mules that night at Blandford.

Owing to the conditions obtaining in Gallipoli only a small part of the transport and mules were required and the remainder of the Train remained in Egypt where they were fully employed at Alexandria, among other duties a party was lent to the R.M.A. Battery (see Chapter 30). Those in Gallipoli took part in all the operations described in chapter 11 and rendered most useful service. Major F. H. Smith, who was by profession a shipbuilder was detailed, whilst in Egypt, to alter the Nile steamers which were being prepared for service in Mesopotamia and his designs and arrangements were fully recognised by the authorities; he himself afterwards served in Mesopotamia and was awarded the O.B.E. and the Order of the Nile.

In November, 1915, when the Salonica Army was being dispatched, a large number of the drivers of the Train were drafted into the 28th Divisional Train; an officer of the Corps relates that one day he was particularly struck by seeing a very smart column of A.S.C. passing through the town of Salonica; on coming nearer them he saw that they were wearing the Globe and Laurel on their caps, and on enquiry they proved to be the drivers of the Train R.M.

After the evacuation of Gallipoli these drivers were recalled and the Train was concentrated for service with the Division in the Aegean Islands. It accompanied the Division to France and was renumbered the 63rd Divisional Train.

Lieut.-Colonel W. Liddell of the A.S.C. relieved Colonel Chaytor in command and a little later Major Holmes also left the Division.

In spite of various attempts on the part of the War Office to transfer them to the A.S.C. these were successfully resisted and they served until the Armistice as Royal Marines, being eventually demobilised with the other units.

As in Gallipoli their doings were bound up with those of the Division and the operations in which they took part will be found in Chapters 11 and 26.

Few of the Corps perhaps realise the arduous duties of the transport in bringing up supplies and ensuring that their Division was properly fed and supplied with ammunition, entailing as it did work at night over broken and muddy roads, often under shell fire with the knowledge that any failure on their part to keep up to time might have most serious effects on the operations.

Later in the War the Army transferred the supply of S.A.A. Ammunition to the A.S.C. from the Artillery so that as happened in one or two cases the Army followed the lead given by the Royal Naval Division, *e.g.* the S.A.A. Column and the Machine Gun Battalion.

On the formation of the 3rd Royal Marine Battalion Captain L. Malcolm was lent for duty as Transport Officer in the Aegean Islands. Later in 1917 when the demand for officers for the R.M.L.I. Battalions was increasing several officers were transferred from the Train to the Battalions, Lieutenant D. J. Aldridge being killed at Passchendaele and A. Wallis at Niergnies. The Train earned a due proportion of the Honours awarded to the Division.

For service in Gallipoli the following were mentioned in Dispatches.

- Major F. Holmes.
- Captain L. Murdoch.
- Lieutenant E. L. Burrell.
- Private P. Doherty.
- Quarter-Master-Sergeant E. Smith (Chatham), R.M.L.I. (attached.)
- Private W. J. Brown (Chatham), R.M.L.I. (attached).

In France-

- O.B.E.-Major F. H. Smith (Egypt).
- Major C. L. Chapman.
- Major W. E. Cooke.
- Captain P. Allard.
- Captain & Adjutant C. G. Murray.
- Lieutenant A. L. Dugon.

Military Medal.-Sergeant G. K. Craik. Sergeant W. Sullivan. Private R Curry.

Meritorious Service Medal.

- Sergeant-Major J. F. T. Ashton.
- Colour-Sergeant G. W. Baker.
- CO. Q.M.S. G. G. Marks.
- Sergeant W. Davidson.
- Sergeant H. W. Pyne.
- Staff Q.M.S. W. A. Read.
- Sergeant N. H. Chubb.

Mentioned in Dispatches.-
    Conductor L. A. Blake.
    Captain A. E. Balfour.
    Qr.-Master & Hon. Lieutenant H. A. Day.
    Lieutenant H. Borthwick.
    Major C. L. Chapman.
    Major W. E. Cook.
    Captain P. Allard.

3. MEDICAL UNIT ROYAL MARINES.

On the formation of the Royal Marine Brigade each Battalion had its own Medical Officer, taken from the surgeons, R.N. serving at the Divisions and Depot, together with some of the Infirmary Staffs, R.M. and reservists who had been trained with them, reinforced by a small number of auxiliary Sick Berth attendants, R.N.

These were the medical arrangements for Ostend and Antwerp, the Naval Battalions being similarly equipped.

Surgeon L. Grieg, R.N. of the Deal Battalion was captured at Morbeke when tending the wounded Royal Marines and it was not till some time later. that he was released.

On the return of the Battalions to England the work of forming a medical unit was taken in hand and commenced in November, 1914. Fleet Surgeon A. Gaskell, R.N. was appointed Assistant Director of Medical Services on the Divisional Staff with Captain F. Casement, R.A.M.C. as his assistant and under these two officers the unit was organised and equipped. The officers were mostly temporary surgeons, R.N. entered for the War, but the Commanding Officers of the Field Ambulances were regular Naval Officers.

After discussion at the Admiralty, it was decided that the personnel should be enlisted as Royal Marines; they were accordingly affiliated to Deal for pay, records, etc. They were borne on the shore strength of the Corps but paid at the same rates of pay and allowances as the R.A.M.C. in the Army, for which a special Order in Council was obtained. The Depot was stationed at Blandford where drafts were trained and dispatched and the personnel manned the Camp Hospital.

To obtain the personnel recourse was had to the St. John's Ambulance Association and with their valuable assistance the numbers were soon voluntarily recruited; the men, who came mostly from the north of England, were already trained technically and their military training was completed at Blandford.

Among them was a large percentage of miners, whose strong physique well fitted them for the heavy work of transporting wounded over the broken heavy ground of Gallipoli and France, but the ranks contained all classes, theological students, clerks and business men.

Each Field Ambulance consisted of nine Medical Officers, one Lieutenant and Quartermaster, one Sergeant-Major and 171 N.C.O.'s and men, with three horsed ambulances and seven motor ambulances.

No.1 Field Ambulance.-
    Commanding Officer. - Staff Surgeon A. F. Fleming, R.N.
    Quartermaster. - Hon. Lieutenant S. T. Scammell, R.A.M.C. (tempy. R.M.).
    Sergeant-Major. - Sergeant-Major A. H. Barnes, R.M., M.U.

No.2 Field Ambulance.-
    Commanding Officer. - Staff Surgeon C. E. Stanford, R.N.
    Quartermaster. - Hon. Lieutenant J. E. Murray, R.M., M.U.
    Sergeant-Major. - Acting Sergeant-Major G. L. Barfield, R.M.L.I.

No.3 Field Ambulance.-
   Commanding Officer. - Fleet Surgeon E. J. Finch, R.N.
   Quartermaster. - Hon. Lieutenant T. E. Grout, R.M.L.I.
   Sergeant-Major. - Acting-Sergeant-Major C. L. Williams,. R.M.L.I.
   Unit-Quartermaster. - Lieutenant G. Morgan, R.M., M.U.
   Paymaster. - Captain D. S. Hitch, R.M., M.U.
   Transport Officer. - Lieutenant H. N. Laws, R.N.V.R. (Captain, R.M.).

The Field Ambulances were formed on the Army model with three sections "A" "B" and "C" each with its own tent and bearer sub-division; the drivers for the ambulances being provided by the Divisional Train. Each Bearer Division had 24 stretcher parties consisting of 96 men, whose work was very hard particularly in Gallipoli, where it was difficult to employ transport and practically impossible to use the motor ambulances.

The hospital staffs of the Royal Marine Divisions proved invaluable in organising and helping on the formation of this unit.

By the end of February, 1915, 500 men had been enlisted and the Field Ambulances were equipped and ready to accompany the Royal Naval Division when they embarked for Gallipoli, and were soon filled up to full strength.

The Bearer Division of the 3rd Field Ambulance was the first unit to land with the Royal Marine Brigade at Anzac on 28th April, 1915, of course without its ambulances and the 1st Field Ambulance followed on the next day with the 1st Brigade at Anzac and the 2nd landed at Cape Helles with the 2nd Royal Naval Brigade.

No separate description of their movements need be given as they were present throughout all the operations described in chapter 11. The 2nd Field Ambulance was lent to the 11th Division and took part with that Division in the landing at Suvla Bay on 6th August and shared all the hard fighting in that area for the next two months, Staff Surgeon Stanford was awarded the D.S.O.

The Field Ambulances established themselves on a site near Caesar's Camp at Helles which was known as the Royal Naval Division Hospital.

At the evacuation, the Medical unit parties were particularly strong, in order to provide bearers for possible casualties and it was even contemplated that it might be necessary to leave a party behind but fortunately this was not necessary.

During the Gallipoli Campaign, the casualties among the medical officers and personnel were heavy and the unit greatly distinguished itself by its gallantry and devotion to duty.

Fleet Surgeon Gaskell was awarded the C.B., and Fleet Surgeon Finch the C.M.G. for their services.

The D.S.O. was awarded to Captain H. N. Laws, the transport officer, Staff Surgeon Stanford and Surgeon Payne, the surgeon of the Portsmouth Battalion. The D.S.M. was awarded to Sergeant N. Roberts and Privates R. Dunkley and P. Lowes. The following were mentioned in Dispatches. Staff-Sergeants D. Booth and B. J. Carr. Sergeant M. Fortescue, R. Holmes, S. T. Getting; Corporal J. H. Crabtree, Privates E. Oates, G. E. Stead, H. Slater (a record has not been kept of the Surgeons).

The 3rd Field Ambulance accompanied the 2nd Royal Naval Brigade to Stavros in February, 1916, and served with them till they returned to Lemnos in April.

The hospital and Training Depot at Blandford were now in full working order at first under Fleet Surgeon E. T. Burton and then under Fleet Surgeon J. H. Pead, R.N.

On the transfer of the Division to France in May, 1916, Fleet Surgeon Gaskell was withdrawn for service afloat, and Surgeon Commander E. J. Finch, C.M.G. became A.D.M.S. of the Division.

[By permission of the Imperial War Museum.]
TRANSPORT CROSSING THE CANAL DU NORD.

[By permission of the Imperial War Museum.]
MEN OF THE ROYAL MARINE MEDICAL UNIT WITH CAPTURED
GERMAN DOCTORS.

The Field Ambulances were renumbered 148, 149 and 150 and were equipped according to the scale in France with horse and motor transport. Each ambulance had seven motor ambulances, three horse ambulances and seven G.S. waggons and also in the event of big engagements had the assistance of the Corps Motor Ambulance Convoys and behind them the Casualty Clearing Stations.

In common with the other units of the Division, when the War Office took over the administration, attempts were made to amalgamate them with the R.A.M.C., but this was resisted and they served to the end as Royal Marines, retaining their individuality of which they were very proud. They became strongly imbued with the traditions of the Corps and were very proud of being enlisted as Royal Marines, and when waiting as reinforcements at the Base Depot, they maintained their position as belonging to the Royal Marines, and when finally towards the end of the War they were ordered to wear the Geneva Cross arm badge and were issued with them, they did not refuse to do so, but insisted on providing themselves at their own expense with the Naval Badge which has a red worsted circle instead of the yellow one worn by the R.A.M.C.

At the beginning of 1917 most of the Naval medical officers were withdrawn for service in the Fleet and were replaced by R.A.M.C. officers. Colonel Clements, R.A.M.C. became A.D.M.S. of the Division and Surgeon Commander Finch was attached to the D.A.G.'s office at the Base to ensure that the necessary Admiralty Regulations were carried out in the case of men invalided, etc.

Sergeant-Major Barfield, R.M.L.I. of the 2nd Ambulance had the unique experience of becoming Regimental Sergeant-Major of No. 15 Convalescent Depot, containing 5000 patients and served there for 12 months, being the only Medical Sergeant-Major to hold such a position as it was usual to appoint Infantry Sergeant-Majors to such posts, but then the Royal Marine combines the two qualifications in his own person.

When the U.S.A. came into the war several American medical officers were appointed to the unit, not the first time that the Royal Marine has served under American Officers (see Volume 2, Pekin).

The Medical Unit served throughout with distinction, and adapted themselves to the Army routine for evacuation of casualties in a most efficient manner, the list of decorations gained by this small unit will bear comparison with any unit in the theatre of war; in every engagement they distinguished themselves and their casualties were heavy.

It has not been possible to obtain a list of the decorations awarded to the Medical Officers, but the attached table gives those of the remainder of the unit.

Sergeant-Majors G. L. Barfield and C. L. Williams, R.M.L.I. were both promoted to Temporary Quartermasters and Lieutenants in the unit, and the latter was mentioned in dispatches in 1918.

The actions in which the decorations were gained have been inserted as far as possible.

Meritorious Service Medal.-

Quartermaster-Sergeant J. B. Carr.	Sergeant J. E. Lord.
Sergeant R. Fitton.	Sergeant-Major D. J. Petit.

Distinguished Conduct Medal.-

Sergeant-Major H. Evans.	Staff-Sergeant D. Booth.

Military Medal.-   BEAUMONT HAMEL.

Private W. Aldred.	Private E. H. Greenwood.
Staff-Sergeant D. Booth.	Sergeant R. Murray.
Lance-Corporal J. Carlyle.	Private A. Senior.

Private J. Davis.
Staff-Sergeant M. Elliot.
Sergeant S. T. Gething.
Lance-Corporal J. E. Green.

Private A. W. Thorp.
Private J. Vernon.
Private J. Woosey.

MIRAMOUNT, ETC.

Private W. Blanchflower.
Private M. Crehan.
Private C. Dean.
Private E. T. Felton.
Private E. Fitton.
Private J. Martin.
Private H. Mangham.
Lance-Corporal J. Pullin.

Private H. Shepherd.
Private T. Simon.
Private P. Smith.
Corporal R. J. Tilley.
Private R. E. F. Wild.
Private M. B. Wilkinson.
Private D. Edmundson.

GAVRELLE AND ARLEUX, ETC.

Private M. Bennett.
Private J. W. Hall.
Private J. Hampson.
Private C. Maundrill.
Private E. Parkinson.
Private J. Singleton.
Private B. Martin.
Private H. C. Micklem.

Private J. E. Singleton.
Private J. Sherman.
Private H. Andrews.
Private J. D. Archibald.
Corporal G. T. Bradley.
Corporal R. King.
Corporal W. Titley.

PASSCHENDAELE.

Sergeant C. P. Brien.
Private S. Clark.
Private R. T. Emmerson.
Private E. Ferriday.

Sergeant J. W. Ferguson.
Private A. Hardy.
Private W. Hodson.
Sergeant J. Holmes.

WELCH RIDGE.

Sergeant A. E. Jackson.
Private M. Johnson.
Private W. J. Jones.
Private F. Masterman.
Private J. K. Merton.
Private J. E. Ramsbottom.
Private M. Robson.

Private J. V. Salisbury.
Private S. Smith.
Private D. J. Thomas.
Private S. Vickers.
Private J. Wild.
Corporal H. N. Taylor.

MARCH RETREAT, 1918.

Private F. Ditchburn.
Lance-Corporal J. Dillon.
Private F. Mills.
Private G. Tamberlin.

Private J. E. Fisher.
Corporal H. Chadwick.
Corporal G. Whiteley.
Private H. Moxon.

BRITISH OFFENSIVE, 1918.

Private N. Marr.

Private G. R Scholes.

Private J. Ward. Private J. Young.

DROCOURT-QUEANT LINE AND SUBSEQUENT OPERATIONS.

Staff-Sergeant J. H. Crabtree. Private P. Read.
Corporal R Compston. Private R Shaw.
Private T. Salisbury. Private W. Wood.
Private J. M. Anderton. Private A. Covell.
Private J. Beesley. Private J. Downie.
Private T. Brooks. Private C. Eastwood.
Private T. W. Cleemy. Private T. E. Moore.
Private S. Holt. Private A. Stott.
Private H. Moxon. Sergeant J. B. Maiden.
Private H. Parr. Private J. Brown.
Private A. Rench. Private J. Crook.
Private F. Sissons. Private H. Fletcher.
Private A. E. Stephenson. Private A. H. Green.
Private W. Waddington. Private T. Johnson.
Corporal F. C. Evans. Private F. Lamb.
Private G. Platt. Private R. Lawton.
Private H. Black. Private R Lee.
Private J. C. Chisholm. Private A. Lord.
Private E. N. Clark. Private E. Morton.
Private R Hilton. Private J. W. Nicholl.
Corporal G. C. Mc Court. Private A. T. Proud.
Corporal M. Meades. Private T. E. Salisbury.
Private R. Paxton. Private F. Wood.

Bars to Military Medal.
Lance-Corporal C. Maundrill. Private J. R Chisholm.
Staff-Sergeant G. Tamberlin. Corporal J. Barran.
Sergeant G. T. Bradley. Sergeant A. Covell.

Mentioned in Dispatches.-
Staff-Sergeant J. H. Crabtree. Sergeant T. Wilson.
Staff-Sergeant W. A. Read. Sergeant C. Brooke.
Sergeant G. Tamberlin. Sergeant M. Fortescue.
Sergeant-Major C. L. Williams, Corporal T. E. Barker.
    R.M.L.I. Sergeant F. Wilson.
Corporal W. J. Jones.

CHAPTER 38.

ROYAL MARINE LABOUR CORPS.

1. France - 2. Home Service.

IN 1916 the increasing numbers of the Army in France with the consequent expansion in the quantity of stores and munitions to be landed was giving great anxiety to the Naval Transport Officers at the Base Ports, whilst the activities of the submarines with the resultant loss of shipping made it essential that there should be no delay in the "turn round" of ships and their quick loading and discharge.

When the troops were first landed the system had been to engage local labour in the ports, but the increasing drain on the French man-power had diminished the supply of labour, which was now becoming totally inadequate to meet the increasing demands.

To meet this difficulty the Army had formed two A.S.C. (Naval Labour) Companies, supplemented by fatigue parties from the troops at the base; these companies were formed of stevedores and men accustomed to the work of loading and discharging ships, but they were under the control of the local A.S.C. officers and Army staffs, and the Naval Transport Officers found great difficulty in obtaining the parties they required, whilst the personnel were frequently changed. Under these circumstances it was proposed to raise R.N.V.R. men under the Admiralty to carry out the work, but the question arose as to whether they would be amenable to the local Military discipline and the orders of the local Commander and the matter was under discussion throughout 1916. Conferences were held at the headquarters of the Inspector General of Communications in France and also in London at which the A.G.R.M. was represented and it was finally decided, after delay, that the Royal Marine system of organisation would best meet the case, for they would be subject to the standing orders and discipline of the ports under the local commanders, but would be entirely at the disposal of the Divisional Naval Transport Officers as regards the control and distribution of their work; a principle which had been settled many years before between the Admiralty and War Office.

Under these circumstances, the Royal Marine Labour Corps came into existence and fully justified its formation.

The personnel of the two A.S.C. Companies were transferred to the Royal Marines on 2nd February, 1917, the Commanding Officer, Major J. F. Cable, A.S.C., an expert in all dock matters, being granted a commission in Royal Marines and appointed to the Staff of the Principal Naval Transport Officer in France, as technical officer in charge Labour; his extensive knowledge of mercantile ports was invaluable in organising the work and equipment of the ports in France.

Major J. G. Home, R.M.L.I. was at first appointed Commanding Officer, but as he was required for important work elsewhere, he was succeeded by Major R. Cator, R.M.L.I. with the temporary rank of Lieutenant-Colonel; a most fortunate selection, as he was an ideal officer for such a post which required tact and firmness with a keen sense of humour and human sympathy, as the men with whom he had to deal were not of the type of those who usually find their way into the service.

Recruiting was opened throughout the ports in England and men poured in; only men over 41 years of age were enlisted (at that time the limit of age for combatant enlistment), and the opportunity of "doing their bit" was gladly seized by many men between 50 and 60, including many ex-Marines and soldiers.

As the officers were required to be experts in the special work, they were appointed from gentlemen, who had served in the Mercantile Marine or who had experience of shipping and ports in England or who were qualified stevedores, many being promoted from the ranks of the Unit.

The Divisional Headquarters were fixed at Deal, where the recruits were sent on enlistment, to be clothed and equipped and given a little drill and discipline; owing to the previous vexatious delays, this time for the first contingent was much curtailed. The Pay Office (they were paid on the Home Base Ledger system at Army Service Corps rates of pay) and records were also kept here, temporary officers being appointed to assist the Paymaster.

Lieutenant-Colonel Cator's Headquarters were established at General Headquarters in France (the post of I.G.C. was now abolished) with the P.N.T.O. Lieutenant J. Carroll, R.M.L.I. was appointed Adjutant and Quartermaster and there was a small staff of clerks. The ports were regularly visited and control maintained over the arrangements and discipline.

The position of the Unit was somewhat difficult as the Army provided all their accommodation, rations (for which the Admiralty paid) and medical attendance, whilst their stores were provided by the Admiralty through the Divisional Naval Transport Officers as a charge to Marine votes[44].

Each port had its own detachment, whose strength was regulated by the work to be done varying from 1,120 at Dunkirk to 50 at St. Valery.

The detachment at each port was commanded by a temporary captain, Royal Marines, with an officer promoted from the ranks of the R.M.L.I. as Adjutant to assist in the duties of discipline and administration, and the number of officers at each port was regulated by the work to be done. The larger ports each had an R.M.L.I. Sergeant-Major (W.O. 1) and Q.M.S. (W.O. 2) and the smaller ports a Company Sergeant-Major (W.O. 2) R.M.L.I. Each port also had an R.M.L.I. Sergeant and one or two selected Lance Corporals for Police and Camp Duties. The larger ports also had their own Labour Corps Company Sergeant-Majors.

As the men had to work in the transports full of troops, it was necessary that they should wear a distinctive uniform and therefore they were dressed in the blue uniform of the Corps but with blue serge trousers without stripes. Cap and collar badges were Globe and Laurel and later the cap badge had a ship in full sail above the Globe in place of the bugle.

        The total strength of the Unit was-
            1 Lieutenant-Colonel.
            12 Captains (afterwards 5 Majors, 7 Captains).
            44 Lieutenants and 2nd Lieutenants.
            5 Company-Sergeant-Majors.
            112 Colour-Sergeants and Sergeants.
            531 Corporals.
            4205 Privates.
with the following R.M.L.I. attached
            1 Major (Acting Lieutenant-Colonel).
            1 Adjutant and Quartermaster.
            5 Lieutenants and Adjutants.

---

44. *Incidentally the rations illustrated the elasticity of the R.M. System; because one of the difficulties which had arisen whilst the Army were supplying the labour, came from the provision of food when the men were employed on all night work; this was got over by the men receiving Army Rations, but when employed at night, they could be authorised to receive extra issues under the King's Regulations and Admiralty Instructions.*

6 Sergeant-Majors.
5 Quartermaster Sergeants.
4 Company-Sergeant-Majors.
2 Sergeants.
8 Lance-Sergeants and Lance-Corporals for Police Duties.

The Home Base Staff was one Assistant Paymaster, one Superintending Clerk and 13 Clerks.

The Unit was distributed as in the following table:

Port	Total Labour	Numbers R.M.L.I.	Commanding Officer.	Adjutant	Sergeant Major.
Havre	977	4	Major W. Cross	Lieut. J. Mackenzie	D. E. Eccles (Chatham)
Rouen	559	4	Major J. A. Paterson	Lieut. R. H. Winne	A. Yarrow (Portsmouth)
Truville	106	1	2nd-Lieut. J. B. Bradly		
Bolougne	726	4	Major E. H. Gill	Lieut. W. Seabrook	E. P. Hann (Plymouth)
Calais	725	4	Major J. Mackay	Lieut. W. Prior	W. G. Hughes (Portsmouth)
Dunkirk	1132	4	Major G. Havelock	Lieut. A. B. Apperley	J. H. Wakeham (Plymouth)
St. Valery	57	1	Lieut. T. W. Howell		
Dieppe	309	2	Captain J. Tait		
Cherbourg	152		Lieut. J. M. Walker		
Other Ports	165		G.H.Q. Sergt-Major William Gregory (Plymouth).		

The Unit quickly grew in numbers and it earned an excellent reputation for good work, particularly at Dunkirk and Calais where they were bombed almost nightly, but the R.M.L.C. stuck to their work and carried on in spite of casualties and damage. Captain Fuller was awarded the D.S.C.. for gallant conduct, when an air raid demolished several huts of the R.M.L.C., in rescuing the wounded and doing everything possible to minimise the damage without regard to his personal safety, and several men were awarded the D.S.M.; whilst C.S.M. L. Smith, Sergt. R. Gooding and Private A. Scott with Private F. Brown (Plymouth) R.M.L.I. were awarded the Meritorious Service Medal for extinguishing a dangerous conflagration at Boulogne on 22nd June, 1918.

With men of this advanced age there was unavoidably a good deal of sickness but they came through the ordeal in a surprising manner.

Though their preliminary connection with the Corps was so slight, they developed a very strong esprit de corps and were very proud and jealous of their position as Royal Marines; though their bearing may not have been altogether pleasing to the eye of the parade soldier, yet they displayed the true soldierly spirit and earned many decorations for gallantry in saving life and for promptitude in emergencies; whilst many officers were mentioned in dispatches and earned decorations for good and efficient service.

The formation of the Corps solved what was threatening to become a very serious problem in the conduct of the war. When the difficulties and loss occasioned by the employment of Greek and other casual labour at other ports are considered and also the diversion of fighting troops in Gallipoli, etc., together with the difficulties experienced in England itself, which were only solved by the employment of Transport Worker Battalions, the desirability of such a Corps as the R.M.L.C. forming part of any scheme of mobilization presents itself.

The following rewards were gained by this unit.

Brevet-Lieutenant-Colonel. - Major R Cator, R.M.L.I.

O.B.E. - Major and Brevet Lieutenant-Colonel R Cator, R.M.L.I.

Lieutenant-Colonel J. F. Cable, R.M.L.C., also promoted Lieutenant-Colonel.
Major W. K. McKay, R.M.L.C.

D.S.C.- Captain H. V. Fuller, R.M.L.C.

D.S.M.- Private M. Boyd. Sergeant R McIntosh.
Sergeant J. W. Cook. Sergeant J. W. Mace.
Sergeant B. Doull. Private J. J. Rate.
Corporal G. E. Hanham.

M.S.M. - Sergeant R Gooding. Sergeant B. L. Steed.
(for gallantry in performance of military duty).

Private A. Scott.
Compy.-Sergeant-Major L. Smith. Sergeant A. S. Traill.
Sergeant S. W. Buckle.

also to the following R.M.L.I. attached.
Private F. Brown (Plymouth). C.S.M. J. H. Wakeham (Plymouth).
C.S.M. D. E. Eccles(Chatham). Sergeant H. J. Eastaway (Plymouth).
C.S.M. C. P. Hann (Chatham).

Mentioned in Dispatches.-
Captain W. K. McKay. Sergeant P. S. W. Buckle.
Captain J. A. Paterson. Sergeant J. P. Purvis.
Major J. F. Cable. Lieutenant E. S. Sutcliffe.
Captain T. H. Gill. 2nd-Lieutenant H. P. Norris.
Captain J. Tait. Private H. J. Williams.
Captain J. White. Captain J. Cooper.
Captain W. Wood. Captain H. V. Fuller.
Lieutenant A. W. Burns. Captain T. A. Harvey.
Lieutenant P. Malarky. Lieutenant R. Horn.
Lieutenant J. Pettigrew. Lieutenant R H. Newton.
Lieutenant W. Thompson. Sergeant J. Beatson.
Sergeant H. Bagge. Sergeant J. Church.
Sergeant J. G. Chapman. Private C. B. Clark.
Sergeant E. Annion. Sergeant J. Dick.
Corporal C. Davidson. Corporal J. English.
Captain (Tempy. Major) J. W. Carroll, R.M.L.I. Sergeant A. B. Fisher.
Lieutenant (A/Captain) J. McKenzie, R.M.A. Sergeant W. Fuller.
Lieutenant (A/Captain) R H. Winne, R.M.L.I. Private T. Hawthorn.
Compy.-Sergeant-Major D. E. Eccles, R.M.L.I. Sergeant R H. Langdown.
Acting Sergeant-Major J. H. Wakeham. Corporal J. Macfarlane.
Sergeant H. N. Ferguson. Sergeant W. J. Millem.
Acting Sergeant-Major T. Henderson. Captain C. Mitchell.
Private P. Mills. Private J. J. R Montague.
Sergeant J. Nimmo (now tempy 2nd-Lieut.) Sergeant A. Nicholson.
Sergeant F. C. Parsons. Private L. Pearson.

Corporal H. Ronald.
Corporal L. Smith (now tempy. 2nd-Lieut.)
Sergeant D. Alexander.
Sergeant E. Baxter.
Company-Sergeant-Major H. J. Peck.
Sergeant W. H. Smee.
Private G. Swire.
Company-Sergeant-Major J. Wishart.

2. HOME SERVICE LABOUR COMPANY.

When the decision was taken in 1917 to greatly increase the mine-laying in the North Sea and adjacent areas, mining Depots were established at Granton and other places under the Admiral in charge of Mining. To handle the mines it was necessary to have disciplined labour and as the Fleet working parties were no longer sufficient the Admiralty decided to raise a Royal Marine Unit called No. 1 (Home Service) Labour Company. Major F. Athow, R.M.L.I. was appointed to command with Lieutenant R. D. Hale, R.M.L.I. as second in command and the establishment was fixed at :-

1 Company-Sergeant-Major, R.M.L.I.	1 Record Clerk, R.M.L.I.
1 Company Quarter-Master-Sergeant, R.M.L.I.	4 Sergeants (Labour).
5 Sergeants, R.M.L.I.	26 Corporals (Labour).
1 Pay Sergeant, R.M.L.I.	200 Privates (Labour).

Recruits were posted by the Minister of National Service by arrangement with the Royal Marine Recruiting Authorities from men over combatant age or of lower medical categories. They were paid at A.S.C. rates and were affiliated to the Chatham Division.

They were quartered in the Mining Depot at Granton on 16th December, 1917, and carried out their work very efficiently, and solved this problem smoothly and without friction. When Major Athow was invalided Lieutenant Hale assumed command and the unit was finally demobilised in 1919.

	Officers.	Warrant Officers.	N.C.O.s and Men.
Administrative H.Q., RM.A. or RM.L.I.	2	1	46
Technical Details, R.M.E.	8		44
Medical Details, R.N.	2		2
	22	1	94

	Officers.	Warrant Officers.	N.C.O.s and Men.
H.Q., R.M.A. or R.M.L.I.	1	1	11
H.Q., R.M.E.	1	3	15
No.1 Platoon, R.M.E.	1	140	
Nos. 2. 3 and 4 Platoons, R.M.E.	3		396
	6	4	562

CHAPTER 39.

ROYAL MARINE ENGINEERS.

AT the end of 1917 and the beginning of 1918 the Director of Works at the Admiralty was experiencing difficulty in obtaining labour for the construction of urgent works in out of the way places such as Scapa Flow where the problem of accommodating and feeding civilian workmen was very difficult; in these circumstances, he invoked the assistance of the Royal Marines with whom his department had always been in close touch through the N.C.O.s and men of the Corps who were trained for the Works at Ascension, Bermuda, etc.

Following on the experience gained with the Labour Corps, schemes were drawn up and approved for Engineer Companies, to be raised and officered by the Royal Marines; the technical officers being the Officials of the Works Department, but before this scheme could be put in operation the Director of Works was replaced by a new Civil Engineer-in-Chief, Sir Alexander Gibb; the scheme at once took on a much larger scope; Sir A. Gibb brought with him a staff of Army officers, Colonel W. James, C.M.G., D.S.O. and Brig.-General H. O. Knox, etc.

Provision was made to raise a large number of companies, each company officered by technical officers (engineers) who were granted temporary commissions in the Corps side by side with Royal Marine officers who were responsible for organisation and discipline.

The organisation of the unit was on the following lines :-

A Divisional Headquarters was established at Chatham consisting of five officers and 19 other ranks, with clerks from the Women's Royal Naval Service.

The following staff was appointed to this unit and was stationed at Chatham :-

Commanding Officer. - Colonel C. H. Willis, R.M.L.I.
Staff Officer I/c Records. - Captain C. A. Hepburn, R.M.L.I.
Quartermaster. - Lieutenant H. Martin, R.M.L.I.
Paymaster.- Lieutenant-Colonel C. E. F. Drake-Brockman, R.M.L.I.
Depot Company. - 1 Lieutenant and 26 N.C.O.s and Men.

The depot received recruits, clothed and equipped them and gave them a certain amount of military training; they were then drafted to companies as required; later the Depot was moved to Bedmenham.

Colonel Willis carried out the duties of a Colonel Commandant of a Division as regards this unit, whose numbers approached 10,000 at the time of the Armistice.

A certain number of mobile Headquarters for charge of the more important works were formed, which could be moved as necessary.

A large mobile headquarter consisted of:-

	Officers.	Warrant Officers.	N.C.O.s and Men.
Administrative H.Q., RM.A. or RM.L.I.	2	1	46
Technical Details, R.M.E.	8		44
Medical Details, R.N.	2		2
	22	1	94

The other personnel were formed into works companies of which there were ten in all.

Each company was composed as follows:-

	Officers.	Warrant Officers.	N.C.O.s and Men.
H.Q., R.M.A. or R.M.L.I.	1	1	11
H.Q., R.M.E.	1	3	15
No.1 Platoon, R.M.E.	1		140
Nos. 2. 3 and 4 Platoons, R.M.E.	3		396
	6	4	562

No. 1 Platoon contained 56 engineers (skilled craftsmen) and 84 pioneers. Nos. 2, 3 and 4 Platoons each contained 48 engineers and 84 pioneers. The pioneers were navvies, cooks, orderlies, etc.

In addition to which there was a miscellaneous Trades Company consisting of:-

	Officers.	Warrant Officers.	Other Ranks.
Headquarters, R.M.A. or R.M.L.I.	1	1	11
Headquarters, R.M.E.	2		4
Engineers and Pioneers, R.M.E.		508 Engineers,	55 Pioneers.

The duty of this company was to reinforce the works companies employed on particular jobs where more skilled craftsmen were required than the company itself possessed.

Each works company was a self-contained unit being complete with its own tools, equipment, etc.

The R.M.A. and R.M.L.I. attached were for administration, care of stores, rations, clothing, etc. and discipline under the mobile headquarters.

The men of the Royal Marine Engineers were largely obtained by transfer from the Inland Water Transport Section of the Royal Engineers, and recruits of categories "B" and "C" together with a certain number of conscientious objectors.

The officers were trained civil and electrical Engineers who were nominated by the Civil Engineer-in-Chief. The R.M.A. and R.M.L.I. officers were mostly Reserve Warrant and N.C.O.'s who were given temporary commissions for the War and who fulfilled their difficult duties with the greatest tact and discretion. many distinguished engineers and architects served in the commissioned ranks of the Unit, among whom besides Sir A. Gibb was Major Sir Gilbert Scott.

The urgency of the work to be performed prevented any attempt at giving the N.C.O.s and the men of the Unit a proper military training, and even with all the efforts to raise the unit hurriedly it was found necessary to reinforce them for a time with parties of the Royal Marine Labour Corps from France.

The Civil Engineer-in-Chief had a certain staff of Army officers at the Admiralty who were not technical officers and in the light of experience gained it is impossible not to conclude that any such officers should be Naval or Marine officers who are acquainted with Admiralty methods.

Officers and men were paid at the same rates as Royal Engineers as had been done in the case of the Divisional Engineers (see Chapter 37).

The most important of these Mobile Headquarters which was organised and commanded by Lieut.-Colonel A. de W. Kitcat, R.M.L.I. was at Southwick near Brighton, where the spacious village green had been turned into a camp where 5000 of the R.M.E. were housed in huts with all the accessories required for such a large number of men; streets were laid out and water and drainage provided and the camp was lit by electric light. Here were constructed the "Mystery Towers"; the object for which they were constructed was never published; only two were completed, one of which has now replaced the Nab Lightship off the Isle of Wight and the other was destroyed.

The other headquarters was established at Bedmenham, between Gosport and Fareham for the units employed on Admiralty Works at Portsmouth; this camp was organised and commanded by Major C. F. O. Graham, R.M.L.I. and here a large hutted camp was constructed which was completed in September, 1918 and soon after its inception the training and disciplinary training was transferred here from Chatham and from this camp drafts were sent out to the various works undertaken by the Unit.

From the two main camps detachments were sent out to carry out any works in other districts, among which were the aerodrome at Scapa Flow and the laying of the oil pipe line from the Clyde to the Forth in conjunction with the skilled American Engineers; this party lived in barges on the Canal during the progress of the work.

After the headquarters at Southwick had been organised and placed on a satisfactory footing by Colonel Kitcat, one of the Technical Officers was placed in command but he was soon after relieved by Lieut.-Colonel A. G. Vincent, R.M.L.I. (retired) who had brought over a battalion of infantry from Nova Scotia.

As soon as the Armistice was signed, the demobilisation of the Unit was commenced, because it was a very expensive unit to maintain; the demobilisation was carried out at Bedmenham Camp, which was singularly free from the unrest of the period.

A party of the unit did duty for several months at Ostend supervising some 2,000 Belgian workmen in making good the damage done by the Germans and clearing the obstructions in the harbour and canal.

A small party raised on similar lines was employed in the destruction of the fortifications on Heligoland under Brig.-General Knox, late A.S.C., and Lieutenant G. H. Littleton, R.M.A.

The value of such a unit was amply proved and many lessons were learnt in its working, and experience shows that such a unit would probably have to be raised in the event of any future war; but to obtain the full value officers and men should have undergone the preliminary military training which would enable them to make the best use of their technical qualifications under war conditions.

PART IX

Administration and Training.

CHAPTER 40.

ADMINISTRATIVE ARRANGEMENTS OF THE CORPS AT HOME.

Numbers - Royal Marine Office - RM. Headquarters – Mobilisation - RM. Acts, 1914 – 1916 – Officers-Recruiting - Records, Pay, etc.- Bands – W.R.N.S. - Equipment - Prisoners of War Comforts Fund -Table of Strengths.

AT the outbreak of the War the voted strength of the Corps was 16,900 R.M.A. and R.M.L.I. with 1,450 Royal Marine Band-total 18,350. The actual serving strength was 3,393 R.M.A., 13,425 R.M.L.I, 1,442 Royal Marine Band making of total of 18,260.

The Reserves consisted of four classes; 401 Immediate Class, 1,676 Class "A," 2,984 Class "B" of the Royal Fleet Reserve and 1,790 Pensioners under 55 years of age, who were not members of the Royal Fleet Reserve.

The Immediate Class were undergoing their month's training afloat in the Third Fleet ships that had been commissioned for the manoeuvres. Volunteers from Classes "A" and "B" had been up for training afloat and at Headquarters during the test mobilisation, but had just been sent home, so that fortunately they had undergone some recent training. The Pensioners were an unknown quantity and consisted largely of senior N.C.O.'s.

For many years training at Headquarters had been carried out under great difficulties, owing to the short time that officers and all ranks were ashore between embarkations, and this had undoubtedly reacted on the military training both artillery and infantry.

There was a most serious shortage of trained officers. Owing to the suspension of entries in 1907 due to the introduction of the Selborne-Fisher scheme there was a deficiency of 19 R.M.A. and 39 R.M.L.I. officers even after including approximately 59 recruit officers in various stages of their training. Two officers only had been entered from Dartmouth under the scheme and in consequence direct entry was reopened in 1912 but on a small scale, however 47 probationary 2nd Lieutenants had been entered in that and the next year who had not yet completed their training at the outbreak of war; an examination had just been held and 53 more were entered in August, 1914. Owing to the slowness of promotion there were 13 R.M.A. and 46 R.M.L.I. captains, who had been promoted at 11 years, who were serving afloat as lieutenants, and several detachments afloat which should have borne one or more officers, Royal Marines were without them, as none were available.

ROYAL MARINE OFFICE.

Though many changes were made in the personnel of the office, there was no great increase in numbers in spite of the increased work.

The addition of the administration of the Royal Naval Division caused a new section to be formed in October, 1914, which remained in one form or another until the end of the war.

In consequence of the great increase in financial work due to separation and other allowances, Major Dimmer was appointed additional for these duties in September, 1915, when he had recovered from his breakdown due to overwork in the earlier days.

Owing to the growing work an attached officer to take a part of the financial work off the shoulders of the A.A.G. was allowed in 1917, and when the Royal Naval Air Service was transferred to the Royal Air Force and the various units that had been under them were transferred to the Adjutant General, viz: The Russian Armoured Car Squadrons, The Tank Testing Squadron, the Chemical Warfare Squadron which were all Admiralty units, an additional D.A.A.G. was allowed.

In 1918 owing to the further increase of special units such as the Labour Corps, Royal Marine Engineers, etc., it was decided to allow an additional A.A.G. and D.A.A.G. for these units and the change was made on 1st July, 1918 when Brig.-General Hutchison relieved Colonel Blumberg, as A.A.G., Colonel C. L. Brooke, R.M.A. being promoted to be the additional A.A.G.

The demobilisation brought a great strain on the office, because the reformation of the Fleet had to be carried out concurrently whilst at the same time the Corps was still being called on to furnish numerous units for active and other operations as described in the foregoing chapters.

Major-General Sir D. Mercer, who had become A.G. in June, 1916 had to bear the burden of this work, and his devotion to duty combined with the effects of the Gallipoli campaign undoubtedly led to his early death in July, 1920.

The holders of the appointments on the Headquarter Staff of the Corps are shown in the Appendix to this chapter.

THE ROYAL MARINE HEADQUARTERS.

When the Royal Marine Brigade was formed the Divisions were much handicapped by the removal of their adjutants and instructional staffs except the Naval Gunnery Instructors for service with the batteries and battalions until Reserve officers and N.C.O.s could be found to carry out the duties at Headquarters; and in the rush of mobilisation the removal of all the company officers for embarkation was a great hindrance to the smooth working. It was demonstrated that the routine at Headquarters was on sound lines as very few modifications were required to meet the war conditions. Reserve officers replaced Active Service officers, who were withdrawn for various duties afloat and overseas and the same principle applied to all ranks and many resumed the duties that they had carried out 20 years previously, of which notable instances were Colonels C. H. Willis and J. Langford who became Office Adjutants (now Brigade Majors) once more at Chatham and Plymouth.

Till the removal of the battalions accommodation was strained to the uttermost and drill sheds, theatres, lecture rooms, etc. were all turned into barrack rooms.

The system of messing by a ration of bread and meat supplemented by purchase of groceries, etc. at the canteen had to be abandoned and a war ration on a generous scale was issued in lieu.

It was remarkable all through the War how the organisation of the Divisions expanded without any difficulty to meet the numerous new demands that arose and after a time battalions and batteries were raised with little more fuss than was required in peace time to send off a draft for embarkation.

MOBILISATION.

The mobilisation arrangements prepared in peace time worked excellently and the active service men were embarked quickly and expeditiously. The reserves were called out on 2nd August and reported themselves immediately; they were clothed, equipped and dispatched to their various duties without a hitch due to the excellent work of the staffs at Headquarters. The response was magnificent and practically all were accounted for within the week, great numbers actually reported on the 2nd and were embarked that day.

The King's Pardon was granted to all deserters who reported themselves for service and a very considerable number surrendered themselves; many interesting stories were unfolded and quite a number of those who were too old to serve reported themselves, and were given protecting certificates; actually one case occurred of a man who wrote from America, who was allowed to report himself to a station in Canada where the certificate was sent as he was too old to serve. One of the most interesting stories was that of a man who had deserted in the East Indies and gone inland to Mexico, he did not hear of the War till six months after it had begun, when on a trip to Vera Cruz; he at once worked his passage home in a ship and being penniless on arrival in Liverpool walked down to join his Division on foot. Several also returned with the Australian Forces.

Offers of service were received from retired officers and Marines of every rank and every age, and in many cases were gladly utilised; in fact in addition to the officers as explained later the bulk of the recruiting staffs and many odd jobs in barracks were replaced by N.C.O.s and men of over 55 years of age. The following letter is typical of the saying "once a Marine, always a Marine."

"Dear Sir,

"There being such a call for men at the present time, I should like if possible, to rejoin for the

"duration of the War

"I am too old for the front I suppose (62 years old), but could take the place of a younger

"man that might be kept in barracks to do certain duties older men could do.

"I would not require setting up drill or backboard (!). say a fortnight for the new rifle, then

"fit for sentry go or any garrison duty. I am not out of a berth, but have a very good one and

"I should require a week or so to put things in order."

ROYAL MARINE ACTS, 1914 AND 1916.

The question at once arose of the retention in the service of men whose time was expiring; the R.M. Mutiny Acts of 1847 provided for the retention of men on foreign stations for a period of two years at the discretion of the Naval Commander-in-Chief and a short Act called the Royal Marines Act, 1914 was obtained extending this regulation to men on home service also at the discretion of the Admiralty. In 1916 as this Act was expiring another Bill called the Royal Marines Act, 1916 was passed through Parliament extending the retention of time-expired men for the duration of the War. This step caused a great block of promotion as the establishment of N.C.O.s was not increased: but the difficulty was met by making all N.C.O.s supernumerary to the establishment on the date when they would have been normally discharged to pension and coupled with acting promotion provided the additional numbers required for the expansion of the Corps.

Later those men who had completed 21 years were discharged to pension and granted their pension, but were continued in the service as mobilised pensioners till the end of the war.

OFFICERS.

As stated before one of the most pressing questions was the provision of officers. The Reserve of Officers was at once called out and utilised as necessary, unfortunately a good many had been earmarked as W.T. censors and were not released for some time. Though many officers over the age for service were accepted, they could not provide all that was necessary, for in this war not only had provision to be made for expansion and the raising of new units, but the casualties sustained particularly in the battalions in the field were beyond all precedent and various expedients for making good the deficiencies were adopted. In spite of the difficulties, the policy was followed of only entering sufficient officers by the direct entry examinations for regular commissions to fill the usual normal vacancies, in order that there should not be a large excess of establishment at the close of the war; it being considered that any deficiency then could be made good by the transfer of temporary officers to the permanent list which was done in 1919.

Temporary officers were commissioned for the duration of the War; the first batch was entered on 20th September, 1914 and was sent to Eastney for training and then allotted to Divisions. This batch numbered 40 but these numbers were soon increased. They were drawn from the Universities and Public Schools; the Inns of Court O.T.C. provided many, and later, after the transfer of the Royal Naval Division to France, officers for the R.M.L.I.. Battalions were drawn from the Officer Cadet Battalions of the Army who volunteered for service with the Royal Marines.

A large number of permanent commissions were given to the warrant and non-commissioned officers of the Corps and practically all the Sergeant-Majors and senior Q.M.S. as well as the Superintending Clerks were promoted to Lieutenant, the experiment was also made of creating acting warrant officers for platoon duties, but the majority were later promoted to Lieutenant and it was not repeated. A considerable number of pensioner and R.F.R. N.C.O.s were also given commissions and a good many were drafted for service with the Naval Battalions of the Royal Naval Division, whilst many gained commissions in the Army in the units to which they had been lent as Instructors (see Appendix 2).

Later a few temporary commissions were given to long service N.C.O.s and those few who survived were mostly retired at the end of the war.

The Corps was deeply indebted to its temporary officers who joined from civil life. They seemed to imbibe its traditions at once and to their gallantry and devotion were due many gallant actions which added so largely to its laurels.

RECRUITING.

Recruits flowed in at once and the Order in Council establishment of 19,845 was soon passed and the resources of the Depots were strained to the uttermost.

It was not until September, 1914 that for the first time in its history, recruiting for short service was opened; the first of these recruits were transfers from the Army (Kitchener's) to the number of 600 men, who were distributed 200 to each Infantry Division; some of them were old soldiers and during the war the record of these men was very fine, many rising to N.C.O. rank. Recruits were then regularly enlisted for duration of the war, and as the long service recruits filled the Depot they were distributed to the Divisions for training. The short service recruits were mostly drafted to the batteries and battalions, as the training of the long service recruits in Naval Gunnery took so long, but after being sent home wounded or invalided short service men were trained in Naval gunnery and utilised afloat or in the various garrisons. Later when the Reserve Battalion R.M.L.I. was formed at Blandford those recruits intended for the Battalions did six weeks at Deal and then were sent to the Reserve Battalion, whilst the short service squads for general Corps duty were trained at the Depot Up to the end of 1916 the Corps had depended on its own recruiting efforts, but with the coming in of National Service and conscription, whilst continuing to voluntarily enlist for long and short service for which the Navy had priority, mostly from lads under 18, a proportion of recruits for the R.M.L.I. Battalions in France were obtained from the Army pool at Reading, who after six weeks at Deal and another six weeks at Blandford were drafted to France.

Recruits for the R.M.A. long and short service, were enlisted direct, and trained at Eastney, where they went through a long and thorough course almost as in peace time.

In 1917 short service recruits of medical categories "B.i" and "C.i" were accepted for R.M.L.I. and received a training of three months at Deal followed by a shortened naval gunnery course to fit them for service in shore defences such as Scapa Flow, Cromarty, etc.

The table at the end of the chapter illustrates the growth of the Corps throughout the War.

In 1917 the Inspector of Marine Recruiting was replaced by the Director of Naval Recruiting with an Assistant Director, the holder of the appointment Brig.-General A. G. Tatham, R.M.A. (retired) being the first Director, with Major R. G. Wharton, R.M.L.I. as his assistant, and Captain Littleton, R.M.A., as Liaison Officer in the Ministry of National Service.

RECORDS AND PAY, ETC.

The Corps organisation for drafting, records, clothing, etc. came triumphantly through the ordeal and the necessary expansions were made smoothly. Never once was there any failure to meet the numerous and varied demands that were made on the Divisions and even later when the offices were staffed by women of the Women's Royal Naval Service, and by old and disabled officers and men, the never ending strain was successfully grappled with.

It is curious to note how elastic the Corps system proved itself, the units being borne according to the nature of the service on which employed. Some units were borne afloat on ships' books under the Naval Discipline Act, others on ships' books but under the Army Act for discipline, whilst others again were borne on the shore strength under the Army Act. Among the first were included the garrisons of Cromarty, Scapa and St. Helena and the R.M.A. Siege Guns; in the second category were included the R.M.L.I. Brigade, the Divisional Train, the North Russian Force; whilst the last included among others the R.M.A. Howitzer and A.A. Brigades, the 3rd and 4th Battalions, East African Batteries, Divisional Engineers, Medical Unit and R.M. Labour Corps.

In addition to their ordinary work a heavy strain was thrown on the Divisional Pay Offices by the institution of the general payment of Separation Allowances. Early in the war the Accountant General's Department found themselves unable to cope with the allotment and separation allowances of dependants; the Corps at once undertook to pay these for themselves, and with improvised staffs made up mostly of pensioners who had previously served in the Pay Offices the tangle transferred from the Admiralty was eventually cleared up and the payment of allowances regularly made. The Corps accounts were particularly complicated, because whilst on shore strength the allowances were paid at Army rates, when embarked they had to be changed to Naval rates, which were considerably less; the explanation of this to angry dependants required no little tact and discretion on the part of those engaged.

The Corps system of pay stood the strain wonderfully well, but it was found better to use a quarterly pay list in place of the weekly one; the introduction of a regular food ration in kind, which was considerably better than the peace arrangement of food plus a messing allowance, simplified matters. For units serving overseas the home base ledger and pay book system was introduced on Army Lines and proved so satisfactory that it was also introduced for men of the defensively armed merchantmen.

The R.M.L.I. Brigade had its own pay staff under Colonel D. L. Barrett (retired) first at Dunkirk, then at Deal and Chatham and finally at Blandford whilst the R.M. units of the R.N.D. each had their own pay staffs affiliated to the R.N.D. Office at Blandford.

In 1918 the first increase of pay, long overdue, was made to N.C.O.'s and men and an increase on the naval scale was made to all rank and file.

[Photo by Swaine.]

LIEUT.-COLONEL AND BREVET-COLONEL H. E. BLUMBERG, R.M.L.I.
D.A.A.G., R.M., 1911-1914; A.A. and Q.M.G., R.N.D., 1914;
A.A.G., R.M. (temp.) Jan.-Nov., 1915 and June, 1916 to June, 1918; C. B., 1916.
Adjutant-General, Royal Marines, Nov., 1920 to March, 1924;
Major-General, 1921; Lieut.-General, 1923; K.C.B., 1923; General, 1924.

DIVISIONAL BANDS.

Towards the end of 1916 the first start was made of sending the several Divisional Bands to be attached to the Royal Naval Division in France for a period of six weeks. The first to be sent was the Portsmouth Division, R.M.L.I. under Major Miller, who was unfortunately taken ill and invalided, but the Band played the Battalions back from the trenches after the battle of Beaumont Hamel and later the Chatham Band were present at the funeral of Brig.-General G. E. Matthews, R.M.L.I. who was killed in the trenches and who had been their adjutant for so many years when a subaltern.

The services of the Bands were Much appreciated, and they played not only to the Division, but for the Howitzers when within reach, at the Base Depot and the Hospitals, headquarter staffs, etc., an example that was afterwards followed by the Guards and other Bands.

W.R.N.S.

No account would be complete without mention of the Women's Royal Naval Service. In 1917 when the question of man-power was becoming acute this service was instituted to replace men employed as clerks, mess waiters, cooks and similar duties by women. In common with other naval establishments the Royal Marine Barracks each received their draft and their neat blue uniform soon became a common sight about the barracks. They performed their work most efficiently, under their own lady officers and the "Wrens" as they were called, though regarded with grave suspicion by the Departmental shell-backs, soon justified their existence.

CLOTHING AND EQUIPMENT.

All the arrangements for equipping and clothing Reservists, etc. worked well, but owing to financial stringency before the war no arrangements had been made to equip the mobile Brigade; no mobilisation stores were available, khaki clothing could not be obtained, web equipment was short, and no assistance could be obtained from the Army. Consequently gear and clothing had to be purchased under the greatest difficulties and it was not until the end of November, 1914 after Antwerp, that the Brigade was fully equipped.

It is regrettable that the way in which the rifle question was handled showed how far the conception of the use of the Marines had altered since 1842, when the Royal Marines were the first troops to be armed with the new percussion muskets. The Corps had to surrender their short Lee-Enfield rifles for the use of the Army and Royal Naval Division, and were re-armed with the old Lee-Metford long rifle which was replaced first by the Japanese rifle and later still by the Canadian Ross rifle which had been discarded by the Canadians; it was only those members of the Corps who were serving with the Expeditionary Forces that kept their short rifles, and for the first time in their history men of the Corps were sent on duty without their own rifles, and were armed on arrival at their place of duty.

Tunics and frocks were early withdrawn, and it was found that the Royal Marine system of annual clothing and issues on repayment were unworkable; arrangements were accordingly made that as clothing was worn out it was replaced by order of the officer commanding the detachment and companies, without charge to the men.

In spite of the expansion of the Corps the master tailors kept pace with it, and it was never necessary to resort to contract for the blue uniforms. The Army inspection of supplies and their provision ceased, and as it was impossible to undertake the inspection of cloth and materials at the Divisions this work was carried out by the store department of the India Office.

PRISONERS OF WAR COMFORTS FUND.

When the several battalions, batteries and units proceeded overseas each Division formed a small Comforts Fund to supply them with articles of warm clothing and to help their funds for a few extra luxuries, Xmas presents, etc; the funds were raised by grants from the canteens and subscriptions from all ranks and their families, and the devoted work of the wives and relatives of members of the Divisions maintained these funds in existence throughout the war, and their gifts were most highly appreciated by all the units.

But soon after the Antwerp expedition it became evident that they would have to undertake a far more serious task, this was the provision of food and clothing parcels for the unfortunate men who had happened to fall into the hands of the Germans as prisoners. Without the work carried out by this organisation it is undoubted that numbers would have died of cold and starvation. The Comforts Fund gradually grew into a bigger and bigger undertaking; it was at first concentrated at Gosport with Major H. N. Houghton, the Gunnery Instructor as secretary, but later when the numbers grew and increased Government supervision owing to arrangements with the enemy became necessary, the Royal Marine Fund was amalgamated with the Royal Naval Division Fund, who became responsible for the provision and dispatch of the parcels, the Royal Marines providing the necessary cost for their own men. All Royal Marines whether captured afloat or ashore were looked after by this Association as well as those interned in the neutral countries.

TABLE OF STRENGTHS.

The following table is interesting as showing the growth of the Corps during the War, 1914-1919.

Date	OFFICERS				N.C.O.s AND MEN.				TOTAL
	Active		Reserve		Active		Reserve		
	Ashore	Afloat	Ashore	Afloat	Ashore	Afloat	Ashore	Afloat	
July 1914	166	241			5090	12737			18234
15th March, 1915	386	259	38	22	12283	13835	2738	3855	33116
15th March, 1916	636	268	39	19	17198	14743	2391	3566	38860
15th March, 1917	553*	278	35	20	17618	15898	2300	4551	40251
15th March, 1918	642	307	36	19	22458	16790	2086	3446	45724†
15th Nov, 1918	699	524	32	16	26831	21031	2469‡	4001‡	55603

NOTE-The shore numbers include the Brigades and Batteries employed in the various theatres of War and also some of the garrisons.
*Divisional Engineers transferred to Army and heavy casualties in France.
†Formation of Labour Corps and commencement of R.M. Engineers.
‡Transfer of time expired men to Reserve and also men for D.A.M.S.

APPENDIX TO CHAPTER 40.
STAFF OF THE ROYAL MARINE OFFICE.

Adjutant General.-

General Sir William C. Nicholls, K.C.B., R.M.A., to 25th June, 1916.

Major-General Sir David Mercer, K.C.B., RM.L.I., 26th June, 1916, to end of War.

Assistant Adjutant General.-

Colonel D. Mercer, R.M.L.I., to 1st January, 1915, to Command of 1st R.N. Brigade.

Lieut.-Colonel H. E. Blumberg, R.M.L.I. (tempy.), 1st January, 1915, to 3rd November, 1915, to Army Staff.

Lieut.-Colonel E. McCarthy, R.M.A. (tempy.), 4th November, 1915, to 5th June, 1916, to D.A.A.G.

Lieut.-Colonel H. E. Blumberg, RM.L.I. (tempy.) 6th June, 1916 to 30th June, 1918, to Aegean.

Brigadier-General A. R H. Hutchison, C.B., C.M.G., D.S.O., R.M.L.I., 1st July, 1918, to end of War.

Lieut.-Colonel C. L. Brooke, R.M.A. (tempy.), 23rd May, 1918, to end of War for special Units.

Deputy Assistant Adjutant-General.-

Lieut.-Colonel H. E. Blumberg, R.M.L.I., to 2nd October, 1914, to R.N.D. Section.

Lieut.-Colonel A. R H. Hutchison, R.M.L.I., 2nd October, 1914 to 31st July, 1915, to 2nd R.M.L.I.

Major M. C. Festing, R.M.L.I. (tempy.), 31st August, 1915, to 5th June, 1916, to 188th Brigade.

Lieut.-Colonel E. McCarthy, R.M.A., 6th June, 1916, to 15th December, 1916, invalided.

Lieut.-Colonel C. L. Brooke, R.M.A., 16th December, 1916, to 22nd May, 1918, to A.A.G.

Major R T. Ford, R.M.A., 1st July, 1918, to end of War.

Major L. Norcock, R.M.L.I., 1st July, 1918, to end of War, for Special Units.

Attached Officers.-

Lieut.-Colonel L. O. Wilson, C.M.G.,D.S.O.,M.P., R.M.L.I.,March 1917 to March 1918, to War Cabinet.

Major L. Norcock, R.M.L.I., March 1918 to 1st July, 1918, to D.A.A.G.

Major J. F. Dimmer, R.M.L.I., September 1916, to end for Finance Duty.

Captain F. W. Mattison, R.M.L.I., 15th November, 1919.

Quartermasters.-

Major J. F. Dimmer till June, 1915, to hospital.

Major W. Synes, R.M.L.I., till end of the War.

Major A. E. Brown, R.M.L.I., 25th June, 1915, till end of the War.

ROYAL NAVAL DIVISION.

Brigadier General.- i/c Administration-

Colonel C. G. Brittan, R.M.L.I. 2-14th October, resigned for ill health.

A.A. and Q.M.G.-

Lieut.-Colonel H. E. Blumberg, R.M.L.I., 2nd October, 1914, to 31st December, 1914, to A.A.G., R.M.

Major E. W. Harding, R.M.A., 1st January, 1915 to 30th April, 1915, to Eastney.

Lieut.-Colonel R F. Foster, R.M.A., 1st May. 1915 to 30th May, 1916, to France. (D.A.A. & Q.M.G. 2nd October, 1914 to 30th April, 1915.)

Quartermasters.-

Major J. Simpson, R.M.L.I., 2nd October, 1914 to 30th May, 1916.

Major J. H. Mitchell, R.M.L.L, 2nd October, 1914 to 30th May, 1916.

Officer in Charge of Records.-

Lieut.-Colonel J. Simpson, R.M.L.I., 1st June, 1916 to end of the War.

CHAPTER 41.

TRAINING ARRANGEMENTS.

Recruit Courses - R.M.A. Brigade Depot - 1st Reserve Battalion, R.M.L.I. - Courses at Headquarters - Physical Training School - School of Musketry - Blandford.

TRAINING for the men destined for the sea service continued at the Divisions on normal lines, but the courses at the Depot, Deal were shortened considerably for the R.M.L.I. recruits, whilst the musketry and field training were also curtailed; later on a general musketry course on the Army lines was substituted for the longer tables "A" and "B." At Eastney the infantry training of the R.M.A. recruits followed much the same lines as in peace, after which they were sent to the sea service battery, the long service recruits did not receive instruction in land service artillery unless actually detailed for the Brigades.

In order to keep the training and drafting for the R.M.A. Brigades distinct from the sea service the Commandant, Sir Geo. Aston, instituted a Brigade Depot at Fort Cumberland commanded by Major G. E. Barnes (retired) with Lieutenant A. Dingli as Adjutant; this Depot trained officers and men in land artillery for the Howitzer and A.A. Brigades and from them men required for coast defences and other similar duties were taken. The short service recruits, after a short course of infantry drill and a short course of gunnery at the sea service battery were sent to the Brigade Depot and there trained for the work for which they proved most suitable; following the Army lines, men were not trained generally as in peace time, but were given intensive training as specialists or gun numbers, so that drafts of the various ratings should always be available. The Brigade Depot also carried out the training of the tractor and lorry drivers required for the various petrol motors with which the Brigades were equipped; Lieutenant Barkley being told off for this branch of the instruction assisted by other M..T. officers waiting draft. In order to familiarise officers and men with the equipments, the detachments of officers and men, whose armaments were not yet ready, accompanied the first units to France and were recalled as their own equipments became available.

In the R.M.L.I. the recruits first required for the Battalions of the Royal Marine Brigade completed their training with them as described in the earlier chapters and after the Brigade had proceeded to Gallipoli were trained at their own headquarters. On the transfer of the Battalions to France, the 1st Reserve Battalion, R.M.L.I. was formed at Blandford, where the reserves of the Royal Naval Division were stationed, to complete the training of recruits and to receive returned officers and men; it also prepared the drafts for France and was responsible for their dispatch.

Recruits for the Battalions, both long and short service, received a training of six weeks at Deal in elementary training, discipline and Corps traditions, and were then transferred to Blandford where they underwent the courses of training, musketry, bayonet and bombing laid down for the Army, lasting about six weeks to two months when the recruits were drafted to the Base Depot in France where they underwent the further training laid down, or else joined the Divisional wing. Temporary officers R.M.L.I. were trained at the Royal Marine Headquarters on the lines that used to be common in the Corps before the institution of the Greenwich course, except that they did not undergo naval gunnery; later, when they were mostly commissioned from the Officer Cadet Battalions of the Army, they only spent a short period at Headquarters to accustom them to Corps routine and tradition and were then sent to the 1st Reserve

Battalion for draft. On return to England sick or wounded they were sent to Blandford for duty or to Royal Marine Headquarters, according to the probability of their fitness for service again with the Battalions or for other services such as Royal Marine garrisons, other battalions, batteries, etc.

The courses for officers entered for permanent service were entirely modified as it was impossible to carry out the normal four year course. These officers were generally sent to Deal for a three months' intensive course of infantry and general knowledge, after which they underwent modified courses in naval gunnery and electricity in H.M.S. *Excellent* and *Vernon*; if successful in passing these courses they underwent a special musketry and machine-gun course at the school at Browndown; they were then given their choice of Divisions according to their positions on the list as a result of the examinations, and were posted to their own Headquarters; here if time permitted they underwent a course of field training (land artillery in case of R.M.A.) and a short course of administrative training and were then drafted to sea, if possible as supernumerary subalterns in a battleship, for a short further training. In the case of the subalterns entered in August 1914, only a portion underwent the above training, the remainder after a short infantry course were drafted to the Brigades at once; on return from Gallipoli wounded, invalided or withdrawn after the evacuation, and in the case of the R.M.A. after a period of service with the A.A. Brigade in France, they underwent the Naval gunnery and other courses and were drafted to sea.

Examinations for promotion were suspended for all ranks, and promotions were made on reports, but in view of the long periods spent afloat the military training of the N.C.O.s necessarily deteriorated. In order to counteract this, with the ready aid of the Commander-in-Chief of the Grand Fleet, a school of instruction was established at Deal, where Corporals and Sergeants, just promoted, and Corporals on the top of the list for promotion were received and under the Depot Staff (Captain H. E. Beere and a Q.M.S.I. of Infantry being specially detailed for the work) they received a thorough grounding; the N.C.O.'s were lent from the Grand Fleet for a period of six weeks or two months and this freshening up, particularly under the inspiring influence of Major W. Garnier and his physical training staff, had very beneficial results not only on the individuals themselves but throughout the Fleet as well. Later the classes were held at the several Royal Marine Headquarters. Similar classes were held at Eastney.

As the Physical Training School at Portsmouth had been closed, the training of instructors was undertaken at Deal with most successful results; N.C.O.s were also lent from the Grand Fleet for these courses. Major Garnier with the utmost devotion and energy, ably assisted by Sergeant-Majors O'Dwyer and Flannagan, raised the school to such a pitch of efficiency that it became a model for all such training in England.

A school of musketry was also instituted in 1916 at Browndown under Lieut.-Colonel F. E. Chichester and the Musketry Staff of the Portsmouth Division, R.M.L.I. where officers and N.C.O.s were trained as rifle and machine-gun instructors; and as the Army School at Hythe could no longer cope with the work, the R.M. school was able to provide instructors in sufficient numbers not only to meet requirements at Headquarters, but also to distribute a considerable number throughout the Fleet and so maintain the musketry efficiency of the Corps in spite of the difficulties of arming and opportunity at a satisfactory level. N.C.O.s from the Fleet also attended these classes.

In the Naval Gun Batteries the principal additional work undertaken was the training of the men for gunlayers of the Defensively Armed Merchant ships; this was a most important duty and the results obtained were very satisfactory, taking into consideration the varied nature of the weapons with which they might be called upon to deal, and the difficult nature of the shooting. When it was decided to train the merchant seamen in elementary gun drill, and classes were formed at the Crystal Palace Depot, R.M. Gunner Wyld and a staff of Royal Marine Gunnery instructors were lent to carry out the instruction, which proved most beneficial.

It was difficult to keep pace with the demands for the largely increased number of higher gunnery ratings required and, to cope with this, likely candidates were lent from the Fleet to undergo the necessary courses at R.M. Headquarters and the Gunnery Schools, and if successful these men were replaced in their ships.

During the war, especially in the Grand Fleet, there was a great demand for increased facilities for educational training and as the Admiralty had largely increased the number of schoolmasters afloat, examinations for educational certificates were resumed and great keenness was displayed and there was no doubt that this training was very useful during the long monotonous days at the Northern Bases.

With the approval of the Commander-in-Chief of the Grand Fleet, a small training staff was sent to Scapa Flow to take charge of the rifle and bayonet ranges, and to assist in the instruction of the detachments, whenever it was possible to land them; and a small staff was also established at Rosyth for the ships based on that place.

BLANDFORD.

Soon after the formation of the Royal Naval Division it was obvious that a training camp must be provided; a very suitable site was selected on Blandford Downs where hutments for 12,000 men were erected by the Admiralty and the Naval Battalions moved into them with the Divisional Engineers, Train, and Medical Unit, R.M. at the end of 1914. There was no accommodation for the R.M.L.I. Brigade who remained at the Royal Marine Headquarters until concentrated in billets at Shillingstone at the end of January, 1915.

On the departure of the Naval Division for Gallipoli, the camp was filled with the Hawke, Benbow and Collingwood Battalions then forming, and Depots were formed for the other Royal Marine units of the Division except the R.M.L.I. Colonel 2nd Commandant C. E. Curtoys, R.M.L.I. was appointed to command with a small R.N.V.R. staff; when he was appointed Commandant of Plymouth Division in June, 1915, he was relieved by Colonel 2nd Commandant E. E. Chown R.M.L.I. The drafts of the Naval Battalions and Divisional Units were furnished from Blandford until after the evacuation of Gallipoli. When the Royal Naval Division was transferred to France and the War Office became responsible for its training and administration, Reserve battalions were formed at Blandford in June and July, 1916.

The 1/Reserve Bn. R.M.L.I. was under Lieut.-Colonel J. B. Finlaison with Captain W. Rutherford as Adjutant, and Captain C. H. Smith as Quartermaster and experienced officers who had been promoted from the ranks were appointed to command the companies and to form the instructional staff. The Reserve Hawke Battalion was commanded by Colonel C. G. Brittan, R.M.L.I. The Reserve Drake by Lieut.-Colonel H. M. Graham, R.M.L.I. and the Reserve Hood by Colonel J. R. Oldfield, R.M.L.I. and the work done by these officers and their assistants was very valuable to the Division in the field.

In 1917 Brig.-General C. McN. Parsons, C.B., relieved Brig.-General Chown in command, as the latter had been appointed to Commandant at Deal, he had also been awarded the C.B. for his services in training the Reserves.

Early in 1918 the Army turned Blandford into the Record Office of the Royal Air Force, and the Royal Naval Division Reserves were transferred to the Wellington Lines at Aldershot, whilst the Command Depot for convalescents under Colonel Oldfield was sent to Tidworth.

By this time owing to the reduction of the Battalions in the Division the Reserve Battalions were now only two, the 1st Reserve, R.M.L.I. and the 2nd Reserve, R.N.V.R. with the depots of the Divisional units. Lieutenant-Colonels H. M. Graham and J. B. Finlaison, R.M.L.I. were awarded the C.M.G. for their services in charge of these training battalions. The training given to the Reserves at Blandford had always been very favourably reported on in France; they had the advantage of several Royal Marine officers and N.C.O.'s who had been trained in the old school and who instilled the principles of discipline and esprit de corps as well as training, and as they had in most cases already served overseas themselves, their teaching bore good fruit.

In May, 1918 Brig.-General G. J. H. Mullins, R.M.L.I. relieved General Parsons who had been appointed Commandant at Deal; the former had already had considerable experience of the training required, for on relinquishing the command of 1/R.M.L.I. he was appointed to command the 63rd Infantry Base Depot in France.

After the Armistice the Royal Naval Division Reserves were moved to Alnwick where demobilisation was carried out in accordance with Army Regulations.

APPENDICES.

APPENDIX 1.
CASUALTIES FROM 4TH AUGUST, 1914 TO 5th APRIL, 1919.

NOTE-It is hoped that this return which has been compiled from Official sources is as complete as possible.

(a) Total Ashore and Afloat.

UNITS	Officers					W.O.s, N.C.O.s & Men					Remarks
	Killed in Action	Died of Wounds	Accidentally killed	Died of Disease	Wounded	Killed in Action	Died of Wounds	Accidentally killed	Died of Disease	Wounded	
R.M Artillery	13	8	2	3	36	431	47	22	164	400	
R.M. Light Infantry											
Distributed as follows :-											
Chatham	41	8	2	1	71	1307	138	19	158	1294	
Portsmouth	35	13		5	78	1321	204	13	144	1736	
Plymouth	42	9		3	51	1007	192	28	157	1946	
Deal						1	2	1	43		
R.N. School of Music						74	2	47	22	2	
R.M. Submarine Miners			1						2		
R.M. Divisional Engineers	4	4		2		27	15	1	5	156	To Royal Engineers, March, 1917
RM. Divisional Train	1			1		6	5	3	12	28	
R.M. Medical Unit						57	39	2	16	555	Surgeons were R. N. Officers
RM. Labour Corps						22	3	14	95		
RM. Engineers								5	31		
Total	136	42	4	13	239	4253	547	155	849	6117	

(b) Casualties sustained Afloat included in (a)

R.M Artillery	4		1			385	7	11	40	6	
R.M. Light Infantry	21	1		4	2	1498	18	42	138	134	
Distributed as follows :-											
Chatham	8		1		1	566	2	12	46	59	
Portsmouth	7	1		3	1	579	11	5	31	23	
Plymouth	6			1		353	5	25	61	52	
R.N. School of Music						74	1		47	12	
Total	25	1	1	5	2	1957	26	100	190	140	

*Note-Officers include R.M. Gunners; other Warrant Officers included with other ranks.

APPENDIX 2.
SERVICES OF ROYAL MARINES WITH UNITS OTHER THAN ROYAL MARINES.

NOTES.

1. In preparing the following record of services, it was thought that they would illustrate what varied parts the training of a Royal Marine renders the individual capable of performing.

2. In this digest the services of officers and others are only included if the units have not been dealt with in previous parts of this volume. Every effort has been made to make them as complete as possible, R.M. Office records have been consulted and information obtained from individuals, but we offer our apologies to any who may have been inadvertently omitted.

3. The ranks given are those on the outbreak of war.

Captain G. F. ABRAHAM, R.M.L.I. Intelligence Officer, Newfoundland, 18/9/14 to 4/2/19. Brevet of Major.
Major and Brevet Lieut.-Colonel St. G. B. ARMSTRONG, R.M.L.I. G.S.O. 2, Milford Haven Defences to Feb.,1915. A.A. and Q.M.G. Lines of Communication Gallipoli 3/6/15 to 18/2/16. Ditto Cairo District and Delta, Egypt to 31/3/16. A.A.G.L. of C. Egyptian E.F. 23/10/16. A.A. & Q.M.G. Northern Canal Section 30/1/17. Ditto. 54th Division 2/5/17. D.A. And Q.M.G. (temp. Brig-Gen.) 21st Army Corps 2/8/17 to end of War. Mentioned in dispatches five times. Awarded C.B., C.M.G. and Brevet of Colonel. Order of Nile 3rd Class and Croix de Guerre (France).
Major F. ATHOW, R.M.L.I. (retired) O.C. W /T. Station, St. Kilda, 11/11/14 to 24/5/15.
Captain A. C. BARNBY, R.M.L.I. Attached R.N.A.S. Commanded Gibraltar Air Station 3/6/15 to 21/3/16. Eastern Mediterranean 16/3/17 to 16/12/17. In charge of Officers and Cadets training wings. Officer of Redeemer of Greece.
Captain G. BARKER, R.M.L.I. (retired) After commanding machine-guns of R.M. Brigade at Antwerp appointed Adjutant of Drake Battalion, killed in the attack of 29th April in Gallipoli.
Sergeant A. J. BANKS. Sergeant-Major of Hawke Battalion. Severely wounded and awarded D.C.M. For Battle of Beaumont Hamel.
Major and Brevet Lieut.-Colonel R. L. BAYLIFF, R.M.L.I. (retired) W /T Censor Malin Head 1/8/14 to 7/2/15.
Major G. L. BEAUMONT R.M.L.I. (retired). After service afloat at the Dardanelles, was appointed Chairman of Board of Control of Ports, etc. in Greece with rank of Brig.-General and later General Staff Officer, South America. Awarded C.B.E. Legion of Honour (France) and Order of Redeemer (Greece).
Major W. E. BINNEY, R.M.L.I. (retired) Assistant W /T Censor Cullercoats and Clifden 16/8/14 to 20/9/17. Valentia to 6/1/19.
Lieut.-Colonel H. E. BLUMBERG, R.M.L.I. From D.A.A.G., R.M. appointed A.A. and Q.M.G. of R.N. Division 2/1/14 to 31/12/14 from A.A. G., R.M. to A.A.G.L. of C. Salonika, 4/11/15 to 6/4/16.
Cr.-Sergeant G. BOULTON, Pensioner, R.M.A. Lent to Rifle Depot. Received commission in Middlesex Regt. Major and 2nd i/c Reserve Battalion.
Colonel C. G. BRITTAN, R.M.L.I. (Reserved List) Brig.-General i/c Administration 2nd to 15th October, 1914. Commanded a Reserve Battalion, R.N. Division, 1915 to 1918. Assistant to Director of Recruiting. Awarded C.B. (Civil).
Captain A. G. BOURNE, R.M.A. After service afloat became G.S.O. 2, 11th Division in France 24/9/17. G.S.0.2 3rd Army H.Q. 24/3/18. G.S.O. 1, 8th Division 14/6/18. G.S.O. 2, X. Corps Rhine Army, 25/3/19. G.S.O. 1, 34th Div. Rhine Army, 4/8/19. Awarded D.S.O. and Chevalier of St. Maurice and St. Lazarus and Italian Silver Medal for valour. Mentioned in Dispatches twice.
Major JOHN BROUGH, R.M.A. Staff Officer to Inspector of West African Forces, Cameroons Campaign. Awarded C.M.G. Lent for command of a Machine-gun Battalion and transferred to Royal Artillery 25/7/16. Brevet of Lieut.-Colonel and mentioned in Dispatches.
Major N. O. BURGE, R.M.L.I. From Cyclist Co., R.M. appointed to command Nelson Battalion, July, 1915. In charge of the Rendezvous at evacuation. Killed at head of his Battalion at Beaumont Hamel 13/11/16. Awarded Brevet of Lieut.-Colonel and mentioned in Dispatches.
Major R. M. BYNE, R.M.L.I. (retired). W /T Censor Cullercoats and Clifden, 13/8/14 to 23/7/1919.
Lieutenant R. M. BRADSHAW, R.M.L.I. (retired). Subaltern in 4th (Uganda) Bn. King's African Rifles in East African campaign.
Lieutenant R. J. CARPENTER, R.M.L.I. Adjutant Nelson Battalion until invalided from Gallipoli. Adjutant Reserve Battalion, Blandford. Awarded Legion of Honour (France).
Lieutenant C. H. COLLET, R.M.A., attached R.N.A.S. Awarded the D.S.O. for dropping bombs successfully on Zeppelin sheds at Dusseldorf 22/9/14. Served in Dardanelles and killed at Imbros owing to aeroplane crashing.
Colonel G. D. DRAKE, R.M.A. (retired). One of the Directors of the Press Bureau in England.
Major-General J. F. DANIELL, R.M.L.I. In command of troops Sierra Leone, providing troops for Togoland and Cameroons. Awarded C.M.G. Intelligence Staff Admiralty 17/1/18 to 30/1/19. Awarded K.C.M.G.

Lieutenant J. H. D'ALBIAC, R.M.A. Served as observer with R.N.A.S. at Dunkirk awarded D.S.O. for reconnaissance and fighting patrols.

Major G. DRAGE, R.M.L.I. (retired). In command of 1/Herefordshire (Territorial Battalion) Suvla Bay landing, wounded, resumed command September 1915. Proceeded to Egypt after evacuation of Gallipoli. Served in Western Desert and on canal. Commanded 158th Brigade at Battle of Romani. First and Second Battles of Gaza. Advance on Beer Sheba, Battle of Kubrilfeh. Counter attack on Jerusalem 27/12/16 and subsequent advance. Awarded D.S.O. Mentioned in Dispatches three times.

Captain L. A. DRAKE-BROCKMAN, R.M.L.I. From Command of Company in R.M. Field Force appointed to command Russian Karelian Battalion, (see Chapter 13).

Captain T. W. DYER, R.M.A. (retired). Served with West African Field Force. September and October, 1914. then joined R.M.A.

Lieut.-Colonel W. B. DAUNTESEY, C.B., R.M.A., (retired). Commanded 9/Cheshire Regt., 1914-1916, 13/ and 14/ K.O.Y.L.I. 1916-1918. Director of Vocational Training, Eastern Command. Awarded C.B.E.

Lieut.-Colonel E. G. EVELEGH, R.M.L.I. from Deal Battalion at Antwerp appointed to command Nelson Battalion; after service at Anzac was killed whilst gallantly leading the attack of his Battalion on 13th July, 1915, mentioned in Dispatches twice.

Captain A. K. EVANS, R.M.L.I. From Adjutant 1/R.M.L.I. appointed G.S.O. 3. R.N. Division, August, 1916. Brigade Major 57th Infantry Brigade February, 1917; G.S.0.2, VI. Corps May, 1917 to August. 1919. Military Cross, O.B.E. Mentioned in Dispatches twice.

Major-General T. J. P. EVANS, C.B., R.M.L.I. (retired). Cable Censor, War Office, 1914-1916. Twice mentioned for valuable services.

Captain J. C. FARMER, R.M.L.I. Liaison Officer in Russian ship *Askold* in China and East Mediterranean. Landed for service with Royal Marine Brigade in Gallipoli 25/5/15. Mentioned in Dispatches. Admiralty Intelligence Staff 1916-1919.

Lieut.-Colonel H. D. FARQUHARSON, R.M.L.I. After service as Staff Officer with R.M. Brigade at Antwerp, appointed to Operations Division of Admiralty; Liaison Officer on staff of French Commander-in-Chief at landing at Dardanelles till June, 1915. Attached Directorate Staff Duties War Office, 1915-1916. G.S.O. 2, 67th Division Home Army, 1917. G.S.O. 1, Western Command 1918-1919. Awarded C.M.G. Croix de Guerre (France).

Captain H. FAWCETT, R.M.L.I. Attached R.N.A.S. Coast Patrol till July 1915 - Dardanelles and France till 23/8/17. Returned to Corps duty-Intelligence Staff, North Russia. Accidentally killed 29/12/18. Mentioned in Dispatches.

Captain M. C. FESTING, R.M.L.I. After service as Brigade Major, R.M. Brigade till June, 1915 when invalided. Appointed Acting D.A.A.G., R.M. till May, 1916 - Brigade Major 188th Brigade France, 1916. G.S.O. 2, 23rd Canadian Division. G.S.O. 1, Canadian Corps till end of war. Mentioned in Dispatches four times.

Brevet Major D.S.O., Croix de Guerre (France).

Colonel C. FIELD, R.M.L.I. (retired). Recruiting S.O. Liverpool and in charge of dazzle painting of ships in that area.

Major C. T. FISHER, R.M.A. Army Ordnance Officer 1st Class, Mesopotamia. Transferred to A.O. Department.

Captain R F. C. FOSTER, R.M.A., D.A.A. and Q.M.G. on Administrative Staff, R.N. Division later A.A. And Q.M.G., 1914-1916, A.A. and Q.M.G., R.N.D. in France, May, 1916-1918. A.Q.M.G. of Corps and later of Army of Rhine. Mentioned in dispatches four times. Brevet of Lieut.-Colonel, C.M.G., D.S.O., Order of Leopold and War Cross (Belgium).

Major A P. LISTON FOULIS, R.M.A. transferred from R.M.A. Howitzer Brigade to command a Brigade of Heavy Artillery. Killed at Gouzeaucourt 3011/17. Mentioned in Dispatches.

Major A. H. FRENCH, R.M.L.I. From Portsmouth Battalion appointed to command Cyclist Company, R.N. Division till disbanded in June, 1916. Appointed Assistant Director of Signals. Chief Officer Signal Corps. Transferred to R. Corps of Signals. Mentioned in Dispatches twice. Awarded D.S.O., Officer of Crown of Italy.

Major F. J. FRENCH, R.M.A. Operations Staff Admiralty 11/8/16 to 5/8/18. On Staff of Caspian Naval Expedition.

Major W. W, GODFREY, R.M.L.I. Naval Staff Officer in H.M.S. Defence, Mediterranean. Transferred to Staff of Commander-in-Chief at Dardanelles. Awarded C.M.G. and Brevet of Lieutenant-Colonel. Chief Staff Officer to Admiral of Patrols, Malta for Convoy and Anti-Submarine Work, 1916-1917. Staff of Vice-Admiral Dover Patrol, 1918. Mentioned in Dispatches twice.

Major E. L. GERRARD, R.M.L.I., attached R.N.A.S. Employed in air operations at Antwerp, Germany and Dunkirk; in Dardanelles. Awarded D.S.O. In command of Eastbourne Air Station, 30/6/16 to end of War. Commanded squadron of aeroplanes that made first invasion of Germany by air, 22/9/14. Mentioned in Dispatches. Awarded C.M.G. Transferred to R.A.F.

Major R. GORDON, R.M.L.I. In command of Air Operations against *Koenigsberg*, East Africa, awarded D.S.O. Present at engagements of Kut and Ctesiphon, Mesopotamia and in command of R.N.A.S. at attempts to relieve Kut, 1916. Eastern Mediterranean 1917 to 1919. In command of operations bombing Constantinople, 1918. In charge of Somali Air Operations, 1920. Mentioned in Dispatches four times. Awarded C.B., C.M.G., D.S.O. Transferred to R.A.F.

Major-General C. L. GORDON, R.M.L.I. After relinquishing Command of Plymouth Division appointed an Inspector of Steel, Ministry of Munitions.

Lieut.-Colonel H. M. GRAHAM, R.M.L.I. Commanded Reserve Battalion at Blandford, training reinforcements. Awarded C.M.G.

Sergeant D. C. GREENING, R.M.L.I. appointed Sergeant-Major, Collingwood Battalion in Gallipoli.

Major L. S. T. HALLIDAY, V.C., C.B., R.M.L.I., G.S.O. 2, Malta, then G.S.O. I, Southern Army Home Defence, 1914

-15. G.S.O. 1, 39th Division in France till invalided in July, 1916. G.S.O. 1, Canadian Training Division till 1917. On reorganisation of Admiralty War Staff appointed Assistant Director of Plans and after Armistice on Staff of British Delegation at Paris Peace Conference.

Lieutenant-Colonel M. P. HANKEY, Secretary of Imperial Committee of Defence and compiled the War Book. Later became Secretary of the War Cabinet. Awarded the G.C.B., Grand Cross of Crown of Italy, Grand Cordon of the Crown of Belgium, Officer of the Legion of Honour. Received grant of £25,000 from Parliament.

Captain R. W. HUTTON, R.M.A. Attached Egyptian Army. Operations against Senussi in Armoured Train. In Darfur 1916. In operations in Nuba Mountains Province, Soudan. Killed in a reconnaissance on the Nile, 3/4/17.

Captain W.L. HUNTINGFORD, R.M.A. Liaison Officer on Staff of French Naval C.-in-C. Mediterranean throughout the War. Important part in all operations in Greece, Adriatic and Corfu. Awarded Brevet Majority and C.B.E., Legion of Honour and Croix de Guerre (France), Officer of Order of Redeemer (Greece).

Major G. R. S. HICKSON, R.M.L.I. After service afloat became Naval General Staff Officer at Gibraltar. Awarded C.B.E. and Officer of Crown of Italy.

Captain C. F. JERRAM, R.M.L.I. Staff Captain R.M. Brigade, 16/12/14. Brigade Major ditto, 18/6/15. D.A.A. and Q.M.G., R.N. Div., 27/12/15. Brigade Major, 190th Brigade 29/7/16, G.S.O. 2, 31st Division 24/1/17, G.S.O.2, XIII. Army Corps, 2/7/17. G.S.O. 1, 46th Division, 23/7/18. In the latter capacity made the arrangements for crossing the Canal de St. Quentin at Bellenglise, the men swimming across the Canal with the aid of the lifebelts of the Cross Channel Steamers. Mentioned in Dispatches five times, awarded C.M.G. and D.S.O., Croix de Guerre (France).

Sergeant K. KELMSLEY, R.M.A. Sergeant. Major 7/Wiltshire Regiment at Salonica. Mentioned in Dispatches.

Major L. C. LAMPEN, R.M.L.I. Naval General Staff Officer at Malta. In charge of the large intelligence organisation of the Allies in that theatre. Awarded Brevet of Lieutenant Colonel, Chevalier of Legion of Honour (France). Commander of Crown of Italy.

Major T. H. HAWKINS, R.M.L.I. Employed on Admiralty War Staff, Trade Division, August, 1914 to 29/10/19. Secretary to Commission for Diversion of Shipping. Member of Port and Transit Executive Committee Largely responsible for raising the various Transport Worker Battalions. Awarded C.M.G. and promoted to Lieutenant Colonel.

Major T. O. H. LEES, R.M.L.I. Served with Imperial Trans - Arctic Expedition, 1914-1916. Lent to Flying Corps 1917 and transferred to R.A.F. Awarded O.B.E. and Air Force Cross.

Lieutenant G. H. LITTLETON, Quartermaster, R.M.A. with Brigades in France. Appointed to Ministry of National Service and after the Armistice Liaison Officer for Naval demobilisation at Ministry of Labour. With Demolition party at Heligoland, destroying the forts. Specially promoted for good service.

Captain C. F. KILNER, R.M.L.I. Attached R.N.A.S. Operations in North Sea, Antwerp and raids on German Coast. Awarded D.S.O. For air raid on Cuxhaven 25/12/14. Dardanelles and Salonica operations 2/2/15 to 5/1/17. Awarded Bar to D.S.O. Mentioned in Dispatches twice. Transferred to R.A.F.

Captain R. D. LOUGH, R.M.L.I. From Adjutant Plymouth Battalion appointed Staff-Captain, R.M .Brigade 18/6/15. Awarded D.S.O. then D.A.A. and Q.M.G., R.N. Division 17/5/16. D.A.A.G. Staff School, Cambridge 16/10/18. D.A.A.G. VI. Corps 12/2/19 to 23/2/20. O.B.E. and Croix de Guerre (France).

Lieutenant E. LOCK, R.M.L.I. Pensioner Sergeant R.M.L.I. Sergeant-Major, Benbow Battalion. Wounded in Gallipoli; Appointed Lieutenant, R.N.V.R. and Adjutant of a Reserve Battalion.

Major F. B. A. LAWRIE, R.M.L.I. From Deal Battalion appointed A.M.L.O. at Suvla; accompanied 10th Division to Salonica, appointed to command 6/Royal Irish Fusiliers and commanded them through brief campaign in Serbia. After a period of service afloat and then service with Royal Marine Battalions in France, appointed to the Command of a Russian Battalion in North Russia till evacuation.

Major S. G. LESLIE, R.M.A. attached A. Ordnance Dept., Suvla and Gallipoli. Awarded D.S.C. D.A.D.O.S. in Mesopotamia. Transferred to Army Ordnance Department.

Captain L. J. INNES, R.M.L.I. (retired). Served with East African Rifles, wounded September, 1914, and invalided home. Appointed to 6/Royal Fusiliers.

Major W. T. C. JONES, R.M.L.I. Admiralty War Staff, 1914-1915, 1916-1919. Assistant Director of Intelligence. Beach Master "X" Beach at Gallipoli. Awarded C.B. and Brevet of Lieutenant-Colonel.

Colonel A. E. MARCHANT, C.B. took over Command of R.M. Brigade at Antwerp. Invalided. After serving as Commandant of Chatham Division, became an Inspector of Steel under Ministry of Munitions.

Lieut.-Colonel G. E. MATTHEWS, C.B., R.M.L.I. After Commanding Plymouth Battalion until invalided in August, 1915, he was appointed to command the 198th Infantry Brigade and proceeded to France February, 1917. He was mortally wounded when visiting the trenches 12th April, 1917 and died the next day. His funeral was attended by the Band of the Chatham Division, R.M.L.I. of which he had been adjutant 1891 to 1896. A very great loss to the Corps where his gallantry was proverbial. Awarded C.M.G. for Gallipoli.

Colonel D. MERCER, R.M.L.I. From A.A.G. R. Marines was appointed to command 1st R Naval Brigade with rank of Brigadier-General Ist January, 1915. He commanded the Brigade throughout the Gallipoli campaign and was awarded the C.B. Appointed Adjutant General Royal Marines, 23rd June, 1916 and died on 1st July, 1920 from the effects of service in Gallipoli. Mentioned in Dispatches twice. Awarded K.C.B. 1918, Croix de Guerre and Commander of Legion of Honour. (France).

Lieut.-Colonel B. A. MILNE, R.M.A. (retired) commanded a platoon in the Volunteers from 1915 to December,1917.

Major H. F. MONTGOMERY, R.M.L.I. Admiralty War Staff till 1915. Brigade Major 90th Infantry Brigade, 21/6/15 to 10/5/16. G.S.O. 2, 34th Division and XIII. Corps 11/5/16 to 26/10/17. G.S.O .1, 19th Division 27/10/17 to 25/5/19. Mentioned in Dispatches six times, awarded C.M.G., D.S.O. And Brevet of Lieutenant-Colonel. G.S.O. 2, IV. Corps

Army of the Rhine 26/3/19 to 6/5/19. G.S.O. 1 London Division to 31/10/19. Appointed to the Staff in Dublin and was murdered by assassins on 21/11/20. Legion of Honour (France).

Captain C. B. MULLINS, R.M.L.I. Naval General Staff Officer, Singapore to 31/3/16. Assisted to quell Mutiny there. Invalided. Admiralty Intelligence Department 1/7/16 to 30/1/19.

Colour Sergeant J. MURPHY, R.M.L.I. Pensioner. Appointed to Chinese Labour Corps as a Lieutenant and later commanded Prisoners of War Camp.

Sergeant J. NEALON, R.M.L.I. Pensioner, Appointed Captain 8/Middlesex Regiment. Draft Conducting Officer; Adjutant of a Training Battalion.

Cr.-Sergeant E. NOBBS, R.M.L.I. Pensioner. Appointed Quartermaster of Hood Battalion serving in Antwerp, Gallipoli and France. Twice wounded and mentioned in Dispatches. Transferred to combatant commission as Lieutenant, R.N.V.R.

Captain R. A. NEVILLE, R.M.L.I. From Captain 1/RM.L.I. appointed G.S.O; 3, RN. Division 27/3/18 to 20/6/19. G.S.O. 3. Army of the Rhine 21/6/19 to 10/6/21. Mentioned in Dispatches.

Major F. C. ORMSBY-JOHNSON, R.M.L.I. (retired). Brigade-Major 1914. Draft Conducting Officer 1915-1919.

Major-General G. T. ONSLOW, C.B., R.M.L.I. Employed on Defences of London 1915-1917.

Colonel J. R. OLDFIELD, R.M.L.I. (Reserve List). Commanded Benbow Battalion. Wounded in Gallipoli on 4th June. Commanded a Reserve Battalion at Blandford till reduction. Then the Command Depot. Mentioned for valuable services in connection with the War. Awarded C.B. (civil).

Lieut.-Colonel C. A. F. OSMASTON, R.M.A. from Command of Anti-Aircraft Brigade appointed Member of the Ordnance Committee, February, 1916, then Member of the Munitions Invention Department, June, 1917. Awarded C.B. and C.B.E., Officer of the Crown of Belgium.

Major H. D. PALMER, R.M.L.I. (retired). After being wounded with Plymouth Battalion in Gallipoli, appointed W /T Censor at the War Office, 20/3/16 to 12/4/17.

Colonel A. PARIS, R.M.A. From Inspector of Marine Recruiting appointed to command of R.M. Brigade and then of R.N. Division in Antwerp with temporary rank of Major-General. Trained Division and Commanded it in Gallipoli. Awarded K.C.B. and promoted to Major General for distinguished service in the Field. Commanded the Division in France until severely wounded on 13/10/16 when. visiting the trenches, his left leg being amputated. Mentioned in Dispatches five times. Commander of Legion of Honour and Croix de guerre (France). Commander of Order of Leopold and Croix de guerre (Belgium).

Captain E. H. PARDOE, R.M.L.I. (retired). Appointed to King's African Rifles and served in East Africa in command of Battalion 3/8/17 to 6/11/17. Mentioned in Dispatches twice and awarded O.B.E.

Colonel C. Mc N. PARSONS, R.M.L.I. from Command of Chatham, R.M.L.I. appointed to command 181st Inf. Brigade which he took to France 5/3/16 to 13/10/16. Commanded R.N. Division Reserves, Blandford, 1917 to 1918 when appointed Commandant at Deal.

Major-General L. T. PEASE, R.M.A. Proceeded to America and Canada to organise the supply of munitions and rendered most valuable service. Later proceeded to Japan for similar duties under the Ministry of Munitions.

Major W. S. POE, R.M.A. From Admiralty Inspector of Steel appointed to the Tank Corps with which he served in France being very severely wounded when gallantly leading an attack at the Battle of the Somme. Awarded the D.S.O.

Sergeant T. PILCHER, R.M.L.I. When serving in a cruiser on East African Station proceeded with a Naval party to Lake Tanganyika where he was given a commission as Lieutenant, RM.L.I. for service with natives Levies on the Lake.

Captain A. PEEL, R.M.L.I. Naval General Staff Officer at Jamaica, where he rendered very valuable service, awarded C.M.G. Promoted Brevet Major for service 25/10/16 Appointed Assistant Director of Intelligence at the Admiralty. Awarded Brevet of Lieutenant Colonel. Legion of Honour (France).

Captain E. F. POWYS-SKETCHLEY, R.M.L.I. From Adjutant of Portsmouth Battalion appointed Brigade-Major, R.M. Brigade at Ostend. G.S.O.2, on formation of R.N. Division at Antwerp and continued throughout Gallipoli campaign and in France until killed by a shell on 13th October, 1916. Awarded D.S.O. Mentioned in Dispatches.

Major F. J. SAUNDERS, R.M.L.I. From 1/R.M.L.I., appointed Brigade-Major, RM. Brigade; on arrival in France appointed to command Anson Battalion and killed in action 13th November, 1916, when gallantly leading his Battalion at Beaumont Hamel.

Major W. G. SIMPSON, R.M.L.I. (retired). Lieutenant-Colonel Commanding 1/24th London Regt. which he commanded in France, awarded D.S.O. When medically unfit for front line appointed Commandant of an Army School till 3/3/18. Awarded C.M.G., and Brevet of Colonel. Mentioned in Dispatches four times.

Major-General J. H. SWANTON, R.M.L.I. (retired). Instructor to young Officers at Plymouth until 1917. Appointed a Staff Lieutenant in France and served as Town Major 14/9/17 to 1/7/19.

Sergeant P. E. SMITH, R.M.L.I. After destruction of H.M.S. Pegasus appointed to Zanzibar Rifles and served in East Africa. Awarded D.S.M. for capture of Bagamoyo.

Captain C. E. H. RATHBONE, R.M.L.I. attached R.N.A.S. In charge of seaplanes from Dunkirk until he joined the Independent Air Force in France. Promoted to Wing Commander 31/12/16. Captured when flying over Germany near Lake Constance in April, 1917. Escaped 23/7/18., Awarded D.S.O. and Bar to D.S.O. 16/12/19.

Captain C. E. RISK, R.M.L.I. attached R.N.A.S. In command of Felixstowe Air Station. Employed with Armoured Car Patrols at Dunkirk 14/9/14 to 28/2/15. Employed in Egypt and landed with Motor Maxim Squadron at Anzac, wounded 30/4/15. Armoured Cars in France in 1915. Command of Dover Air Station 1915, to March, 1916. Isle of Grain Station, etc. Awarded D.S.O. and Order of the Nile. Mentioned in Dispatches.

Lieutenant C. E. ROBINSON, RM.L.I. attached R.N.A.S. Employed in Dardanelles Operations. Shot down and seriously wounded November, 1915. Taken prisoner, and died of wounds in hands of the Turks.

Captain N. F. E. G. SAMPSON-WAY, R.M.L.I. (retired). Assistant W/T Censor, Clifden, 1/8/14 to 1917. Poldhu and Rame Head 1917 to 29/6/19.

Captain E. J. B. TAGG, R.M.L.I. From Adjutant Deal Battalion and 1/R.M.L.I. Appointed Staff-Captain H.Q. units R.N.D. 17/5/16 and then Staff-Captain 190th Brigade. D.A.Q.M.G. XIX. Corps 13/2/17. Transferred to Durham Light Infantry 9/1/19. Awarded D.S.O. Croix de Guerre (France). Mentioned in Dispatches four times. Wounded 30/6/15.

Major R C. TEMPLE, R.M.A. After H.M.S. Ocean was sunk appointed Military Governor of Tenedos, March to May, 1915. Appointed Staff Officer in charge of Intelligence Eastern Mediterranean 4/8/15 to 13/1/19. In charge of arrangements for arranging surrender of Forts and mines at Dardanelles, 1918. Afterwards in similar capacity in Black Sea until invalided. Brevet of Lieutenant-Colonel and O.B.E.. Legion of Honour (France).

Major F. V. TEMPLE, R.M.L.I. Naval Intelligence Division at Admiralty till May, 1918. Then appointed Director of Intelligence Mediterranean, May, 1918 to October, 1919, with temporary rank of Brigadier-General. Awarded Brevet of Lieutenant-Colonel and C.M.G.

Captain A. S. TETLEY, R.M.L.I. From 2/RM.L.I. was appointed to command the Drake Battalion, May, 1916, with temporary rank of Lieutenant-Colonel. Was seriously wounded whilst gallantly leading this Battalion at the Battle of Beaumont Hamel and died of wounds 13/11/16.

Major C. J. THOROTON, R.M.L.I. Naval Intelligence Officer at Gibraltar, 1914 to 1919. Promoted Brevet Lieutenant-Colonel, C.M.G. Officer of Legion of Honour (France), Commander of Crown of Italy, Commander of Order of Ouissam Alaouite (Morocco).

Cr.-Sergeant E. G. TIMS, R.M.A. (retired). Served as Quartermaster of 6/Hants Regiment in India. Awarded M.B.E.

Captain E. F. TREW, R.M.L.I. From Adjutant 2/R.M.L.I., appointed Brigade-Major 125th Infantry Brigade, 11/9/15. D.A.A. and Q.M.G. 54th Division 20/9/15 and in similar capacity to NO.3 Section of Suez Canal Defences 5/10/16. D.A. and Q.M.G..with rank of Brigadier-General of Desert Corps in Palestine Campaign, 2/8/17 to 23/5/19. Mentioned in Dispatches four times. Brevet of Lieutenant-Colonel. C.M.G., and D.S.O.

Captain W. H. L. TRIPP, R.M.A. From the South African Heavy Artillery (Chapter 34) appointed to command a Brigade of Heavy Artillery in France. Mentioned in Dispatches four times. Awarded D.S.O. and M.C.

Major N. F. TROTMAN, R.M.A. On inspection Staff at Woolwich Arsenal 1/4/14 to 31/7/19. Brevet of Lieutenant-Colonel.

Colonel C. N. TROTMAN, R.M.L.I. From Command of R.M. Brigade and 2nd R.N. Brigade, appointed to command 190th Infantry Brigade, July, 1916 until recalled to England to command Portsmouth Division, R.M.L.I. in November, 1916. Mentioned in Dispatches twice, C.B., Croix de Guerre and Legion of Honour (France).

Colonel J. A. TUPMAN, R.M.L.I. Relinquished Paymaster at Deal to join Deal Bn. R.M.L.I. Appointed Brigade Major 1st R.N. Brigade 30/5/15 and served with them until I8/4/16. Appointed to command 2/4 Gloucester Regiment in France until invalided and then commanded Reserve and Training Battalions of King's Regiment, Lincolns, and Durham L.I.; the 51st Bn. of latter he took to join the Army of the Rhine until 14/4/19. Mentioned in Dispatches twice. Brevet of Lieutenant-Colonel, and O.B.E.

Major and Bt. Lieut.-Colonel A. G. B. URMSTON, R.M.L.I. (retired). Appointed to command 15/Royal Scots which he trained and took to France. After the Battle of the Somme, July, 1916 the Battalions of the Brigade were re-organised. and he returned home having attained the age of 56. Awarded the D.S.O. Appointed to command 13/Highland L.I. and on this unit being demobilised in February,1918 was attached to the Staff of XI. Corps serving with it in Italy and France. In April, 1915 appointed to command "E" Machine Gun Corps Training Battalion until demobilised. Mentioned in Dispatches.

Lieut.-Colonel A. G. VINCENT, R.M.L.I. (retired) commanded 40th Bn. Canadian Expeditionary Force, 18/5/15 to 2/1/17 and 26th Canadian Reserve Battalion to May, 1917. Appointed to command troops at Southwick November, 1915. Awarded C.B.E. Mentioned for valuable services in war.

Sergeant P. L. WEBB. R.M.L.I. became Quartermaster 18/London Regiment. After Battle of Loos appointed to a combatant commission, rose to the rank of Major and commanded a Battalion for some weeks. Appointed Act. Staff Captain 141St Brigade. Mentioned in Dispatches. Awarded M.C.

Colonel F. WHITE, D.S.O., R.M.L.I. (retired) served as Draft Conducting Officer 19/5/15 to 20/3/19.

Sergeant J. J. WILKINSON, R.M.L.I. (Pensioner) appointed Sergeant-Major, Depot, West York Regiment and received a commission in that regiment and served with them in the Mediterranean.

Captain F. S. WILSON, R.M.L.I. From Adjutant, Depot, Royal Marines, was appointed second in Command of Drake Battalion and served with them at Antwerp. Appointed Brigade Major 1st RN. Brigade and served with that unit in Egypt, Anzac and Cape Helles. He was killed in the trenches on 24th May, 1915.

Major L. O. WILSON, D.S.O., R.M.L.I. (retired) M.P. for Reading. From Berkshire Royal Horse Artillery appointed to command Hawke Battalion which he raised and trained and commanded in Gallipoli from 2/6/15 to evacuation. Awarded C.M.G. In temporary command 1st RN. Brigade February to May, 1916. Commanded the Battalion in France until seriously wounded at Beaumont Hamel. Mentioned in Dispatches; Brevet of Lieut.-Colonel. Served at R.M.O. in 1917 and was then appointed to Secretariat of the War Cabinet. Now Governor of Bombay.

Captain J. D. Wyley, R.M.A. (retired). Assistant W /T Censor, Clifden and Malin Head. Awarded O.B.E.

APPENDIX 3.
DECORATIONS-BRITISH AND FOREIGN.

NOTE.-List of D.S.M. and Military Medal have been given at end of cognate Chapters.

1-BRITISH DECORATIONS.

VICTORIA CROSS.

Lance-Corporal W. R. Parker, R.M.L.I.
Major F. J. W. Harvey, R.M.L.I.
Major F. W. Lumsden, D.S.O., R.M.A.
Captain E. Bamford, D.S.O., R M.L.I.
Sergeant N. A. Finch, R.M.A.

ORDER OF THE BATH.

Knight Grand Cross. (Civil Division)-Lieutenant-Colonel Sir M. P. A. Hankey, R.M.A.

Knight Commander -

Major-General Sir Archibald Paris, R.M.A.
Major-General Sir David Mercer, R.M.L.I.

Companions (Military Division).-

Brigadier-General C. N. Trotman, R.M.L.I.
Brigadier-General D. Mercer, R.M.L.I.
Lieutenant-Colonel C. McN. Parsons, R.M.L.I.
Lieutenant-Colonel C. A. F. Osmaston, R.M.A.
Lieutenant-Colonel C. E. Collard, R.M.L.I.
Lieutenant-Colonel L. Conway-Gordon, R.M.A.
Brigadier-General E. E. Chown, R.M.L.I.
Lieut.-Col. A. R H. Hutchison, C.M.G., D.S.O., R.M.L.I.
Brig.-General F. W. Lumsden, V.C., D.S.O., R.M.A.
Major B. G. Weller, D.S.C., R.M.L.I.
Lieut.-Colonel G. J. H. Mullins, R.M.L.I.
Colonel St. G. B. Armstrong, C.M.G., R.M.L.I.
Lieutenant-Colonel W. T. C. Jones, D.S.O., R.M.L.I.

Companions (Civil Division)-

Lieutenant-Colonel H. E. Blumberg, R.M.L.I.
Brigadier-General H. S. N. White, R.M.L.I.
Brigadier-General C. E. Curtoys, R.M.L.I.
Brigadier-General C. G. Brittan, R.M.L.I.
Colonel A. G. Tatham, R.M.A.
Colonel J. R. H. Oldfield, R.M.L.I.
Colonel C. H. Willis, R.M.L.I.
Lieutenant-Colonel C. L. Brooke, R.M.A.
Brigadier-General G. M. Campbell, R.M.A.
Major B. C. Gardiner, R.M.L.I.
Major R. H. Willis, R.M.L.I.

ORDER OF ST. MICHAEL AND ST. GEORGE.

*Knight Commander-*Major-General Sir J. F. Daniell, R.M.L.I.

Companions-

Colonel G. E. Matthews, C.B., R.M.L.I.
Major J. Brough, R.M.A.
Major W. W. Godfrey, R.M.L.I.
Major A. E. Bewes, R.M.L.I.
Lieut.-Colonel E. J. Stroud, R.M.L.I.
Bt.-Lieut.-Colonel C. J. Thoroton, R.M.L.I.
Lieut.-Colonel F. D. Bridges, R.M.L.I.
Major H. C. Benett, R.M.L.I.
Lieut.-Colonel A. R. H. Hutchison, R.M.L.I.
Lieut.-Colonel L. O. Wilson, D.S.O., M.P., R.M.L.I.
T/Colonel F. H. Sykes, R.M. (attd. R.N.A.S.).
Lieut.-Colonel G. R. Poole, R.M.A.
Lieut.-Colonel T. H. Hawkins, R.M.L.I.
Lieut.-Colonel E. L. Gerrard, R.M.L.I. (attd. R.N.A.S.)
Lieut.-Colonel R. Gordon, R.M.L.I. (attd. R.N.A.S.).
Lieut.-Colonel W. Dixon, R.M.A

Colonel H. M. C. W. Graham, R.M.L.I.
Brigadier-General E. F. Trew, D.S.O., R.M.L.I.
Major R. J. Saumarez, R.M.L.I.
Major A. G. Little, R.M.L.I.
Lieutenant-Colonel Pryce Peacock, R.M.A.
Brigadier-General St. G. B. Armstrong, R.M.L.I.
Colonel P Phillips, RMA

Major F. V. Temple, R.M.L.I.
Colonel H. D. Farquharson, R.M.L.I.
Lieut.-Colonel J. B. Finlaison, R.M.L.I.
Major H. F. Montgomery, D.S.O., R.M.L.I.
Major J. A. M. A. Clark, R.M.L.I.
Major C. F. Jerram, D.S.O., R.M.L.I.
Major A. Peel, R.M.L.I.

ORDER OF THE BRITISH EMPIRE.

Knight Commander - T/Brig.-General Sir Alexander Gibb, R.M.E.

Commanders -

Colonel G. N. A. Harris, R.M.A.
Major G. E. Barnes, R.M.A.
Colonel D. L. Barrett, R.M.L.I.
Colonel W. P. Drury, R.M.L.I.
T/Lieut.-Colonel Hon. C. James, R.M.

Lieut.-Colonel C. A. F. Osmaston, C.B., R.M.A.
Major G. R S. Hickson, R.M.L.I.
Lieut.-Col. J. R H. Homfray,
Major H. D. E. O'Sullivan, R.M.L.I.
Lt.-Col. W. B. Dauntesey, C.B., R.M.A.

Lieut.-Colonel R V. T. Ford, R.M.A.
Major W. L. Huntingford, R.M.A.
Major S. C. Wace, R.M.A.
Hon. Lieut.-Col. H. M. Airey, R.M.
Major A. G..Vincent, R.M.L.I.

Officers -

Major R M. Byne, R.M.L.I.
Lieut.-Colonel J. F. Dimmer, R.M.L.I.
T/Captain R. H. Fowler, R.M.A.
T/Lieut.-Colonel J. F. Cable, R.M.L.C.
Captain G. F. Haszard, D.S.C., R.M.A.
Major H. L. Jones, R.M.L.I.
Lieut.-Colonel J. Simpson, R.M.L.I.
Major C. W. Slaney, R.M.L.I.
T/Major F. H. Smith (Div. Train)
Major W. G. Sparrow, R.M.A.
Major W. Symes, R.M.L.I.
Major A. K. Evans, M.C., RM.L.I.
Major R. D. H. Lough, D.S.O., R.M.L.I.
Major F. W. Eady, R.M.L.I.
Major D. A. Hailes, R.M.L.I.
T/Captain C. G. Murray (Div. Train).
Captain A. E. Syson, R.M.L.I.
Major R G. Wharton, R.M.L.I.
Major R O. Paterson, R.M.A.
T/Captain P. W. Allard (Div. Train).
T/Major W. E. Cook (Div. Train).
T/Lieut. A. L. Dugon (Div. Train).

T/Captain F. T. Blumberg, R.M.S.M.
T/Captain J. H. Morgan, R.M.S.M.
T/Major A. Dingli, R.M.A.
Captain H. A. C. Webber, R.M.L.I.
Captain A. M. Craig, R.M.L.I.
T/Captain A. S. Innes, R.M.S.M.
T/Major P. A. Smith, R.M.S.M.
Major J. D. N. Wyley, R.M.A.
Major A. F. Simson, R.M.A.
Hon. Lieut.-Col. J. Causton, R.M.E.
Captain E. Jukes - Hughes, R.M.L.I.
Captain C. A. C. Lucas, R.M.L.I.
Major P. W. Ma1colm, R.M.L.I.
Major G. C. Woodcock, R.M.A.
Lieut.-Col. J. A. Tupman, R.M.L.I.
2nd-Lieut. E. B. Harries, R.M.L.I.
Captain C. T. Brown, R.M.A.
Hon. Major W. C. T. Hammond, R.M.
Major G. L. Beaumont, R.M.L.I.
Brevet-Lieut.-Col. R Cator, R.M,.L.I.
Brevet-Colonel C. Clarke, R.M.L.I.
Major C. Franklin.

Major C. F. O. Graham, R.M.L.I.
Lieut.-Colonel J. L. Homer, R.M.A.
Brevet-Major T. L. Hunton, R.M.L.I.
Lieut.-Col. J. H. Lambert, R.M.L.I.
T/Capt. E. M. Compton-Mackenzie, R.M.
Colonel H. Slessor, R.M.A.
Major J. W. Snepp, R.M.L.I.
T/Major W. K. McKay, R.M.L.C.
Major T. O. H. Lees, R.M.L.I. (attd. RA.F)
Major H. E. Gillespie, R.M.L.I.
Captain H. R. Haines, R.M.L.I.
Captain J. V. Lovatt, R.M.E.
Major K. E. Lawrence, R.M.L.I.
Captain M. R Yeo, R.M.L.I.
Major G. H. Jollye, R.M.A.
Major R C. Temple, R.M.A.
Major A. E. Rann, R.M.A.
Captain A. I. Bell, R.M.L.I.
Major W. Blackman, R.M.L.I.
Hon. Lieut.-Col. C. E. C. Eliot, R.M.
Lieut.-Colonel. J. R Garrett.
Lieut.-Col. I. T. Courtney, R.M.L.I. (attached R.N.A.S.)

Members of the Order-

Major A. E. Rann, R.M.A.
Captain G. Harrington, R.M.A.
Lieutenant H. G. Burrage, R.M.A.

R.M. Gunner, J. Cameron.
R.M. Gunner E. Kimber.

R.M. Gunner F. G. Botterill.
Bandmaster J. G. Welsh, R.M. Band.

Medal of the Order- Sergt. A. E. Hawkes (Po.) R.M.L.I. Mr. C. H. Cross (late Barrack Sergt., R.M.L.I.)

DISTINGUISHED SERVICE ORDER.

Lieut. C. H. Collet, R.M.A. (R.N.A.S.)
Major E. F. P. Sketchley, R.M.L.I.
Maj. C. F. Kilner, R.M.L.I. (R.N.A.S.) and Bar.

Major A. H. French, R.M.L.I.

T/Lieut. J. H. D'Albiac, R.M.A. (R.N.A.S.)
Captain A. L. Forster, R.M.A.
Captain H. C. Harrison, R.M.A.

Captain E: Bamford, R.M.L.I.

Maj. H. F. Montgomery, R.M.L.I.
T/Lt.-Col. R. T. McCready, R.M.L.I.
Lieut.- Col. A. G. B. Urmston, R.M.L.I. Royal Scots).

Major C. D. O'Harmar, R.M.L.I.

Royal Marines in the War of 1914-1919

T/Lt.-Col. Kennedy – Crauford - Stuart, R.M.

T/Capt. H. N. Laws (Med. Unit)

Captain. B. N. Elliot, R.M.L.I.

Capt. R Gordon, R.M.L.I. (R.N.A.S.)

Captain E. H. Barr, R.M.A.

T/Capt. H. M. Leaf, R.M. (Mtr. Trans.)

Captain E. Gillespie, R.M.L.I.

Brevet-Major E. L. Gerrard, R.M.L.I. (R.N.A.S.)

Captain J. H. Howell-Jones, R.M.A. (A.O.D.)

Captain G. H. Seath, R.M.L.I.

Major A. G. B. Bourne, R.M.A.

Bt.-Lt.-Col. R F. C. Foster, R.M.A.

Captain A. R Chater, R.M.L.I.

Captain R. A. Dallas-Brooks, R.M.A.

Lieut. T. F. V. Cooke, R.M.L.I.

Major N. S. Clutterbuck, R.M.L.I.

Captain H. Blount, R.M.A.

Major R H. Darwall, R.M.L.I.

Major G. Drage, R.M.L.I. (Territorials)

Lieut.-Colonel A. R. H. Hutchison, C.M.G., R.M.L.I.

Lt.-Col. F. J. W. Cartwright, R.M.L.I

Captain C. E. Eagles, R.M.L.I.

T/Lieut.-Col. G. H. Harrison (Div. Engineers), R.M.

T/Capt. W. R. Ledgard, R.M.A.

Major F. W. Lumsden, R.M.A. (and 3 Bars).

Lt.-Col. J. Markham-Rose, R.M.A.

T/Capt. D. L. Robinson, R.M.A. (Tank Corps).

Lieut.-Colonel G. R Poole, R.M.A.

T/Major C. Micklem, R.M.A.

Captain R H. D. Lough, R.M.L.I.

Captain T. H. Jameson, R.M.L.I.

Major C. E. Risk, R.M.L.I. (R.N.A.S.)

T/Capt. Hon. L. S. Montagu, R.M. (Hood Bn.)

Major H. Ozanne, R.M.L.I.

Act - Maj. T. S. Dick, R.M.A. (Tk. Cps.)

Major E. F. Trew, R.M.L.I.

Major W. H. L. Tripp, R.M.A.

T/Major V. H. Cartwright, R.M.A.

Major M. C. Festing, R.M.L.I.

Major R E. Kilvert, R.M.A.

Capt. E. J. B. Tagg, R.M.L.I.

T/Maj. G. L. Wilks, R.M.A.(Tank Cps.)

Major W. S. Poe R.M.A. (Tank Corps)

Capt. C. E. H. Rathbone, R.M.L.I. R.N.A.S.

Major P. Sandilands, R.M.L.I.

Major H. E. W. Iremonger, R.M.A.

Major T. B. Luard, R.M.L.I.

Maj. E. K. Fletcher, R.M.L.I. (and Bar)

DISTINGUISHED SERVICE CROSS.

Lieutenant D. J. Gowney, R.M.L.I.

Lieutenant J. Cheetham, R.M.L.I.

Lieut. A. B. F. Alcock, R.M.L.I.

Lieut. E. H. Lamb (Divn. Engineers).

Lieut. R H. Roe (Divn. Engineers).

Lieutenant G. P. Lathbury, R.M.L.I.

Lieutenant F. C. Law, R.M.L.I.

Lieutenant M. C. Browne, R.M.L.I.

Captain B. G. Weller, R.M.L.I.

Captain G. Carpenter, R.M.L.I.

Lieutenant F. H. Thomas, R.M.L.I.

Captain G. L. Raikes, R.M.A.

Captain W. N. Stokes, R.M.A.

Lieutenant H.R Lambert, R.M.A.

Captain D. L. Aman, R.M.A.

Captain G. Evans, R.M.A.

Captain T. Cuming, R.M.A.

Capt. F. Summers (R.M. Transport Co.)

Lieut. G. N. Riley (Divn. Engineers.)

Captain J. E. Reynolds, R.M.A.

Lieut. G. F. Haszard, R.M.A.

Captain H. Peck, R.M.A.

Lieutenant B. Baseby, R.M.A.

Capt. J. M. Palmer, R.M.L.I. (and Bar)

Capt. C. R. W. Lamplough, R.M.L.I.

Captain G. Underhill, R.M.L.I.

Sergt.-Major C. J. Thatcher, R.M.

Co.-Sgt.-Major E. E. Kelly, R.M.L.I.

Captain H. V. Fuller, R.M.L.C.

Captain R. Burton, R.M.L.I.

Captain V. C. Brown, R.M.A.

Lieut. C. M. Sergeant, R.M.L.I.

Lieutenant J. A. Bath, R.M.L.I.

2nd-Lieut. D. Harding, R.M.A.

Captain W. G. A. Shadwell, R.M.A.

ALBERT MEDAL.

Private J. E. Brown, R.M.L.I.

Lieut. H. M. Day, R.M.L.I.

MILITARY CROSS.

Lieutenant D. L. Robinson, R.M.A.

Lieutenant H. N. Elphick, R.M.A.

Lieutenant J. Franklyn, R.M.A.

Lt. A. C. St. Clair - Morford, R.M.

Captain A. E. Rann, R.M.A.

Lieut. B. C. V. Weeks, R.M.L.I.

Lieutenant T. Westby, R.M.L.I.

2nd-Lt. W. C. Williamson, R.M.L.I.

Captain T. H. Burton, R.M.L.I.

Captain J. F. Ellison, R.M.L.I.

Lieutenant J. C. Guy, R.M.A.

Major C. G. Farquharson, R.M.L.I.

Captain R. H. P. West, R.M.L.I.

Lieutenant G. J. Wharf, R.M.L.I.

Capt. W. H. L. Tripp, D.S.O., R.M.A.

Major L. L. Foster, R.M.A.

Captain R H. Vance, R.M.L.I.

Lieutenant M. H. Collett, R.M.A.

Lieut. H. V. Scott-Willcox, R.M.L.I
Captain H. B. Inman, R.M.L.I.
Captain J. Pearson, R.M.L.I.
Captain A. K. Evans, R.M.L.I.
2nd-Lieut. E. A. Godfrey, R.M.L.I.
Captain E. J. Huskisson, R.M.L.I.
2nd-Lieut. G. A. Newling, R.M.L.I (and bar).
Lieutenant S. H. Wood, R.M.A.
Lieut. G. R. Goldingham, R.M.L.I. (and bar).
Capt. H. B. Van Praagh, R.M.L.I.
Lieut. A. G. Bareham, R.M.L.I.

Captain T. R. McCready, R.M.L.I.
Lieutenant E. W. Collier, R.M.L.I.
Lieutenant W. Russell, R.M.A.
Lieutenant T. A. Ryder, R.M.A.
Lieutenant W. D. Hart, R.M.A.
2nd-Lieut. C. H. Bailey, R.M.L.I.
Lieut. T. Buckley, R.M.L.I. (and two Bars).
Captain R. H. Campbell, R.M.L.I.
Captain F. G. Eliot, R.M.L.I.
Lieutenant J. W. Middleton, R.M.L.I.
Lieutenant F. A. Proffitt, R.M.L.I.

Lieutenant R. H. Sawyer, R.M.A.
Lieut. J. A. P. Curran, R.M.L.I.
Lieut. H. L. Hardisty, R.M.L.I.
Lieutenant A. E. Holton, R.M.A.
Lieutenant R W. Spraggett, R.M.L.I.
Lieut. T. G. Stewart, D.C.M., R.M.L.I.
2nd-Lieut. A. G. Stone, R.M.L.I.
Captain C. Carus-Wilson, R.M.A.
Lieut. H. Churchill Smith, R.M.L.I.
Lieut. L. H. Wrangham, R.M.L.I.
Lieutenant W. A. M. Hanson, R.M.L.I.

CONSPICUOUS GALLANTRY MEDAL.

Cr.-Sgt. C. Mayes (Po.), R.M.L.I.
Sgt. C. Braddock (Ch.), R.M.L.I.
Bugler E. Sillence (Ch.), R.M.L.I.
A/Cpl. E. A. Grindley (Po.), R.M.L.I.
Private M. Turner (Po.), R.M.L.I.

L/Corpl. J. G. Way (Po.), R.M.L.I.
Corpl. F. Pilgrim (Po.), R.M.L.I.
Cr.-Sgt. A. Spooner, R.M.A.
Corpl. E. V. Dean (Ply.), R.M.L.I.
Sgt. J. F. McLoughlin (Po.), R.M.L.I.

Pte. H. G. Bartlett (Po.), R.M.L.I.
Pte. W. Hopewell (Ply.), R.M.L.I.
Sergeant F. J. Knill, R.M.A.
Pte. J. D. L. Press (Po.), R.M.L.I.

DISTINGUISHED CONDUCT MEDAL.

Corpl. W. J. Stone, R.M.A.
Private L. J. Elliott (Ch.), R.M.L.I.
Batt.-Sgt.-Maj. S. G. Dacombe, R.M.A.
Sergeant W. Guest, R.M.A.
Cr.-Sgt. (Act.-Sgt.-Maj.) A. J. Banks (Ply.), R.M.L.I.
Batt.-Sgt.-Maj. W. Davis, R.M.A.
Cr.-Sgt. W. G. Scott (Ply.), R.M.L.I.
Corpl. R E. Payne, R.M.A.
Staff - Sgt. (Mech.) H. Williams, R.M.A.
Private G. Davies (Ply.), R.M.L.I.
L/Cpl. T. Salt (Ch.), R.M.L.I.

Corpl. F. Cross, R.M.A.
Sergt. E. C. Tye, R.M.A.
Sergt. A. C. Woodhouse, R.M.A.
Batt.-Sgt.-Maj. C. Dadd, R.M.A.
Corpl. E. Forsyth, R.M.A.
Act.-Cpl. W. A. Watts, M.M. (Ply.), R.M.L.I.
Staff.-Sgt. D. Booth (Med. Unit).
Batt.-Sergt.- Major C. Usborne, R.M.L.I.
C.S.M. A. H. Sands (Ply.), R.M.L.I.
A/Sgt. G. A. Priestley (Ch.), RM.L.I.

L/Cpl. H. Sadd (Po.), R.M..L.I.
Sergt. H. J. Trigg (Ply.), R.M.L.I.
Sergt. A. Paterson (Ply.), R.M.L.I
Sergt. G. H. Hastings, M.M. (Ply.) R.M.L.I.
Private W. Brindley.(Ch.), R.M.L.I.
Corpl. W. S. Carey (Ch.), R.M.L.I.
Corpl. L. Insley, M.M. (Ch.), R.M.L.I.
A/Cpl. J.W. Coulthard.(Ply.), R.M.L.I.
L/Cpl. P. W. Childs (Po.), R.M.L.I.
Private T. Pyle (Ch.), R.M.L.I.

For D.S.M. and M.M. see Chapters jn previous parts.

MERITORIOUS SERVICE MEDAL.

A/Supt. Clerk F. Cook (Chatham).

Sergwt. B. G. Tomkins (Chatham).

Conductor L. A. Blake, Divn. Train.

Colour - Sergt. J. Jones (Plymouth).

Gunner T. J. Lee, R.M.A.

Cr.-Sergeant C. J. Miller, R.M.A.

Corpl. (A/Sergt.-Maj.) A. J. Spry (Ply.)

Farrier - Sergt.-Major R. A. Wright (Divn. Train).

Sergt. (Acting B.S.M.) V. C. Willcox, R.M.A.

Colour - Sergt. J. Amos (Portsmouth)

Sergeant A. A. Atwood, R.M.A.

Staff-Sergt. F. Baseley (Med. Unit).

Colour - Sergt. W. G. Cooper, R.M.A.

A/S.-Sergt. J. H. Crabtree (Med. Unit)

Sergt.-Major J. Benson (Ch.)

A/Sergt. G. W. Baker (Divn..Train).

Sergt. W. A. Watts (Ply.), D.C.M. M.M. (Trench Mortars).

Q.M. Sergt. Instructor B. Wilson (Chatham).

Co.-Sergt.-Major L. Smith, R.M.L.C.

Sergeant R. Gooding, R.M.L.C.

Private A. Scott, R.M.L.C.

Private F. Brown (Ply.) (att. R.M.L.C.)

Q.M. Sergeant W. Saunders, R.M.A.

Staff-Sergt. H. J. Russell (Divn. Train).

Sergt. E. Duckworth (Medical Unit).

Sergeant G. Moyce, R.M.A.

B.Q.M.S. W. J. Pilcher, RMA

Q.M. Sergt. G. W. Rayner (Chatham).

Cr.-Sergeant J. J. Russell (Ch.)

Sergeant B. G. Vicars (Plymouth).

Sergt. B. S. Wilson (Divn. Train)

Corpl. H. R Frankland (Plymouth).

Lce.-Corpl. H. B. Spencer (Po.)

Private A. N. Waters (Chatham).

C.Q.M.S. H. Antrobus (Plymouth), attd. R.M.L.C.

Private F. Guy (Portsmouth).

Sergeant R. H. Ingoe (Portsmouth).

Sergeant J. Brown (Plymouth).

Private M. Graham (Chatham).

Colour - Sergt. J. King (Portsmouth).

Colour - Sergt. W. T. Reeves (Po.)

Private S. Caird, R.M.S.M.

Private A. W. Balsom (Chatham). (R.N. Transport Service).

Colour - Sergt. J. J. Child (Portsmouth) (R.N. Transport Service).

Corporal E. Merritt (Portsmouth). (RN. Transport Service).

Sergeant A. S. Traill, R.M.L.C. (R.N. Transport Service).

Gunner D. Bullard, R.M.A.

A/Sergt.-Major W. Carlton, R.M.A.

Sergeant W. H. Chubb (Divn. Train).
A/Co.-Sergt.-Major W. George (Ply.).
Co.-Sergt.-Major W. Pascoe (Ply.).
Sergt.-Major D. J. Pettit (Med. Unit).
Sergt. L. A. Scott (Portsmouth).
Cr.-Sergt. A. G. Squibb (Portsmouth).
Private J. Brown (Portsmouth).
Private A. Haile (Plymouth).
Corporal G. H. Odey (Portsmouth).
Private M. J. Netherway (Plymouth).
Lce.-Corpl. D. J. Stepney (Po.)
Private E. N. Stevenson (Po.)
Private F. J. Williamson (Ply.)
Private (Act. Sergt.-Maj.) J. J. Edwards (Chatham).
A/Co. Qr.-master - Sergt. R. A. Golding (Divn. Train).
Colour - Sergt. (Act./Sergt.-Major) F. R. Graham (Plymouth).
Gunner F. J. Haynes, R.M.A.
A/Corporal A. G. Howe (Po.)
Corporal H. Mann, R.M.A.
Sergeant P. R. McLeish, R.M.A.
Sergeant J. H. Meade, R.M.A.
Private J. Moore (Portsmouth).
Private F. A. Norris (Chatham).
Private B. Ortlieb (Chatham).
Sergt. (Act. Sergt.-Major) F. G. Weight (Chatham).
Co.-Sergt.-Major W. White (Ch.)
Lce.-Bombdr. W. O. Croft, R.M.A.
Corporal J. W. Lawson, R.M.A.
Private J. S. Stalham (Portsmouth).
Private Snellgrove (Plymouth).
Private A. H. Chaffe (Plymouth).
Private E. J. Friend (Chatham).
Private F. A. J. Parsons (Plymouth).
Private J. W. Smith (Plymouth).
Private A. J. Still (Chatham).
Private H. L. Weaver (Plymouth).
Private W. Wolstenholme (Ply.)
Supt. Clerk G. W. Barwick (Po.)
Sergt. O. J. Colan (Portsmouth).
Supt. Clerk H. Darlow (Chatham).
Act. Supt. Clerk W. J. Darlow (Ch.)
Sergt. W. H. Meatyard, M.M. (Ply.)
Supt. Clerk W. Owen (Portsmouth).
Cr.-Sergt. J. Milton (Plymouth).
Cr.-Sergt. T. Sillitoe (Plymouth).
Cr.-Sergt. J. Turnbull (Chatham).
Cr.-Sergt. E. J. Wood (Chatham).
Cr.-Sergt. A. Young (Plymouth).
Lce.-Sergt. W. A. Gouge (Po.)
Lce.-Sergt. J. Hook (Portsmouth).
Lce.-Sergt. F. A. Peasnell (Po.)
Corporal H. Briggs, RM.A.

Corporal J. W. Padley (Plymouth).
Private D. N. Allan (Portsmouth).
Gunr. A. Allgood, R.M.A.
Co.-Sergt.-Major E. E. Edwards, R.M.A.
Driver A. Hicks, R.M.A.
Corpl.-Driver O. Sutton, R.M.A.
Colour - Sergt. A. Baugh (Plymouth)
Colour - Sergt. A. Hill (Plymouth).
Sergt. B. E. Lawson (Ch.)
Private J W Haynes, R.M.S.M
Sergt.-Major H. J. Hill (Deal).
Scrgt.-Maj. II. W. Marshall, R.M.A.
Sergt. G. Adams (Plymouth).
Private W. H. Oakes (Portsmouth).
Colour - Sergt. C. H. Reepe (Ch.)
Colour - Sergt. C. Bryan, R.M.A.
Q.M. Sergeant H. R. Underhay (Ports).
Colour - Sergt. G. A. Lawford (Ch.)
Staff-Sergt. F. B. Niblett, R.M.A. (Mech.)
Sergt.-Maj. J. F. Ashton (Divn. Train).
Sergt.-Maj. J. F. Ashton (Divn. Train).
Q.M. Sergt. J. B. Carr (Med. Unit).
Colour - Sergt. G. J. Cooper (Ply.)
S/Q.M. Sergeant W. A. Read (Divn.Train).
Co.-Sergt.-Major D. E. Eccles (Ch.) attd. R.M.L.C.
Co.-Sergt.-Major C. P. Hann (Ch.) attd. R.M.L.C.
Co.-Sergt.-Major J. H. Wakeham (Plymouth). attd. R.M.L.C.
Q.M. Sergt. A. M. Butler (Plymouth).
C.Q.M.S. A. M. Eade (Ch.) R.M.L.C.
Colour - Sergt. E. F. Hobbs (Po.)
Corpl. A. E. Cowton (Plymouth).
C.Q.M.S. J. Herbert (Po.) R.M.L.C.
C.Q.M.S. G. Marsh (Divn. Train).
Sergt. P. S. W. Buckle, R.M.L.C.
Sergt. J. Clark (Portsmouth).
Sergt. A. Sharp (Portsmouth).
Sergt. W. Davidson (Divn. Train).
Sergt. R Fulton (Medical Unit).
Sergt. W. H. Pyne (Divn. Train).
Q.M. Sergt. W. Snape (Plymouth).
Sergt. B. L. Steed, RM.L.C.
Sergt. A. Dewhurst (Portsmouth).
Q.M. Sergt. E. Diggle (Portsmouth).
Private A. H. W. Dowding (Po.)
Corporal J. E. Lord, (Med. Unit).
Q.M.S.I. C. F. Coward (Chatham).
Q.M.S.I. C. Ellis, R.M.A.
Q.M.S. T. C. Gardner (Plymouth).
Q.M.S.I. F. H. Green (Plymouth).
Q.M.S. F. M. Masters (Deal).
Q.M.S. W. Watling, R.M.A.
Q.M.S. J. Werry (Plymouth).

Gunner S. J. Cattle, R.M.A.
Gunner H. W. Gates, R.M.A.
Colour -Sergt. E. F. Godsell, R.M.A.
Cr.-Sergt. T. E. Stevens, R.M.A.
C.S.M. J. R. Welch, R.M.A.
C.S.M. C. J. Blythe, R.M.A.
Sergt. W. Broadbridge, R.M.A.
Colour - Sergt. H. Burnley, R.M.A.
Colour - Sergt. G. J. Cooper (Ply.)
Bd.-master H. Lodge, R.M.B.
Sergt. F. Tulk (Portsmouth).
Corpl. A. E. Cowton (Plymouth).
C.S.M. J. Greenhalgh, R.M.A.
Colour - Sergt. E. F. Hobbs (Po.)
Colour - Sergt. W. Lee, R.M.A.
Supt. Clerk S. A. Allison, R.M.A.
Supt. Clerk W. McK. Brown (Ply.)
Supt. Clerk Geo. Burt (Portsmouth).
Supt. Clerk F. J. Garbe (Plymouth)
Supt. Clerk E. C. Green, R.M.A.
Supt. Clerk R. B. Holland (Plymouth)
Supt. Clerk T. C. Kelsey, R.M.A.
A/Supt. Clerk A. W. Ordish, R.M.A.
A/Supt. Clerk H. J. Osborne, R.M.A.
A/Supt. Clerk C. F. Parfitt (Ch.)
A/Supt. Clerk W. Pearce, R.N.D. attd. R.M.L.C. Office.
Supt. Clerk F. W. Phillips (Po.)
Supt. Clerk A. G. Sanderson, R.M.A.
Supt. Clerk J. W. Smith (Po.).
Supt. Clerk E. W. Speed (Plymouth).
Supt. Clerk H. M. Watkis (Ch.)
Supt. Clerk W. E. Webber (Chatham).
Staff Clerk E. Evans, R.M.A.
Staff Clerk F. A. Freeman (Ch.)
Staff Clerk Geo. Moody (Portsmouth)
Co.-Sergt.-Major D. E. Eccles (Ch.)
A/Staff Clerk A. J. M. Munro (Po.)
Staff Clerk A. J. D. Robinson (Ply.)
Staff Clerk W. Townsend (Po.)
Cr.-Sergt. W. R. Bury (Chatham).
Cr.-Sergt. C. Dodd (Portsmouth).
Cr.-Sergt. T. E. Hanlon (Chatham).
Cr.-Sergt. G. Lee (Chatham).
Sergeant W. E. Driscoll, R.M.A.
Sergeant H. J. Eastaway (Plymouth).
Sergeant W. J. Hall (Chatham).
Sergeant M. Hawes (Plymouth).
Sergeant H. Martin (Plymouth).
Sergeant W. A. T. Martin (Po.)
Sergeant Jas. Ponsford (Plymouth).
Sergeant C. R. Potter (Plymouth).
Sergeant W. P. Rist (Chatham).

Corporal A. H. Daniell (Plymouth).
Corporal P. J. de Carle (Po.)
Corporal J. Henderson (Plymouth).
A/Corporal J. Nolan (Plymouth).
Sergt.-Major W. J. Flannagan (Deal).
Sergt.-Major C. E. Maton, R.M.A.
Sergeant F. Crawley (Plymouth).
A/Sergt. Frank Smith (Chatham).
Sergeant V. L. Cox (Chatham)

Q.M.S. C. Wild (Plymouth).
C.S.M. F. Cook, R.M.A.
C.S.M. J. J. Hughes, D.S.M. (Po.)
C.S.M. C. G. Salter, R.M.A.
C.S.M. J. P. Strevens (Portsmouth).
Sergeant B. Baxter (Chatham).
Sergeant W. E. C. Blackman, R.M.A.
Sergeant F. M. E. Boulton, R.M.A.
A/Sergt.-Major A. G. Smith (Ch.)

Sergeant W. J. Thornton (Po.)
Sergeant E. G. Williams (Po.)
Corporal J. W. Preston (Chatham).
Corporal A. W. F. Putnam (Po.)
Corporal C. H. Withers (Po.)
Lce.- Copl. G. A. Keefe, D.S.M. (Po.)
Private Jas. Johns (Portsmouth).
Private F. H. Narracott (Plymouth).

2.-FOREIGN DECORATIONS.
BELGIUM.
ORDER OF THE CROWN.

Chevalier - T/Lieut. C. W. Comyns, R.M.A.   T/Lieutenant T. W. Lewis, R.M.A.   T/Captain J. H. Percy, R.M.A.

ORDER OF LEOPOLD WITH SWORDS.

Commander - Major-General Sir Archibald Paris, K.C.B.. R.M.A.

Officer - Brevet Lieut.-Colonel R. F. C. Foster, C.M.G., D.S.O., R.M.A.

Chevalier - Major E. L. Gerrard, D.S.O., R.M.L.I. (RN.A.S.)   Sergt. F. Hill, R.M.A.   Corporal J. Robinson, R.M.A

DECORATION MILITAIRE.-Corporal G. Bate (Med. Unit), R.M.

CROIX DE GUERRE-

T/Lieutenant C. W. Comyns, R.M.A.
T/Lieutenant T. W. Lewis, R.M.A.
T/Captain J. H. Percy, R.M.A.
Gunner J. H. Butler, R.M.A.
Sergeant F. Hill, R.M.A.
Sergt. (Driver) J. J. Honner, R.M.A.
Gunner W. J. Jerram, R.M.A.
Corpl. (Driver) A. P. Levy, R.M.A.
T/Lieutenant M. F. Cope, R.M.A.
T/2nd-Lieut. H. L. Hunt, R.M.A.
Brig.-Gen. F. W. Lumsden, V.C., C.B., D.S.O., R.M.A.
T/Captain F. G. Eliot, R.M.L.I.
Pte. H. Bardsley (Medical Unit).
Sergeant W. Clewes (Medical Unit)
Gunner W. Green, R.M.A.
Private C. F. Cumiskey, R.M.L.I.
Sergeant R F. Hurford (Div. Train)
Corporal J. Sherman (Chat.), R.M.L.I.
A/Sergt. W. Young (Ply.), R.M.L.I.
Brevet-Lieut.-Colonel R. F. C. Foster, C.M.G., D.S.O., R.M.A.
Maj.-Gen. Sir A. Paris, K.C.B., R.M.A.
Brevet-Lieut.-Col. H. E. W. Iremonger, R.M.A.
Maj. J. B. Chancellor, R.M.A. (S. Tn.)
Capt. R A. G. Stewart, R.M.A. (S. Tn).
Capt. E. W. Husey, R.M.A. (S. Tn.)
Capt. M. H. Webb-Bowen, R.M.A. (Siege Train).
Capt. T. F. Connew, R.M.A. (S. Tn.)
Capt. R. F. Reynolds R.M.A. (S. Tn.)
Capt. S. T. Mattheison, R.M.A. (S. Tn.)

Capt. J. T. Hollingsworth, R.M.A. (Siege Train).
Lieut. C. A. Pearce, R.M.A. (S. Tn.)
2nd-Lt. C. A. Bishop, R.M.A. (S. Tn.)
Lieut. E. L. Clogg, R.M.A. (S Tn.)
2nd-Lt. D. Harding, D.S.C. (S. Tn.)
Chief R.M. Gunner W. E. Petley, R.M.A. (Siege Train).
Q.M.S. G. Barton, R.M.A. (S. Train)
Sergt. J. Brookbank, R.M.A. (S. Tn.)
Gnr. E. G. Brown, R.M.A. (S. Train)
Gnr. E. Sutton, R.M.A. (Siege Train)
Gnr. D. Burke, R.M.A. (Siege Train)
Gnr. J. Cooper, R.M.A. (Siege Train)
Gnr. R. W. Cox, R.M.A. (Siege Train)
Gnr. L. W. Dale, R.M.A. (Siege Train)
Gnr. M. G. Daley, R.M.A. (Siege Train)
Gnr. J. Drape, R.M.A. (Siege Train)
Gnr. A. G. Dunstall, R.M.A. (S. Train)
Q.M.S. E. Edward, R.M.A. (S. Train)
Gnr. H. S. Goodwin, R.M.A. (S. Tn.)
Gnr. A. Gray, R.M.A. (Siege Train)
Gnr. T. W. Gurney, R.M.A.
Gnr. G. F. Hickman, R.M.A. (S. Train)
Corpl. T. H. Hucker, R.M.A. (Siege Train)
Sergt. J. E. Kersey, R.M.A. (S. Train)
Cpl. T. McCudle, R.M.A. (S. Train)
Cpl. E. H. Martin (Ply.), R.M.L.I.
C.S.M. W. H. Rann, R.M.A. (S. Train)
Gnr. W. George, R.M.A. (Siege Train)
Gnr. H. C. Rendall, R.M.A. (S. Train)
Gnr. E. E. Sadler R.M.A. (S. Train)

Sergt.-Maj. E. Rolf, R.M.A. (S. Train)
Sergt. L. H. Simmons, R.M.A. (S. Tn.)
Gnr. A. Smith, R.M.A. (Siege Train)
Gnr. G. W. Starbuck, R.M.A. (S. Train)
Sgt. J. Ward, R.M.A. (Siege Train)
Sgt. A. Waring, R.M.A. (Siege Train)
Gnr. J. R. Warrington, R.M.A. (S. Tn.)
Gnr. A. Watson, R.M.A. (S. Train)
Gnr. A. Webb, R.M.A. (Siege Train)
Lieut.-Colonel Pryce Peacock, C.M.G., R.M.A. (Siege Train)
Lieut. B. Baseby, R.M.A. (Siege Train)
Sergt. A. C. Chave, R.M.A. (S. Train)
Gnr. E. Bennett, R.M.A. (Siege Train)
Gnr. G. Crosby, R.M.A. (Siege Train)
Gnr. G. Morton, R.M.A. (Siege Train)
Cpl. F. Gray, RM.A. (Siege Train)
Gnr. E. Popplewell, R.M.A. (S. Train)
Gnr. E. J. Randall, R.M.A. (S. Train)
Cpl. E. G. Rook, R.M.A. (Siege Train)
Gnr. L. Siebert, R.M.A. (Siege Train)
Gnr. F. S. Willis, R.M.A. (Siege Train)
A/Sergt.-Major G. H. Bruce, (Ch.), R.M.L.I.
Sergt. T. McGubbin, R.M.A. (S. Train)
Cr.-Sgt. W. J. Cook, D.S.M. (Ply.),
Sgt. W. J. Darlow (Ch.), R.M.L.I.
Sgt. T. C. Franks (Ch.), R.M.L.I.
Pte. G. H. Hall, (Ch.), R.M.L.I.
Cr.-Sgt. R Hill (Ply.), R.M.L.I.
Captain C. B. Conybeare, R.M.L.I.
Cr.-Sgt. H. Camfield (Po.), R.M.L.I.

Royal Marines in the War of 1914-1919

EGYPT.
ORDER OF THE NILE (2nd Class)-

Major H. D. Palmer. R.M.L.I.
Major H. D. E. O'Sullivan. R.M.L.I.

Major T. B. Luard, D.S.O., R.M.L.I.
Brig.-Gen. St. G. B. Armstrong, C.B., C.M.G., R.M.L.I.

ORDER OF THE NILE (3rd Class)-

Major H. W. Channer, R.M.L.I.
Major R S. Gibson, R.M.L.I.

Brevet-Lieut.-Colonel R. H. Darwall, D.S.O., C.B.E., R.M.L.I.
Lieut.-Col. C. E. Risk, D.S.O., R.M.L.I. (R.N.A.S.)

ORDER OF THE NILE (4th Class)-

T /Major F. H. Smith (Div. Train) R.M.
Major J. J. Bramble, R.M.L.I.
Major G. H. H. Prynne, R.M.L.I.

FRANCE.
LEGION OF HONOUR.
Commander-

Maj.-Gen. Sir A Paris, K.C.B., R.M.A.

Major-Gen. Sir D. Mercer, K.C.B., R.M.L.I.

Officer-

Bt.-Lieut.-Col. C. J. Thoroton, C.M.G. R.M.L.I.
Capt. I. T. Courtney, R.M.L.I.
Brig.-General C. N. Trotman, C.B., R.M.L.I.

Colonel H. E. Blumberg, C.B., R.M.L.I.
Bt.-Lieut.-Colonel H. F. Montgomery, C.M.G., D.S.O., R.M.L.I.

T/Lieut. Col. H.M. Grayson, R.M.
Maj. E. Bamford, V.C., D.S.O., R.M.L.I.

Chevalier-

Captain J. A. F. Cuffe, R.M.L.I.

Brevet-Major T. L. Hunton, R.M.L.I.

Bt.-Lieut.-Colonel W. W. Godfrey, C.M.G., R.M.L.I.

Lieutenant R J. Carpenter, R.M.L.I.
Lieutenant C. H. Congdon, R.M.L.I.
Bt.-Lt.-Col. L. C. Larnpen, R.M.L.I.
Major W. L. Huntingford, R.M.A.
Major S. C. Wace, R.M.A.
Major C. d'O. Harmar, R.M.L.I.
Captain J. M. Palmer, R.M.L.I.
T/Major W. J. Douglas, R.M.

Captain L. E. Innes - Baillie, R.M.A.
T/Major C. E. Binns, R.M.
T /Capt. E. M. Compton-Mackenzie, R.M.
T /Captain L. F. Orde, R.M.A.
Captain R. C.A. Glunicke.
Major A. Peel, R.M.L.I.
T/Lieut. C. H. F. Woolley, R.M.L.I.

Major A. S. Cantrell, R.M.A.
Major H. E. W. Iremonger, D.S.O. R.M.A.
Bt.-Lt.-Col. R. C. Temple, R.M.A.
Captain L. S. Wilkinson, R.M.L.I.
Major R C. S. Waller, R.M.L.I.

MEDAILLE MILITAIRE-

Lce - Sergt. F. Radford, (Ply.).
Private W. G. Pitt (Ply.).
Cr.-Sergt. R G. Salter (Ply.).
Cr.-Sergt. S. Woolbridge (Ports.)
Cr.-Sergt. R. Milne (Portsmouth).

Corpl. A. E. Ganner (Portsmouth).
Lce - Corpl. R McDowall (Portsmouth).
Bugler F. P. Chapman (Portsmouth).
Sergeant L. Oakey (Chatham).

Sergt. F. Lefevre (Plymouth).
Corporal C. Butler, R.M.A.
Sergeant G. R Vale (Chatham).
Private H. Atkins (Chatham).
Private G. T. James (Plymouth).

Private J. A. Short (Plymouth).
Colour-Sergeant P. J. Strachan (Ch.)
Corporal T. H. Wedge (Plymouth).
Pte. T. H. Symons, D.S.M. (Ply.)

Cr.-Sergt. E. F. Hobbs (Portsmouth).
Sergt. H. Mann, R.M.A.
Sergt. H. Usborne, D.C.M., R.M.A.
Private H. G. Bartlett, C.G.M. (Po.)
Sergt. J. F. McLoughlin, C.G.M. (Portsmouth).
Sergt. C. Mayes, C.G.M. (Po.)
Cr.-Sgt. A. Spooner, C.G.M., R.M.A.
Sergt. A. Tushaw (Chatham).

CROIX DE GUERRE-

Lt.-Col. H. D. Farquharson, R.M.L.I.Cr.-
Gunner Wm. Woodman, R.M.A.
Gunner J. W. Pooley, R.M.A.
Capt. G. P. Lathbury, D.S.C.,
Lieut. C. B. Conybeare, R.M.L.I.
Lieutenant F. C. Law, R.M.L.I.
Captain E. J. B. Tagg, R.M.L.I.
Major-General Sir A. Paris, R.M.A.
Brig.-Gen. D. Mercer, R.M.L.I.

Lieut.-Col. J. W. Carroll, R.M.L.I.
Lieutenant A. R Chater, R.M.L.I.
Lieutenant E. G. M. Roe, R.M.L.I.
Lieutenant R. A. Dallas-Brooks, R.M.A. (late R.M.L.I.).
Private E. Adam (Plymouth).
Sergt. F. W. Dash (Plymouth).
Private E. A. Grindley (Portsmouth).
Corporal J. McDowell (Plymouth).

Sergt. P. J. Strachan (Ch.)
Private J. A. Short (Plymouth).
Private J. Cook (Chatham).
Private T. Gorman (Plymouth).
Private A. Whittle (Plymouth).
Private G. T. James (Plymouth).
Private J. Jones (Chatham).
Lce - Corpl. C. F. G. Gilbert (Ch.)
Major V. H. Cartwright, R.M.A.

Brig.-Gen. C. N. Trotman, R.M.L.I.
Captain A. E. Syson, R.M.L.I.
Capt. R. D. H. Lough, D.S.O., R.M.L.I.
Captain A. S. Tetley, R.M.L.I.
Lieut.-Col. G. J. H. Mullins, R.M.L.I.
Bt.-Lt.-Col. J. A. M. A. Clark, R.M.L.I.
Major H. W. Channer, R.M.L.I.
Major M. C. Festing, R.M.L.I.
Brig.-Gen. St. G. B. Armstrong, C.M.G., R.M.L.I.
Lt. & Q.M. G.H. Littleton, R.M.A.
Lieut. W. Russell, R.M.A.
Bt - Lieut.-Colonel B. G. Weller, C.B. D.S.C., R.M.L.I.
Bt.-Maj. T. F. V. Cook, D.S.O., R.M.L.I.
Pte. W. Hopewell, C.G.M. (Plymouth).
Capt. J. A. Bath, D.S.C., R.M.L.I.

Sergt. D. McKay (Plymouth).
Corporal J. Mulligan (Plymouth).
Sergt. F. Pilgrim, C.G.M. (Portsmouth).
Private H. Willons (Plymouth).
Sergeant B. I. Wilson (Chatham).
Major C. d'O. Harmar, R.M.L.I.
Captain J. M. Palmer, R.M.L.I.
Corpl. T. H. Wedge (Ply.) R.M.L.I.
Sergeant F. J. Knill, C.G.M., R.M.A.
Pte. J. D. L. Press, C.G.M., R.M.L.I.
Gunner W. Brown, R.M.A.
Major R. C. Morison - Scott, D.S.O., R.M.A.
Corpl. E. V. Deane, C.G.M. (Plymouth).
Lieut. D. L. Robinson, D.S.O., R.M.A.

Capt. G. F. Haszard, R.M.
Lieut. R. H. Sawyer, R.M.A.
Corporal D. A. Archer, R.M.A.
Corporal E. Parish, R.M.A.
Gunner A. J. Sawyer, R.M.A.
Gunner W. H. Yeates, R.M.A.
Sergeant H. C. Barlow, R.M.A.
Sergeant F. Cox, R.M.A.
Sergeant G. Fry, R.M.A.
Corporal C. P. Harris (Plymouth).
Captain H. Hutchison, R.M.A.
Captain H. B. Vincent, R.M.A.
Lieut. H. F. Angold, R.M.A.
Major C. F. Jerram, C.M.G., D.S.O. R.M.L.I.

GREECE.
ORDER OF THE REDEEMER.
Commander

Major G. L. Beaumont, R.M.L.I.

Major R Gordon, D.S.O., R.M.L.I.

Brigdr.- General H. E. Blumberg, C.B., R.M.L.I.

Officer

Bt.-Lieut.-Col. W. W. Godfrey, C.M.G., R.M.L.I.

Major A. C. Barnby, R.M.L. (R.N.A.S.)

Major W. L. Huntingford, R.M.A.

MEDAILLE OF THE "MARINE CAISSE DES INVALIDES."

Sergeant A. C. Wilkins, R.M.A.

Gunner F. Johnson, R.M.A.
Lieut. E. L. Moore, R.M.A.

Corporal W. A. Leurigndon, R.M.A.

ITALY.
ORDER OF THE CROWN.
Commander

Bt.-Lieut.-Col. L. C. Lampen, R.M.L.I.

Bt.-Lieut.-Col. C.J. Thornton, RM.L.I.
Major G. R. S. Hickson, R.M.L.I.

Lieut.-Col. H. M. Grayson, R.M.

Officer

Major S. C. Wace, R.M.A.

Captain I. T. Courtney, R.M.L.I. (RN.A.S.)

Lieut.-Colonel A. H. French, D.S.O., R.M.L.I. (R.C. of Signals).

Cavalier.

Capt. A. J. Mellor, R.M.L.I., W/T.

Hon. Capt. C. T. Rolland, R.M.
Major F. Holmes (Divn. Train), R.M.

Hon. Major. A. B. Wilson, R.M.

ORDER OF ST. MAURICE AND ST. LAZARUS.
Cavalier.

Major A. G. B. Bourne, D.S.O., R.M.A.

Major C. E. Binns, R.M.

SILVER MEDAL FOR MILITARY VALOUR.

Major A. G. B. Bourne, R.M.A.
Private E. J. Nutt (Plymouth).

Major H. St. G. Morgan, R.M.A.

Gunner C. Beard, R.M.A.

BRONZE MEDAL FOR MILITARY VALOUR.

Capt. L. S. Wilkinson, R.M.L.I.
Capt. J. Geldard, R.M.L.I., W/T.

Sergeant H. J. Jordan, R.M.A.
Sergeant W. A. Morey (Chatham).

Private E. Eldridge (Chatham).
Sergeant B. E. Lawson (Chatham).

CROCE DI GUERRA.- Sergeant J. W. Syer (Ply.), R.M.L.I.

Royal Marines in the War of 1914-1919

JAPAN.
ORDER OF THE "RISING SUN." 4th Class

Major F. H. Griffiths, R.M.L.I.	Bt.-Lieut.-Col. W. W. Godfrey, R.M.L.I.	Major St. G. F. G. Caulfeild, R.M.A.
Major H. L. Jones, R.M.L.I.	Major R. Sinclair, R.M.L.I.	

ORDER OF THE "RISING SUN."5th Class - Captain H. E. Ravenshaw.

RUSSIA.
ST. STANISLASS. 2ND CLASS WITH SWORDS.

Bt.-Lieut.-Col. F. L. Dibblee, R.M.A.	Major H. Blount, R.M.A.	Major L. D. Briscoe, R.M.A.
Brevet-Lieut.-Col. A. G. Troup, R.M.A	Lieut.-Col. C. E. Collard, R.M..L.I.	Major A. P. Grattan, R.M.L.I.
Major F. G. Tanqueray-Willaume, R.M.A.	Major H. Ozanne, R.M.L.I.	Major G. C. Wainwright, R.M.L.I.

ST. STANISLASS. 3RD CLASS WITH SWORDS.
Lieutenant N. K. Jolley, R.M.L.I.

ST. ANNE WITH SWORDS

Captain J. C. Farmer, R.M.L.I.	Capt. I.T. Courtney, R.M.L.I.(R.N.A.S.)	Capt. A. G. W. Greirson, R.M.L.I. W/T
Capt. E. Bamford, D.S.O., R.M.L.I.	Capt. F. W. Home, R.M.L.I., W/T.	

MEDAL OF ORDER-
R.M. Gunner S.T. Washburn

ST. GEORGE'S CROSS (4TH CLASS)

Sergeant A. W. Balcombe (Ch.)	Sergeant J..Hall, R.M.A.	Lce.-Corporal A. Palmer (Plymouth)
Sergeant F. W. Bird, R.M.A	Private W. Hamilton (Chatham).	.Corporal T. Parrott, R.M.A.
Sergt. A. H. Goulding (Chatham).	Private J. W. Hawkins (Portsmouth)	Gunner W. G. Partridge, R.M.A.
Bandmstr. T. H. Hawkins, R.M.B.	Gunner H. N. Hardy, R.M.A.	Gunner J. W. Peacock, R.M.A.
Colour - Sergt. T. H. Mitchell, R.M.A.	Musician P. R Hardy, R.M.B..	Gunner J. Penfold, R.M.A.
Corporal A. Phipps (Portsmouth).	Gunner W. J. Harmes, R.M.A.	Private G. Phillips (Chatham)
Sergeant G. R. Westlake (Plymouth).	Private B. E. Hartley (Plymouth.)	Musician W. H. J. Pickard, R.M.B.
Corporal A. S. Aheir, R.M.A.	Cr.-Sergt. F. Hawkesworth, R.M.A.	Sergeant W. H. Prince-Cox, R.M.A.
Private B. Anderson (Plymouth).	Gunner J. Haydon, R.M.A.	Colour - Sergt. J. Reid (Po.)
Sergeant H. C. Barton, R.M.A.	Private E. W. Haynes (Chatham).	Sergeant W. Riseley (Portsmouth).
Gunner F. C. Batt, R.M.A.	Corporal W. Heath, R.M.A.	Private F. J. Scutt (Chatham).
Gunner P. Blackley, R.M.A.	Private G. R. Hubert (Chatham).	Gunner W. Sellen, R.M.A.
Sergeant J. T. Burley, R.M.A.	Colour - Sergt. A. Hill (Plymouth).	Gunner S. Shipp, R.M.A.
Sergeant C. Butler, R.M.A.	Private D. Holland (Portsmouth).	Private H. T. Silk (Chatham).
Gunner E. Button, R.M.A.	Musician M. P. Howard, R.M.B.	Gunner A. E. Skuce, R.M.A.
Private E. Cassell (Portsmouth).	Private G. Huxtable (Chatham)	Private J. E. Slater (Plymouth).
Gunner C. H. Cheesman, R.M.A.	Sergeant W. Jackson, R.M.A.	Musician J. A. Somerville, R.M.B.
Gunner J. Cooper, R.M.A.	Private C. Jarvis (Portsmouth).	Gunner W. Stallard. R.M.A.
Gunner E. A. Cuff, R.M.A.	Musician R. W. Johnson, R.M.B.	Colour - Sergt. W. Still (Chatham)
Colour - Sergt. F. N. Davis, R.M.A.	Private T. Jones (Portsmouth).	Sergeant J. N. Stone (Plymouth).
Sergeant F. J. Denash (Plymouth).	Private H. A. King (Portsmouth)	Q.M.S.I. W. A. Stratton (Po.)
Sergeant D. T. Dunn (Chatham).	Private T. W. Lambert (Plymouth).	Private. R. E. Swinden (Plymouth).
Lce.-Sergt. R. Edmunds (Chatham).	Private A. L. Lawley (Portsmouth).	Lce.-Sergeant C. W. Tugwell (Ply.)
Private J. Ellis (Chatham).	Musician E. E. McAlister, R.M.B.	Gunner J. A. Wainwright, R.M.A.
A/Bombdr. J. W. Field, R.M.A.	Private G. W. Macdonald (Po.)	Colour - Sergt. R. W. Ward, R.M.A.
Sergeant H. Fisher, R.M.A.	Private W. Mack (Chatham).	Colour - Sergt. C. J. Watts (Po.)
Band Corporal L. Forbes, R.M.B.	Gunner D. McVicker, R.M.A.	Musician R F. White, R.M.B.
Gunner R Forbes, R.M.A.	Co.-Sergt.-Maj. R Magson, R.M.A.	Gunner W. N. Wilson, R.M.A.
Gunner H. Frost, R.M.A.	Gunner J. H. Marshall, R.M.A.	Sergeant G. Workman, R.M.A.
Cr.- Sergt. W. J. Frost, R.M.L.I. (Plymouth)	Band-Corporal J. M. Messer, R.M.B.	Gunner J. Hart, R.M.A.
Gunner A. Miller, R.M.A.	A/Bombdr. A. Lincoln, R.M.A.	Gunner W. Fry, R.M.A.
Gunner J. C. Morris, R.M.A.	Bombdr. C. G. Looker, R.M.A.	Lce.- Bombdr. A. Underhay, R.M.A.

Co.-Sergt.-Major J. F. German, R.M.A.   Private H. Morton (Portsmouth).   Private. M. Underhill (Portsmouth)
Private W. Green (Chatham)   Gunner R J. Mudge, R.M.A.

SERBIA.
WHITE EAGLE. 4th Class-Captain B. N. Elliot D.S.O., R.M.L.I.
WHITE EAGLE. 5th Class-T/Captain E. M. Compton-Mackenzie, R.M.
ST. SAVA. 3rd Class-Captain B. N. Elliot, D.S.O., R.M.L.I.
St. SA VA. 4th Class-Lieutenant G. Bullock, R.M.L.I.

GOLD MEDAL FOR BRAVERY

Lieutenant G. Bullock, R.M.L.I   Sergeant C. A. Pearce, R.M.A.   Sergeant A. H. Turner, R.M.A.

SILVER MEDAL FOR BRAVERY

Gunner D. Wass, R.M.A.   Gunner H. J. Carter, R.M.A.   Gunner S. E. Davies, R.M.A.
Gunner A. E. K. Fish, R.M.A.

GOLD MEDAL FOR ZEALOUS SERVICE

Sergt. H. Bolton, R.M.L.I. (Plymouth) (killed).   Gunner R. H. Oates, R.M.A.   Private F. Turner (Plymouth) R.M.L.I.
Gunner J. Ransom, R.M.A.   Private F. Fry (Portsmouth), R.M.L.I.

GOLD MEDAL FOR MILITARY VIRTUE.-Sergeant C. A. Pearce, R.M.A.

SILVER MEDAL FOR ZEALOUS SERVICE

Corporal A. H. Turner, R.M.A.   Private F. Fry (Po.), R.M.L.I.   Gunner R. H. Oates, R.M.A.
Gunner D. Wass, R.M.A.   Private F. Turner (Ply.) R.M.L.I.   Gunner J. R. Ransom, R.M.A.
Gunner A. T. H. Fish, R.M.A.   Private C. E. Bird (Ply.) R.M.L.I.   Private A. E. Joyner (Chatham),R.M.L.I.
Gunner S. E. Davies, R.M.A.   Gunner H. J. Carter, R.M.A.

MISCELLANEOUS

Brevet-Lieut.-Colonel C. J. Thoroton, R.M.L.I. *(Ouassan Alouit, Morocco.)*
Lieut.-Col. C. G. Crawley, R.M.A. *(Order of Avis, 2nd Class, Portugal.)*
Major T. L. Hunton, R.M.L.I. *(Chevalier of Star of Roumania.)*
Major J. C. Farmer, R.M.L.I. *(Officer of Crown of Roumania.)*
Major H. L. Jones, R.M.L.I. *(Order of Avis, 2nd Class, Portugal.)*
Sergeant H. Jinks, R.M.L.I. *(Cross of Military Virtue, 2nd Class, Roumania.)*
Staff-Sergeant A. E. Jackson, M.M. *(Medical Unit) (Cross of Military Virtue, 1st Class, Roumania.)*
Sergeant E. J. Banks (Portsmouth), R.M.L.I. *(D.C.M., 1st Class, Roumania.)*
Lce.-Corporal L. Peach, (Portsmouth), R.M.L.I. *(D.C.M., 3rd Class, Roumania.)*
Private L. H. Sands (Chatham), R.M.L.I. *(D.C.M., 3rd Class, Roumania.)*
Brig.-General Sir A. Gibb, R.M. Engineers *(D.S.M., U.S.A.)*

INDEX.

Albert, King of Belgian, 403
Albert Medal
  Lieutenant H M Day, 60, 458
  Private J E Brown, 68, 458
American Land Forces, 77, 187, 189, 192, 293, 341, 342, 421, 431
Amet, Vice-Admiral, (French Navy), 59, 249
Andrew, Prince of Greece, 212
Armistice, 4, 58, 59, 60, 83, 146, 243, 247, 249, 253, 256
Armoured Trains, 83, 86, 195
Askaris, 228, 232
Australian Forces, 27, 29, 34, 119, 120, 121, 122, 125, 128, 276, 407, 437
  1st Australian Brigade, 119, 122, 124
  3rd Australian Brigade, 119, 121,
  4th Australian Brigade, 122, 124, 126
  Australian Light Horse Brigade, 127, 389
  9th Australian Battalion, 120
  12th Australian Battalion, 120
  13th Australian Battalion, 124
  14th Australian Battalion, 121
  16th Australian Battalion, 124, 126
Belgian Forces, 65, 103, 104, 106,107, 108, 110, 285, 286, 342, 289, 402, 403
  4th Belgian Division, 98
  6th Belgian Division, 290, 398
  7th Belgian Regiment, 107
  21st Belgian Regiment, 102
Belgian Artillery, 104, 106, 397, 399, 401
Belgian Engineers, 107
Belgian Fortress Troops, 108
Bolsheviks, 58, 63, 64, 73-76, 79-85, 88-91, 184, 187, 192, 196, 198-199, 257, 405-406

British and Empire Army Formations and Units
  First Army, 267, 336, 337, 342, 348
  Second Army, 289, 290, 378
  Third Army, 108, 289, 331, 337, 342, 347, 353
  Fourth Army, 331, 342, 347
  II Corps, 298, 300
  IV Corps, 295, 297, 331
  V Corps, 286, 288, 298, 300, 320, 321, 330, 331, 348
  VI Corps, 331, 337, 342, 348
  VII Corps, 289
  VIII Corps, 141, 313, 314
  XXII Corps, 330, 354, 355
  XIII Corps, 313
  XVII Corps, 336, 337, 338, 341, 342, 345, 348, 352, 353
  XVIII Corps, 313, 314
  XXII Corps, 330, 354, 355
  Machine Gun Corps, 196, 197, 198, 199
  1st Division, 347
  2nd Division, 300, 319, 322, 323, 325, 326, 327, 348, 351, 352, 365
  3rd Division, 366
  3rd Cavalry Division, 102, 103, 373
  5th Division, 313, 331, 334
  7th Infantry Division, 103
  9th Division, 315

10th Division, 38
11th Division, 354, 419
12th Division, 325, 326
37th Brigade, 326
53rd Brigade, 325
13th Division, 143, 146
17th Division, 323, 324, 325, 326
19th Division, 318, 319
27th Division, 149
80th Brigade, 149
28th Division, 286, 296, 404, 417
29th Division, 29, 31, 128, 139, 144
31st Division, 300, 313, 318
32nd Division , 282
14th Brigade, 282
Major Lumsden's VC, 282-284
37th Division, 298, 304, 331, 334
42nd Division, 128, 132, 139, 334, 336
46th Division, 347
47th Division, 286, 297, 319, 322, 323, 324, 325
51st Division , 300, 301, 303
52nd Division, 135, 136, 137, 138, 337, 338, 342, 343, 347
155th Brigade, 135, 138
157th Brigade, 135, 136
56th Division, 354
57th Division, 336, 337, 338, 341, 342, 345, 348, 351, 353
172nd Brigade, 338
58th Division, 315
62nd Division, 318
Guards Division, 276, 318, 339, 342
3rd Brigade, Signal Section, 414
37th Brigade, 326
53rd Brigade, 325
87th Infantry Brigade, 116
155th Brigade, 135, 138
157th Brigade, 135, 136
168th Brigade, 354
188th Brigade, (see Royal Naval Division)
189th Brigade, (see Royal Naval Division)
190th Brigade, (see Royal Naval Division)
236th Brigade, 190
Army Service Corps (ASC), 246, 415, 416, 425
Artists, 322, 341, 343
Baluchi Battalion, 232
Bedfords, 295, 299, 328, 330, 341, 343
Berar Native Infantry, 217
Border Regiment, 32, 116
British West India Regiment, 252
Carbineers, 106
Cheshire Regiment, 452
Dorset Regiment, 215
Duke of Cornwall's Light Infantry, 13
Durham Light Infantry, 455
Dragoon Guards, 102
East African Brigade, 366
East African Batteries, 439
East African Rifles, 453
East Surrey Regiment, 196, 352
Essex Regiment, 309
Gold Coast Regiment, 225
Gordon Highlanders, 300, 304

Hampshire Regiment, 31
Herefordshire Regiment (Territorials), 452
Highland Light Infantry (HLI), 135, 137, 282
Honorable Artillery Company (HAC), 295, 304, 308, 309, 311, 314
Ghurkas, 257
King's African Rifles, 232, 364, 365, 451, 454
Kings Own Scottish Borderers (KOSB), 116, 117, 118
Kings Royal Rifle Corps(KRRC), 193, 318, 351
King's Shropshire Light Infantry, 287
Lancashire Fusiliers, 32, 128,
London Electrical Engineers (Territorials), 374
London Regiment (Territorials), 143, 144, 297, 328, 452, 455
Loyal North Lancashire Regiment, 365
Manchester Regiment, 85, 134, 336
Middlesex Regiment, 84, 85, 193, 305, 327, 328, 451, 454
Native Infantry, 215, 217, 227, 406
Oxfordshire Hussars Yeomanry, 101, 102, 416
Oxford and Bucks Light Infantry, 112, 322
Queen's, (Royal West Surrey) Regiment, 325
Queen's Westminster Rifles, 393
Rhodesian Rifles, 365
Rifle Brigade, 149, 308, 334
Royal Artillery (RA), 17, 286, 365, 377, 397
26th Heavy Artillery Group, 264, 269
Royal Dublin Fusiliers, 31, 295, 299
Royal Engineers (RE), 102, 162, 244, 292, 346, 413, 414, 415, 430
Royal Field Artillery (RFA), 149
Royal Fusiliers, 32, 116, 295, 322, 323, 327, 328, 333, 339, 343, 346, 356, 370
Royal Garrison Artillery (RGA), 240, 244, 377, 379, 388
Royal Horse Artillery (RHA), 367
Royal Inniskilling Fusiliers, 32, 116
Royal Irish Regiment, 329, 335, 337, 338, 343, 346, 348, 349, 350, 351, 355
Royal Malta Artillery, 389
Royal Munster and Royal Dublin Fusiliers, 31
Royal Scots, 76, 77, 315,
Royal Scots Fusiliers, 347
Royal East Kent Regiment (The Buffs), 325
Royal West Kent Regiment, 327
Sherwood Foresters, 305
South African Heavy Artillery, 390, 391
Cape Garrison Artillery, 390
South Wales Borderers, 13, 31, 116, 117, 118
Tank Corps, 376
Tyne Electrical Engineers, 411
West African Field Force, 452
West African Frontier Force, 220, 225

466

Index

West African Regiment, 232
Wiltshire Regiment, 453
Zanzibar Rifles, 228

British and Empire Army Officers
 Albert, Colonel (South African Forces), 391
 Allenby Sir E, General, 59
 Aspinall C, Lieutenant Colonel(Royal Munster Fusiliers), 295
 Athlone, The Earl of, Brigadier-General, 285
 Bangor Lord, Major, (RA), 112, 413
 Beves, General, 369
 Birdwood, General, 35, 120, 143
 Blacklock C A, Major-General (KRRC), 336, 355
 Bromfield, Lieutenant Colonel (Leicester Regiment), 318
 Botha, General, 18, 391
 Boyle R C, Major-General, 388
 Bridges W T, Major-General (Australian), 120
 Burne, Colonel (South African Forces), 367
 Byng Sir J, General, 328, 353
 Cable J F, Lieutenant Colonel (ASC), 424, 427, 457
 Campbell J S, Captain (RFA), 314
 Capper Sir T, General, 102
 Carey A B, Major (RE)(Temp Lieutenant Colonel RM) 112, 413, 414,
 Casement F, Captain (RAMC), 112, 418
 Chaytor E C, Lieutenant Colonel, (NZ forces), 103, 416, 417
 Clements, Colonel (RAMC), 421
 Coleridge J F, Brigadier-General (Indian Army), 318, 324, 326, 328
 Cox, General (Indian Army), 15,
 Crowe, Brigadier-General (Royal Artillery), 365, 366
 Cunliffe, General (Nigeria), 226
 Dark, 2nd Lieutenant (Royal West Kent Regiment), 328
 Davies F J, General, 141
 Delamain, General (Indian Army), 215
 Denikin, General, 64, 250
 Deventer, General, 366
 de Rougemont C H, Brigadier-General (RA), 296, 413
 Dobell C M, Major-General, 220
 Dunsterville L C, Major-General, 255
 Fergusson Sir C. Lieutenant-General, 336, 341, 353
 Floyd, Captain (RA), 369
 Forestier-Walker, Colonel (RA), 366, 367
 French Sir J, General, 373
 Freyberg B C, Colonel (Royal West Surrey Regiment) (see also Freyberg B C, Lieutenant RNVR), 301, 303
 Gaskill, Major (RGA), 377
 Gibb Sir A, Brigadier-General, 429, 430, 457, 465
 Gilpin, General (RASC), 374
 Gough, General, 317
 Grogan, Brigadier-General, 78, 80
 Haig Sir D, General, 58, 273, 299
 Hamilton Sir I, General, 28, 29, 35, 38, 116, 118, 141, 245

 Helyar, Lieutenant (RFA), 365
 Heneker, General, 299
 Hunter-Weston Sir A, General, 141
 Jack J, General, 91
 James W, Colonel, 429
 Kennedy-Craufurd-Stuart, Lieutenant Colonel (Indian Army), 132, 157
 Kitchener, Lord, 23, 38, 111
 Knox H O, Brigadier-General, (ASC), 429, 431
 Lawrie C E, Major-General (RA), 314, 336, 373
 Lecky, Colonel, 192
 Leslie, Brigadier-General, 330, 356
 Liddell A, Lieutenant Colonel (RASC), 296
 Liddell W, Lieutenant Colonel (ASC), 417
 Liddington W R, Captain (Oxfordshire Hussars), 416
 Mackenzie J H, Lieutenant Colonel, (Royal Scots), 336
 MacKenzie, General, 391
 Malleson, General, 365
 Marsh, Colonel, 189
 Maxwell W L, Major (Indian Army), 112
 Maynard E M M, Major-General, 73, 189, 193
 Milne, General, 59
 Monro Sir H (or C), General, 38, 139, 141
 Moore M C, Major (RGA), 378
 Morshead, Lieutenant Colonel, (West African Forces), 31
 North P W, Major, (Royal Berkshire Regiment), 285
 Oliver, Major (RGA), 378
 Ollivant A H, Lieutenant Colonel (RA), 103, 107, 111, 149
 O'Grady, General, 371
 Paris A C, Captain, (Oxford and Bucks Light Infantry), 112
 Poole Sir F C, Major-General, 73, 189
 Prentice G E, Brigadier-General (HLI), 295, 303, 307, 318
 Pretorious, Major, 369
 Pryce, Brigadier-General, 192
 Rarding, Lieutenant Colonel (69th Punjabis), 15
 Rawlinson, Lord H, General, 82, 103, 108, 194, 195, 199
 Richardson G S, Lieutenant Colonel, (NZ Forces), 106, 107, 112, 149
 Robinson, Battery Sergeant Major (RA), 378
 Rooke, Captain (RE), 106, 414
 Ryan, Major (RGA), 379
 Sadleir-Jackson L W, Brigadier-General, 78, 80, 81, 82, 83
 Saunders M, Major (Indian Army), 112
 Scammell Hon S T, Lieutenant (RAMC), 418
 Shimold, Lieutenant (Middlesex Regiment), 328
 Shute C D, Major-General, 298, 303
 Smith G, Major (KOSB), 251
 Smith H R, Second Lieutenant, (Royal West Kents), 328
 Smith-Dorrien Sir H, General, 364, 365
 Smuts Sir J C, General, 365, 367

 Smythe R R, Lieutenant Colonel, 336, 353
 Sparling, (Indian Army), 132
 Spragon, 2nd Lieutenant (Middlesex Regiment), 328
 Spinney, Lieutenant (Intelligence Corps), 305
 Strover, Major (RGA), 197
 Townshend Sir C, General, 59
 Tufnell, Brigadier-General, 144
 Twystleton-Wykeham-Fiennes (Oxford Hussars), 112
 Vibart M C, Captain, (RE), 327
 Walmesley G J T, Captain, (Berkshire Yeomanry), 112, 160
 Walter, Captain (Middlesex Regiment), 328
 Ward J, Colonel (Middlesex Regiment), 84, 85
 Wilberforce R. Major (Royal West Kent), 112
 Williams, Major, 196, 198
 Wintle, Major (96th Berar Native Infantry), 217
 Wrangel, General, 250,
 Wylie, Colonel (South African forces), 391
Browndown, 56, 97, 113, 163, 445
Bulgarians, 58, 149, 207, 384, 385

Canadian Forces, 18, 275, 278, 282, 308, 336, 337, 342, 353, 354, 355, 396
 1st Division, 338, 339
 3rd Division, 8th Brigade, 315, 316, 317
 4th Division, 342
 10th Brigade, 243
 40th Battalion, Canadian Expeditionary Force, 455
 Reserve Battalion, 455
Canadian Ross Rifle, 185, 441
Cape Helles, 27, 36, 39, 66, 116, 148, 245, 414, 419
Carson Sir E, 295
Casement Sir R, 394
Casualties, 1914 to 1919, Appendix 1, 450
Cato, Conrad, Preface
Chancellor Sir J (Governor of Trinidad), 252
Chemical Warfare Squadron, 436
Churchill, Winston, 101, 103, 104, 374
Clasps to the War Medal, Battles qualifying for issue , 92
Connaught, HRH The Duke of, 272, 403
Cross C H,Mr (Late Sergeant RMLI), 406, 457

Dartige du Tournet, Admiral (French Navy), 207
de Lacy, Mr, Preface, 175
de Fregate Millot, Capitaine (French Navy), 208
de Vaisseau Pugliesi-Conte, Capitaine (French Navy), 208
Deve, Lieutenant, (French Army), 210
Didier, General (Belgian Army), 403
Dowager Empress of Russia, 64
Durrant Smyth, A, 283

Elope Force, 77, 189, 190
Egyptian Army, 453

467

Falkland Islands, 6, 11, 16
Fierdoroff, Captain (Russian), 86
Finnish forces, 186, 187
   Finnish Legion, 184, 189, 190
   White Finns, 188
   Red Guards, 187, 188
Foch, General, 58, 330, 341
Foot, Mr A, 112
French Forces, 22, 29, 59, 64, 73, 75, 76, 84, 101, 103, 128, 134, 138, 143, 192, 208, 209, 210, 211, 212, 224, 225, 226, 342, 397, 404, 405, 406
   First French Army, 340
   1st French Division, 135, 144
   2nd French Division, 135, 144
   French Artillery, 137, 139, 143, 397, 401
   34th French Colonial Infantry, 208
   1st Battalion, 208
   2nd Battalion, 208
   3rd Battalion, 208
   French Marines, 187

Geddes E (First Lord of the Admiralty), 339
German Marine Corps, 13, 371, 399
Gouraud H, General (French Army), 341, 342
Greek Army Corps, 212
   Greek Division, 149
   Greek Labour Corps, 249

Hartlepool, 17, 237
Honours and Rewards
   All Decorations except DSM and MM, 23, 456-461
   All Foreign Decorations, 461-465
   Antwerp and Dunkirk Operations, 110-111
   Archangel, 83
   After Armistice for service in the Grand Fleet, 62-63
   Caspian Sea, 257
   Dardanelles per Mare, 39
   East Africa, 371-372
   France 1915-1918, 358-363
   Gallipoli, 157-160
   Kama River, 91
   Serbia, 386-387
   Siberia, 91
Horse Marines, 366
Hungarian, White Army, 406
Hussein, King of the Hedjaz, 213

Ibbet C E, Mr, 251
Imbros, 24, 27, 35, 36, 37, 38, 39, 58, 114, 141, 148, 244, 245, 246, 249, 250, 404, 405
Indian Forces, 17, 59, 213, 214, 215, 375
   29th Indian Brigade, 15, 35, 128
   21st Indian Cavalry, 366
   Indian Expeditionary Force, 17
   Indian Sappers and Miners, 369

Jackson, Sir John, 82
Japanese Forces, 13, 84
Japanese Rifle, 21, 441

Kama River (see River Operations)
Karelian Forces, 190, 193, 452
Kolchak, Admiral, (Russion Navy), 86

Lemnos, 24, 29, 112, 113, 114-147, 242-244, 248, 402, 417
Lowestoft, Bombardment of, 23

Malay States Volunteers, 407
Malta, 12, 24, 28, 29, 36, 113, 114, 244, 249, 363, 383, 385, 388
Maxim Gun, 65, 97, 139, 185, 205, 215, 218, 226, 296, 375, 376
Mead (Cricket Challenge) Cup, 143
Messina, 11, 12, 203
Michaeloopoulos, Mr, 247
Miles Cup, 56
Motor Maxim Squadron (RNAS), 120, 454
Mudros, 22, 24, 27, 29, 32, 35 39, 55, 58-59, 115-116, 148-149, 244-250, 256, 267, 295, 404, 406
Munro D.J. Captain, Cromarty Harbour Master, 237

New Zealand Forces, 127, 334
   New Zealand Brigade, 128, 345
   Otago Battalion, 124
Nicholas, The Grand Duke of Russia, 64
Noble, Mr (Dominica Civil Engineer), 252
Norper (North Persian) Force, 256

Polish Contingent, 189

Queen Alexandra, 139

Reuter von, Rear-Admiral (German Navy), 60
Roumanian Army, 406
Royal Fleet Reserve, 97, 435

Royal Marines Officers and Other Ranks
   Abigail, Lieutenant, 291
   Abraham G F, Captain, 451
   Ackerman A C, Lieutenant, 194
   Adair C W, Lieutenant, 51
   Adam E, Private, 462
   Adam J E, Lieutenant, 415
   Adams G, Sergeant, 460
   Adams J W, Private, 180
   Adams S R, Major, 112, 413
   Adamson M C, Captain, 139, 152
   Ainsworth S, Sergeant, 414
   Aheir A S, Corporal, 464
   Airey Hon H M, Lieutenant Colonel, 457
   Aitken R, Private, 224
   Albert, Colonel, 391
   Albury F A, Sergeant, 83
   Albury L F, Lieutenant, 343, 347
   Alcock A B F, Lieutenant, 120-122, 152, 155, 158, 159, 458
   Aldred W, Private, 421
   Aldridge D J, Lieutenant, 316, 417
   Alexander D, Sergeant, 428
   Alexander E K, Captain, 269
   Allan D N, Private, 460
   Allan G, Gunner, (promoted to Lieutenant), 48, 50
   Allard P, Captain, 417, 418
   Allard P W, Captain, 457
   Allen A E, Private, 69
   Allen J, Band Corporal, 160

   Allgood A, Gunner, 460
   Allison S A, Superintending Clerk, 460
   Allman F, Sergeant, 371, 372
   Aman D L, Captain, 285, 286, 289, 291, 293, 458
   Amos H C, Lieutenant, 155
   Amos J, Colour Sergeant, 362, 459
   Anderson B, Private, 464
   Anderton J M, Private, 423
   Andrews B G, Captain, 148, 329, 332, 334, 336, 362, 393
   Andrews C B, Captain, 114, 118, 128, 153, 154
   Andrews E L, Captain, 155, 328, 329, 336
   Andrews H, Private, 422
   Andrews S B, Sergeant, 414
   Angold H F, Lieutenant, 463
   Annion E, Sergeant, 427
   Antrobus H C, Quarter Master Sergeant, 459
   Apperley A B, Lieutenant, 426
   Archilbald J D, Private, 422
   Arkill J W, Gunner, 180
   Armstrong St G B, Lieutenant Colonel, 39, 160, 451, 456, 457, 462, 463
   Armstrong H G B, Major, 100, 102, 126, 151, 154, 159
   Armstrong O H, Lieutenant, 265
   Arnold W A, Sergeant, 66
   Arnold W C, Private, 361
   Artis W, Private, 361
   Ash W R, Gunner, 402
   Ashton J F T, Sergeant Major, 417, 460
   Aston Sir Geo, Brigadier-General, 98, 99, 100, 102, 103, 444
   Athow F, Major, 428, 451
   Atkins C J, Corporal, 458
   Atkins H, Private, 160, 462
   Atkinson H C, Captain, 364, 365, 366
   Atkinson T G, Lieutenant, 281, 311
   Attryde G H, Private, 69
   Attwood C, Major, Preface, 405
   Atwood A A, Sergeant, 459
   Aveling T C, Lieutenant Colonel, 112, 414, 415
   Avery H M, Mechanic, 281
   Avery, Quarter Master Sergeant, 276
   Bach S M J, Battery Sergeant Major, Preface, 364, 365, 367-370, 372
   Backhouse W J, Lieutenant, 377
   Backhouse, Sergeant, 392
   Bacon R H, Colonel (see also Rear Admiral Bacon), 261, 267, 269, 270
   Baddeley, Staff Paymaster, 170
   Bagge H, Sergeant, 427
   Bagot R W, Captain, 56
   Bailey C H, Lieutenant, 328, 358, 459
   Bailey J H, Sergeant, 180
   Baird J, Private, 360
   Baker C W E, Colour Sergeant, 160
   Baker F, Driver, 293
   Baker G W, Colour Sergeant, 417, 459
   Baker H, Lieutenant, 341
   Baker J, Driver, 290, 402
   Baker R F D, Lieutenant, 388, 389
   Baker W J, Sergeant, 180
   Baker-Carr, Major, 376
   Balcombe F C, 2nd Lieutenant, 316

Index

Balcombe A W, Sergeant, 464
Balfour A E, Captain, 418
Balsom A W, Private, 459
Bamber J B, Lance Sergeant, 360
Bamford E, Captain (VC), 42, 48, 52, 165, 167, 168, 172, 173, 178, 179, 456, 457, 462, 464
Banks A J, Sergeant Major, 359, 451, 459
Banks E J, Sergeant, 465
Barber C A, 2ns Lieutenant, 336
Barber C F, Major, 154
Barber J, Captain, 36
Barber, Lieutenant, 332
Bardsley H, Private, 461
Bareham A G, Lieutenant, 347, 352, 359, 393, 459
Barfield G L, Quarter Master Sergeant, Preface, 418, 421
Barford S W, Lance Corporal, 69
Barker A E, Private, 360, 421
Barker G, Captain, 102, 111, 128, 150, 154, 451
Barker T E, Corporal, 423
Barkley, Lieutenant, 444
Barlow H C, Sergeant, 48, 463
Barnard E D 'A, Lieutenant, 318, 341
Barnby A C, Captain, 194, 198 451, 463
Barnes A H, Sergeant Major, 418
Barnes G E, Major, 444, 457
Barnes J S (or J C), Lieutenant, 128 152, 154
Barnes W, Driver, 281
Barnes, Lieutenant, 289 291, 398
Barr E H, Major, 285, 290, 293, 458
Barraclough F, Private, 257
Barran J, Corporal, 423
Barrett D L, Colonel, 103, 439, 457
Barrington-Ward C W, Lieutenant, 270
Bartlett H G, Private, 214, 459, 462
Barton G, Company Sergeant Major, 402, 461
Barton H C, Sergeant, 464
Barwick G W, Superintending Clerk, 460
Baseby B, Lieutenant, 399, 402, 458, 461
Baseley F, Staff Sergeant, 459
Bassett S J, Captain, 250
Bastin E, Captain, 143, 159, 296, 301
Bastin E, Acting Sergeant Major, 154
Bate G, Corporal, 461
Bates J R, Lieutenant, 341
Bath J A, Captain, 50, 84, 86, 458, 463
Batt F C, Gunner, 464
Battin J, Lieutenant, 97, 152
Baugh A, Colour Sergeant, 460
Baverstock, Driver, 281
Baxter B, Sergeant, 461
Baxter E, Sergeant, 428
Bayliff R L, Lieutenant Colonel, 451
Beale B P, Sergeant, 402
Beard C H, Gunner, 48, 463
Beasley G W, Lieutenant, 194
Beatson J, Sergeant, 427
Beaumont G L, Major, 451, 457, 463
Bebgie W H, Lieutenant, 388
Beer W C, Private, 361
Beere A J, Lieutenant, 279
Beere H E, Captain, 250, 445
Beith R D, Lieutenant Colonel, 100, 104, 116

Bell A E, Private, 361
Bell A I, Captain, 457
Bell C R, Private, 158, 160
Bell E T, Private, 361
Bell G W, Private, 361
Bell J, Gunner, 39
Bell R, Acting Sergeant Major, 158, 160
Bell R, Lieutenant, 363
Bell, Captain, 393
Beloe W, Lieutenant, 415
Bendyshe R N, Lieutenant Colonel, 111, 116, 122, 124, 153, 154
Benett H C, Major, 252, 454
Benham F E, Lieutenant, 391
Bennett E, Gunner, 281, 461
Bennett M F, Major, 56
Bennett M, Private, 422
Bennett W N, Sergeant, 360
Bennie H E, Lieutenant, 307, 393, 394
Benning S E, Private, 69
Benson J, Sergeant Major, 459
Beresford, Lord C, Hon Colonel (see also Admiral Beresford), 313
Beresford E, Corporal, 361
Beresford J, Gunner, 294
Berger, 2nd Lieutenant, 328
Berrington J, Lieutenant, 286
Berrington D, Lieutenant, 288
Berry E, Private, 159, 360
Berry H A P de, Lieutenant, 167, 168, 173, 180
Berry P, Private, 158
Berry S, Corporal, 281
Best E, Sapper, 415
Bevan E A, Gunner, 281
Bewes A E, Major, 39, 106, 111, 115, 117, 118, 153, 155, 157, 160, 456
Bickford, Colonel, 397
Billing C G, Captain, 130, 154, 254
Bing, 2nd Lieutenant, 328
Binney A F, Major, 240
Binney W E Major, 451
Binns C E, Major, 462, 463
Bird C E, Private, 387, 465
Bird F W, Sergeant, 464
Bishop A G, Lieutenant, 21
Bishop C A, 2nd Lieutenant, 461
Bishop E L, Lieutenant, 50
Bisiker W J, Lieutenant, 194
Bissett O D, Lieutenant, 152
Black H, Private, 423
Black C J T, Lieutenant, 151
Black H C T, Lieutenant, 154
Black J C, Lieutenant, 124
Blackburn R, 2nd Lieutenant, 327
Blackley P, Gunner, 464
Blackman W, Major, 457
Blackman W E C, Sergeant, 461
Blake C S, Corporal, 415
Blake L A, Conductor, 418, 459
Blanchflower W, Private, 422
Bland R, Corporal, 281
Blount H, Major, 48, 51, 458, 464
Bloxsom W C 2nd Lieutenant, 167, 168, 176
Blumberg F T, Captain, 412, 457
Blumberg H E, Colonel, 107, 247, 250, 393, 436, 440, 443, 451, 456, 462, 463
Blundell W G, Corporal, 275, 281

Blunt C A, Lieutenant, 50, 57, 265, 279
Blythe C J, Company Sergeant Major, 460
Blythe F, Private, 361
Board D, Sergeant Major, 194, 198
Bockett-Pugh E H, Captain, 246
Boffey H, Lieutenant, 269, 270, 281
Boffey H, RM Gunner, 405
Boffey T W, Colour Sergeant, 23
Boissier G M, Lieutenant, 265, 270
Bolan J H, Lance Corporal, 360
Bollam C, Lieutenant, 415
Bolton E T, Private, 193
Bolton H, Sergeant, 384, 386, 465
Bolton, Gunner, 369
Bonnet E C, Sergeant, 134, 158,
Bonnett E C, Lieutenant, 316
Booth D, Staff Sergeant, 419, 421, 459
Booth E, Private, 360
Booth R W, Private, 360
Borthwick H, Lieutenant, 418
Botterill F O, R.M. Gunner, 51, 62, 457
Bottomley W, Sapper, 414
Boucher, Lieutenant, 329
Boultbee W R, Captain, 194, 254
Boulton F M E, Sergeant, 461
Boulton G, Colour Sergeant, 451
Bourne A G B, Major, 51, 451, 458, 463
Bowen A E, Sergeant, 62, 67
Bowen F C, Lieutenant, 111
Boxall W H, 2nd Lieutenant, 167, 168
Boyd M, Private, 427
Boyle A, Lieutenant, 393, 394
Brace C D, Private, 39
Braddock C J, Acting Sergeant, 122, 158, 159, 459
Bradley G T, Corporal, 422, 423
Bradley W, Lance Corporal, 230
Bradly J B, 2nd Lieutenant, 426
Bradshaw R M, Lieutenant, 364, 451
Braid, Lieutenant, 328
Bramall F M, Lieutenant, 194
Bramble J J, Major, 462
Branch A C, Sergeant, 415
Branske R B, Gunner, 13
Branston G P, Corporal, 224, 372
Brattle S W, Gunner, 69
Brett F J, Captain, 253
Brewer H R, Major, 17, 78, 83
Bridge C D, Major, 270
Bridges F D, Lieutenant Colonel, 130, 132, 246, 404, 405, 415, 416, 456
Brien C P, Sergeant, 422
Briggs H, Corporal, 461
Brighten F J, Bombardier, 276, 281
Brindley E A, Lieutenant, 347
Brindley W, Private, 334, 359, 459
Briscoe L D, Major, Preface, 49, 293, 464
Bristow A H, Gunner, 292, 293
Brittan C G, Colonel, 107, 443, 446, 451, 456
Britton J, Sergeant Major, 153, 157
Broadbridge W, Sergeant, 49, 460
Broadwood D, Lieutenant, 162, 165, 167, 168, 174, 180
Brockman E St J, Lieutenant, 194, 198
Brogan T W, 2nd Lieutenant, 317
Brookbank J, Sergeant, 461

469

Brooke C, Sergeant, 423
Brooke C L, Colonel, 240, 436, 443, 456
Brookes H J, Gunner, 400
Brooks J H, Colour Sergeant, 256, 254
Brooke-Short C, Lieutenant, 151, 156
Brooks R, R.M. Gunner, 50
Brooks T, Private, 423
Brough J, Major, 451, 456
Broughton A W D, Captain, 47, 51
Brown, Bombardier, 40
Brown A E, Major, 443
Brown C T, Captain, Preface, 50, 187, 185, 457
Brown E G, Gunner, 461
Brown F, Private, 426, 427, 459
Brown H C, 2nd Lieutenant, 306
Brown H M, Lieutenant, 51
Brown J, Private, 91, 460
Brown J, Sergeant, 36, 459
Brown J E, Private, 68, 458
Brown N F, Corporal, 281
Brown V C, Captain, 185, 186, 388, 389, 396, 458
Brown W, Lance Corporal, 68, 69
Brown W, Gunner, 463
Brown W C, Lance Corporal, 5
Brown W J, Private, 417, 423
Brown W McK, Superintending Clerk, 460
Browne M C, Captain, 137, 143, 152, 155, 157, 160, 300, 458
Brown-King J, Private, 12
Brownlow, Colonel, 407
Brownrigg A H, Lieutenant, 281
Bruce G H, Sergeant, 111, 159, 461
Brugnier P E, Private, 160
Bryan C, Battery Sergeant Major, 188, 193, 294, 460
Bryan W R, Colour Sergeant, 402
Bryant, Lieutenant, 401
Buckland F, RM. Gunner, 50
Buckle P S W, Sergeant, 427, 460
Buckle, Lieutenant Colonel
Buckley T, Captain, 322, 329, 332, 334, 335, 336, 339, 341, 345, 356, 358, 459
Bucknall S W, Captain, Preface, 240, 242
Budd A J, Sergeant, 17
Budd C P, Acting Sergeant, 174, 180
Bull S, Sergeant, 294
Bullard D, Gunner, 459
Bullen W H, Private, 360
Bullock G, Lieutenant, 72, 383, 384, 385, 386, 465
Bunyan D'Arcy, Lieutenant, 249, 406
Burchell J H P, Sapper, 415
Burge N O, Major, 107, 111, 138, 146, 150, 158, 159, 296, 301, 451
Burke D, Gunner, 461
Burley G, Colour Sergeant, 23
Burley J T, Sergeant, 464
Burn G A, Sergeant, 415
Burnett E E, Corporal, 361
Burnley H, Colour Sergeant, 460
Burns A W, Lieutenant, 427
Burns R, Private, 62
Burnside F M, Captain, 269, 279, 279
Burnsside (or Burnside) G E M, Lieutenant, 281, 277, 279

Burrage H J or G, Lieutenant, 242, 457
Burrell E L, Lieutenant, 417
Burt G, Superintending Clerk, 458
Burt R C, Sergeant, 178
Burton C R, 2nd Lieutenant, 306
Burton R G, Captain, 26, 28, 76, 78, 154, 194, 197, 198, 318, 320, 456
Burton T H, Captain, 100, 143, 153, 160, 295, 329, 331, 356, 358, 458
Burton-Fanning N E, Captain, 152, 311
Bury W R, Colour Sergeant, 460
Bush J, Captain, 121, 153
Bushnell J, Sergeant Major, 360
Butchers A S, Gunner, 281
Butler A M, Quarter Master Sergeant, 362, 460
Butler C, Sergeant, 188, 190, 460, 462, 464
Butler J H, Gunner, 461
Butt S W V, Private, 160
Button E, Gunner, 464
Byne R M, Major, 451, 457
Caffyn, Lieutenant, 406
Cailes S E, 2nd Lieutenant, 327
Caird S, Private, 459
Callaway H C B, Corporal, 294
Cameron J, R.M. Gunner, 17, 51, 62, 457
Camfield H, Colour Sergeant, 461
Campbell A, Gunner, 402
Campbell G M, Lieutenant Colonel, 97, 110, 456
Campbell J, Lieutenant, 304, 311
Campbell R H, Captain, 50, 327, 328, 330, 332, 336, 358, 459
Cantrell A S, Major, 50, 55, 462
Carey W S, Sergeant, 351, 359, 459
Carle P L de, Corporal, 461
Carlton W, Acting Sergeant Major, 459
Carlyle J, Lance Corporal, 421
Carpenter E B, Lieutenant, 128, 141, 152, 154, 155
Carpenter G, Captain, Preface, 216, 217, 218, 458
Carpenter R J, Captain, 111, 132, 150, 159, 451, 562
Carr B J (or J B), Staff Sergeant, 419, 421, 460
Carroll J W, Lieutenant, 155, 423, 425, 462
Carron J, Lieutenant, 150
Carter D B, Captain, 152, 194, 197
Carter H, Sergeant, 230
Carter H J, Gunner, 384, 386, 387, 465
Carter J H, Sergeant, 361
Cartwright F J W, Lieutenant Colonel, 293, 295, 298, 299, 301, 302, 304, 307, 309, 311, 360, 456
Cartwright V H, Colonel, 283, 285, 286, 289, 290, 291 293, 456, 460
Carus-Wilson C C, Captain, 269, 280, 459
Carvell R C, 2nd Lieutenant, 188, 190
Cassell E, Private, 464
Castley H, Private, 360
Catley C, R.M. Gunner, 17, 41, 47, 51
Cator R, Lieutenant Colonel, 240, 242, 424, 425, 426, 457
Cattle S J, Gunner, 460
Caulfield St G F G, Major, 464

Causton, Hon J, Lieutenant Colonel, 457
Chadwick H, Corporal, 422
Chaffe A H, Private, 460
Chamberlain E G, Gunner, 293
Champness R E, 2nd Lieutenant, 306
Chancellor J B, Major, 397, 398, 402, 461
Channer H W, Major, Preface, 130, 132, 135, 137, 155, 159, 462, 463
Chapman C L, Major, 417, 418
Chapman F P, Sergeant, 209
Chapman F P, Bugler, 462
Chapman F S, Sergeant, 211, 294
Chapman J G, Sergeant, 427
Chapman, Sergeant Major, 311
Chater A R, Captain, 110, 132, 150, 159, 161, 166, 167, 168, 172, 180, 458, 462
Chater H E, Lieutenant, 347
Chatfield A, Sergeant, 281
Chave A C, Sergeant, 461
Chave W, Colour Sergeant, 281
Cheesman C H, Gunner, 464
Cheetham J, Lieutenant, 122, 134,151,156,156, 159, 393, 458
Chichester F E, Colonel, 56, 103, 161, 445
Child J J, Colour Sergeant, 459
Child (or Childs) T W, Lance Corporal, 351, 359
Childs P W, Lance Corporal, 459
Chisholm J C (or J R), Private, 423
Chivers A J (or A T), Major, 112, 413
Chivers F J, Lieutenant, 243
Chouffot A, Sergeant, 376
Chown E E, Colonel, 446, 456
Chubb N H (or W H), Sergeant, 415, 458
Church J, Sergeant, 427
Churchill-Smith H, Lieutenant, 459
Churchyard, Lieutenant, 373, 374, 375
Clanchy, Lieutenant, 247
Clark C B, Private, 427
Clark E N, Private, 423
Clark F G, Private, 23
Clark J, Sergeant, 372, 460
Clark J A, Major, 120, 124, 126, 159, 404, 405
Clark J A M A, Major, Preface, 124, 152, 155, 158, 246, 393, 394, 393, 457, 463
Clark S, Private, 422
Clark W de T L, Captain, 137, 155, 246
Clarke A G, Private, 173, 180
Clarke C, Lieutenant Colonel, 457
Clarke F G, Private
Clarke M, R.M.Gunner, 50
Clarke T H, Acting Sergeant Major, 153
Clarke W E, Private, 361
Clarke W T, Battery Sergeant Major, 290, 293
Clarke, Captain, 299
Claudet B S, Lieutenant, 167, 168
Cleemy T W, Private, 423
Clements W S, Lance Corporal, 69
Clerk C F, Private, 69
Clerk J, Sergeant, 48
Clewes W, Sergeant, 461
Clogg E L, Lieutenant, 461
Clutterbuck N S, Major, 51, 319, 320, 323, 325, 328, 334, 355, 358, 362, 458
Coen W J, Colour Sergeant, 402
Cohen E, Lieutenant, 143, 300

INDEX

Colan O J, Sergeant, 134, 460
Colgan, Gunner, 188
Collard C E, Colonel, 20, 21, 47, 50, 242, 243, 456, 464
Collet C H, Captain, 18, 37, 155, 451, 457
Collet M H, Captain, 269, 279, 280, 458
Colley P H, Captain, 50
Collier E W, Lieutenant, 320, 321, 327, 358, 459
Collier, Corporal, 36
Collins F T, Company Sergeant Major, 359
Collinson J, Private, 360
Colquhom R C, Major, 16
Compston R, Corporal, 423
Compton-Mackenzie E M, Captain, 457, 462, 465
Comyns C W, Lieutenant, 461
Congdon C H, Lieutenant, 18, 32, 50, 130, 462
Connew T F(or F T), Lieutenant, 230,232, 367, 397, 402, 461
Connolly A M, Major, 18
Conway-Gordon L, Lieutenant Colonel, 237, 456
Conybeare C B(or C G), Captain, 102, 139, 153, 155, 159, 162, 165, 168, 173, 176, 461, 462
Coode C H, Lieutenant, Preface, 98, 99, 100, 108, 317, 318, 319, 391
Cook , Sergeant, Preface, 115
Cook F, Superintending-Clerk, 362, 459
Cook F, Company Sergeant Major, 461
Cook J, Private, 211, 212, 462
Cook J W, Sergeant, 427
Cook (or Cooke) W E, Major, 417, 418, 457
Cook W J, Colour Sergeant, 111, 461
Cooke T V F(or T F V), Lieutenant, 167, 168, 172, 173, 176, 180, 458, 463
Cooper A, Private, 363
Cooper F, Private, 361
Cooper G J, Colour Sergeant, 460
Cooper J, Captain, 427
Cooper J, Gunner, 461, 464
Cooper W, Private, 227
Cooper W G, Colour Sergeant, 459
Cope M F, Lieutenant, 461
Cope, Lieutenant, 402
Copland E G, Sergeant, 461
Cordner A A, Major, 161, 167, 168, 172, 176, 180
Cornish J E, Lieutenant, 316
Costa D, 2nd Lieutenant, 251
Coulson E G, 2nd Lieutenant, 306
Coulthard J W, Corporal, 345, 359, 463
Courtney I T, Lieutenant Colonel, 457, 462, 463, 464
Covell A, Sergeant, 423
Coward C F, Quarter Master Sergeant, 460
Cowton A E, Corporal, 460
Cox A B, Sergeant, 62
Cox C, Lance Corporal, 363
Cox F, Sergeant, 49, 463
Cox R W, Gunner, 461
Cox V L, Sergeant, 461
Coyne P, Private, 360

Crabtree J H, Sergeant, 419, 423, 459
Crafts A E, Private, 257
Craig A M, Captain, 457
Craig F, Private, 363
Craig W, Corporal, 181
Craig W D, Major, 63, 184, 188, 189, 190, 191
Craik G K, Sergeant, 417
Cramer, Captain, 411, 412
Craven C, Captain, 269, 270, 278, 279
Crawley C G, Captain, 6,
Crawley C G, Lieutenant Colonel, 465
Crawley E A, Gunner, 48
Crawley F, Sergeant, 461, 459
Creed A E, Lieutenant, 336
Creedon J, R.M. Gunner, 50
Crehan M, Private, 422
Crick C, Lieutenant, 215
Crick G M, Lieutenant, 29, 393, 394, 395
Cridland J P, Corporal, 84, 86, 222, 224
Croft W O, Bombardier, 371, 372, 460
Croke W D, Sergeant, 361
Crook A E, Private, 360
Crook J, Private, 423
Crosby G, Gunner, 461
Cross F, Corporal, 280, 459
Cross W, Major, 426
Cruddas S, Captain, 50
Cuff E A, Gunner, 464
Cuffe J A F, Captain, 462
Cullimore, Captain, 407
Cuming T C, Captain, 269, 269, 281, 458
Cumiskey C F, Corporal, 360, 461
Cunningham T, Colour Sergeant, 111
Cunnington G H, Private, 69
Curran J C P, Lieutenant, 332, 336, 356, 359, 459
Curry R, Private, 417
Curtin M, Lieutenant, 108, 111, 122, 124, 151, 154
Curtis G R, Lieutenant, 111, 150, 155
Curtis J O, Lieutenant, 313
Curtis S M, Bombardier, 281
Curtis S W, Bombardier, 69
Curtis W E, Sapper, 415
Curtis W M, Lieutenant, 362
Curtoys C E, Colonel, 446, 456
Cutcher G E, Captain, 305, 307, 362
Daborn W, Private, 159
Dacombe S G, Battery Sergeant Major, 391, 392, 459
Dadd C, Battery Sergeant Major, 280, 459
D'Albiac J H, Lieutenant, 452, 457
Dale L W, Gunner, 461
Daley M G, Gunner, 461
Dallas-Brooks R A, Major, 121, 151, 155, 159, 161, 162, 165, 167, 168, 171, 172, 180, 458, 462
Damant E L, Sapper, 415
Dance W, Gunner, 181
Daniell A H, Corporal, 461
Daniell J F, Major-General, 220, 451, 456
Darlow H, Superintending Clerk, 460
Darlow W J, Acting Superintending Clerk, 460
Darlow W J, Actng Sergeant Major, 160, 461
Darwall R H, Lieutenant Colonel, 458, 462

Dash F W, Sergeant, 462
Dashwood E, Lieutenant, 265
Dauntesey W B, Lieutenant Colonel, 452, 457
Davidson C, Corporal, 427
Davidson W, Sergeant, 417, 460
Davies G, Private, 311, 359, 459
Davies S E, Gunner, 386, 387, 465
Davis, Gunner, 384
Davis F N, Colour Sergeant, 464
Davis J, Private, 422
Davis W, Battery Sergeant Major, 391, 392, 459
Dawson A P, Captain, 232
Day H A, Quartermaster & Honorary Lieutenant, 418
Day H M, Lieutenant, 60, 458
de Strother R L, Captain, 50, 167, 168, 176
Dean C, Private, 422
Dean (or Deane) E V, Corporal, 230, 459, 463
Dean, 2nd Lieutenant, 329
Dean, Private, 206
Deane T A D, 2nd Lieutenant, 126, 151, 154
Deaton F, 2nd Lieutenant, 327
Deed J C, Captain, 19
Delves-Broughton A W, Captain, 46
Denash F J, Sergeant, 464
Denman-Dean G W, Lieutenant, 318
Dennis W, Private, 228, 230
Dennison J D, Captain, 240, 242
Denyer D G, Lance Corporal, 158
Devitt J, Colour Sergeant, 148
Dewar L J, Lieutenant, 301
Dewar P, Lieutenant, 300
Dewhurst A, Sergeant, 460
Dewhurst F W, Lieutenant, 153, 160
Dewhurst R, Sergeant, 362
Dibblee F L, Lieutenant Colonel, 50, 464
Dick J, Sergeant, 427
Dick T S, Major, 280, 458
Diggle E, Quarter Master Sergeant, 362, 460
Dillon J, Lance Corporal, 422
Dimmer J F, Lieutenant Colonel, 435, 443, 457
Dingli A, Major, 444, 457
Ditchburn F, Private, 422
Dix J, Sergeant, 62
Dixon E, Corporal, 361
Dixon W, Lieutenant Colonel, 253, 456
Dobson F H, Lance Corporal, 360
Dockett F, Private, 69
Dodd C, Colour Sergeant 460
Doherty R, Private, 417
Dollery W H, 2nd Lieutenant, 167, 168, 176
Domville C G T, Lieutenant, 152
Donkin J, Private, 360
Donne A C, Lieutenant, 143, 300, 306
Donovan F E, Corporal, 362
Dougherty E C B (or E B C), Lieutenant, 137, 152, 154, 160
Douglas W J, Major, 462
Doull B, Sergeant, 427
Dowding A H(or A W), Private, 362, 460

471

Dowding B, Major, 57, 393
Downey S, Private, 159
Downie J, Lance Corporal, 362, 423
Downing, Captain, 251
Dowson E, Private, 160
Drage G, Major, 452, 458
Drake G D, Colonel, 451
Drake-Brockman C E F, Lieutenant Colonel, 429
Drake-Brockman L A, Captain, 188, 190, 193, 452
Drape J, Gunner, 461
Driscoll W E, Sergeant, 460
Druce J S, Gunner, 36, 39
Drury W P, Colonel, 457
Duckling G H W, Private, 459
Duckworth A R, Private, 159
Duckworth E, Sergeant, 459
Dugon A L, Lieutenant, 417, 457
Duke W J, Private, 360
Dumble, Lieutenant Colonel, 373, 375
Dunkley R, Private, 419
Dunkley, Lieutenant, 289
Dunn D T, Sergeant, 464
Dunn H H, Private, 69
Dunn J C, Sergeantm 158, 160, 300
Dunstall A G, Gunner, 461
Durham F H, Lieutenant, 377
Durrant C M, Captain, 242
Dutton A B L, Sergeant, 415
Dutton D, Private, 359
Dyer T W, Captain, 452
Dyer W P, Captain, 396
Dyer W S, Sergeant, 13
Eade A M, Quarter Master Sergeant, 460
Eady F W, Major, 457
Eagles C E, Major, 130, 145, 165, 168, 174, 176, 180, 295, 298, 301, 358, 362, 458
Eastaway H J, Sergeant, 427, 460
Easterbrook S S, 2nd Lieutenant, 316
Easterman E J, Lieutenant, 51
Eastman H S G, Lieutenant, 194
Eastwood C, Private, 423
Eaves A T, Sergeant, 360
Eccles D E, Company Sergeant Major, 426, 427, 460
Eddisbury G, Corporal, 148
Edmunds H W, RM Gunner, 50
Edmunds R, Serbeatn, 464
Edmundson D, Private, 422
Edward E, Quarter Master Sergeant, 461
Edwards E E, Company Sergeant Major, 402, 460
Edwards F C, Lieutenant Colonel, 243
Edwards J J, Acting Sergeant Major, 362, 460
Edwards T, Captain, 114, 145, 153, 155, 201, 317
Edwin C F, Lieutenant, 414
Egan C V, 2nd Lieutenant, 327
Eldridge E, Private, 463
Eliot, Hon C E C, Lieutenant Colonel, 164
Eliot F G, Captain, 324, 329, 343, 347, 359, 362, 459, 462
Elliot B N, Lieutenant Colonel, 161, 164, 165, 167, 168, 172, 176, 178, 180, 383-386, 458, 465

Elliot C E C, Lieutenant Colonel, 457
Elliot M, Staff Sergeant, 422
Elliott A E, RM Gunner, 51
Elliott G W, Private, 360
Elliott L J, Private, 297, 359, 459
Elliott W C A, Lieutenant, 297
Elliott W S, Sergeant, 23
Ellis C, Quarter Master Sergeant, 460
Ellis F, Gunner, 372
Ellis G H, Lance Corporal, 361
Ellis H, Private, 69
Ellis J, Private, 464
Ellison J F, Lieutenant, Preface, 152, 155, 364, 365, 367, 370, 371, 372, 458
Elmes W G, Lieutenant, 352
Elphick H N, Lieutenant, 265, 280, 458
Emmerson R T, Private, 422
Emmett R, Lance Corporal, 23
Empson R W H, Lieutenant, 120, 121, 124, 152, 154, 159
Englefield T C, Gunner, 281
English J, Corporal, 427
Epton J, Private, 69
Erskine F A, 2nd Lieutenant, 126, 152, 154, 160
Esson W, Major, 23
Evans A K, Major, 130, 143, 160, 295, 358, 363, 452, 457, 459
Evans E, Staff Clerk, 460
Evans F C, Corporal, 423
Evans G, Captain, 285, 287, 288, 291, 293, 458
Evans H, Sergeant Major, 421
Evans H C, Major, 242
Evans H L, Sergeant, 361
Evans J, Private, 181
Evans T J P, Major-General, 452
Evans, Lieutenant, 311
Evanson B G, Captain, 318
Evelegh E G, Lieutenant Colonel, 100, 111, 124, 127, 132, 137, 138, 150, 154, 159, 452
Eveleigh P F, Corporal, 87
Everill, Motor Cyclist, 287
Eves C E, Lieutenant, 347
Facer H E, Lance Corporal, 69
Fairs W H, Sergeant, 48
Faithful W E, Bandmaster, 116, 159
Farmer F, Private, 159
Farmer J C, Major, 6, 130, 160, 452, 464, 465
Farquarson (or Farquharson) C G, Captain, 139, 145, 159, 295, 301, 303, 313, 318, 319, 327, 358, 458
Farquharson H D, Lieutenant Colonel, 97, 98, 100, 107, 321, 452, 457, 462
Fathers J B, Corporal, 414
Fawcett E C, Lieutenant, 153, 389
Fawcett H, Major, 184, 185, 452
Feeny C J, Sergeant Major, 415
Fell, Battery Sergeant Major, 379
Feltham S H, Private, 361
Felton E T, Private, 422
Fenton A, Gunner, 62
Ferguson H N, Sergeant, 427
Ferguson J W, Sergeant, 422
Ferguson-Davie F G, 2nd Lieutenant, 124, 151, 154

Ferriday E, Private, 422
Festing M C, Major, 98, 107, 111, 112, 126, 134, 150, 158, 159, 295, 358, 362, 443, 452, 458, 463
Field C, Colonel, Preface, 13, 177, 452
Field G H, RM Gunner, 41, 47, 51
Field J W, Bombardier, 464
Field S A, Lieutenant, 50
Fielden, 2nd Lieutenant, 320
Fielding J, Lieutenant, 362
Fields J W, Private, 372
Fiennes C W, Lieutenant, 143, 153, 160
Filmer-Bennett M, Major, Preface, 50
Finch G, Corporal, 23
Finch N A, Sergeant (VC), 172, 178, 183, 456
Finlaison J B, Brigadier-General,17, 250, 393, 395, 446, 447, 457
Finnegan W W, Colour Sergeant, 49
Firth F, Private, 257
Fish A E K, Gunner, 465
Fish H T H (or A T H), Gunner, 386, 387, 465
Fisher A B, Sergeant, 427
Fisher C T, Major, 452
Fisher H, Sergeant, 464
Fisher J E, Private, 422
Fitton E, Private, 422
Fitton R, Sergeant, 421
Flannagan W J, Sergeant Major, 445, 461
Flawn F, Sergeant Major
Flaye E, Lieutenant, 265
Flaye, Sergeant Major , 391
Fleet C J, Private, 111
Fletcher C, Private, 361
Fletcher E K, Lieutenant Colonel, 50, 313, 319, 320, 325, 327-334, 336, 358, 362, 458
Fletcher H, Private, 423
Flippence A G S, Musician, 48
Flower J E, Lieutenant (former RM Gunner), 48, 51, 247, 329, 336
Foote C G, Lieutenant, 102,106, 110, 111
Ford A R, Corporal, 363
Ford R T, Lieutenant Colonel, 398, 402, 443, 457
Ford W H, Lieutenant, 353
Forsyth T (or E), Corporal, 280, 459
Fortescue M, Sergeant, 419, 423
Forster A L, Captain, Preface, 97, 285, 286, 287, 289, 290, 293, 457
Foster L L, Captain, 269, 280, 281, 458
Foster R, Private, 362
Foster R F C, Colonel, 107, 295, 336, 358, 362, 443, 452, 458, 461
Foster, Lieutenant, 277
Foster, Major, 279
Fouracre W J, Colour Sergeant, 230
Fowler R H, Captain, 457
Fox R H, Lieutenant, 285, 289
France W H, Sergeant, 62
Frankis W W, Major, 31, 39
Frankland H R S, Corporal, 363, 459
Franklin C, Major, 457
Franklyn J, Lieutenant, 194, 269, 280, 458
Franks H M, Captain, 5, 48
Franks T C, Sergeant, 111, 461
Freeman F A, Staff Clerk, 460

Index

French A H, Lieutenant Colonel, 110, 111, 112, 150, 160 , 452, 457, 463
French B, Corporal, 148
French F J, Major, 364, 365, 366, 452
French J N, Gunner, 69
Frew W, Gunner, 281
Friend G J (or E J), Private, 78, 460
Frossard H L, Lieutenant, 153, 156
Fry F, Private, 386, 387, 465
Fry G, Sergeant, 463
Fry W, Gunner, 464
Fuller H V, Captain, 426, 427, 458
Fuller W, Sergeant, 427
Fulton, J H C, Lieutenant, 126, 151, 154
Fulton R, Gunner, 281
Fulton R, Sergeant, 460
Gaitskell S, Lieutenant Colonel, 253
Galliford J T, Sergeant Major, 111, 150
Galloway F, Private, 227
Gamble C A, Driver, 281
Gannon G W, Corporal, 360
Ganner A E, Corporal, 462
Garbe F J, Superintending Clerk, 460
Gardiner B C, Lieutenant Colonel, 5, 55, 56, 62, 456
Gardner E C, Sergeant Major, 362
Gardner G, Sergeant, 160
Gardner H, 2nd Lieutenant, Preface, 169, 230, 232, 238, 367, 370, 371, 372
Gardner T C, Quarter Master Sergeant, 460
Gardner W H, Corporal, 361
Garnett, Lieutenant, 301
Garnham W F, Sergeant, 415
Garnier W, Major, 445
Garrett G D, Lieutenant, 134,151
Garrett J R, Lieutenant Colonel, 457
Gates H W, Gunner, 460
Gates J A, Lieutenant, 160
Gayner, Lieutenant, 319
Gazeley W, RM Gunner, 50
Geary W G, Private, 63, 193
Geldart J, Captain, 5, 39
Gellatly E W, Driver, 281
George W, Acting Sergeant Major, 460
George W, RM Gunner, 48, 461
Gerrard E L, Lieutenant Colonel, 37, 157, 452, 456, 458, 461
Getting S T, Sergeant, 419
Gibbons C, Captain, 322, 327
Gibbs C J, Acting Sergeant Major, 152, 157, 159
Gibson A, Lieutenant, 97
Gibson F M, 2nd Lieutenant, 238
Gibson R S, Major, 462
Gilbert C F G, Private, 360, 462
Gilbert M K, 2nd Lieutenant, 427
Gill E, Private, 360
Gill E H, Major, 426, 427
Gill J, Private, 70
Gillespie H E, Major, 5, 23, 50, 62, 457, 458
Gillespie W, Private, 180
Gilliat J, 2nd Lieutenant, 375
Gillman J G W, Lieutenant, 263
Gingell H, Private, 193
Girdlestone W C, 2nd Lieutenant, 306
Glass, Driver, 293, 294

Glunicke R C A, Captain, Preface, 18, 364, 365, 366, 372, 462
Godfray A D B, Captain
Godfrey C G de B, Lieutenant, 194
Godfrey E A, 2nd Lieutenant, 311, 358, 459
Godfrey F R, Lieutenant Colonel, 87, 103, 130, 135, 138, 150
Godfrey H, Private, 360
Godfrey W W, Lieutenant Colonel, 6, 39, 452, 456, 462, 463,464
Godsell E F, Colour Sergeant, 460
Goff E J, Bombardier, 281
Goldie F, 2nd Lieutenant, 300, 362
Golding R, Acting Quarter Master Sergeant, 460
Goldingham G R, Lieutenant, 296, 301, 317, 358, 362, 459
Goldring T A, Sergeant Major , 153
Goldring T A, Captain, 160, 301
Goldsmith, J, Captain, 219, 220, 222, 223, 224, 308, 309, 311
Goodden C P, Lieutenant, 71, 153
Gog R, Sergeant, 426, 427, 459
Goodwin H S, Gunner, 461
Goodwin S, 2nd Lieutenant, 355, 356
Gordon C L, Major-Genera, 452,456l
Gordon F, Lieutenant, 347
Gordon R, Lieutenant Colonel, 21, 58, 452, 456, 458, 463
Gorman F T, Private, 212, 462
Gorringe H D, Private,363
Goss J H, RM Gunner, 47, 51
Gouge W A, Lance Sergeant, 460
Goulding A H, Sergeant, 464
Gowney D J, Captain, 110, 111, 134, 137, 138, 145, 151, 155, 159, 303, 304, 363, 458
Grady J H, Gunner, 181
Graham C F O, Major, Preface, 100, 101, 102, 121, 151, 155, 431, 457
Graham F R, Sergeant Major, 329, 338, 362, 460
Graham H M C W, Lieutenant Colonel, 446, 447, 452, 457
Graham M, Private, 459
Grainger A R, Corporal, 158, 160
Grant A, Lance Corporal, 69
Grant D L, Private, 361
Grant H, Major, 254
Grantham, Corporal, 292
Grattan A P, Major, 48, 50, 56, 71, 464
Gray A, Gunner, 461
Gray F, 2nd Lieutenant, 327
Gray F, Corporal, 461
Grayson H M, Lieutenant Colonel, 462, 463
Grayson, 2nd Lieutenant, 301
Green A H, Private, 423
Green A S, Private, 361
Green E C, Superintending Clerk, 469
Green F H, Quarter Master Sergeant, 460
Green J E, Lance Corporal, 422
Green W, Gunner, 461
Green W, Private, 465
Greenhalgh J, Company Sergeant Major, 460
Greening D C, Sergeant, 452

Greenwood E H, Private, 421
Greenwood, Lieutenant, 328
Gregory A W, Lieutenant, 347
Gregory W, Sergeant Major, 426
Greig W, RM Gunner, 51
Grierson A G W, Captain, 5, 48
Grierson R, Captain, 415
Griffiths C, Corporal, 193
Griffiths D, Corporal, 63
Griffiths F H, Major, 464
Griffiths, Lance Corporal, 158
Grimshaw J, Private, 461
Grindey E A, Corporal, 459, 462
Grinling C S, Lieutenant, 124, 151, 154
Grinham T, Private   Preface
Grout, Hon T E, Lieutenant, 419
Grover G W M, Lieutenant, 153
Grover J, Major, 130, 134, 154
Groves F W, Corporal, 69
Guest W, Battery Sergeant Major, 391, 392, 459
Gumm R, Lieutenant, 250
Gumm R J, RM Gunner, 51
Gurney T W, Gunner, 461
Guttridge L F, Bugler, 180
Guy F, Private, 459
Guy J C, Lieutenant, 364, 365, 367, 370, 370, 371, 372, 458
Gwynne W, Acting Sergeant Major, 159
Gwynne W C, Lieutenant, 327
Haddon J H, Lieutenant, 151, 156
Haile A, Private, 91, 460
Hailes D A, Major, 457
Haines H R H, Captain, 50, 62, 457
Halden J, Gunner, 281
Hale R D, Lance Corporal, 62.
Hale R D, Lieutenant, 428
Hall A V, Lieutenant, 194
Hall C, Major, 228
Hall C L, Captain, 220, 223, 224, 225, 228
Hall C R, Private, 224
Hall D W R, Lieutenant, 327
Hall F H H, Major, 250
Hall G H, Private, 111, 461
Hall G W, Private, 181
Hall H W, Lieutenant, 306
Hall J, Sergeant, 464
Hall J W, Private, 422
Hall W J, Sergeant, 460
Halliday L S T, Lieutenant Colonel, (VC), 6, 452
Hamer F A, Captain, 50, 246, 249
Hamilton A D P, Lieutenant, 42, 47, 51
Hamilton W A, Private, 49, 464
Hamilton, 2nd Lieutenant, 251
Hamilton-Cox H J, Lieutenant, 50, 402
Hammond J, Lieutenant, 97, 110, 111
Hammond J, Private, 226
Hammond, Hon W C T, Major, 78, 457
Hampson J, Private, 322
Hanham G E, Corporal, 427
Hankey Sir M P A, Lieutenant Colonel, 453, 456
Hanlon T E, Colour Sergeant, 460
Hann E P (or C P), Sergeant Major, 426, 427, 460
Hann W, Private, 361

473

Hansler J H, Corporal, 257
Hanson F J, Lieutenant, 143, 300
Hanson W A N, Lieutenant, 194, 198, 459
Harden E J, Lieutenant, 137, 153
Harding D, 2nd Lieutenant, 399, 458, 461
Harding E W, Major, 262, 388, 443
Hardisty H L, Lieutenant, 326, 336, 339, 341, 355, 356, 359, 459
Hardy A, Private, 422
Hardy H N, Gunner, 464
Hardy P R, Lieutenant, 307, 311
Hardy P R, Musician, 464
Harmar C D'O, Major, Preface, 207, 208, 209, 210, 211, 212, 457, 462, 463
Harmes W J, Gunner, 464
Harries E B, Lieutenant, 188, 189, 190, 193, 457
Harries L H, Lieutenant, 73, 76, 78, 265, 275
Harrington G, QMS/Lieutenant/Captain, 239, 242, 457
Harris C P, Corporal, 463
Harris G N A, Lieutenant Colonel, 239, 242, 457
Harris J, Lieutenant, 393
Harris R L, Lieutenant, 194
Harrison G H, Lieutenant Colonel, 296, 413, 414, 415, 458
Harrison H C, Captain, 391, 392, 457
Hart J, Gunner, 464
Hart W D, Lieutenant, 265, 278, 281, 459
Hartley B E, Private, 464
Harvey F J W, Major (VC), 40, 41,43,47, 48, 51, 456
Harvey T A, Captain, 427
Hastings G H, Sergeant, 332, 359, 361, 459
Haszard G F, Captain, 290, 292, 293, 457, 458, 463
Hatcher B W, Sergeant, 63
Hathorn G V, Lieutenant, 19
Hatton E A, Captain, 120, 121, 124, 151, 154
Havelock G, Major, 426
Hawes B S, 2nd Lieutenant, 364, 365, 367, 369
Hawes M, Sergeant, 460
Hawkes A E, Sergean, 158, 457
Hawkesworth F, Colour Sergeant, 464
Hawkesworth J F, Private, 181
Hawkins J W, Private, 464
Hawkins T H, Lieutenant Colonel, 6, 453, 456
Hawkins T H, Bandmaster, 464
Haworth-Borth O M, Lieutenant, 50
Hawthorn T, Private, 427
Haydon J, Gunner, 464
Hayes H, Sergeant, 62
Haynes E W, Private, 464
Haynes F J, Gunner, 460
Haynes J W, Private
Hayward A F, Regimental Sergeant Major (Ty Lieutenant), 122, 124, 150, 154
Hazel J, Major, 50
Hazell C H, Lieutenant, 270
Hazeon C S, Captain, , 23, 51, 242
Heard, Sergeant, 256

Hearn E, Gunner, 172, 180
Heath W, Corporal, 464
Heaton E A, 2nd Lieutenant (Local Captain), 187, 188, 190
Heaton J, Sergeant, 281
Hefferman C, Lance Corporal Bugler, 174, 181
Hemmings F W, Corporal, 226
Henderson J, Corporal, 461
Henderson T, Acting Sergeant Major, 427
Henschell V, 2nd Lieutenant, 251
Hepburn C A, Captain, 159, 429
Herbert J C, Quarter Master Sergeant, 460
Herford B H, Lieutenant, 124, 150, 154
Herford G M, Captain, 16
Heriot G M, Major, 26, 39, 130
Heselton A W, Corporal, 360
Hewitt G J, Sergeant, 174, 180
Hickman G F, Gunner, 461
Hicks A, Driver, 402, 460
Hicks J S, Lieutenant, 52
Hickson G R S, Major, 42, 453, 457, 463
Higgins K A L, Lieutenant, 124, 139, 154
Hilditch G F, Lieutenant, 415
Hill A, Colour Sergeant, 460, 464
Hill C E, Captain, 50
Hill F, Sergeant, 461
Hill F E, Corporal, 87
Hill H J, Sergeant Major, 460
Hill J H, Lance Corporal, 69
Hill R, Colour Sergeant, 461
Hill R, Sergeant, 111
Hills J W, Captain, 242
Hillsley S, Private, 159
Hilton R, Private, 423
Hinchliffe L, Bombardier, 281
Hipkiss, Sergeant, 255, 256
Hissock J, Sergeant, 361
Hitch D S, Captain, 419
Hoare H, Captain, 143, 300
Hoare H, Colour Sergeant, 159
Hoath H W, Private, 181
Hobbs E F, Colour Sergeant, 460, 462
Hobson G S, Captain, 17
Hodding W H, Lieutenant, 300
Hodson W, Private, 422
Hoite C, Corporal, Preface
Holden E V, Private, 361
Hollamby G R B, Lieutenant, 329, 343, 347
Holland D, Private, 464
Holland R B, Superintending Clerk, 460
Holles L C, Lieutenant, 51
Hollingsworth J H (or J T), Captain, 396, 397, 461
Holloway 2nd Lieutenant, 301
Holloway W, Lieutenant, 398
Holmes F, Major, 416, 417, 463
Holmes J, Sergeant, 422
Holmes R, Sergeant, 419
Holt S, Private, 423
Holton A E, Lieutenant, 280, 459
Holway E, Lance Corporal, 361
Home F W, Captain, 464
Home J G, Captain, 244, 424
Homer J L, Lieutenant Colonel, 457
Homfray J R H, Colonel, 251, 252, 253, 457

Honner J J, Sergeant, 461
Hook L, Lance Sergeant, 460
Hooper S, Bombardier, 281
Hope A J, Lieutenant , 279
Hopps E, Private, 69
Hopwell W, Private, 173, 180, 459, 463
Hore F J, Lieutenant, 161, 167, 168, 176, 295
Horn R, Lieutenant, 427
Horne, 2nd Lieutenant, 328
Horne H R, RM Gunner, 50
Horne J G, Major, 13, 36, 247
Horton W, Lance Bombardier, 69
Hoskins T H, Private, 122, 158, 160
Hoskyns-Abrahall C H, Major, 111, 126, 151, 154
Hotham, Lieutenant, 328
Houghton H N, Major, 442
How F C, Lieutenant, 316
Howard A E, Sergeant, 294
Howard, Hon G, Captain, 373, 374, 375
Howard M P, Musician, 464
Howarth J, Gunner, 281
Howe A E, Private, 362
Howe A G, Corporal, 460
Howell T W, Lieutenant, 426
Howell-Jones J H, Captain, 157, 458
Howells W, Gunner, 402
Hubbard J E, Private, 360
Hubert G R, Private, 464
Hucker T H, Corporal, 461
Hudleston F J, Lieutenant Colonel, 194, 237
Hudleston J W, Captain, 237
Hudson J G, Private, 83
Hughes A E, Lieutenant, 311
Hughes J J, Sergeant, 158, 461
Hughes W G, Sergeant Major, 426
Hughes W H, 2nd Lieutenant, 327
Hull A H, Lance Sergeant, 257
Hulme R J, Private, 359
Hulme T E, Lieutenant, 402
Hunt A H, Sergeant
Hunt F, Private, 158
Hunt H L, 2nd Lieutenant, 461
Hunt W T, Sergeant, 49
Hunt, Lieutenant, 402
Hunting A H, Sergeant, 158, 160
Huntingford W L, Major, 6, 207,212, 247, 452, 457, 462, 463
Hunton T L, Major, 51, 404, 457, 462, 465
Hurford A, Sergeant Major, 159
Hurford R F, Sergeant, 461
Husey E W, Captain, 50, 461
Huskisson E J, Major, Preface, 304, 306, 307, 308, 309, 319, 358, 459
Hutchings S J, Private (Acting Sergeant), 148, 159
Hutchins W, Corporal, 402
Hutchison A, Gunner, 281
Hutchison A R H, Major-General, Preface, 139, 144, 145, 148, 157, 160, 295, 298, 299, 301, 302, 303, 304, 309, 311, 313, 324, 328, 330, 358, 362, 436, 443, 456, 458
Hutchison H, Captain, 463
Hutton A F, Private, 360
Hutton R W, Captain, 453

INDEX

Huxtable G, Private, 464
Hyland J F (or J E), Lieutenant, 126, 151, 154
Ilton G H, Lieutenant Quarter Master, 71
Ingoe R H, Sergeant, 459
Ingram G, Corporal, 361
Ingram W T, Private, 158
Inman C, Sergeant, 277, 281
Inman H B, Captain, 304, 305, 307, 358, 459
Innes A, Lieutenant, 242
Innes A S, Captain, 412, 457
Innes J A, Corporal, 360
Innes L J, Captain, 364, 453
Innes-Baillie L E, Captain, 462
Inskip S H E, Lieutenant
Insley L, Sergeant, 351, 359, 360, 459
Iremonger H E W, Captain, 51, 397, 398, 402, 458, 461, 462
Irwin H J, 2nd Lieutenant, 327
Jackman W, Gunner, 402
Jackson A E, Staff Sergeant, 422, 465
Jackson J, Lieutenant, 167, 168
Jackson S, Private, 360
Jackson W, Musician, 464
Jacobs L R, Sergeant, 402
James A, Private, 360
James, Hon C, Lieutenant Colonel, 457
James D J, Private, 359
James G T, Private, 212, 462
James R, 2nd Lieutenant, 352
Jameson A, Lance Corporal, 69
Jameson A, Lieutenant, 246
Jameson T H, Captain, 86, 87, 91, 111, 150, 156, 160, 458
Janes A E, Private, 360
Jarman H H, Gunner, 281
Jarman H H, Lieutenant, 269, 279
Jarvis C, Private, 464
Jayne W H, Sergeant, 415
Jeffcoate H R, Sergeant, 39
Jefferey E, Private, 361
Jeffery N S, Private, 181
Jeffery W S C, Bombardier, 281
Jenkins, Private,198
Jenner A J, Private, 49
Jennings A, Gunner, 281
Jenvey, Sergeant Major (later Lieutenant), 390, 391
Jermain P L, 2nd Lieutenant, 134, 154
Jerram C F, Lieutenant Colonel, Preface, 111, 112, 134, 136, 138, 141, 150, 159, 295, 347, 358, 362, 453, 457, 463
Jerram W J, Gunner, 461
Jervis S, 2nd Lieutenant, 188, 189, 190, 193
Jinks R, Sergeant, 56
Jinks H, Sergeant, 465
Johns J, Private, 461
Johnson E E (or E K), Lieutenant, 50, 269
Johnson F, Gunner, 463
Johnson K McK, Sergeant, 372
Johnson M, Private, 422
Johnson R H, Private, 160
Johnson R W, Musician, 464
Johnson T, Private, 423
Johnston G, Driver, 281
Jolley N K, Lieutenant, 20, 50, 464
Jolley W A, Captain, 51
Jollye G H, Major, 51, 62, 457
Jones F, Corporal, 148
Jones F, Private, 361
Jones F R, Captain, Preface, 40, 51
Jones G B, Private, 361
Jones H, 2nd Lieutenant, 247, 318
Jones H J, Lieutenant
Jones H L, Major, 457, 464, 465
Jones H M, Lieutenant, 404
Jones J, Colour Sergeant, 459
Jones J, Captain, 242
Jones J, Private, 212, 462
Jones L O, Lieutenant, 194
Jones S, Quarter Master Sergeant, 362
Jones T, Private, 361, 464
Jones T E, Private, 159
Jones V H, Captain, 308, 309, 311
Jones W J, Private, 422, 423
Jones W T C, Lieutenant Colonel, 39, 116, 453, 456
Jordan F T (or F H), Sergeant (Temporary 2nd Lieutenant), Preface, 188, 190, 191
Jordan H J, Sergeant, 463
Joyner A E, Private, 387, 465
Jukes-Hughes E J, Captain, 50, 62, 457
Kearney, Lieutenant, 311
Kearslake A J, Sergeant, 460
Keating J, Private, 361
Keating T, Private, 69
Keefe G A, Private, 206, 461
Keirby T, Lance Sergeant, 49
Kelly E E, Company Sergeant Major, 180, 458
Kelmsley K, Sergeant, 453
Kelsey T C, Superintending Clerk, 460
Kemp A V, RM Gunner, 50
Kemp, Driver, 287
Kendle G H, Captain, 50
Kenny G J, Lieutenant, 151, 158, 311
Kenny J, Quarter Master Sergeant, 111
Kerr A D, Lance Corporal, 415
Kersey J E, Sergeant, 402, 461
Kibbler C, Private, 361
Kilner C F, Captain, 18, 453, 457
Kilvert R E, Major, 48, 50, 397, 398, 458
Kimber E, RM Gunner, 62, 457
Kimber H R, Sergeant, 39
King B, RM Gunner, 50
King H A, Private, 464
King J, Colour Sergeant, 459
King J R, Lance Sergeant, 49
King R, Corporal, 422
Kingdom C, Corporal, 84
Kingshott W, Corporal, 173, 180
Kirbell W, Lance Corporal, 159
Kirby E E, Colour Sergeant, 180
Kirkpatrick, Lieutenant Colonel, 324
Kiste, Van der, Captain, 242, 393
Kitcat A.de.W, Lieutenant Colonel, 194, 195, 430, 431
Kitchin D H, Lieutenant, 51
Knight F, Major, 242
Knight J H, Captain, 117, 118, 156, 240
Knight S C, Lieutenant, 285, 287
Knight W O, Sergeant, 359
Knill F J, Sergeant, 172, 180, 459, 463
Knott G H, Captain, 238, 240, 242
Kyle A G, Lieutenant, 143, 156, 300, 362
Ladd F W, Sergeant, 63, 66
Laing R J, Captain, 17
Laing R W, Major, 194
Lake W A, Lieutenant, 311
Lamacraft E J, Sergeant, 159
Lamb E H, Lieutenant, 414, 415, 458
Lamb F, Private, 423
Lambert H R, Lieutenant, 285, 289, 293, 458
Lambert J, Captain, 242
Lambert J H, Lieutenant Colonel, 457
Lambert T W, Private, 464
Lampen L C, Lieutenant Colonel, 453, 463
Lamplough C R W, Lieutenant, 153, 156, 167, 168, 172, 174, 180, 458
Lane C R, RM Gunner, 50
Lane C R, Lieutenant, 188, 189, 190, 191, 192
Lane L I, Private, 180
Lang J G, Lieutenant, 279
Lang S, Private, 111
Langdown R H, Sergeant, 427
Langford J, Colonel, 436
Larter J, Corporal, 361
Last W J, Corporal, 63, 193
Lathbury G P, Lieutenant, 100, 102, 103, 126, 139, 152, 157, 160, 393, 458, 462
Law F C, Lieutenant, 118, 152, 156, 157, 160, 393, 394, 458, 462
Lawford G A, Colour Sergeant, 460
Lawley A L, Private, 464
Lawrence C H, 2nd Lieutenant, 327
Lawrence K E, Major, 457
Lawrie F B A, Major, 121, 153, 328, 329, 330, 355, 453
Laws H N, Captain (Lieutenant RNVR), 157, 419, 458
Lawson B E, Sergeant, 460, 463
Lawson J H, Captain, 415
Lawson J W, Corporal, 371, 460
Lawson J W, Bombardier, 366, 372
Lawton R, Private, 423
Lea W C, Corporal, 424
Leaf, H M, Captain, Preface, 265, 373, 374, 375, 376, 458
Ledgard W R, Captain, 267, 269, 270, 273, 280, 281, 388, 458
Lee A V, Private,180
Lee G, Colour Sergeant, 460
Lee J C, Lieutenant, 320, 329, 362
Lee J S, Lieutenant, 307
Lee R, Private, 423
Lee T J, Gunner, 459
Lee T J, Sergeant, 281
Lee W, Colour Sergeant, 460
Lees T O H, Major, 453, 457
Lefevre F, Sergeant, 49, 462
Leith A, Private, 69
Le Selleur J,(or T), Lieutenant, 16, 47, 51
Leslie S G, Major, 453
Leuringdon W A, Corporal, 463
Levett A, Sergeant, 63, 193
Levy A P, Corporal, 461
Lewington W E, Private, 63, 193
Lewis E S, Sergeant, 293

475

Lewis T W, Lieutenant, 279, 281, 329, 350, 461
Lidstone A W, Private, 69
Ligertwood P, Captain, 317, 393
Lincoln A, Bombardier, 464
Lintott J, Quarter Master Sergeant, 414
Lion N, Lieutenant, 309
Liston-Foulis A P, Major, 269, 270, 272, 281, 452
Little A G, Major, Preface, 55, 56, 62, 457
Littleton G H, Captain, Preface, 291, 363, 397, 398, 431, 439, 453, 463
Lock C A, Private, 361
Lock E, Lieutenant, 453
Lock H J, Lieutenant, 17
Lock J, Private, 361
Lock W J, Sergeant, 360
Lockley T C, Corporal, 281
Lodge H, Bandmaster, 49, 460
London, Private, 311
Long J, Sergeant Major (promoted to Lieutenant), 411, 412
Longust-Higgins K A, Lieutenant
Looker C G, Bombardier, 464
Lord A, Private, 423
Lord J E, Sergeant, 421, 460
Lord J V, 2nd Lieutenant, 363
Lough R H D, Major, 118, 134, 152, 157, 159, 295, 358, 362, 453, 457, 458, 463
Lovatt E C, Lieutenant, 157
Lovatt H B, 2nd Lieutenant, 167, 168, 176
Lovatt J V, Captain, 457
Lovatt, Lieutenant, 416
Love W W, Company Sergeant Major, 304, 311, 318, 359
Lowdell G D, Lieutenant, 156
Lowe J C, Driver, 281
Lowes P, Private, 419
Loxley V D, Major, 141, 143, 159, 300
Luard F W, Colonel, 97, 109, 119, 124, 126, 135, 137, 151, 154, 156, 159
Luard T B, Lieutenant Colonel, 67, 458, 462
Lucas C A C, Captain, 50, 62, 457
Lucas H R, Sergeant, 48
Ludbrooke E R, Sergeant, 360
Lukis W F B, Lieutenant, 153, 156
Lumsden F W, Brigadier-General (VC), 257, 263, 265, 266, 280, 281, 282, 283, 457, 459, 462 (see also 14th Brigade above)
Luxmore C G, Lieutenant, 194
Lyne, Lieutenant, 393
Lyson J, Private, 360
Lywood E G, Lieutenant Colonel, 97
Macdonald G W, Private, 464
Macdonnell, Lieutenant, 121
Mace J W, Sergeant, 427
Macfarlane J, Corporal, 427
Mack W, Private, 464
Mackay J, Major, 426
Mackenzie D, Private, 360
Mackenzie J, Lieutenant, 426
Mackenzie R C, Lieutenant, 50, 152
Maconochie H, RM Gunner, 50
Magson R, Colour Sergeant, 48, 464
Maiden J B, Sergeant, 423
Malarky P, Lieutenant, 427
Malcolm L, Captain, 246, 417

Malcolm P W, Major, Preface, 254, 255, 256, 257
Malden C H, Major, 6, 17, 254
Mangham H, Private, 422
Mann A B, Private, 181
Mann H, Sergeant, 392, 460, 462
Mann W G, Private, 372
March B O, Lieutenant, 285, 287
March S J, Sergeant Major, 338, 356, 363
Marchant A E, Colonel, 107, 110, 453
Marchant J, Lance Corporal, 69
Markham H E, Lieutenant, 311
Markham-Rose J, Colonel, 390, 458
Marks G G, Quarter Master Sergeant, 417
Marlow E E, Colour Sergeant, 159
Marlow, Sergeant, 251
Marr N, Private, 422
Marriott W, Private, 63
Marsden W, Lance Corporal, 360
Marsh S G, Quarter Master Sergeant
Marsh T E, Lieutenant, 23
Marshall E A, Lieutenant, 153, 156
Marshall E J, Gunner, 402
Marshall H W, Sergeant Major, 460
Marshall J H, Gunner, 464
Marshall J S, Captain, 157, 414
Marshall P, Private, 361
Marshman M H, Captain, 246
Marsland R H, Lieutenant, 311, 362
Marston J S, Corporal, 360
Martin B, Private, 422
Martin C W, 2nd Lieutenant, 300
Martin E, Corporal, 111
Martin E, Private, 361
Martin E H, Corporal, 461
Martin H, Lieutenant, 429
Martin H, Sergeant, 460
Martin J, Lieutenant Colonel, 411, 412
Martin J, Private, 422
Martin W A T, Sergeant, 460
Martyn C H, Private, 174, 180
Mascall G P Y, Lieutenant, 135, 153
Mason A H, Gunner, 402
Masterman F, Private, 422
Masters F, Colour Sergeant, 159
Masters F M, Quarter Master Sergeant, 460
Masterton J, RM Gunner, 51
Mathieson S T, Captain, 397
Matthew G, Major, 253, 269, 281
Matthews G E, Brigadier-General, 97, 104, 109, 115-118, 136, 138, 139, 152, 156, 157, 159, 363, 441, 453, 456
Matthews J K, Private, 360
Matthews R, Lieutenant, 50
Matthews W, 2nd Lieutenant, 336
Mattison F W, Captain, 443
Matts S, 2nd Lieutenant, 188, 190
Maundrill C, Private, 422, 423
May A G, Private, 386
May J F, Lieutenant, 115, 118, 152, 154, 159
Mayes C, Colour Sergeant, 16, 459, 462
McAdam A C, Lieutenant, 341
McAlister E E, Musician, 464
McBride J, Lieutenant, 347
McBryde, Lieutenant, 343
McCarthy E, Lieutenant Colonel, 443

McCausland E L, Major-General, 48, 50, 97
McCormack G J, Corporal, 361
Mc Court G C, Corporal423
McCready T R, Lieutenant Colonel, 301, 320, 323, 346, 358, 363, 457, 459
McCudle T, Corporal, 461
McCullough W S, Sergeant, 361
McCurrack R G, Gunner, 290, 293
McDonnell R, Lieutenant, 151
McDowell J, Corporal, 158, 462
McDowell R, Corporal, 160
McFarland H, 2nd Lieutenant, 188, 190, 191
McGubbin T, Sergeant, 461
McIlveny R, Private, 160
McIntosh R, Sergeant, 427
McIntyre W R, Corporal, 15
McKay D, Sergeant, 463
McKay F M, Lieutenant, 240
McKay W K, Major, 242, 427, 457
McKeand, 2nd Lieutenant, 316
McKenzie J, Lieutenant, 427
McKheand C L, Captain, 320
McLeish P R, Sergeant, 160, 275, 460
McLoughlin J F, Sergeant, 213, 459, 462
McMillan, Private, 101
McNair-Smith J, Captain, 50
McNeil, Sergeant, 291
McPhee M N
McVicker D, Gunner, 464
Mead C F, Lieutenant, 143, 153, 154, 156
Mead, Lieutenant, 102, 106, 393, 394
Meade J H, Sergeant, 460
Meades M, Corporal, 423
Meatyard W H, Sergeant, Preface, 117, 303, 304, 360, 460
Meese J, Lance Corporal, 361
Mellor A J, Captain, 17, 463
Mennell C E, Lieutenant, 316
Mercer Sir D, Major-General, 111, 112, 116, 120, 127, 130, 138, 143, 147, 148, 150, 157, 159, 163, 181, 239, 373, 436, 443, 453, 456, 462
Merchant L, Lieutenant, 73, 78, 188, 189, 190
Merckel F, Battery Sergeant Major, 290, 293
Merton J K, Private, 422
Messer J M, Band Corporal, 464
Messum J H, Gunner, 290, 293
Metcalfs J H, Private, 193
Micklem C, Major, 269, 274, 280, 281, 458
Micklem H C, Private, 422
Middleton J W, Lieutenant, 324, 359, 262, 459
Miles H W, Captain, 20, 50, 56, 57
Mill W H, Sergeant, 372
Millem W J, Sergeant, 427
Miller A, Gunner, 464
Miller A C, Lieutenant, 156
Miller A C, Acting Sergeant Major, 153
Miller C J, Colour Sergeant, 281, 459
Miller L W, Lieutenant Colonel, 298, 305, 313, 362, 441
Millett H, Lieutenant, 139, 154
Mills F, Private, 422
Mills H, Private, 158, 160

Mills P, Private, 427
Mills W, Lance Corporal, 361
Milne B A, Lieutenant Colonel, 453
Milne J, Quarter Master Sergeant, 363
Milne R, Company Sergeant Major, 360, 462
Milne R, Private, 158
Milson A C, Sergeant, 281
Milton J, Colour Sergeant, 460
Minter M W, Sergeant, 78, 158, 160
Mitchell A H, 2nd Lieutenant, 327
Mitchell C, Captain, 427
Mitchell J H, Major, 107, 443
Mitchell T H, Colour Sergeant, 464
Moffatt A, Bandmaster, 50
Monk G T, Captain, 329, 363
Montague, Hon L S, Lieutenant, 413
Montague J J R, Private, 427
Montgomery H F, Major, 453, 457, 462
Moody G, Staff Clerk, 460
Moore D T, Colour Sergeant (promoted Lieutenant RNVR), 242
Moore E L, Lieutenant, 463
Moore I, Corporal, 362
Moore J, Private, 362, 460
Moore T E, Private, 423
Morey W A, Sergeant, 463
Morgan G, Lieutenant, 419
Morgan H St G, *2, 51, 463
Morgan C, Private,
Morgan J H, Captain, 412, 457
Morgan R H, Lieutenant Colonel, 58, 71
Morres E, Lieutenant, 364, 365
Morris F A, Private, 360, 362
Morris J, Bombardier, 277, 281
Morris J C, Gunner, 464
Morris J D, Lieutenant, 58
Morrison A, Corporal, 361
Morrison F J, Private, 69
Morrison-Scott R C, Major, 269, 280, 281, 398
Morriss S, Corporal, 23, 66
Morsley J, Lieutenant (late RA), 413
Morton C E H, Captain, 111, 126, 151, 154
Morton E, Private, 423
Morton G, Gunner, 461
Morton H, Private, 465
Morton H C, Captain, 17
Moss H, Private, 159
Moxham J F, Lieutenant, 121, 124, 153, 154
Moxon H, Private, 422, 423
Moyce G, Sergeant, 459
Mudge R J, Gunner, 465
Mulholland, Hon H, Lieutenant, 375
Muller G F, Major, 121, 124, 153, 154
Mulligan J, Corporal, 48, 463
Mullins C B, Major, 406, 407, 454
Mullins G J H, Brigadier-General, 141, 143, 149, 160, 245, 296, 363, 447, 456, 463
Mulraney J, Bombardier, 48
Mumford, Sergeant, 197, 198
Munday F W, Private, 181
Munday W, Corporal, 159
Munro A J M, Acting Staff Clerk, 460
Muntz C L, Captain, 298, 299, 300, 303
Murdoch J, RM Gunner, 50

Murdoch L, Captain, 417
Murdoch-Browne, Lieutenant, 137
Murfitt J, Sergeant Major (promoted to Lieutenant), 375
Murphy J, Colour Sergeant, 454
Murray C G, Captain, 417, 457
Murray, Hon J E, Lieutenant, 418
Murray J H, Sapper, 414, 415
Murray R, Sergeant, 421
Murrell A E, Sergeant, 48
Naitby, Corporal, 392
Narracott F H, Private, 461
Nash H W, Private, 360
Nash R S, Private, 69
Nealon J, Sergeant, 454
Netherway J, Private, 91, 460
Neville R A, Captain, 50, 327, 363, 454
Newbold G T, Lieutenant, 52
Newling G A, Captain, 311, 317, 318, 328, 336, 358, 363, 459
Newman F D K, Driver, 402
Newton R H, Lieutenant, 427
Niblett F B, Staff Sergeant, 460
Nichol E J, Sergeant, 48
Nicholl J W, Private, 423
Nicholls Sir W, General, 148, 443
Nicholson A, Sergeant, 427
Nimmo J, Sergeant (promoted 2nd Lieutenant), 427
Nind J P, Major, Preface, 194, 197, 199
Nixon E A, Gunner, 44
Nobbs E, Colour Sergeant (promoted Lieutenant Quartermaster), 111, 150, 156, 160, 454
Nolan J, Acting Corporal, 461
Norcock L, Major, 32, 39, 393, 443
Norrie R S, Sapper, 415
Norris A G, 2nd Lieutenant, 167, 168, 180, 184, 188, 190, 190, 193
Norris F A, Private, 460
Norris H P, 2nd Lieutenant, 427
Northrop, Lieutenant, 296, 301
Nottingham-Palmer E, Captain, 249
Nourse, Lieutenant, 143, 304
Noyes E J B, Captain, Preface, 50, 194, 197, 198
Nutt E J, Private, 463
Oakden A M, Lieutenant, 155, 414
Oakes F J, Lance Sergeant, 224
Oakes W H, Private, 460
Oakey L, Sergeant, 126, 159, 462
Oates E, Private, 419
Oates P H (or R H), Gunner, 386, 387, 465
Odey G H, Acting Sergeant, 86, 91, 460
O'Dwyer, Sergeant Major, 445
Ogston, Lieutenant, 253
O'Harmar C D, Major, 457
O'Kell A A, 2nd Lieutenant, 306
Oldfield J R H, Colonel, 130, 132, 156, 446, 454, 456
Ollier G V, Sergeant, 159
Onslow G T, Major-General, 454
Orde-Browne, Captain(late RA), 365
Orde L F, Captain, 462
Ordish A W, Acting Sergeant Clerk, 460
Orfeur R F, Lieutenant, 318
Ormsby R D, Lieutenant Colonel, 194, 246

Ormsby-Johnson F C, Major, 454
Ortlieb B, Private, 362, 460
Osborne W T, Private
Osmaston C A F, Lieutenant Colonel, 97, 110, 262, 285, 286, 289, 290, 293, 454, 456, 457
Osment, Major, 251
O'Sullivan H D E, Major, 457, 462
Ottignon J D, Colour Sergeant, 494
Owen W, Superintending Clerk, 460
Owens R E, Private, 158
Ozanne H, Colonel, Preface, 13, 51, 298, 306, 307, 313, 316, 318, 358, 362, 458, 464
Pace H J, Lieutenant, 29, 155
Padley J W, Corporal, 459
Padwick W H, Sergeant, 62, 67
Page G H, Private, 362
Palmer A, Lance Corporal, 464
Palmer C C, 2nd Lieutenant, 307
Palmer H D, Major, 111, 114, 117, 118, 152, 156, 454, 462
Palmer J M, Captain, 165, 167, 168, 172, 174, 176, 181, 181, 208, 211, 212, 458, 462, 463
Panton, Captain, 26
Pardoe E H, Captain, 364, 454
Parfitt C F, Acting Superintending Clerk, 460
Paris Sir A, Major-General, 35, 103, 104, 105, 107, 108, 111, 127, 128, 135, 138, 143, 148, 149, 150, 157, 159, 295, 297, 298, 373, 454, 456, 461, 462
Parish E, Bombardier, 281, 463
Parker E M, Lieutenant, 31
Parker E M C, Captain, 63
Parker H J, Sergeant, 181
Parker S C, Gunner, 39
Parker W R, Lance Corporal (VC), 122, 123, 157, 456
Parkes F H, Gunner, 281
Parkes G W, Lance Sergeant, 361
Parkinson E, Private, 422
Parr H, Private, 423
Parrott T, Corporal, 464
Parry G L, Lieutenant Colonel, 50, 313, 318, 319
Parson F C, Seargeant, 427
Parsons C McN, Brigadier-General, 97, 104, 107, 110, 111, 135, 139, 150, 156, 157, 159, 446, 447, 454, 456
Parsons C Q, Lieutenant, 134, 153, 156
Parsons F A J, Private, 78, 460
Partington D, Corporal, 361
Partridge C B, Captain, 16
Partridge J, Private, 361
Partridge W G, Gunner, 464
Parvin, Lieutenant, 393
Pascoe W, Company Sergeant Major, 460
Paterson A, Sergeant, 333, 359, 459
Paterson J A, Major, 426, 427
Paterson R C, Colonel, 58, 188, 189, 190, 193
Paterson R O, Major, 457
Paton J, Sapper, 415
Patterson W J, Private, 42, 49
Paull F S, Private, 62, 148, 159
Paxton R, Private, 423

Payne R E, Corporal, 270, 280, 459
Payne, Sergeant, 256
Peach L, Lance Corporal, 69, 465
Peach, Private, 303
Peacock J W, Gunner, 464
Peacock P, Lieutenant Colonel, Preface, 391, 398, 400, 491, 402, 457, 461
Pearce C A, Lieutenant, Preface, 461
Pearce F A, Sergeant (later Lieutenant), 360, 383, 386, 387, 465
Pearce S E, Gunner, 281
Pearce W, Acting Superintending Clerk, 460
Pearse H N, Lieutenant, 152
Pearson J, Captain, 143,160, 247, 306, 307, 311, 358, 459
Pearson L, Private, 427
Pease L T, Major-General, 454
Peasnell F A, Lance Sergeant, 460
Peck H, Captain, 396, 397, 399, 458
Peck H J, Company Sergeant Major, 428
Peckham A T, Gunner, 69
Peel A, Lieutenant Colonel, 6, 454, 457, 462
Peel, Hon A V, Major, 160
Penfold J, Gunner, 464
Penny F G, Private, 361
Percy J H, Captain, 269, 281, 461
Perkins G S, Lieutenant, 153, 154
Perkins W, Sergeant, 39
Perry A S, Lieutenant, 327, 328
Perry F W A, 2nd Lieutenant, 306, 311
Perry, Lance Sergeant, 227
Peters W E, Private, 63
Peters W G, Private, 193
Petit D J, Sergeant Major, 421
Petley W E, RM Gunner, 50, 461
Pettigrew J, Lieutenant, 427
Pettman A H, 2nd Lieutenant, 320
Phillipps P, Lieutenant Colonel, 364, 365, 366
Phillips F T, Lieutenant Colonel, 97, 109, 242
Phillips F W, Superintendng Clerk, 460
Phillips G, Private, 464
Phillips J W, Private, 69
Phillips P, Colonel, 457
Phillips W G, Private, 361
Phillips, Sergeant, 188
Phipps A, Corporal,48, 464
Pickard W H J, Musician, 464
Pickering J L, Sergeant, 159
Pidduck G, Corporal, 368
Pike H, Bombardier, 273, 280
Pilcher T, Sergeant, 454
Pilcher W J, Battery Quarter Master Sergeant,459
Pilgrim F, Sergeant, 143, 158, 160, 459, 463
Pinkerton W A, Acting Sergeant Major, 153
Pinkerton W A, Lieutenant, 55, 362
Pipe D A, Captain, 316
Piper C T, Sergeant (promoted to Lieutenant, RNVR), 242
Pippet B C, 2nd Lieutenant, 316, 327
Pitt W G, Private, 462
Platt G, Private, 423

Platts E L, Lieutenant, 300, 393, 394
Poe W S, Major, 454, 458
Poland R A, Major, 51, 319, 328, 330, 332, 334, 336
Ponsford J, Sergeant, 460
Poole G R, Major-General, 73, 189, 239, 261, 263, 264, 267, 269, 280, 281, 456, 458
Pooley J W, Gunner, 462
Pope H C, Captain, 393
Popplewell E, Gunner, 461
Pordage J, Lieutenant, 294
Porteous J, RM Gunner, 50
Postin J, Private, 360
Potter C R, Sergeant, 480
Potter W H, Colour Sergeant, 48
Pound J M, Captain, 300
Powell (A man named), 311
Powers M, Sergeant, 372
Powys-Sketchley E F, Major, 160, 454
Praagh H B Van, Captain, 300, 304, 308, 316, 358, 459
Press J D L, Private, 173, 180, 459, 463
Preston J W, Corporal, 461
Previte K B, Lieutenant, 194, 197
Price, Lieutenant Colonel, 228
Price W, Lieutenant, 279
Priestley G A, Sergeant, 317, 359
Primrose D, Captain, 398, 402
Prince A, Private, 160
Prince-Cox W H, Sergeant, 464
Prior W, Lieutenant, 426
Priscott F O, Acting Sergeant Major, 139, 152
Proctor A V, Sergeant, 62
Proctor H C, Private, 180
Proffitt F A, Lieutenant, 328, 359, 459
Proud A T, Private, 423
Prunell, Lieutenant, 329
Pryce-Browne W H, Major, 106. 110, 111
Prynne G H H, Major, 462
Puckle K A, Lieutenant, 111, 150
Pullin J, Lance Corporal, 422
Purdie J A, Corporal, 84
Purser H R, Captain, 364, 365, 366, 369, 372, 390, 391
Purvis J P, Sergeant, 427
Putnam A F W, Corporal, 461
Puttock Driver, 294
Puxley, RM Gunner, 50
Pyle T, Private, 198, 459
Pym J B, Lieutenant Colonel, 139
Pyne H W (or W H), Sergeant, 417, 460
Quill M D, Lieutenant, 285, 287, 288, 289
Quill R H, Lieutenant, 153
Radford F, Lance Sergeant, 180, 462
Raikes G L, Major, Preface, 14, 239, 261, 269, 270, 279, 280, 281, 458
Ramsbottom J E, Private, 422
Ramsey A, Private, 218
Randall E J, Gunner, 461
Randell E, Sergeant, 83
Rann A E, Major, Preface, 390, 391, 392, 457, 458
Rann W H, Company Sergeant Major, 402, 461
Ransome J, Gunner, 386, 387

Ranson W, Gunner, 181
Rapkin, Corporal, 130
Rate J J, Private, 427
Rathbone C E H, Captain, 454, 458
Ravenshaw H E, Captain, 50, 464
Rayner F W, Private, 218
Rayner G W, Quarter Master Sergeant, 362, 459
Rayson E W, Gunner, 402
Read P, Private, 423
Read T W, Company Sergeant Major, 361
Read W A, Quarter Master Sergeant, 417, 423, 460
Read, Private, 214
Reading, Captain, 63
Redhead E, Private, 21
Redman E J, Bombardier, 281
Reed A E, Corporal, 69
Reed S C, Bugler, 19
Reeley H, Bandmaster, 51
Reepe C H, Colour Sergeant, 460
Reeves W T, Colour Sergeant, 459
Regan A J, Corporal, 257
Regnart C H, Captain, 238
Reid J, Sergeant, 49, 464
Rench A, Private, 423
Rendell A, Lieutenant, 51
Revell J W, Captain, 414
Reynold W, Private, 23
Reynolds J E, Captain, 391, 458
Reynolds R F, Captain, 397, 461
Reynolds, Sergeant Major (later Commissioned), 390
Richards F S, Captain, 285, 286, 287, 289
Richards J F, Lieutenant, 153
Richards J W, 2nd Lieutenant, 300
Richards W H P, Captain, 97, 111, 126, 132, 150, 155, 159
Richter A, Corporal, 224
Ridings A G, Major, 50
Ridings A W, Major, 56, 194, 195, 197, 398
Rigby C N, Lieutenant, 161, 162, 165, 167, 168, 171, 172, 176, 178, 270, 273, 281
Riley T N (or G N), Lieutenant, 414, 415, 458
Riman C S, Sergeant, 360
Rimmer W, Sergeant, 148, 159
Riseley W, Sergeant, 464
Risk C E, Lieutenant Colonel, 100, , 120, 156, 454, 458, 462
Rist W P, Sergeant, 461
Roberts H W, Lance Corporal, 69
Roberts L D, Colour Sergeant, 48
Roberts N, Sergeant, 419
Roberts, Lieutenant, 311
Robertson, Lieutenant, 257
Robins T, Private, 36, 39
Robins W T, Corporal, 281
Robinson A J D, Staff Clerk, 450
Robinson C E, Captain, 37, 155, 454
Robinson D L, Captain, 458, 463
Robinson F L, Lieutenant, 270, 280, 281
Robinson J, Corporal, 461
Robinson L W, Lieutenant, 306
Robinson W, Private, 70
Robson J C, Sergeant, 361

Robson K, Private, 360
Robson M, Private, 422
Robson, RM Gunner, 50
Robus, 2nd Lieutenant, 336
Rodger W, Private, 360
Roe A H, Lieutenant, 157
Roe E G M, Lieutenant, 151, 159, 462
Roe R H, Lieutenant, 414, 415, 458
Rogers A L, Private, 222, 224
Rogers R C, Colour Sergeant, 360
Rogers R F, Lieutenant, 242
Rogers W H, Lieutenant, 249, 293
Rogers W H, Sergeant
Rogers W H C, Acting Sergeant Major, 309, 364, 366
Rogers W R, Lieutenant , 406
Rolf E, Sergeant Major, 461
Rolland C T, Captain, 463
Rombulow-Pearse A E, Major, 146, 244
Ronald H, Corporal, 428
Rook E G, Corporal, 361
Room L C T, Lieutenant, 159
Rooney G C, Major, 41, 47, 51
Ross H, Sergeant, 48
Roxby E H, Gunner, 281
Rudd, Driver, 287
Ruffles, Lieutenant, 398
Rugg C W, 2nd Lieutenant, 306
Rugg L H, Captain, 415
Russell F, Lieutenant, 388, 389
Russell G Y, Major, 242, 364, 365, 367, 370, 371
Russell H J, Staff Sergeant, 459
Russell J J, Colour Sergeant, 362
Russell W, Captain, 292, 293, 459, 463
Rutherford G, Lieutenant, 111, 151, 159, 393, 394
Rutherford W, Captain, 446
Rutland A C, Lance Corporal, 226
Rutledge G, Major, 50, 237
Ryan E St.V, Lieutenant, 51, 155
Ryder T A, Lieutenant, 280, 459
Ryman C W, RM Gunner, 50
Sadd A (or H), Lance Corporal, 359, 459
Sadler E E, Gunner, 461
Salisbury J V, Private, 422
Salisbury T, Private, 423
Salisbury T E, Private, 423
Salt T, Lance Corporal, 311, 359, 360, 459
Salter C G, Company Sergeant Major, 461, 462
Sampson-Way N F E G, Captain, 455
Sanders J M, Sergeant, 360
Sanders W H, Lieutenant, 126, 152, 155, 159
Sanderson A G, Superintending Clerk, 460
Sanderson E, 2nd Lieutenant, 306
Sandilands P, Colonel, Preface, 328, 330, 334, 345, 346, 355, 356, 358, 362, 458
Sands A H,Company Sergeant Major, 359, 459
Sands L H, Private, 220, 465
Saumarez R J, Major, 39, 457
Saunders F J, Major, 139, 141, 161, 296, 301, 362, 454
Saunders W J, Quarter Master Sergeant, 293, 402, 459

Saunders, 2nd Lieutenant, 320
Savage F, 2nd Lieutenant, 306
Sawyer A J, Gunner, 463
Sawyer R H, Lieutenant, 291, 293, 459, 463
Saxton E, Private, 222, 224
Scholes G R, Private, 422
Scott A, Private, 426, 427, 459
Scott B F, Lieutenant, 148
Scott C, Sergeant, 360
Scott E, Private, 360
Scott F G, Colonel, 411, 412
Scott L A, Sergeant, 78, 460
Scott N A W, Major, 364
Scott W, Private, 160
Scott W G, Colour Sergeant, 307, 359, 459
Scott Sir Gilbert, Major, 430
Scott-Wilcox H V, Lieutenant, 358, 459
Scutt F J, Private, 464
Seabrook W, Colour Sergeant, 23
Seabrook W, Lieutenant, 426
Sears N, Colour Sergeant, 62
Seath G H, Major, 22, 35, 39, 66, 67, 458
Sellen W, Gunner, 464
Senior A, Private, 421
Sergeant C M, Lieutenant, Preface, 78, 458
Sessions E C, Sergeant, 402
Sewell W A, Gunner, 402
Seyd G, RM Gunner, 50
Shadwell W G A, Captain, 55, 56, 289, 290, 293, 458
Sharp A, Sergeant, 462, 460
Sharrock N, Corporal, 181
Shaw R, Private, 423
Shaw W E, Sergeant, 49
Shearer J M, Lieutenant, 240
Shelton C, Captain, 393
Shepherd D H, Private, 422
Shepherdson A, Bombardier, 281
Sherman J, Corporal, 360, 422, 461
Sherwood W A, Sergeant, 159
Sherwood-Kelly, Colonel, 80
Shipp S, Private, 464
Short G, Lance Corporal, 62
Short J A, Private, 211, 212, 462
Shubrick C L, Major, 106, 111, 135, 150
Shuttleworth F, Corporal, 361
Siebert L, Gunner, 461
Silk H T, Private, 464
Sillence E, Bugler, 126, 158, 159, 459
Sillitoe T, Colour Sergeant, 460
Sillitoe W E, 2nd Lieutenant, 162, 165, 167, 168, 174, 176
Simmons L H, Sergeant, 461
Simms A, Bombardier, 372
Simon P R, Captain, 242
Simon T, Private, 422,
Simonds E, Lieutenant, 151, 156
Simonds, Private, 188
Simpson G W, Corporal, 361
Simpson H W, Lieutenant, 121, 151, 156
Simpson J, Lieutenant Colonel, 107, 443, 457
Simpson J H, Major
Simpson W G,Major, 454
Simson A F, Major, 239, 240, 242, 457

Sinclair R, Major, 17, 51, 464
Singleton J, Private, 422
Singleton J E, Private, 422
Sissons F, Private, 423
Sitwell, Lieutenant, 135
Skerry W G, Private, 70
Sketchley E F P, Major, 98, 100, 107, 111, 136, 150, 157, 160, 295, 298, 362, 454, 457
Skinner, Lieutenant, 251
Skuce A E, Gunner, 464
Slaney C W, Major, 457
Slater H, Private, 419
Slater J E, Private, 464
Slessor J W, Colonel, 457
Smee W H, Sergeant, 428
Smeethe V G, Corporal, 361
Smith A, Gunner, 461
Smith A G, Acting Sergeant Major, 461
Smith A J H, Captain, 364
Smith C H, Captain, 150, 446
Smith D M, Lieutenant, 336
Smith E, Private, 361
Smith E, Quarter Master Sergeant, 417
Smith F, Acting Sergeant, 461
Smith F H, Major, 416, 417, 457, 462
Smith F R, Corporal, 414
Smith G, Sergeant, 361
Smith G, Private, 158, 160
Smith H C, Lieutenant, 359, 363
Smith H J, Sergeant, 361
Smith H S, Sergeant, 414
Smith J, Private, 360
Smith J A, 2nd Lieutenant, 327
Smith J W, Superintending Clerk, 460
Smith J W, Private, 78, 460
Smith L, Company Sergeant Major, 426, 427, 459
Smith L, Corporal(later Ty. 2nd Lieutenant), 428
Smith O S, Lieutenant, 377
Smith P, Private, 422
Smith P A, Major, 412, 457
Smith P E, Colour Sergeant, 228, 230, 454
Smith P E A, Company Sergeant Major, 363
Smith S, Private, 422
Smith T W, Corporal, 359
Smith W, Private, 49
Smith W J, Corporal, 415
Smith W N E, Major, 224
Smith-Hill P R, Lieutenant, Preface, 194, 196, 198
Snape W, Quarter Master Sergeant, 460
Snellgrove, Private, 460
Snepp J W, Major, 205, 206, 250, 457
Somerville J A, Musician, 464
South A G, Corporal, 360
Soutry, Lieutenant Colonel, 336
Sparrow C P, Lieutenant, 51, 194
Sparrow W G, Major, 183, 457
Speed E W, Superintending Clerk, 460
Spencer H B, Lance Corporal, 362, 459
Spicer M H, Lieutenant, 55, 56, 137, 152, 156, 207, 208, 211, 212
Spittle G H, Major, 112, 413, 415
Spooner A, Colour Sergeant, 44, 48, 459, 462

479

Spraggett R W, Lieutenant, Preface, 329, 331, 333, 356, 359, 459
Spry A J, Sergeant Major, 329, 362, 459
Squibb A G, Colour Sergeant, 78, 460
St Clair-Morford A, Lieutenant Colonel, 297, 458
Stacey A G, Lieutenant, 205
Staite R J, Corporal, 159
Stalham J S, Private, 460
Stallard W, Gunner, 464
Stanger S, 2nd Lieutenant, 240
Stanton G K, Corporal, 360
Stanton G W, Driver, 402
Stanton R G O, Lieutenant, 167, 168, 176
Starbuck G W, Gunner, 461
Staughton A W, Sergeant Major, 139, 153
Staughton, Captain, 301
Stead G E, Private, 419
Steed B L, Sergeant, 427, 460
Steele J D A, 2nd Lieutenant, 336
Steinthal G R, Lieutenant, 46, 47, 51
Stephens H W, 2nd Lieutenant, 188, 190, 191
Stephenson A E, Private, 423
Stepney D G (or D J), Private, 91, 460
Stevens A E, Sergeant, 49
Stevens T E, Colour Sergeant, 460
Stevenson E N, Private, 91, 460
Stevenson F, Private, 86
Stevenson J M, Private, 63
Stewart A B, Lieutenant, 50, 414
Stewart R A, Lieutenant
Stewart R A G, Captain, 461
Stewart T G, Lieutenant, 332, 336, 356, 359, 397, 459
Stiles C W, Lieutenant, 377
Still A J, Private, 78, 460
Still W, Colour Sergeant, 464
Stock C A, Lieutenant, 151, 156, 281, 364, 369
Stock F C G, Lieutenant, 111
Stockham E, Private, 159
Stockley H H F, Captain, 124, 151, 156, 159
Stoddart S A, Captain, 134, 151, 156
Stokes W N, Captain, 458
Stokes, 2nd Lieutenant, 301
Stone A G, 2nd Lieutenant, 333, 336, 352, 359, 459
Stone J N, Sergeant, 464
Stone W L (or W J), Corporal, 287, 293, 459
Stott A, Private, 423
Strachan P J, Colour Sergeant, 212, 462
Stratton W A, Quarter Master Sergeant, 464
Strevens J P, Company Sergeant Major, 461
Strother R L del, Captain, 50, 167, 168, 176
Stroud E J, Brigadier-General, 139, 141, 143, 149, 157, 160, 246, 247, 295, 296, 297, 456
Strugnell, Lieutenant, 22
Stuart W G, 2nd Lieutenant, 327
Stuart W J, Lieutenant, 156, 393, 394
Stuart W J, Sergeant Major, 152
Sturges R G, Lieutenant, 50

Sturges R L, Lieutenant, 130
Sulivan G H, Captain, 300
Sullivan E, Lieutenant, 97
Sullivan E J, Lieutenant, 151
Sullivan W, Sergeant, 417
Sully W E J, Corporal, 360
Summers F, 2nd Lieutenant (later Tank Corps), 373, 375, 376, 458
Summers L F, Sapper, 415
Sumner J, Private, 361
Sutcliffe E S, Lieutenant, 427
Sutcliffe F J, Lieutenant, 137
Sutcliffe J F, Sergeant Major, 151
Sutton E, Gunner, 461
Sutton C, Corporal Driver, 402, 460
Swanney C E, Captain, 240
Swanton J H, Major-General, 454
Swinden R E, Private, 464
Swire G, Private, 428
Syer J W, Sergeant, 463
Sykes F H, Colonel, 37, 157, 456
Symes W. Major, 457
Symons T M, Private, 212
Symons T H, Private, 462
Synes W, Major, 443
Syson A E, Captain, 126, 152, 156, 159, 457, 463
Tagg E J B, Captain, 100, 139, 143, 153, 159, 295, 358, 362, 455, 458, 462
Tait J, Captain, 426, 427
Tamberlin G, Private, 422
Tamberlin G, Staff Sergeant, 423
Tanqueray-Willaume F J (or F G), Major, 51, 464
Taplin H A, Lieutenant, 307
Tapper W B, RM Gunner, 51
Tapsall, Sergeant, 211
Tarbottom H, Sergeant, 281
Tatham A G, Brigadier-General, 439, 456
Tayler L F W, Lieutenant, 137, 151, 156, 393, 394
Taylor A, Sergeant, 87, 91
Taylor E, Company Sergeant Major, 180
Taylor E A, Lieutenant, 265, 276
Taylor E H, RM Gunner, 50
Taylor H N, Corporal, 422
Taylor J A, Gunner, 402
Taylor M E, 2nd Lieutenant, 327
Taylor R, Private, 69
Taylor W H, Sergeant, 181
Taylor W J, Lieutenant, 413
Teague J C, Captain, 124, 151, 155
Teale J W, Major, 414
Temple F V, Major, 455, 457
Temple R, Colonel, Preface, 247, 404
Temple R C, Major, 29, 59, 215, 245, 455, 457, 462
Tennyson C A, Captain, 50
Tetley A S, Lieutenant Colonel
Tetley A S, Lieutenant Colonel, 118, 128, 145, 148, 152, 156, 159, 296, 301, 362, 455, 463
Thatcher C J, Regimental Sergeant Major, 161, 168, 173, 180, 458
Thirkell, Lieutenant, 190, 191
Thomas D J, Private, 422
Thomas F H, Captain, 39, 66, 227, 228, 230, 458

Thomas J T, Lieutenant, 301
Thomas J W, Lieutenant, 311
Thomas V D, Lieutenant, 51
Thompson F M, Colour Sergeant, 62
Thompson H D, Lance Sergeant, 360
Thompson J E, Driver, 290, 294
Thompson M J, Sergeant, 180
Thompson R O C, Sergeant, 415
Thompson W, Lieutenant, 427
Thompson W, Sergeant, 173
Thompson, Major, 324, 327
Thomson R J T, Lieutenant, 153
Thorburn A J E, Sergeant, 293, 402
Thorne G W, Private, 69
Thorneley J S S, Lieutenant, 137, 151
Thornton C, Company Sergeant Major, 414
Thorton C J, Lieutenant Colonel, 463
Thornton E G, RM Gunner, 51
Thornton W J, Sergeant, 461
Thorold, Lieutenant, 301
Thorp A W, Private, 422
Threlfall, Private, 155
Throssell E, Private, 39
Tildesley W, Corporal, 361
Tildesley, Lieutenant, 243
Tilley R, Corporal, 422
Timmins T, Major, 47
Timmins, Bugler, 57
Tims E G, Colour Sergeant, 455
Todd J T, Private, 363
Todd W T, Sergeant, 360
Tollast R O, Lieutenant, 155
Tomkins B G, Colour Sergeant, 362, 459
Tomlin L H, Corporal, 294
Tomlinson J, Private, 361
Tootell, Captain, 225, 226
Toulmin, Captain, 22
Townsend W, Staff Clerk, 460
Tracey S J, Lieutenant, 153, 393, 395
Traill A S, Sergeant, 427, 459
Tregedga, 2nd Lieutenant, 328
Trench B F, Captain, 12
Trew E F, Brigadier-General, 138, 455, 457, 458
Trigg H J, Sergeant, 333, 359, 459
Tripp W H L, Major, 390, 391, 392, 455, 458
Trollope E, Private, 39
Trotman C N, Brigadier-General, 24, 111, 126, 129, 135, 136, 138, 141, 149, 150, 156, 157, 159, 295, 295, 296, 298, 299, 362, 455, 456, 462, 463
Trotman, 2nd Lieutenant, 316
Trotman N F, Major, 455
Troup A G, Lieutenant Colonel, 48, 51, 55, 269, 464
Trowse B, Private, 69
Trusler H, Sergeant, 361
Tucker, Sergeant, Preface
Tuckey C P, Lieutenant, 143, 152, 167, 168, 176, 393
Tugwell C W, Lance Sergeant, 464
Tulk F, Sergeant, 460
Tulley H, Lieutenant, 347
Tupman J A, Colonel, Preface, 111, 116, 121, 122, 127, 130, 153, 156, 158, 159, 362, 455, 457

Index

Turnbull, Colour Sergeant, 26, 363, 460
Turner A B, Driver, 281
Turner A H, Corporal, 383, 386, 387, 465
Turner C O, Private, 304
Turner F, Private, 386, 387, 465
Turner J H, Sergeant, 415
Turner M, Private, 141, 158, 160, 459
Turner R L, Lance Bombardier, 402
Tushaw A, Sergeant, 462
Twigg, Lieutenant, 203
Twiss H L, Captain, 239, 242
Twiss H R, Lieutenant, 388, 389
Tye E C, Sergeant, 280, 459
Underhay A, Lance Bombardier, 464
Underhay H R, Quarter Master Sergeant, 193, 460
Underhill G, Lieutenant, 167, 168, 173, 180, 393, 394, 458
Underhill M, Private, 465
Underwood W A, Gunner, 402
Unwin L A, 2nd Lieutenant, 156
Unwin, Lieutenant, 406
Upham H E, 2nd Lieutenant, 300
Uren, RM Gunner, 243
Urmston A G B, Lieutenant Colonel, 455, 457
Urquhart T, Private, 360
Usborne C, Battery Sergeant Major, 391, 392, 459
Usborne H, Sergeant, 462
Vale G R, Sergeant, 462
Vale H L, Sergeant, 49
Vance R H, Captain, 332, 336, 359, 458
Vernon J, Private, 422
Vicars B G, Sergeant, 459
Vickers S, Private, 422
Vincent A G, Lieutenant Colonel, 431, 455, 457
Vincent H, Captain, 281
Vincent H B, Captain, 463
Vincent W E, Lieutenant, 347
Vinnell E A, Sergeant, 281
Wace S C, Major, 457, 462, 463
Waddington W, Private, 423
Wadsworth W, Private, 13
Wagner L B, Sergeant, 360
Wainwright G, Private, 69
Wainwright G C, Lieutenant Colonel, 313, 318, 464
Wainwright G E, Captain, 51
Wainwright J A, Gunner, 464
Waite H H, Private, 360
Wakefield W J, Private, 173, 180
Wakeham J H, Company Sergeant Major, 426, 427, 460
Walker N, Bandmaster, 50
Walker D H, Lieutenant, 311
Walker H, Captain, 251, 252
Walker H S, Lieutenant, 16
Walker J M, Lieutenant, 426
Walker N B, Lieutenant, 300
Walker, Gunner, 292
Wall H G, Sergeant, 218
Wallace, Private, 203
Waller R C S, Major, 5, 48, 462
Walley H, Lance Corporal, 69
Wallis A, Lieutenant, 352, 417
Wallis E F, Corporal, 84, 86

Wallis H B, Lieutenant, 413
Walsh T J, Lieutenant, 347
Walters, Eductation Officer, 194
Walters E, Lieutenant, 285, 289
Waltham A W, Acting Bombardier, 193
Walton H, Sergeant, 378
Warburton, Corporal, 203
Ward J, Private, 423
Ward J, Sergeant, 461
Ward N B, Lieutenant, 50
Ward R W, Colour Sergeant, 464
Ward W W, Captain, 265, 269, 270, 280, 281
Warder B G, Major, 242
Waring A, Sergeant, 461
Warman, Lieutenant, 265, 279
Warren G H, Private, 360
Warrington J R, Gunner, 461
Watkis H M, Superintending Clerk, 460
Washburn S T, RM Gunner, 50, 464
Wass D, Gunner, 386, 387, 465
Waterloo H, Lance Sergeant, 48
Waters A N, Private, 362, 459
Waters F C, RM Gunner, 50
Waters W J, Company Sergeant Major, 361
Watkins C, Lieutenant, 300
Watling W, Quarter Master Sergeant, 460
Watson A, Gunner, 461
Watson C W, Lieutenant, 296, 301, 347, 393
Watson J W, Private, 83
Watson R, Gunner, 379
Watts C J, Company Sergeant Major, 180, 464
Watts J, Staff Sergeant
Watts P S, Lieutenant, 327
Watts R H, Captain, 139, 151, 156, 194
Watts W A, Sergeant, 311, 359, 459
Watts W H, Corporal, 360
Way J G, Lance Corporal, 136, 158, 459
Weaver H L, Private, 78, 460
Webb A, Gunner, 461
Webb F J, Private, 363
Webb P L, Sergeant, 455
Webb-Bowen M H, Captain, 253, 397, 461
Webber H A C, Captain, Preface, 50, 63, 457
Webber W E, Superintending Clerk, 460
Webley W T, Lieutenant, 270, 281, 388
Wedge T H, Corporal, 212, 462, 463
Weeks B C V, Lieutenant, 358, 458
Weight F G, Regimental Sergeant Major, 338, 460
Weir, Lieutenant, 232
Welch J R, Company Sergeant Major, 460
Weller B G, Major, 136, 138, 157, 160, 165, 167, 168, 172, 173, 180, 456, 458, 463
Wellington A, Gunner, 69
Wellington W, Lieutenant, 269
Wells B, Corporal, 173, 180
Wells E, Sergeant, 219, 224
Welman, 2nd Lieutenant, 301
Welsh D, Private, 193
Welsh J G, Bandmaster, 62, 457
Welsh J J, Sergeant, 159

Went H S D, Captain, 50
Werry J, Quarter Master Sergeant, 460
West D O, Sergeant, 361
West R, Lieutenant, 301
West R H, Lieutenant,
West R H P, Captain, Preface, 143, 325, 329, 333, 349, 350, 355, 356, 359, 363, 458
Westall J H, Private, 39
Westall T C, Bombardier, 69, 372
Westby T, Lieutenant, 317, 319, 358, 362, 458
Westenra, Hon R, 2nd Lieutenant, 373
Westlake G R, Lance Sergeant, 49, 464
Weston E W, Sergeant, 48
Wetton G, Sergeant, 460
Whale H L, Lieutenant, 241, 388, 389
Wharf G J, Lieutenant, 325, 327, 359, 458
Wharton R G, Major, 439, 457
Whatley A V, Private, 49
Wheeler G, Sergeant Major, 152, 155, 159
Wheeler W, Driver, 281
Whelan J J, Private, 160
White C, Lieutenant, 130, 155, 159
White C, Quarter Master Sergeant, 126, 160
White E, Private, 69
White E C, Sergeant, 63, 193
White F, Colonel, 455
White H S N, Brigadier-General, 456
White J, Major, 240, 242, 427
White "Jock", Private
White R F, Musician, 464
White R N, Captain, 130, 135, 138, 246
White W, Company Sergeant Major, 362, 460
Whiteley G, Corporal, 422
Whittle A, Private, 212, 462
Widdington F P, Sergeant, 415
Wigley T H, Private, 63
Wilby H W, Lieutenant, 130, 156
Wilcox F E V, Private (Acting Sergeant), 158, 159
Wild C, Quarter Master Sergeant, 460
Wild J, Private, 422
Wild R E F, Private, 422
Wilde P M C, Captain, 41, 47, 51
Wilding, Lieutenant, 103, 373
Wilkes G L, Lieutenant, 270
Wilkie R S, Captain, 296, 311
Wilkins A C, Sergeant, 463
Wilkinson J J, Sergeant, 455
Wilkinson L S, Captain, Preface, 55, 203, 204, 462, 463
Wilkinson M B, Private, 422
Wilks G L, Major, 458
Wilks J H, Private, 160
Willcox V C, Battery Sergeant Major, 365, 367, 371, 459
Willes F C, Captain, 50, 191
Willett P J, Private, 360
Willey W, Lieutenant, 250
Williams A N, Lieutenant, 114, 153, 156, 393
Williams C, Major, 13, 238
Williams C L, Sergeant Major (promoted to Lieutenant), 419, 421, 423
Williams E G, Sergeant, 461
Williams E J, Lieutenant, 51

481

Williams G W, Private, 361
Williams H, Staff Sergeant Mechanic, 280, 402, 459
Williams H J, Private, 427
Williams M, Captain, 100, 101, 265, 269, 270, 272, 281
Williams R J, Captain, 307, 327
Williamson F J, Private, 460
Williamson J, Private, 91
Williamson W C (or W A), 2nd Lieutenant, 316, 358, 458
Willis C H, Lieutenant Colonel, 429, 429, 456
Willis F S, Gunner, 461
Willis G L, Gunner, 281
Willis R.ff, Lieutenant Colonel, 6, 429
Willons H, Private, 463
Willoughby J H, Lieutenant, 151
Willows H, Private, 49
Wills G E, Sergeant, 159
Wills G L, Captain, 280
Willsher C D, Sergeant Major, 151, 155
Wilmot-Sitwell S D, Lieutenant, 137, 151, 155
Wilson A B, Major, 463
Wilson B, Quarter Master Sergeant, 459
Wilson B I, Sergeant, 463
Wilson B S, Sergeant, 459
Wilson D, Private, 70
Wilson F, Sergeant, 423
Wilson F B, Private, 361
Wilson F S, Major, 111, 112, 130, 150, 155, 159, 159, 455, 455, 456
Wilson G, Lieutenant, 281
Wilson J, Private, 62
Wilson L, Colonel
Wilson L O, Lieutenant Colonel, 132, 148, 157, 296, 301, 443
Wilson T, Sergeant, 423
Wilson W A, Lance Corporal, 160
Wilson W N, Gunner, 464
Windybank F, Company Sergeant Major, 335, 359
Wingfield J F, Acting Sergeant Major, 152, 156
Winne R H, Lieutenant, 426, 427
Winwood H, Lance Corporal, 69
Wishart J, Company Sergeant Major, 428
Withers C H, Corporal, 461
Witting S N, 2nd Lieutenant, 327
Wolstenholme F, Colour Sergeant, 158, 160
Wolstenholme W, Private, 78, 460
Wolstenholme, Lieutenant, 329
Wood E J, Colour Sergeant, 460
Wood F, Private, 423
Wood G E, Corporal, 281
Wood S H, Lieutenant, 265, 280, 459
Wood T W, Lieutenant, 194
Wood W, Captain, 427
Wood W, Private, 361, 423
Woodard, Corporal, 279
Woodcock G C, Major, 249, 269, 272, 275, 281, 404, 406, 457
Woodhouse A C, Sergeant, 280, 459
Woodman W, Gunner, 462
Wood-Roberts J, Lieutenant, 50
Woodroffe L W, Lieutenant, 151
Woodrow T H, Gunner, 281

Woods J M, Lieutenant, 316
Woods, Colonel, 190
Woodward G W, Sergeant, 359
Woolbridge A (or S), Colour Sergeant, 158, 462
Woolley C H F, Lieutenant, 137, 152, 156, 160, 397, 462
Woosey J, Private, 422
Workman G, Sergeant, 464
Wormold A, Private, 360
Worthington H, Lieutenant Colonel, 269
Wrangham L H, Captain, 301, 321, 327, 345, 347, 359, 393, 459
Wray E, Major, 17, 56
Wrenn, Lieutenant, 305
Wright F G, Quarter Master Sergeant, 362
Wright G D, Corporal, 69
Wright H, Corporal, 224
Wright H, Sergeant, 181
Wright R A, Farrier Sergeant Major, 459
Wright T G, Lieutenant, 281
Wright W, Gunner, 281
Wyatt A W, Private, 360
Wyld F C, RM Gunner, 50, 446
Wyld, Colour Sergeant, 255, 255
Wylde E A, Major-General, 407
Wyley J D N, Major, 455, 457
Yarrow A, Sergeant Major, 160, 426
Yates G, Private, 218
Yeldham C F, Lieutenant, 320
Yeo M R, Captain, 393, 394, 457
Young A, Colour Sergeant, 460
Young J, Private, 423
Young W, Acting Sergeant, 461
Young W A, RM Gunner, 50

Royal Marines serving with units other than RM, 451-455
Royal Marine Formations
  Table of Strengths 1914 to 1919, 442
  Casualties August 1914 to April 1919, 450
  Chatham Division RMLI, 302, 357, , 411, 453
  Plymouth Division RMLI, 446, 452
  Portsmouth Division RMLI, 250, 299, 301, 352, 441, 445
RM Brigade
  Formation of, 97
  Expediton to Ostend, 97-99
  Reorganisation, 100
  Chatham Battalion, 12, 97, 98, 102, 103, 108, 113, 115, 126, 132, 137, 138, 150
  Deal Battalion, 113, 115, 119, 121, 122, 128, 130, 134, 138, 153
  Plymouth Battalion, 27, 29, 98, 109, 113, 114, 116-118, 119, 128, 135, 138, 141, 148, 152
  Portsmouth Battalion, 103, 106, 107, 108, 109, 113, 115, 124, 126, 137, 138, 151
  RMA Battalion, 97, 100
RMLI Brigade (see also 188th and 189th Brigades in the Royal Naval Division below)
  Formation, 100
  At Dunkirk and Antwerp, 100-112
  Casualties, 110
1st RMLI, 58, 295-357
  Reorganisation, 295, 296, 299
  Demobilisation and Inspection by Prince

of Wales, 357
2nd RMLI, 295-330
  Re-organisation, 295, 296
  RMLI operations in Belgium and France, 1916-1918 in sequence
    Somme, First Battle of, 321-327
    Albert, Battle of, 262, 264, 268, 276, 290, 294, 323, 325, 330
    Ancre (Beaumont Hamel), Battle of, 300-304
    Ancre, Operations on the Ancre, 305
    Miraumont, Actions of, 306-308
    Vimy Ridge, 308
    Arras, Battle of, 308
    Scarpe, Second Battle of, 308
    Gavrelle, Capture of
    Arleux, (Capture of Gavrelle Windmill), Battle of, 308- 314
    Ypres, Battles of, 314-318
    Passchendaele, Second Battle of, 314-318
    Welch Ridge, Action of, 318-319
    St Quentin, Battle of , 321-322
    Bapaume, First Battle of, 323-324
    Martinsart, March retreat to, 324-327
    Losses, 327
    Aveluy Woods, 327-328
    Amalgamationj of 1/RMLI and 2/RMLI, April 1918, 329-330
    Somme, Second Battle of, Albert and Logeast Wood, 331-334
    Loupart Wood and Le Barque, 334-336
    Casualties, 336
    Arras, Second Battle of, 336-342
    Drocourt-Quéant Line, Battle of, 337-342
    Canal du Nord, Battle of, 342-345
    Canal de L'Escaut, crossing of, 345-347
    Cambrai, Battle of, 347-353
    Mons, Pursuit to, 353-355
    Armistice, Positons at, 355-357
    Rewards in Belgium and France 1916-1918, 358-363
3rd RM Battalion, 58, 59, 148, 244, 245-250, 321, 404, 405, 406
4th RM Battalion, (See Zeebrugge below)
5th RM Battalion, 58, 71-72, 412
6th RM Battalion, 194-199
  Officers, 194
7th RM Battalion, 194
RM Battalion for Service in Ireland, 393-395
  Officers, 393
8th RM Battalion, 395
RMLI Reserve Battalions, 296, 438, 444, 446, 447, 452, 454
Royal Marine Artillery
  RMA Battalion, 97, 100, 239, 261
  Howitzer Brigade, 55, 261-267
  Howitzer Brigade Battles, 58, 226, 239, 268
  Commanding Officers, 269
  Extracts from Battery Diaries, 270-280
  Honours & Rewards, 280-281
  Anti-Aircraft Brigade, 100, 261, 285-294
  Honours & Rewards, 293, 294
  Heavy Siege Train, 58, 163
  At Dunkirk, 396-403
  Honours and Rewards, 402
  Siege Batteries, 58, 253, 265, 267, 329
  RMA attached to the Royal Garrison

482

Index

Artillery, 377-379
  Batteries in East Africa, 364-372
  Honours, 371, 372
  Battery in Egypt, 388-389
  RMA Contingent in South Africa, 390-392
RM Submarine Miners, 70, 237, 242, 411-412
RM Labour Corps, 424-428
  Honours and Rewards, 427-428
RM Engineers, 429-431
RM Motor Transport Company, 261, 262, 373-376
  Honours, 376
RM Band (RN School of Music), 4, 116, 308, 435
  Divisonal Bands, 441
  Signal Company, 112, 127, 296, 413
  Honours, 415
RM Signallers, 5, 71, 103, 190, 245, 304, 311
RM Field Force, 58, 73, 76, 78, 188-193
  Glory 111, 188, 191
  Honours and Rewards, 193
Cyclist Company, 111, 113, 132, 138, 149, 295, 296
Divisional Bombers, 132
Examination Service, 5, 11
Home Service Labour Company, 428
London Picquet, 7
Medical Units (See also RND Divisional Train), 418-423
Motor Owner Drivers, 103
Special Orderlies, 6-7
Transport Staffs, 6
Wireless Staffs, 5-6
RM Administration and Training
  Royal Marine Office, Preface, 435-436, 443
  Royal Marine Headquarters, 436
  Mobilisation, 436-437
  King's Pardon, 436
  Royal Marine Mutiny Act of 1847
  Royal Marine Acts 1914 and 1916, 437
  Officers, 437
  Recruiting, 438
  Records and Pay, 439
  Clothing and Equipment, 441
  Prisoner of War Comforts Fund, 442
  Table of Strengths, 442
  Training Arrangements, 444-446
  Blandford, 446-447
  Shilingstone, 446
RM Strengths, 1914-1918, 442
RM Casualties August 1914 to April 1919, 450
RM Serving with units other than RM, 451-455
RM British Decorations, 456-461
RM Foreign Decorations, 461-465

RM Operations/Battles except Belgium and France 1916-1918
  Aegean Islands, 244-250
  Akaba, Gulf of, 205-206
  Archangel, 73, 75, 78, 79, 83, 184, 189, 190
  Ascension, 6, 254

Bagamoyo, Capture of, 228-232
Cameroons 1914-1916, 219-226
Buea Operation, 223-224
Edea Expedition, 220, 223
Dardanelles per Terram, 113-160
  RM officers & Staff landed April 1915, 150-154
  RM officer casualties, 154-157
  Achi Baba Nullah, 135
  Anzac, 119-121
  L/Cpl Parker's VC, 122
  Chessboard, attack on, 124
  Casualties, 24th April to 13th May, 127
  The Helles Sector, 128
  Krithia, Second battle of,
  Krithia, Third battle of, 132128
  'Y' Beach, 116-118
  Stavros, Macedonia, 149
  Reorganisation of RM Brigade into 1st and 2nd RMLI, 138
  Evacuation, 38-39, 66, 143, 146-148
  Honours and Rewards (See also Gallipoli), 157-160
Expedition to Siberia, 86-91
  Honours, 91
Falkland Islands, 6, 16
  List of RM Officers, 16-17
Greece, 207-212
Long Island, Smyrna, 149, 204-205
Mediterranean & Red Sea, 203-214
North Russia, 73, 184-199
Ostend, 97-99
Persian Gulf, 215-218
  Fao, 215-216
  Dilwar, 216-218
  Bushire, 218
Post Armistice Operations, 61-62, 90
Red Sea, Action at Salif, 213-214
Salonica, 14, 22, 37, 38, 55, 59, 67, 143, 149, 207, 245, 388, 404, 417
Serbia, 250, 383-387
  Belgrade, Battle of, 384-385
  Honours and Rewards, 386-387
St Helena, 253-254
Vladivostock and Volga Front, 83-86
West Indies, 250-253
  Post Armistice Operations, 63-64

Royal Naval Air Service (RNAS), 14, 21, 98, 99, 100, 101, 120, 374

Royal Naval Officers and Ratings
  Altham E, Captain RN, 73, 78, 79, 187
  Anderson, Lieutenant RNVR, 323
  Arbuthnot Sir R, Rear-Admiral, 40, 42
  Arnold, Sub-Lieutenant RN, 21
  Asquith, Commander RN,
  Backhouse O, Commodore RN, 112, 138
  Bacon R H, Rear-Admiral (see also Colonel Bacon), 57, 66, 261, 267, 396
  Baddeley, Staff-Paymaster, 170
  Barnes H N, Gunners Mate, 86, 91
  Battenberg, Prince Louis of, Admiral, 97
  Bayly Sir Lewis, Admiral, 393, 394, 395
  Beadon, Petty Officer, 213
  Beak, Commander RN, 338
  Beatty Sir D, Admiral, 5, 19, 40, 41, 44, 48, 55

Beatty-Pownall, Captain RN, 220, 223
Bent, Lieutenant RN, 36, 66
Beresford, Lord Charles, Admiral, 313
Bethell, Admiral. 98
Bigger, Surgeon RN, 293, 402
Bingham, Commander RN, 41
Bishop, Captain RN, 397
Boyle, Hon A D H, Rear-Admiral, 194
Boyle, Captain RN, 213
Burton E T, Fleet Surgeon RN, 419
Bradford, Lieutenant RN, 174
Braithwaite, Captain RN, 223
Braithwaite, Commander RN, 223, 224
Brewill, Lieutenant Commander RN, 397
Briggs A W, Chaplain RN, 194
Brock Sir O de B, Rear-Admiral, 55
Brounger, Commander RN, 204
Browning Sir M E, Admiral, 56, 60
Buckle, Lieutenant Commander RN, 319, 351
Buller H T, Captain RN, 12
Burney, Admiral, 44, 46
Campbell S H, Lieutenant Commander RN, 164
Campbell A, Lieutenant RNVR, 296, 319
Carden, Vice-Admiral, 24, 28
Carpenter A F B, Captan RN (VC), 163, 164, 171, 172, 176, 180, 399
Chapman, Lieutenant RN, 228
Charsley, Lieutenant Commander RN, 255
Christian A H, Admiral, 98
Clark C W, Gunner RN, 87, 91
Collard, Commander RN, 36
Colville Sir S, Admiral, 240
Cornwell Boy (VC), 42
Colston H St G, Surgeon-Lieutenant, 168, 176
Coote, Lieutenant Commander RNVR, 321, 325
Cradock C, Rear-Admiral, 15
Crossman, Lieutenant, 110
Cull, Commander RNAS, 21
Culme-Seymour M, Admiral, 59, 59, 404
Curry, Rear-Admiral, 98
Dampier C F, Rear-Admiral, 412
Dannreuther, Commander RN, 44
Davidson A P, Captain RN, 31, 170
de Robeck Sir J, Admiral, 26, 28, 35, 38, 61
Dent D L, Captain RN, 38, 66, 146
Dickenson, Lieutenant RN, 164, 165
Dorman, Lieutenant Commander, 218, 218
Eykyn F B, Surgeon, 300
Finch E J, Fleet Surgeon, 293, 419, 421
Fisher, Lord, 65, 164, 411
Fitch, Paymaster-Lieutenant, 383
Fitzmaurice M S, Captain RN, 13, 15
Fleming A F, Staff-Surgeon RN, 112, 418
Freemantle Sir S, Admiral, 247
Fox, Captain RN, 12
Fraser, Captain RN, 411, 412
Freyberg B C, Lieutenant RNVR [see also Colonel (Royal West Surrey Regiment)] (VC), 34, 301, 303
Fuller, Captain RN, 219, 220, 223, 224
Fullerton E J, Captain RN, 21

483

Gaskell A, Fleet Surgeon, 112, 296, 418, 419
Georgiadas, Lieutenant RNVR, 249
Gibbs V, Commander RN, 164, 174
Gilliland, Lieutenant Commander, 303
Gaskell A, Fleet Surgeon RN, 112, 296, 418, 419
Glossop, Captain RN, 15
Goodenough, Commodore RN, 40
Gough-Calthorpe Sir S, Admiral, 59, 404, 405
Grant N, Captain RN, 13
Grieg L, Surgeon Lieutenant RN, 110
Grieve, Sick Berth Attendant, 211
Guest, Hon L, Lieutenant RNVR, 375, 376
Guy, Commander RN (VC), 256
Halahan F C, Captain RN, 66, 164, 172, 396
Hamilton, Lieutenant RN, 220, 223
Harrison A L, Lieutenant RN (VC), 180
Haselfoot, Lieutenant Commander RN, 67
Hawkins, Lieutenant RN, 174
Hayes-Sadler, Rear-Admiral, 207
Heath H L, Rear-Admiral, 40
Herbert, Lieutenant RN, 70
Hobbs A, Sub-Lieutenant RNVR, 363
Hood, Rear-Admiral, 42, 44, 57, 65
Hughes, Commander RNR, 223, 226
Jellicoe Sir John, Admiral, 11, 45, 46, 55, 239, 240
Jerram T M, Vice-Admiral, 40, 406
Joyce H C, Surgeon Lieutenant, 87, 91
Kelly W A H, Captain RN, 12
Kemp, Rear-Admiral, 73, 184
Ker C A, Lieutenant Commander RN, 383
Keyes Sir R, Admiral, 58, 163, 168, 170, 171, 174, 178
King H D, Captain RNVR, 138
King-Hall, Admiral, 21
Lambert C F, Rear-Admiral, 247
Lambert R, Captain RN, 227
Larken F, Captain RN, 203, 204
Laws H N, Lieutenant RNVR (see also Captain RM), 419
Laurence, Commander RN, 55
Lawson R N, Captain RN, 42
Le Mesurier, Commodore RN, 40
Lewin, Commander RN, 55
Littlejohns, Lieutenant RN, 396
Loder-Symonds, Captain RN, 23
Loxley A N, Captain RN, 19
Luckach, Lieutenant RNVR, 244
Madden Sir C, Admiral, 55
Manning, Sub-Lieutenant RNR, 228
Martyn-Jones, Chaplain RN, 347
McBean-Ross J, Surgeon, 141, 301, 304, 318, 359
McCutcheon, Surgeon-Commander, 176
McKenzie, Seaman (VC), 180
Miller F S, Rear-Admiral, 240
Milligan, Surgeon Lieutenant, 211
Milne, Admiral, 24
Moffatt Mr, Gunner RN, 84
Molteno, Captain RN, 42
Morgan, Surgeon RN, 316
Myles T W, Sugeon-Commander, 247, 250

Nicholls E C, Surgeon Lieutenant Commander, 194
Nicholson B, Lieutenant RNVR, 298, 373
Nicholson S, Rear-Admiral, 22
Norris D T, Commodore RN, 255, 256, 257
Oldham, Sub-Lieutenant RNVR, 328
Oliver E C, Assistant Paymaster, 270
Pakenham Sir W, Admiral, 55
Palliser, Lieutenant RN, 208
Parnell, Commander RN, 256
Payne, Surgeon, 141, 419
Pead J H, Fleet Surgeon RN, 419
Pearce-Gould, Surgeon RN, 319, 329
Peirse, Vice-Admiral, 27
Peshall C J, Chaplain RN, 170
Piercey B H, Lieutenant Commander RN, 29
Pillar, Captain RN, 19
Pocock, Surgeon Lieutenant RN, 167, 168, 176
Ponsford, Lieutenant Commander RNVR, 259
Priestly, Lieutenant RN, 208, 209
Rees F H, Surgeon RN, 155
Ritchie H P, Commander RN, 18
Robertson, Lieutenant RN, 257
Robinson, Commander RN (VC), 257
Rombulow-Pearse, Captain RN, 244
Rymer, Captain RN, 250
Salmond, Commander RN, 213
Samson C R, Commander RNAS, 37, 98, 100, 101, 102, 373
Sandford, Lieutenant RN, 174
Saunders, Ship's Steward, 170
Simpson, Commodore RN, 251
Sloan, Lieutenant RN, 407
Smith A B, Lieutenant RNR (VC), 69
Sneyd, Lieutenant Commander RN, 220, 224
Spearman A Y, Commander RN, 130
Spencer, Lieutenant RNR, 174
Stanford C E, Staff Surgeon RN, 112, 418, 419
Steele, Lieutenant RNR, 70
Stirling, Commodore RN, 46
Sturdee Sir F D, Vice- Admiral, 5, 16, 20, 48, 56
Swabey, Commander RN, 66
Troubridge, Rear-Admiral, 383, 386
Tweedie, Commodore RN, 60
Twigg, Lieutenant RN, 203
Twyrrhit R Y, Commodore RN, 19, 23, 57
Unthank, Surgeon RN, 306
Unwin, Commander RN, 31
Wake D St A, Captain RN, 20, 216
Wardle T E, Captain RN, 22
Warleigh, Captain RN, 205
Watson, Commander RN, 230
Weir S F, Engineer Lieutenant RN, 60
Wemyss Sir R E S, Rear-Admiral
Wemyss, Lord Wester, Admiral, 15, 24, 29, 38, 113, 244
Wilkinson R A, Surgeon Commander RN, 194
Wilson, Commander RN, 21
Wise, Lieutenant RN, 65
Wollaston, Surgeon RN, 365, 369
Wolfe-Murray, Commander RN, 84

Wood, Yeoman of Signals, 218
Woods A R, Commander RN, 213, 214
Yendell, Chief Gunner, 170
Young T, Chief Sick Berth Attendant, 402

Royal Naval Division Formations (later 63rd [(Royal Naval] Division)
Staff, 111-112
1st Royal Naval Brigade
  (later 188th Brigade) 295, 297, 303, 305, 306, 308, 313, 314, 315, 316, 318, 320, 321, 322, 326, 327, 329, 3330, 334, 336, 337, 339, 342, 343, 346, 347, 348, 350, 354, 355
2nd Royal Naval Brigade
  (later 189th Brigade) 296, 305, 324, 326, 332, 333, 335. 338, 339, 345, 346, 348, 348, 354, 355,
190th Brigade, 295, 296, 297, 298, 299, 300, 303, 307, 308, 313, 319, 321, 323, 322, 327, 330, 332, 335, 339, 341, 342, 346, 348, 354
Anson Battalion, 29, 31, 34, 132, 138, 149, 296, 300, 301, 303, 304, 309, 316, 319, 320, 322, 323, 324, 326, 328, 329, 330, 331, 334, 335, 343, 345, 346, 348, 349, 351, 355
Benbow Battalion, 130, 132, 414, 446
Collingwood Battalion, 130, 132, 446
Drake Battalion, 35, 109, 116, 128, 136, 138, 146, 148, 320, 322, 331, 332, 335, 337, 338, 339, 343, 345, 346, 348, 350, 354
Drake, Reserve, 446
Hawke Battalion, 130, 134, 138, 146, 148, 296, 300, 301, 313, 315, 317, 320, 322, 323, 326, 329, 335, 337, 338, 339, 343, 346, 348, 351, 352, 354, 446
Hawke, Reserve, 446
Hood Battalion, 34, 138, 146, 148, 300, 301, 303, 307, 313, 315, 317, 322, 324, 328, 330, 331, 335, 337, 338, 339, 341, 346, 348, 351, 352, 354, 356
Hood, Reserve, 446
Howe Battalion, 138, 141, 143, 146, 149, 299, 300, 301, 304, 306, 311, 316, 317, 318, 319
Nelson Battalion, 121, 124, 127, 136, 137, 138, 296, 299, 300, 301
Machine Gun Battalion, 320, 321, 337, 345, 346, 348, 354
Divisional Engineers, 112, 113, 130, 134, 296, 325, 346, 352, 413-415
Signal Company (later 63rd Division Signal Company), 112, 296, 413, 415
1, 2 & 3 Field Companies (later 247, 248 & 249 Field Companies), 127, 296, 413, 415
Divisional Train, 4, 296, 415-418, 419
Honours and Rewards, 421-423
Divisional Labour Company, 305
Divisional Ordnance Company RM, 4, 413
Medical Unit
1st Field Ambulance (later 148), 418
2nd Field Ambulance (later 149), 418
3rd Field Ambulance (later 159), 419-423
No 15 Convalescent Depot, 421
Honours and Rewards, 321-423
Motor Maxim Squadron, 121

Index

Division Infantry Base Depot, 363
Horse Show, 313
Reorganisation (February 1918), 319

Royal Fleet Reserve, 97, 435
Royal Naval Siege Guns, 66, 396, 397
Royal Naval Staff Officers, 6

Russian Forces, 76, 77, 185, 189, 194, 196, 197, 198, 255
  Russian Armoured Car Squadron, 436
  Russian Black Sea Fleet, 59, 64, 404
  White Russians, 78, 79, 80, 81, 195

Scarborough, 17
Schleswig-Holstein, 194, 195
Scottish Women's Hospitals, 383
Serbian troops, 186, 189, 383, 384, 385
Shackleton, Sir E, 191

Ships:
  Royal Navy:
    Abdiel, 46
    Abercrombie, 37, 38
    Aboukir, 13, 98
    Achilles, 46, 92
    Active, 40, 52
    Adventure, 65
    Agamemnon, 23, 26, 27, 28, 30, 35, 36, 38, 39, 59, 114
    Agincourt, 4, 14, 41, 50, 54
    Ajax, 41, 50, 406
    Albemarle Class, 13
    Albion, 18, 22, 26, 27, 28, 30, 31, 32, 36, 390, 394
    Amethyst, 26, 27, 28, 30, 34, 36, 66, 114, 116, 117
    Amphion, 12
    Andes, 23
    Arethusa, 12, 13, 18, 19, 22
    Ark Royal, 30
    Astraea, 18, 225
    Attentive, 65, 73, 75, 187, 190
    Attentive, 11, 397
    Audacious, 13
    Aurora, 19
    Bacchante, 30, 35, 37
    Baralong, 70
    Barham, 41, 44, 51
    Bellerophon, 41, 50
    Bellona, 40, 52
    Benbow, 41, 47, 50
    Berwick, 12, 18
    Birmingham, 13, 19, 52
    Birkenhead, 52
    Black Prince, 11, 42, 46, 51
    Blanche, 40, 52, 61
    Blenheim, 15
    Blonde, 61
    Bluebell, 394
    Boadicea, 40, 52, 61
    Bristol, 12, 16, 17, 57
    Britannia, 59
    Broke, 56, 92
    Bryony, 250
    Bulwark, 17
    Bustard (Gunnery School Tender),, 65
    Cadmus, 406, 407
    Caesar, 98

Calliope, 45, 52
Calypso, 57, 64
Canada, 41, 50
Canopus, 16, 17, 27, 28, 30, 34, 36, 114
Canterbury, 440, 42. 52
Caradoc, 57, 64
Cardiff, 57, 60, 61, 64
Carlisle, 91
Carnarvon, 16, 17
Caroline, 52
Cassandra, 57, 63
Castor, 46, 52, 60, 61
Centaur, 64
Centurion, 41, 50
Ceres, 57, 63
Challenger, 220, 223, 224, 225, 228, 230, 232, 364, 367
Chatham, 12, 15, 37, 38
Chelmer, 35
Chester, 40, 42, 52, 54
Childers (Tug), 21
Cicala (River Gunboat), 78
Cleopatra, 23
Cochrane, 51, 185, 186
Cockchafer (River Gunboat), 78
Comus, 23, 52
Collingwood, 41, 50
Colne, 35
Colossus, 41, 45, 50
Colombo, 91
Comus, 23, 52
Constance, 52
Conqueror, 41, 50
Cordelia, 52
Cornwall, 16, 17
Cornwallis, 26, 27, 30, 31, 36, 55, 114, 116
Crescent, 14, 22, 239
Cressy, 13
Cricket (River Gunboat), 78, 81
Cumberland, 219, 220, 223, 224
Cyclops, 78
Daffodil (Mersey Ferry Boat), 164, 168, 171, 172, 173, 174, 175
Dartmouth, 15, 27, 30, 34, 35, 36, 38, 57, 114, 386
Defence, 11, 42, 45, 46, 51
Diana, 205, 255, 398
Dominion, 170
Doris, 30, 34, 38, 66, 203, 204
Dreadnought, 20
Dublin, 11, 12, 15, 27, 30, 32, 38, 46, 52, 54, 114, 116, 250
Duke of Edinburgh, 11, 15, 42, 51
Duncan, 207
Dundee (Armed Boarding Steamer), 56, 92
Dwarf, 219, 220, 223
Earl of Peterborough, 38
Echo (Whaler), 21
Edgar, 37, 38
Egmont, 383, 385
Eileen, 251
Emperor of India, 56, 64, 250
Empress, 100
Endeavour, 18
Endymion, 22, 37, 38, 67
Engadine, 40, 42
Erebus (Monitor), 163
Erin, 4, 14, 41, 50, 54

Espiegle, 213, 214
Essex, 18
Euryalus, 12, 27, 29, 30, 32, 98
Exmouth, 22, 37, 55, 207, 211, 213, 385
Falmouth, 12, 52, 54
Fandango (Minesweeper), 79
Fearless, 13, 52, 61
Fly (Whaler), 21
Foresight, 65
Formidable, 18, 98
Forward, 207
Fox, 15, 17, 18, 79, 256
Fullah, 225
Furious, 57, 61
Galatea, 23, 40, 52
General Crauford, 163
Glasgow, 15, 16, 17
Glorious, 57
Glory, 37, 58, 73, 184, 185, 186, 187, 188
Glory 1V, 13, 75, 187
Gloucester, 12, 15, 52
Glow-worm (River Gunboat), 78
Goliath, 17, 18, 27, 30, 32, 34, 36, 66, 98, 116, 118
Good Hope, 15, 16
Grafton, 22, 37, 38, 67
Grasshopper, 148
Hampshire, 23, 51, 242
Hannibal, 14, 37, 239, 388
Havelock, 37, 38
Hawke, 14
Hazard (Gunnery School Tender),, 65
Helmuth (Tug), 14, 17, 228
Hercules, 41, 45, 50, 60
Hermes, 14
Hibernia, 22, 38, 39
Highflyer, 12
Himalaya, 230
Hindustan, 165, 168, 170
Hogue, 13
Hope, 405
Humber (Monitor), 37, 65, 78, 80, 81, 82
Hyacinth, 15, 18, 21, 232, 364, 366, 390
Hyderabad, 78
Illustrious, 238
Implacable, 29, 30, 32, 34, 35, 36, 66
Inconstant, 52
Indefatigable, 11, 15, 41, 44, 51
India, 54
Indomitable, 11, 15, 19, 44, 51
Inflexible, 16, 17, 24, 26, 27, 28, 29, 44, 51, 114, 244
Intrepid, 164
Invincible, 12, 16, 44, 51
Iphigenia, 164
Irresistible, 26, 27, 28, 29, 98, 114, 115, 245
Iris (Mersey Ferry Boat), 164, 165, 171, 174, 176, 177, 393, 394, 395
Iron Duke, 11, 41, 44, 45, 50, 55, 64
Juno, 216, 217, 218, 255
Jupiter, 18, 20, 184
Kathleen (Steam yacht), 77
Kent, 16, 17, 85, 86, 88 (see also Russian Ships)
King Edward V11, 22
King George V, 41, 44, 50, 54, 61
Lancaster, 18
Lanconia, 364

485

Lion, 5, 12, 19, 40, 42, 44, 51, 61
Liverpool, 13, 59
Lizard, 58
London, 29, 30, 32, 34, 36
Lord Clive, 163
Lord Nelson, 27, 28, 30, 35, 36, 59, 64, 114, 141, 245
Lowestoft, 12, 19
Magnificent, 14, 37
Majestic, 26, 27, 29, 30, 34, 35, 36
Malaya, 41, 51
Manica (Kite Balloon Ship), 30, 34, 227, 228
Mantis (River Gunboat), 78, 256
Margaret Elizabeth, 224, 225
Marlborough, 41, 44, 45, 46, 50, 64
Mars, 37
Marshal Soult, 163
Mersey (Monitor), 92, 227, 228, 21, 65
Minerva, 20, 299, 30, 205, 232
Minotaur, 51, 61
Monarch, 41, 50
Monitors,
  18, 38
  23, 78
  25, 76, 77, 78, 82
  27, 78, 81, 82
  28, 58, 78
  31, 31, 38, 81
  33, 38, 81
Monmouth, 15, 16
Morris Dance (Minesweeper), 79
Moth (River Gunboat), 78, 256
Motor Launches
  M.L. 1, 77
  M.L. 2, 76, 77
  M.L. 3, 77
Nairana (Seaplane Ship), 73, 75, 77
Natal, 18, 23
Neptune, 41, 48, 50
Nestor, 41
Newbridge (Collier), 15
New Zealand, 12, 19, 41, 44, 48, 51
Nomad, 41
Nottingham, 12, 19, 52, 54
Ocean, 27, 28, 29, 215, 216, 245
Odin, 213, 215
Orama, 16
Orbita, 364
Orion, 41, 48, 50, 54
Osiris, 244
Patrol, 17
Pegasus, 14, 15, 79, 365
Pelican, 54
Porpoise, 54
Phaeton, 23, 52, 60, 61
Primrose, 394
Prince Eugene, 163
Prince George, 22, 27, 28, 30, 35, 37, 98, 148
Prince of Wales, 29, 30, 32, 34, 35, 36, 98
Princess Margaret, 63
Princess Royal, 12, 19, 51
Pyramus, 21, 216, 217, 218
Queen, 29, 30, 32, 36
Queen Elizabeth, 26, 27, 28, 29, 34, 36, 54, 55, 61
Queen Mary, 41, 51
Raglan (Monitor), 37, 38, 58, 245

Remus, 223
Renown, 54
Repulse, 54, 57
Revenge (renamed Redoubtable), 12, 41, 45, 46, 50, 54, 55, 65
Rinaldo (Gunnery School Tender), 65, 225, 232
Roberts, 37, 38
Royal Arthur, 14, 22, 239
Royal Edward, 168
Royal George, 246
Royalist, 52
Royal Oak, 41, 50
Russell, 23, 38, 39
Sapphire, 27, 30, 65, 66, 116, 117
Sakata (Sternwheel Gunboat), 224
Savage (Torpedo Boat Destroyer), 205
Scourge (Torpedo Boat Destroyer), 205
Sentinel, 207
Severn (Monitor), 21, 65, 92, 227, 228, 364
Shannon, 51
Sirius (Gunnery School Tender), 65, 225
Sir T. Picton, 38
Southampton, 12, 19, 40, 41, 46, 52
Step Dance (Minesweeper), 79
St. Vincent, 41, 50
Suffolk, 18, 83, 84, 86 (see also Russian Ships)
Superb, 41, 50, 59, 64, 404, 405
Swift, 56, 92
Swiftsure, 20, 27, 28, 29, 30, 32, 36, 37, 396
Sword Dance (Minesweeper), 79, 83
Talbot, 30, 37, 66, 227, 228, 230, 232
Tamar, 13
Temeraire, 41, 50, 59, 64, 405
Terrible, 37
Terror (Monitor), 163
Theseus, 37, 38
Thetis, 164
Thistle, 227, 232, 370
Thunderer, 41, 50
Tiger, 14, 19, 20, 51
Tigress, 58
Topaze, 213
Torpedo Boat Destroyers (T.P.Ds),11, 31, 207, 247
Torpedo Boat Destroyer (E.23), 54
Trent, 230, 564
Triad, 31
Triumph, 13, 26, 27, 28, 30, 32, 35, 36, 114, 244
Tweedmouth, 21
Undaunted, 14, 19, 23
Valiant, 41, 51
Vanguard, 20, 41, 50, 56, 57
Venerable, 36, 37, 65, 98
Vengeance, 24, 26, 27, 28, 30, 36, 37, 98, 114, 227, 228, 230, 232, 364, 367
Venus, 256
Vestal (Gunnery School Tender), 65
Vindictive, 20, 163-176, 178, 184
Warrior, 11, 42, 44, 45, 51
Warspite, 41, 44, 51, 334
Weymouth, 12, 15, 21
Wildfire (Gunnery School Tender), 65
Wolverine, 114
Zealandia, 22

RN Shore Stations
  Excellent, 445
  Vernon, 445
  Victory, 112, 416
Royal Australian Navy:
  Brisbane, 405
  Sydney, 15, 92
  Warrego, 405
French Ships:
  Admiral Aube, 60, 73, 75, 184
  Bruix, 223
  Charlemagne, 26
  Condorcet, 211
  Diderot Class, 59
  Dupleix, 17
  Kleber, 38
  Mirabeau, 208, 211
  Provence, 211
  Suffren, 15, 26, 27
  Surprise, 223
  Vergniaud, 208, 209
  Veriti, 15
Greek Ships
  Averoff, 59, 207
  Kilkis, 207
  Lemnos, 59, 207
Italian Ships
  Piemonte, 59
  Torpedo Boat Destroyers, 57
Nigerian Ships
  Ivy, 219, 223, 224, 225
Royal Indian Marine Ships
  Dalhousie, 217
  Hardinge, 20
  Lawrence, 216
  Minto, 213
  Northbrook, 213
Russian Ships:
  Black Sea Fleet, 59, 63, 54, 404
  Advokat (Paddle Steamer), 75, 76, 77
  Askold (later Glory 1V), 13, 38, 75, 184, 187
  Borodino (River Paddle Steamer), 78, 79, 80
  Chasavry (Bolshevik Caspian Flotilla), 88, 257
  Elburz (Bolshevik Caspian Flotilla), 88, 257
  Gorodok (Paddle Steamer), 75
  Grogin(Kama River Operation with Kent and Suffolk), 89
  Magoochy(Paddle Steamer),77
  Radzlyff, 77
  Retvisan, 76
  Roosal (Bolshevik Caspian Flotilla), 88
  Sviagator (Ive Breaker), 79
  Tchesma, 187
  A Tug (named Kent, one of two ships of the Russian Naval Flotilla on the Kama River), 86, 87, 88, 89, 90
  A Barge (named Suffolk one of two ships of the Russian Naval Flotilla on the Kama River), 86, 87, 88
  Van (Bolshevik Caspian Flotilla), 88
Turkish Ships
  Barbarossa, 36
United States Ships
  American Battle Squadron, 58, 60
  Arkhansas, 58

Florida, 58
New York, 58
Olympia, 73, 184
Texas, 58
Wyoming, 58
Armed Merchant Cruisers
  Alcantara, 22, 23
  Armadale Castle, 364
  Bayano, 21
  Carmania, 13, 92
  Kinfauns Castle, 15
  Laurentic, 224
  Rhydwen, 68
  Viknor, 21
Armed Boarding Steamers, 5,
Defensively Armed Merchantmen
  Otranto, 15
  Otway, 5
  Otaki, 69
  Tremorvah, 68, 69
Merchant Ships
  Alnwick Castle, 113, 127
  Arabic, 70
  Aragon, 295
  Archangel, 393
  Bharata, 17
  Braemar Castle, 113, 117
  Cawdor Castle, 113, 116, 127
  City of Edinburgh, 102
  Connaught, 395
  Czar, 194
  Durham Castle, 364
  Franconia, 113
  Gloucester Castle, 113, 116
  Great Southern, 394, 395
  Innisfallen, 393
  Kildonan Castle, 391
  King Orry, 60,61
  Lake Michigan, 102
  Lusitania, 21
  Lydia, 267
  Manitou, 29
  Minnewaska, 388
  Nicosian, 70
  Olympic, 251
  Porto, 188
  Providence (Brixham Trawler), 19
  Somali, 113
  Thracia, 20
  River Clyde, 30, 31
  Saxon, 364, 390
Caspian Sea Operations
  Alla Verdi, 256, 257
  Asia, 256, 257
  Bibi Abat, 256, 257
  Emile Nobel, 256, 257
  Kruger, 255, 256, 257
  Kursk, 255, 256
  Orlionock, 257
  Slava, 256
  Sergie, 257
  Venture, 256, 257
  Windsor Castle, 257
  Zoroaster, 256, 257
Austrian Ships
  Battleships, 12
  Battle Cruisers, 12
  Light Cruisers, 56
  Monitors, 383, 384

German Ships
  Ariadne, 12
  Bayern, 57, 60, 61
  Blucher, 19
  Bremse, 60
  Breslau, 11, 58, 247
  Brumme, 60
  Cap Trafalgar (Armed Merchantman), 13, 92
  Coln, 60
  Derfflinger, 19, 45, 47, 53, 60
  Dresden, 16
  Deutschland, 46, 53
  Elbing, 47, 53
  Emden, 14, 15, 60, 92, 216
  Feldmarschall, 17, 18
  Frankfurt, 53, 60,
  Frauenlobe, 46, 47
  Frederich der Grosse, 42, 53, 60
  Gneisenau, 15, 16
  Goeben, 11, 34, 35, 58, 59, 245, 247
  Greif, 22, 23
  Grosser Kurfurst, 53, 61
  Hamburg, 53
  Hannover, 53
  Helgoland, 53
  Herzogin Elizabeth, 219, 224
  Hessen, 53
  Hindenburg, 60
  Kaiser Class, 44, 45, 46, 55, 60
  Kaiser, 53
  Kaiserin, 53
  Kaiser Wilhelm 11
  Kaiser Wilhelm der Grosse, 12, 18
  Karlsruhe, 12, 60
  Koenigsberg, 14, 15, 21, 92
  Kolberg, 19
  Koln, 12
  Konig Class, 44, 45, 60
  Konig, 17, 18, 44, 53
  Konigin Luise, 12
  Kronprinz, 53, 61
  Kronprinz Wilhelm (Armed Merchant Cruiser), 21
  Leipzic, 15, 16
  Leopard, 56, 92
  Lutzow, 45, 47, 53
  Mainz, 12
  Markgraf, 53, 61
  Moewe, 69, 71
  Moltke, 19, 53, 60
  Munchen, 53
  Nachtigal, 220
  Nassau, 53
  Nurnberg, 16, 60
  Oldenburg, 53
  Ostfriesland, 53
  Pillau, 53
  Pommern, 46, 47, 53
  Posen, 53
  Prinz Regent Luitpold, 53
  Regensburg, 53
  Rheinland, 53
  Rostock, 47, 53
  Scharnhorst, 15, 16
  Schlesien, 53
  Schleswig Holstein, 53
  Seydlitz, 19, 47, 53, 60
  Spreewald (Armed Merchantman) 12

  Stettin, 53
  Stralsund Class, 57
  Stuttgart, 53
  Thuringen, 53
  Torpedo Boat Destroyers (T.B.Ds), 14, 19, 23, 41, 173, 257
  Torpedo Boat Destroyer V187, 12
  U9, 13
  U29, 20
  Van der Tann, 60
  Westfalen, 53
  Wiesbaden, 42, 45, 47
  Yorck, 15

Scottish Bases
  Aultbea, 238
  Cromarty, 11, 20, 40, 54, 70, 237, 238, 411, 439
  Inverness & Kyles of Loch Alsh, 238
  Orkneys, 17, 23, 70, 239, 240, 242
  Scapa Flow, 14, 21, 40, 61, 237, 238, 239, 261, 411, 412, 429, 431, 439, 446
  Shetlands, 17, 70, 239, 240, 242
Smirnoff, Admiral (Russian), 86, 87, 89
Somers, Marie (Belgian Nurse), 110
South African Forces, 390, 391
South African Heavy Artillery, 390-392
Stavros, Macedonia, 22, 66, 149, 414, 419
Stevens' Telephones, 132
St John's Ambulance, 418
Stokes Trench Mortars, 162, 163, 164, 165, 171, 311, 367, 370
Surrender of German High Seas Fleet, 60-61
Syren Force, 73, 189

Tank Testing Squadron, 436
Tenedos, 24, 26, 27, 29, 114, 115, 141, 148, 244, 245, 246, 249, 250, 404
Tickler's Bombs, 138,
Transport Worker Battalions, 426

United States Marine Corps, 58
Ussuri River, 83, 84

Various or miscellaneous incidents
  Dardanelles and Bosphorus 1918, 404
  Buda Pesth, 406
  New Guinea, 407
  Sevastopol, 405
  Singapore, 406-407
  Vladivostock, 83, 85. 86, 91
Von Lettow-Vorbeck, Colonel (German Marine Corps), 371
Von Reuter, (German Navy), 60
Von Spee, Admiral, 11, 15, 18, 253
Vulte N P, Major (USMC), 58

War at Sea
  Actions and Incidents 1914-1916, 11-23
  Actions and Incidents 1916-1919, 54-63
  Anti-Submarine War, 68-72
  Bombardments from the Sea, 65-67
  Caspian Sea operations, 244-255
  Coronel, Battle of, 15-16
  Cuxhaven, Air attack on, 18, 451
  Dardanelles – Per Mare, 24-39
  Dardanelles, Bombardment of, 24-28
  Dogger Bank, Battle of, 19-20

Falkland Islands, Battle of, 11, 16
   RMs embarked, 16-17
Hampshire, loss of, 23
Heligoland Bight, Battle of, 12, 54, 57
Jutland, Battle of, 40-53
   RM Losses and comparison with Trafalgar, 47
   Total RM numbers engaged, 47
   Major Harvey's VC
   Honours and Rewards, 47-49
   RM detachments (Table A), 50-52
   German Ships engaged, 53
East Africa, Coastal Operations, 227-232
Red Sea Action at Salif, 213-214
River Operations, 73-91
   Suffolk Detachment expedition into Siberia, 83-86
   Dwina River, 73-79
   Kama River, 86-91
   Modyuski Island, 73, 75
   Rufigi River, 15, 113, 119, 364, 367, 368, 369
   Ussuri River, 83, 84
Single Ship Actions, 5, 13, 22, 92
Surrender of German Fleet, 60, 61

Wassmuss, Herr (German ex-Consul), 216, 218
Weddigen, (Submarine Captain, German Navy), 13
Whippet Tanks, 332
Women's Royal Naval Service, 429, 439, 441

Yarmouth, 57

Zeebrugge, 161-182
   4th Battalion, formation and strength, 161
   Battalion officers, 167, 168
   Inspection by the King, 163
   Lt Col Elliot's Battalion Orders, 165-166
   The operation, 171-174
   Casualties, 176
   VC Ballot, 178
   Honours and Rewards, 180-181